A HISTORICAL GUIDE TO
THE UNITED STATES

A HISTORICAL GUIDE TO THE United States

PREPARED BY THE AMERICAN
ASSOCIATION FOR STATE AND
LOCAL HISTORY

W · W · NORTON & COMPANY
NEW YORK   LONDON

Published simultaneously in Canada by Penguin Books Canada Ltd., 2801 John
Street, Markham, Ontario L3R 1B4.
Printed in the United States of America.

The text of this book is composed in 9/11 Garamond Light, with display type
set in ITC Garamond Book. Composition by the Vail-Ballou Press, Inc.
Manufacturing by the Murray Printing Company.

First Edition

Library of Congress Cataloging-in-Publication Data

A Historical guide to the United States.

   Collected essays previously published in the American Association for State
and Local History's States and the nation series.
   Edited by James B. Gardner and Timothy C. Jacobson.
   1. Historic sites—United States—Guide-books. 2. United States—
Description and travel—1981–   —Guide-books. I. Gardner, James B.,
1950–   III. American Association for State and Local History.
E159.H718   1986   917.3′04927   86–12881

ISBN 0-393-02383-4

W. W. Norton & Company, Inc., 500 Fifth Avenue, New York, N. Y. 10110
W. W. Norton & Company Ltd., 37 Great Russell Street, London WC1B 3NU

1 2 3 4 5 6 7 8 9 0

The costs of writing and editing this book were met mainly by grants from the National Endowment for the Humanities, a federal agency, to the American Association for State and Local History, a non-profit educational organization, which alone is responsible for the information and opinions expressed in the text.

HISTORICAL GUIDE TO
THE UNITED STATES

INTRODUCTION

Historic sites have always fascinated travelers. As human beings, we feel somehow drawn to places where others have thought, fought, triumphed, or endured in a way that made history. To explore Monticello where the genius of Thomas Jefferson can still be seen; to cross the Cumberland Gap where many of our ancestors made their way with high hopes to find new lives; to walk beside the time-weathered walls of mission churches in the Southwest, built centuries ago—such contact with the "real thing" can inspire, thrill, and humble us, or deeply move us in a way we can hardly define.

The history books we studied in school sometimes made the Civil War or the Battle of the Little Bighorn seem abstract; Lincoln and Lee or Crazy Horse and Custer unreal, except as revered memories. But when one actually stands on the battlefield at Gettysburg, or out on the plains where Custer made his last stand, the significance to both sides— indeed to all Americans—of what happened there can make history come vividly alive.

Whether you are planning a trip or recalling places you have already seen, whether traveling by car, R.V., or armchair, we hope to enhance your enjoyment and appreciation of the American history that is still to be found in the local historic sites of every state.

This guide provides essays on certain major historic sites in each state, plus an annotated listing of additional places of historical interest. The entries are representative rather than exhaustive. Included, however, are not only sites where important events occurred, but historic houses where prominant people once lived, and museums exhibiting historically significant artifacts. To use the book for traveling, consult the sections on the states you plan to visit and use the entries to help select places to stop for sight-seeing. If you've already chosen sights to visit, use this information to prepare yourself for what you are going to see. And if you know a site, but not its location, a complete index will help you.

The essays collected here were prepared for publication state by state in a series of history books that can also be helpful to travelers and general readers. The *States and the Nation* series is made up of short, readable histories of the fifty states, plus the District of Columbia, prepared by the American Association for State and Local History and co-published by W. W. Norton & Company.

James B. Gardner and Timothy C. Jacobson, historians at the American Association for State and Local History, authored the essays and compiled the reference lists. The editors of the Association take complete responsibility for the selection of sites and the informational descriptions. Nonetheless, we owe thanks to many individuals and historical organizations, including those listed, for generously providing information and advice. Our thanks also go to the National Endowment for the Humanities which granted funds for the writing and editing of the materials in this book, as it did for the *States and the Nation* series. We all wish you many enjoyable and rewarding journeys!

Gerald George, Director
American Association for State
and Local History

ALABAMA

OVERTON FARMSTEAD four miles northwest of Hodges. Contrary to popular tales of moonlight and magnolias, most Alabamians—and most Southerners—prior to the Civil War lived not on grand plantations but on small farms much like those north of the Mason-Dixon line. While the log cabins of the state's "plain folk" do not rival the grandeur of its columned mansions, the former do illustrate an essential part of the Alabama experience. One of the best surviving examples is the Overton Farmstead, a log dogtrot cabin and outbuildings located in the Bear Creek Education Center near Russellville.

The typical white Alabamian was neither a cotton aristocrat nor "poor white trash" but a middle- or lower-middle-class farmer, who owned and cultivated a modest self-sufficient farm. He had few if any slaves and usually lived outside the wealthy Black Belt. He probably grew tobacco or cotton as a cash crop, but his mainstay was corn, which provided food for his family, feed for his livestock, and mash for his whiskey. While this scale of operations did not promise wealth and social mobility, it was sufficient to meet the needs of the frontier farmer and his family.

One such farmer was Abner Overton, a native of Raleigh, North Carolina, who joined the stream of emigrants across the Appalachians after the War of 1812. Overton first visited the Alabama region in 1815, while peddling a wagon load of tobacco. On a similar trip two years later, he spotted an attractive parcel of land along Bear Creek. Since Alabama was still part of Mississippi Territory, he had to go to Pontitoc, Mississippi to secure a deed to the 160-acre section. Back in Alabama, he soon built a small shed on the property, but it was 1819 before he began construction of a one-room cabin for himself and his bride, Judy May. As their family grew in the years that followed, the Overtons added on to the house one room at a time and eventually had a five-room cabin. Nearby stood the typical outbuildings of a north Alabama farmstead: a corn crib, a blacksmith and tool shed, a seed and feed shed, a horse and mule barn, two cattle barns, a fruit and potato house, and a smokehouse. Here Overton and his wife lived until their deaths in 1877 and 1876 respectively, and their descendants continued to reside there until 1946.

In 1969 the Tennessee Valley Authority acquired the farm as part of the Bear Creek Water Control Project, encompassing 371 acres bordered on three sides by the curving creek. Today the Bear Creek Development Authority owns the property, but it is maintained by the Bear Creek Education Project, a cooperative effort by surrounding school systems to develop the site for educational purposes. The farmstead includes the Overtons' log home and various outbuildings reconstructed from timbers salvaged from other area farms. Visitors can see

Abner Overton's log dogtrot house

a corn crib, a three-stall animal barn, a potato house, a smokehouse, and a chicken house. The split-rail fences are not original, but the well and family cemetery do date from the Overton family's residence.

The focus of the complex is the log dogtrot house. The structure was apparently erected in the first half of the nineteenth century, and local accounts date the oldest portion from 1819. Only three of the five rooms constructed by the Overtons remain now. Each reflects a different stage in the family's growth and development. The oldest crib on the west side features saddle-notch construction, a dirt floor, a shuttered window, and a broad-chimneyed fireplace used for both cooking and heating. Across the nine-foot-wide breezeway or dogtrot is a later addition of dovetail-notch construction. The third room forms an "L" and demonstrates still another log construction technique, the ridge-lock notch. Moving from one room to another, the visitor sees the changes that transpired between the first crude frontier structure and the more settled farmstead of later years.

Other examples of early log construction in Alabama include the Looney House at Ashville, the Owen Pioneer Home and the McAdory Pioneer Home at Bessemer, and a series of old pioneer homes at Tannehill Historical State Park at McCalla. These and the other frontier structures that still stand in the state testify to Alabama's frontier heritage and offer a much-needed corrective to the time-worn image of the plantation South.

DEXTER AVENUE KING MEMORIAL BAPTIST CHURCH *454 Dexter Avenue, Montgomery.* For over a century, black Alabamians have taken pride in the accomplishments of Booker T. Washington and the Tuskegee Institute. The noted Negro leader and the normal and agricultural school he organized in 1881 have become popular symbols of racial self-help in the face of white prejudice and discrimination. But although twentieth-century black Americans have honored Washington's early advocacy of the Negro cause, they have not embraced the racial conservatism he espoused. His policies of accommodation and compromise failed in the long run to come to grips with persistent racial injustice and inequality in American society. No one addressed those issues more ably than Martin Luther King, Jr. The young Baptist minister's advocacy of nonviolent resistance to white racism attracted national attention during the Montgomery bus boycott in 1955–1956 and made him the pivotal figure in the emerging struggle for political and social equality. Indeed, King virtually launched the modern civil-rights movement from his pulpit at Montgomery's Dexter Avenue Baptist Church. That church stands today as a symbol of King, his work, and the thousands of black Alabamians who shared his dream of social justice and racial equality.

In the decades that followed the Civil War, Alabama's black citizens experienced the same prejudice, discrimination, and violence that plagued the lives of former slaves elsewhere in the unreconstructed South. Despite the hopes and plans of Republican Reconstruction, black Alabamians found themselves powerless against the white majority and could do nothing to halt the abridgement of political rights or the discriminatory Jim Crow practices in employment, housing, education, transportation, and nearly every other aspect of life in the late nineteenth century. Thus isolated from the larger society by restrictions and proscriptions, they retreated into segregated communities and by the close of the century had established strong, independent businesses and institutions apart

Restored Dexter Avenue Church

from the hostile white world. Foremost among the community institutions stood the black churches.

Alabama Negroes organized numerous Methodist, Presbyterian, and Episcopal congregations, yet none rivaled the size or influence of the Baptist churches established across the state. The first black Baptist church was established in Alabama in the early nineteenth century, but a black Baptist convention was not organized until after the Civil War. Within just a few decades, zealous missionary activity led to the proliferation of new Baptist congregations across the state. Among these was the Second Colored Baptist Church of Montgomery. Mission workers established the Second Baptist Sunday School in February 1877, but several months passed before the organization of the church itself in a meeting at the home of Samuel Philips on High Street. With only meager finances, the congregation met for several years in whatever building was available and for a time held services in a former slave trader's pen on Dexter Avenue. A lot was purchased on that street in 1879, although construction did not begin on a new church building until 1883. The first worship services were held in the church basement two years later, and the sanctuary was completed in time for Thanksgiving Day services in 1889. By that time, the church's name had been changed to Dexter Avenue Baptist Church.

Over succeeding decades, Dexter Avenue became a leading institution in black Montgomery, but nothing compared to its pivotal role during the tenure of Dr. Martin Luther King, Jr. King's acceptance of the Dexter Avenue pastorate came during a particularly strained period of race relations in Alabama and throughout the South. For decades, discontent had been mounting within the black community over continued discrimination and segregation, but few actually expected to see an end to the old racial barriers. Then on May 17, 1954, just a few months before King arrived in Montgomery, the United States Supreme Court broke with the past and declared racial segregation in public schools unconstitutional. Although the landmark decision did not lead to immediate redress of long-term grievances, it did arouse black hopes and expectations and added further fuel to white racist fears. When King began his pastorate in October 1954, he faced the real possibility of open conflict between Montgomery's black and white communities.

That confrontation did not come, however, until December of 1955, when Mrs. Rosa Parks, a black seamstress, refused to relinquish her seat to a white passenger and move to the back of a city bus. Her arrest for violation of the city's and the state's segregation statutes aroused black Montgomery and gave rise to a community-wide meeting that same night at Dexter Avenue Baptist Church. Determined to take action against such abuses, the city's black citizens formed the Montgomery Improvement Association with Dr. King as president. Addressing the group that first night, King exhorted them: "If you will protest courageously, and yet with dignity and Christian love, when the history books are written in future generations, the historians will have to pause and say, 'There lived a great people—a black people—who injected new meaning and dignity into the veins of civilization.' "

By that time, King was strongly committed to nonviolent resistance, and the MIA endorsed his call for a boycott of the bus system as long as segregated use continued. King immediately took charge of organizing the black community. He held mass meetings at Dexter Avenue and other locations and arranged voluntary motor pools to meet transportation needs. His success in achieving the boycott surprised and outraged much of the white community. Membership in the White Citizens Council rose, white employers fired boycotters, and King's home was bombed. Determined to break the boycott, city authorities uncovered an old anti-boycott ordinance from the 1920s and arrested King. Still the boycott continued, lasting a total of 381 days. It finally ended on December 21, 1956, when the United States Supreme Court ruled bus segregation illegal.

The Montgomery bus boycott served as the starting point for the modern civil-rights movement. Later characteristics of the movement first appeared there. Obviously Montgomery demonstrated the viability of nonviolent tactics, but equally significant were community-wide organization and the central role of the black church. Indeed the anthem of the movement was an old hymn, "We Shall Overcome." But the key was the charismatic leadership provided by King. Indeed, it is hard to imagine the early years of the civil-rights movement without King, for he articulated the issues in a way no one else could do and gave the movement focus and direction through the difficult decade that followed Montgomery.

King stayed on at Dexter Avenue Baptist Church until 1960, when he returned to his home church in Atlanta. His efforts at Birmingham and Selma in the mid-sixties testified, however, to his continued interest in Alabama. He returned to Dexter Avenue for the last time on December 10, 1967, four months before his assassination in Memphis, Tennessee. A decade later, as part of its centennial observances, the church officially changed its name to Dexter Avenue King Memorial Baptist Church in honor of its most illustrious pastor.

The church stands today at 454 Dexter Avenue, about a block from the State Capitol and facing the Alabama Supreme Court Building. Restored to its original appearance, the red brick edifice features an eclectic combination of Late English Renaissance, Classic, and Gothic details. No other site so embodies the black experience in twentieth-century Alabama.

GAINESWOOD Morgan Street, Demopolis. The Big House of the pre-Civil War plantation constitutes the most enduring symbol of Alabama's history. Although more Alabamians descend from plain folk than from aristocrats, the romantic imagery of the Old South has prevailed over the historical realities of life in pioneer Alabama. Of the few grand antebellum mansions remaining in the state, the most impressive is Gaineswood, in Demopolis. Completed in 1860, this Black Belt plantation house illustrates the romantic ideal and provides insight into life in Alabama's planter aristocracy.

Exiled French followers of Napoleon Bonaparte established the town of Demopolis in 1817 on the banks of the Tombigbee River. The aristocratic founders of this "city of the people" intended to plant vineyards and olive groves as an economic base for their colony, but their plans soon proved unfeasible. The colony disbanded, and by the 1820s most of the original settlers had left. The land was not abandoned for long, however: the fertile soil and accessibility to river transportation that had attracted the French settlers proved equally appealing to cotton planters, who began moving into the area within the decade. The cotton economy proved viable, and by 1830 a prosperous plantation society flourished around Demopolis. With rich black soil and a high concen-

Nathan Bryan Whitfield's Gaineswood

tration of black slave labor, Marengo County became a key component of Alabama's Black Belt region in the years prior to the Civil War.

While visiting a relative's plantation in the early 1830s, Nathan Bryan Whitfield, a successful North Carolina politician and businessman, became convinced of the economic advantages of Marengo County and decided to buy land and move his family out from North Carolina. By 1834 he had purchased over two thousand acres of land, and the next year his family moved to Chatham plantation near Jefferson, fifteen miles from Demopolis. Whitfield prospered over the next decade, but by 1843 he apparently decided that the health of his family necessitated moving to a new location. Consequently he bought 480 acres of land near Demopolis from George S. Gaines, a factor to the Choctaw. As soon as the deal was completed, the Whitfield family moved into a small log cabin already standing on the property. They called their new home Marlmont.

As was typical of many Southern women in the period, Whitfield's wife, Elizabeth, remained in the background throughout their married life. During her husband's trips to Alabama prior to 1834, she stayed at home with the children in Lenoir County, North Carolina, just as she had during his tenure in the state legislature. While he was absent, she ran their sizable household, which in 1830 included seventy-one slaves. One constant throughout her married life was children, for she gave birth every two to three years until her death. Of her twelve children, only six survived her. The deaths of three within five weeks during the summer of 1842 prompted the move from Chatham to Demopolis. After a lengthy illness, she died at Marlmont on November 4, 1846, apparently before Whitfield began his remodeling of their Demopolis home. Her successor as mistress of the house was her daughter Mary Elizabeth, who stayed on at Marlmont with her husband after their marriage in 1847. She and her husband moved to Mississippi by 1853, and Marlmont then had no mistress until 1857, when Whitfield married again. His second wife, Bettie, played no more conspicuous a role than had his first. Apparently none of the mistresses of Marlmont, or Gaineswood as it was called by 1856, had any significant role in the planning or design of the house. The Whitfield home, like many of its contemporaries, was essentially a product of the taste and interests of the Southern planter and not the Southern lady.

Whitfield began adding on to the original structure at Marlmont in about 1847. He functioned as his own architect, consulting various architectural handbooks and incorporating those features he liked, whether Greek Revival, Renaissance Revival, or Italianate. He expanded and elaborated the structure over a decade and a half, using slave labor in his own carpentry and plaster shops and kilns to produce an imposing structure rich in detail and craftsmanship. When completed in 1860, the two-story stone mansion with columned porticoes and elaborately landscaped grounds was truly one of the most magnificent homes in the Black Belt. Gaineswood reached its zenith in 1860, when Whitfield presided over an estate that included 1,400 acres around Gaineswood, 5,690 acres at the Chatham plantation, and over 250 slaves. A product of the cotton culture and a social center for the Black Belt plantation society, Whitfield's Big House stood as a symbol of the Old South on the eve of the Civil War.

Although Gaineswood survived the Civil War without damage, the plantation era had come to a close. In 1865 Whitfield's declining health forced him to sell his Marengo County property to his son. Three years later, on December 27, 1868, he died. Gaineswood deteriorated under a succession of owners before its purchase by the state of Alabama in 1966. In 1971 the Alabama Historical Commission assumed control of the property. After years of careful research and restoration, Gaineswood now appears much as it did on the eve of the Civil War, with original furniture and accessories throughout the twenty columned, galleried, domed, and medallioned rooms. The property is now open to the public daily as a state historic site.

ALABAMA CAPITOL head of Dexter Avenue, Montgomery. Main part of building erected 1851. Served as Confederate capitol briefly in 1861.

ALABAMA DEPARTMENT OF ARCHIVES AND HISTORY   Washington Avenue, Montgomery. War Memorial Building, constructed of marble, houses all official state documents, records, and historical materials as well as collections from every era in the state's history.

ALABAMA SPACE AND ROCKET CENTER Tranquility Base, Huntsville. An aeronautics and space museum with exhibits on space technology and solar energy, including the Saturn V launch vehicle that sent the first men to the moon.

ARLINGTON HISTORIC HOUSE AND GARDENS 331 Cotton Avenue, S.W., Birmingham. Greek Revival home built in 1822; with antiques and period gardens.

BATTLE-FRIEDMAN HOME 1010 Greensboro Avenue, Tuscaloosa. An 1835 house now used as a civic and cultural center.

BELLINGRATH GARDENS AND HOME Theodore, near Mobile. Year-round flora along the Isle-aux-Oies River and a home with antique furnishings and art.

BLUFF HALL 405 North Commissioners Avenue, Demopolis. Built on a river bluff in 1832; period furnishings and collection of clothing.

CAHABA Dallas County road 2, four miles south of state 22. Ruins and cemeteries remaining from the first capital of Alabama, 1820–1826.

CHURCH OF ST. MICHAEL AND ALL ANGELS Eighteenth Street and Cobb Avenue, Anniston. Romanesque church that has been called one of the most beautiful in the United States.

CLARKSON COVERED BRIDGE U.S. 278 West, nine miles off I-65 near Cullman. Built in 1904, with a span of 250 feet; site of Battle of Hog Mountain, 1863.

CONSTITUTION HALL PARK corner of Gates Avenue and Franklin Street, Huntsville. An authentic reconstruction of twelve buildings that existed in the Huntsville of 1819, including Constitution Hall, where the first state constitution was ratified.

DOCTOR FRANCIS MEDICAL MUSEUM AND APOTHECARY 100 Gayle Street, Jacksonville. Contains medical supplies and surgical instruments of a country doctor from before the Civil War. Open by appointment only.

FENDALL HALL 917 West Barbour Street, Eufaula. Built in 1854 by a merchant and banker. Has Italian Villa elements and hand-stencilled interior. Open by appointment only.

FIRST WHITE HOUSE OF THE CONFEDERACY Union and Washington streets, Montgomery. Home of Jefferson Davis during the early days of the Confederacy, with many items from the Davis family.

FORT CONDE Royal Street, Mobile. Reconstructed French fort of the 1700s on the original site, with remnants of foundations and brick walls.

The center of French, British, and American activities in the area for 100 years.

FORT MORGAN *Mobile Point, near Gulf Shores.* Constructed 1833–1834, patterned after sixteenth-century fort designed by Michelangelo. Where Union Admiral David Farragut won a victory in the Civil War.

GORGAS HOUSE *University of Alabama campus, Tuscaloosa.* Built in 1829 as the college hotel. Now contains furniture and silver of the Gorgas family.

GOVERNOR'S MANSION *1142 South Perry Street, Montgomery.* Neoclassic Revival house.

HORSESHOE BEND NATIONAL MILITARY PARK *state 49, twelve miles north of Dadeville.* Where Andrew Jackson defeated the Creek Indians in 1814.

IVY GREEN *300 West North Commons, Tuscumbia.* Birthplace and museum of Helen Keller, with performances of *The Miracle Worker* in the summer.

KIRKWOOD *111 Kirkwood Drive, Eutaw.* Built just before the Civil War with an interesting combination of Italianate and Greek Revival elements; original furnishings. Open by appointment only.

MAGNOLIA GROVE *state 14, Greensboro.* An 1835 home that was the birthplace of Richmond Pearson Hobson, Spanish-American War hero.

MOUND STATE MONUMENT *state 69 at Moundville.* Reconstructed temple on site occupied A.D. 1000–1500; with twenty mounds.

MUSEUMS OF THE CITY OF MOBILE *355 Government Street, Mobile.* Comprehensive history of the region, including French, British, early American, Indian, and Civil War history, with decorative arts, fire-fighting equipment, Creole house.

OAKLEIGH *350 Oakleigh Place, Mobile.* Small antebellum Greek Revival house, built 1831–1832, in a historic district with many other fine buildings from the 1800s near the heart of the city.

OLD NORTH HULL HISTORIC DISTRICT *220 North Hull Street, Montgomery.* Recreated village of the 1800s, with a tavern, log cabins, church, and cottages, all furnished with period items.

REDSTONE TEST STAND *southwest of Huntsville on Dodd Road at Redstone Arsenal.* Rocket launch stand, built in 1953, where testing was done for first long-range firing of United States ballistic missile and first flight of an American in space; interpretive exhibit.

RUSSELL CAVE NATIONAL MONUMENT *eight miles west of U.S. 72 near Bridgeport.* Visitor center at cave where people from 7000 B.C. to A.D. 1000 stayed while hunting and farming.

SHOAL CREEK CHURCH *four miles northwest of Edwardsville, Forest Service Road 553.* Rare hand-hewn log church from the 1880s in Talladega National Forest. Exterior viewing only.

SLOSS BLAST FURNACE *First Avenue at 32nd Street, Birmingham.* Remains of a blast-furnace complex whose first parts were built in the 1880s; the oldest blast furnace in the area.

TANNEHILL HISTORICAL STATE PARK *3 miles east of I-59 at the Busksville exit between Birmingham and Tuscaloosa.* Site of major ironworks destroyed during the Civil War; also grist mill, pioneer homes, and other historic structures moved to park.

TUMBLING WATERS MUSEUM OF FLAGS *131 S. Perry Street, Montgomery.* Flags and banners from countries around the world.

TUSKEGEE INSTITUTE NATIONAL HISTORIC SITE *339 Old Montgomery Road, Tuskegee.* Includes George Washington Carver Museum, home of Booker T. Washington, and other buildings.

TWICKENHAM HISTORIC DISTRICT *bounded by Clinton and Hermitage avenues and Madison and California streets, Huntsville.* Residential houses dating from 1814 in the heart of the old city.

U.S. ARMY AVIATION MUSEUM *Building 6007, Fort Rucker.* Fixed- and rotary-wing aircraft and memorabilia.

WATER AVENUE HISTORIC DISTRICT *Water Avenue between Franklin and Lauderdale streets on the Alabama River, Selma.* A five-block area that reflects the different architectural styles of an antebellum riverfront street.

WHEELER HOME *state 565 three miles east of Courtland.* Home of Confederate Gen. Joe Wheeler. Has rare porcelain china.

WILSON DAM *state 133, Florence.* One of the earliest Tennessee Valley Authority dams.

ALASKA

SITKA NATIONAL HISTORICAL PARK Sitka. The history of relations between America and Russia is dominated by images from recent times. As the two superpowers, the United States and Soviet Russia have dominated world affairs since World War II. Each predominates in the other's vision of the world; each represents to the other a competing, different, and hostile way of life. This was not always so. For most of its history Russia was not Soviet, and for hundreds of years it was a land isolated by choice from the rest of the world. The United States was not even a nation until 1776, and not for decades more did it reach to the Pacific coast. Thus the historical probability was slight that these two nations should ever be thrown together as they are today. But there were earlier contacts.

During the 1770s and 1780s the Russia of Catherine the Great adopted maritime policies favorable to the struggling American colonies. The weak new nation on the other side of the world could not have figured very importantly in the minds of Russian policy makers. But the North American continent did. Part of it, the northwest Pacific Coast, was closer to Russia than to the thirteen fledgling states. The region seemed for a time a natural enough interest for Russia, and it also seemed for a time that the Russians had come there to stay.

Their interest was furs, that great fascination of eighteenth- and nineteenth-century Europeans. The search for them brought the Russians into contact with others with similar ideas (and with the Indians), and it eventually brought them to Sitka. The Alaskan coast had been sighted and claimed for Russia by Vitus Bering in 1741. Over the next decades Russian trading expeditions made regular calls in Alaska, and a permanent settlement of the Russian-American Company was established on Kodiak Island. From there the rich pelts of otter, beaver, marten, and mink were sent west, many to markets in China. It was a great age of political and economic empire-building and of competition for territory and influence among the great powers of Europe, and the extension of the Russian presence south to Sitka was part of that larger story.

Russia's agent in Alaska as the eighteenth century drew to a close was Alexander Baranov. An enterprising empire-builder who arrived at the Russian settlement at Three Saints Bay on Kodiak Island in 1791, Baranov determinedly subdued the competition and consolidated the position of the Russian-American Company. But he knew that Russian fur hunters were not alone in the North Pacific, and that if Russian profits and influence with the Indians were to be secured he must forestall further penetration northward by British and American traders and trappers. Thus he cast his eye on the Alexander Archipelago, west of the lower coast of modern Alaska, as a potential Russian buffer against the English-speaking trappers moving in from Charlotte Island to the south.

Trail to 1804 fort site and battleground

He made his first move in May 1799, taking a small expedition from Kodiak east to the site of Old Sitka. There he bargained for a building site with the local Tlingit chief, Katlean, and commenced building a fort. As he did so, the captain of an American trading ship anchored nearby in Sitka Sound warned Baranov to keep constantly alert for a Tlingit attack.

The warning was well-founded, for two years later St. Michael (as Old Sitka was called) was attacked and destroyed by the Tlingits. Baranov, who had left a deputy in charge, remained determined to regain Russia's foothold at Sitka. He succeeded in 1804. With fresh men and supplies from Siberia and with the added help of Russian naval vessels sent around the world from St. Petersburg, he returned to Sitka in force, arriving September 19. His immediate object was the substantial fort the Tlingit had built about eight miles south of St. Michael. The Sitka National Historical Park marks the site of the ensuing confrontation. Some 700 Tlingit took refuge in the fort and were well prepared to resist. Baranov first negotiated for their surrender and, failing, tried to take the place by storm. An assault by Baranov and 150 Russians, Aleuts, and Kodiaks failed dramatically: ten Russians were killed and Baranov himself was shot in the arm. Probably only the heavy guns on the naval vessels prevented another massacre. Bombardment and more negotiation followed, until during the night of October 6 the Tlingit slipped away and fled to the southern part of the island. The next day the Russians moved in, stripped the fort of valuables, and burned it to the ground.

Straightaway they began building a new Sitka, which they named New Archangel. This time they built to last, and over the years a prosperous and reasonably well-appointed trading town grew up. Around a central fort and barracks rose the warehouses that stored the rich piles of furs and of ivory from walrus herds that were Sitka's reason for being. Handsome private homes were built; five schools educated the young; a library and a museum sprang up in the Alaska wilderness. In 1836 a large mansion, locally known as Baranov Castle (though Baranov was long dead), rose on a prominent hilltop; ten years later appeared Sitka's most famous building: the Russian Orthodox Cathedral of St. Michael. Under the able guidance of Baranov and his successors, Sitka gained a wide reputation as the metropolis of the North Pacific. Americans, British, and other Europeans regularly called and traded there, and by the mid-nineteenth century even the Tlingit, whose fathers had fought Baranov in the Battle of Sitka, began to make their homes there. It all remained Russian until 1867 when the United States, now a reunited and truly continental power, purchased all of Alaska for $7.2 million. But Sitka did not become Americanized overnight, and to this day it bears reminders of its distinctive Russian colonial past.

The park itself occupies some 107 acres on Sitka Sound and the Indian River. Several miles of forest walkways connect a visitor center with the site of the Tlingit fort and the Battle of Sitka and, across the river, with the Russian Memorial. Adjacent to the park visitor center is the Southeast Alaska Indian Cultural Center, a workshop demonstration center where Tlingit artists demonstrate the skills and arts of their people. Perhaps the most famous artifacts of their culture are the totem poles, numerous examples of which dot the park. Stately cedar monuments standing up to eighty feet high, the poles served many purposes in Tlingit society and are today perhaps its most compelling monument. The poles are products of a subtle culture that over the years was urged to abandon much of its traditional way of life, and they are today sometimes difficult to interpret; the history and legend they record are lost with the people who carved them. But from their mystery comes much of their power.

The Russians knew about mystery too and left behind two especially notable monuments to their kind of faith in powers beyond themselves. The Russian Bishops' House (which has been elaborately restored) was pivotal in the work of the Orthodox Church during the years of Russian rule. It housed a consistory, school, and dormitory for the bishop's staff, the bishop's own residence and his chapel. Today it occupies a separate unit of the park. In the town of Sitka, St. Michael's Cathedral was the seat of the Orthodox diocese serving the vast Alaska-Bering Sea region. Though the original burned in 1966, the onion-domed church has been authentically reconstructed and is a living reminder of lasting Russian religious ties in an Americanized Alaska. Today the Russians are known by other images than icons and onion domes. Sitka preserves something of the time when those were their chief symbols for Americans.

KLONDIKE GOLD RUSH NATIONAL HISTORICAL PARK   *Skagway.* The nineteenth century was an adventurous time. In the western world it was a century of unprecedented economic growth and development. The Industrial Revolution—man's latest device for creating wealth from his own talents and nature's resources—swept across Europe and America. It brought at least the hope of prosperity to millions whose mere survival would barely have been possible in an essentially agricultural world. New nations, like Germany, were forged from old confederations. Others, like the United States, reaffirmed their political unity. Some, like Canada, created theirs. Empires dwarfing Caesar's and Alexander's embraced the world, Britain's above all. Whether cause or effect, enormous self-esteem accompanied such economic success and political competence. The cultural confidence of the western peoples was at its zenith. Never since have they manifested such exuberance; never since has their claim to power, wealth, and dominion been so undisputed.

The United States partook fully of this good fortune. Indeed, it was in the last decades of the century that America dramatically emerged as an economic giant and, though sometimes reluctant to admit it, a great power among the nations. The process of so becoming was filled with great adventures. History and legend tend to blur about some of them. But whether fact or fiction, they all have become part of the national heritage: the Pony Express, the building of the transcontinental railroad, the Indian wars, the building and rebuilding of Chicago, lumbering in the North Woods, cattle-ranching in the Southwest. It is a heritage also filled with great adventurers: Kit Carson, the mountain man; William F. Cody, better known as Buffalo Bill; George Armstrong Custer, remembered for his "last stand"; Jim Hill, the empire builder.

But there was one special kind of adventure that seemed to distill the exuberance and optimism of that most optimistic of centuries: the gold rush. Most of its adventurers did not become famous, and their names are lost to history. Their renown is collective. It was born at midcentury in California, where thousands of "Forty-Niners" hurried to make their fortunes. Through the next decades it grew continually as prospectors scampered over the West on the trail of the latest rumor of precious metal. Colorado, Nevada, Idaho, Montana, and South Dakota all felt their presence. Mining defined one of the West's several frontiers—which, like other frontiers, eventually settled down and became businesslike. But in its early stages, it attracted thousands who braved high risks in the hope of getting rich quick. One of their last chances came, fittingly, in the very last years of the century, and it brought them to the United States' last frontier: Alaska.

Gold had been discovered before in this far northern territory, purchased from Russia only in 1867. In 1880 a major strike brought thousands to the southeastern coast around Juneau. Another in 1886 brought miners to the Forty Mile River region straddling the Alaska-Yukon border. The early 1890s found them deep in Alaska's interior, on Birch Creek, some 240 miles down the Yukon River from Forty Mile. In the greatest of the Alaska gold rushes, ironically, the gold lay not in Alaska at all, but in Canada. Getting to it, however, meant getting first to Alaska. Gold was discovered in 1896 on a tributary of the Klondike River in Canada's Yukon Territory, and by the next summer one of the world's greatest gold rushes was on. Nature had seldom put gold in places especially easy to get to, but in this instance she could hardly have found a place more remote or better suited to testing the strength of would-be argonauts. Dawson City was their goal, and it lay 600 long miles inland in Canada's far North.

There were three routes. The easiest and most expensive (and the least traveled) was by water, from Seattle or San Francisco northwest across the Pacific, into the Bering Sea to St. Michael. From there, river steamers chugged up the mighty Yukon River to Dawson. There was also an all-land route from the northwestern United States through British Columbia and the Northwest Territories, but it was so tortuous that relatively few who started ever reached the gold fields. The great majority of gold seekers (20,000 to 30,000 in the first year alone) trekked over the Chilkoot and White Pass trails in southeastern Alaska, and even there they encountered hardships such as few had ever known before. On the way they created two roaring boom towns in Skagway and Dyea, which bore all the marks of places that existed because they were on the way to someplace else. When the stampeders finally reached their destination, fulfilled dreams and blasted hopes apportioned themselves about as they had in other gold fields.

Today the Klondike Gold Rush National Historical Park preserves the physical setting that greeted the gold seekers years ago. Its many sites now draw thousands seeking treasures other than gold. At the end of their voyage from America's west coast, ships bearing the hopeful sailed up Taya Inlet to dock at Skagway or its rival, Dyea, nine miles farther north. Dyea has vanished; the railroad to White Pass, completed by the turn of the century, passed it by. All that remain of Dyea, the jumping-off point for the arduous Chilkoot Trail, are a few foundations, the rotting stumps of its once-extensive wharves, and a cemetery containing sixty victims of an avalanche long ago. Skagway survives and prospers, offering in its historic district a glimpse of what an Alaska boomtown was like during the gold rush. The town is small, and a walking tour reveals it best. Numerous buildings date from the turn of the century, including the depot and general offices of the White Pass and Yukon Route Railroad, the Pacific Clipper Line office, the city hall and museum, and the Pantheon and Mascot saloons. The old Arctic Brotherhood Hall

Mascot Saloon

serves as the park's visitor center and is a good place to start a tour.

But Skagway was just the beginning. Once a prospector had bought his kit, he set out for Lake Lindeman or Lake Bennett on the other side of the Coast Range of mountains. From there he still had to float and paddle the 560 or so remaining miles to the Klondike and gold. Deceptively short—just thirty-three miles—that first leg of the journey was a back-breaker and a heart-breaker. The hopeful trudged back and forth, for a total of hundreds of miles, in order to get the required year's worth of supplies up to the lakes. There were two trails connecting the tidewater with the lakes: the White Pass from Skagway and the more famous Chilkoot from Dyea. The Chilkoot Trail is maintained for hikers by the United States and Canadian national park services as part of the Klondike Gold Rush historical park. For the fit and well-equipped visitor, a hike along its thirty-three-mile length is probably the best way to recapture the experience of the long-vanished gold seekers. The trip takes an average of three days and is not easy. From sea level it rises at Chilkoot Pass to some 3,700 feet, and the final ascent between Scales and the summit rises at a grade of forty-five degrees. The summit also marks the international boundary. Here the Royal Northwest Mounted Police (the legendary red-coated "Mounties") enforced the requirement that stampeders carry with them into the Yukon a year's supply of food, a regulation that kept many from starving once they reached the gold fields.

There is another, less arduous but still historic, way over the mountains. In 1899 the White Pass and Yukon Route Railroad was completed between Skagway and Bennett, British Columbia, over White Pass; a year later it reached White Horse in Yukon Territory. Today the trains still run, carrying passengers, freight, and automobiles through some of Alaska's and Canada's most magnificent scenery. There are few such train rides left, which makes this one—as befits the great nineteenth-century adventure that gave birth to the line itself—an adventure too. No one, of course, goes north from Skagway anymore to pan for gold and get rich quick. Today's adventures take other forms, and it is not likely that men will confront one like this ever again.

INDEPENDENCE MINE STATE PARK *Hatcher Pass.* Accounts of gold mining in Alaska all too often center on the dramatic placer strikes and colorful gold-rush years at the close of the nineteenth century and ignore subsequent expansion and development of the mining industry during the first half of the twentieth century. Although placer deposits were worked out early, hard-rock gold mining remained profitable for decades despite the substantial capital required for the more complex and expensive process. Typical of the later large-scale operations was the Alaska-Pacific Consolidated Mining Company, which owned both the Independence and the Alaska Free Gold mines in the Willow Creek district. The Independence Mine State Historic Park preserves the remnants of the company's operations and offers a unique opportunity to learn about hard rock gold mining and the men who worked the rich lodes of south-central Alaska.

The Willow Creek mining district encompasses about fifty square miles along the southern border of the Talkeetna Mountains. Placer deposits were discovered in the region at the turn of the century, but mining activity proved relatively unprofitable during the famous Klondike gold rush era. The mountains' rich veins of ore were not discovered until 1906, when Lee Hatcher staked the first lode claim at what was to become the Alaska Free Gold mine. The following year Eugene and William Barthoff discovered another lode on the east slope of Granite Mountain—the future Independence mine. The ore from these finds proved exceedingly rich, with assay values ten times higher than those from the larger Juneau mines. As word spread, fortune hunters moved into the remote area. They staked twenty-four mines and prospects in the Willow Creek region between 1906 and 1916.

Despite the numerous claims, only five mines actually began producing gold during that first decade. The explanation for this lack of activity was simple: few could afford the expense entailed in mining the gold-bearing quartz veins located deep in bedrock. While individuals with little capital could undertake placer mining, hard rock mining required expensive tunnels, tramways, and processing plants. Cooperative efforts proved necessary, and small companies began combining efforts to work neighboring claims. The next step was even larger companies that consolidated numerous claims and undertook efficient, large-scale mining.

Thus the Barthoff brothers sold their Independence claims in 1908 to a group of Oklahoma capitalists, who began operations as the Alaska

Independence mining camp

Gold Quartz Mining Company. The company installed the district's first stamp mill that same year and continued to expand mining facilities and operations until 1914, when the property was sold to the Independence Gold Mining Company. The latter operated only until 1917 and then shut down. The mine remained inactive until 1920, when the Kelly Mining Company leased it. In 1924 the mine shut down again and remained closed until the mid-1930s, when Alaska-Pacific Mines, Inc., reactivated mining operations. The level of activity and production hinged on the current gold market. When prices fell, mines closed and production dropped. And when prospects improved, as they did in 1933, mining operations expanded. By 1936, when Alaska-Pacific began consolidating claims, the district had produced over ten tons of gold valued at more than seven million dollars. Several maneuvers, mergers, and transactions followed, and in 1937 the Alaska-Pacific Consolidated Mining Company emerged as the owner of both the Independence and the Alaska Free Gold (which had been owned since 1912 by the Alaska Free Gold Mining Company). This new company became the largest producing lode gold mining operation in the district, the second largest in Alaska, and the eleventh largest in the United States. The new company's peak production year came in 1941, when the consolidated Independence mines produced 48,194 ounces of gold worth $1,686,790.

The two hundred men who operated the Independence during that time lived in what many considered to be the finest mining camp in the district. For single miners, the company provided bunkhouses with heating, plumbing, and electricity—unheard-of luxuries in many camps at that time. Other amenities included a recreation room, a library, and a movie room. Miners with families were allowed to build homes nearby in "Boom Town" or Independence Village, and their children attended a company school. Managers and foremen also had appropriate accommodations. A mess hall completed in 1941 included not only a kitchen and dining hall but also a bakery, scullery, and butcher shop. The camp even had its own store. In short, Alaska-Pacific built a self-sufficient community to support its extensive mining and milling operations.

The company's expansion was cut short by World War II and the War Production Board's decision that gold mining was non-essential. Although the board closed most mines, the Independence was allowed to remain open because of the presence of scheelite, a tungsten ore used in making tool steel. Controversy arose about the scheelite operations, however, and in 1943 the mine was virtually closed down. After the war Alaska-Pacific tried to resume operations, but in January 1951 the Independence closed for good. The company retained ownership of the property until the 1970s, when it went into receivership. After several years of negotiation, the state of Alaska secured title to the site in January 1980 and established the Independence Mine State Historic Park, encompassing 271 of the company's original 1,350 surface acres.

Visitors to the park today can view exhibits on hard-rock gold mining and take a walking tour of the Independence mill site. The latter encompasses a variety of structures dating from between 1936 and 1941, some still in sound condition but others collapsed. Included are the "new" bunk house, the "old" bunk house, the timber shed, warehouse, remnants of the "old" mess hall, the administrative offices/commissary, the "new" mess hall, the apartment building, plumbing/sheet metal shops, and the collapsed mill. Interpretive signs tell the story of the Independence's mining and milling operations and daily life in a hard rock mining camp. Located about ten miles north of the cities of Wasilla and Palmer, Independence Mine State Historic Park preserves an important chapter in the history of modern-day Alaska.

ALASKA HISTORICAL AND TRANSPORTATION MUSEUM *Glenn Highway, Mile 40.2, Palmer.* Antique planes, kayaks, dog sleds, mine railroad cars, and other transportation equipment.
ALASKA INDIAN ARTS *22 Fort Seward, Haines.* Living village with Tlingit costumes, art, and dance recitals.
ALASKA STATE MUSEUM *Juneau.* Alaskan history from 100 B.C. to the present, including maritime, Russian, industrial, and natural history.
ANCHORAGE HISTORICAL AND FINE ARTS MUSEUM *121 W. Seventh Avenue, Anchorage.* Art and artifacts from Alaska history, including

material on Eskimo, Aleut, Tlingit, and Athabascan crafts and Russian-American art and architecture.

***BALLAINE HOUSE** 437 Third Avenue, Seward.* The residence of Frank L. Ballaine, founder of the community of Seward and central figure in the creation of the Alaska Central Railway; built in 1905.

***CAPE NOME ROADHOUSE** Nome-Council Highway east of Nome at Mile 14.* Loghouse built during Nome Gold Rush and stop-over for dog teams traveling between Nome and Fairbanks; used as store, orphanage, FAA station. Privately owned.

***CAPE ST. ELIAS LIGHTHOUSE** Kayak Island south of Katalla.* Two-story light and signal station, built in 1915–1916 and still in use.

***CHURCH OF THE ASSUMPTION OF THE VIRGIN MARY** east shore of Cook Inlet, Kenai.* Russian Orthodox mission church built between 1894 and 1896; with front tower and metal onion dome.

***CHURCH OF THE HOLY ASCENSION AND BISHOP'S HOUSE** Unalaska, Aleutian Islands.* Central portion of the church dates from 1825–1826 and is a fine example of nineteenth-century church built on cruciform plan; Bishop's House also restored.

***CIRCLE DISTRICT HISTORICAL MUSEUM** 128 Mile Steese Highway, Central.* Materials on mining, farming, lumbering, native life, and pioneer life.

***DUNCAN'S COTTAGE** Fifth Avenue and Atkinson Street, Metlakatla, Annette Island.* Built about 1891 for Anglican missionary who founded a cooperative.

***EAGLE HISTORIC DISTRICT** Eagle.* More than 100 buildings of the 1800s and 1900s, including remains of Fort Egbert, log houses, and stores with false fronts.

***ERSKINE HOUSE** near Main and Mission Road, Kodiak.* Built about 1793 by Alexander Baranov as fur-storage and office building; called the oldest Russian building in the United States.

***FORT ST. NICHOLAS (FORT REDOUBT) SITE** Kenai.* Site where Russians built a fur-trading post in 1791.

***FORT YUKON** 140 miles northeast of Fairbanks in interior Alaska, one mile north of the Arctic Circle.* Founded in 1847 by Hudson's Bay Company; called oldest English-speaking settlement in Alaska; now a trading post famous for native crafts and furs.

***GOVERNOR'S MANSION** 716 Calhoun Street, Juneau.* Built 1912–1913, first public building erected after Juneau became permanent capital.

***HERITAGE MUSEUM OF THE ARCTIC** Kotzebue.* An Eskimo museum with arts, crafts, and artifacts; daily show during the summer.

***IMMACULATE CONCEPTION CHURCH** 115 North Cushman, Fairbanks.* Wooden church dating from 1904, still in use.

***IPIUTAK NATIONAL HISTORIC LANDMARK** next to Point Hope.* Remains of large Eskimo community at zenith, about A.D. 300, with burial area and ruins of log and stone buildings.

(THE) KINK east of Fairbanks on the north fork of Fortymile River.
Remains of a mining camp and channel blasted through rock, forcing
kink in river.

KNIK SITE about fifteen miles southwest of Wasilla on Knik Road. Frame
building erected between 1898 and 1911 and used as a roadhouse and
store; with a museum.

*LAST CHANCE MINING MUSEUM AND HISTORICAL PARK end of
Basin Road, Juneau.* Tools and equipment from the gold mine days;
includes a 1912 Alaska-Juneau Gold Mining building.

NENANA Alaskaland, Fairbanks. Sternwheel riverboat built in 1933;
restoration in process.

RAINEY'S CABIN University of Alaska Campus, Fairbanks. One-story
log house with rear cache elevated on poles for food storage; built in
1936 for first professor of anthropology at the university.

*SAINT NICHOLAS RUSSIAN ORTHODOX CHURCH 326 Fifth Street,
Juneau.* Octagonal structure with onion dome; built in 1893 for Indian
converts.

SHAKES ISLAND HISTORIC SITE Wrangell harbor. Island reached by
footbridge from mainland, with replica of Tlingit Tribal House of the
Bear and 200-year-old totems.

SHELDON JACKSON MUSEUM Sitka. Tlingit, Haida, Eskimo, and Athabascan items, including fine collection of masks and canoes and kayaks.

SHELDON MUSEUM AND CULTURAL CENTER Haines. Includes
Indian art, Eskimo carvings, and items from pioneer days.

*SKAGWAY HISTORIC DISTRICT AND WHITE PASS head of Taiya
Inlet on Lynn Canal, Skagway area.* Mining town from late 1800s, with
railroad depot and narrow-gauge railway through pass.

TALKEETNA HISTORICAL MUSEUM Talkeetna. Old mining equipment, Alaskan art, and photos of early Alaska, housed in an old schoolhouse.

THOMAS MEMORIAL LIBRARY 901 First Avenue, Fairbanks. Log
building erected 1909 for early Anglican missionaries.

*TONGASS HISTORICAL SOCIETY MUSEUM 629 Dock Street, Ket-
chikan.* Artifacts from Tlingit, Haida, and Tsimshian cultures, as well as
history of mining, fishing, and logging industries.

*TOTEM BIGHT STATE HISTORIC SITE on Tongass Highway ten miles
north of Ketchikan.* Replica of a nineteenth-century chief's house, with
collection of Haida and Tlingit totems.

TOTEM VILLAGE Port Chilkoot. Replicas of a Chilkat tribal house and
of a trapper's cabin, with several totems.

UNIVERSITY OF ALASKA MUSEUM University of Alaska, Fairbanks.
General museum with anthropology and other exhibits on early human
life.

VALDEZ HERITAGE CENTER Valdez. Excellent displays on the history of Valdez, the Richardson Highway, and the surrounding area.

WASILLA MUSEUM AND HISTORICAL PARK   *Wasilla.*   Museum housed in original Wasilla Community Hall; exhibits on gold mining and the Alaska Railroad.

WICKERSHAM HOUSE *213 Seventh Street, Juneau.* An 1899 clapboard house that was the home of James V. Wickersham, early judge and territorial delegate and the man who introduced the first Alaska statehood bill into Congress; with a museum.

YUGTARVIK-REGIONAL MUSEUM *Bethel.* Artifacts of the Yupik Eskimos, with authentic Eskimo arts and crafts for sale.

ARIZONA

MISSION SAN XAVIER DEL BAC Santa Cruz Valley, route 11 nine miles south of Tucson. Despite the significant cultural changes that accompanied the United States' acquisition of the region over a century and a quarter ago, present-day Arizona still reflects strongly the influence of its earlier Indian, Spanish, and Mexican inhabitants. One of the most notable symbols of this heritage is Mission San Xavier del Bac, located in the Santa Cruz Valley nine miles south of Tucson. Established by Father Eusebio Francisco Kino in 1700 to serve the largest community of Pima Indians in the region, San Xavier testifies to the centrality of Jesuit and Franciscan missionary activity to the exploration and settlement of the Spanish Southwest.

No other individual proved as central to the development of the Southwest as Father Kino, an Italian Jesuit assigned by his order to do missionary work among the region's Indians. Kino arrived in Mexico in the early 1680s and in 1683 embarked upon his first missionary expedition to Baja California. Efforts to establish colonies at La Paz and San Bruno failed, but the priest remained intrigued by the potential of the California region even after he turned his attention to Pimería Alta, a region that included Sonora in northern Mexico and part of present-day Arizona. Moving west in 1687 from the Spanish outpost at Cucurpe, Kino first established the mission of Nuestra Señora de los Dolores at the village of Cosari and over the next two and a half decades built a seventy-five-mile chain of missions that dramatically pushed back the Spanish frontier. While Christianizing the Pima Indians remained his central purpose, Kino also promoted agricultural development and worked to establish an alliance among the various tribes of the region. Rumors of his ambitions caused occasional concern, but reviewers sent by the church found the Jesuit's work in Pimería Alta impressive.

In 1697 the church granted Kino's request to expand his missionary activities into California. Over the next fourteen years he made a series of *entradas* into the region to the west, making contact with the Indian inhabitants and exploring new routes. But the northernmost of Father Kino's mission chain was Mission San Xavier del Bac, established in 1700 at the most populous Pima Indian settlement in Pimería Alta. Kino laid the original church's foundation and named it San Xavier in honor of St. Francis Xavier, his patron saint. Although he reportedly planned for Bac to be the base for his western entradas, he never moved his headquarters from Dolores. One particularly significant event took place at the mission, however. In 1700 Kino convened there the "Blue Shell Conference," a meeting of Indian chiefs to determine the origin of blue abalone shells given to the Jesuit during his travels. Kino concluded that the shells came from the Pacific and had been traded hand to hand from California to Pimería Alta. This ran counter to earlier assumptions

San Xavier Mission, ca. 1910

that California was an island and inspired a series of expeditions that took the priest as far west as the Colorado River and demonstrated the feasibility of a land route to California. These arduous trips across the desert Southwest consumed most of Kino's time during the last decade of his life. Even incomplete records indicate he traveled over eight thousand miles on horseback during this period. His last trip ended in March 1711 at Magdalena, where he stopped to dedicate a new chapel to St. Francis Xavier. While celebrating mass, the revered priest fell ill; he died on March 15.

Mission San Xavier del Bac languished for two decades after Kino's death. It did not even have a resident missionary until 1732, when Father Philip Segesser, a Swedish priest, accepted the assignment. His stay was relatively brief, however, and it was 1740 before San Xavier had a priest in residence for even a full year. The mission limped along in this fashion for decades. Then after the Pima rebellion ended in 1751 and the Spanish government garrisoned the presidio at nearby Tubac, activity at the mission increased dramatically. This revival proved rather short-lived, however, for in 1767 King Charles III expelled the Jesuit order from all Spanish territories. San Xavier del Bac survived, but under the control of the Franciscans, who took over their predecessors' work by 1768.

After an Apache raid destroyed the old Jesuit complex, the Franciscans decided to relocate about two miles from the site of Kino's original church and between 1783 and 1797 erected the present mission structure. The architect and artisans are unknown, but the mission reflects an exceptionally fine blending of Moorish, Byzantine, and late Mexican Renaissance styles. Constructed of burned adobe brick and lime plaster, the structure features a Latin Cross plan, a pair of octagonal towers resting on two-story square bases, a high, central dome, and an elaborately detailed portal. Rich reredos and frescoes decorate the interior. So exceptional is this structure that it is considered perhaps the finest example of Spanish mission architecture in the United States.

Although secularized by Spain in 1813 and abandoned by the fathers during the Mexican regime, Mission San Xavier del Bac was reoccupied by the Franciscans in 1857, after the Arizona territory had been annexed to the United States. The "White Dove of the Desert" remains today an active parish, with a predominantly Indian congregation, and a living symbol of Arizona's mission heritage.

BISBEE MINING AND HISTORICAL MUSEUM *5 Copper Queen Plaza, Bisbee.* The discovery of copper in Arizona in the late nineteenth century fueled the territory's economic development and influenced the region's political and social life for nearly a century. The undisputed corporate leader during copper's long reign was the Phelps Dodge Company, whose Copper Queen Mine at Bisbee was Arizona's richest and most productive operation. The company's former headquarters still stands today in Bisbee as a monument to this industry and its impact on modern Arizona history.

The Phelps Dodge Company's roots lay in the mercantile economy that prospered along the Atlantic seaboard in the early nineteenth century. By the 1850s it had become a leading New York mercantile house and the largest importer of metals (primarily tin and tin plate) in the United States. Without yielding its recognized leadership in the export-import trade, Phelps Dodge then began to shift capital acquired in its commercial ventures into manufacturing, railroads, timber, and other enterprises designed to take advantage of the United States' expanding economy in the last half of the nineteenth century. For example, the firm became a leading supplier of copper wire, tin cans, and other metal wares basic to the technological advances of the post-Civil War period. Then in the 1880s Phelps Dodge underwent a basic reorientation, embarking upon one of the first copper-mining ventures in Arizona— and thereby moving into the mainstream of the new industrialized economy and helping lead the way in expansion of the trans-Mississippi West. The company's copper venture eventually led to a total cessation of all its earlier mercantile activities and a shift of its major interests nearly three-fourths of the way across the continent.

The man most responsible for the company's new direction was James Douglas, a Canadian metallurgist and mining engineer and later president of Phelps Dodge's mining enterprises. Phelps Dodge executives had discussed the newly found copper resources in Arizona with the owners of the Clifton-Morenci mine, the first copper mine to be developed in the state (1877). But it was Douglas' reports on the Arizona copper mines and his enthusiasm about the potentials of the Bisbee area that persuaded the company to make its initial investment in 1881.

The first copper discovery in the Bisbee area had been made as early as 1875, but no claim was actually established until 1877, when an army scout named Jack Dunn staked out what later became known as the Copper Queen Mine. Before the end of the decade the title passed into the hands of a group of San Francisco financiers, who began active mining in 1880 as the Copper Queen Mining Company. Douglas convinced Phelps Dodge to buy the adjoining Atlanta claim in 1881, but by

Former Phelps Dodge headquarters

1884 it was evident that continuing conflicts over mineral rights and boundaries would hinder full exploitation of the evidently rich copper deposits. Consequently, in 1885 a merger was accomplished under the auspices of Phelps, Dodge, and Company, and the legendary Copper Queen Consolidated Mining Company came into being.

Phelps Dodge's Copper Queen venture marked the beginning of the great Arizona copper mining era. Individual mining operations simply could not equal the scope of this corporate undertaking, which called for expanding existing mining operations, authorizing intensive exploration, constructing and enlarging smelters, and purchasing other properties. The corporation's influence and power were formidable. For example, when faced by the reluctance of both the Southern Pacific Railroad and the Atchison, Topeka, and Santa Fe Railroad to construct the connecting tracks essential for economical transportation of newly mined copper, Phelps, Dodge, and Company simply constructed its own line. By 1924, when it finally sold out to the Southern Pacific, the company had built nearly 1,200 miles of track, with connections to three transcontinental American railroads and two major Mexican lines. Phelps Dodge's influence was fully evident in the town of Bisbee as well. Before 1885 Bisbee had been a typical rowdy western mining camp; after Phelps Dodge moved in, it became a company town, presided over by the Phelps Dodge General Office Building constructed in the heart of the town in 1895. The company's determination to dominate the mining area and the town became most pronounced in its opposition to labor organization and its support of the Bisbee Deportation, a notorious violation of civil liberties that received wide publicity throughout the country. On July 12, 1917, 1,186 men, reputedly members of the Industrial Workers of the World, were rounded up by the sheriff and a group of citizens, put in Phelps Dodge boxcars, hauled into the desert, and denied reentrance to the town. The clout of the company was never more clearly illustrated.

The focus of Phelps, Dodge, and Company on its copper mining and refining operations became even more evident in 1906, when the firm publicly ceased its trade activities after a final shipment of tin from England. Recognizing the potential profits from the new age of electricity, the firm focused its full attention on the Arizona copper industry, which in the next year took the lead in domestic production of the metal. In the years after World War I, the company expanded its operations further and acquired such former competitors as Calumet and Arizona in 1931. Ever aware of the necessity of maintaining new sources, Phelps Dodge also turned to new methods for extracting copper from the remaining low-grade ores, most notably in the strip-mining operations at Sacramento Hill and the Lavender Pit in Arizona. By 1950, the company was considered one of the "Big Four" copper producers responsible for mining 90 percent of the United States' copper. But as copper prices declined and new sources opened up in South America and Africa, further operations at the Copper Queen became unprofitable, and in 1975 the mines were closed.

The Phelps Dodge General Office Building still stands on Queen's Plaza as it did during the peak years of mining activity. The two-story, red brick, gable-roofed structure housed the company's offices for sixty-six years after its construction in 1895, but in the 1970s the Bisbee Council on the Arts and Humanities assumed control of the historic structure. Now restored to its early twentieth-century appearance, the building houses the Bisbee Mining and Historical Museum. Visitors can view the restored and furnished general manager's office, a collection of old mining equipment donated by Phelps Dodge, and a series of exhibits and dioramas that depict the history of the Arizona mining industry.

Located at the entrance to Bisbee's famed Brewery Gulch, the old office is one of several structures that remain from the copper mining era. Particularly notable is the nearby Copper Queen Hotel, built by the company in 1902 and now also restored. Visitors to Bisbee can also visit the Mulheim Heritage House, the former home of an important saloon keeper and mining entrepreneur, and arrange for tours of nearby mining operations. The "Queen of the Mining Camps" offers a variety of opportunities to learn more about this era in the state's history. None, however, surpass the Phelps Dodge General Office Building as a symbol of the industry and its far-reaching impact on the Arizona experience.

SALT RIVER PROJECT *Sylva House Museum, 628 E. Adams, Phoenix.* Water—or the lack thereof—has played a major role in the Arizona experience. Nowhere is this more evident than in the central part of the state around Phoenix. The harnessing of the Salt and Verde rivers in the late nineteenth and early twentieth centuries made possible the development of this once drought-stricken region into one of the nation's most productive agricultural centers. Now decidedly more urban and industrial, the greater Phoenix area still depends on the water and hydroelectric power provided by the Salt River Project, which operates the historic Roosevelt Dam, completed in 1911, and the other facilities in the massive reclamation development. As part of its service to the region, the SRP operates a History Center and the Sylva House Museum, both dedicated to telling the story of the valley's dramatic transformation.

The Salt River Valley encompasses nearly a half-million acres in central Arizona. While the valley's alluvial soil had significant agricultural potential, the semi-arid climate and irregular rainfall hindered development. The ancient Hohokam people apparently began irrigation efforts as early as 200 B.C. and eventually dug as many as 250 miles of canals before they mysteriously abandoned the region about 1400 A.D. Traces of those early canals remained visible over four and a half centuries later, when John W. "Jack" Swilling arrived in the Salt River Valley. Always on the lookout for a profitable opportunity, Swilling recognized the region's potential and in 1867 organized the Swilling Irrigating and Canal Company. During the winter of 1867–68, he and sixteen other men dug the first modern irrigation canal in the valley. The first crops were planted that spring, and by the following fall the community of Phoenix numbered one hundred.

Development of the Salt River region proceeded rapidly over the next decades. A second canal, the Maricopa, was dug in 1868, followed by the San Francisco in 1820, the Tempe in 1871, the Grand and the Mesa in 1878, the Arizona in 1883, and the Highland in 1888. In the late 1880s, the Arizona Improvement Company began consolidating canals on the north side of the river into a more unified system, and a similar effort unified the southside canals in the next decade. Construction of this elaborate delivery network dramatically increased the valley's productive potential. Only 600 acres were farmed in 1868, but new canal

Roosevelt Dam

construction made it possible to bring more and more acreage under cultivation. By 1870, 1,800 acres were being farmed; that increased to 8,100 by 1872 and jumped to over 100,000 by 1888.

Although the valley had made impressive gains in just three decades, major obstacles remained. For one thing, conflicting claims to water rights and time-consuming litigation hindered full development of the region's potential. Even more serious, however, was the lack of a stable water supply. Both floods and droughts plagued the valley. The solution was obvious: dams that would hold back flood waters in reservoirs until the inevitable dry years. Early brush and rock constructions had proved worthless, however, easily washed away by high water. In 1900, after three straight drought-ridden winters, the Maricopa County Board of Trade established a committee to study the water storage problem. Two opposing views emerged. One group, headed by Territorial Governor Nathan O. Murphy, emphasized the need for local authority over any irrigation and land reclamation project and vehemently opposed relinquishing control to the federal government. On the other side were Benjamin A. Fowler, head of the committee, and other advocates of federal reclamation. Their proposal was that the federal government take charge of the project using funds from the sale of public lands. This plan gained several influential supporters, including George Maxwell of the National Irrigation Association, Representative Francis G. Newlands of Nevada, and President Theodore Roosevelt. Their combined efforts led to the National Reclamation Act of 1902.

With passage of the Reclamation Act, plans for local development were abandoned, and county leaders turned to the task of meeting federal guidelines. Since Washington would not deal with individual landowners, the Salt River Valley Water Users' Association was incorporated on February 7, 1903. This association mediated conflicting differences between landowners, took care of assessments to repay the construction debt, and handled negotiations with the U.S. Reclamation Service. On June 25, 1904, officials representing both Arizona and the federal government signed an agreement for the first multipurpose reclamation project authorized under the 1902 act.

The project centered on the construction of a high dam across the Salt River. An 1889 surveying team had located a likely site just above the junction of the river and Tonto Creek, the federal engineers concurred in that selection for the new project. Construction began by 1904 and proceeded for seven years under the supervision of Louis C. Hill. When completed in 1911, the 280-foot-high structure was the world's highest masonry dam. On March 18 of that year, the dam was dedicated by former President Theodore Roosevelt, for whom it was named.

By that time, the question of prior water rights had also been solved. The Kent Decree of 1910, issued by the Chief Justice of the Territory, determined the relative water rights and priorities of the valley landowners/water users. This decree still constitutes the basis of the service area's right to the water from the Salt and Verde watershed.

In 1917, the Salt River Valley Water Users' Association took over the operation of the Salt River Project. Subsequent developments have included the construction of new dams on both the Salt and the Verde and significant expansion of the project's hydroelectric generating capacity. Reorganization in 1937 established the Salt River Project Agricultural Improvement and Power District, and it and the older Association together operate the Salt River Project.

At its administration building on Project Drive in Tempe, the Salt River Project's History Center provides exhibits on irrigation projects from the Hohokam era through the early twentieth century. The SRP also operates the Sylva House Museum at 628 E. Adams in Phoenix. This Victorian structure, erected around 1900, houses exhibits on the history of water and irrigation in the region in the twentieth century. Of particular interest is a room furnished to depict a Salt River Valley Water Users' Association office in the early 1900s. Together these facilities offer the visitor the opportunity to learn more about the nation's oldest water reclamation project and its central role in the dramatic growth and development of twentieth-century Arizona.

AMERIND FOUNDATION Dragoon. Archeology and ethnology museum with exhibits on the Southwest, Mexico, Great Plains, Eastern Woodlands, California, and Arctic.

ARIZONA HERITAGE CENTER 949 E. Second Street, Tucson. Exhibits on Spanish Colonial, Mexican, and American military periods of state history; with a mining hall showing how copper ore is dug, smelted, and refined.

ARIZONA STATE MUSEUM University of Arizona, Tucson. Collections of Indian arts and crafts as well as manuscripts and other materials on the Southwest.
CANYON de CHELLY off state 63 at Chinle. Where the Anasazi lived a thousand years ago. The epitome of the cliff dwelling.
CASA GRANDE state 87 two miles north of Coolidge. A multistory rammed-adobe structure with an uncertain use and unknown builders; probably dating from 1100s or 1200s, possibly a temple or granary.
CENTRAL ARIZONA MUSEUM 1242 N. Central, Phoenix. Items displaying history of the state and of central Arizona in particular, including clothing, toys, photos, and other material on farming, transportation, business, and ethnic life.
CENTURY HOUSE MUSEUM 240 S. Madison Ave., Yuma. Collections related to the history of Yuma and the Colorado River.
COLORADO RIVER INDIAN TRIBES MUSEUM Parker. Exhibits on the Mojave, Chemehuevi, Navajo, and Hopi as well as earlier Mogollon, Anasazi, Hohokam, and Patayan.
CORONADO NATIONAL MEMORIAL off state 92 thirty miles west of Bisbee. Notes the approximate point of entry into present Arizona of the Spanish explorer in 1540. Includes a museum.
EL TOVAR south rim of Grand Canyon, Grand Canyon National Park. One of the most famous tourist hotels in America, built in 1905 of Douglas fir and Coconino sandstone.
FORT VERDE STATE HISTORIC PARK Camp Verde. Restored officers' quarters and administrative building of a fort active in the Indian wars, 1866–1891; with artifacts from military days in a museum.
HEARD MUSEUM 22 E. Monte Vista Road, Phoenix. Anthropology and art museum with exhibits on North American Indians as well as primitive people from Africa, Asia, Oceania, and the Amazon.
HUBBELL TRADING POST Ganado. An active trading post established in 1876; with historic buildings from the 1800s and early 1900s as well as Indian arts and crafts.
JEROME city of Jerome. A ghost town come to life, with preservationists and arts and crafts lovers at work where copper miners lived in the late 1800s and early 1900s.
JUDAICA MUSEUM OF TEMPLE BETH ISRAEL 3310 N. Tenth Avenue, Phoenix. Art and ritual items from the seventeenth century in the temple of the oldest congregation of Jews in Phoenix.
MESA MUSEUM OF HISTORY AND ARCHAEOLOGY 53 N. Macdonald, Mesa. Exhibits on early Indians and settlers of Mesa and east valley.
MUSEUM OF NORTHERN ARIZONA Fort Valley Road, Flagstaff. Natural history museum with Indian and southwestern art and crafts; particularly fine collection of Hopi artifacts and literature.
NAVAJO NATIONAL MONUMENT off state 64 thirty-two miles southwest of Kayenta. Large cliff dwellings built in the thirteenth century—

Betatakin, with 135 rooms, Keet Seel, 350 rooms, and Inscription House, 75 rooms.

NAVAJO TRIBAL MUSEUM *Window Rock.* Navajo history, arts, crafts, and artifacts.

NORTHERN ARIZONA PIONEERS HISTORICAL MUSEUM *Fort Valley Road, Flagstaff.* Includes materials related to astronomer Percival Lowell, the movie cameras and photos of the Kolb brothers' first trip down the Colorado, history of Oak Creek and other areas near to Flagstaff.

OLD MAIN *University of Arizona campus, Tucson.* First building of the new (1885) university, of eclectic design, completed in 1891.

OLD ORAIBI *state 264 three miles west of Oraibi.* Mesa pueblo of Hopis since about 1150; vying with Acoma pueblo in New Mexico as oldest continuously occupied site in North America.

PAINTED DESERT INN *west of Navajo in Petrified Forest National Park.* Rubble and stucco house built for the National Park Service by the Civilian Conservation Corps, with art by Hopi artist Fred Kabott.

PIONEER ARIZONA *I-17 and Pioneer Road, Phoenix.* Living history museum with homes and shops of 1800s showing Arizona pioneer life and farming.

PIPE SPRING *off U.S. 89 fifteen miles southwest of Fredonia.* Mormon outpost established in 1863 in the Arizona Strip, still with strong ties to Utah.

PUEBLO GRANDE RUIN *Pueblo Grande City Park, Phoenix.* Hohokam building, on the Salt River, from between A.D. 900 and 1450, showing significance of water to the culture of all Arizonians.

SHARLOT HALL MUSEUM *415 West Gurley Street, Prescott.* Material on the history of early Arizona, including medicine, mineralogy, and information on several historic buildings: Old Governor's Mansion, log cabin of 1864, and Fort Misery, 1864.

TALIESIN WEST *north of junction of Shea Boulevard and 108th Street, Scottsdale.* Winter workshop of architect Frank Lloyd Wright and students, built in 1937; now working center for architects; privately held.

TEMPE HISTORICAL MUSEUM *3500 S. Rural Road, Tempe.* Material relating to Senators Carl Hayden and Barry Goldwater, and farm, ranch, and home items from the 1800s.

TOMBSTONE COURTHOUSE STATE HISTORIC PARK *219 Toughnut Street, Tombstone.* Tombstone history interpreted in the 1882 Cochise County Courthouse.

TUBAC PRESIDIO STATE HISTORIC PARK *I-19, forty-five miles south of Tucson.* First Spanish armed camp in area, founded in 1753 athwart an Apache raiding trail into Mexico. Launching area for the de Anza mission of 1775 that resulted in founding of San Francisco. Includes a museum.

TUZIGOOT *off U.S. 89A about thirty-three miles southwest of Flagstaff.*

A prehistoric site on the Verde River at the geographical heart of Arizona, restored in 1934 by the WPA.

WALNUT CANYON *I-40, eight miles east of Flagstaff.* Museum near 300 cliff dwellings of the Sinagua, dating from the eleventh through twelfth centuries.

WESTERN ARCHEOLOGICAL CENTER *1415 N. Sixth Avenue, Tucson.* Southwestern culture, with photographs and artifacts.

WUPATKI NATIONAL MONUMENT *U.S. 89 about twenty-five miles northeast of Flagstaff.* More than 800 ruins dating from the twelfth century. Displays of artifacts.

YUMA CROSSING *U.S. 95, banks of the Colorado River.* Where de Anza expedition of several hundred colonists, with livestock and provisions, forded the river on their way to California in 1775.

ZANE GREY LODGE *off state 260 north of Kohl's Ranch.* Stick-style house built in 1922 for the western writer. Includes a museum.

ARKANSAS

ARKANSAS POST NATIONAL MEMORIAL eight miles southeast of Gillett on state highway 1 and 169. In 1686, near the mouth of the Arkansas River, the French explorer Henri de Tonti established the first European outpost in the lower Mississippi Valley. Despite repeated flooding, European colonial rivalries, and other hindrances, the settlement known as Arkansas Post survived to become the birthplace of present-day Arkansas. Today the Arkansas Post National Memorial preserves the few remaining traces of the early French, Spanish, and American presence and commemorates the post's central role in the settlement of Arkansas and the trans-Mississippi West.

The Akansa or Quawpaw had inhabited the Arkansas River-Mississippi River region long before the French arrived in the late seventeenth century. The location was attractive to the first residents for much the same reasons that Europeans later found it inviting—fertile soil, a moderate climate, accessibility to navigable rivers, and a wealth of game, fish, hardwood, and other resources. But the French also recognized the site's special commercial and strategic advantages. A trading post near the confluence of the Arkansas and the Mississippi could exploit trade with the Spanish West and provide a base halfway between older settlements in Illinois and projected colonies along the Gulf of Mexico. René Robert Cavelier, Sieur de la Salle, envisioned a vast inland empire when he claimed the region for France in 1682. His plans required fortifying the Gulf coast, but his efforts to do so ended with his death in 1687. Henri de Tonti, la Salle's friend and trusted lieutenant, proved more successful in establishing the French presence in the lower Mississippi Valley. La Salle had granted him land and a trading concession in the region around the mouth of the Arkansas River, and Tonti confirmed his claim in 1686 by detaching six men from his expedition to establish a trading post there. The station was known as *Poste de Arkansea* or Arkansas Post.

Colonial rivalries and adverse economic factors forestalled the development of la Salle's trading empire; Tonti's outpost soon languished for lack of activity and by 1700 was abandoned. In the early eighteenth century, however, interest in the area revived as the French consolidated control in both the Great Lakes-Illinois region and Louisiana. Arkansas Post was ideally situated to protect transportation and communications between the two imperial centers. A Scottish speculator named John Law developed a grand scheme to settle the region and enrich both himself and the French crown. He aggressively recruited settlers, and in 1721 some two hundred Germans arrived at Arkansas Post. But news soon followed that Law's speculative venture had collapsed, and by 1725 few of the settlers remained. For the next several

Arkansas Post

decades, the small military outpost and trading station struggled to survive.

The Treaty of Aix-la-Chapelle in 1748 ended the War of Austrian Succession (or King George's War, as it was known in America), but the peace that followed between France and England was uneasy at best. Preparing for the worst, Louisiana's Governor Baron de Kerlerac decided that defense of New Orleans required fortifying Arkansas Post. In 1752 and 1753, Lieutenant Chevalier de la Houssaye built a new fort on higher ground at the southeast edge of the Grand Prairie. His fort included a barracks, powder magazine, warehouse, and other structures and served not only as a military garrison but as a fur-trading center, a church mission, and a focus of efforts to counter British influence with Indians in the region. War between France and Britain did resume in 1755, but Arkansas Post played no significant role in the conflict. Nevertheless, as part of the Treaty of Paris that brought the war to an end in 1763, France ceded Louisiana to Spain, and Arkansas Post ceased to fly the French flag.

The French actually continued to operate the post until the Spanish commander arrived in 1770. By that time, the fort had been relocated again, about thirty-five miles closer to the mouth of the Arkansas River. Flooding at the new site, however, necessitated a return to the site of la Houssaye's fort. In 1779 the Spanish erected a new fort there and named it San Carlos III. The new fortification testified to the Spanish interest in Arkansas Post as an Indian trading center and as the starting point on the route west along the Arkansas, Canadian, and Cimarron rivers to Santa Fe and Taos. The Spanish were especially eager to undermine British influence and competition in the Mississippi River Valley and consequently sided with the American colonies in their revolt against England. This alliance led to the only Revolutionary War engagement in Arkansas. On April 17, 1783, James Colbert led a force of British and Chickasaw in an attack on the village and the fort at Arkansas Post. The unsuccessful raid made little difference, however, for it came a year and a half after the British surrender at Yorktown.

In 1796 the Spanish relocated the fort again—about a half-mile to the northwest—and renamed it Fuerto San Estevan de Arkansas. Four years later, Spain ceded Louisiana back to France, then ruled by Napoleon Bonaparte, who planned to re-establish the French empire in America. Napoleon's plans fell through, however, and in 1803 the French sold the entire Louisiana territory to the United States. In March 1804, the United States flag was raised at Arkansas Post for the first time.

By the early nineteenth century, the Arkansas Post community included some sixty or seventy families, some living in the small village at the fort and others on adjoining farms. Located at the juncture of the major north-south trade route and the first significant trail west, Arkansas Post prospered under American rule. When Missouri Territory was organized in 1813, the town was made the seat of government for Arkansas County. Efforts to secure Missouri statehood led to the establishment of a separate Arkansas Territory in 1819 with Arkansas Post as its capital. The town reached the zenith of its political and economic importance during its brief tenure as territorial capital but remained relatively prosperous after the government moved upriver to Little Rock in 1821. Railroad construction cut into river commerce by the 1850s, however, and Arkansas Post began to decline; the county seat was relocated to DeWitt in 1855. The town experienced one last brief revival during the Civil War, when the Confederates erected Fort Hindman there to protect the Arkansas River and Little Rock. On January 10, 1863, Union troops seized the earthen fortification, destroying much of the town in the process.

The historic site was essentially abandoned until the state established a park there in 1929. In the 1960s, the Arkansas Post National Memorial was established under the National Park Service. The park now encompasses over three hundred acres and includes a visitor center and a trail with wayside exhibits. Although the site of Tonti's post and the Law settlement are not within the park boundaries, archeological remains mark the sites of the other forts and communities in Arkansas Post's long history. No other site so effectively tells the story of the exploration and settlement of frontier Arkansas.

ARKANSAS TERRITORIAL RESTORATION AND THE OLD STATE HOUSE *Little Rock.* In 1821 the Arkansas legislature moved the territorial capital up the Arkansas River from Arkansas Post to the frontier community of Little Rock. Designation as territorial and later state capital provided the catalyst for the town's growth and development into the political, economic, and cultural center of nineteenth-century Arkansas. The Arkansas Territorial Restoration and the Old State House in Little Rock preserve the most significant remnants of that era and bring to life the colorful history of Arkansas in its transition from territory to state.

The selection of Little Rock as the second territorial capital reflected both its location near the geographic center of the territory and the lobbying efforts of land speculators hoping to cash in on the inevitable real-estate boom. Named for a landmark on the Arkansas River, Little Rock was scarcely more than a village with less than a dozen houses when the territorial legislature made its decision in 1820 to relocate there. The population increased by 1824 to about forty families, and by 1827 some sixty buildings stood in the river settlement. Although there were several brick and frame structures, the majority were of log construction typical of frontier Arkansas. By the close of the first decade, the population stood at 430.

Although violence, drunkenness, and lawlessness remained persistent problems, Little Rock showed signs of becoming a more settled and mature community. Local businesses, including a tailor, a hat store, a coffee house, a cabinetry shop, a bakery, a bookbindery, and an assortment of other enterprises, brought a semblance of civilization to the territorial outpost by 1831. Residents also established churches during the decade, the first school opened in 1823, and the Little Rock Debating Society was established in 1822. William E. Woodruff began publishing his *Arkansas Gazette* at Arkansas Post in 1819 and moved his operations to the new capital in 1821. By 1824 he had set up operations adjoining his home at the corner of Markham and Cumberland streets in what is now the Arkansas Territorial Restoration. Still in publication, the *Gazette* is the oldest newspaper west of the Mississippi River. A rival paper, the *Arkansas Advocate,* began publication in 1830. Both depended on information from eastern newspapers, and transportation problems often meant that "news" would be twenty to thirty days late. The first steamboat to land at Little Rock—the *Eagle*—arrived in 1822, but the hazards of river transportation hampered regular service. The old road from St. Louis provided another transportation route, and in 1826 construction began on a road to Memphis. Transportation and communication remained, however, rudimentary at best.

By 1835, when the population of Little Rock had reached 700, a danc-

McVicar-Conway House

ing school had opened and the Thalian Society had sponsored the town's first theatrical performance. Living conditions remained fairly primitive, however. In 1832 a board of health was established to deal with recurring epidemics of smallpox and to head off a much feared wave of cholera. When Arkansas became a state in 1836, Little Rock was made the state capital. Construction had begun on a permanent capitol building in 1833 and was well under way before the 1834 constitutional convention that paved the way for the paired admission to the Union of both slave-state Arkansas and free-state Michigan. The statehouse was not completed until 1842, by which time the town's population had reached more than 1,500.

The area encompassed by the Arkansas Territorial Restoration is the only significant remnant from the territorial and early statehood years still standing in Little Rock. The half-block of block 32 of the original town plot was restored between 1939 and 1941 by the Works Progress Administration in cooperation with the state government. Three structures stand on their original sites, and a fourth was relocated within the half-block bounded by Markham, Cumberland, Third, and Scott streets.

The oldest structure in the complex, and in fact within the city, is the Hinderliter House at Third and Cumberland. This two-story structure was erected between 1826 and 1828 with hand-hewn logs and clay chinking. Red-heart, hand-beaded cypress siding was added in 1834, as were a rear porch and stairway. Original ceiling beams, a hand-carved mantel, wall boards, and flooring are still visible. Little is known about the owner, Jesse Hinderliter, or about the grog shop or tavern that he operated on the ground floor prior to his death in 1834. Taverns usually served several important functions in frontier towns like Little Rock. In addition to lodging, food, and drink, the tavern provided a public meeting place, served as a center for the exchange of information, and functioned as the focus of community social life. According to tradition, the Arkansas territorial legislature even met at the Hinderliter House in 1835.

To the north of the Hinderliter House on Cumberland stands the Brownlee-Noland House, built before 1860 by Robert Brownlee. Brownlee, a Scottish stonemason, arrived in Little Rock in 1837 to work on the new capitol building. He and his partner James McVicar subsequently worked on the state bank and the state penitentiary, but in the late 1840s he was lured away by the discovery of gold in California. His brother James, a blacksmith, continued to live in the house until R. L. Dodge purchased it in 1852. The brick structure has a wide rear porch and is furnished to suit the more refined tastes of residents in the years between 1846 and 1850.

Brownlee's partner James McVicar built the house at Scott and Markham at about the same time. The structure apparently stood originally between the Hinderliter House and the Brownlee House. McVicar was also a Scottish stonemason and came to Little Rock for the same reasons as Brownlee. After he and Brownlee completed work on the state penitentiary in 1842, he became warden of the institution. That same year he bought a lot in block 32. When gold fever hit at the end of the decade, he headed the Little Rock Company's venture in California, but he returned to Arkansas in 1856. The house is also connected with Elias Conway, a territorial auditor and the state's fifth governor. His brother, James S. Conway, was elected Arkansas' first governor in 1836. The Conways were part of the "Dynasty" that dominated early state politics. This frame house is furnished to reflect the wealth and influence of the McVicar and Conway families.

The fourth house stands at the corner of Markham and Cumberland. The original sections of the house date from 1823, when William E. Woodruff moved his family and newspaper business to this location. Successive owners have altered the house, but it still provides an excellent opportunity to learn about life in nineteenth-century Little Rock.

Also included in the Arkansas Territorial Restoration are several reconstructed outbuildings, a log cabin used for education programs, and, on the adjoining half-block, a modern reception center that houses exhibits, the Arkansas Artists Gallery, and a craft store. Programs include guided tours, exhibits, films, the Pioneer Education Programs for students, and several special events. The site is administered by the

Department of Arkansas Natural and Cultural Heritage.

What remains of the original "little rock" can be found a short distance away in a riverfront park. The outcropping was so named in 1722 by Bernard de la Harpe, one of the first Europeans to ascend the Arkansas River to that point. It served as a starting point for early land surveys.

About a block west of the Arkansas Territorial Restoration on the north side of Markham stands the Old State House. Erected between 1833 and 1842, this stuccoed brick Greek Revivial structure has a pedimented portico, gabled roof, and two-story central block with side wings. The state government occupied this historic structure until 1911, when a new capitol was completed. Renovated in 1885 and then restored between 1947 and 1950, the building has housed a state museum since 1951. The museum today has both exhibits and period rooms that interpret the state's history.

Situated in the heart of a bustling metropolitan center, these historic sites preserve the last significant remnants of Little Rock's colorful frontier heritage. The Arkansas Territorial Restoration and the Old State House provide a unique opportunity to learn about the history of Arkansas from territory to statehood.

PEA RIDGE NATIONAL MILITARY PARK *Pea Ridge.* Arkansas' most important Civil War battle—and perhaps the war's most decisive engagement west of the Mississippi River—was the Battle of Pea Ridge on March 7 and 8, 1862. The Union victory in Arkansas was fortuitous, for disappointments in the East had begun to undermine the Northern morale during that first year of conflict. Pea Ridge and the other campaigns in the West began the process of opening up the Mississippi Valley and splitting the Confederacy, a strategy that ultimately proved crucial to the Union cause. The Pea Ridge National Military Park preserves the main battlefield and effectively commemorates this significant episode in Arkansas history.

When the Civil War broke out in 1861, Arkansas joined the Confederacy; but its neighbor to the north, Missouri, did not secede from the Union despite a sizable slave population and a significant body of Southern sympathizers. President Abraham Lincoln and his advisers recognized the importance of keeping border states like Missouri in the Union and were concerned about an apparent shift in popular sentiment toward secession as the first year of the war progressed. Concern turned to alarm when secessionist legislators mobilized the Missouri State Guard under the command of Major General Sterling Price, and Federal troops took action to secure the state for the Union. Initially, the pro-Southerners had the advantage, and they defeated the Union army in the Battle of Wilson's Creek on August 10, 1861. Dissension within leadership, however, prevented the pro-Southerners from following up on that initial victory, and by the winter of 1861–62 a new Union commander was pushing his opponents southwest into Arkansas.

The opposing armies basically followed Telegraph Road south from

West overlook on Pea Ridge

Springfield into Arkansas. The road, also known as Old Wire Road, was the main artery connecting St. Louis and Fort Smith and became the focal point of the Pea Ridge campaign. The first skirmishes within the Arkansas borders were at Cross Timber Hollow on February 16 and the following day at Dunagin's farm near present-day Brightwater. The pro-Southerners continued to retreat to the south after a skirmish at Cross Hollow on February 22, but their ranks were swelled significantly by the addition of Confederate troops under the command of Brigadier General Ben McCulloch. The combined forces set up camp on Cove Creek in the Boston Mountains southwest of Fayetteville at the end of the month and began planning strategy to push the Union forces back.

Price and McCulloch could not, however, agree on a plan of action, and on March 3 Major General Earl Van Dorn took command of the combined Confederate armies. Van Dorn's troops numbered over sixteen thousand and included Price's Missourians, a Confederate contingent led by McCulloch, and three regiments of Cherokee Indians commanded by Brigadier General Albert Pike. The new Confederate commander knew his forces significantly outnumbered the opposition and on March 4 ordered the troops to move northward against the Federal encampment at Cross Hollow. The Union commander, Brigadier General Samuel R. Curtis, then pulled his troops back to Little Sugar Creek and began preparing for battle.

Curtis positioned his troops along the bluffs on the north side of Little Sugar Creek and established clear control over access along both the creek and Telegraph Road. Under such circumstances a frontal attack by the Confederate troops would be suicidal, and Van Dorn developed an alternative plan of attack. He decided to swing his troops to the north along a bypass and surprise the Federal army from the rear.

Hoping to deceive Curtis, Van Dorn ordered his men to set up camp at Little Sugar Creek on March 6 as if intending to stay the night. Meanwhile Price and the Missouri State Guard initiated a flanking movement up the Bentonville-Keetsville Road to Cross Timber Hollow, where the detour intersected Telegraph Road. By the morning of March 7, only Price's troops had made it to Cross Timber, so Van Dorn revised his battle plan in favor of a two-prong attack on the Union forces. Meanwhile, Curtis learned of the Confederates' plan to attack from the rear and began repositioning his men for the impending engagement.

The Battle of Pea Ridge began on March 7 on two separate fronts. On the east, fighting centered on Elkhorn Tavern, a stage stop used by Curtis's troops as a supply center. Price's Missouri State Guard successfully pushed the Federal forces back, took possession of the tavern, and established headquarters there. The Confederates at Leetown on the west flank proved far less successful. The deaths of McCulloch and General James McIntosh left the Confederate troops in disarray, and on the following day the Leetown survivors joined their comrades at Elkhorn. The battle on March 8 proved shortlived: the Confederates quickly ran out of ammunition and were forced to retreat. Fighting ended by 11 a.m. that morning, as the Confederates withdrew to the east along Huntsville Road.

The Battle of Pea Ridge was one of the most decisive engagements west of the Mississippi River. The Confederate defeat assured Federal control over Missouri and contributed to the success of the Union campaign in the West. The price in casualties was high, however. The total of men killed, wounded, and missing was 2,384, and another 300 were captured. The surviving Confederate troops hastily retreated and shortly left the state to support the Southern cause elsewhere. Their departure left Arkansas undefended, and Curtis' Union troops consolidated their victory by moving on to occupy Batesville and Helena.

In 1960, the state of Arkansas purchased the property around Leetown and Elkhorn Tavern and donated it to the federal government for the establishment of a national park. Now administered by the National Park Service, the Pea Ridge National Military Park encompasses about 4,700 acres of the original battlefield. A self-guiding tour begins on Telegraph Road at a modern visitor center and includes the site of Curtis' headquarters just before the battle, the Leetown site, Pea Ridge overlooks, Elkhorn Tavern, and earthworks built by the Union troops at Little Sugar Creek. The focus of the park is Elkhorn Tavern, named for elkhorns mounted on the ridgepole of the roof in the late 1850s. The original structure, erected in the 1830s by William Reddick, served at various times as a trading post, a post office, a stage stop, a military telegraph office, and even a church. The building burned in 1863, but the Cox family, which operated the tavern through the war period, rebuilt it shortly thereafter on the original foundations. The structure was restored in 1965 and 1966 and now appears much as the original tavern did during the war.

While not the only Civil War-related site in Arkansas, Pea Ridge is perhaps the most significant. No other site conveys so effectively the human drama of the war or commemorates so ably the state's commitment to the Confederate cause.

ARKANSAS COUNTY AGRICULTURAL MUSEUM E. *Fourth Street, Stuttgart.* Farm equipment, home furnishings; replica of 1890 prairie home, 1914 schoolhouse.

ARKANSAS HISTORY COMMISSION 1 Capitol Mall, Little Rock. Library with manuscript collections on Arkansas; portrait collection.

ARKANSAS STATE UNIVERSITY Arkansas Room, Dean B. Ellis Library, State University. Materials related to Arkansas state history.

BOB BURNS HOUSE 821 Jefferson Street, Van Buren. An 1885 clapboard house, the home of radio comedian Burns (who also invented the musical bazooka).

CRATER OF DIAMONDS STATE PARK Murfreesboro. A 72-acre dike containing diamonds, first discovered in 1906. Includes a museum.

FORT SMITH NATIONAL HISTORIC SITE Rogers Avenue between Second and Third streets, Fort Smith. Visitor center and museum on site of fort established in 1817. Includes restoration of courtroom of Judge Isaac C. Parker, who served for twenty-one years after being appointed by President Ulysses S. Grant.

GANN BUILDING 218 S. Market Street, Benton. An 1893 doctor's building that is the only known structure built out of bauxite.

HAMPSON MUSEUM STATE PARK Lake Drive at state highway 61, Wilson. Archeology museum with materials from the Late Mississippian and Ozark Bluff Dwellers periods.

HOT SPRINGS NATIONAL PARK NATURAL HISTORY MUSEUM Hot Springs. Includes Indian artifacts, archeology, and other historical materials.

JACKSONPORT STATE PARK on state highway 69 three miles northwest of Newport. Museum in an 1861 courthouse, with an old river steamboat permanently moored on the White River nearby.

JACOB WOLF HOUSE on state highway 5 west of the fork of the White and North Fork rivers, Norfolk. Dogtrot log house built about 1825, one of the state's few remaining log buildings. Includes a museum.

McCOLLUM-CHIDESTER HOUSE MUSEUM 926 Washington Street,

N.W., Camden. An 1850 building with furniture, china, glassware, silver, clothing, and pictures.

MAMMOTH SPRING STATE PARK Mammoth Spring. History museum in an 1885 railroad depot; railroad memorabilia and early history of Mammoth Spring.

MID-AMERICA MUSEUM 400 Mid-America Boulevard, Hot Springs National Park, Hot Springs. A general museum with materials relating to the history of the region.

MUSEUM OF SCIENCE AND HISTORY MacArthur Park, Little Rock. General museum with natural and human history; in the U.S. Arsenal Building built 1838–1840, occupied by Confederates 1861–1863, and the birthplace of Douglas MacArthur in 1880.

OLD WASHINGTON HISTORIC STATE PARK Washington. History museum located in one of state's oldest towns; with several houses of early 1800s.

ORR SCHOOL 831 Laurel Street, Texarkana. An 1880 clapboard building with bungalow elements; only extant building related to the Texarkana childhood of famed ragtime composer Scott Joplin.

OZARK FOLK CENTER Mountain View. Folk art museum with crafts of the Ozarks, early sheet music, and recordings of Ozark folklore.

PRAIRIE GROVE BATTLEFIELD PARK between North Road on the northwest and U.S. 62 on the south. Historical houses and a museum on the site where Confederates tried but failed to stop the Union advance through Arkansas in 1862.

STATE CAPITOL Little Rock. Portraits of governors and supreme court judges and other exhibits, as well as the living history of dynamic legislative action.

SHILOH MUSEUM 118 W. Johnson, Springdale. Local and regional history museum.

TEBBETTS HOUSE 118 E. Dickson Street, Fayetteville. House built in 1853 by a Union sympathizer and occupied by both Union and Confederate officers during the Civil War; still shows bullethole from battle of Fayetteville, 1863.

TEN MILE HOUSE east side of state highway 5, ten miles southwest of Little Rock. Georgian brick house built in the early 1800s on the Old Southwest Trail and occupied by Union troops during the Civil War; privately owned.

TOLTEC MOUNDS STATE PARK 15 miles southwest of North Little Rock off highway 130 on Arkansas 386. Archeological site.

UNIVERSITY OF ARKANSAS MUSEUM Fayetteville. General museum with artifacts on Arkansas Indians and Americana.

VAN BUREN HISTORIC DISTRICT Main Street, bounded by Cane Hills Street and the Arkansas River, Van Buren. Late-nineteenth-century commercial buildings in many styles.

VILLA MARRE 1321 Scott Street, Little Rock. Granite Second Empire

house, built 1882, the home of Arkansas governor and United States senator Jeff Davis. Museum furnished with period pieces and art.
WHITE COUNTY PIONEER MUSEUM *Searcy.* Early farm implements and nineteenth-century buildings.

CALIFORNIA

LA PURISIMA MISSION STATE HISTORIC PARK four miles east of Lompoc, near junction of California 1 and 150. The settlement of North America is commonly regarded as an east-to-west affair. Europeans landed along the Atlantic seaboard, settled a string of coastal colonies, and then slowly pushed into the interior. This slow process took until the end of the eighteenth century to reach much beyond the Appalachian Mountains, and until the end of the nineteenth to conquer and settle the awesome spaces between the Mississippi and the Pacific. It was a dramatic, perhaps even epic, story whose action and characters every school child knows well: covered wagons lumbering over the Oregon Trail; cavalry chasing Indians through red rock canyons; cowboys rounding up cattle; miners panning for gold; homesteaders breaking prairie sod. Fact and fancy freely mix, which is one of the things that makes the story so exciting.

But while all that was happening, American settlement was also proceeding along another axis. From the south where Spain's colonial empire had long been established came settlers who hardly fit the usual image. They were not people yearning especially for greater economic opportunity or for political and religious freedom. On the contrary, they were priests of Rome. The Catholic Church played an important part in Spain's imperial effort; together sword and cross marched triumphantly over two-thirds of the Western hemisphere in the years after Hernán Cortez landed in Mexico in 1519. Despite their fierce reputation, the Spanish were not merely conquerors. They were farmers, ranchers, and missionaries, bent on creating a variant of European civilization in the New World. To that end the mission system, whose purpose was both to save souls and to consolidate Spanish power, was a useful tool.

It reached the area that would become the state of California in 1769, six years before the Revolutionary War began 3000 miles to the east. The first head of the California Mission, Father Junipero Serra, had grand plans to build a chain of missions extending north from San Diego Bay, each within a day's walk of the next. The first were Mission San Diego de Alcala (1769) and San Carlos Borromeo at Monterey (1770, later moved to Carmel). By the time of Serra's death in 1784, nine were complete; by 1823 his successors had established a total of twenty-one, completing the chain.

La Purisima Mission (its full name was the Mission of the Immaculate Conception of the Most Holy Mary), first located at the base of some low hills just south of the Santa Ynez River within the present-day city of Lompoc, was the eleventh established. Construction began in 1788, and growth in the early years was impressive. La Purisima was one of three missions designed particularly to control the Chumash Indians who lived in the coastal area along the Santa Barbara Channel, and from

Padres' Residence at
La Purisima

that tribe the Franciscan fathers at the mission won many willing converts. Mission holdings were large, as were adjoining rancheros, which meant that the Indians gradually abandoned their old ways and grew dependent on the mission. Both they and the Spaniards seemed pleased. Indians driven from the Channel Islands by the activities of hunters and traders swelled the population. Baptisms kept pace, and by 1804 the mission settlement counted more than 1,500 Indians within its bounds. The same year Father Mariano Payeras took charge of La Purisima and nurtured it to a high level of prosperity. He devised important improvements in the mission's water supply and irrigation system and then improved its food supply. Mission industries prospered, too: soap, candles, wool, leather products were produced in abundance. Meanwhile, the fathers diligently tended their spiritual duties, winning and keeping souls for their Savior.

The prosperity was not, however, unmarred. Smallpox, measles, and other diseases to which the Indian had no resistance took a heavy toll after 1804; in the next three years 500 died. Some of the survivors ran away to the hills, and new converts became harder and harder to attract. Earthquakes in 1812 made things worse, destroying La Purisima's major buildings and most of the Indian houses. Drenching rains and floods finally destroyed the mission beyond recovery. Rebuilding, which began almost immediately, was on a site several miles to the north in a small canyon known to the Spaniards as "the canyon of the watercress." It had several advantages: abundant spring water, good soil, and a low mesa that offered some protection from strong ocean winds. "El Camino Real," the King's Highway, also passed nearby, making the hazardous crossing of the Santa Ynez River unnecessary.

The choice was a good one, and the next years saw a large measure of prosperity return to La Purisima. The mission's physical plant, today elaborately restored, was impressive. The centerpiece was a 300-foot-long tile-roofed residence building, which incorporated design features that the priests hoped would render it safe from earthquake damage. Its main walls were four feet thick, made of adobe and reinforced with parallel columns and, at the south end, a massive sandstone buttress. Completed in 1815, it housed the priests' living quarters, office space and a store, guest and dining rooms, and a small chapel. The building stood for nearly a century with little maintenance, long after the mission effort itself had come to an end.

The mission's main church was a long narrow building decorated with colorful paintings and large enough to accommodate all the mission residents and a thousand Indian neophytes. Bells of the campanario, cast in Lima, Peru, in 1817 and 1818, regularly called the faithful to worship. The altar was wood inlaid with mother-of-pearl. But the building was undermined by a spring near the northwest corner, which caused its collapse in 1836. Afterward the priests' private chapel was enlarged to become the mission's main place of worship.

Between the church and the residence building was the shops and quarters building, the center of the mission's craft activities. Here master weavers turned out wool and cotton cloth. The friars also developed shops for producing pottery and leather work from abundant local raw materials. An elaborate water system was vital to the mission. A small white building received spring water from the nearby hills that was then filtered slowly through sand and charcoal and piped in ceramic tile pipelines to the central fountain and two *lavenderias,* or washing and rinsing basins. Waste water and water caught in a cistern irrigated surrounding fields.

La Purisima's prosperity was a victim of the political upheavals that swept through Spanish America in the 1820s. The Mexican revolution disrupted Spanish government support for the mission system, which found itself under ever heavier financial burdens. Disruption of civil and military authority led to an Indian revolt in 1824 which, though unsuccessful, was an indication that the disillusionment of the once proud and independent Chumash people was profound. Death rates among them remained high. The year of the revolt their numbers had already dropped to 662. In 1832 the mission counted 372; in 1846 only about 160 were left there. The final blow came in 1834 when the Mexican authorities decreed the secularization of the missions, placing them under civil rather than religious control. *Mayordomos* were assigned to the missions and charged with dispersing their holdings; the last two resident priests at La Purisima, meanwhile, moved to Santa Ynez. Regular services ended after 1835, though for another fifteen years or so there were occasional baptisms and funerals.

Its reason for existence gone, the once peaceful, prosperous La Purisima eventually became a ruin. Successive private owners used it as a sheep and cattle ranch. A fire in 1880 damaged the roof; the residence became a stable. In 1904 the roof tiles were removed to prevent total collapse, but the rains soon dissolved the thick adobe walls so that by the 1930s the stately old mission had been reduced to some shapeless mounds of overground adobe. Restoration efforts began in the 1930s with labor supplied by the Civilian Conservation Corps under the supervision of the National Park Service. State and local government and private citizen groups also participated. The mission was reopened to the public in 1941 and has been administered ever since by the California Department of Parks and Recreation. At present the state historic park comprises an area of 966 acres that, though only a small part of La Purisima's property, preserves the pastoral setting of the original mission. Nineteen of the original structures have been restored; others are exhibited as ruins. A walk through them best reveals what the California mission frontier once was like. Only the Spanish priests and Indian neophytes are missing—just like the miners, homesteaders, cowboys, and cavalry in the other more familiar images of the West. But amid these impressive old buildings, the history-minded visitor will have little difficulty conjuring up their presence.

MARSHALL GOLD DISCOVERY STATE HISTORIC PARK   *Coloma.* Few Americans initially took much interest in the United States' acquisition of California in the Mexican War. Located 1,800 miles west of "civilization," the new territory was simply out of sight and out of mind. Then on January 24, 1848, James Marshall discovered gold along the South Fork of the American River, about forty-five miles east of Sacramento. News of Marshall's find spread quickly, touching off a gold frenzy that swept the nation and spread to South America, Europe, Asia, and Australia. Eighty thousand would-be millionaires streamed into the territory in 1849, and the next year California became the nation's thirty-first state. Marshall's find was the catalyst for California's growth and development in the mid-nineteenth century and thus constitutes a major watershed in the state's history. The Marshall Gold Discovery State Historic Park commemorates that pivotal event and the gold fever that followed.

In the late 1840s, James Marshall worked as a handyman, carpenter, and millwright for John Sutter at his New Helvetia settlement, the predecessor of present-day Sacramento. Sutter needed lumber for his expanding central California empire and negotiated a partnership with Marshall: he would provide the necessary capital if Marshall would build and operate a sawmill. The latter readily agreed and soon found a likely site along the South Fork of the Sacramento River in the Sierra foothills east of Sutter's fort. The river would provide the necessary water power, and nearby stands of pine would keep the mill busy and profitable.

Construction of the sawmill began in late 1847. Marshall had never actually built a mill before, but he had worked in one and was familiar with the basic principles. Indian laborers built a diversion dam and dug a raceway, and Marshall hired Mormon workers to erect the mill, using heavy hand-adzed timbers and oak pins. By the first of the year, the structure was nearly completed, and the waterwheel was put into place. But to Marshall's dismay, the wheel would not turn properly in the shallow tailrace. With some difficulty, he and his men excavated deeper

Reconstruction of Sutter's Mill

under the wheel. While inspecting the deepened tailrace on January 24, Marshall spotted the glittery bits of metal that soon had California swarming with treasure hunters.

In the rush of events that followed, neither Marshall nor Sutter struck it rich. Bonanza claims and easy fortunes eluded both, and each ended up trying to make a living in any way possible. Marshall and two partners reopened the famous sawmill in 1849: although it was not completed at the time of the gold discovery in 1848, Marshall and his men had finished the project soon thereafter. But once gold fever hit, there was no one left to run the mill, and it closed down. When reopened, the mill provided lumber for the rash of construction at the neighboring town of Coloma.

The central California village boomed overnight into a city of 10,000 with churches, schools, banks, and other fine structures. As the center of the rich mining country, the "Queen of the Mines" attracted not only miners but storekeepers, doctors, prostitutes, lawyers, gamblers, and ministers, all expecting to profit indirectly from gold fever. As the chief suppliers of lumber, Marshall and his partners charged high prices and expected substantial profits, but poor management and bad debts forced the mill to close again in 1851. The discoverer of California's gold proved no more successful at subsequent business ventures and died penniless in 1885.

Coloma remained active for several years after Marshall's sawmill finally closed, but by the mid-1850s it became evident that richer deposits were to be found elsewhere. When the El Dorado County seat was transferred to another mining city, Placerville, in 1857, only a few Chinese miners still searched for placer gold at the discovery site.

The Marshall Gold Discovery State Historic Park was established in 1927 to preserve the site of this famous event in the state's history. The park encompasses about 220 acres, some 70 percent of old Coloma. Visitors to the park can take a self-guided tour that includes the discovery site, the mill site on the American River, a replica of the mill, exhibits on California's gold-rush history, and a variety of stores and other structures along Coloma's Main Street. Appropriately, the tour ends with the James W. Marshall Monument that marks the grave of the gold discoverer. Erected by the California state legislature in 1890, the monument stands on a hill about a half-mile from the cabin Marshall lived in during the 1850s and 1860s. Standing atop a granite base, a larger-than-life bronze statue of Marshall points toward the American River and the site of his 1848 discovery.

Throughout the Mother Lode country stand other remnants of the gold-rush era. One of the best preserved mining towns is Colombia, and visitors to the Columbia State Historical Park can see a variety of stores, saloons, and other structures that date from the peak years of the 1850s. Other nearby mining towns include Placerville, Auburn, Volcano, Murphys, Angels Camp, Jackson, Mokelumne Hill, and Sonora. But although its heyday was brief, Coloma was clearly the "Queen of the Mines." The Marshall Gold Discovery State Historic Park appropriately commemorates James Marshall's discovery and brings to life this exciting era in the history of the Golden State.

JOHN MUIR NATIONAL HISTORIC SITE *4202 Alhambra Avenue, Martinez.* Half a millennium ago, when Europeans first began to cast eyes toward the North American continent, they saw or thought they saw many riches. It seemed a land filled with gold and silver—an El Dorado; a land of milk and honey—a Promised Land; a land filled with wild beasts and wilder men—a wilderness. Of gold and silver there was relatively little. The milk and honey awaited long years of patient nurture. The wilderness, however, was there in abundance from the very beginning. There are famous pictures of pilgrims in Massachusetts and adventurers in Virginia perched precariously at its edge, while to the west stretched an endless thicket of trees. Exploration confirmed the image of a forest filled with hostile creatures. But the trees themselves were the greatest obstacle between the Europeans and what they came for: greater prosperity than they had ever known. In that agricultural age, prosperity for most men meant owning or at least having access to cleared land for farming. The trees, or at least some of them, had to go, both to make way for crops and to build barns, houses, and churches.

At first the number of settlers was small and their tools, driven by muscle power, were adequate to the job. But after the Civil War, when the nation surged across the trans-Mississippi West, different conditions led to different results—and elicited from some, like John Muir, a different response. Everything moved faster. It was the age of steam-powered machinery in transportation and industry. Burgeoning eastern cities demanded food, fiber, and building materials and in the West's ranches, farms, and forests found a natural supply. Emigrants from other lands swelled population and multiplied many times the human talents—and appetite—of the American nation. But the West was more than a great treasure trove of natural resources. It was also a very beautiful place whose high mountains, rugged canyons, towering waterfalls, and exotic geysers were unlike anything Americans had seen before. And such beauty raised problems. It demanded, in some at least, a changed understanding of wilderness.

Because it had already stood for so many years as an obstacle to settlement, "wild" nature had traditionally been understood as an enemy. To conquer it was to win the land for civilization, to open it to development and the creation of wealth. Wilderness resources were, in this view, something to be used. At first, when the West seemed boundless, they were sometimes used recklessly. Later, as limits became more apparent, careful management for long-term use became a common theme. In either case, use in an economic sense governed. But John Muir and his followers understood use in another sense. Wilderness, they said, had redeeming aesthetic and even spiritual qualities quite apart from its economic value. Wilderness, they said, was fragile and must be preserved at all costs from thoughtless human despoliation.

John Muir, who first made the preservationist view respectable, dramatically lived his conviction. His lifetime spanned the great Victorian age, perhaps one of the most hopeful in human history. His optimism and gentle cheerfulness were in keeping with those times; his gospel of wilderness was probably ahead of them. He was born in Scotland in 1838, a year after Queen Victoria came to the throne. He died in 1914, the year World War I began, and was buried in his beloved Alhambra Valley in California. From his earliest days he was drawn to nature and was remembered as a boy scampering over the rough Scottish landscape. When he was eleven, his family immigrated to America and made a new home on what was then the Wisconsin frontier. There he helped his father, a farmer and preacher, clear the land, plant crops, and establish an outpost of civilization. As thousands of his contemporaries then were doing in westward-moving America, Muir helped tame a small part of the wilderness. In the early 1860s he attended the University of Wisconsin but did not graduate. He later did odd jobs in Canada and worked in a carriage factory in Indianapolis, where an accident nearly cost him his eyesight. From that point on, he went his own distinctive wilderness way. He set out on a 1,000-mile walk from the Ohio River through Kentucky, Tennessee, Georgia, and Florida to the Gulf of Mexico. He then wandered to California, discovering for himself the Yosemite Valley and the Sierra Nevada mountains. He tended sheep, worked in a sawmill, and—most important—spent long periods wandering in

John Muir's Alhambra Valley home

solitude, acquainting himself as no other man yet had with the Yosemite Valley wilderness.

In 1880 he married Louise Strentzel, daughter of a prosperous Alhambra Valley horticulturalist and fruit-grower. Over the next eight years they had two children, and Muir secured a modest fortune as a fruit-grower. His true calling, though, lay elsewhere. Even as he worked diligently in those orchards and vineyards, he was drawn periodically back to the wilderness, and after he had securely provided for his family his wanderings took him to wilderness around the globe from Alaska to Africa. Back in his beloved Sierra, meanwhile, the pressures of development threatened the virgin wilderness he had known there. And in the late 1880s and 1890s Muir set out on his true calling as skilled publicist and campaigner for the cause of wilderness preservation. With the help of well-connected friends like Robert Underwood Johnson, editor of the influential *Century Magazine* and Theodore Roosevelt, he helped build a powerful wave of public enthusiasm for preservation. The excesses of cattlemen, sheepmen, and loggers in the Yosemite Valley and Mariposa Grove especially angered him, and early success came with the creation in 1890 of Yosemite (a state park since 1864), General Grant, and Sequoia national parks. Two years later he was a key in the founding of the Sierra Club, and he served as its president until he died. His life as a writer and campaigner grew busier, but still he was known to become physically ill when he stayed away from the wilderness too long. "The mountains are calling and I must go," he once wrote.

He did not win all his battles, however. Despite his efforts, the beautiful Hetch Hetchy Valley became a reservoir for the city of San Francisco, and much wilderness was destined to succumb in the years after his death. But his specific victories and defeats may be less important than his success in implanting in America's public consciousness his new view of wilderness. Whatever compromises there later had to be, Muir's own vision was absolute. As he put it: "Wilderness is a necessity. Mountain parks and reservations are useful not only as fountains of timbers and irrigating rivers, but as fountains of life." It was a vision that unfortunately became easy to trivialize and reduce to caricature. Muir did not counsel people to forsake the modern world and literally move back to nature. (He himself lived in a comfortable Victorian house set amid a farm, not a forest.) He declared only that wilderness should always be there to lend its quiet inspiration to people destined to live in a very different world.

So the John Muir National Historic Site testifies. It is not a log cabin in the High Sierra but a seventeen-room, two-story Victorian house built in 1882 that today overlooks the freeways, subdivisions, and industries of Martinez. He inherited the house from his father-in-law in 1890 when it was still the center of a 2,600-acre fruit ranch. Today fewer than nine acres surround it. The house has been restored to the period when Muir lived and wrote here, and trees around the house that date from Muir's years there have been identified so that landscaping too can appear as it did then. No primitive, he had installed a telephone and electric lights, as befit a prosperous (and by his death famous) man. Most of his voluminous writing was done in the study here. He wrote and polished laboriously by hand; his daughter Wanda faithfully typed the manuscripts. John Muir would surely be saddened to see much of what has grown up around his once-palatial estate. He would also be gratified that off to the east in the Sierra, much of his precious wilderness still survives.

BODIE HISTORIC DISTRICT *seven miles south of Bridgeport, east of U.S. 395.* Ghost town from gold rush of 1859 with 170 original buildings.

CABRILLO NATIONAL MONUMENT *tip of Point Loma, San Diego.*

Commemorates the discovery of the American West Coast by Portuguese explorer Juan Rodriguez Cabrillo in 1542.

COLUMBIA HISTORIC DISTRICT *four miles north of Sonora off state 49.* Restored and reconstructed downtown buildings in a gold-rush town of 1850.

DONNER CAMP STATE PARK *two and a half miles west of Truckee, Nevada, off I-80.* Where the snowbound Donner emigrant party in the winter of 1846–1847 resorted to cannibalism to allow forty-seven to survive.

EL MOLINO VIEJO MUSEUM *1120 Old Mill Road, San Marino.* Art and California history.

EL PUEBLO DE LOS ANGELES STATE HISTORIC PARK *between Los Angeles and Main streets, Arcadia and Macy streets, Los Angeles.* Site where Los Angeles was founded in 1781. Old Mission Church and other historic buildings nearby.

FORT HUMBOLDT STATE HISTORIC PARK *U.S. 101, 3431 Fort Avenue, Eureka.* Site of a fort established in 1853 to protect settlers from Indians; now with logging exhibits.

FORT POINT *the Presidio, San Francisco.* Fort built 1853–1861 on the site where, in 1776, explorer Juan Bautista de Anza claimed territory for Spain and began construction of the Presidio. Three forts have been built here to protect San Francisco harbor.

FORT ROSS *state 1 thirteen miles north of Jenner.* Restored stockade, blockade, commander's house, and Russian Orthodox chapel from the Russian trading post built here beginning in 1812.

HEARST SAN SIMEON STATE HISTORIC PARK *state 1 north of Morro Bay.* Publisher William Randolph Hearst's palatial estate, including La Casa Grande and 123 acres of gardens and grounds.

HISTORY CENTER *California Historical Society, 6300 Wilshire Boulevard, Los Angeles.* History museum with art collection, historical photos, archives, and library.

HUNTINGTON LIBRARY, ART GALLERY, AND BOTANICAL GARDENS *1151 Oxford Road, San Marino.* Research library with rare books and manuscripts in English and American history and literature, 130-acre botanical garden, and eighteenth-century British and French art.

LONDON RANCH *off state 12 west of Glen Ellen.* Built as a memorial to writer Jack London by his widow in 1919. Includes memorabilia and London's grave.

LOS ANGELES COUNTY MUSEUM OF NATURAL HISTORY *Exposition Park, Los Angeles.* Exhibits on California and western American history and North American habitats.

LOS ENCINOS STATE HISTORIC PARK *16756 Moor Park Street, Encino.* Site where Spanish first settled in 1769. Includes Osa Adobe, built 1849 and later a station for the Butterfield Stage, and Garnier House, built 1872.

LUMMIS HOUSE 200 E. Avenue 43, Los Angeles. Concrete and stone house in Mission style built 1897–1912 by an author, editor, and historian. Contains a museum of archeology, ethnology, Indian artifacts, and photography.

MARIN MIWOK MUSEUM 2200 Novato Boulevard, Novato. Extensive collections on native Americans from Alaska to Peru, including photos of California Indians and Edward S. Curtis photogravures. Also a thirty-five acre park with nature trails.

MISSION SAN ANTONIO DE PADUA off U.S. 101 twenty miles southwest of King City. Restored mission built in 1771, the third built by Father Junipero Serra.

MISSION SAN CARLOS BORROMEO DEL RIO CARMELO off state 1 at Rio Road, Carmel. Restored church built 1793–1797 by Father Junipero Serra, who is buried here.

MISSION SAN DIEGO DE ALCALA seven miles east of downtown San Diego in Mission Valley. The "mother mission" of twenty-one Spanish missions built in California in the 1700s, founded in 1769 and relocated in 1774; where the first irrigation system in California was developed and the first palm and olive trees rooted.

MISSION SAN GABRIEL ARCANGEL Junipero Street and West Mission Drive, San Gabriel. Restored church established in 1771. The first winery in California established here; today has what is called the largest grapevine in the world.

MISSION SAN JUAN CAPISTRANO Camino Capistrano and Ortega Highway, San Juan Capistrano. Ruin of one church and restored chapel of another from late 1700s, famous for the swallows that arrive every March 19 and depart October 23.

MISSION SAN LUIS REY Mission Road, four miles east of Oceanside. Founded in 1798. Combines Mexican, Moorish, and Spanish architectural elements. Now a Franciscan seminary.

MISSION SAN MIGUEL ARCANGEL on U.S. 101, San Miguel. Established 1797. One of the best-preserved missions, with many original decorations.

MONTEREY OLD TOWN 210 Oliver Street, Monterey Original capital of Spanish California, founded 1802. Includes eight historic buildings from the 1800s, including the Custom House, oldest government building in California.

NATIONAL MARITIME PARK Aquatic Park, foot of Polk Street, San Francisco. Four restored wooden vessels from the late 1800s and early 1900s, and a museum and library of maritime history.

OAK GROVE BUTTERFIELD STAGE STATION on state highway 79 thirteen miles northwest of Warner Hot Springs. A well-preserved adobe building of 1858 that is one of the few remaining stage stations on the Butterfield Overland Mail Route, 1858–1861.

OAKLAND MUSEUM 1000 Oak Street, Oakland. Art, history, and natural-science museum, with materials on western Americana.

OLD AUBURN HISTORIC DISTRICT on I-80 near Auburn. Remaining buildings of a gold town of 1848.

OLD U.S. MINT Fifth and Mission streets, San Francisco. Built 1869–1874. The first mint established outside Philadelphia and one of the few buildings to survive the 1906 earthquake and fire.

PETALUMA ADOBE Casa Grande Road four miles east of Petaluma. Built 1836–1846. One of the largest Mexican adobe buildings extant.

RANCHOS LOS ALAMITOS 6400 Bixby Hills Road, Long Beach. An 1806 Mexican ranch with period furniture, tools, and gardens.

RANCHOS LOS CERRITOS 4600 Virginia Road, Long Beach. An 1844 adobe ranch house with furniture, tools, and gardens.

SAN DIEGO HISTORICAL SOCIETY 2727 Presidio Drive, San Diego. Materials on San Diego, California, and western America; includes Serra Museum and Villa Montezuma; also research facilities and post-Mexican period exhibits in Electrical Building, Balboa Park.

SAN JUAN BAUTISTA STATE HISTORIC PARK three miles east of U.S. 101 near San Juan Bautista. Active mission, founded in 1797, with a town of buildings built in the 1800s.

SHERMAN LIBRARY AND GARDENS 2647 E. Coast Highway, Corona del Mar. Research institute for the Pacific Southwest, with gardens containing cacti and tropicana.

SONOMA PUEBLO state 12, Sonoma. Established as the only Mexican Franciscan mission in 1823, with largest plaza in California. Scene of the Bear Flag Revolt in 1846. Complex includes other historic homes of the 1800s.

SOUTHWEST MUSEUM 234 Museum Drive, Los Angeles. Collections on prehistoric and historic peoples of North, South, and Central America and the Spanish Colonial and Mexican eras.

WEAVERVILLE JOSS STATE HISTORIC PARK on U.S. 299 in Weaverville. Taoist temple, built in 1874, and other buildings showing the Chinese influence in California.

WELLS FARGO BANK HISTORY ROOM 420 Montgomery Street, San Francisco. Concord stagecoach, gold ore, and relics of the Pony Express and Wells Fargo. Also Wells Fargo museum at 444 S. Flower, Los Angeles.

WILL ROGERS STATE PARK 14253 Sunset Boulevard, Pacific Palisades. Ranch where Rogers lived and worked 1928–1932, with his memorabilia.

YOSEMITE COLLECTIONS Yosemite National park. Collections on anthropology, archeology, and natural history, with several historic houses.

COLORADO

BENT'S OLD FORT NATIONAL HISTORIC SITE eight miles west of Las Animas on Colorado 194, La Junta. "The outside exactly fills my idea of an ancient castle," wrote the eastern-born nineteen-year-old wife of a Santa Fe trader of Bent's Old Fort in 1846. "The walls are very high and very thick with rounding corners." So this key western outpost appeared during its heyday in the 1830s and 1840s and so, reconstructed by the National Park Service, it appears today: a massive adobe-walled structure reminiscent of much of the history and legend of the old Southwest.

Bent's Old Fort truly fits the popular image of what such a western outpost was like. High walls are perforated by musket loopholes, forbidding bastions mount artillery, a heavy wooden gate controls entry to the interior where the supplies and facilities to make the place self-sufficient are found. But no one popular image could possibly encompass all the actual forts that dotted the American West in the nineteenth century. Bent's Old Fort, for instance, lacked right up until the end of its career one of the key ingredients in the Hollywood image: hard-riding, blue-coated troopers. Like some other famous forts, at least in the beginning (Forts Laramie and Bridger in Wyoming are examples), this was a civilian rather than a military operation; the motives of its builders more economic than political. Pursuit of profit, not empire, accounted for its existence, though in the end it became a stepping stone along the path of America's westward expansion.

The Bent brothers hailed from St. Louis, in the 1820s a place on the edge of the great West. Ambitious, talented, and brave, Charles and William Bent set out to make their fortune in the West's then only known resource: furs. They ranged far to the northwest but found only slim prospects in the face of competition from the giants of the business: the American Fur Company, the North West Company, and the legendary British Hudson's Bay Company. Turning southward, they found the opportunity that would make them rich and famous. Early in the 1820s the Santa Fe Trail, running from Independence, Missouri, across Kansas southwestward to New Mexico, had opened trade with the old and prosperous Spanish settlements of the upper Rio Grande Valley, most notably Sante Fe. Down the trail to New Mexico went wagon trains bearing the manufactured merchandise of the East; back came silver, turquoise, and Navajo blankets. All along the way were various Indian tribes eager to trade buffalo robes and other pelts for axes, guns, whiskey, and other wonders of the white man's world.

For the Bents (and for fellow St. Louisan Ceran St. Vrain who was soon to be their partner) it was a wonderful chance. They brought to it, in the best nineteenth-century tradition, entrepreneurial skills of a high order, good sense, and luck. They began by dividing the tasks: St. Vrain did the sales work in New Mexico and farther south in Chihuahua. Brother William dealt with the Indians. Brother Charles handled purchasing and transportation from the Missouri end. There were two immediate tangible results: "Bent, St. Vrain & Company," as they called their new enterprise, and the fort in southeastern Colorado that became its headquarters.

The site for that fort was carefully chosen. For nearly half its length, the Santa Fe Trail was actually two routes. It divided in southwestern Kansas at the Cimarron Crossing of the Arkansas River. The south branch, called the Cimarron Cutoff, led directly southwest across the future panhandle of Oklahoma and into New Mexico to a point near present-day Watrous. The north branch, called the Mountain Branch, followed the Arkansas River to beyond the Purgatoire River in Colorado and thence

Reconstruction of Bent's Old Fort

southwest through Raton Pass. The two branches then merged and formed a single route into Sante Fe. Though it was longer, the northern route was also safer and more traveled, and the Bents decided to put their fort along its path. Determined to extract the most from their venture, they considered more than the traffic passing along the trail. They also needed a place close both to the buffalo-hunting Indians of the Great Plains and to the mountain men who trapped the beaver on the streams of the Rockies. They found it on the north bank of the Arkansas River near present-day La Junta, Colorado. Here the wagon trains turned south for the final tortuous 300-mile trek over the Raton Mountains to Santa Fe. Here too would come the Cheyennes, Arapahos, Utes, Comanches, Crows, Shoshonis—and mountain men.

The Bents probably began their outpost in 1832, and they knew it must also be a fort. They used adobe, not timber, and they built generously. One hundred fifty masons were brought up from Taos in New Mexico; pine and cottonwood logs were dragged and floated in for roof beams and doors. By early 1834 it was finished, and from the Mississippi to the Pacific there was nothing else quite like it. At its zenith in the 1840s the fort had grown to a trapezoid 130 by 175 by 185 feet, enclosed by walls that averaged twenty-seven inches thick and were fourteen feet high. One astounded eastern visitor wrote in 1839 that it was "as though an air-built castle had dropped to earth ... in the midst of the vast desert." Inside there were thirty-eight rooms on two stories, twenty-two fireplaces, and just about everything necessary for survival in the wilderness.

If it was a "castle," it was, as befit the country around it, a crude one. Floors were dirt, walls whitewashed adobe, bedding Spanish blankets and pallets of straw. During the day it hosted a great and varied throng of humanity come there to rest, deal, and trade. But at night the Indians among them were always escorted outside the walls and the massive ironstudded gates slammed shut. Today only tourists throng there, for the fort's purpose is long gone. What they see there, however, is faithful to what people saw long ago. A trader's room contained an array of staples and luxuries from the East to be exchanged for buffalo robes, beaver pelts, and horses. Blacksmith and carpenter shops offered services constantly needed by the wagon trains that passed through, and the ring of the blacksmith's hammer was one of the fort's most familiar sounds. There were separate quarters for Mexican laborers and their families and for the fur trappers who once a year came down from the mountains with their pelts. Warehouses, wellroom, and powder magazine accommodated frontier necessities.

More commodious, though still far from fancy, were the rooms reserved for William Bent and, on the second floor, for his partner St. Vrain. Two rooms did bring a touch of more settled civilization to this remote castle in the desert. The dining room (with adjacent cook's room and kitchen) was the scene of much hearty eating. Cook Charlotte Green's buffalo-hump roasts, slapjacks, and pumpkin pies were renowned for miles around. And on occasions when distinguished eastern visitors were present, sumptuous fare and French wines were served. Historian Francis Parkman, author of the *California and Oregon Trail,* was delighted to find a table laid with a white cloth. Across the plaza, meanwhile, a billiard room (the original table was brought from St. Louis in the 1830s) was the scene of gaming, smoking, and drinking.

For a decade the Bents' influence spread far beyond their imposing fort. They helped keep peace among the Indians and between the Indians and the whites (William Bent married a well-born Cheyenne). Their prosperity was as famous as their hospitality. It was also short-lived—a victim of the rush of national expansion that brought war with Mexico and vastly longer columns of white men to the West. Army troops, gold-seekers, settlers, and adventurers destroyed the buffalo and angered the Indians, whose hostility from the late 1840s on brought the end of the great trading days for people like the Bents and St. Vrain. Charles died in an Indian revolt in Taos. St. Vrain moved to New Mexico. William, discouraged at the sad changes he saw coming, abandoned (and some say set fire to and blew up) his famous fort and moved thirty-eight miles down the Arkansas in an ill-fated attempt to try again. Today's reconstructed Bent's Old Fort is a monument to their ambition and the trading empire that resulted—and to a fleeting episode in western history.

GEORGETOWN LOOP *Georgetown-Silver Plume Historic District, Georgetown.* In 1859, James Buchanan of Pennsylvania was still in the White House, the new Republican Party was preparing for the fateful presidential election of 1860, and the southern states were growing ever more restive with the Union. That Union still numbered just thirty-three states, of which only two, California and Oregon, were in the great American West. Wagon trains had been reaching out across the plains, bound for any number of promised lands, for nearly twenty years. But the great fulcrum of American history still lay decisively in the East, as the Civil War would soon show. Most Americans lived there, and for years to come nearly all of the nation's newly built industrial power—and not a little of its much older agricultural wealth—was to be found in the eastern states.

Another kind of wealth lay elsewhere, visions of which lured America's earliest explorers. Gold and silver—metals which, men had long believed, had "natural" value—accounted for many a fabulous adventure. Unlike other less tangible sources of wealth (a business enterprise, for example) this wealth could be held in one's hands, possessed and enjoyed with little tending. Even the dullest imagination knew that having enough of it made a man rich. But it was seldom the dullest who became rich. Nature usually makes this wealth hard to get, locking it away in mountains and desert fastness. That is a difficulty that could of course be overcome by stealing (as many romantic and some not-so-romantic western outlaws did, and as the Spanish conquistadores did in Central and South America). But for the honest man who craved it, there was no substitute for first finding it and then digging it up.

That meant prospecting and mining, two words indelibly associated with the West. By the 1850s, when most of American history was still being made elsewhere, the West's mining frontier began to move. The most famous episode was the California gold rush that began in 1849. But over the remainder of the nineteenth century, discovery of gold and silver throughout the vast interior of the West set thousands of gold-seekers digging, created a good many fabulous fortunes, and helped create several western states. Colorado was among the first; Georgetown was one of its first mining districts and is today one of the best-preserved mining districts in the West.

Gold was discovered in Georgetown in 1859 by two brothers, George and David Griffith, who had prospected along a cold mountain stream aptly called Clear Creek. In two days they panned and washed out $100 worth of gold dust. They naturally named the place the Griffith District, then platted out a townsite and named it for brother George. As in other

mining districts throughout the West, in the early days before any formal authority had arrived the prospectors organized their own miners'
courts. They wrote their own laws to protect mineral claims and to
ensure a modicum of law and order in isolated communities. When
Colorado became a territory in 1861 and a state in 1876, many of these
informal rules, revised and codified, found their way into its formally
enacted legal code. Georgetown is an especially good example of this
process and remains today governed by laws some of which derive
from the old mining frontier. Its chief administrative official or "police
judge" performs functions similar to those of his predecessor, the judge
of the miners' court.

Though gold that could be panned from rivers and streams was the
chief attraction in the beginning years, silver soon displaced it. Georgetown's miners burrowed deep into the surrounding mountains and were
soon removing millions of dollars' worth of silver ore. Many mines
were opened in the Clear Creek Valley, and one of the most important,
the Lebanon, has been restored as part of the Georgetown Loop Historic Area. It is one of the oldest tunnels in Colorado; its interior is dry,
the original supports are still sound, and it still contains ore deposits.
Also being restored are the above-ground facilities typical of silver mining. A water-powered crushing mill (part of it used as late as 1949)
began the process of ore recovery; a blacksmith shop built and repaired
equipment and tools; a changing room provided a place for miners to
don their work clothes and a place to store them at the end of their
shift. A mine office kept track of the whole operation. For a number of
years Clear Creek Valley (and similar districts like Leadville, which in
time eclipsed it) hummed with such activity.

An important part of that activity was the railroad, after whose
remarkable "loop" the area is named. By 1877 the Colorado Central
connected Georgetown with Denver. But in 1884, the Georgetown,
Breckenridge, and Leadville Railway (a subsidiary of the Union Pacific)
extended service to another mining settlement, Silver Plume. This route,
which ran four and a half miles to connect two towns only two miles
apart, constituted the famous loop. There were actually several loops
that wound across the valley climbing 638 feet in elevation on a maximum grade of three and a half percent. Along the way the line passed
through a tunnel and over four trestles, including the Devil's Gate Via-
duct, a 300-foot span that towered 95 feet above Clear Creek.

Though the narrow-gauge line never got to Leadville as once planned,
it carried ore, freight, and passengers between Silver Plume and
Georgetown for fifty-five years until highway competition forced abandonment of the line. Some of the passengers were residents or people
with business in the area, but many were tourists. Indeed, the tourists
arrived just after the miners, and long outlasted them. As soon as the
railroad connected Georgetown with Denver, tourists became big business. Hired liveries carried visitors eager for a taste of the mountains'

Pin truss bridge on the Georgetown loop

wonders on day excursions to scenic peaks and lakes. Completion of the loop increased the region's attractiveness, enabling tourists both to gaze comfortably at the scenery and to marvel at man's genius in taming it. At the peak six trains a day carried passengers over the line on the twenty-five-minute run from Georgetown to Silver Plume.

Georgetown itself grew with the silver boom into an attractive mountain town. Its prosperous merchants, bankers, and mine operators built handsome houses reflecting their success and the fashion of the times. Among the best examples are the Hamill house, built by a mining millionaire in the eighties, and the Frank Maxwell house, an especially fine representation of the Victorian style. Grace Episcopal Church dates from the late 1860s, the stone Presbyterian church from 1873. A distinguished office block rose in 1867, a public school a few years later. The watchtower of the Alpine Hose Company guarded it all against fire, one of the worst enemies of such wooden frontier towns. In fact, unlike many other mining settlements, Georgetown never burned, and as a result it stands today as one of the prettiest and best-preserved of Colorado's famous mining camps. With the railroad loop (on which steam trains again carry tourists) and the Lebanon Mine (also open for inspection), Georgetown offers the visitor an excellent view of what the West's mining frontier once looked like.

Like the West's other frontiers, this one also passed—making places like Georgetown, Leadville, and Cripple Creek, curiosities, once the centers of men's search for wealth, now historical curiosities. Whatever silver's "inherent natural worth," it was its market value that either spurred or deterred the search for it. And when silver's heyday passed with the repeal of the Sherman Silver Purchase Act in 1893, places like Georgetown fell from eminence and from man's imagination. Fortunately, unlike some others, Georgetown did not disappear. Some people stayed and a goodly number still live there. The silver boom may be long gone, but Georgetown remains a living and inviting reminder of the wealth that helped create Colorado.

MOLLY BROWN HOUSE MUSEUM, PEARCE-McALLISTER COT- TAGE, AND GRANT-HUMPHREYS MANSION Denver. On a topo- graphical map, Colorado is made up of plains, peaks, and passes. Much of Colorado's history is hard to imagine against any other backdrop. The plains were at first an obstacle between easterners and attractions farther west: gold, green valleys, and adventure. Later the plains grew rich with cattle and wheat. The peaks and passes guarded mineral wealth that lured thousands who hoped to strike it rich. Colorado's was a set- ting whose remoteness and harshness inspired all the fact and fancy of the frontier. Intrepid mountain men and trappers, exotic tribes and dauntless cavalry, determined prospectors and railroad builders: all seemed naturally at home there. It was no doubt once a very exciting place to be.

But Coloradans, like everybody else, could not survive on adventure alone. As years passed, frontiers inevitably passed with them. Those who stayed built lives that transcended their often rude beginnings. As they grew wealthy, their pretensions to grace and style took form in their buildings. Ornate Victorian hotels, substantial banks and business blocks, and elegant private houses proclaimed their success—and pro- claimed that they had settled down. Hamlets became towns, and towns cities. Denver was the largest and most famous.

In the years after statehood in 1876, Denver boldly emerged from the chaos of frontier days into a city of some distinction. A place with money and a powerful need to be noticed, it offered fresh new oppor- tunities to architects and builders. An early example of their work was the Tabor Block on Larimer Street, a five-story "Temple to Progress, worthy of any city in the world." It was followed a few years later by the million-dollar Tabor Grand Opera House. The magnificent triangular Brown Palace Hotel at Seventh and Broadway opened for business in 1892 at a cost of $1.6 million. It still welcomes guests. Five hundred architects competed to design the state capitol, which was completed in 1908 as it stands today for $3.5 million.

But it was not all grand commercial and public building that changed the face of Colorado's first city. The upwardly mobile and newly rich whose fortunes poured down from the mines of Leadville and Cripple Creek required private residences befitting their and Denver's exalted new status. Some of these residences still stand; three in particular, preserved as historic-house museums, offer a glimpse of how Denver's gentry once lived. The most legendary is the Molly Brown House on Pennsylvania Street in the Capitol Hill area, one of Denver's most fash- ionable neighborhoods in the late nineteenth century. Hardly unique for that time and place, it is a massive Victorian structure with a dazzle

Denver's Pearce-McAllister Cottage

of rooflines, chimneys, and porches, faced in lava stone and trimmed with intricate woodwork. Its fame derives from its occupants, James Joseph and Margaret ("Molly") Brown, who moved in five years after the house was built. Like so many wealthy Coloradans, Brown came from the East and made his fortune in mining. He met Molly, who had come from Pennsylvania, in Leadville and they were married in 1886. They had a son and daughter there, and in 1894 moved from Leadville down to Denver. They paid a respectable $30,000 for their stylish residence, joined the right clubs, and stepped out confidently in Denver's high society. The Browns made numerous changes to their house, which has been restored according to photographs of the interior taken in 1910. The Browns traveled extensively and in their absence rented it to several prominent tenants, including in 1902 Colorado Governor James B. Orman—thus distinguishing their house as the governor's mansion for one year. Molly won national renown for her relief work with immigrant women and children who survived the sinking of the *Titanic* in 1912 and later became an active preservationist, purchasing the house of poet Eugene Field and giving it to Denver as a memorial. Later preservationists, organized as Historic Denver, Inc., saved her own house, which had passed out of family hands after Molly's death in 1932.

Two other Denver houses (both properties of the Colorado Historical Society), though dating from the same era, reflect other tastes. The Pearce-McAllister Cottage on Gaylord Street just west of City Park was built in 1899. Though it is more modest than the Brown House, it too is associated with several prominent families whose names are tied to Denver and Colorado. It was built by Englishman Richard Pearce, a well-known metallurgist and manager of a large smelter, for his son,

Harold. Harold's wife was the daughter of William A. Bell, a founder of the Denver & Rio Grande Western Railroad. In 1907 the house passed to Henry McAllister, Jr., whose family was prominent in real estate, mining, and farming ventures. McAllister himself served as Denver District Attorney and later as counsel for the D&RGW. Their house could hardly be more different from Molly Brown's. With a gambrel roof, dormer windows, inviting front porch, and gold, green, and cream color scheme, it is an excellent example of America's turn-of-the-century fascination with the colonial architecture of the East Coast, and one can easily imagine still living in it. The now curious term "cottage" then distinguished even a decent-sized free-standing house such as this one from the rowhouses and townhouses typical of urban residential building. Its designer, Frederick J. Sterner, was like Richard Pearce an Englishman and was also an influential Denver architect. His other larger and more famous work included General William Jackson Palmer's spacious house, "Glen Eyrie," and the old Antlers Hotel, both in Colorado Springs.

The Grant-Humphreys Mansion on Pennsylvania Street, begun the year after the Pearce-McAllister Cottage, also housed some prominent Denverites but in a more pretentious fashion. Its builder was James B. Grant, a native southerner who came west, made his fortune in smelting in Leadville and Denver, and served as Colorado's third governor in 1883–1884. Declining to run for a second term, he remained a powerful influence in Denver for years to come, helping found Colorado Women's College and the Denver National Bank and serving as president of the American Smelting and Refining Corporation. His forty-two room house on Quality Hill, then Denver's most elegant section, cost him about $35,000 and measured the large distance he had come since arriving in Leadville nearly a quarter-century before. Its architect, F. Louis Harnois, designed a superb beaux-arts classical house whose grand proportions, imposing columned facade, balustraded porches, and detailed stone finishes proclaimed this as the seat of a Denver mogul. Inside there were large spaces and all the amenities: on the first floor, drawing, reception, dining, and billiard rooms, breakfast porch, library, kitchen, butler's pantry, and servants' hall. Above were seven bedrooms, all opening onto a skylit sitting area; playroom and two more bedrooms occupied the third floor. The basement level contained a ballroom, a stage, and a bowling alley. The fittings were all appropriately deluxe: there were an elaborate intercom system of speaking tubes, rosewood and mahogany moldings, silk wall coverings, an electrically back-lit marble fireplace, and a secret vault.

Grant died in 1911. The next owner, Albert E. Humphreys, a self-made oil millionaire, made a number of changes that only added to the house's elegance. The billiard room became a sunroom; new parquet floor was laid; windows became French doors. The bowling alley gave way to a shooting gallery, and a new Chippendale dining-room table and chairs were custom made to match the room's mahogany panelling.

Mechanically there were three additions: an electrified cold room in the kitchen, three new bathrooms on the second floor (bringing the total for the house to eleven), and steam heat for the whole house. Thus elegant and up-to-date for the 1920s, the mansion remained virtually unchanged. In 1976 Ira Humphreys willed it and its 2½ acres of grounds to the Colorado Historical Society. Historic Denver, Inc. presently manages it as a historic-house museum. Carefully furnished and maintained, it is a place its first tycoon owners might still be proud of.

BACA HOUSE-BLOOM HOUSE-PIONEER MUSEUM *Main Street, Trinidad.* Two historic houses from the late nineteenth century and a museum on the history of the Santa Fe Trail, Trinidad, and the open-range cattle days.

BELMAR MUSEUM OF THE CITY OF LAKEWOOD *797 S. Wadsworth Boulevard, Lakewood.* Special focus on the agricultural history of the foothills area of the Eastern Slope of Colorado.

BOULDER HISTORICAL SOCIETY MUSEUM *1655 Broadway at Arapahoe, Boulder.* Exhibits and programs on local and western history.

BUFFALO BILL MEMORIAL MUSEUM *Route 5, Golden.* Museum founded by a close friend of Buffalo Bill and member of his Wild West Show.

CENTENNIAL VILLAGE *14th Avenue and B Street, Greeley.* Village museum illustrating the city's growth.

CENTRAL CITY HISTORIC DISTRICT *Central City.* Historic mining town. Includes Central City Opera House, erected in 1878 and the state's oldest opera house, and the Teller House, a famous hotel built in 1872 by Henry M. Teller, U.S. Senator and Secretary of the Interior, and his brother, Willard.

COLORADO HISTORICAL SOCIETY *Colorado Heritage Center, 1300 Broadway, Denver.* Museum of Colorado history.

COLORADO RAILROAD MUSEUM *17155 West 44th Avenue, Golden.* Exhibits and programs highlighting the history of railroading in the state.

COLORADO SKI MUSEUM-SKI HALL OF FAME *15 Vail Road, Vail.* Exhibits pertaining to the popular sport and the Colorado recreation industry.

COLORADO STATE CAPITOL *Capitol Hill, Denver.* Three-story granite capitol constructed between 1890 and 1907.

DENVER MINT *W. Colfax Avenue and Delaware Street, Denver.* Erected in 1897 to house a branch office of the U.S. Bureau of the Mint.

EL PUEBLO MUSEUM *905 S. Prairie Avenue, Pueblo.* Includes a reproduction of the Pueblo trading post and exhibits on the history of the region.

FORT COLLINS MUSEUM *200 Mathews, Fort Collins.* Local history museum.

FORT MORGAN HERITAGE FOUNDATION *Fort Morgan.* Focuses on Morgan County and northeastern Colorado.

FORT VASQUEZ *U.S. Highway 85, Platteville.* Museum and reconstruction of 1835 fur-trading post.

FOUR MILE HISTORIC PARK *715 South Forest Street, Denver.* Log house erected in the late 1850s, at one time a stop on the Wells Fargo-Butterfield Stage line.

HEALY HOUSE-DEXTER CABIN *912 Harrison Avenue, Leadville.* Two structures that date from the late-1870s silver bonanza.

HERITAGE MUSEUM *102 E. Ninth Street at Harrison Avenue, Leadville.* Museum and historic structures located in the Leadville Historic District.

HOTEL DE PARIS *Alpine Street, Georgetown.* One of the great luxury hotels of the late nineteenth century, erected in 1875 by Frenchman Louis Dupuy.

HOVENWEEP NATIONAL MONUMENT *McElmo Route, Cortez.* Six groups of pre-Columbian dwellings.

LITTLETON HISTORICAL MUSEUM *6028 Gallup, Littleton.* General museum, historic buildings, and historic farm.

LONGMONT PIONEER MUSEUM *375 Kimbark, Longmont.* History museum focusing on the St. Vrain Valley.

MEEKER HOUSE *1324 9th Avenue, Greeley.* Adobe residence built in 1870 for Nathan C. Meeker, who founded Greeley as a cooperative agricultural colony.

MESA VERDE NATIONAL PARK *U.S. 160, Cortez.* Museum and archaeological remains of pre-Columbian dwellings abandoned at the end of the thirteenth century.

MUSEUM OF WESTERN COLORADO *4th and Ute streets, Grand Junction.* History and natural history museum focusing on western Colorado.

OLD FORT GARLAND *Colorado 159, Fort Garland.* Restoration of fort erected in 1858 to protect settlers from the Ute Indians; at one time commanded by Kit Carson.

OVERLAND TRAIL MUSEUM *Junction I-76 and Highway 6 East, Sterling.* General museum located on the route of the Overland Trail.

ROCKY MOUNTAIN NATIONAL PARK *Estes Park.* Established in 1915 as a result of the efforts of Enos Mills, Colorado naturalist and early spokesman for conservation.

PIONEERS' MUSEUM *215 S. Tejon, Colorado Springs.* Museum housed in old El Paso County Courthouse and focusing on the history of the Pike's Peak region.

SOUTH PARK CITY MUSEUM *Fairplay.* Historic-village museum, including brewery and saloon that date from the 1870s.

WESTERN MUSEUM OF MINING AND INDUSTRY *1025 Northgate Road, Colorado Springs.* Exhibits on mining technology, including western hard rock mining and placer mining.

CONNECTICUT

HENRY WHITFIELD STATE HISTORICAL MUSEUM   Old Whitfield Street, Guilford. English Puritans dominated the settlement of Guilford in 1639 much as they did earlier colonization efforts at Hartford and New Haven. These settlers, part of the great Puritan migration of the early seventeenth century, remained faithful to their religion and to English customs and traditions in the establishment of their New World communities. Erected in a traditional English style for the Puritan clergyman who led the community, the Henry Whitfield State Historical Museum of Guilford reflects these influences and serves as an important symbol of colonial Connecticut.

Although educated for a career in law, Henry Whitfield decided to enter the ministry and was ordained by the Church of England in 1618. That same year he married Dorothy Shaeffe and became Vicar of St. Margaret's Church at Ockley. For the next twenty years, he served the parish faithfully and lived a life of relative ease, made all the more comfortable by an inheritance from his father. Content with his situation, Whitfield at first did not join the dissidents who protested against the papist tendencies of the Church of England during the reign of King Charles I. But as the strictures of Archbishop William Laud became less tolerable, the Ockley clergyman became a convert to the cause of reform. After the High Commission Court censured him for his support of the Puritan cause, Whitfield resigned his position at St. Margaret's and resolved to join the Puritan migration to America.

In 1638 Whitfield recruited twenty-five families to join him in establishing a plantation in the southern part of New England, where his friends John Davenport and George Fenwick had recently founded new colonies. During the long voyage, Whitfield drew up an agreement of mutual support for all the heads of families to sign. Known as the Guilford Covenant, this compact reflected the Puritan concern with social order and provided a basis for organizing the new settlement.

The Whitfield group landed first at Quinnipiac or New Haven, where the Reverend John Davenport and other settlers greeted them. The new emigrants consulted with Davenport and with George Fenwick of the Saybrook colony and decided to locate halfway between the two coastal settlements. In September 1639, on behalf of the entire group, Whitfield purchased from Shaumpishuh, the Sachem of the Menuncatuck Indians, a track of land that extended from the East River to Stony Creek. Here they established the Plantation of Menuncatuck, now known as Guilford.

With winter fast approaching, the settlers erected temporary shelters for the most part but also began construction of a more substantial home for Whitfield. Transporting stone from a site about a quarter of a mile east, they probably completed that fall only the north chimney and part of the main hall, perhaps enclosing the south side with a temporary timber wall. Work resumed the next spring, and the two-a-half-story stone structure was completed. The walls, constructed of local stone in a coursed rubble pattern with mortar made of yellow clay and pulverized oyster shells, tapered from a thirty-inch base to a thickness of eighteen inches at the roofline. Joists and rafters were hand-hewn oaken timbers, and pine and whitewood were used for inside partitions. Other features included a steeply pitched roof, corbeled end chimneys, stone lintels, and a separate stair tower. Although most of the settlers came from Surrey and Kent, the Whitfield house was more similar in style to that of the Cotswolds further north—perhaps an indication of the influence of William Leete, one of the few emigrants from that region and later a prominent leader in the New Haven Colony.

The rather imposing structure not only housed the Whitfields, their seven children, and several servants, but also served as a community meetinghouse, a place of worship, a garrison, and even a resting place for New England travelers. The center of activity was the Great Room, a thirty-three-by-fifteen-foot chamber that occupied the entire first floor. An enormous fireplace at each end heated the Great Room. The north fireplace was ten feet, four inches wide and required a divided flue for structural stability. Here family meals were prepared and eaten, servants did their work, children played, and the other routine activities of a large household were carried out. On Sundays, the Great Room was used for worship services conducted by the Reverend Mr. Whitfield, and on other occasions it was used for public meetings and celebrations—including a wedding feast for one of Whitfield's daughters.

Henry Whitfield's stone house

An ell was added to the rear a few years later. Isolated from the activity in the Great Room, this Hall or Parlour Chamber probably served Whitfield as a combination study-sleeping chamber, a quiet place where he could prepare sermons and meet with parishioners. A separate stair tower, a feature typical of English houses, led to the upper chambers. Over the Great Hall was a single large sleeping chamber, and a second, smaller one occupied the rear ell. The garret provided additional sleeping space as well as storage.

Whitfield remained in Guilford until 1650 or 1651, when he returned to England. It is not clear why he left the colony or why his wife and several of his children remained behind. Whitfield took a parish in the Diocese of Winchester and died in 1657 without having returned to America. His wife left Guilford in 1659 to return to England, where she died a decade later.

The Town of Guilford considered purchasing the Whitfield house for use as a school, but in 1659 a family friend bought the structure from the Whitfield heirs. Assorted tenants occupied the house until 1772, when Joseph Pynchon bought it for use as his own residence. A prominent figure in both town and colony politics prior to the Revolution, Pynchon in turn sold the stone structure to Jasper Griffing, whose descendants owned it until about 1900.

By the late nineteenth century, Whitfield's house had undergone significant alteration. After a fire in 1865, the owners changed the pitch of the roof, covered the exterior in stucco, and removed the south chimney and fireplaces. These alterations and the general deterioration of the building toward the end of the nineteenth century came to the attention of the Connecticut Society of the Colonial Dames of America, who led a successful campaign for state purchase of the historic building. The house was purchased in 1900 with funds from the state, Guilford, the Colonial Dames, and others. Administered by a board of trustees and operated by the Colonial Dames, the Whitfield house opened to the public as a museum in 1903. In 1930 and 1931 the Hall or Parlour Chamber was reconstructed, and between 1935 and 1937 a major restoration project returned the structure to its mid-seventeenth-century appearance.

Now administered by the Connecticut Historical Commission, the Whitfield house recreates what life must have been like in the young colony at Guilford. While the Henry Whitfield State Historical Museum is significant simply as the oldest remaining house in Connecticut and the oldest stone house still standing in New England, the structure and its history have broader meaning for the Connecticut experience. It provides a strong link to the state's origins in the English Puritan migration of the early seventeenth century.

OLD STATE HOUSE *800 Main Street, Hartford.* In laying out the town of Hartford in 1636, Thomas Hooker and his followers began with the selection of a site for the community's meeting house. Known first as

Hartford's Old State House

Meeting House Square and later as Old State House Square, this small parcel of land served as the center of Connecticut government and politics for nearly two and a half centuries. The Old State House, erected on the square in 1792, is the oldest surviving state capitol erected under the federal constitution and stands today as a fitting symbol of Connecticut's early statehood.

The Hooker colony erected Hartford's first Meeting House in 1638. Situated on a ridge overlooking the Connecticut River, the small structure served the community and the Connecticut colony until 1720. The most significant event of that first century occurred on May 31, 1638, shortly after the completion of the building, when the Reverend Mr. Hooker delivered his famous sermon establishing the framework for the colony's Fundamental Orders of 1639, the earliest written constitution in America. That compact then served as the basis for the Charter of 1662, which confirmed the legal basis of the Connecticut colony and insured its continued self-government. This constitution remained in effect for the next one hundred fifty years, providing continuity from the colonial period into the early nineteenth century and buttressing the power of the Puritan Congregational establishment in both the colony and the state.

Hartford's rival to the south, New Haven, joined the Connecticut colony in 1665, but the rivalry between the two cities did not abate. With great reluctance, the prosperous coastal city initially accepted the continued designation of Hartford as the colony's capital; but the need for a new capitol building reopened the debate in the early eighteenth century. The old Hartford Meeting House did not have sufficient space for the growing colonial legislature, and proposals were made for construction of a larger edifice on the same site. Counter-proposals then called for relocation of the capital to New Haven, the colony's most populous city. In 1720 the opposing sides reached a compromise: Hartford would remain the capital in exchange for the establishment of Yale College at New Haven.

Thus a second, larger Meeting House rose on Meeting House Square in 1720. This structure served the colony until the American Revolution and became the state's first capitol under the new nation. During the celebration of the end of the war and the signing of the Treaty of Paris in 1783, the Meeting House caught fire and burned. Although repaired shortly thereafter, the frame structure was simply too small and inadequate for the state's needs. After years of debate and study, the Connecticut legislature in 1792 finally authorized construction of a new state capitol at Hartford.

Various delays and funding problems jeopardized completion of the project. The legislature's building committee recognized immediately that initial funding would not cover the expected construction costs, but in 1793 the assembly authorized a lottery to make up the difference. The committee had the old structure moved off the site, and construction of the new capitol began under the supervision of John Leffingwell, the city's most important master builder. The lottery, however, failed, and completion of the project appeared impossible. Two local entrepreneurs then came up with a financing proposal that provided for both personal profit and completion of the building. Although the scheme actually proved financially ruinous for the two, the new State House was completed in time for the opening of the state legislature in May 1796.

Noted Boston architect Charles Bulfinch reportedly drew up the design for the structure, and its fine Federal details certainly support that claim. When completed in 1796, the rectangular brick and brownstone edifice rose three stories to a low hipped roof, without the balustrade and cupola added in the early nineteenth century. An open arcade through the width of the building provided access. Columned and pedimented porticoes surmounted the arcades on the west and east facades. The interior reflected traditional English design, with a large central hall separating the people's court and the lower house at one end from the executive offices and upper house at the other. As the first state capitol erected after the adoption and ratification of the United States Constitution, the new structure was an impressive statement of Connecticut's faith in the permanence of the young republic.

Because of the continued rivalry between Hartford and New Haven, the state found itself with two capital cities for a time, and the legislature met in the new state house only every other session from 1796 to 1875.

Although Connecticut politics remained rather stable through the nineteenth century, the years 1814 through 1818 proved particularly significant for the state's historical development. The War of 1812 and consequent curtailment of American commerce caused considerable economic distress in Connecticut, as in most of mercantile New England. The Federalist-dominated state government railed against "Mr. Madison's War" and refused to cooperate with the Republican president. In December of 1814 Connecticut Federalists joined with representatives of other New England states in a closed meeting held in Hartford's State House. This "Hartford Convention" considered ways of preventing similar abuses of power in the future. The signing of the Treaty of Ghent on December 24 eliminated the focus of their complaints, however, and in the exhilaration of victory the whole proceeding took on an unpatriotic cast. Republican opponents then used charges of unpatriotic behavior to undermine the Federalists' dominance in state politics. Defections from the Federalist ranks began in 1815, and by 1818 the opposition controlled the governorship and both legislative houses. The breaking of the Federalist–Congregationalist hegemony amounted to a virtual political revolution.

Republican control of the state government resulted in another significant event: the state constitutional convention of 1818. Meeting at the Hartford State House, the convention significantly reworked the constitution along more liberal lines. The Constitution of 1818 remained in effect until 1965, when another convention was called. In a symbolic gesture, the 1965 convention also held its opening session in the State House.

Throughout this period, the Connecticut government moved back and forth between Hartford and New Haven. The issue finally came to a head in 1873, when voters selected Hartford as the capital in a statewide referendum. The State House was too small for the growing state government, so plans proceeded for a new and larger structure. The state legislature held its last session in the historic building in May 1878.

Upon the state government's departure, the City of Hartford converted the Old State House for use as a city hall. By that time construction had begun on a new federal building on the east lawn, twenty feet from the main entrance to the older structure; so the entrance was switched to the west side, and the main staircase was reversed as well. The city made numerous other alterations prior to moving to a new structure in 1915. After over a century of use, the old State House stood empty, its future uncertain.

Efforts to preserve the vacant structure culminated in a major restoration project in 1918 and 1919. When the building was reopened on January 1, 1921, the staircase had been returned to its original position, new structural supports had been added, and the interior was restored as closely as possible to the original. In 1934 the neighboring federal building was demolished and the square was restored to its former park-like appearance. The structure was used for a variety of purposes until 1959, when the Connecticut Historical Society assumed its management. In the wake of severe cutbacks in government support, administration of the site shifted in 1975 to the Old State House Association, a private non-profit organization. A subsequent restoration program has further insured the authenticity of the building's appearance as well as its structural stability.

In addition to guided tours, lectures and talks, and a museum shop, the Old State House Association sponsors a variety of special cultural and historical programs and activities in the building and on the grounds. After over three hundred fifty years, Meeting House Square remains a focal point for community life and a symbol of Connecticut's political development from colony to state.

MYSTIC SEAPORT *route 27, Mystic.* Connecticuters first began building ships in the seventeenth century; but the industry did not develop fully until the nineteenth century, when limited agricultural opportunities necessitated economic diversification. By the 1820s the community of Mystic stood at the center of a thriving maritime commerce along the state's Atlantic coast. Although the era of great wooden sailing ships ended before the close of the century, Connecticut's maritime past has been carefully preserved at the Mystic Seaport museum complex. An impressive collection of historic ships and small boats, a recreated maritime community, and a variety of exhibits and special programs at Mystic Seaport provide a unique opportunity to learn about the history of coastal Connecticut and the seafaring heritage of New England.

The earliest shipbuilders along the Mystic River devoted only part of their time to maritime activity and continued to farm during the summers. Increased coastwise commerce and trade with the West Indies expanded the market for their sloops and schooners in the late seventeenth and eighteenth centuries, but the industry did not really burgeon in the Mystic region until the 1820s. The discovery of Antarctica in 1820 by the captain of a Mystic ship brought fame to the community, but routine whaling expeditions provided the catalyst for substantial growth and development prior to 1850. The demand for whaleships encouraged entrepreneurs like George, Clark, and Thomas Greenman to open new shipyards at Mystic. Some even became directly involved in whaling: during the peak years 1845–1846 local merchants owned eighteen whalers, an impressive number for this relatively small port.

Between 1850 and 1860 the romance of the clipper ship shifted attention away from the whalers. Developed originally for the China trade, these long, narrow, high-masted ships provided the fastest transportation available to the gold fields of California. Between 1850 and 1860, Mystic shipyards constructed twenty-two of these beautiful sailing ships, including the *David Crockett,* a record-setting clipper built at the Greenman yards. The era of the great clipper ships was brief, however, yielding to the greater efficiency and speed of steam and rail in the last half of the nineteenth century. Although local yards continued to build small boats, barges, and schooners into the twentieth century, production at Mystic never again reached the level of the 1850s.

Interest in preserving Connecticut's maritime past led to the establishment of the Marine Historical Association in 1929. Two years later the organization acquired one of the original Greenman shipyard buildings and an actual sailing vessel, the sandbagger sloop *Annie*. From these came Mystic Seaport, which now includes over sixty buildings and a forty-acre site along the Mystic River.

From the beginning, a primary concern has been the preservation and restoration of historic ships and small boats. Mystic's collection now numbers over two hundred. The centerpiece of this collection is the

Seaport Street in Mystic

Charles W. Morgan, the last surviving nineteenth-century wooden whaleship. Named for its principal owner, the vessel was built in 1841, during the peak decade for the whaling industry before the introduction of petroleum products. Twenty-one different masters commanded the *Morgan* on thirty-seven whaling expeditions between 1841 and 1921, when the ship was retired. Visitors today can tour the upper and lower decks of the fully restored whaler.

Two other major vessels are the *Joseph Conrad,* a full-rigged training ship built in 1882, and the *L. A. Dunton,* a rare example of a New England fishing schooner. Mystic Seaport also has a fine example of what replaced the great sailing ships—the steamboat *Sabino,* the last remaining coal-fired, steam-powered passenger ferry in operation. Small-craft exhibits include a variety of sail, power, and rowing crafts, both domestic and foreign made. Examples include the *Emma C. Berry,* a Noank smack built on the Mystic River in 1866; *Estella A.,* a Friendship sloop used by Maine fishermen and lobstermen; the *Glory Anna II,* a reproduction of a nineteenth-century Block Island Cowhorn; and the *Nellie,* a Long Island oyster sloop.

Mystic Seaport has also meticulously recreated a nineteenth-century maritime community. While some of the structures are original to the site, many have been moved in to depict various aspects of shipbuilding and community life. These include a variety of maritime craft shops, typical New England businesses and community institutions, and several representative residences.

In addition to the ships and boats and the village, Mystic Seaport maintains exhibits on a variety of related topics. For example, the Mallory Buildings feature exhibits on shipbuilding, a fine collection of maritime art and artifacts is displayed in the Stillman Building, and the Noyes Building focuses on offshore and onshore fisheries. The complex includes some twenty galleries and exhibit spaces that deal with maritime history and life in coastal New England.

Finally, Mystic Seaport provides a wide range of programs for all ages. In addition to regularly scheduled demonstrations, gallery talks, and lectures, the museum conducts special tours and programs for school groups, sponsors a varied publications program, and actively supports continued research in maritime history. More than fifty years after its establishment, Mystic Seaport remains committed to preserving New England's maritime history. Through historic vessels, the village, exhibits, and public programs, the museum brings to life this critical aspect of the Connecticut experience.

AMERICAN CLOCK AND WATCH MUSEUM 100 Maple Street, Bristol. Exhibits of clocks, watches, and other horological artifacts.

AMERICAN INDIAN ARCHEOLOGICAL INSTITUTE   state   199, Washington. Artifacts from prehistoric cultures in the northeastern United States.

AUDUBON SOCIETY OF THE STATE OF CONNECTICUT 2325 Burr Street, Fairfield. Natural science museum with thousands of mounted specimens of Connecticut birds.

BARNUM MUSEUM 820 Main Street, Bridgeport. Memorabilia of circus king P. T. Barnum, with items related to Tom Thumb and Jenny Lind and a model five-ring circus.

BUTLER–McCOOK HOMESTEAD 396 Main Street, Hartford. Clapboard house of 1782 altered by classical and Victorian additions; branch museum of Antiquarian and Landmarks Society of Connecticut.

CONNECTICUT ELECTRIC RAILWAY MUSEUM 58 North Road, East Windsor. Electric locomotives, interurban and suburban passenger cars, railway cars, and steam locomotives, 1880–1947.

CONNECTICUT HISTORICAL SOCIETY MUSEUM 1 Elizabeth Street, Hartford. Furniture and other items from early American history, with some art and Indian artifacts.

CONNECTICUT STATE LIBRARY *231 Capitol Avenue, Hartford.* A museum of Connecticut history that includes the royal charter signed by Charles II in 1662, Colt firearms, portraits, and items manufactured in the state.

DANBURY SCOTT–FANTON MUSEUM *43 Main Street, Danbury.* Charles Ives memorabilia and information on the 1780 Ives House in Danbury; hatting exhibit; and eighteenth-century furnishings.

GLEBE HOUSE *Hollow Road, Woodbury.* Where Samuel Seabury was elected first bishop of the American Episcopal Church in 1783, launching the new church; with a museum.

HALE BIRTHPLACE *South Street, Coventry.* Site of birth of patriot Nathan Hale; with a 1776 house built by his father, furnished with period pieces.

JOSHUA HEMPSTEAD HOUSE *11 Hempstead Street, New London.* Restored clapboard house with Colonial elements built about 1678, and one of the state's oldest houses; administered by the Antiquarian and Landmarks Society of Connecticut.

LEFFINGWELL INN *348 Washington Street, Norwalk.* Local headquarters for patriots during the American Revolution; visited by Washington.

LITCHFIELD HISTORIC DISTRICT *Litchfield.* One of the most picturesque and best-preserved eighteenth-century New England towns; where Aaron Burr, John C. Calhoun, and numerous other American leaders went to law school.

LYMAN ALLYN MUSEUM *625 Williams Street, New London.* Includes American and English art, furniture, and ceramics; also nearby Deshon–Allyn house, constructed in 1829.

MASSACOH PLANTATION *800 Hopmeadow Street, Simsbury.* Includes fuse machinery, sleighs, tools from three centuries, and several historic buildings dating from 1683.

NEW BRITAIN MUSEUM OF AMERICAN ART *56 Lexington Street, New Britain.* Colonial and contemporary American art, including sculpture and graphics.

NEW CANAAN HISTORICAL MUSEUM *13 Oenoke Ridge, New Canaan.* Exhibits on local history, with information on several historic buildings in New Canaan from the 1700s and 1800s.

NEWGATE PRISON AND GRANBY COPPER MINES *East Granby.* Supposedly the first copper mines in British America, dating from 1707, and the colony prison during the Revolutionary War, with ruins of other prison buildings from the 1800s.

NEW HAVEN COLONY HISTORICAL SOCIETY *114 Whitney Avenue, New Haven.* Museum with art and photographs on the history of New Haven.

NEW HAVEN GREEN *New Haven.* Where the Puritans planned a marketplace in 1638; three churches built about 1815, including the United Church where Henry Ward Beecher held forth.

OLD WETHERSFIELD HISTORIC DISTRICT *bounded by the rail-*

road, I-91, and Wethersfield Cove. Seventeenth-century houses, including the restored Buttolph–Williams House, built 1692.

PUTNAM MEMORIAL STATE PARK state 58, Redding. Where Revolutionary War American soldiers spent the winter of 1778–79; with remnants of chimneys from the barracks and a museum.

REVOLUTIONARY WAR OFFICE West Town Street, Lebanon. Renovated and restored office where John Trumbull, only colonial governor to break with the British, and Committee of Safety met.

ROGERS STUDIO 10 Cherry Street, New Canaan. Where sculptor John Rogers worked from 1877 to 1914; with exhibits of his work.

SLOAN–STANLEY MUSEUM U.S. 7, Kent. Exhibits of early American tools and ruins of the Kent Iron Furnace.

STAMFORD HISTORY MUSEUM 713 Bedford Street, Stamford. Includes Americana from 1700s and 1800s, farm implements, pottery, and crafts; in a 1699 farmhouse.

STANLEY–WHITMAN HOUSE 37 High Street, Farmington. Clapboard house built about 1660, partially restored; rare example of house with medieval English elements.

STOWE–DAY FOUNDATION Nook Farm, 77 Forest Street, Hartford. Neighborhood of 1800s where Harriet Beecher Stowe, Mark Twain, and other notables lived; with Stowe House and memorabilia.

TRUMBULL HOUSE the Common, Lebanon. Home of Revolutionary War governor Jonathan Trumbull, built about 1735 and the birthplace of artist John Trumbull; with a museum.

TWAIN HOUSE 351 Farmington Avenue, Hartford. Built in 1874 for Samuel Clemens, in variety of Victorian styles; where Clemens wrote *Huckleberry Finn* and other novels; with a museum.

U.S. COAST GUARD MUSEUM Coast Guard Academy, New London. Maritime museum with artifacts relating to the Revenue-Cutter Service, Lighthouse Service, and Life-Saving Service.

WADSWORTH ATHENEUM 600 Main Street, Hartford. Art museum that includes early American furniture, European and American paintings from 1400, pre-Columbian artifacts, and decorative arts.

WEBB HOUSE 211 Main Street, Wethersfield. Clapboard house, built in 1752, where Washington and French commander de Rochambeau planned the campaign against Cornwallis.

WEBSTER HOUSE 227 S. Main, West Hartford. Saltbox built about 1676 where Noah Webster was born; with a museum containing his books and manuscripts.

YALE UNIVERSITY College Street and environs, New Haven. Founded in 1713; with Connecticut Hall (built 1750–1752) and other historic structures, museums, and libraries.

DELAWARE

ELEUTHERIAN MILLS-HAGLEY FOUNDATION, INC. Wilmington.
Delaware's Brandywine Creek was one of the leading manufacturing centers in America in the late eighteenth and early nineteenth centuries. Foremost among the Brandywine entrepreneurs stood Eleuthère Irénée duPont, a French emigré who purchased a mill site in 1802 and shortly thereafter began manufacturing black powder. His company became the nation's largest powder manufactory in the nineteenth century and precursor of the twentieth-century DuPont chemical empire. Certainly no other company has had greater impact on Delaware's economic growth and development, and no other family has become so powerful in the state, influencing everything from schools and roads to banks and politics. The Eleutherian Mills-Hagley Foundation preserves and interprets the original duPont industrial site and reflects the integral role played by the family and the company in Delaware's history.

Fleeing the uncertainties of post-Revolutionary France, Pierre Samuel duPont de Nemours, his sons Victor and Eleuthère Irénée, and their families arrived in the United States in 1800. The elder duPont, a noted French bureaucrat and economist, hoped to establish a rural colony based on physiocratic theories of the economic supremacy of land and agriculture. When such plans proved unfeasible, the family sought other alternatives. Since he had experience in powder manufacturing as an apprentice to chemist Antoine Lavoisier, Irénée proposed to establish a black-powder factory. With the family's financial backing, he considered a variety of sites before locating in Delaware along the Brandywine, a thriving center for milling and manufacturing by the beginning of the nineteenth century. Early industrial development in America depended on the availability of waterpower, and Brandywine Creek proved an excellent source for the flour, textile, paper, and iron mills that located along the millstream after the Revolution. In 1802 duPont purchased a mill site from Jacob Broom, who had established the area's first cotton spinning mill in 1795. Shortly thereafter, Irénée and his family moved into a small cabin built by Broom and construction began on the first manufacturing plant for E. I. duPont de Nemours and Company.

DuPont named the new mill complex Eleutherian Mills. In addition to a refinery and other factory buildings, the complex included a barn for farming activity and the duPont family residence. Constructed in stone and stucco in 1803, the latter overlooked the powder yards, allowing duPont to manage the business from his home but also exposing him and his family to the same dangers as his employees. Explosions were a fact of life in powder manufacturing, and over the next decades the damage from such accidents necessitated major rebuilding and renovation of the house as well as the other structures at Eleutherian Mills.

Refinement of saltpeter began at the mill in 1803, and in the spring of the next year the first shipment of black powder went to New York. Within six years Eleutherian Mills became the largest powder factory in America. As the need for gunpowder increased with the War of 1812, the duPonts expanded still further by purchasing an adjoining tract, called Hagley (and they retained the name given the property by its previous owners). The duPonts erected new mills at Hagley that doubled the company's output.

The nineteenth-century duPont powder yards included a variety of structures, each with its own specialized function in the powder-making process. From the refinery, the saltpeter, sulphur, and charcoal went to the composition house and the roll mills for mixing. At the press house, the powder was pressed hydraulically to increase its density before being reduced to grains in the graining mills. Finishing processes took the powder to glazing mills, the dry house or dry tables, and finally the pack house. In hopes of directing the inevitable accidental explosions away from the complex toward the water, the mill buildings were constructed with three heavy stone walls but a light roof and a light fourth wall that would give way toward the creek in an explosion. Water remained the principal source of power for these mills throughout the nineteenth century. Each originally incorporated a waterwheel, but by the 1880s the wheels had been replaced with turbines. The first steam engine was installed in 1855, and in 1883–84 a central steam plant was constructed, followed in 1900 by a water turbine-powered electrical generator. The Hagley complex also included a machine shop, a blacksmith shop, a stone quarry, and a narrow-gauge railroad. As the manufacturing process changed and new power sources came into use, older buildings were renovated and new structures erected, creating a seemingly random pattern across the powder yard.

Residential communities adjoined the powder yards. The small houses left by Jacob Broom on the Eleutherian Mills property apparently housed workers at one time, but the duPonts also erected new housing, especially around the Hagley yard. Row houses for workers with families and dormitories for single workers clustered on the hillsides overlooking the powder yard. Also part of the worker community was the Brandywine Manufacturers' Sunday School, erected in 1817 for the education of the mill workers' children.

Irénée duPont headed the family powder works until his death in 1834. Through the rest of the century, the family retained control over the company and expanded its operations. In 1902 the company celebrated its centennial and began a new era of consolidation and expansion under the leadership of duPont's great-grandsons T. Coleman duPont and Pierre S. duPont. Under their aggressive leadership, the company expanded internationally and underwent a massive reorganization that shifted its focus from gunpowder to a range of chemical products. The relocation of the company's headquarters to Wilmington in 1906 and the closing down of the Brandywine powder yards in 1921 were indicative of the broader changes in the company's direction in the twentieth century. With expansion and diversification, Irénée duPont's one-product company evolved into a phenomenal worldwide chemical empire.

As part of its one hundred fiftieth anniversary celebration in 1952, the company chartered and endowed the Eleutherian Mills-Hagley Foundation, named for the two adjoining properties that made up the early-nineteenth-century powder-manufacturing complex. The Brandywine property had been sold by the company to family members in 1921 and they donated it to the foundation, which had the responsibility of maintaining and interpreting the site to the public. The indoor-outdoor historic complex first opened to the public in 1957 and has expanded to include some two hundred acres, a variety of industrial and domestic buildings, and an ambitious interpretive program of exhibits, dioramas, working models, audiovisual presentations, guided and self-guided tours, demonstrations, museum school programs, publications, and scholarly activities.

Just inside the entrance to the complex stands the Hagley Museum, which houses exhibits on the development of industry in the region and the nation. The museum building is a three-story stone structure erected in 1814–15 as a cotton spinning mill. Adjoining it is a picker house, a small stone building that now houses the museum store. Further upstream in the Hagley powder yard stand several restored mill buildings that illustrate the manufacturing process and the various power sources. These include the Eagle Roll Mills, the Birkenhead Roll Mills, the Engine House, and the New Century Power House. Of particular interest is the millwright shop, which recreates the working environment of an 1875 machine shop. Adjoining the Hagley yard are the remnants of the nineteenth-century residential community, including the

Birkenhead Mills at Hagley

Brandywine Manufacturers' Sunday School and the Gibbons House, the only remaining worker house. The latter effectively interprets the home life of a working man and his family around 1870.

Further upstream stands Eleutherian Mills, duPont's first mill complex. Only the foundations of the original mills remain, but visitors can tour the duPont residence, the company office from 1837 to 1890, the barn, and a small chemist's workshop. The residence dates from 1803 but underwent a number of renovations, some necessitated by powder explosions and others simply by the need for more space. The Georgian house was the hub of the family's business operations and social life throughout the nineteenth century and reflects the changing tastes and interests of the five generations of duPonts that lived there. To the north of the house stands the Eleutherian Mills Historical Library, a research institution concerned with the economic, industrial, and technological history of the mid-Atlantic region.

Brandywine Creek was one of the birthplaces of American industry, and the duPonts' activities there constitute an important chapter in the history of industrialization and big business in the United States. The Eleutherian Mills-Hagley Foundation provides a variety of opportunities to learn more about this history and about the history of Delaware in the nineteenth and twentieth centuries.

HOLY TRINITY CHURCH *606 Church Street, Wilmington.* The first permanent European settlement in Delaware was the New Sweden colony, established on the Christina River in 1638. Swedish hegemony in the region proved shortlived: in 1655 the Dutch took control of the faltering settlement. The only survivor of the early Swedish presence is Wilmington's Holy Trinity (Old Swedes) Church, which dates back to the first worship services at Fort Christina in 1638. The church commemorates the first of many immigrant groups that came to Delaware and symbolizes the diversity of peoples and cultures that characterizes the state today.

In 1637 Dutch adventurer Peter Minuit convinced the Swedish government to sponsor a colonization venture along the South River. Under the supervision of the government-chartered New Sweden Company, Minuit led the first shiploads of Swedish, Finnish, and Dutch colonists to the Delaware region in 1638. They settled initially on the South River, which they renamed the Christina River in honor of the Swedish queen, and erected Fort Christina, the progenitor of present-day Wilmington. Although the economic functions of the colony were given highest priority, worship services were conducted during the first year to meet the colonists' spiritual needs. The arrival in 1640 of Reorus Torkillus, a Swedish Lutheran minister, testified to the importance placed on establishing the Swedish national church in the new colony. When the Swedes relinquished control to the Dutch in 1655 and they in turn to the English in 1664, the Swedish Lutheran Church remained as the only formal link between the early colonists and their homeland.

The Swedes held their church services initially at Fort Christina, but as the settlement spread across the river into New Jersey and south towards New Castle, a new church was built just below the mouth of the Christina in an area known as Cranehook. Erected in 1667, this log church served the congregation for the next three decades. Lars Lokenius, the last minister-missionary sent by the Swedish government prior to 1655, served the small congregation until 1688. His health was so poor in the later years, however, that the church secured the services of Jacob Fabritius, a Dutch minister at Wicoca (present-day Philadelphia), who added Cranehook to his itinerary despite his blindness. Fabritius died in 1691, and the church found itself without an ordained minister. Charles Christophersson Springer and other laymen continued to hold church services, but the congregation had no one to conduct weddings and funerals or administer the sacraments. Repeated appeals to the Swedish government and the Swedish Lutheran Church went unanswered until 1696, when King Charles the Eleventh authorized the establishment of the Swedish Missionary Society to provide ministers to Swedish congregations in America. The first group arrived the following year, and Reverend Eric Bjork assumed leadership of the Cranehook congregation.

Bjork's first project was the erection of a new church building to replace the dilapidated and poorly located Cranehook structure. A committee considered several proposals for a new site and finally agreed to build next to the old burying ground at Fort Christina. The church secured additional land from an adjoining farm and in late 1697 began contracting for the construction of a simple stone and brick edifice. Church members hauled granite stones from the Brandywine River region, and

Old Swedes Church and cemetery

on May 28, 1698, the foundation stone was laid. Members of the congregation supplied most of the other materials in addition to donating labor and money and providing board for the stonemasons, bricklayers, carpenters, plasterers, and other laborers employed on the project during the next year. The new edifice was completed in late May 1699 and dedicated on Trinity Sunday, June 4, 1699.

Bjork named the new church Helgo Trefaldighetz Kyrckia, or Holy Trinity Church. The interior of the rectangular structure measured sixty by thirty feet. The stone walls were three feet thick up to the windows and two feet thick from there up to the clipped gable roof. The main entrance was on the west facade with a second entrance on the south and two small doors on the north. There were two windows each on the north and on the south sides and a larger window in the chancel area at the east end. The floors were brick, and the pine box pews were assigned by Bjork to individual families. A black walnut pulpit and canopy stood against the north wall.

For nearly a century after the church's dedication, the Swedish Missionary Society provided Holy Trinity with ministers, including Israel Acrelius and Lars Girelius. A major concern of the church leaders throughout the period was a trend toward assimilation of the Swedish community into the larger society. Most of the Swedish-Americans in the community were born in America and found less and less use for the old-country customs and language. The clergy even yielded to Anglicization by preaching in English as well as Swedish and by working with their counterparts in the Church of England. The climax came in 1791, when the vestry of Holy Trinity selected an Episcopalian as Girelius' successor. The appointment of Joseph Clarkson terminated the church's tie to the Swedish Lutheran Church and placed it under the jurisdiction of the Protestant Episcopal Church.

The church building underwent several alterations in the eighteenth and nineteenth centuries. When the north and south walls began to buckle in the late 1740s, two gabled porticoes were added to buttress the north side, and several years later a single large porch was added on the south. The two on the north were enclosed at some point to provide a sacristy and a vesting room, but the other portico remained a vestibule. When a gallery was added in the 1770s to accommodate increased membership, the stairs were located in the south portico. In 1802 a brick belfry with open cupola and frame base was erected over the west entrance. This tower housed a bell purchased in 1772.

The congregation decided in 1830 to build a chapel more conveniently located in Wilmington. Although they intended to use the new structure only during the winter months, few services were held in the old church for the next twelve years. By that time Holy Trinity had become somewhat delapidated, so the congregation had the church refurbished, including the addition of a wooden floor and bench pews. Services resumed and in 1847 an agreement was worked out that called for both churches to function as Trinity Parish, with the rector at the newer Trinity Church and the vicar at Holy Trinity or Old Swedes Church.

As part of its two hundredth anniversary in 1898–1899, Old Swedes was restored to its pre-1842 appearance. Although recent stained-glass windows were retained, the wooden floor was removed, and box pews replaced the more modern benches. The pulpit returned to its north-wall site. The original altar was encased in a new marble altar given in memory of the church's Swedish ministers.

The church stands adjacent to the old Fort Christina cemetery, where the oldest identifiable gravestone dates from 1718. The Parish House, erected in 1893, houses the Christina Cultural Arts Center. In 1959, the Hendrickson House, a 1690 Swedish stone edifice, was moved to the property. It now houses a small museum, the church library and archives, and the church offices. About two blocks away is the Fort Christina Monument and Park, operated by the Delaware Division of Historical and Cultural Affairs.

Other historic Delaware churches that reflect the state's pluralist history include the Welsh Tract Baptist Church in Newark, Old St. Anne's in Middletown, the Appoquinimink Friends Meetinghouse in Odessa, Barratt's Chapel in Frederica, and St. Joseph's on the Brandywine in Greenville. Old Swedes' Church, however, remains the oldest and most significant symbol of the state's diverse ethnic, racial, and religious heritage.

NEW CASTLE COURT HOUSE AND DOVER STATE HOUSE *New Castle and Dover.* The Delaware General Assembly now occupies a structure that dates back only to 1932 and 1933, but two preceding capitols from the eighteenth and nineteenth centuries still stand. Erected in 1732, the New Castle Court House served as the capitol of colonial Delaware and housed the state's first constitutional convention and first legislative session before the seat of government shifted to Dover in 1777. Dover's State House was built between 1788 and 1792, and the state legislature met there until the completion of its new quarters in the 1930s. Each commemorates a significant era in Delaware history; together they provide a unique opportunity to learn about politics and government in "The First State."

Quaker proprietor William Penn chose New Castle as the seat of the "three lower counties" he acquired from the Duke of York in 1682. Clashes between these territories and the larger colony of Pennsylvania led to the establishment of a separate province of Delaware in 1704. Although the governor of Pennsylvania continued to rule the Delaware region until the Revolution, the three counties held their own assembly separate from that of their neighbor to the north. The General Assembly's original meeting place, erected about 1690, burned in the 1720s, but a new two-and-a-half-story brick structure was built on the same site

Dover's
State House

in 1732. From its octagonal cupola surveyors plotted the twelve-mile circle that still marks the boundary between Delaware and Pennsylvania.

The General Assembly continued to meet in this structure until July 1776, when the legislators severed Delaware's ties to Great Britain and approved the Declaration of Independence. The following September a constitutional convention convened in the same building and adopted the first constitution of "Delaware State." The first state legislature assembled there on October 28, 1776, and on February 12, 1777, chose John McKinly as the first "President of the Delaware State." After the British captured McKinly later that year, state leaders abandoned New Castle for a safer inland capital. The New Castle County government then occupied the historic structure until 1881, when the county seat moved to Wilmington.

The state legislature did not have a permanent home again until 1792, when construction was completed on a two-story brick state house in Dover. The new structure stood on the same lot as a courthouse erected in 1722, and materials from that structure were incorporated in the new construction. State government was then still a small operation, so the legislature only occupied the second floor, leaving the rest of the building for the Kent County government. After the county constructed a new courthouse in 1873, the state occupied the entire structure. Although the General Assembly moved into new quarters in 1934, the historic structure remains a symbol of Delaware's government.

Both of the early capitols were altered at one time or another, but they have now been carefully restored to their former appearances. The New Castle Court House was enlarged with the construction of two small wings in 1765, and in 1771 a new gambrel roof and cupola were constructed to replace similar features destroyed in a fire. In 1802, the small east wing was enlarged to two stories, but the corresponding west addition remained intact until replaced by a slightly larger wing in 1845. About that same time, the structure's Flemish bond brickwork and glazed headers were covered with stucco. By the time restoration began in the 1950s, much of the interior had been rearranged as well. Through painstaking research, however, the New Castle Historic Buildings Commission managed to restore the historic courthouse to its eighteenth-century appearance. Standing on the edge of the Green laid out by order of Peter Stuyvesant in the mid-seventeenth century, the structure provides a focal point for the New Castle National Historic Landmark District, which includes the Old Academy, Immanuel Church, the Presbyterian Church, the Old Arsenal, the Old Dutch House, and numerous other fine examples of eighteenth and nineteenth-century architecture.

The State House also underwent several remodelings. A two-story wing was added to the rear in 1836, and further enlargements were made in 1896, 1910, and 1925 and 1926. More damaging to the structure were the construction of a new mansard roof in place of the flat gambrel roof and cupola and the addition of a projecting square tower to the front facade between 1873 and 1875. Interior alterations included removal of the double stairs, changes in the floor level, replacement of the original woodwork, and other modifications fashionable in the late nineteenth century. The exterior was restored in 1909 and 1910, but it was 1972 before work began on the interior. Careful historical and archeological research made possible a faithful restoration and furnishing of the structure. A courtroom, a ceremonial Governor's office, legislative chambers, and county offices are now open to the public. Near the State House and the Green stand the Delaware State Museum, the Hall of Records, and the visitor center, which provides an audiovisual show on other Kent County historic sites.

These two structures provided the setting within which Delaware's leaders resolved pressing political and governmental issues basic to the state's survival. Both clearly rank among the preeminent historic landmarks of the nation's "First State."

BARRATT'S CHAPEL U.S. 113 one mile north of Fredericka. Where Francis Asbury and Thomas Coke first administered the sacraments for the new Methodist Church in America.

BELMONT HALL U.S. 13 one mile south of Smyrna. Georgian mansion begun in 1689, home of the first American governor of Delaware; where the state legislature met in 1777.

BOWERS BEACH MARITIME MUSEUM Cooper Avenue, North Bowers Beach, Fredericka. Includes artifacts from ships and shore of Delaware Bay, and art.

BRANDYWINE VILLAGE HISTORIC DISTRICT bounded by Tatnall Street, Twenty-second Street, Vandever Avenue, Mabel Street, and Brandywine Creek, Wilmington. Where the Dutch settled in the 1600s, to be followed by the Swedes; a mill provided flour for American soldiers in the Revolution.

CAMDEN HISTORIC DISTRICT both sides of Camden-Wyoming Avenue and Main Street, Camden. Buildings of various styles built 1780–1820 in a center of Quaker abolitionism.

CHESAPEAKE AND DELAWARE CANAL Battery Park, Delaware City. Eastern lock of the 1829 canal, improved in the 1850s and 1919–1927; one end filled, the other still open for boats.

COOCH'S BRIDGE Christiana Creek, two miles southeast of Newark, one mile east of state 896. Where the only Revolutionary War fight in Delaware occurred—a 1777 skirmish in which American troops attacked British marching on Philadelphia.

CORBIT-SHARP HOUSE southwest corner of Main and Second streets, Odessa. Georgian house built 1772–1774 with a richly finished interior; now with a museum.

DELAWARE ART MUSEUM 2301 Kentmore Parkway, Wilmington. American and English paintings, including Wyeth family collections, and photography, graphics, and sculpture.

DICKINSON HOUSE Kitts Hummock Road, just east of U.S. 113 five miles southeast of Dover. Early home of Revolutionary and constitutional leader John Dickinson; rebuilt after an 1804 fire and today furnished with period items, some from the Dickinson family.

FORT DELAWARE STATE PARK on Pea Patch Island near Delaware City. Fort, completed in 1860, that served as prison for Confederates during Civil War; now includes a military museum.

GOVERNOR'S MANSION Kings Highway, Dover. Brick house built about 1790 that exemplifies fine late-eighteenth-century Georgian-style houses; period items within.

HALE-BYRNES HOUSE intersection of state 4 and 7, Stanton. Restored Georgian house, built about 1750, where Washington and Lafayette met in 1777 just before the Battle of the Brandywine.

HALL OF RECORDS Legislative Avenue and Court Street, Dover. Historic documents, including royal charter of Charles II giving Delaware to Duke of York, William Penn papers, and papers from 1787 related to Delaware's becoming the first state to sign the Constitution.

IMMANUEL CHURCH Market and Harmony streets, New Castle Green. An Anglican-style church built in 1703 and enlarged ca. 1840; on the site where William Penn participated in a ceremony granting him owner-ship of Delaware.

ISLAND FIELD SITE near South Bowers, one-half mile southeast of Bowers Beach. Archeological exhibits on the site of burials of Indians who lived there A.D. 600 to 1000; later occupied by precursors of the Leni Lenape.

LEWES HISTORICAL MUSEUM 119 W. Third Street, Lewes. Includes early Sussex County furniture, early log cabin furnished as in the period, country store, and children's museum.

McINTIRE HOUSE 8 Strand, New Castle. Built about 1690 and proba-bly the oldest in New Castle; nice example of the small townhouse of the period. Privately owned.

MASON-DIXON LINE boundary line between Delaware and Mary-land and between Delaware and Pennsylvania. Surveyed in 1768 to resolve border disputes and marked with more than 90 markers; with a monument marking the southwestern boundary of Delaware on state 54 west of Delmar.

NEW CASTLE HISTORIC DISTRICT bordered by Harmony Street, the Strand, Third Street, and Delaware Street, New Castle. Contains houses dating from 1740s onward in the town founded in 1651 by the Dutch, captured by both Swedes and English; where William Penn arrived in 1682.

NEW CASTLE HISTORICAL SOCIETY 2 E. Fourth Street, New Castle. Early Dutch and eighteenth-century furnishings, with tours of historic Amstel House, 1730, and Dutch House, about 1700, which has a collec-tion of Dutch furniture.

OCTAGONAL SCHOOLHOUSE off state 9 east of Cowgill's Corner. Stone and stucco structure built about 1836; one of state's earliest remaining educational buildings.

ODESSA HISTORIC DISTRICT bounded by Appoquinimink Creek and High, Fourth, and Main streets. Many examples of architecture from the 1700s and 1800s in an agricultural shipping area.

OLD WELSH TRACT BAPTIST CHURCH about six miles from New-ark, near Cooch's Bridge. Oldest Baptist church in America, built in 1746; hit by cannon during the battle at Cooch's Bridge.

PORT PENN MUSEUM Port Penn. Originally a public school built in the mid-1880s, now housing exhibits on one-room schools, local his-tory, and trapping and fishing along the Delaware River.

ROCKWOOD MUSEUM 610 Shipley Road, Wilmington. Located in a Victorian country estate, built 1851–1857, and now restored; with family furnishings and decorative arts.

SAINT MARY OF THE IMMACULATE CONCEPTION CHURCH Sixth

and Pine streets, Wilmington. Romanesque Revival church built in 1858 and associated with Bishop John Neuman, Philadelphia cleric now a candidate for canonization.

ZWAANENDAEL MUSEUM *Savannah Road and King's Highway, Lewes.* Historical exhibits on the Lower Delaware, including first Dutch settlements.

FLORIDA

HISTORIC ST. AUGUSTINE St. Augustine. Forty-two years before English colonists established Jamestown and fifty-five years before the Pilgrims landed at Plymouth Rock, the Spanish planted their first colony in present-day Florida. The founding of St. Augustine in 1565 secured Spain's claim to Florida and provided an important strategic base for the European imperial power for nearly two and a half centuries. Although the United States took possession in 1821, the Spanish influence remained strong, contributing to Florida's distinctive historical character. Now fully restored, the old city of St. Augustine and the Castillo de San Marcos vividly bring to life this Spanish heritage.

The Spanish crown established St. Augustine in an effort to stop French encroachment on territory first claimed by Ponce de León in 1513. The specific target was Fort Caroline, a French outpost established in 1564 on the St. Johns River. Spain viewed the fort as a threat to its control over shipping lanes between Nueva España and the home country and authorized Admiral Pedro Menéndez de Avilés to lead an expedition to eliminate the intruders. Menéndez arrived on the west Florida coast in August 1565 and shortly thereafter established a colonial settlement on the small peninsula formed by Matanzas Bay and the San Sebastian River. Since he had spotted the site on August 28, St. Augustine's Day, he named the new colony after the early Christian saint. With an outpost established, Menéndez then turned to the task of eliminating the French intruders. Within two weeks, he took Fort Caroline and reestablished Spain's claim to the Florida peninsula.

In the decades that followed, St. Augustine became the focus of efforts to expand and consolidate the influence of Catholic Spain in the New World. As a military outpost, St. Augustine protected Spanish commerce and blocked the expansion of English colonies established to the north along the Atlantic coast in the seventeenth century. At the same time, the colony provided a base for missionary activities by the Roman Catholic Church. The Church's efforts among the region's Indians expanded Spain's control to the north and the west, beyond the confines of the original colony. Yet despite its function in the imperial system, St. Augustine was long neglected by the Spanish crown. Instead of erecting a permanent installation, the Spaniards financed a succession of wooden forts scarcely defensible against any concerted attack. The outpost's vulnerability was largely ignored, however, until 1668, when pirates raided the town. The next year Queen Mariana, regent for her son King Carlos II, ordered construction of a permanent fortification.

To carry out these orders, a new governor was dispatched to Florida. Don Manuel de Cendoya arrived in St. Augustine in July 1671 and within a month had laborers at work quarrying coquina, a natural shell rock, at Anastasia Island and preparing for construction to begin. On October

2 ground was broken, and the first stone was laid at the end of the month. An assortment of Indian laborers, Spanish peons, convicts, and slaves proceeded with work on the new fort and by mid-summer of 1673 the east wall had reached twelve feet in height. Work continued slowly, however, plagued by numerous delays and chronic shortages of funds. Construction was not completed until August 1695—over twenty years after Cendoya initiated the project. Castillo de San Marcos, as the fort was named, reflected Spanish principles of fortification transplanted and adapted to the New World. The square citadel featured diamond-shaped extensions or bastions at each corner, a ravelin protecting the gate, and a surrounding moat, and its thick stone walls enclosed a magazine, storerooms, a chapel, and quarters for the soldiers on duty.

The first test of the new fort's strength came in 1702, when the War of the Spanish Succession spread to America. England had declared war on Spain and France in 1701, and English colonists in the Carolinas decided to follow suit and move against St. Augustine. The Carolinians raided north Florida, occupied the town, and attacked the Castillo, retreating only when Spanish reinforcements arrived. The stone citadel stood impregnable, but the invaders burned St. Augustine to the ground. In an effort to secure the town against a repeat invasion, the Spanish erected earthworks, palisades, and redoubts on its exposed sides. The first of these—the Cubo Line—extended from the fort west to the San Sebastian River, thus controlling the only land route onto the peninsula on which both the town and the fort stood. This defense measure made St. Augustine a virtual walled city.

The new fortifications were completed before another major attack by the English in 1740. Commercial rivalry between England and Spain had erupted in 1739 in the War of Jenkins' Ear, and St. Augustine became

Moat at Castillo de San Marcos

a target of British strategy to gain control of the Caribbean. British warships laid siege to the Castillo for thirty-eight days, but problems within the English command made it possible for the Spanish to break the blockade and stymie the takeover effort. Experience again proved an excellent teacher, and the Spaniards proceeded in the 1750s and 1760s to rework and strengthen the old garrison. Masonry vaults, higher walls, and stronger outworks prepared the Castillo for yet another major assault, but the Spanish ended up yielding the fort without a fight. In the Treaty of Paris that concluded the French and Indian Wars, defeated Spain ceded Florida to Britain in order to regain Havana. When the English arrived to take possession of the old Spanish outpost, both the military and the civilian population departed.

The British renamed the Castillo Fort St. Mark and used it as a base of operations for twenty-one years. In a second Treaty of Paris, which ended the Revolutionary War in 1783, Florida once again reverted to Spanish ownership. The former empire had declined considerably by then, however, and involvement in the Napoleonic Wars further weakened the Spanish crown. In 1821 Spain yielded to diplomatic pressure and ceded Florida to the United States. The latter renamed the Castillo Fort Marion and used it as a coastal fortification and military prison until 1900. Declared a national monument in 1924, the old Spanish garrison in 1935 came under the administration of the National Park Service, which today provides tours, talks, and exhibits on the history of the fort and Spanish Florida.

The Castillo's history is integrally tied to that of St. Augustine, and both must be visited in order to gain a better perspective on the blend of military and civilian life in Spanish Florida. As the fort has changed over the centuries, so has the city. For example, residents shifted from traditional board-and-thatch construction to masonry because of the availability of surplus material from the fort project. When Spain's imperial quarrels led to conflict, the city often suffered the worst. This necessitated periodic reconstruction of war-damaged structures and eventually the erection of perimeter fortifications that virtually walled in the eighteenth-century city. But despite such changes, the basic physical form of the community remained relatively constant after 1598, when the governor established the present city plan and laid out the public square in the heart of the still-young settlement.

Nearly four centuries later, St. Augustine is still in many ways a typical Spanish colonial town. Visitors can pass through the old city gates, walk along the narrow, winding streets, and view old coquina and wood structures that date back to the seventeenth and eighteenth centuries. Among the many significant structures are the Gonzalez-Alvarez House, constructed about 1623 and reputedly the oldest house in America; the Llambias House, a late eighteenth-century edifice; the Old Spanish Treasury; and the Cathedral of St. Augustine, erected in 1797 by the oldest Roman Catholic parish in the nation, established in 1594. Within the historic section of the city, the St. Augustine Historical Society operates several historic-house museums, and the Historic St. Augustine Preservation Board owns and administers over twenty original and reconstructed structures. The latter's programs include living history, crafts, exhibits, and publications.

Of course, the Spanish influence was not confined solely to St. Augustine; other cities and regions of Florida celebrate their Spanish origins as well. But the Castillo de San Marcos and St. Augustine clearly functioned as the center of Spanish imperial activity on the Florida peninsula and today provide the most exciting opportunities to relive this colorful chapter in the state's history.

BULOW PLANTATION RUINS STATE HISTORIC SITE   nine   miles southeast of Bunnell. The tradition of moonlight and magnolias is as important to Florida history as it is to that of the rest of the South. A plantation society complete with slavery and a code of chivalry thrived in Florida in the decades after Spanish cession of the territory to the United States. One of the most magnificent and extensive antebellum estates was Bulow Plantation or Bulowville, situated some forty miles below St. Augustine near the east coast. The Bulow family's sugar and cotton operations lasted only about fifteen years, until the Seminole Indians destroyed the plantation in early 1836 during the Second Seminole War. The Bulow Plantation Ruins State Historic Site thus commemorates both Florida's plantation heritage and resistance to the infamous Indian removal policy of the United States government.

James Russell began in 1812 the initial development of what would later be known as Bulow Plantation. The 2,500 acres of land that he named "Good Retreat" had been given to him as payment for a schooner he sold to the Spanish government soon after he and his household arrived at St. Augustine from the Bahamas. He did not make much progress in clearing the dense growth of hardwood trees prior to his death in 1815, and in 1820 his heirs sold the property to Charles Wilhelm Bulow, a Charleston, South Carolina, planter and politician. Bulow was a descendant of Baron Joachim Von Bulow, who had been sent by the Elector of Wurtemburg to establish the Lutheran church in the Carolina colonies. By the early nineteenth century the Bulow family owned Savannah Plantation, Ashley Hall in Charleston, and numerous other properties. Bulow was one of many wealthy Southerners who augmented their extensive landholdings with new plantations in Florida about the time the Spanish ceded the territory to the United States. With land prices low and sugar and cotton prices up, these planters expected high profits from the newest addition to the plantation South.

Altogether Bulow purchased between four and six thousand acres along Smith's Creek. Using slave labor, he proceeded with Russell's plan to clear the densely wooded area and soon planted the first sugarcane, cotton, and indigo crops. With wood and coquina (a soft limestone formed of shells) available on the property, he constructed a

Ruins at Bulow Plantation

residence, slave quarters, and other essential outbuildings. But like Russell, Bulow died before he could see his plans to fruition. At his death in 1823, the property passed to his son and heir John Joachim Bulow. Since the younger Bulow was still a minor, however, trustees operated the estate until about 1828, when John Bulow completed his European education and returned to the United States to succeed his father as Master of Bulowville.

Under John Bulow's management, the plantation developed into one of the largest and most profitable in the area. Although he planted about 1,000 acres of cotton, 1,500 acres of sugarcane became the key to the plantation's operations. The plantation sugar mill may have been the largest in the Florida territory. Here the cane stalks were crushed to extract the juice, which was then reduced to a thick syrup, crystalized, and stored. The mill complex included a crushing house, steam boiler, kettle room, wooden vats, curing room, and storage sheds. Transportation of the sugar and by-product molasses also required boat slips on Smith's or Bulow Creek, where flats or barges could load up for the eleven-mile trip down to the Halifax River and on to Mosquito Inlet to make connections for shipment to distant markets. Other support structures typical of a working plantation included a barn, corn house, gin house, poultry house, cooperage, blacksmith shop, and fodder houses.

A plantation of this scale depended on slave labor. The three hundred slaves owned by Bulow lived in forty houses arranged in a semicircle about two hundred yards from their master's home. These twelve-by-sixteen-foot wooden structures apparently had wooden floors, a rare feature in slave quarters, and were furnished adequately by Bulow. He was reportedly a good master. Although he only gave the slaves ground corn each week, they had enough time on their own to hunt, fish, and cultivate small garden plots.

Bulow himself apparently lived in grand style in the plantation's Big House. Piazzas encircled the two-story coquina structure, and the house had an especially fine library. Bulow, who had spent several years in Paris, became known as a lavish host. The numerous empty ale and wine bottles from his parties were used to reinforce the sides of the boat slips at which he kept canoes and skiffs for fishing and hunting expeditions along interior waterways. Bulow Plantation's hospitality and accessibility to transportation made it a perfect home base for John James Audubon when he visited the area in 1831.

John Bulow maintained good relations with the Seminole Indians in the region and did not support the government's removal policy. During the Second Seminole War, he opposed the army's presence, but Major Benjamin Putnam and his Mosquito Raiders took the plantation by force and set up headquarters there in late December of 1835. With Bulow kept under guard, the army built a small fort of palm logs and fortified the Big House and slave quarters with stacks of baled cotton. Meanwhile Seminole raids were reported closer and closer to the Bulow estate. After Putnam and a sizable number of his men were wounded in a skirmish at Dunlawton plantation in January, such reports caused considerable alarm. Unable to resist attack, Putnam ordered all to abandon the plantation and retreat to St. Augustine on January 23. Although the exact date is not known, within the next week the Seminoles raided and burned the plantation. Bulow died in Paris a few months later at the age of twenty-seven.

With the plantation in ruins, the woods again took over the once profitable fields. When the state secured the property, only the ruins of the mansion, the sugar mill, the spring house, and the slave quarters remained. The Division of Recreation and Parks of the Florida Department of Natural Resources now administers the 109-acre state park. The ruins provide a visual link to Florida's plantation past and a reminder of the infamous Second Seminole War. Related sites include two other examples of antebellum plantations, the Gamble Plantation State Historic Site at Ellenton and the Kingsley Plantation State Historic Site at Ft. George, and the Dade Battlefield State Historic Site at Bushnell, the location of the opening conflict of the Second Seminole War.

HENRY MORRISON FLAGLER MUSEUM *Cocoanut Row, Palm Beach.* No one more deserves to be called "the Father of Florida" than Henry M. Flagler, the central figure in the development of the state's east coast in the late nineteenth and early twentieth centuries. His East Coast Railway opened up new areas to developers, provided the transportation network essential to exploiting the state's agricultural potential, and, together with his hotels, launched the modern tourist industry on Florida's "gold coast." The preeminent symbol of Flagler's wealth and influ-

Flagler's Whitehall

ence is Whitehall, his elaborate Palm Beach home. Now preserved as the Henry Morrison Flagler Museum, it reflects both Flagler's role in developing Palm Beach as a legendary gathering place for America's wealthy and famous and his greater impact on the history of Florida.

When Flagler first became interested in developing Florida in the 1880s, he had already established himself as one of the nation's leading entrepreneurs. His most notable business venture was a partnership with John D. Rockefeller in 1870 to form the Standard Oil Company, one of the world's richest and most powerful corporations. He demonstrated the same business acumen in 1883 when, while honeymooning with his second wife in St. Augustine, he became intrigued by the city's potential as a resort. Struck by the lack of modern facilities, he commissioned architects John M. Carrère and Thomas Hastings to design a luxury hotel in keeping with the city's European background and traditions. The lavish Spanish revival Ponce de Leon Hotel opened in 1888. Flagler soon expanded his operations to the Cordova and Alcazar hotels as well. To insure accessibility and the success of his hotels, he also acquired and improved the East Coast Railway from Jacksonville to St. Augustine. His instincts proved correct, and the historic city soon flourished as a fashionable winter resort.

In the decades that followed, Flagler extended his railroad southward through purchase and construction and added to his chain of luxury resort hotels. First he extended his railroad to Daytona Beach, where he bought and enlarged the Ormond Beach Hotel. Then in 1894 the line reached Palm Beach, a small coastal-island settlement some two hundred miles south of Daytona. The island was named for its palm groves, which date from the wreck of a coconut-laden Spanish ship in 1878. Flagler found the island and its temperate climate well suited to development and in 1893 began work on what would soon become one of America's most famous resorts.

Construction began on the royal Poinciana Hotel before the railroad even reached Palm Beach. Completed in 1894 on a thirty-two acre site along the shore of Lake Worth, the 1,150-room frame building was one of the world's largest wooden structures and the largest resort hotel in existence. For the construction workers and hotel employees, Flagler directed the layout of the adjoining town of West Palm Beach, complete with water system, paved streets, and landscaping. The East Coast Railway line reached West Palm Beach in 1894, and a railroad bridge across Lake Worth was completed later that year. Shortly thereafter private railroad cars began arriving, bearing the wealthy and famous Americans who would make Palm Beach the country's most fashionable winter gathering place.

As the resort's popularity increased, Flagler added new wings to the Royal Poinciana and in 1896 opened the Palm Beach Inn, which he later enlarged, renovated, and renamed the Breakers. Another landmark of the early years was Bradley's Beach Club, an exclusive gambling casino established in 1899 by Colonel Edward Reilly Bradley. A later addition was the Everglades Club, the first of the famous Boom Spanish structures designed by Addison Mizner for the resort community. Mizner also designed extravagant mansions for the Stotesburys and Wanamakers of Philadelphia and other socially prominent families, who preferred to stay in their own homes rather than hotels during the two months of Palm Beach's winter season. One particularly notable example is Mar-A-Lago, the opulent home of the late Marjorie Merriweather Post and now a national historic site.

In 1901 Flagler erected Palm Beach's most lavish mansion as a wedding present for his third wife, Mary Lily Kenan. Designed and built in just eighteen months at a cost of two and a half million dollars, Whitehall, as the Flagler home was known, stood south of the Royal Poinciana on a six-acre site at the edge of Lake Worth. Architects Carrère and Hastings incorporated both Spanish and Classical elements in their design. The red tiled roof, stuccoed exterior, and interior courtyard reflected the Spanish influence, but Whitehall's Doric columns and porches were more typical of Southern Greek Revival homes. In addition to designing the Ponce de Leon Hotel for Flagler, Carrère and Hastings became well known as the architects of the New York Public Library, the old Metropolitan Opera House, the Frick Mansion, and the U.S. Senate Office Building. Upon completion of the mansion, the Flaglers spent another one and a half million dollars on furnishings. From 1902 until Flagler's death in 1913, the couple spent their winters there, entertaining lavishly in the style that became synonymous with Palm Beach society.

Palm Beach was not the end of the line for Flagler's East Coast Railway. By 1896, his line extended to Miami, where he again played a central role in establishing a popular resort community. His Royal Palm hotel was the first such establishment in the city now renowned for its resort hotels. The last leg of his railroad construction project took much longer, for his goal of reaching Key West required bridging miles of swampland, barren coral, and ocean. This 156-mile engineering marvel took seven years and twenty million dollars to complete. On January 22, 1912, Flagler rode into Key West on the first train that crossed the overseas bridges to the islands. In a brief speech, the aging entrepreneur declared, "Now I can die happy; my dream is fulfilled." He died less than a year and a half later, on May 20, 1913, and was buried in a mausoleum adjacent to St. Augustine's Memorial Presbyterian Church, which he had built in 1890 in memory of his daughter.

Mrs. Flagler opened Whitehall only one more season before her death in 1917. Subsequently the house was used as a private club and then in 1925 opened as a luxury resort hotel. The mansion itself was used for public rooms and luxury suites, and a ten-story tower provided three hundred sleeping rooms. In 1959 the house was purchased for the Henry Morrison Flagler Museum, and it was opened to the public the following year. Careful restoration and furnishing have returned the house to the elegance of the Flagler era. Visitors can now tour the magnificent marble entrance hall, the walnut-panelled library, the music room where the Flaglers held weekly musicales, the billiard room, the ornate gold and white ballroom, the breakfast room, the dining room, the salon, and a courtyard on the first floor. Second-floor rooms include the master suite with its original Louis XV style furniture, Mrs. Flagler's morning room, and several of the fourteen guest rooms. The lower floors of the 1925 hotel addition have been retained for exhibits, meetings, and community events.

Flagler's private railroad car, "Rambler," also stands on the grounds. Flagler had the car built in 1886 and used it throughout the remainder of his life, including his inaugural trip to Key West in 1912. Later used as a tenant farmer's shack, the car was found and restored in 1967. The exterior bears the yellow and maroon colors of the East Coast Railway, and the interior lounge, stateroom, berths, and kitchen have been accurately restored to the Flagler period.

Whitehall is an impressive symbol of Henry M. Flagler's wealth and influence. His pioneering development of Florida's east coast provided the basis for the boom of the 1920s and firmly established the resort industry that has become so integral a part of the state's economic growth and development. His Palm Beach home and the exhibits and programs of the Henry Morrison Flagler Museum provide a unique opportunity to experience the lavish lifestyle of one of America's most famous resort communities and to learn more about the history of modern Florida.

DADE BATTLEFIELD SITE AND MUSEUM state 476 just west of U.S. 301, Bushnell. Exhibits and artifacts of the 1835 battle in which Seminoles killed more than 100 U.S. soldiers.

De SOTO NATIONAL MEMORIAL five miles west and two miles north on 75th Street W., Bradenton. Site visited by De Soto in 1539, with visitor center where costumed interpreters demonstrate crossbow and arquebus.

FLORIDA STATE MUSEUM University of Florida, Gainesville. Exhibits on archeology and anthropology from prehistoric times to the present; extensive natural history exhibits.

FORT CAROLINE NATIONAL MEMORIAL ten miles east of Jacksonville and five miles north of state 10. Museum near the site of the French settlement of 1564, the first European settlement on the North American continent.

FORT GEORGE ISLAND twenty-five miles east of Jacksonville. Several historic sites, including the Huguenot Memorial honoring the French landing in 1562; Fort Saint George, 1736; and Kingsley Plantation, 1817.

FORT JEFFERSON NATIONAL MEMORIAL Dry Tortugas Islands, sixty-eight miles west of Key West in the Gulf of Mexico. Incompleted United States fort begun in 1846, now a ruin.

FORT MATANZAS NATIONAL MONUMENT fourteen miles south of St. Augustine. Site where the Spanish massacred (matanzas–Sp. *slaughters*) the French in 1565 and constructed a fort in 1740–1742, of which only a remnant stands.

GAMBLE PLANTATION U.S. 301, Ellenton. Greek Revival house built 1845–1850, where Confederate Secretary of State Judah Benjamin hid before escaping to England. Contains antebellum furnishings.

GULF ISLANDS NATIONAL SEASHORE south of Pensacola on state 399 on Santa Rosa Island and at the U.S. Naval Air Station, Pensacola. Includes Fort Pickens, built 1829–1835, where Geronimo was imprisoned 1886–1888; Battery San Antonio, built by the Spanish about 1797; Fort Barrancas (1834–1844); the Pensacola Lighthouse (1858); and the Advanced Redoubt of Barrancas (1840s).

HERITAGE PARK Largo. A reconstructed town, including residences, a store, a depot, and a church, all dating from the late nineteenth and early twentieth centuries.

HISTORICAL MUSEUM OF SOUTHERN FLORIDA Miami. General history museum with exhibits on history of the region, including the Caribbean.

INTERNATIONAL SWIMMING HALL OF FAME One Hall of Fame Drive, Fort Lauderdale. Photos, murals, Olympic medals.

JACKSONVILLE MUSEUM OF ARTS AND SCIENCES 1025 Gulf Life Drive, Jacksonville. Antique and ethnic dolls; exhibits on pre-Columbian and Florida Indians and early white Florida history.

KEY WEST HISTORIC DISTRICT Key West. Includes the Audubon

House, where the painter stayed in 1832; Hemingway House, home of writer Ernest Hemingway from 1931 to 1960; and Civil War forts.

LAUNCH COMPLEX 39, KENNEDY SPACE CENTER Titusville area. Where the first manned voyage to the moon was launched in 1969.

LIGHTNER MUSEUM City Hall-Museum Complex, King Street, St. Augustine. Housed in the 1889 Alcazar Hotel, built for Henry Flagler; with decorative arts, Tiffany glass, Victorian art glass, and other nineteenth-century material arts.

MARJORIE KINNAN RAWLINGS HOUSE state 325 south of Cross Creek, Cross Creek. Late-nineteenth-century farmhouse, home of the author of *The Yearling.*

MARY McLEOD BETHUNE HOME Bethune-Cookman College campus, Daytona Beach. Clapboard house built in the 1920s, the home of black leader and founder of the college; contains a museum.

MORIKAMI MUSEUM OF JAPANESE CULTURE 4000 Morikami Park Road, Delray Beach. Exhibits on the Yamato Colony of Japanese farmers, including bonsai collection and folk art.

MUSEUM OF FLORIDA HISTORY R. A. Gray Building, Tallahassee. General history museum with exhibits on life in Florida, including Spanish trade and maritime artifacts.

OKEECHOBEE BATTLEFIELD four miles southeast of Okeechobee on U.S. 441. Where Zachary Taylor defeated Seminole and Mikasuki soldiers in 1837 in the Second Seminole War.

PELICAN ISLAND NATIONAL WILDLIFE REFUGE east of Sebastian in the Indian River. First federal sanctuary to protect wildlife, established in 1903 by Theodore Roosevelt for the brown pelican.

PENSACOLA HISTORIC DISTRICT bounded by Chase Street, Ninth Avenue, Pensacola Bay, and Palafox Street. Includes houses and buildings from 1800s and 1900s, Museum of West Florida History, Plaza Ferdinand VII, Seville Square, and the Clara Barkley Dorr house.

PENSACOLA HISTORICAL MUSEUM 405 S. Adams Street, Pensacola. Local history, including family silver, men's and women's accessories and household items from 1800s, fine art glass, and glass negatives.

ROCHELLE SCHOOL off state 234, Rochelle. An 1885 clapboard school in use until 1935, with Italianate elements; one of few remaining buildings from town's early period.

SAN MARCOS de APALACHE on state 363 about two miles south of U.S. 98 just south of St. Marks. Where the Spanish built three forts between 1565 and 1763; with a portion of the stonework remaining and a museum.

TALLAHASSEE JUNIOR MUSEUM 3945 Museum Drive, Tallahassee. Includes an excellent "cracker" homestead with support buildings.

TARPON SPRINGS SPONGE EXCHANGE Dodecanese Street, Tarpon Springs. Greek community and center of United States sponge industry.

TEMPLE MOUND MUSEUM 139 Miraclestrip Parkway, S.E., Fort

Walton Beach. Interpretive center next to Temple mound of Fort Walton culture; with rock and ceramic artifacts from the area.

TOMOKA MUSEUM *Tomoka State Park, Ormond Beach.* Exhibits and art on the site of Timucuan village extant in 1605.

VIZCAYA *3251 S. Miami Avenue, Miami.* Concrete and stucco mansion with formal gardens; the home of industrialist James Deering.

YBOR CITY HISTORIC DISTRICT *Tampa.* Cuban community, once a famous cigar-making center.

GEORGIA

SAVANNAH NATIONAL HISTORIC LANDMARK DISTRICT Savannah. Savannah, Georgia, is a well-known symbol of the urban elegance of the cotton South prior to the Civil War, but its history actually extends back to the founding of the colony by James Oglethorpe in 1733. Oglethorpe laid out the original town plan that exists today and contributes to the unique character of the city's historic district. The houses and public buildings that line Oglethorpe's broad avenues and squares, however, date primarily from the end of the eighteenth century and the first half of the nineteenth century, when the lucrative cotton trade brought wealth and influence to the port city. Through the efforts of the Historic Savannah Foundation, both the town plan and the structures have been preserved as the Savannah National Historic Landmark District, one of the nation's largest urban historic districts. The district and the tours and programs of Historic Savannah together make possible a fuller understanding of Savannah's central role in early Georgia history.

James Edward Oglethorpe, an English gentleman and member of Parliament, conceived of the colonization of Georgia as a philanthropic venture. Repulsed by conditions in England's debtors' prisons, he sought to give poor but deserving men and women a chance to start over in the New World. King George II did not share his altruism, but he did perceive the imperial advantages of a new southern colony and in 1732 granted Oglethorpe and his associates a twenty-one-year charter. Oglethorpe carefully selected the first group of settlers and within the year set sail for America. On February 12, 1733, the first shipload disembarked on the banks of the Savannah River just below the bluff that Oglethorpe had chosen as the site for his new city.

For the next decade Oglethorpe spoke for the colony's trustees in establishing and governing the new colony. With the assistance of Colonel William Bull, he immediately began laying out the town of Savannah according to a plan that he apparently worked out before leaving England. The plan called for a series of residential wards, each focused on an open square. The new settlement initially consisted of four such squares, each flanked by trust lots for churches and public buildings and residential blocks marked off into sixty-by-ninety-foot lots. The plan also included a ten-acre trustees' garden for experimental cultivation of products and plants needed in England, including grapes for wine, mulberry trees for silk production, fruit, spices, herbs, and cotton. Other gardens and farmland were located on the outskirts of the settlement. For the next hundred years, Oglethorpe's original town plan determined the growth and development of the city.

From the first, Oglethorpe and the trustees encountered problems with their colonization venture. Internal political and religious conflicts, financial difficulties, and opposition to the trustees' prohibition of rum and slavery plagued the project's first decade. Oglethorpe's attempts to mediate between the increasingly independent-minded colonists and the distant trustees failed, and in 1743 he finally gave up and returned to England. The trustees continued to grapple with the colony's problems and in 1751 even yielded to the colonists' demands for slavery and rum. But the next year the frustrated trustees finally gave up and surrendered their charter to the crown, a year before it was due to expire.

As the maturing colony became more productive and commercial activity flourished, the economic problems that had plagued the trustees eased. The colony's healthy prosperity under royal rule fostered a conservatism that frustrated radical calls for independence from England. Georgians finally joined the revolutionary ranks in 1775 but had little direct involvement in the war until the siege of Savannah in 1778–79. The defeat of American and French forces at Savannah shifted control of the strategic port city back to the British until 1782 and the end of the war.

Eli Whitney's invention of the cotton gin in 1793 at Mulberry Grove, a plantation near Savannah, provided the key to postwar economic recovery in Georgia and the rest of the South. Of minor importance prior to the war, cotton became the region's dominant cash crop in the early nineteenth century. As Georgia's great rice plantations of the colonial period yielded to King Cotton, the plantation system and slavery became even more deeply imbedded in the economic and social life of the state. Nowhere was this more evident than in Savannah, the hub of shipping and brokerage in the southeast and a stronghold of the cotton elite. The city's wealth reflected the volume of its import-export business, which began developing along the river bank in 1744. Commission merchants erected the first commercial row in 1789, and by 1810 the blocks of warehouses along the river's edge were known as Factors' Walk. Factors were the planters' agents or middlemen, who managed the sale of crops, provided credit and supplies, and performed a variety of other services essential to the operation of the cotton economy. Their warehouses stood on the river's edge with iron and plank walkways and ramps to the bluff above and the city itself. Eleven blocks of the nineteenth-century Factors' Walk remain today in the Savannah historic district. One structure houses the Ships of the Sea Museum and its exhibits on the city's maritime and commercial history.

The elegant homes of Savannah's historic district testify to the profitability of the cotton economy in the first half of the nineteenth century. Early residents erected modest frame cottages on Oglethorpe's narrow residential lots, but construction after the fire of 1796 reflected the greater wealth and more refined tastes of the cotton planters and merchants of the antebellum period. The tall, narrow brick, stucco, and frame rowhouses of the later period reflect a variety of architectural styles, including Georgian, Greek Revival, Italianate, and Gothic Revival. Some were based on designs found in imported architectural handbooks, while others were the products of architects such as William Jay. Common features included high ceilings, thick walls to combat the summer heat, and living quarters one story above the dust and dirt of the ground level.

Savannah's wealth and influence depended on the continued vitality of the cotton economy and plantation society of the Southeast. Secession and the Civil War brought both to a standstill. Although Savannah escaped the physical destruction of the war in the early years, the curtailment of trade brought severe economic hardships to the port city. In December 1864 General William T. Sherman and his Union forces occupied the city to complete his now famous march across Georgia to the sea. The city endured Union occupation for only a few months, for the next spring the war came to a close. But although cotton production and trade resumed after the war, Savannah never fully recovered.

Except for such individual projects as the Savannah Gas Company's renovation of the Trustees' Garden Village and the Girl Scouts' restoration of the Juliette Gordon Low Birthplace, vacancy, decay, and demolition characterized Savannah's historic areas in the first half of this century. Disturbed by the demolition of the City Market in 1954 and the scheduled demolition of the Isaiah Davenport House, in 1955 seven Savannah women founded the Historic Savannah Foundation, an organization dedicated to preserving the city's architectural heritage. Significant programs and activities have included a revolving fund to purchase endangered structures for resale, federal designation of the historic district, a building-by-building inventory of the district, a tour service, a variety of redevelopment and commercial revitalization projects, design

Isaiah Davenport House

and technical assistance, a furnishings reproduction program, and Georgia Week, a celebration and commemoration of the city's and the state's birth and history.

The Savannah National Historic Landmark District encompasses 2.2 square miles in the heart of the city, including the central business district, the riverfront, and residential neighborhoods. This superb collection of eighteenth- and nineteenth-century structures preserves the history of old Savannah, from the initial town plan of Oglethorpe to the elegant houses of the city's antebellum elite.

GEORGIA STATE CAPITOL *Capitol Square, Atlanta.* Atlanta, Georgia, stood as the capital of the New South in the decades that followed the end of Reconstruction. The city's growth and industrial development in the 1880s and 1890s epitomized the region's hopes for building a new, dynamic economic order to supplant the restrictive plantation cotton economy of the prewar years. The most significant remaining symbol of Atlanta in this post-Reconstruction era is the Georgia State Capitol. Erected between 1884 and 1889, the capitol then signified Atlanta's political and economic ascendancy and stands today as an expression of the spirit of the Gilded Age in the New South.

Atlanta's history begins in 1837, when a stake was driven marking the terminus of the Western and Atlantic Railroad. The state-owned line intersected at this point with the Georgia Railroad from Augusta and the Central of Georgia from Macon. Originally called "Terminus" and then "Marthasville," the settlement that grew up there in the decades before the Civil War remained tied to the railroads and did not become a part of the larger plantation society. The street pattern of the town reflected this, with businesses and homes wedged between the radiating rail lines and wagon trails that made it a hub of transportation. When the Civil War came, this transportation network proved crucial in supplying the Confederate army and in turn made the city a principal target of Union strategy. In 1864 Atlanta fell to Union forces under the command of General William Tecumseh Sherman, who evacuated and burned the city before proceeding on his infamous march to the sea in November and December 1864.

The rebuilding of Atlanta after the war took place within the larger context of Georgia's social, political, and economic reconstruction. Conservative leaders initially tried to regain control of the state government, but hopes for an immediate restoration of the old order faded in the face of military rule, a new "radical" constitution, a Republican governor, and even a new state capital. The latter designation made Atlanta Georgia's fifth capital, preceded by Savannah, Augusta, Louisville, and Milledgeville. The state legislature met in the city for the first time on January 10, 1869, in an unfinished opera house at Forsyth and Marietta streets. The owner of the building was Hannibal I. Kimball, an associate of Governor Rufus B. Bullock and a controversial entrepreneur of the Reconstruction era. When Georgia's readmission to the Union in 1870

Georgia State Capitol

finally cleared the way for conservative "redemption" of the state, evidence of shady financial dealings involving Kimball and Bullock fueled Democratic charges of carpetbag corruption and Republican misrule.

Despite the political turmoil and corruption of the 1860s and 1870s, Atlanta underwent rapid rebirth. The railroads again proved crucial, making possible a quick resumption of trade and hence a dramatic revival in the city's economy. Although commercial activity continued to predominate for decades to follow, Atlanta entrepreneurs also recognized the need for diversification and began developing other sectors of the economy. The capital accumulated in commerce provided the basis for Atlanta's emergence as the financial center of the state, and by the 1880s manufacturing and industry also contributed significantly to the city's phenomenal growth and development.

As the economy revived, new construction replaced wartime destruction. Some of the structures erected in downtown Atlanta in the late nineteenth century for commercial, service, and industrial use still stand. Underground Atlanta and the Terminus District reveal the impact of the complex network of railroad lines on the city's growth. The Fairlie-Poplar District, in contrast, preserves more impressive commercial structures that illustrate the wealth of the city's business community. Also related to the city's growth is the Inman Park neighborhood, a suburban residential community that developed after 1889 and attests to the affluence of Atlanta at the end of the nineteenth century. Tours of Fairlie-Poplar and Inman Park are available through the Atlanta Preservation Center.

The Atlanta World's Fair and Great International Cotton Exposition of 1881, the South's first such event, provided an opportunity to publicize this successful rebirth. The Piedmont Exposition of 1887 and the Cotton States and International Exposition of 1895 also highlighted the city's achievements in commerce and industry. But the most eloquent and persuasive spokesman for Atlanta and the New South was Henry W. Grady, editor of the Atlanta *Constitution* from 1879 until his death in 1889. Grady's vision of a "New South" called for a new economic order based on business and industry and exemplified in the growth and prosperity of Atlanta. According to Grady and other New South advocates, this new economic order was crucial to the region's reentry into the mainstream of American life.

The withdrawal of the last federal troops from the former Confederate states in 1877 signified the end to Reconstruction and the beginning of a new era of reconciliation between the South and the rest of the nation. For Georgians, 1877 also brought a new constitution to replace the 1868 "Radical Republican" document. Since the Republicans had also engineered the relocation of the state capital to Atlanta a decade before, a referendum was held to allow the voters to voice their will. The voters affirmed the choice of Atlanta, and legislators began considering the construction of a new, larger capitol building. In 1883 the legislature appropriated one million dollars for the construction project. The five-acre city hall lot was chosen as the site, and demolition of the thirty-year-old city hall and county courthouse began soon thereafter. The Capitol Commission chose Chicago architects Willoughby J. Edbrooke and Franklin P. Burnham to design the new building. Construction began in 1884, the cornerstone was laid in 1885, and the structure was completed by mid-1889. Situated on what is now known as Capitol Square, bounded by Capitol Avenue and Mitchell, Washington, and Hunter streets, the Neo-Classical Revival structure rises three full stories to a large central dome. The front facade on Washington Street, constructed of gray Indiana limestone, features a two-story Corinthian pedimented portico supported by six rusticated piers. A bronze female figure holding a torch and a sword stands atop the gold leafed dome. White Georgia marble predominates in the interior. Two-story galleried lobbies flank the galleried rotunda on the north and south, and on the east and west sides stand the Senate and the House chambers. In the latter, the oak panelling features Florentine Renaissance motifs with an Eastlake Victorian flavor. On the grounds surrounding the Capitol stand statues of famous Georgians, including Civil War governor Joseph E. Brown and agrarian leader Tom Watson.

When completed in 1889, the Georgia State Capitol reflected the New South ideal. New and modern, the structure expressed the optimism of the state's leaders in a strong and prosperous Georgia. It was deliberately similar in style to the United States Capitol, evoking a neo-nationalism and signifying the reentry of the state and the South into the mainstream of American life. No other structure in the state more clearly evokes the spirit of the Gilded Age in the South. Today guided tours and a variety of special programs and exhibits throughout the year provide opportunities to learn more about the Capitol and the broader context of Georgia history.

MARTIN LUTHER KING, JR. NATIONAL HISTORIC SITE Atlanta. In the first decades of the twentieth century, black Georgians looked to Atlanta's Sweet Auburn community as a source of opportunity and model of social and economic success. Named for Auburn Avenue, the community's main street, this business, cultural, and residential district developed independent of the city's larger white society and typified black community development in the segregated urban South prior to 1930. Sweet Auburn's most famous native son was Martin Luther King, Jr., born in 1929 in his grandparent's home on Auburn Avenue. In the 1950s and 1960s King became the leader of the civil rights movement in the United States and a symbol of the struggle for racial equality and social justice worldwide. The Martin Luther King, Jr., National Historic Site was established to preserve the properties most closely associated with King's life and work and forms the core of a larger preservation district that protects the most significant remaining areas of the Sweet Auburn community. Together the site and the preservation district provide a unique opportunity to learn about the twentieth-century experience of black Georgians and a pivotal figure in the history of American race relations.

The community that originally developed along Auburn Avenue in the 1880s and early 1890s was not a racial enclave. Although no one would claim that the community was integrated, blacks and whites did live in close proximity and maintained routine business contacts. The racial composition of the neighborhood began to change in the mid-1890s, however, with the rise of white supremacy and legalized segregation in Georgia. Jim Crow legislation preceded the adoption of the white primary in 1897, and virtual disfranchisement of black Georgians followed by 1908. As opportunities in the larger white community narrowed, blacks pulled back into more secure, segregated communities. Black businesses that earlier had been located in downtown Atlanta began to relocate along Auburn Avenue, while white residents and businesses moved from there to predominantly white areas of the city. The real turning point was the race riot of 1906, the most violent in the city's history and a devastating illustration of the depth of white hostility toward black Atlantans. In the aftermath of that riot, building a strong, independent black community became imperative.

A variety of businesses, financial organizations, service institutions, fraternal orders, and churches proved crucial to the community's growth and development in the decades that followed. Black entrepreneurs opened barbershops, beauty shops, funeral homes, restaurants, and other small businesses in the Auburn Avenue neighborhood as early as the 1890s. These establishments provided essential goods and services and became important neighborhood gathering places where residents could exchange news and information. More formal lines of communication existed as well, including WERD, the nation's first black-owned and -operated radio station, and several newspapers, especially the *Atlanta Age,* the *Atlanta Post,* and the *Atlanta Daily World,* the oldest black-owned daily in the United States. The most visible symbols of the growth and development of Sweet Auburn were its financial institutions, which provided the capital essential to economic independence. Foremost among these were the Citizen's Trust Bank, Mutual Federal Savings and Loan, and the Atlanta Life Insurance Company. Alonzo F. Herndon founded the last in 1905 by merging nine faltering mutual aid societies. Atlanta Life eventually became the city's largest black business and a model of sound financial management.

The oldest community service institution in Sweet Auburn is the Butler Street YMCA, located on a side street just off Auburn Avenue. Organized in 1894 in the basement of Wheat Street Baptist Church, the YMCA has provided night-school classes, lectures, sports and craft activities, and a variety of other programs designed to meet the community's changing needs. It has also served as a focus for community organizations, including the Atlanta Negro Voters League and the Hungry Club Forum. Fraternal orders played significant roles in community life as well. The largest and wealthiest fraternal order during Sweet Auburn's early years was the Odd Fellows, whose imposing headquarters on Auburn Avenue, completed in 1912, became a symbol of black pride and accomplishment. The name "Sweet Auburn" was coined by John Wesley Dobbs, for decades the leader of the Prince Hall Masons, another major black fraternal order. Both the Odd Fellows and the Masons began as mutual aid and fellowship organizations and developed into centers of community leadership.

But unquestionably Sweet Auburn's churches have had the greatest impact on the community's growth and development. The churches have sponsored programs for community welfare and improvement, served as meeting centers, and proved important sources of power and leadership. Big Bethel A.M.E. Church, First Congregational Church, Wheat Street Baptist Church, and Ebenezer Baptist Church have been the most prominent. Originally known as the Bethel Tabernacle, Big Bethel established the first black school in Atlanta shortly after the Civil War. First Congregational was founded in 1867 with a racially mixed congregation and a white pastor but became all black in the 1890s as the racial composition of the community changed. The church's first black pastor, Dr. Henry Hugh Proctor, became a leading advocate of the development of Sweet Auburn after the 1906 race riot. The role of the churches

Ebenezer Baptist Church

in more recent community development is effectively illustrated by Wheat Street Baptist's civic improvement projects, including the Wheat Street Garden Apartment Complex, the Wheat Street Credit Union, and the Wheat Street Towers for senior citizens.

The most famous of Sweet Auburn's churches is Ebenezer Baptist Church. Founded in 1886, Ebenezer Baptist came to national attention in the 1950s and 1960s as the home church of Martin Luther King, Jr. King's grandfather, Adam D. Williams, and his father, Martin Luther King, Sr., served as Ebenezer's pastors from 1894 to 1931 and from 1932 on respectively, so the younger King spent much of his childhood in and around the church. His ties to Ebenezer remained strong even after he left Atlanta to attend school and then to assume his own pastorate in Montgomery, Alabama, in the 1950s. Of particular significance was his return to the Auburn Avenue church in 1957 to hold the first meeting of the Southern Christian Leadership Conference, an organization he hoped would provide the leadership essential to ending racial discrimination and segregation. In 1960 he became co-pastor of Ebenezer Baptist, a position he held until his death in 1968.

King was born at 501 Auburn Avenue, about a block east of Ebenezer Baptist Church, The houses in Sweet Auburn range from simple one-story shotgun dwellings typical of rental property for blacks in the 1920s to two-story Victorian homes like the King birthplace, a Queen Anne-style frame structure erected in 1895. The first black owner and occupant of the house was King's grandfather, Adam D. Williams, who lived there from 1909 until his death in 1931. After their marriage in 1925, Williams' daughter and her husband, Martin Luther King, Sr., moved into the Auburn Avenue house as well. There they raised their three children, including Sweet Auburn's most famous son.

King rose to national and international prominence as the focus and symbol of the movement for civil rights and social justice in the United States in the 1950s and 1960s. Calling for non-violent social change, he led the Montgomery bus boycott of 1955–1956, founded the Southern Christian Leadership Conference in 1957, and inspired the sit-ins and freedom rides of 1959–1960. He continued his efforts through the mid-1960s as an organizer of the Birmingham marches, the March on Washington, and the Selma marches, which focused nationwide attention on the civil rights movement and the racial injustice that still persisted a decade after the Supreme Court's 1954 desegration ruling. The Civil Rights Act of 1964 and the Voting Rights Act of 1965 addressed the legal and political disabilities that concerned King and his followers, but social and economic inequality persisted. As frustration increased, rising black militancy after 1965 threatened King's hopes for non-violent change. Nevertheless, he remained the preeminent leader of black Americans until his assassination on April 4, 1968. His body was returned to Sweet Auburn for burial in a memorial park just east of Ebenezer Baptist Church. The marble crypt bears the now familiar words: "Free at last, free at last, thank God almighty, I'm free at last."

The Martin Luther King, Jr., National Historic Site preserves the Auburn Avenue neighborhood where King lived and worked, including his birthplace and childhood home, Ebenezer Baptist Church, the King Memorial, and Freedom Hall, the headquarters of the Martin Luther King, Jr., Center for Non-Violent Social Change. This is only a portion of the larger Sweet Auburn community that is included in the preservation district. The district comprises a variety of residential, business, and public buildings associated with the community's historical development. No other historic area conveys so effectively the history of the modern civil rights movement and the larger context of the twentieth-century black experience.

ANDERSONVILLE PRISON *state 49 one mile east of Andersonville.* Site of the stockade and surrounding fortifications of the infamous prison where 33,000 Union soldiers were held; escape tunnels made by inmates still visible.

ATLANTA HISTORICAL SOCIETY *3101 Andrews Drive, N.W., Atlanta.* Modern museum and research facility housing Margaret Mitchell memorabilia and other collections. Tulie Smith House (1840s) and Swan House (1927–1928) also on grounds.

CHICKAMAUGA-CHATTANOOGA NATIONAL MILITARY PARK *Fort Oglethorpe.* Military museum with an extensive collection of shoulder arms of the American military.

CYCLORAMA *Grant Park, Boulevard at Atlanta, Atlanta.* Constructed

in 1887 and recently restored; depicts the Battle of Atlanta, July 22, 1864.
DAHLONEGA COURTHOUSE GOLD MUSEUM *Old Lumpkin County Courthouse, public square, Dahlonega.* Museum at site of the nation's first gold rush, 1829, and where the gold that gilds the state capitol was mined.
FORT AUGUSTA SITE *churchyard of St. Paul's Episcopal Church, Augusta.* Where Oglethorpe first marked off the town in 1735.
FORT FREDERICA *Saint Simons Island.* Ruins of English barracks, fort, and house foundations dating from 1736–1746.
FORT McALLISTER *state 67 ten miles east of Richmond Hill.* Confederate earthworks that withstood navel assault in 1861 but were overrun by Sherman in 1864.
FORT PULASKI *Cockspur Island, seventeen miles east of Savannah by U.S. 80.* Site of John Wesley's mission to the Indians, 1736; a fort built 1829–1847 was occupied by Confederates then taken by Union forces in 1862.
GEORGIA AGRIRAMA *Interstate 75 exit 20 at 8th St., Tifton.* Outdoor agricultural museum focusing on the wiregrass region of South Georgia in the 1880s and 1890s.
GEORGIA HISTORICAL SOCIETY *501 Whitaker Street, Savannah.* Museum with books, manuscripts, maps, photographs, art, and artifacts on Savannah and Georgia.
HAY HOUSE *934 Georgia Avenue, Macon.* One of many fine antebellum residences still standing in this historic city.
JARRELL PLANTATION *Jarrell Plantation Road, Juliette.* Farm with visitor center showing Georgia agriculture from the 1840s to the 1940s, including gristmill and cotton gin.
KENNESAW MOUNTAIN NATIONAL BATTLEFIELD PARK *off U.S. 41 two miles north of Marietta.* Site of several battles and skirmishes between Union and Confederate forces under Sherman and Johnston, respectively, in 1864.
LAPHAM-PATTERSON HOUSE STATE HISTORIC SITE *626 N. Dawson Street, Thomasville.* Restored Victorian resort home, built in 1885 by a Chicago merchant.
MACKAY HOUSE *1822 Broad Street, Augusta.* A 1760 house that was site of a Revolutionary War battle in 1780 after which the British hanged several American prisoners.
MILLEDGEVILLE *on U.S. 441.* State capital 1807–1868; includes the Old State Capitol, 1940s reconstruction of 1807 capitol, and Old Governor's Mansion (1838).
MILLIONAIRES VILLAGE *375 Riverview Drive, Jekyll Island.* Several historic houses built by millionaires at the turn of the century; contain period furnishings and other items.
NEW ECHOTA STATE HISTORIC SITE *Route 3, Calhoun.* Capital of the Cherokee Nation, 1825; includes restored mission and tavern and reconstructed courthouse and print shop.

OCMULGEE NATIONAL MONUMENT *U.S. 80E and 129, east edge of Macon.* Museum displaying artifacts found on the site from Mississippian cultures active A.D. 900–1100; also mounds.

OKEFENOKEE HERITAGE CENTER *Waycross.* History museum complex showing life in the areas around the swamp.

STEPHENS MEMORIAL STATE PARK *off U.S. 278, Crawfordsville.* Confederate museum and antebellum residence of Alexander H. Stephens, Confederate vice president.

STONE MOUNTAIN PARK *Stone Mountain.* Includes historic houses, water-powered grist mill, covered bridge, and Georgia Heritage Museum.

WARM SPRINGS LITTLE WHITE HOUSE *off U.S. 27A, Warm Springs.* House Franklin Delano Roosevelt built in 1932 as retreat; where he died in 1945.

WESTVILLE HISTORIC HANDICRAFTS, INC. *Troutman Road, Lumpkin.* Re-creation of a mid-nineteenth-century southwestern Georgia town.

HAWAII

PU'UHONUA O HŌNAUNAU NATIONAL HISTORICAL PARK
Hōnaunau, Kona. The royal line of *alii* or chiefs and the sacred laws of *kapu* dominated Hawaiian culture before the arrival of foreign settlers and missionaries in the early nineteenth century. As representatives of the gods, the *alii* presided over the elaborately detailed *kapu* system that regulated everyday life and buttressed the ancient Hawaiian religion. The punishment for breaking *kapu* was death, unless the violator could reach a refuge sanctified by the *mana* or spiritual power of deified chiefs. The most sacred and best preserved such asylum is Pu'uhonua o Hōnaunau on the island of Hawaii. Now maintained as the Pu'uhonua o Hōnaunau National Historical Park, this place of refuge and the adjoining ancestral home of the Hawaiian royal family together constitute an impressive reminder of the way life used to be in Hawaii.

The *kapu* system formed the structure of Hawaiian life for perhaps a thousand years. This ancient code prescribed the proper conduct for everything from land ownership to sexual relations. Dietary prohibitions were particularly strict, extending to what foods women could eat and dictating separate food preparation and dining by the sexes. Because these laws were believed to be divinely given, violation was an offense to the gods and thus required punishment by death lest an offended god take his revenge out on everyone. No matter what the circumstances or how minor the violation, breaking *kapu* brought a sentence of death, unless the offender escaped to a place of refuge like that at Pu'uhonua o Hōnaunau.

The concept of a refuge or asylum hinged on the Hawaiians' reverence for *mana,* the special spiritual power of the high chiefs. The chiefs' *mana* pervaded not just their persons but their possessions and even the ground they walked on. Respect for *mana* prohibited commoners from walking in a chief's footsteps, touching his possessions, or letting their shadows fall on the palace grounds. As with other *kapu,* violation would lead to death. Yet the sanctity of *mana* also provided the basis for the *pu'uhonua* or place of refuge. *Mana* remained in the bones of dead chiefs and hence sanctified the mausoleum temple or *heiau* in which these bones were placed. Protected by the dead chiefs' *mana,* these temples came to be regarded as sanctuaries or refuges for breakers of *kapu.* After a ceremony of absolution performed by the priest or *kahuna,* the violator could then return home safely, free from danger. Others who sought refuge included defeated warriors awaiting the outcome of battle and noncombatants—the aged, the young, those unable to protect themselves during the fierce island wars.

Pu'uhonua o Hōnaunau was one of six such refuges on the island of Hawaii. The sanctuary adjoined the ancestral home of the royal lineage that produced Kamehameha, the great Kohala chief who united all the

Restored temple house of Hale-O-Keawe

islands in the early nineteenth century. The palace grounds included a collection of thatched buildings, royal fish ponds, and a royal canoe landing, all forbidden to commoners and protected by warriors. Separating the palace grounds from the refuge was a massive stone wall approximately one thousand feet long, ten feet high, and seventeen feet wide. This wall was erected about 1550, perhaps as a monument to Keawe-ku-i-ke-ka'ai, the ruling chief at the time. After his death, a *heiau* was erected to house his remains. Since his *mana* remained in his bones, this mausoleum temple sanctified the area. The sacredness of the Hale o Keawe *heiau* increased further with the burial of at least twenty-two more Kona chiefs over the next two and a half centuries, ending with the deification of a son of Kamehameha in the early nineteenth century.

According to legend, Kaahumanu, the favorite wife of Kamehameha, took refuge at the Pu'uhonua o Hōnaunau after a quarrel with the great chief. Her pet dog revealed her hiding place, however, and she and Kamehameha reconciled. At his death in 1819, she became *kuhina nui*— a sort of executive officer, with more power than a prime minister—to his heir and exerted enormous influence over the affairs of the kingdom. In particular, she instigated the break with *kapu* later that same year. At her encouragement, Kamehameha II defied the sacred laws of *kapu* and deliberately committed taboos long forbidden by the old religion. This defiance of the power of the gods marked the end of *kapu* and signalled a basic change in Hawaiian culture. Their perspectives broadened by decades of foreign contact, the Hawaiians refused to submit any longer to the religious tyranny of their ancestors. In the wake of this development, *pu'uhonua* ceased to function as well, and *heiau* were dismantled throughout the islands. The *heiau* at Pu'uhonua o Hōnaunau survived because of continued veneration of the remains of Kamehameha's ancestors, but after the bones were removed in 1829, this temple was also demolished.

The Hawaiian royal family retained ownership of the palace and temple grounds until the late nineteenth century. In the 1890s Charles R. Bishop purchased the property and added it to his estate. In 1961, the 180-acre site became a national historical park under the administration of the National Park Service. Now restored to its appearance in the late eighteenth century, the Pu'uhonua o Hōnaunau National Historical Park is open to visitors daily.

The focus of the park is the palace-refuge complex. The palace grounds include several examples of early housing construction, a special stone on which the chiefs played the game of *kōnane,* the *keone' ele* or royal canoe landing, and a royal fish pond or *he-lei-pālalu.* The massive L-shaped stone wall that separates the palace from the *pu'uhonua* has survived virtually intact for over four centuries, although it was repaired in 1902 and again in 1963–1964. At its north end stands the reconstructed Hale o Keawe *heiau.* An 1823 sketch by the Reverend William Ellis, an American missionary, made possible an accurate reconstruction of the structure on the original stone platform. The remnants of two earlier *heiau* also remain in the refuge, as well as a *kōnane* stone and the Keoua stone, according to legend the favorite resting place of a Kona chief. The Kaahumanu stone marks the location where Kaahumanu hid during her flight from Kamehameha. Elsewhere in the park are other temple foundations, a village site, burial caves, petroglyphs, and sledding tracks used for recreation by the chiefs. Park programs include orientation talks by park interpreters, a self-guided tour of the refuge and palace grounds, and a living-history program of traditional Hawaiian crafts and skills.

The Pu'uhonua o Hōnaunau National Historical Park preserves the most historically significant remnant of the traditional society that reigned in Hawaii prior to the arrival of outsiders at the close of the eighteenth century. It offers a rich opportunity to learn about and experience that ancient island culture.

MISSION HOUSES MUSEUM *553 South King Street, Honolulu, Oahu.* When Hiram Bingham and his fellow missionaries journeyed from New England to Hawaii in 1819 and 1820, not even the most optimistic anticipated the profound impact their work was to have on the island kingdom. While they were sent principally to bring the Christian religion to the native residents, over the forty years that followed their influence extended to politics and government, the economy, education, and social customs. The missionaries filled the void created by the crumbling of the traditional island culture and provided direction and purpose essential to the emergence of modern Hawaii. The three structures that served as the mission's headquarters have been preserved as the Mission Houses Museum, a fitting monument to these men and women and their pivotal roles in shaping nineteenth-century Hawaiian society.

In 1819, the American Board of Commissioners for Foreign Missions, a Congregational organization, dispatched Bingham and his associates to establish the Sandwich Islands Mission. The Pioneer Company included seven married couples, five children, and three young Hawaiians who had been educated at the Foreign Mission School in Connecticut. After a six month voyage aboard the *Thaddeus,* the group arrived in the Hawaiian islands in April 1820 and shortly thereafter established the first mission station—four grass houses just outside Honolulu. These temporary structures not only provided shelter for the missionary families but also served as a focus for mission activities during the first year and a half. Although a prefabricated house arrived by ship from Boston on Christmas day, 1820, it was August of the following year before the first family moved into it. The residence was not the island's first frame structure, but it was certainly the largest and required the king's permission to construct. Once King Liholiho consented, the missionaries erected the four-bedroom structure, supplementing the pre-cut lumber with salvaged ship timbers and native materials. When completed, the simple frame house stood as an oasis of New England culture within the foreign land.

In addition to providing much-needed residential space, the new structure served as a center for mission programs. Principal among these

Missionaries' frame house

was Christianizing the Hawaiians. During their first couple of years, the Americans made little headway, but the conversion of Kaahumanu, the new young king's chief advisor (and his late father's favorite wife), in 1823 won broader acceptance for their teachings. Under the influence of Bingham, the mission's leader, the island kingdom became a virtual theocracy; New England Protestantism took the place of the old *kapu* system in ordering the lives of the Hawaiians. The missionaries' influence soon extended as well to the nation's diplomatic relations, political development, and economic direction. The symbol of the mission's central role in Hawaiian life was Kawaiahao Church, a massive stone New England-style church designed by Bingham and constructed between 1839 and 1842. Adjoining the mission station, the new structure dominated the city long after the mission closed.

Another major goal of the Sandwich Islands Mission was to bring literacy to the islands. The Hawaiian language had never been committed to writing, so the missionaries faced an unenviable task. Although it took years of work to establish a phonetic standard, the first spelling sheet in Hawaiian was printed in 1822, when the mission press first began operations. The missionaries had brought the small second-hand Ramage press with them on board the *Thaddeus,* but other duties prevented printer Elisha Loomis from setting up shop until January 1822. In the years that followed, the press turned out volumes of printed material in the Hawaiian language, ranging from a translation of the Bible to textbooks and handbills. The press thus became the cornerstone of the mission's education program, providing the materials for a network of schools extending to every district in the islands. By the mid-1840s, Hawaii had one of the highest literacy rates in the world.

The establishment of a network of seventeen mission stations testified to the expansion of activities in the mission's first two decades. To staff these, the ABCFM dispatched twelve more companies of missionaries, including ministers, doctors, printers, teachers, and business agents. The size of the mission operations complicated the work of the Honolulu headquarters. For example, someone had to coordinate the distribution of food, clothing, furniture, and other supplies required by the Americans. When grass huts proved unsuitable as warehouses, Levi Chamberlain, the mission's business agent, began construction of a more permanent facility in 1830. The two-story coral-block structure, not completed until December 1831, provided space for a business office, storage, and living quarters for the Chamberlain family. Between it and the frame house, the mission in 1841 erected a bedroom wing—thus completing the present-day complex of mission houses.

The Sandwich Islands Mission proved enormously successful in its work, and the ABCFM began in the late 1840s to encourage the independence of the Hawaiian churches. Finally in 1863 the board withdrew its financial support and closed the mission. Some of the missionaries returned to the United States; but others stayed on, continuing the mission's work or taking active roles in island politics and business. The mission property remained in private hands until the early twentieth century, when the three main buildings became the property of the Hawaiian Mission Children's Society, a genealogical society made up of the missionaries' descendants.

The Mission Houses Museum now stands as the oldest and most significant symbol of the role of Protestant missionaries in nineteenth-century Hawaii. The restored frame house erected in 1821, open to visitors, includes parlors, bedrooms, kitchens, and cellar and reflects the missionaries' New England roots and their communal living arrangements during the early years. Furnishings include items imported from the United States, China, and elsewhere, a variety of native crafts, and even some pieces hand-made by the missionaries—a mixed collection that illustrates the various cultural influences in Hawaiian society. On the other side of the museum complex stands the Chamberlain house. Of particular interest are the dutch doors and block-and-tackle, which recall the structure's earlier function as a storehouse. Between the two buildings is the bedroom wing to the frame house. Erected about 1841, the small coral building now houses the museum's printing exhibits.

In addition to tours of the historic properties in the complex, the museum sponsors formal exhibits, school programs, and research facilities. It also provides a walking tour of historic sites in downtown Honolulu, including Kawaiahao Church and Iolani Palace. Although the city has many sites associated with the history of Hawaii in the nineteenth and early twentieth centuries, none surpass the Mission Houses Museum in illuminating the forces that shaped the Hawaiian nation in the mid-nineteenth century.

U.S.S. ARIZONA MEMORIAL *Arizona Memorial Drive, Honolulu, Oahu.* Few events in recent history rival in significance the Japanese attack on the United States naval base at Pearl Harbor on December 7, 1941. The immediate consequence was the United States' entry into World War II, but perhaps more significant in the long term was how that event altered the course of American social, economic, and political life and influenced the structure of international relations. What is often ignored, however, is the impact of the event on Hawaiian history. In the wake of the attack, the American territory underwent a controversial period of tight military rule that had enormous impact on the shaping of contemporary Hawaii. The U.S.S. *Arizona* Memorial commemorates this pivotal event and honors the thousands who lost their lives there.

Pearl Harbor comprises a series of natural locks on the south coast of Oahu near Honolulu. Named for the pearl oysters that grew in the water there, the harbor went undeveloped until the late nineteenth century. In 1884 the United States obtained exclusive rights to establish a fuel and supply base there, but it was 1902 before dredging operations removed part of a coral bar that limited full access by deep-draft ships.

Memorial at Pearl Harbor

With that obstacle out of the way, the United States proceeded with plans to develop the harbor as a strategic base for American naval operations in the Pacific. In 1916 Pearl Harbor was made the headquarters of the Fourteenth Naval District.

Over the next twenty-five years, the United States invested considerable sums of money in building up the installation. By 1941 the base included a battleship dock, a floating drydock, a large repair basin, a fuel depot, a submarine base, a section base, the district headquarters, and the Naval Air Station on Ford Island. The installation's facilities and strategic location gained significance for the United States in 1940 and 1941, when deteriorating relations with Japan threatened American interests in the Pacific. Recognizing that the Hawaii-based Pacific Fleet was the key to United States military strength in the region, the Japanese government apparently began making plans to attack the Pearl Harbor installation as early as December 1940. Negotiations with the United States continued into November 1941, but by mid-October the Japanese Navy General Staff had approved attack plans, expecting a quick decisive victory that would cripple the United States. On November 26, the Japanese navy began moving into place, and by December 7 the warships had arrived at the planned launch position 275 miles north of Oahu. At 6:00 a.m. the first wave of fighters, bombers, and torpedo planes headed for their target.

Despite cautionary alerts from Washington and defense preparations by local civilian officials, the naval base at Pearl Harbor was not prepared for the Japanese attack, which first hit at 7:55 a.m. In two waves of bombing that lasted until about 9:45 a.m., the Japanese either sank or seriously damaged eighteen American warships, including six Pacific Fleet battleships moored on "Battleship Row," and destroyed or damaged nearly two hundred fifty aircraft. Deaths totaled 2,403, including

Navy, Army and Marine personnel and sixty-eight civilians, and over a thousand more were wounded. The Navy lost in the one attack three times as many men as in the Spanish-American War and World War I combined. In contrast to the devastating American losses, their assailants had only 164 casualties and lost only twenty-nine planes, five midget submarines, and one I-Class sub.

Over half the American fatalities came from the bombing of the U.S.S. *Arizona*. Launched in 1915 and modernized in 1929, the thirty-one-thousand-ton battleship was one of the six units in the Pacific Fleet Battle Force moored on the southeast shore of Ford Island. The *Arizona* was one of the first targets of the Japanese: only fifteen minutes into the attack a 1,600 pound armor-piercing bomb ripped into the vessel and set off a massive explosion in the powder magazine. Within nine minutes, the ship broke in half and sank to the bottom of the harbor. Of the 1,550 men on board, only 289 survived. After the attack ended, only about 150 bodies could be pulled from the wreckage, leaving the bodies of approximately 1,100 Navy and Marine personnel entombed there.

Luckily for the United States, its aircraft carriers were not in port and escaped damage. Of the battleships, only the *Arizona*, the *Utah*, and the *Oklahoma* were not salvaged. The shipyards, fuel storage areas, and submarine base suffered only slight damage. While certainly crippling American military strength in the Pacific, the Pearl Harbor attack did not knock the United States out of the picture. On December 8, the United States declared war on Japan, thereby entering World War II. The details of the war and its impact on American life and world order are familiar to many, but few understand the problems Hawaii endured during the course of the war. Military rule severely abridged civilian rights, and the injustices of that era had significant repercussions for Hawaiian politics and society in the postwar era.

The *Arizona* remains today at the bottom of Pearl Harbor as a tomb for those interred in its hull and as a memorial to the 1941 tragedy. In 1962, a white concrete memorial was erected over the sunken battleship. Resting on pilings driven deep into the coral rock harbor floor, the memorial includes a bell room housing the ship's bell, a semi-open room for ceremonies and observation, and a shrine room, where the names of the 1,177 sailors and Marines killed on the ship have been engraved on a white marble wall. A flagpole affixed to the mainmast of the *Arizona* still flies the American flag, a privilege extended by the Navy to no other inactive ship. On the shoreline overlooking the harbor is a visitor center erected in 1980. This structure provides a variety of support facilities, including a theater where visitors can view a documentary film on Pearl Harbor and a museum that provides exhibits on the *Arizona* and the Japanese assault. All are located within the boundaries of the Pearl Harbor Naval Base, which still remains the headquarters of the United States Pacific Fleet.

Visitors to present-day Hawaii are usually most intrigued by the state's exotic Polynesian heritage and its luxury resort atmosphere. They often fail to realize that this island paradise has had its own share of the social, economic, and political problems that vacationers think they have left behind. The U.S.S. *Arizona* dramatically calls attention to one tragic event and the obstacles and challenges it posed for twentieth-century Hawaii.

ALA MOANA HOTEL 2365 Kalakaua Avenue, Honolulu, Oahu. The oldest hotel in Waikiki, built 1901.

ALOHA TOWER Pier 9, Honolulu Harbor, Honolulu, Oahu. Ten-story building constructed in 1926 and symbolic of early tourism industry; used by the military in World War II.

BERNICE P. BISHOP MUSEUM 1355 Kalhiki Street, Honolulu, Oahu. Natural and human history, with rare examples of canoes, shields, head-dresses, ceremonial objects, featherwork, and other artifacts from Hawaiian life pre-contact to modern era.

CHINATOWN HISTORIC DISTRICT bounded approximately by Beretania Street, Nuuanu Stream, Nuuanu Avenue, and Honolulu Harbor, Honolulu, Oahu. Center of Chinese life, with early-twentieth-century buildings and Hawaii Chinese History Center at 111 N. King Street.

COOK LANDING SITE two miles southwest of state 50, southwest section of Waimea Bay, Kauai. Where Capt. James Cook, the first Western visitor to the islands, disembarked in 1778.

FALLS OF CLYDE Pier 5, Honolulu Harbor, Honolulu, Oahu. An 1878 four-masted sailing ship used as a freighter, passenger ship, oil tanker, and now a floating museum taking passengers on rides in Mamala Bay.

GROVE FARM HOMESTEAD MUSEUM state 58 one mile southeast of Lihue, Kauai. Sugar complex begun in 1854 and in use until 1978.

HALE HOIKEIKE (OLD BAILEY HOUSE) Iao Valley Road, Wailuku, Maui. Example of architecture of early missionary houses, begun in 1833 and built of lava rock and stucco; includes a museum.

HANALEI MUSEUM Hanalei, Kauai. Rice implements and furniture of different ethnic groups living on the island, in an 1880s plantation-style house.

HAWAII VOLCANOES NATIONAL PARK Hawaii. Fossil footprints of men, women, children, and hogs left after a 1790 eruption of Kiluanea volcano; visitor center.

HONOLULU ACADEMY OF ARTS 900 S. Beretania Street, Honolulu, Oahu. Traditional arts of Oceania, collection of Japanese prints, Asian art (including bronzes and furniture), and traditional and contemporary Western art.

HULIHEE PALACE Alii Drive, Kailua-Kona, Hawaii. Restored lava and stucco house begun in 1838, with later alterations; built for early island governor and later owned by King Kalakaua. Museum with exhibits of tapa and featherwork.

IOLANI PALACE 364 S. King Street, Honolulu, Oahu. Elegant seat of Hawaiian government after 1893, with ornate carved woods and plaster cornices; occupied by King Kalakaua and Queen Liliuokalani and later the territorial capitol.

KALAUPAPA NATIONAL HISTORIC PARK Molokai. Located on peninsula where Father Damien De Veuster, a Belgian priest, gave his life caring for victims of Hansen's disease (leprosy) in the late nineteenth century.

KAMAKAHONU northwest edge of Kailua Bay north and west of Kailua Wharf, Kailua-Kona, Hawaii. Temple remains, stone walls, and royal platform from last residence of King Kamehameha in early nineteenth century.

KAUAI MUSEUM 4428 Rice Street, Lihue, Kauai. Exhibits of items from Hawaii, with emphasis on Kauai, and ethnic displays.

KEIAWA HEIAU Aeia Heights Drive, Aeia, Oahu. Small prehistoric structure surrounded by low walls, used as temple of healing.

LAHAINA HISTORIC DISTRICT west side of Maui on state 30. Seaport that was center of whaling industry in 1800s and capital of Maui. Includes Baldwin House, 1835; Hale Paahao Prison, 1851; Lahainaluna missionary school, founded 1831; and Hale Pa'i Printing House.

LYMAN HOUSE MEMORIAL MUSEUM 276 Haili Street, Hilo, Hawaii. Restored Lyman house, built in 1839 for missionaries; adjacent modern natural-history museum with Hawaiiana, missionary, and ethnic collections.

MOOKINI HEIAU northern tip of Hawaii one mile west of Upolu Point Airport, near Hawi, Hawaii. Remains of sacrificial temple, with twenty-foot stone walls and birthstone of Kamehameha I.

OLD RUSSIAN FORT state 50, 200 yards southwest of Waimea River bridge, Kauai. Remains of outer walls and foundations of Russian fort built 1816–1817.

PUU-KOHOLA HEIAU NATIONAL HISTORIC SITE north end of Hawaii off state 26, about one mile southeast of Kawaihae, Hawaii. Stone temple and wall built by Kamehameha I and center of his effort to unify the islands.

PUU O MAHUKA HEIAU state 83, four miles northeast of Haleiwa, Oahu. Built before contact with Westerners; largest temple on island and reputed to be where Vancouver's men were sacrificed.

QUEEN EMMA SUMMER PALACE 2913 Pali Highway, Honolulu, Oahu. Restored home of Emma and Kamehameha IV, with furnishings and memorabilia of family, including tapa, featherwork, and quilts; built 1847.

ROYAL MAUSOLEUM 2261 Nuuanu Avenue, Honolulu, Oahu. Completed in 1865, chapel added 1922; where Kamehameha family members and ancient chiefs are interred.

ULA PO HEIAU off Kailua Road, Kailua, Oahu. Prehistoric terrace temple with small enclosures and stone mounds.

U.S. ARMY MUSEUM *Battery Randolph, Kalia Road, Fort DeRussy, Honolulu, Oahu.* Military exhibits related to activity of U.S. Army in the Pacific; in a pre-World War I coast artillery defense bastion.

WAIOLI MISSION DISTRICT *off state 56, Hanalei, Kauai.* Complex of church, community hall, mission house, and other structures related to missionary activity begun in the 1830s; an early restoration effort in 1921 with unusual mixture of Western and Polynesian styles of architecture.

WASHINGTON PLACE *320 S. Beretania Street, Honolulu, Oahu.* Built about 1846; where Hawaiian governors have lived since 1921.

IDAHO

NEZ PERCE NATIONAL HISTORICAL PARK U.S. 95, Spalding. The history of Idaho is incomplete without the Native American experience. Perhaps the most famous of the Indian tribes are the Nez Perce, whose lands at one time encompassed much of Oregon and Washington as well as northern Idaho. Their first encounter with white men occurred when the Lewis and Clark expedition passed through the region in 1805, and for nearly six decades thereafter the Nez Perce remained on relatively good terms with the explorers and settlers who ventured into their ancestral lands. The discovery of gold in 1860, however, unleashed white greed for the Indians' land, and tribal members who resisted were eventually defeated in the Nez Perce War of 1877. The Nez Perce National Historical Park in northern Idaho includes twenty-three historic sites that preserve the history of the Nez Perce Indians and their disastrous encounter with white America.

The original territory of the Nez Perce may have encompassed as much as 27,000 square miles in the Pacific Northwest. Scattered across this vast territory were numerous small bands or villages, each with its own leader or chief. Their principal activities included hunting, gathering, and fishing, all necessary for their subsistence, but the Nez Perce also developed trading relations with other tribes and became known as excellent horse breeders.

The first white men to venture into Nez Perce territory were the Lewis and Clark expedition, dispatched in 1803 by President Thomas Jefferson to explore the newly acquired Louisiana Purchase and search for a route west to the Pacific. The most arduous portion of their westward journey took them along the Lolo Trail over the Bitterroot Mountains in September 1805. This was the same route used by the Nez Perce when traveling to and from buffalo hunting grounds in Montana. The trail's western terminus was the Weippe Prairie, one of the Nez Perce's favorite places to gather camas roots for food, and there on September 20 William Clark and a small advance party first encountered the Nez Perce. During the expedition's brief stop in the Idaho region, the Indians proved very helpful, supplying them with food, helping them build log canoes on the Clearwater, and keeping their horses until they returned from the Pacific coast the next June en route back to St. Louis.

In 1831 a delegation of Nez Perce traveled to St. Louis, reportedly seeking knowledge of the white man's religion. The American Board of Commissioners for Foreign Missions interpreted that as an invitation to establish missions and assigned Henry and Eliza Spalding and Dr. Marcus and Narcissa Whitman to the Pacific Northwest. In 1837 the Whitmans established a mission among the Cayuse Indians near present-day Walla Walla. The Spaldings set up another among the Nez Perce at Lapwai, although they soon found the summer heat and mosquitoes at Lapwai unbearable and moved two miles north. There they built a meeting house, school, mission church, residence, saw and grist mills, and other buildings. The construction program proved more successful than the missionary work, however; Henry Spalding had several unpleasant encounters with the Indians in the area and never managed to involve many of the Nez Perce in mission activities. After the Whitmans were killed at Waiilatpu on November 29, 1847, by a band of angry Indians, Spalding deemed it wise to close down the Lapwai Mission and withdraw to Oregon. He returned twice in later years, with somewhat more success, and died while working at the mission in 1874.

Despite Spalding's fears, Indian-white relations remained amicable through the decade that followed his first departure from the Nez Perce country. In 1855 the United States government and the Nez Perce tribe signed a treaty opening up 12,230 square miles of the Indians' accustomed territory to white settlers and establishing a system of reservations on the remaining 5,122 square miles. As part of this agreement, the federal government established the Nez Perce Indian Agency in 1860 on the site of the old Spalding Mission. That same year, however, Captain Elias D. Pierce's discovery of gold on the Clearwater River set off a chain of developments that proved disastrous for the Nez Perce people. When word of Pierce's discovery spread, miners swarmed into the area, ignoring the fact that they were trespassing on Nez Perce land. The Indians protested, and government agents tried to mediate. In 1862 the army was brought in to restore order. Then, succumbing to white clamor for more land, the federal government decided in 1863 to further reduce the size of the Indian reservation. A new treaty took over seven million acres, leaving the Nez Perce only 757,000.

While many tribal chiefs signed the new agreement, one faction refused, becoming known thereby as the "non-Treaty" Nez Perce. They simply refused to move from their ancestral lands to the Idaho reservation. After a meeting with the Indian leadership at Fort Lapwai in 1876, the government concluded that force would be necessary to gain compliance with the treaty. Joseph, the leader of the non-Treaty faction, and his followers finally yielded to pressure and began the move to the reservation in February 1877. Then in mid-June, a small group of young Nez Perce men murdered four whites near the Salmon River. General O. O. Howard, in charge of moving the Indians onto the reservation, dispatched the cavalry to restore order. The soldiers finally caught up with the Nez Perce warriors on June 17, and the Battle of White Bird Canyon ensued. The cavalry lost thirty-four men, the Indians none.

The initial victory at White Bird Canyon buoyed the hopes of the non-Treaty faction, but subsequent encounters were not so successful. Less than one month later, the Nez Perce faced the army again at the Battle of the Clearwater. Although the engagement ended in a draw, the Nez Perce lost several chiefs and warriors and decided to withdraw to the east along the Lolo Trail, hoping to find safety over the mountains in Montana Territory or Canada. In two and a half months, they traveled 1,700 miles and managed to elude the pursuing army. Their flight ended in early October 1877, when most of the weary Nez Perce surrendered at the Bear Paw in Montana.

Those of the non-Treaty faction who did not flee to Canada lived in exile in the Indian Territory until 1885, when they moved to a reservation in Washington Territory. But while those who accepted the treaty escaped defeat and exile, they did not evade the white man's continuing greed for land. At the close of the nineteenth century, the federal government's allotment policy further dispersed tribal land. Thus, by the end of their first century of contact with the white man, the Nez Perce's land holdings totaled only 87,879 acres—less than 12 percent of the portion included in the 1855 treaty.

The Nez Perce National Historical Park includes twelve thousand square miles of the tribe's ancestral lands and twenty-three historic sites chiefly associated with their history and culture. Although administered by the National Park Service, the park is actually a cooperative effort involving as well the Forest Service, the Bureau of Indian Affairs, the Idaho State Historical Society, the Nez Perce Tribe of Idaho, and several individuals and private organizations.

The park's sites reflect various aspects of the Nez Perce experience. Coyote's Fishnet, Ant and Yellow Jacket, and the Heart of the Monster are natural formations important to the religion and legends of the Nez Perce. Visitors can also see Camas Prairie and Musselshell Meadow, where the tribe gathered camas roots, an important part of their food supply. Also within the park are Weis Rockshelter and Lenore, two archeological sites that testify to centuries of Native American occupation of the region. Sites associated with the Lewis and Clark expedition include the Lolo Trail, Weippe Prairie, Long Camp, and Canoe Camp, where the Nez

Tribe's legendary "place of beginning"

Perce helped the explorers build canoes for the next leg of their journey west. The site of Donald Mackenzie's Pacific Fur Company post recalls early fur-trading activity, and the mission period is commemorated at the site of the Spalding home, the Craig Donation Land Claim, St. Joseph's Mission, the Asa Smith Mission, and the town of Spalding, the park's headquarters. The town of Pierce represents the gold discovery era, and the Northern Idaho Indian Agency and Fort Lapwai sites recall the Indians' relations with the federal government in subsequent decades. Three sites focus on the Nez Perce War: the White Bird Battlefield, the Cottonwood Skirmishes, and the Clearwater Battlefield. The Spalding Visitor Center provides a tour map of the park as well as a brief audio-visual program on the Nez Perce culture, a museum, and cultural demonstrations by members of the Nez Perce tribe. Together these sites and programs provide a unique opportunity to learn about an important and controversial chapter in the history of frontier Idaho and the Northwest.

CITY OF ROCKS STATE PARK Almo. In the 1840s and 1850s thousands of emigrants followed the Oregon and California trails across the Rocky Mountains to new homes in the American West. The two roads actually followed the same routes into Idaho, but between Fort Hall and the Raft River travelers had to choose between continuing on to Fort Boise and hence to Oregon and breaking off to the south along the California Trail. The City of Rocks near Almo is one of the major landmarks along the latter and commemorates Idaho's pivotal role in the great westward migration of the mid-nineteenth century.

"Oregon fever" preceded "California fever," so the initial trail west had the Oregon country as its destination. Although a few pioneers made the trip in the 1830s, the first substantial caravan of covered wagons did not follow until 1841. Activity increased dramatically in the next couple of years, and by 1845 an estimated five thousand emigrants had made the trek west along the Oregon Trail. The route originated at St. Joseph and Independence, Missouri, where wagon trains formed to follow the Platte and North Platte rivers into southern Wyoming. The wagon caravans then crossed the Rocky Mountains at South Pass, followed the Snake River across Idaho, and then cut across to the Columbia River and the Willamette Valley. Although the Idaho region was part of Oregon, travelers usually only stopped long enough to rest themselves and their stock and secure provisions at Fort Hall and Fort Boise, fur-trading posts established in 1834 and operated by the Hudson's Bay Company. Until the discovery of gold in the region in the 1860s, few emigrants thought of Idaho as more than just a transportation corridor to other destinations.

The Bidwell-Bartleson party, which opened up the Oregon Trail in 1841, had planned originally to head for California, but when the group reached the bend of Bear River in Idaho, half changed their minds and continued on to the Willamette Valley. The California-bound contingent

The Lizard rock formation

turned to the south and took an arduous route through Utah and Nevada to their destination. The next year Joseph B. Chiles, a member of the Bidwell-Bartleson group, led a return party east from California along the Humboldt, across to Fort Hall, and back along the Oregon Trail to Missouri. A significant improvement over the 1841 route, Chiles' road soon became known as the California Trail. The new route did not undergo heavy use until the California gold rush. Then in 1849 some 22,500 emigrants followed the trail to the new gold fields. The total rose to an estimated 165,000 in the next eight years. The volume of traffic peaked during the 1850s and all but disappeared after the completion of the transcontinental railroad in 1869.

One of the most prominent landmarks on the California Trail was the City of Rocks, a mass of soft granite formations in southern Idaho. Emigrants followed the Raft River southwest from the Oregon Trail to this site and then swung through Granite Pass into Nevada, along the Humboldt, and into California. Called City of Rocks as early as 1850, the landmark became a popular campsite for the forty-niners, and many travelers even carved their names in the rock formations. Visitors today can still see wagon-wheel ruts left by thousands of emigrant wagons over a hundred years ago. Now designated a National Historic Landmark, the City of Rocks recalls the era of westward expansion and the diverging trails followed by pioneer emigrants across Idaho to their new homes in Oregon and California.

OLD ASSAY OFFICE 210 Main Street, Boise. In the early 1860s the population of the Idaho region boomed as thousands of would-be millionaires rushed to find new gold bonanzas. The initial focus of activity was in the north, around Lewiston, but by 1864 the population center

*Former
United States
Assay Office*

shifted south to Boise—a military outpost and supply base established the year after the 1862 gold strike in the nearby Boise Basin. As territorial and then state capital, the city has remained at the heart of the Idaho experience ever since. Although Boise is no longer a gold-mining boom town, its Old Assay Office still stands as a reminder of the pivotal role of mining in the history of both the city and the region.

Idaho's first gold rush began with the discovery of gold on the Clearwater River in 1860. Prospectors paid little heed to the protests of the Nez Perce, who owned the land, and by 1861 swarmed across northern Idaho. The discovery of a new placer deposit on the Salmon River near Florence followed. Then in August 1862 Moses Splawn opened a new mining district in the Boise Basin far to the south. All these mines initially proved highly productive. Clearwater yielded nearly seven million dollars in gold by 1866, the Salmon River another sixteen million by 1867, and the Boise Basin twenty-four million by 1866. The gold output for Idaho's mines totaled over fifty million dollars between 1861 and 1866—or about 19 percent of the nation's total production during the same period. Only California and Nevada exceeded Idaho in gold production by the mid-1860s.

Impressed by the region's dramatic population increase and its great mineral wealth, Congress organized the Idaho Territory on March 4, 1863. Lewiston initially served as the territorial capital and resisted for a time efforts to move the government to Boise, which by 1864 eclipsed the northern town in both size and influence. The controversy ended in 1865 when, following legislative action to move the capital south, the territorial governor had the seal and archives removed from Lewiston to Boise. The latter's influence increased in 1869, when Congress appropriated $75,000 for the erection of a U.S. Assay Office there. The decision came at the end of a long campaign aimed at eliminating high shipping costs to the San Francisco mint and thereby expediting exploitation of the region's mineral resources.

Congress approved the appropriation in February 1869, a local citizen donated a site for the project later that year, but construction did not begin until July 1870. John R. McBride, a former congressman from Oregon and chief justice of Idaho Territory, finally convinced the Treasury Department to move ahead by offering to take charge of the construction project. Alfred B. Mullet, Supervising Architect of the Treasury, oversaw the plans and specifications, which called for a two-story sandstone structure with a low hipped roof and ventilator. When completed in July 1871, the structure was an impressive sight, the most important example of public architecture in Idaho until the twentieth century.

The office did not actually open until the following year, when all the necessary machinery finally had been put in place. The first assay was made on March 2, 1872. By that time, however, the placer mines had been largely worked out, and gold production fell into a slump that lasted until 1883 and a new strike in the Coeur d'Alene region in northern Idaho. In the next year, 1884, gold production doubled; by the end of the decade an infusion of capital from out of state further expanded the scope of operations. Deep mining, new stamp mills and smelters, and silver and lead mining enabled fuller exploitation of the region's resources. In 1895 deposits in the Boise Assay office passed the million dollar mark, and the deposits for the next eleven consecutive years averaged one and a half million dollars annually. By 1917, total production from Idaho mines had reached four hundred million dollars: one-quarter in gold, one-quarter in silver, and one-half in lead.

Mining declined over the next decade and a half, however, and the need for assaying services decreased. The Assay Office finally discontinued its operations on June 30, 1933, and turned the building over to the Forest Service, which used it as headquarters for the Boise National Forest. Since 1970 the building has housed a museum and offices of the Idaho Historical Society. Now designated a National Historic Landmark, this venerable structure ably symbolizes Idaho's gold-rush era and Boise's emergence as a metropolitan center.

ARROWROCK DAM *about ten miles east of Boise on U.S. Forest Service roads, Middle Fork of Boise River.* Concrete, built 1910–1916, with later alterations; at 354 feet the highest dam in the world when completed.

BEAR RIVER BATTLEGROUND *northwest of Preston off U.S. 91.* Site of massacre of 400 Shoshoni men, women, and children by United States troops in 1863 (greatest Indian massacre in the country's history).

BOISE GALLERY OF ART *670 S. Julia Davis Drive, Boise.* Works of Idaho and other American artists as well as crafts and Asian art.

BONNEVILLE POINT, OREGON TRAIL *ten miles southeast of Boise off I-84.* Interpretive exhibits on a stretch of the trail used from the 1840s to 1880s.

CATALDO MISSION *I-90 about 28 miles east of Coeur d'Alene.* Built 1848–1853 by Indians to whom Roman Catholic missionaries had gone; has Greek Revival elements. Oldest structure in the state.

CLEARWATER HISTORICAL SOCIETY MUSEUM *315 College Avenue, Orofino.* Exhibits on early days of logging using horsepower and on early mining in the area.

COEUR D'ALENE DISTRICT MINING MUSEUM *507 Bank Street, Wallace.* Early history of mining in area, including stock certificates and annual reports of mining companies for sale.

CONGREGATION BETH ISRAEL SYNAGOGUE *1102 State Street, Boise.* An 1895 frame building that houses the oldest synagogue in the state, which had as a leader Boise mayor and Idaho governor Moses Alexander.

CUSTER MUSEUM *Yankee Fork Ranger District, Clayton.* Gold-rush mining equipment and turn-of-the-century buildings on the site of an 1870 rush.

EGYPTIAN THEATER *700 Main Street, Boise.* Movie theater of 1927 with unusual and striking Egyptian elements, outside and inside, and a large theater organ.

EXPERIMENTAL BREEDER REACTOR NO. 1 *National Reactor Testing Station, Arco.* Where the demonstration took place showing that nonfissionable uranium could produce more fissionable material than it consumed; decommissioned in 1964. Museum at site open to public. National landmark.

FORT BOISE *Fifth and Fort streets, Boise.* City park and several remaining buildings on the site of the 1863 post established by the United States Army to protect miners and others.

IDAHO CITY *state 21.* Major settlement in Boise Basin, where an 1862 gold rush occurred; once the largest city in the Northwest. An 1867 Wells Fargo express office houses a museum.

IDAHO MUSEUM OF NATURAL HISTORY *Idaho State University, Pocatello.* Manuscripts and photos of Northern Rockies, flint-working collection, and other materials on primitive people in North and South America.

IDAHO STATE HISTORICAL MUSEUM *610 N. Julia Davis Drive, Boise.* Exhibits on Idaho and Northwest prehistory and history.

LEESBURG *west of Salmon at Napias Creek in Salmon National Forest.* Ghost town active 1866–1900, with several log cabins remaining from early gold rush.

McCONNELL HOUSE *110 S. Adams Street, Moscow.* An 1886 clapboard house that was the home of William J. McConnell, first United States senator from Idaho. Home of Latah County Historical Society.

MASSACRE ROCKS STATE PARK *U.S. 30 west of American Falls.* Pioneer, Oregon Trail, and Indian items.

MUSEUM OF NORTH IDAHO *Coeur d'Alene.* Devoted to logging and lumbering artifacts; in the center of lumbering industry.

NEZ PERCE COUNTY HISTORICAL SOCIETY MUSEUM *Third and C streets, Lewiston.* Items from pioneer and Indian history in an art-deco building.

NORTHERN PACIFIC RAILWAY DEPOT *off U.S. 10, Wallace.* Built on a formula by the railroad in 1901, with brick, half-timber, and concrete; beautiful example of its type.

OLD IDAHO PENITENTIARY *2200 Warm Springs Avenue, Boise.* Territorial and state prison 1870–1973. Self-guided tour. Electricity and transportation museums within the compound.

PIERCE COURTHOUSE *Pierce.* An 1862 log and board-and-batten courthouse still standing on the site of a gold-rush town of the early 1860s.

SHOSHONE HISTORIC DISTRICT *from the northern bank of the Little Wood River and West D Street from S. Cherry Street to S. Alta Street, Shoshone.* Mixture of architectural styles on buildings from the late 1800s and early 1900s in a rail, farm, and ranch center.

SILVER CITY *unpaved road twenty-five miles southwest of Murphy.* More than thirty well-preserved buildings still standing in a town dating from the 1860s.

UNION PACIFIC MAINLINE DEPOT *1701 Eastover Terrace, Boise.* Spanish Colonial Revival style on a depot built 1924–1925.

UNIVERSITY OF IDAHO MUSEUM *Moscow.* Items from Idaho agricultural history as well as from around the world.

VAN SYLKE MUSEUM *Caldwell Memorial Park, Caldwell.* Has tools and equipment from pioneer agriculture days and several historic houses.

ILLINOIS

LINCOLN'S NEW SALEM STATE PARK Petersburg. The early settlement of Illinois was dominated by migrants from Kentucky, Tennessee, the Carolinas, and Virginia. Establishing small subsistence farms throughout the southern third of the territory, these pioneers maintained the distinctive life style, values, and beliefs of the traditional agrarian society from which they came. As the focus of settlement gradually shifted north in the 1830s and pioneers from more diverse backgrounds joined them, this traditional society began to yield to modern values and patterns of thought. The village of New Salem, a mid-state community rooted in agrarian traditionalism yet clearly more progressive than the older settlements to the south, was typical of this transitional period. Indeed, out of it came Abraham Lincoln, the leading spokesman for modern values in nineteenth-century Illinois. Lincoln's New Salem State Park recreates the historic village and brings to life the state's pioneer past.

John M. Camron and his uncle, South Carolinian James Rutledge, initially constructed a saw and grist mill on the tract of land they purchased along the Sangamon River in 1828, but in 1829 they decided to develop the promising location as a town. Several families moved into the area within the first year, and the town of New Salem became a reality. Samuel Hill and John McNeil opened the village's first store and post office, Kentuckian Henry Onstot opened a cooper shop, and William Clary opened a second store. Clary appraised the tastes of his fellow settlers and wisely stocked his establishment with gin, wine, rum, and whiskey. On their way to and from the nearby mill, the male residents of the rural settlement regularly stopped at his establishment for a half pint and some entertainment—perhaps a gander pull, a cock fight, or wrestling.

New Salem flourished over the next couple of years as new arrivals erected homes and established businesses. Like other early Illinois communities, the town attracted migrants from the Southern uplands and particularly from Kentucky. Residents with ties to the latter included Isaac Burner, Isaac Gulihur, Peter Lukins, James and Rowan Herndon, Denton Offutt, and Abraham Lincoln, who was employed by Offutt in 1831 to operate a store at New Salem. The village also had a few Yankee residents, notably John Allen and Francis Regnier, physicians from Vermont and Ohio respectively. Educated, middle-class, and ambitious, the two were conspicuous representatives of modern values in the still largely traditional Illinois society. With typical Presbyterian reforming zeal, Allen even organized a temperance society to counter the hard-drinking habits of his fellow settlers.

Both traditional craft occupations and entrepreneurial activity contributed to the town's economic growth and diversification. Joshua Miller, a blacksmith, and Martin Waddle, a hatter, were typical craftsmen who practiced age-old skills learned as apprentices. Henry Onstot, a cooper, and Peter Lukins, a cobbler, also practiced their trades, but both had wider interests as well that revealed their ambitions for upward mobility. Not content with just his cooperage business, Onstot and his wife for a time operated the New Salem Tavern and in 1840 moved on to a more prosperous neighboring town. Lukins did not stay in New Salem long either, for he and George Warburton left in 1832 to develop the nearby town of Petersburg, a successful speculative venture. Other prominent entrepreneurs were James and Rowan Herndon, who opened a store in 1831; Samuel Hill, a merchant who built a carding mill and wool house in 1835; and Jacob and Hardin Bale, who eventually owned the saw and grist mill, the carding mill and wool house, the New Salem Tavern, and the ferry. The most famous businessman in New Salem, however, was Abraham Lincoln.

Lincoln first came through New Salem in April 1831, while poling a

New Salem village

flatboat of farm produce down the Sangamon River for Denton Offutt. While temporarily stranded at the village, Offutt decided it was a promising site for a store and hired Lincoln to run it. The two delivered their cargo to New Orleans and returned that August to set up Offutt's new business. The enterprise did not, however, last even a year. Offutt left, but his former clerk stayed on. He, Isaac Gulihur, and Alexander Trent served in the Black Hawk War in the late spring of 1832, and later that summer Lincoln made an unsuccessful bid for a seat in the state legislature. He then became a partner with William Berry in a store established in New Salem the year before by the Herndon brothers.

In 1833 Berry and Lincoln moved their business across the road to the Warburton building, and Lincoln took on the additional duties of town postmaster. Not content with life as a small-town merchant, he made a second bid for a seat in the state legislature in 1834, won, and was reelected again in 1836. Meanwhile, he studied law and secured admission to the bar in March 1837. Convinced that New Salem held no further opportunities for him, he then moved to Springfield, the new state capital. Lincoln's roots were in the traditionalist upland South, but his values, beliefs, and aspirations were clearly those of a modern man.

The riverboat *Talisman* arrived in New Salem in the spring of 1832, and residents hoped that more river traffic and prosperity would soon follow. But the Sangamon River proved unnavigable, and the town did not become the bustling port envisioned. New Salem remained an agrarian village of crude log structures, and business continued to depend on simple barter and trade. The population had increased at first despite a high turnover, but by 1836 no new residents were taking the places of those that departed. Put simply, New Salem stagnated while other towns prospered. In 1836 the post office was moved to Petersburg, and then in 1839 the latter became the county seat as well. By the close of the decade, New Salem was a virtual ghost town.

In the late nineteenth and early twentieth centuries, the Old Salem Chautauqua Association held annual summer meetings at New Salem and convinced newspaper publisher William Randolph Hearst to purchase the site for preservation. He did so and conveyed the property in trust to the association, which in turn gave title to the state of Illinois in 1919. Under the state's supervision, the village was carefully reconstructed in the 1930s and 1940s, and all structures have been appropriately furnished with respect to the period, their owners, and their use. Lincoln's New Salem State Park now includes twelve timber houses, eleven other reconstructed buildings, a museum, and various park support facilities.

Visitors to Lincoln's New Salem can tour the re-created village, ride a replica of the *Talisman,* view museum exhibits, and attend outdoor dramas at the Kelso Hollow Amphitheater. The park also includes concessions, campgrounds, picnicking facilities, and a nature trail. Finally, the park sponsors a variety of special events and programs throughout the year. Together the park's varied offerings provide a unique opportunity to experience early Illinois history.

LINCOLN HOME NATIONAL HISTORIC SITE *426 South Seventh Street, Springfield.* The preeminent symbol of modern values in nineteenth-century Illinois was Abraham Lincoln. Articulating the modern commitment to free labor, he rose from relative obscurity in the 1850s to election as the nation's first Republican president in 1860. His victory did not end the conflict between opposing value systems but rather precipitated a more devastating confrontation—the Civil War. Under Lincoln's uncompromising leadership, the nation survived the war and emerged more committed to modernization and more certain of America's mission to transform the world. During his rise to national prominence, the Illinois politician and his family lived in a modest frame house in Springfield at the corner of Eighth and Jackson streets. Now preserved as the Lincoln Home National Historic Site, the residence

Lincoln's Springfield home

reflects the family's adherence to modern middle-class concepts of home and family and aptly symbolizes Lincoln's broader commitment to modern values.

Abraham and Mary Todd Lincoln purchased their Springfield home in 1844 from the Episcopal minister who had married them two years before. During the seventeen years they lived there, the aspiring politician won election to Congress, established his legal practice, built support within the fledgling Republican party, and in 1858 made an unsuccessful bid for Stephen A. Douglas' seat in the United States Senate. His political career drew strength from the rising tide of modernism in Illinois in the 1850s, and he quickly attained national prominence with his forceful articulation of the modern man's faith in reason and progress and his persuasive rallying cry for the free labor doctrine. When the Republican party selected him as its standard-bearer in the 1860 presidential race, Lincoln received the convention's notification committee in the front parlor of his Springfield residence. Through much of the campaign that followed, he remained at home, receiving delegations and political leaders, basking in the enthusiasm of rallies and other demonstrations of public support, and leaving travel and speeches to others. There he also learned of his victory and began planning for the challenge ahead. The following February, he and Mrs. Lincoln held a final reception for friends and supporters at their home before packing up for the move to Washington.

But Lincoln's Springfield home has significance beyond its associations with his political career, for it reflects as well the Lincoln family's basic commitment to modern middle-class values. Erected in 1839 in a fashionable area on the edge of the city, the modest but substantial frame structure provided Lincoln, his wife, and one son a comfortable and roomy home and suggested to the community the success of the young lawyer's legal practice. Ambitious and hard-working, he apparently took pride in his rise from rather humble origins to the comfortable middle class. As his family grew and his standing in the community rose, Lincoln made several improvements, including enlargement of the house from a story and a half to a full two stories in 1856. Although simple and lacking in elaborate architectural details, the large residence certainly befitted an aspiring lawyer and politician.

Perhaps even more indicative of the Lincolns' modern values was the way they lived within the house. When the Lincolns purchased it in 1844, they had little money and had to live on a rather tight budget. That meant that the young lawyer cared for his own horse, milked his own cow, and even chopped wood. His wife took responsibility for sewing, cooking, housework, and childrearing, occasionally with the help of a female domestic. Clearly, the Lincolns functioned in separate spheres—he the public figure responsible for the family's economic well-being as well as for outdoor chores, she the dominant figure in the private world of the home and family. These separate but equally important spheres of responsibility indicated a rejection of traditional male supremacy and a strong commitment to nineteenth-century notions of sexual equality.

Although traditional in many of her attitudes and ways of thinking, Mary Todd Lincoln embraced modernity within the woman's sphere. As ambitious and aspiring as her husband, she always endeavored to maintain an appearance of good taste and breeding, a requisite of middle-class status in nineteenth-century America. She decorated her home as fashionably as the family budget would allow, paying close attention to the details that bespoke refinement and style. Furniture, flowers, pictures, curtains, and other household ornaments reflected the fashions of the day without being pretentious, and her personal touches provided the residence with the air of homeyness and comfort that Victorians associated with love of home, family, and marriage.

Her eagerness to keep up with fashion and with the latest developments in household management typified the modernizer. She read popular domestic manuals like *The House Book, or, A Manual of Domestic Economy for Town and Country* and doubtless aspired to the efficient household described in such volumes. Given this penchant for progress and modernity, it should come as no surprise that, when cast-iron stoves came into vogue, the Lincolns dutifully closed up their fireplaces and installed the more efficient heating sources.

Modern values also influenced parent-child relationships. The modernizers' mission to transform the world began with their own children, and the Lincolns were typical modern parents concerned with childrearing, schooling, and other matters. Both deeply loved their four sons and lavished attention on them. Parties, games, and other activities kept the house alive and testified to the central role the children played in their parents' lives.

Clearly, the Lincolns' home had great significance for their lives, and it must have been difficult to break up housekeeping for the move to Washington in 1861. Some possessions were packed in trunks for shipment to the White House, others were stored, but much of the accumulation of seventeen years was sold privately that January. When the Lincolns left Springfield for Washington, they left the last home they would ever know as a family.

At Lincoln's death, his wife and two surviving sons inherited the Springfield house. The structure was rented out for several years and at one point housed a museum of Lincoln memorabilia. In 1887 Robert Todd Lincoln, the only remaining heir, deeded the historic structure to the state of Illinois as a memorial to his father. In succeeding decades, various attempts were made to restore and furnish the Lincoln house, but no careful historical and archaeological research was conducted until the 1950s. Now administered by the National Park Service, the house has been restored and furnished as accurately as possible to depict the Lincoln years. Although the state abounds with sites associated with Lincoln, none equals the Lincoln home in providing insight into the values and beliefs basic to both his private life and his public career.

JANE ADDAMS' HULL-HOUSE 800 South Halsted Street, Chicago. The influence of agrarian traditionalism in Illinois' politics and society had faded by the close of the nineteenth century, but those trying to modernize still had to contend with persistent traditionalism in the state's urban areas. Nowhere was this urban traditionalism more evident than in the slums and tenements of Chicago's Near West Side, a transitional community that experienced successive waves of immigrant settlement in the late nineteenth and early twentieth centuries. Trapped in urban poverty rather than subsistence agriculture, the Italians, Poles, Russians, Greeks, and other ethnic groups that swelled Chicago's population in this era maintained within their isolated neighborhoods the traditional values of their backgrounds. Ever eager to transform mankind, modernizers sought to uplift this working-class culture through a variety of philanthropic efforts and reform activities.

At the forefront of this movement stood Hull-House, the famous settlement house established on the Near West Side in 1889 by Jane Addams and Ellen Gates Starr. An aggressive pioneer in social, educational, humanitarian, and civic reform, the Halsted Street settlement became the preeminent symbol of modern reform in urban and industrial America. Jane Addams' Hull-House preserves two structures from the historic complex and effectively tells the story of the interaction of modern values and urban traditionalism in this port-of-entry neighborhood.

By the 1880s and 1890s, the Near West Side was Chicago's most densely populated district. Originally settled by old-stock Americans in the 1830s,

*Original
Hull mansion
on Halsted*

the rural suburb was soon engulfed in the rapid growth that made Chicago one of the nation's largest cities. Old stock residents gave way to German and Irish workers employed in nearby railroad yards, mills, and foundries, and the population increased dramatically. Soon industrial expansion and the encroachment of factories and warehouses from the Loop lowered property values and initiated a general decline in the residential neighborhood. The older German and Irish immigrants then moved on to better communities, and speculators took over, dividing up the one-and two-family cottages to house a huge influx of immigrants from southern and eastern Europe. The Near West Side became the port of entry for thousands of illiterate, unskilled Poles, Russian Jews, Greeks, and Italians, whose lack of resources forced them to crowd into the slums that filled the area by the late 1880s.

Within the district bounded on the east by the Chicago River, on the west by Ashland Avenue, on the north by Lake Street, and on the south by 16th Street, the various ethnic groups established well-defined neighborhoods apart from the larger city. Here they found continuity and community, a haven from the alien and often bewildering experiences of urban and industrial America. The Irish community centered on Holy Family Roman Catholic Church at May Street and Roosevelt Road; the Italians occupied the area north of Taylor, first to the east and later to the west of Halsted; the Jews crowded into "the Ghetto" south of Taylor; the Greeks clustered at the "three points" where Blue island, Halsted, and Harrison meet; and pockets of Turks, Bulgarians, Serbians, and other groups scattered through the district. Each faced its own peculiar dilemmas in adjusting and adapting to American society, but all shared the common plight of urban poverty and exploitation.

Convinced that something should be done to alleviate the problems of urban life that confronted these immigrant families, Jane Addams and Ellen Gates Starr decided to establish a settlement house modeled on London's Toynbee Hall. The settlement house, staffed with resident social workers, would provide a refuge in the midst of urban poverty addressing both the immediate day-to-day problems of the immigrant community and the larger issues of urban life. Addams and Starr decided to focus their efforts on Chicago's Near West Side and in 1889 rented a portion of a Halsted Street mansion once owned by Chicago business-man Charles J. Hull. The house was in the heart of the slum district and had served at various times as a hospital, a saloon, a livery stable, a tene-ment, and the offices of a desk factory. It stood between a funeral par-lor and a livery stable on one side and an Irish saloon, a German bakery, and a Jewish junk shop on the other. Furnishing the house with the same walnut and mahogany furniture they would have used in their own homes, the women made the once-fine country residence an oasis of middle-class culture and values in the middle of the city's worst slums.

Hull-House officially opened on September 18, 1889. The first pro-gram was a kindergarten for area children, established that October in the Hull-House reception room. In the years that followed, the settle-ment's activities expanded dramatically. Addams, Starr, and the other social workers that joined them set up numerous programs obviously designed to modernize and Americanize their immigrant neighbors. Art classes and exhibitions, music instruction, dramatic presentations, con-certs, public lectures and discussion, extension courses, and a variety of other services reflected their determination to remake the slum-dwellers in their own middle-class image.

Residence in the middle of the city's poorest and most densely pop-ulated district inspired more significant reform activity as well. Responding to the conditions they witnessed daily, Hull-House's workers estab-lished the city's first public bathhouse and first public playground, opened an employment bureau, and sponsored the Jane Club, a cooperative effort to provide housing to working girls. The fruits of their efforts also included the Immigrants Protective League, the Juvenile Protective Association, the Institute for Juvenile Research, and the Illinois Child Labor Committee. Residents championed the inspection of alleys, sani-tation reform, child-labor laws, new school construction, compulsory school attendance legislation, and an eight-hour day for women. As their frustration increased, they turned to political activity as well and pro-vided meeting space for trade union groups attempting to organize the unskilled immigrant workers. Indeed, Hull-House became the most aggressive and influential reform institution in the nation. Addams and her associates played a central role in initiating and organizing the broad movement for urban reform central to the progressive movement of the early twentieth century.

Hull–House continued in operation at the original site until 1963. Over the years, the settlement expanded to fill thirteen buildings, cov-ering the entire city block upon which Hull's house stood. All but the house and the 1905 dining hall were torn down in the mid-1960s to make room for the campus of the University of Illinois at Chicago Cir-cle. Now decentralized through the city, the Hull-House Association continues the work begun nearly a century ago.

The University of Illinois at Chicago Circle has restored and opened to the public the two remaining structures, the Hull mansion and the old dining hall. Visitors can see many original furnishings, paintings, photographs, and documents and several rotating exhibits. In addition to tours of the historic structures, Jane Addams' Hull-House sponsors a variety of special programs and exhibits and works with the remaining residents of the community to preserve the history of the ethnic neighborhoods that Hull-House served.

Hull-House epitomized the middle-class reforming zeal of Illinois' nineteenth- and twentieth-century modernizers. The settlement house aptly suited the reformers' plans to introduce to the urban poor the values and life styles of modern America. But Hull-House soon moved beyond that limited vision to stand at the forefront of pioneering efforts for social justice in urban and industrial America. Jane Addams' Hull-House preserves the site where it all began and commemorates Addams, her fellow residents, and the community they served.

ALTGELD HALL *University of Illinois, Urbana.* A Richardsonian Romanesque building, built 1896–1897, housing the third-largest university library in the country.

BISHOP HILL *Bishop Hill.* Houses, Colony Church, hotel, and artifacts of a colony of Swedish dissenters active here 1846–1862.

BLACK HAWK STATE PARK *off U.S. 67 and state 2, Rock Island.* Commemorates the Black Hawk War of 1832, in which the Sauk and Fox resisted in vain white efforts to occupy their land.

BRYANT COTTAGE *146 E. Wilson Avenue, Bement.* Tours and exhibits of the place where the Lincoln-Douglas debates were agreed to; contains period furnishings.

CAHOKIA COURTHOUSE *214 W. First Street, Cahokia.* A 1737 French residence used as a courthouse 1793–1814.

CARL SANDBURG BIRTHPLACE *331 E. Third Street, Galesburg.* Cottage built about 1870, now with antique furniture and other family items of the famous writer.

CARSON, PIRIE, SCOTT AND COMPANY *1 S. State Street, Chicago.* Designed by Louis Sullivan and built 1899, 1903–1904; his last commercial building, an outstanding example of his work, and a building still being used.

CHICAGO AVENUE WATER TOWER AND PUMPING STATION *both sides of N. Michigan Avenue between E. Chicago and E. Pearson streets, Chicago.* Limestone structures built 1866–1869 that were the only buildings to survive the 1871 fire.

CHICAGO HISTORICAL SOCIETY *Clark Street at North Avenue, Chicago.* Extensive collections with exhibits and tours on Chicago and Illinois history; including American folk art, photos of early Chicago, and Civil War material.

CHICAGO PUBLIC LIBRARY CULTURAL CENTER 78 *E. Washington Street, Chicago.* Includes collections other than books, such as military items relating to the Civil War, contemporary art, and cultural traditions.

CLOVER LAWN Bloomington. Italianate home of David Davis, United States Supreme Court justice and confidant and campaign manager of Lincoln; constructed 1870–1872 and furnished with many original family antiques.

DICKSON MOUNDS MUSEUM Lewistown. Museum that interprets the life of inhabitants on this site from Paleo-Indian to Mississippian periods, with one large mound and several smaller.

EVANSTON HISTORICAL SOCIETY 225 Greenwood Street, Evanston. Materials on Charles G. Dawes, vice president 1925–1929 and Nobel Peace Prize winner, in the Dawes Mansion, built 1894.

FIRST SELF-SUSTAINING NUCLEAR REACTION SITE S. Ellis Avenue, Chicago. Where the first self-sustaining nuclear reaction occurred in 1942 under the direction of Enrico Fermi; now a grass plot between two tennis courts on University of Chicago campus.

FORT de CHARTRES HISTORIC SITE MUSEUM Prairie du Rocher. Site of the French stone fort, built 1753–1758, that was the center of French government in early Illinois country.

FORT KASKASKIA STATE PARK off state 3 ten miles north of Chester. Site of the French fort erected 1736 and captured by George Rogers Clark in 1778.

FORT MASSAC STATE PARK AND HISTORIC SITE Metropolis. Site of a military fort built by the French in 1757, then occupied by the British and Americans.

FRANK LLOYD WRIGHT HOME AND STUDIO Chicago and Forest avenues, Oak Park. A museum in the residence of the famous architect, who lived here 1889–1911.

ILLINOIS RAILWAY MUSEUM Olson road, Union. Collection of 150 railway cars, locomotives, and interurban and trolley cars; in an 1851 depot.

ILLINOIS STATE MUSEUM Spring and Edward streets, Springfield. A natural science and art museum, with exhibits on anthropology, archeology, paleontology, and Illinois decorative arts.

JOHN DEERE HOUSE AND SHOP Grand Detour. Clapboard house built about 1836 where John Deere invented the revolutionary steel plow.

LINCOLN LOG CABIN STATE HISTORIC SITE AND MOORE HOME Lerna. Reconstructed home of Thomas and Sara Lincoln on site where they lived, with museum and living farm; nearby is home of Matilda Moore, Abraham Lincoln's step-sister.

LINCOLN'S TOMB STATE HISTORIC SITE Oak Ridge Cemetery, Springfield. Grave of Lincoln.

METAMORA COURTHOUSE 113 E. Partridge, Metamora. Museum

in an 1844 courthouse where Lincoln practiced law on a circuit. *MUSEUM OF SCIENCE AND INDUSTRY 57th Street and Lake Shore Drive, Chicago.* Includes a coal mine moved to the site and materials on the historical development of various forms of energy and technology. *NAUVOO HISTORIC DISTRICT Nauvoo.* Several buildings from the Mormon period, 1839–1846, including the Joseph Smith Homestead. *OLD MARKET HOUSE STATE HISTORIC SITE Market Square, Galena.* Exhibits on architecture, mining, and economics from nineteenth-century Galena; in an 1845 Greek Revival house. *OLD STATE CAPITOL Fifth and Adams streets, Springfield.* Museum in the restored Greek Revival capitol, built 1837–1853; the fifth capitol of Illinois, where Lincoln served in the legislature, delivered the "House Divided" speech, and argued before state supreme court. *PIERRE MENARD HOME Ellis Grove.* Finest example of southern French architecture in the central Mississippi Valley; construction begun in 1802 for Menard, a late-eighteenth-century trader and first lieutenant governor of Illinois. *POLISH MUSEUM OF AMERICA 984 N. Milwaukee Avenue, Chicago.* Art, costumes, religious artifacts, military items, and memorabilia of Kosciuszko and Paderewski. *POSTVILLE COURTHOUSE STATE MEMORIAL AND MUSEUM 914 Forth Street, Lincoln.* Replica of the Logan County Courthouse where Lincoln practiced law; antiques from the period. *PULLMAN HISTORIC DISTRICT bounded by 103rd Street, C.S.S. and S.B. Railroad tracks, 115th Street, and Cottage Grove Avenue, Chicago.* Where industrialist George M. Pullman developed a self-contained company community in 1880; many buildings with unaltered exteriors. *ULYSSES S. GRANT'S HOME STATE HISTORIC SITE Bouthillier Street, Galena.* Exhibits on Grant's life in Galena, Victorian furnishings, Grant mementos; in house given to Grant by Galena in 1865. *VANDALIA STATE HOUSE HISTORIC SITE 315 W. Gallin Street, Vandalia.* The fourth state capitol, built in 1836–1839 and restored in the interior to that period and in the exterior to the late-1800s appearance; contains a museum. *WILLARD HOUSE 1730 Chicago Avenue, Evanston.* Home of temperance leader and socialist Frances Willard, built in 1865; contains a museum.

INDIANA

GEORGE ROGERS CLARK NATIONAL HISTORICAL PARK
401 South Second Street, south of U.S. 50, Vincennes. History is full of
fascinating "might have beens." Frequently they involve the bold actions
of individuals, or single dramatic events. What might have Reconstruction been like if John Wilkes Booth had not murdered Abraham Lincoln? Might Hitler have triumphed in 1940 if Winston Churchill had not
rallied the British to stand alone? Had there been no First World War,
might the Russian Revolution never have happened? Had the Japanese
not attacked Pearl Harbor, might the United States have stayed out of
World War II?

Such questions entail conjectures about things that did not in fact
happen, and therefore they are questions that historians sometimes are
reluctant to deal with. There are no firm answers. Still, they are useful
questions because they compel us to think about individual action in
history. Can one individual, at a specific place and time, really make a
difference? Or are the larger forces of history so complex that individuals really have little influence on the course of events? The life of
George Rogers Clark, which is memorialized today on the banks of the
Wabash in Vincennes, Indiana, raises such questions. In Clark's career
a specific action was followed by related events of great historical
importance. Did his action cause those events, or would they have happened anyway?

The specifics are these. The Revolutionary War was a long and costly
conflict fought over an immense area. The most famous and most decisive action took place east of the Appalachian Mountains, where, in the
1770s and 1780s, most Americans still lived: Saratoga, Trenton, Camden,
Kings Mountain, Yorktown. In 150 years the English colonies had pushed
inland hardly as many miles. Theirs was still largely an Atlantic world
dominated by the mercantile and naval power of England. But England's
power also stretched inland, and there as to the east it clashed with
American ambitions.

At the end of the French and Indian War in 1763, the victorious
English became masters of what once had been New France, an enormous and vaguely defined empire reaching from the mouth of the St.
Lawrence west through the Great Lakes and south down the Ohio and
Mississippi to lands where few white men had ever been. They inherited and occupied the network of outposts established by the French,
and from them they pursued the fur trade and cemented alliances with
the Indians. American settlement meanwhile was slowly but surely
probing past the mountain barrier into the rich lands of the interior.
Virginians and Carolinians moved in small but determined bands into
what would become Tennessee and especially Kentucky. Daniel Boone's

George Rogers Clark Memorial

Wilderness Road through the Cumberland Gap carried many, bound for the storied Bluegrass country.

When the war broke out, their remote settlements at Boonesborough, Harrodsburg, and Fort Logan faced an insecure and sometimes bloody future. From their headquarters at Detroit, the British in 1777 incited their Indian allies to raid the white settlements all through the backcountry in the hope that George Washington would send forces from his Continental Army to the West. It was a brutal business. The British rewarded the Indians according to the number of scalps they brought in—a practice that earned Lieutenant Colonel Henry Hamilton, the commandant at Detroit, the nickname "Hair Buyer."

Washington did not divide his forces, but other Americans did rise to the challenge in the West. Virginia claimed as hers all the land of the Old Northwest (the future states of Ohio, Indiana, Illinois, Michigan, and Wisconsin) plus Kentucky. Virginian George Rogers Clark appealed to Virginia Governor Patrick Henry for the authority and the resources to mount a campaign against the British bases in the Northwest. A persuasive man, he came away from Williamsburg with £1200 of overvalued colonial currency, the rank of lieutenant colonel, and the authority to recruit 350 men for his expedition. He also received two sets of orders. The public ones ordered him simply to defend Kentucky from the British and the Indians. The secret ones directed him more boldly to attack British strongholds to the north: Kaskaskia, Vincennes, and if possible Detroit itself.

Clark was a natural leader, and what followed became one of the more legendary chapters in the military history of the Revolution. Armed with the authority to secure boats, provisions, and ammunition at Fort Pitt, Clark gathered men in western Pennsylvania and set sail down the Ohio in the spring of 1778. He paused at Corn Island, opposite present-day Louisville, to drill and train his band of frontier fighters and in June sailed again, this time for the Illinois country. Intelligence was poor over such a vast area, and Clark did not know with any precision the strength of the enemy forces he would confront. Surprise, therefore, was important and he strove to avoid detection by British scouts and hostile Indians. But luck was with him. A party of American hunters appeared who had been at Kaskaskia just a week before, and they reported it to be lightly held. As an extra precaution, Clark and his little army, which numbered 170 men, left the river and struck out overland across the southwestern tip of Illinois toward Kaskaskia on the Mississippi. The tactic worked. Surprise was complete, and the British commander there surrendered without a fight.

Knowing that his small command was far from any reinforcement, Clark tried hard to win over the local French settlers to the American cause, and thus make easier the next step of his strategy: the capture of Vincennes. In this he was aided by knowledge of the just concluded alliance between France and the rebellious colonies. Restive under British rule ever since 1763, many French at Kaskaskia responded eagerly to the Virginians and encouraged their fellows at Cahokia and Vincennes to come over to the American side. Clark's luck held, and by mid-July 1778 his friendship with the French plus the fact that no British troops were stationed there put Vincennes too in his hands.

Unfortunately, the British mounted an expedition from Detroit and in December took it back. Settling in for the winter, Henry Hamilton planned to attack Rogers at Kaskaskia in the spring. But Clark did not wait for spring: after an arduous February march across flooded southern Illinois, he attacked Fort Sackville in Vincennes. Surprised, and believing the American force much larger than it actually was (127 men, 50 of whom were French), Hamilton surrendered on February 25. The Americans never again left the region north of the Ohio and west of the Appalachians.

By the peace treaty that formally ended the Revolutionary War in 1783, Britain conceded to the United States all of the lands north of the Ohio to the Great Lakes and west as far as the Mississippi. It was an enormous concession, considering that most of the territory still lay securely in their hands. (Clark never got to Detroit.) But Clark's daring thrust had unquestionably suggested to the British that holding those vast lands in the future might be very difficult. Whether they would have made the same judgment had Clark stayed in Kentucky (or even at Kaskaskia) remains a matter of conjecture.

Only this much is certain. Clark and his Virginians took Vincennes, and the British gave up the northwestern country to the new American nation. From it in time five new states were created, according to the orderly state-making process established in the Northwest Ordinance of 1787. George Rogers Clark himself never knew such glory again, and misfortune, poverty, and unhappiness dogged him for the rest of his life. (His younger brother William, however, kept the family torch lit when with Meriwether Lewis he led the most famous of all exploring expeditions across the American continent twenty years later.) But had Clark not acted as he did and when he did, it is at least possible that the future states of Ohio, Indiana, Illinois, Michigan, and Wisconsin might have stayed British in 1783, and that to this day the American-Canadian boundary might be the Ohio and Mississippi rivers. It is at least an interesting "might have been."

HISTORIC NEW HARMONY *Church and West streets, New Harmony.* Southern Indiana seems an odd place to find a town once famous as a Utopian experiment in communal living. The region is largely agricultural, its people an independent-minded lot—many with roots in Kentucky and Tennessee. During the Civil War it was "copperhead country," a place of strong Southern sympathies and many Democrats. Social conservatism and traditional religion shaped its character, as they did that of other places much farther south.

The story of New Harmony, however, reaches back to an earlier time, when much of Indiana Territory (especially the western parts along the Wabash) had no character but that which nature gave it. In 1814 it was still largely wilderness, very much on America's frontier. Stories are legion of how the frontier attracted hardy individualists eager to pioneer a new life and build a better future. More rare were people of other convictions who saw in the same wilderness a chance not to improve an old way of life, but rather to establish a radically new one. These in general were the two groups that made New Harmony famous and made it different.

The first were a group of separatist Lutherans originally from Wurttemburg in Germany. Lead by Father George Rapp (and hence known as "Rappites") they were believers in the imminence of Christ's second coming. To prepare for that millenial event, they believed in subjugating all individual desires to the needs of the community. Obedient to those parts of the New Testament that spoke of holding goods in common, Rapp and his followers practiced a truly communitarian life based on piety and self-denial. They moved from Butler County, Pennsylvania, in 1814 to 30,000 acres of Indiana wilderness that Rapp had chosen as an even better place to wait for the Lord. They called it, hopefully, "New Harmony" and diligently took up the challenge of building something that God might once again be proud of.

Strong faith and strong muscles produced some remarkable results. They brought 2,000 acres under cultivation and raised a town better designed and more solidly built than most. Their grain, produce, and livestock were plenteous; there were orchards, vineyards, and a greenhouse for raising lemons and oranges. At its peak New Harmony boasted two distilleries and a brewery; woolen, hemp, cotton, and saw mills; a mechanics' shop; a tannery; a shoe factory. The faithful lived in an array of sturdy log, frame, and masonry buildings. Single men and women (Rappites practiced celibacy both as a form of self-denial and because

Christ's imminent coming made another generation superfluous) lived in four large dormitories; those already married were provided separate houses but were also to practice abstinence. Streets were sensibly named and laid out. East and South streets, Tavern and Brewery streets meant exactly what they said.

Such diligence and much hard work produced real material success. It was estimated that New Harmony's per capita wealth substantially exceeded the national average, and the colony's crops and manufactured goods enjoyed wide and lucrative markets. But hard work and pious living could not, it seemed, hasten the blessed event the New Harmonists longed for. Christ did not come again. Instead, the hard work of building a town out of the wilderness being finished, the Harmonists began to show disturbing signs of disharmony. To keep them together, Rapp led them back to Pennsylvania to start all over again. Their New Harmony had lasted just ten years.

Rapp did not leave his village to revert to the wilderness but sold it, for $190,000, to another man whose values could hardly have been more different from his own. Rapp and his followers were devout Christians, only with their own peculiar understanding of when their Lord would come again and of the kind of life that required. They were odd, but not unorthodox. Robert Owen, the Welsh industrialist who succeeded them at New Harmony, had no religion at all. He did have a faith, quite as encompassing as theirs had been. A self-made man in the best nineteenth-century tradition, Owen had risen to control of a well-equipped cotton mill in the village of New Lanark in Scotland. There he introduced a number of pioneering reforms designed both to improve the lot of the workers (many of whom were young children) and to make the place run more efficiently. The results were gratifying and suggestive of the principle ever since associated with the name of Robert Owen. He set it down in 1813 in his book, *A New View of Society,* whose argument to orthodox Christians (Rappites presumably included) was plainly heretical. Owen held that human character was formed in early childhood and was formed entirely by environment. Redemption from evil surroundings, not redemption from an evil will, he said, was mankind's great need and the key to a good society.

Acting on his beliefs, Owen at first campaigned for factory reform in England. When the results were disappointing, he turned away from government and took up agitating against organized religion and for various sorts of social cooperation and socialism. The once successful philanthropic entrepreneur soon went from one experiment to another. The first was New Harmony. With money from his New Lanark mills, he bought the Rappite town in 1825 and issued an invitation to "the industrious and well-disposed of all nations" to join him there in the establishment of an "empire of good sense." Unfortunately not all of those who came were "well-disposed," and the colony did not last. But during his brief tutelage, New Harmony was changed from an experiment in

1830 Owen House

religious piety to a social laboratory for solving the problems of this world. William Maclure, a Scot and fellow leader of the colony, responded to Owen's hopeful if secular vision by assembling for a time at least some remarkable people: naturalists Thomas Say and Charles-Alexandre Lesueur; Gerard Troost, a Dutch geologist; and Francis Wright, an early advocate of women's rights. New Harmony sprouted a women's club, a trade school, a free public library, and the kindergarten and public school system that lay at the heart of Owen's scheme to benevolently shape the character of young children and hence of the adults they would become.

Believing that thus the greater part of man's misery could be removed, Owen had a faith greater than the ability of New Harmony actually to remove it. After only a few years Owen returned to England to fight his own good fight in other ways. But he left behind at New Harmony his sons and daughter and, through them, a legacy of intellectual activity. One son, David Dale Owen, turned to geology, and at New Harmony established important scientific laboratories. His older brother, Robert Dale Owen, served in Congress and sponsored the legislation establishing the Smithsonian Institution, where he served as an early regent. For the rest of the antebellum era, the old reformist quality of the town endured in what has been called the "afterglow" of earlier glory days.

But those days grew inevitably more remote and the spirit that had made them ever harder to conjure. Only a deliberate effort could save the historical character of New Harmony, and happily one was successfully mounted in the 1970s. Historic New Harmony, Inc., has carried out a comprehensive plan of restoration and community revitalization in keeping with the town's historical character, and together with New Harmony State Memorial has brought new life to this old and once very lively place. What cannot be restored, of course, are the religious piety and the utopian vision of New Harmony's founders. Indeed it is a fair guess that Robert Owen, who had no use at all for history, would scoff at the careful restoration of his old community. But it is also a fair guess that neither Owen nor Rapp, very different from each other and very different from today's New Harmonists, would scoff at the happy vitality and ferment that once again make New Harmony different. Probably they would smile.

CONNER PRAIRIE PIONEER SETTLEMENT 13400 *Allisonville Road, Noblesville.* The rural world, thought by countless people a century or a century and a half ago to be the natural order of things, is now largely lost to their descendants. A drive along some of America's back roads still holds wonderful vistas of farmland and forest not unlike those that people long ago once knew. The traveler along such roads will still pass through scores of small villages and towns—not as many as once, for sure, but still a goodly number—whose tree-lined streets, courthouse squares, and white clapboard houses attract the eye and momentarily stir the imagination. Real people still live in them, some are farmers, others merchants and professionals who depend on farmers. They are friendly places that welcome visitors, perhaps in part because they see relatively few.

But though present, such places and people are no longer pervasive. In the twentieth century, other geographies have replaced them. Urban and suburban, engaged in manufacturing or a burgeoning array of ser-

William Conner House

vice industries, more "modern" Americans demonstrate the tendency since the Industrial Revolution toward the ever greater division of labor and the ever greater production of wealth. Unlike their ancestors who founded, and some of whose descendants still live in, the small towns along the back roads, they see their lives as part of a vast web of complex economic, political, and technological forces. They take their values, so sociologists say, from the things around them. One of the consequences is that the distinctions of place diminish. Characteristics once thought determining become merely curious.

From all this, Indiana has been no more immune than busier, richer states. The lives of most of its people today, like those of their fellows in New York and California, move to markedly different rhythms from those of their ancestors: the people who made the first farms where once the forests stood and who built the small country towns. But in Indiana there is a place where modern Hoosiers can be transported back to an earlier age, when Indiana was a frontier and when its people lived necessarily on the land close to nature. The Conner Prairie Pioneer Settlement, four miles south of Noblesville, is an outdoor village museum that affords a unique opportunity to experience something of Indiana's nineteenth-century rural beginnings. It also helps measure how much Indianans and other Americans have changed since then.

The recorded history of Conner Prairie goes back to 1802, just a year after Thomas Jefferson became president, a year before the Louisiana Purchase, and when Indiana was still part of a large territory that reached west to the Mississippi and north to the Lake of the Woods. In that year, William Conner, who was something of a frontier entrepreneur, established a trading post on the White River twenty miles north of present-day Indianapolis. There he went into business with the Indians, bartering trade goods for furs. Conner had grown up among the Delaware tribe and married the daughter of a prominent Delaware chief. His reputation as an honest trader and reliable guide established him as an important figure in the new territory.

In 1818, two years after Indiana became a state, politics forced a change in Conner's domestic arrangements. The Delaware in 1817 relinquished by treaty their claim to a large piece of Indiana called the "New Purchase" and agreed to relocate west of the Mississippi. When they went, Conner's wife and six children went with them. Conner, however, stayed and adjusted his own life to what he saw as a fast-changing Indiana. He married a white woman, Elizabeth Chapman, who gave him another ten children. Meanwhile, settlers from the south and east quickly replaced the Indians, and as quickly William Conner moved to service their needs and moved himself to a place of influence among them.

Commissioners met in 1820 at Conner's trading post to select the site for a state capital more centrally located than Corydon, near the Ohio River. In 1823 Conner founded and platted the town of Noblesville and replaced his log house with a substantial brick one, one of the first in the New Purchase. It was used as the first post office in Hamilton County and as a courthouse before one was built in Noblesville. He became active in state and local politics and served three terms in the state house of representatives. He died in Noblesville in 1855. His seventy-eight years had spanned the momentous era from the Revolutionary War to the years just before the Civil War—years that saw Indiana change from a trackless wilderness into a settled agricultural civilization.

That civilization is preserved, as if locked in time, at the Conner Prairie Pioneer Settlement. The preservation effort itself has a considerable history. For nearly a century after the Conner family moved out, their old brick house passed through numerous hands and fell into considerable disrepair. In 1934 Eli Lilly, grandson of the pharmaceutical magnate, rediscovered the old home and determined to restore it as a monument to Indiana's early settlers. Walls were strengthened; the kitchen was rebuilt; and period furnishing returned it to an appearance that William Conner might have recognized. In addition, Lilly also purchased several log buildings in Brown County that were moved near the Conner house, which still sits on the original foundation. It was Lilly's idea to depict the outbuildings that would have surrounded Conner's 1820 house: barn, spring house, log cabin, distillery, and trading post. The site was then opened to private groups on a limited basis. In 1964, the Conner settlement was given to nearby Earlham College to be operated as an outdoor rural museum. More building and restoration have been undertaken.

An elaborate educational program also has been designed that, through the use of costumed guides who play the role of the pioneers themselves, transport visitors back to the rural Indiana of the 1830s. Visitors are invited into the daily lives of Indiana settlers—to talk with them about names, places, and a way of life long since forgotten. The degree to which that way of life moved to rhythms different from our own soon becomes obvious. This was a rural world, where most people were farmers or the families of farmers. The land and the weather directly shaped their lives as it does for few Hoosiers and other Americans today. Spring was planting time, when the women started a kitchen garden and the men prepared the fields. Summer saw continued cultivation, tending of livestock, and some happy diversions. The Fourth of July always occasioned hearty celebration. There were weddings, visits by the circuit-riding preacher, and court days when a justice of the peace held forth. In the fall crops had to be harvested and preparations made for winter. Corn, wheat, and barley were gathered, hay put aside. Wool was dyed and winter clothing put in good order. Autumn was also election season, and like the settler who lived in Conner Prairie long ago, visitors are invited to cast their votes in the presidential contest of 1836, which pitted Jacksonian Martin Van Buren against several Whig candidates. Wintertime saw the pace of life slow down in a rural community, and it did in Conner Prairie. Smoke rose constantly from cabin chimneys, beef and hogs were butchered, repairs made to farm implements and tools. Christmas was kept in varying ways, though even on that special day life here remained plain and simple.

As life was then, so activity at the museum today is seasonal. Weaving, dyeing, sheep-shearing, the forging of wrought iron in the blacksmith shop, firing a kiln to make pottery, constructing furniture in the carpenter's shop, fireplace cooking, and winter butchering are all things that the visitor might witness here.

The settlement now comprises twenty-five buildings on fifty-five acres and includes the historic Conner home, a blacksmith shop, a potter's complex, the Nichols farm, a frontier school, a doctor's house, a weaver's house, and a country store. Visitors are encouraged to wander through the settlement at their own pace, talking at their leisure with the staff who pose as pioneers.

If they do, they will be impressed by several things. One is that there will always be a certain romance about the way our pioneer ancestors lived: log cabins, homespun, food cooked on an open fireplace. Conner Prairie partly confirms this. But it also reminds us of something else: how remote and different from us these people truly were. Partly, they were remote from each other. They lived on a farming frontier in the age of primitive communication and transportation. But also their values were sprung from the soil that sustained them, which was something they could clearly see and which few men today can remember.

ANGEL MOUNDS STATE MEMORIAL *8215 Pollack Avenue, Evansville.* Restored village of the Middle Mississippian Indians, A.D. 1300–1500.

AUBURN-CORD-DUESENBERG MUSEUM *1600 S. Wayne Street, Auburn.* Antique and classic cars and radios, photos, and other material related to the cars.

CHILDREN'S MUSEUM *30th and Meridian, Indianapolis.* A natural-history museum with toys and dolls as well as exhibits in geology, archeology, and other sciences related to the study of the human past.

CORYDON CAPITAL STATE MEMORIAL *202 E. Walnut, Corydon.* Site of the first state capitol, 1816.

DISCOVERY HALL MUSEUM *120 S. St. Joseph St., South Bend.* Especially noted for its collection of Studebaker carriages, wagons, and automobiles, 1824–1966.

ELI LILLY AND COMPANY ARCHIVES *893 S. Delaware, Indianapolis.* A pharmacology museum displays material related to the company's work since 1876.

EVANSVILLE MUSEUM OF ARTS AND SCIENCE *411 S.E. Riverside*

Drive, Evansville. Arts and artifacts on transportation and anthropology; re-creation of a nineteenth-century village street.

HISTORIC FORT WAYNE *107 S. Clinton Street, Fort Wayne.* A reconstructed fort and military museum, illustrating frontier life in 1816.

HISTORIC LANDMARKS FOUNDATION OF INDIANA *3402 Boulevard Place, Indianapolis.* A historic preservation foundation, housed in an 1885 waiting station in Crown Hill Cemetery; with a museum and tours to several historic homes.

HISTORIC MADISON *500 West Street, Madison.* A preservation organization with collections and tours of historic homes and a hospital.

HOWARD STEAMBOAT MUSEUM *1101 East Market Street, Jeffersonville.* Furnishings and steamboat artifacts in the home of shipyard owner Edmunds J. Howard.

HUDDLESTON FARMHOUSE INN MUSEUM *Cambridge City.* A Federal-style three-story brick farmhouse dating from about 1840.

INDIANA DUNES NATIONAL LAKESHORE *1100 N. Mineral Springs Road, Porter.* Dunes as high as 180 feet on the shores of Lake Michigan, adjacent to beaches, bogs, and restored 1822 homestead and 1900 family farm.

INDIANA STATE MUSEUM *202 N. Alabama Street, Indianapolis.* Housed in the former Indianapolis City Hall, 1909; with artifacts and materials from natural history, Hoosier art, nineteenth-century life, and Indian life.

INDIANAPOLIS MOTOR SPEEDWAY HALL OF FAME MUSEUM *4790 W. 16th Street, Indianapolis.* Includes not only racing cars but antique and classic passenger cars.

LINCOLN BOYHOOD NATIONAL MEMORIAL *Lincoln City.* Where Abraham Lincoln grew from childhood to maturity.

MUSEUM OF INDIAN HERITAGE *6040 DeLong Road, Eagle Creek Park, Indianapolis.* Collections on archeology and ethnology.

SPRING MILL STATE PARK PIONEER VILLAGE *Mitchell.* On the site of a village settled in the early 1800s; with an 1817 grist mill and space-age artifacts in the Virgil I. Grissom State Memorial.

TIPPECANOE BATTLEFIELD MUSEUM *Tippecanoe and Railroad streets, Battle Ground.* Contains materials related to the Battle of Tippecanoe, the election of 1840, and 1850s Methodist campground experiences.

WAYNE COUNTY HISTORICAL MUSEUM *1150 North "A" Street, Richmond.* Housed in an 1864 Friends Meeting House, with antiques, costumes, fire-fighting equipment, guns, toys, and other artifacts.

WHITEWATER CANAL STATE MEMORIAL *Metamora.* Restored canal locks, boat, and aqueduct from the 1840s.

WILLIAM HENRY HARRISON MANSION *3 W. Scott Street, Vincennes.* Furniture and contemporary pieces displayed in the Harrison mansion, "Grouseland," built 1803–1804.

IOWA

GARDNER LOG CABIN Arnolds Park west of Estherville on U.S. 71.
Conflict between Native Americans and white settlers over possession
of the land pervades the history of frontier Iowa. Decades of broken
treaties, opposing claims, and misunderstanding frustrated Native
Americans and aggravated their resentment toward white intruders. This
interracial contest climaxed in 1856 in the legendary Spirit Lake Massacre in northwest Iowa. The Gardner Cabin at Arnolds Park marks the
site of the massacre and calls attention to this controversial dimension
of the pioneer experience.

Long-term grievances and immediate circumstances combined to
produce a highly volatile situation. After years of broken treaty prom-
ises, forced concessions, and other injustices, the Sioux in Iowa had
little reason to trust white intruders. The relocation of eastern tribes to
the Iowa grasslands in the 1820s had deprived the Sioux of part of their
traditional hunting grounds, and in 1851 they had relinquished claims
to the rest. Unwilling to accept the cession, several small renegade bands
continued to hunt as they always had in the northwest portion of the
state, but ignoring the treaty did not stop white settlement and consequent ruin of the hunting grounds. Farms and communities could do
what treaties could not: render the land spoiled and useless to the people who had hunted there for generations. Problems were com-
pounded by the government's indifference toward the plight of Native
Americans and the outright treachery of some settlers and traders in
their individual dealings with the Indians. The murder of Sidominado-
tah, a Sioux chief, in 1854 and the failure of the white government to
punish his killer, a white trader, confirmed the Sioux's doubts and sus-
picions.

The leader of one of these Sioux hunting parties was Inkpaduta, an
outlaw Wahpekute chief. Inkpaduta's band numbered about thirty-five,
including fourteen or fifteen warriors and their families. Their initial
contact with the isolated white settlements along the Little Sioux River
proved cordial, and few settlers or government officials recognized the
extend of Inkpaduta's anger or expected any substantial problems with
him or any of the other Native Americans still in the region. In 1853,
the federal government even removed the troops who had been stationed at Fort Dodge to protect the settlers. None foresaw the violent
interracial conflict that erupted in the winter of 1856–57.

The immediate cause of conflict was the weather. Neither Inkpaduta
and his fellow Sioux nor the white settlers on the Little Sioux River had
prepared adequately for the harsh winter that virtually paralyzed northwestern Iowa in 1856–57. When food became scarce and the whites
grew reluctant to share, tempers flared. Finally white vigilantes attempted
to disarm the Sioux band and then forced them to move on. Traveling

north up the Little Sioux River, Inkpaduta and his band retaliated by breaking into cabins, terrorizing settlers, and taking whatever food, weapons, and ammunition they needed. Although they destroyed property and terrified the isolated settlers, the Sioux warriors did not kill anyone prior to their arrival in the Spirit Lake region in early March 1857.

Spirit Lake is the largest of the "Great Lakes" on the northern border of Iowa. To the south of Spirit Lake extend East and West Okoboji lakes, the other two principal "Great Lakes." By the time Inkpaduta arrived in 1857, about forty people had settled in the immediate area. Their six cabins stood on the western edge of white settlement, virtually isolated in what had long been considered Indian domain. Pioneers like Rowland Gardner were attracted to this unknown and uninhabited region by the availability of open prairie and rich virgin soil. The elusive search

Rowland Gardner's cabin at Spirit Lake

for good, cheap farmland had already taken the Gardners from New York to Ohio, to Indiana, and then to Shell Rock and Clear Lake, Iowa, before they finally reached Spirit Lake in July 1856. Shortly after their arrival, they selected a site along West Okoboji and, before winter set in, erected a simple one-room log cabin with a dirt floor, shake roof, and puncheon door.

The Gardners and the other Spirit Lake settlers found themselves unprepared for the harsh winter of 1856–57. Rowland Gardner's son-in-law Harvey Luce and another resident traveled east to Waterloo to secure additional supplies, and Gardner planned to begin a second expedition despite the encampment of Inkpaduta and his band nearby during the first week in March. Then on the morning of March 8, as Gardner was preparing for his trip, the Sioux appeared at the family's cabin. Although no one was harmed, the confrontation alarmed the Gardners, and Luce and another man set out that afternoon to warn their neighbors. Inkpaduta and his warriors apparently intercepted and killed the two men and then proceeded to the Gardner cabin, where the killing continued. With the exception of thirteen-year-old Abbie Gardner, the entire household was slaughtered. Taking Abbie as a hostage, Inkpaduta moved on to two other cabins. The death toll reached twenty by the end of the day. The massacre continued the next morning at two other nearby cabins, the inhabitants of which had no knowledge of the previous day's events. The Sioux took two more female hostages and left twelve more men, women, and children dead. They did not reach the last cabin on Spirit Lake until March 13. There they took Mrs. Margaret Marble hostage and killed her husband, bringing the toll to thirty-three dead and four captive.

News of the Spirit Lake massacre spread quickly to Fort Dodge and nearby Springfield, Minnesota, the next target for Inkpaduta and his warriors. With the element of surprise gone, however, the carnage at Springfield was less, and the Sioux soon fled to South Dakota. Efforts to capture and punish the renegades proved futile, but friendly Indians managed to ransom the only two of the four hostages who survived captivity. Mrs. Marble was released first, and then in late May, four months after the massacre, Inkpaduta agreed on a ransom for Abbie Gardner.

Abbie Gardner married Casville Sharp in August 1857 and lived in various locations in Iowa, Missouri, and Kansas until 1891, when she returned to Spirit Lake and purchased the cabin in which her family had been killed. For the next thirty years she operated the cabin as a tourist attraction, making her living from admission charges, a souvenir stand, and the sale of her own account of the massacre. After her death in 1921, her grandson, Albert Sharp, managed the property for a time. The site was sold to the state in 1943 and administered by the State Conservation Commission until 1959, when the responsibility shifted to the Iowa State Historical Department. The latter agency constructed a visitor center for displays and exhibits and in the mid-1970s undertook a painstaking restoration and reconstruction of the cabin. Now restored and furnished as closely as possible to its appearance in 1856, the Gardner Cabin typifies pioneer life on the Iowa frontier and serves as a reminder of a memorable episode in the state's early history.

OLD CAPITOL *University of Iowa campus, Clinton Street and Iowa Avenue, Iowa City.* No structure has more significance for Iowa history than the Old Capitol at Iowa City. Erected between 1840 and 1858, this Greek Revival building served as Iowa's third and last territorial capitol, the first state capitol, and the first home of the University of Iowa. Now restored and open to the public, the Old Capitol brings to life the history of Iowa in the crucial transition from territory to statehood.

Disagreement over the location of a permanent capital for Iowa erupted soon after the first territorial legislature met at Burlington in 1838. Altogether some twenty-seven towns and villages were considered as the future site of the government, but the legislators could

Iowa's first state capitol

not agree on any of them. Rivalry among the Mississippi River towns of Burlington, Davenport, and Dubuque proved particularly intense. To break the deadlock, Colonel Thomas Cox proposed locating the capital on unoccupied public land, a solution used to settle a similar controversy in Illinois twenty years before. Although his proposal met defeat, another legislator, Stephen Hempstead, used much the same concept in proposing the location of the capital on public land in Johnson County in the interior of the state. His motion passed both houses on January 3, 1839. A supplemental bill named the new capital Iowa City.

The territorial legislature established a three-member commission to select the actual town site and carry out plans for a permanent capitol. Commissioner Chauncey Swan of Dubuque took charge and on May 4, 1839, selected a townsite—a grove of oaks overlooking the Iowa River about two miles north of the village of Napoleon. Here he planned to establish a fitting capital city, with a four-block Capitol Square, a Governor's Square, broad avenues, and special reserved lots for schools, churches, a park, a college green, markets, and even a riverfront promenade. Although all of Swan's ambitious plans were not carried out, streets and lot lines were established, and in August of that year the commission held the first sale of Iowa City lots.

The income from the sale of city lots was earmarked for the construction of a permanent capitol. In addition to the proceeds from these land sales, funding for the project included a $20,000 appropriation from the United States Congress and a series of small appropriations from the territorial and state legislatures. Although Iowa legislators insisted on keeping costs down and set a $51,000 limit on the cost of constructing the new building, the total cost of the structure probably exceeded $125,000. A final accounting is difficult because of numerous small appropriations, the last of which was made in 1858—a year after the state government moved to Des Moines.

The commission advertised for construction bids for the capitol on the same day a site was selected. The contract went to John F. Rague, a New Jersey-born architect who had also designed the Illinois capitol in Springfield. Although hired as both architect and construction contractor, Rague terminated his role in the project in mid-July 1840, only nine days after Territorial Governor Robert Lucas laid the cornerstone. Rague claimed that he was concerned about the inferior quality of the locally quarried limestone, but the financial uncertainty of the project also played an important role in his resignation. Swan took over Rague's construction duties and attempted to carry out the architect's original plans. He and his successors during the next eighteen years, however, faced financial restrictions that dictated modifications in Rague's Greek Revival design.

Rague designed a simple rectangular three-story structure constructed of native Devonian limestone. The structure rested on six-foot-thick foundations. The elevated basement and ground-floor walls were four feet thick, and the walls of the upper two stories were two to three feet thick. Other construction details included native oak floor joists, timber roof trusses, a roof of pine shingles on oak sheeting, gutters and downspouts cut from walnut logs, granite steps, a wooden portico, and a central wooden cupola with a copper-clad roof. Rague planned porticoes for both the east and the west facade, but although the necessary steps, platform, pediment, and recessed cornice were constructed on both sides, only the east one was completed. Financial considerations also dictated plain rather than decorated cornices and wood instead of stone pillars. For the same reason, the central reverse spiral stairway rose from the first to the second floor but did not descend to the ground level. The interior also had plastered walls, white pine trim, oak flooring, and both stoves and fireplaces for heat. The plan for the first floor included offices for the secretary of state, the governor, the auditor, and the treasurer as well as space for the supreme court and the territorial library. The senate and the house chambers filled the second floor. Although plans were made for use of the basement as well, it remained unoccupied by the government during this period.

The territorial legislature met in Iowa City for the first time in December 1841. Since the capitol was not ready yet, the meeting was held in a nearby two-story frame building later called Butler's Capitol. When the legislature convened in the new building on December 5, 1842, only four first-floor rooms were ready for occupancy. The legislature later moved into the more spacious second-floor chambers, which were also used for church meetings and community functions. The unfinished basement became home for the Iowa City Fire Company No. 1 in 1844.

Paired as a free state with slave-state Florida, Iowa secured conditional admission to the Union on March 3, 1845, pending approval of a state constitution. A constitutional convention had met in 1844, but voters rejected its product. A second meeting began at the capitol on May 4, 1846, and in August voters finally approved a state constitution. On November 30 the first session of the Iowa General Assembly convened, and on December 2 Ansel Briggs was innaugurated as the state's first governor. All of this became official on December 28, 1846, when President James K. Polk signed legislation making Iowa the twenty-ninth state.

The state government occupied the Iowa City capitol for another decade, until a series of political developments led to relocation of the capital to Des Moines. Support in Iowa for the free-soil movement increased with passage of the Kansas-Nebraska Action in 1854, and by 1856 antislavery forces banded together to organize the state Republican party, the first meeting of which was held in the capitol. Backed by overwhelming electoral victories in 1856, the Republicans pushed for a new state constitution. When the constitutional convention convened at the capitol in 1852, support developed for relocation of the capital to Des Moines, which was more centrally located. As part of the bargain, the University of Iowa was to remain the only state university and to be permanently located in Iowa City. By a narrow margin, Iowa voters subsequently ratified the new constitution, the same one in effect today.

Upon the state government's move to Des Moines in December 1857, ownership of the Old Capitol passed to the University of Iowa. The state legislature had chartered the university on February 25, 1847, but the first classes did not actually meet until 1855. The university occupied a rented building until taking over the Old Capitol and the ten acres of land surrounding it. For the next 113 years, the building provided offices and classrooms for the university. For example, from 1868 to 1910, the structure housed the College of Law, the first law school west of the Mississippi River. As the university developed into one of the nation's leading institutions of higher learning, the Old Capitol became a symbol if its history and traditions.

Between 1921 and 1924, the university renovated the aging structure. To strengthen the building and make it fireproof, steel beams replaced the old oak beams, and the cupola was rebuilt with concealed steel supports. The west portico was finally constructed, but the exterior otherwise remained unchanged. Interior changes included reconstruction of the spiral stairway and its extension to the ground floor. While some of the alterations caused problems for a later restoration project, these efforts insured the preservation of the Old Capitol.

In 1970 the university announced that its administrative offices would be moved out of the building and that the Old Capitol would be fully restored as an historic site open to the public. Six years of extensive research and painstaking restoration followed. This diligence paid off in the discovery of original chairs and desks from the house chamber, in the assembling of over a thousand of the original volumes in the territorial-state library, and in the uncovering of structural evidence for the reconstruction of the House gallery. This attention to detail insured that the restoration of the Old Capitol would be as accurate historically as possible.

The restored Old Capitol opened to the public on July 3, 1976. The structure reflects three eras: the territorial period from 1842 to 1846, the state period from 1846 to 1857, and the university years, focusing on the 1920s. The senate chamber and the university president's office illustrate the recent period, while the remaining rooms have been furnished in keeping with the building's use in the mid-nineteenth century. The latter include the offices of the governor, the auditor, and the treasurer, the territorial-state library, the supreme court chamber, and the house chamber. No other historic site so effectively symbolizes Iowa's transition from frontier territory to mature statehood.

LIVING HISTORY FARMS *Des Moines.* The central factor in Iowa's historical development has been the land. The availability of rich, fertile farm land attracted the first white settlers before the Civil War, and by the turn of the century agriculture ruled the state's economy. Even today, rural and small-town life dominates the Iowa experience. Living History Farms, an open-air museum near Des Moines, preserves this heritage of farming and agriculture and offers visitors the opportunity to relive Iowa's rural past.

Agriculture has changed considerably since the first farms were established in Iowa nearly a century and a half ago. Technological improvements and the application of scientific techniques have virtually revolutionized farming and farm products and have influenced as well the quality of life in rural America. As the self-sufficient farmer has yielded to large-scale agriculture, farms and small towns have become more interdependent, and the basic needs and daily routines of life have changed.

Relatively isolated from one another, farm families on the Iowa frontier became largely self-sufficient. On modest plots of fertile prairie soil, farmers grew enough food for their families and feed to support a few head of livestock as well. Although teams of oxen were used initially to break the tough prairie sod and for other heavy work, most settlers relied on hand labor for routine planting and harvesting. Meeting the family's other basic needs similarly required considerable physical activity. The regular chores included tending the livestock and garden, cooking on an open hearth, washing, sewing, and making butter, cheese, and soap. What few necessities the family could not produce itself could be purchased on occasional trips to the local store, which also served as the post office, inn, and stage stop for the area.

*Barn
at the
1900
Farm*

The frontier disappeared from Iowa rather quickly. By 1880 nearly all of the state's land was under cultivation. Although perhaps two-thirds of the state's citizens lived on farms, a sizable proportion lived in small towns. The numerous small towns and villages that dotted the Iowa landscape by the 1870s and 1880s played key roles in the evolution of farming and agriculture. As the self-sufficient farm began to yield to small-scale commercial agriculture, rural communities became indispensable market outlets and sources of goods and services. While the farms needed the towns, the towns in turn depended on the business activity brought in by neighboring farmers. An interdependent relationship developed between the farms and the towns of rural Iowa.

Commercial agriculture secured an even stronger hold on rural Iowa by the close of the nineteenth century. Profit-conscious farmers turned in increasing numbers to corn and hog production and began utilizing new machinery and advanced farm technology. Most relied on horse-drawn equipment for plowing, planting, and cultivating, but the first steam engines were in use by the 1890s. Other improvements followed in the early twentieth century, including scientific advances in livestock and poultry breeding, the development of commercial hybrid corn, changes in farming techniques, and further mechanization. These changes had significant impact not only on agricultural productivity and the organization of farm work but also on the quality of life in rural Iowa. The self-sufficient frontier farm had been replaced by a modern agricultural enterprise.

The sites that make up Living History Farms reflect these changes in agriculture and rural life. The oldest site, the Ioway Indian encampment, actually dates back to before the arrival of white settlers and reminds visitors that the inhabitants of the region have farmed for at least a thousand years. The site includes gardens, storage areas, and cooking areas that illustrate traditional Indian foodways.

The complex also includes a pioneer farm that reflects rural life in the 1840s. Visitors can see a typical log home and outbuildings, including a corn crib, barn, smokehouse, root cellar, and shelter for the oxen. The split rail fences are also typical of the era before the invention of barbed wire. Costumed interpreters demonstrate daily farming and domestic activities, ranging from plowing fields with oxen to cooking on the open hearth. Also part of this site is the Oak Grove Stage Stop, a log structure that typifies the small rural stores and inns of the early nineteenth century.

In sharp contrast stands the developing community at Walnut Hill, a small town typical of the 1870s. While still essentially rural in character, Walnut Hill boasts a number of businesses and institutions that testify to its important role in an evolving economic order. Visitors can see the blacksmith's shop, the potter's shed, a carpentry shop, a general store, a veterinary infirmary, a one-room schoolhouse, a lawyer's office, a doctor's office, and of course a church. All served farm families in the surrounding hinterland. Of particular interest is an Italianate mansion that presides over the city. Martin Flynn, a local businessman and banker, erected this impressive residence with the wealth he accumulated in a variety of well-calculated ventures that took advantage of the developing rural economy.

A fourth site, a circa-1900 farm, incorporates later advances in farm machinery and agricultural technology. Visitors find in contrast to the pioneer farm, a simple white frame house with a white picket fence, a fine barn, and a windmill. Demonstrations of routine activities also reflect the changes in rural life, including the shift away from self-sufficiency and the use of labor-saving devices.

The Henry Wallace Farm of Today and Tomorrow and Crop Museum brings the evolution of agriculture and rural life up to the present. This modern facility demonstrates the latest developments and techniques, with special focus on contemporary problems of conservation, energy use, and high-yield technology.

Established in 1967, Living History Farms is one of the nation's largest outdoor museums, encompassing six hundred acres in the center of the Corn Belt. Open from mid-April until October, the complex sponsors a variety of special events and educational programs in addition to its daily schedule of activities. No other site provides so exciting an opportunity to experience the varieties of Iowa's rural past.

BETTENDORF ROOM *Bettendorf Museum, 533 Sixteenth Street, Bettendorf.* Exhibits in a manufacturing plant that at one time was the largest railroad car shop west of the Mississippi.

CZECH VILLAGE *59 Sixteenth Avenue, S.W., Cedar Rapids.* Shops and stores in an ethnic center.

DES MOINES CENTER OF SCIENCE AND INDUSTRY *4500 Grand Avenue, Greenwood-Ashworth Park, Des Moines.* Exhibits and laboratory workshops on the history of science and industry.

DODGE HOUSE *605 Third Street, Council Bluffs.* Restored 1869 mansion that was the home of Grenville M. Dodge, financier and railroad builder and confidant of presidents.

FLOYD MONUMENT *near I-29 south of Sioux City.* Stone obelisk 100 feet high marking the grave of Sgt. Charles Floyd, only member of Lewis and Clark expedition to die on trip, 1804.

FORT DODGE MUSEUM *Museum Road and U.S. 20, Fort Dodge.* Replica of the 1850 fort built to protect settlers against Indians, about one mile from original site along the Des Moines River.

FREMONT COUNTY HISTORICAL MUSEUM *Sidney.* Local history, including information on old trails and Indian camps.

GROUT MUSEUM OF HISTORY AND SCIENCE *Park Avenue at South Street, Waterloo.* General history museum with exhibits on arts and crafts, musical instruments, and period costumes of 1800s and early 1900s.

HAM HOUSE MUSEUM *2241 Lincoln Avenue, Dubuque.* General history museum located in an 1857 Victorian mansion on bluff; with the Newman log cabin, pre-dating 1827 and supposedly the oldest extant building in Iowa, on grounds.

HERBERT HOOVER PRESIDENTIAL LIBRARY AND MUSEUM *West Branch.* Hoover papers, gravesite, and birthplace cottage, restored to its 1870 appearance, on original site.

HOWARD COUNTY HISTORICAL MUSEUM *324 Fourth Avenue West, Cresco.* Period furnishings in an 1880 Second Empire mansion built by English immigrant and local businessman.

ICE HOUSE MUSEUM *17 North Franklin Street, Cedar Falls.* Displays items used in the cutting, harvesting, storing, and selling of natural ice; in a 1922 building.

KEOKUK RIVER MUSEUM *housed in George M. Verity, Mississippi River steamboat, Victory Park at foot of John Street, Keokuk.* Upper Mississippi River history in a 1927 paddlewheeler.

KINNEY PIONEER MUSEUM *entrance to Mason City airport on U.S. 18.* General museum on history of north central Iowa.

LEE COUNTY HISTORIC CENTER *old Santa Fe Railroad depot, Fort Madison.* Local history, including information on the 1842 Lee County Courthouse, one of oldest Iowa courthouses in continuous use, and nearby Santa Fe bridge, called the longest double-deck swing-span bridge in the world.

LITTLE BROWN CHURCH IN THE VALE Bradford. Built in 1864 and reputedly the church in the famous song.

MAMIE DOUD EISENHOWER BIRTHPLACE 709 Carroll Street, Boone. Restored home (moved from original location) where Mamie Doud, wife of Dwight D. Eisenhower, was born in 1890; with furnishings and memorabilia of Doud family.

MILLS COUNTY HISTORICAL MUSEUM Glenwood Lake Park, Glenwood, Iowa. Local history with a country store and country school.

MONTAUK one mile north of Clermont on U.S. 18. The 1874 brick and limestone home of William Larrabee, Iowa governor 1886–1890; with original furnishings and family memorabilia.

MORMON HANDCART HISTORICAL SITE three miles west of Iowa City on U.S. 6. Bronze marker noting camp where Mormons constructed handcarts for use on their journey to Utah in 1846.

MUSEUM OF AMANA HISTORY Main Street just east of state 149, Amana. Exhibits on the religious community established here in 1855; with information on the Amana Villages, seven Amana towns in the area, and tours through factories and access to restaurants serving family-style meals.

MUSEUM OF NATURAL HISTORY Macbride Hall, University of Iowa, Iowa City. Specimens of Iowa birds as well as exhibits on wildlife around the world, including Indian artifacts from Iowa River.

NELSON HOMESTEAD Glendale Road, Oskaloosa. Pioneer craft and farm museum in an 1852 farmhouse and farm buildings; log cabin, school, and country store moved from other sites.

NORWEGIAN-AMERICAN MUSEUM 520 West Water Street, Decorah. Exhibits on Norwegian immigrant life located in early luxury hotel in center of Norwegian community established in 1850; with nearby stone mill, blacksmith shop, church, and other pioneer buildings.

PLUM GROVE 1030 Carroll Street at Kirkwood Avenue, Iowa City. Home built in 1844 by Robert Lucas, first territorial governor.

POLK COUNTY HERITAGE GALLERY First and Walnut, Des Moines. Exhibits of art and historic material in a restored 1908 post office.

POTTAWATOMIE COUNTY JAIL 226 Pearl Street, Council Bluffs. Circular jail built 1885 and referred to as "the human squirrel cage."

PUTNAM MUSEUM 1717 W. Twelfth Street, Davenport. Local, regional, and river history, including the original Black Hawk Treaty, and art.

SANFORD MUSEUM AND PLANETARIUM 117 E. Willow, Cherokee. General museum with local history.

SEMINOLE VALLEY FARM Seminole Valley Park, five miles northwest of downtown Cedar Rapids. Restored farm and grounds of the 1880s.

SHELBY COUNTY MUSEUM Potters Park, Harlan. Local history and exhibits in several log cabins; includes World War II correspondent Ernie Pyle's press jeep.

SIOUX CITY PUBLIC MUSEUM 2901 Jackson Street, Sioux City. General history museum in an 1890 mansion.

TERRACE HILL *2300 Grand Avenue, Des Moines.* An 1869 Victorian mansion with a ninety-foot tower and extensive grounds.

TOOLSBORO INDIAN MOUNDS *Toolsboro.* Burial mounds from the Hopewell and Middle Woodland periods, 500 B.C. to A.D. 300; with visitor center and demonstration prairie plot of grasses and wildflowers. Overlooks site where Joliet and Marquette stopped in 1673 and where Sac and Fox Indians met to plan Black Hawk War.

WAYNE COUNTY HISTORICAL MUSEUM *state 2, Corydon.* Local history, including the cage and safe from a bank robbed by Jesse James in 1871 and materials on the 1846 Mormon trek.

KANSAS

JOHN BROWN MEMORIAL MUSEUM 10th and Main streets, Osawatomie. No other territory in the nation underwent an experience comparable to that of Kansas between 1854 and 1859. During those five years the unyielding determination of opposing groups to prevail in the debate over the extension of slavery gave rise to unprecedented violence and conflict. The leading advocate of armed resistance to proslavery forces and unquestioned symbol of "Bleeding Kansas" was John Brown, a Yankee free-soiler whose "divine mission" to abolish slavery eventually ended in defeat at Harpers Ferry, Virginia, in 1859. The Kansas State Historical Society maintains the John Brown Museum at Osawatomie as a memorial to this controversial figure and his central role in perhaps the most dramatic era in Kansas history.

According to tradition, John Brown's commitment to abolitionism dated back to the age of twelve, when he became angered at the harsh treatment of a black youth and resolved to fight slavery and racism wherever he encountered it. Whatever good intentions he might have had, Brown found little time for his crusade during the four decades that followed. His father trained him as a tanner, but he proved no more successful at that trade than at the various others at which he tried his hand. He relocated at least ten times during his adulthood, each move coinciding with a new business venture and futile plans for recouping past losses. With each sporadic move from the Midwest to New England and back again, Brown uprooted his growing family, which included seven children from his first marriage and thirteen from his second.

In 1849 Brown's travels and commitment to abolitionism took him to North Elba, New York, where wealthy abolitionist Gerrit Smith planned to establish a farming community for free blacks. The project proved unsuccessful, but Brown found the Adirondack region to his liking and decided to make his permanent home there. Despite occasional temporary moves over the next decade, the North Elba farm remained his home until his death in 1859. It was there that he left his wife and small children in the fall of 1855.

John Brown's five older sons, Frederick, Salmon, Oliver, Owen, and John, Jr., had moved to Kansas in the spring of 1855 and joined the growing number of free-soilers determined to block the extension of slavery into the western territories. They settled at Osawatomie on the Marais des Cygnes River and soon became the targets of raids by proslavery ruffians from nearby Missouri. Convinced of the necessity of armed resistance, their father loaded up a wagon with guns, knives, and ammunition and headed for Kansas that fall. In October he moved in with his brother-in-law, the Reverend Samuel L. Adair, and quickly assumed a leading role in the free-state movement. More cautious leaders quelled Brown's initial calls for revenge, but the arrests of numerous free-state leaders and an attack on Lawrence by proslavers in May 1856 spurred him to action. On the night of May 23, Brown led seven other men in an attack on the cabins of two proslavery families, the Doyles and the Wilkinsons. The raiding party killed five men in what became known as the Pottawatomie Creek Massacre. This atrocity demonstrated Brown's conviction that he was God's instrument of revenge and initiated months of guerilla warfare in eastern Kansas.

The Battle of Osawatomie on August 30 capped the summer of violence. Alarmed at the growing strength of the free-state movement and the weaknesses of the proslavery territorial government, Missouri Senator David R. Atchison organized some four hundred pro-slavery sympathizers in one last attempt to oust the anti-slavery faction. Atchison and his band attacked the free-state stronghold at Osawatomie on the morning of August 30. The first casualty was John Brown's son Fred, shot by a scouting party. Determined to fight off the invaders, the elder Brown quickly assembled about forty volunteers, but they were no match

John Brown Museum

for Atchison's army. After forcing Brown and his men to retreat across the Marais des Cygnes, the proslavers invaded Osawatomie, plundering and burning all but two houses in the village.

The free-staters continued to gain strength that fall despite the defeat at Osawatomie. Although violence continued in the southeast for some time, a referendum in 1857 decided the controversy in favor of the anti-slavery group. Brown left the territory in 1857, returning only in 1858 to lead a slave liberation raid into Missouri. By that time, he had turned his attention to the larger problem of slavery in the South and had begun developing a scheme to incite a general slave revolt throughout the region. The conclusion to his abolitionist crusade came in 1859, when he led an unsuccessful raid on the United States arsenal at Harpers Ferry. The widespread slave uprising that he expected did not materialize, and Brown and his small band of followers soon yielded to federal troops. Convicted of treason, he was executed on December 2, 1859. A martyr and hero to Northern abolitionists, Brown exhibited an irrational fanaticism that alarmed the South and aggravated sectional tension in the years just prior to the Civil War.

John Brown lived in Kansas for only twenty months but left a lasting impression on its history. None more clearly symbolized the moral commitment of Yankee abolitionists to a free Kansas, and none contributed more to the image of "Bleeding Kansas." The John Brown Museum and the John Brown Memorial Park in Osawatomie commemorate Brown's role in Kansas' territorial history. The focal point is the cabin in which he lived during his stay in Kansas. Erected in 1854, the cabin was moved from its original site to the park location in 1912 and a pergola was erected in 1928 to protect the structure. The small log building has been furnished much as it was in Brown's day. The main room contains a few pieces of original furniture, and a bed used by the Brown family can be seen in the sleeping loft. A small rear room to the north still features the loose floor boards that reportedly disguised an underground haven for fugitive slaves. The simple structure stands as a symbol of the conflict and moral purpose fundamental to early Kansas history.

CARRY A. NATION HOME MEMORIAL 211 W. Fowler, Medicine Lodge. The small farming community of Medicine Lodge, Kansas, produced two of the most famous symbols of the political ferment and moral purpose that characterized the state's history in the late nineteenth and early twentieth centuries. Medicine Lodge's Jerry Simpson could not even afford socks after the failure of his Barber County farm in the 1880s, but as "Sockless Jerry," he became one of the state's most successful Populist leaders and an effective spokesman for the plight of small farmers. Militant prohibitionist Carry A. Nation became equally famous for her saloon-destroying hatchet. In her home in Medicine Lodge, Nation experienced the "divine call" that inspired her unprecedented antisaloon campaign in the first decade of the twentieth century. The Carry A. Nation Home Memorial effectively symbolizes this critical era and the religious idealism and Puritan moralism basic to Kansas history.

Prohibition was not a new issue in Kansas politics when Carry Nation began swinging her hatchet at the turn of the century. The state constitutional convention avoided the issue in 1859, but a "women's crusade" in the 1870s led to amendment of the state constitution to prohibit the sale of alcoholic beverages in the state. Constitutional prohibition did not dry up the state, however, for "joints" continued to sell alcohol openly. Faced with this laxity of enforcement, Carry Nation decided in 1899 to take matters into her own hands and close the saloons in Medicine Lodge.

Nation and her husband had lived in the community for a decade. Born in Kentucky in 1846, she grew up in Texas and Missouri. Her first husband, Charles Gloyd, was a young physician who died of alcoholism in 1870, leaving her a widow with a small child. In 1874 she married David Nation, a widower nineteen years older than she. He was var-

Carry Nation's home in Medicine Lodge

iously a newspaper editor, a lawyer, and a minister. The last career took
the couple to Medicine Lodge in 1889, when he accepted the pastorate
of the community's Christian church. In December of that year the Nations
paid $2,500 for a small brick house on Fowler Avenue.

Mrs. Nation became involved in a variety of religious and reform
causes in the next decade and was one of the founders of the local
chapter of the Women's Christian Temperance Union. Their campaign
for the closing of the community's seven illegally operating saloons
culminated in a public demonstration in 1899. After singing hymns outside one establishment, Mrs. Nation led an attack, swinging her black
umbrella. Their tactics proved successful: the saloons soon closed down.

About that same time, Carry Nation claimed that a "divine call" directed
her to extend her antisaloon campaign to the community of Kiowa,
some twenty miles to the south on the Kansas-Oklahoma border. In the
summer of 1900, she wrecked the community's three saloons by hurl-
ing bricks wrapped in newspapers. That incident paled, however, in
comparison to her Wichita campaign in December 1900. Her assault on
the Hotel Carey bar resulted in $2,000 damage, a two-week stay in jail,
and national recognition for Mrs. Nation and her crusade.

With the hatchet as her weapon and symbol, she then carried her
cause to Topeka and Enterprise, Her demonstrations began with public
prayers, hymns, and exhortations on the evil of alcohol, and then Nation,
swinging her hatchet, would lead her followers in an attack on the
offending establishment. Her activities received extensive press cover-
age, and she began to organize her new recruits as the Home Defenders
and the Hatchet Brigade. For a time she even published a newspaper,
The Smasher's Mail. To raise funds to extend her campaign, Nation also
sold miniature hatchets, the symbol of the prohibition cause.

Nation's activities inspired similar antisaloon violence across the country, and she personally took her campaign to Chicago, St. Louis, Denver, San Francisco, and New York. Arrested over thirty times for her exploits, she used the money from the sale of hatchets and fees from her speaking engagements to pay her fines. Meanwhile, her husband filed for divorce on the grounds that she had deserted him to pursue her crusade. After the divorce was granted in 1902, she sold their Medicine Lodge house for $800 and used the money to establish a refuge in Kansas City for drunkard's wives.

Convinced that the sale of alcoholic beverages was a national problem, Nation went to Washington in 1903. She failed to secure a meeting with President Theodore Roosevelt, but her disruption of the Senate attracted attention to her cause. In 1904 she wrote her autobiography, *The Use and the Need of the Life of Carry A. Nation*. The following year she moved to Oklahoma and started a new magazine, *The Hatchet*. Another trip to Washington and then a speaking tour of Great Britain followed. Although she bought a small farm at Eureka Springs, Arkansas, as a place to rest, Nation maintained a heavy schedule of speaking engagements until felled by a stroke in 1911. She died shortly thereafter and did not live to see the fruition of her crusade, the Eighteenth Amendment to the United States Constitution.

Carry Nation's Medicine Lodge home was erected in 1882. She resided there from 1889 to 1902, the most significant period in her life. Here she experienced the "divine call" that inspired her nationwide crusade. The Women's Christian Temperance Union purchased the house in 1950 as a memorial to Nation. Now open to the public as an historic-house museum, the simple one-story brick house appears much as it did during Nation's day. Original furnishings include her organ, her cupboard, her desk, and such personal items as a bonnet and a valise.

Carry Nation was the best known agitator in the prohibition cause at the turn of the century. Her campaign reflected the perennial moral debates basic to Kansas' political development and history. Her home thus stands as a symbol of both her militant crusade and a significant dimension of Kansas history.

EISENHOWER CENTER *Abilene*. Located at the juncture of the Chisholm Trail and the Union Pacific Railroad, Abilene was the first and most famous of the rowdy cowtowns that sprang up across the West in the 1860s and 1870s. By the time Dwight D. Eisenhower and his family moved there in the 1890s, however, the era of Wild Bill Hickok and the Texas cattle trade had yielded to a more settled existence. Throughout his life, Eisenhower identified closely with the quiet central Kansas town where he grew up. As soldier and president, he exemplified the "middleness" of twentieth-century Kansas character and brought national and international attention to his home state. His boyhood home still stands today as part of the Eisenhower Center, an impressive complex that includes the Dwight D. Eisenhower Library, the Eisenhower Museum, the Place of Meditation where he and his wife are buried, and a visitor center.

When David and Ida Eisenhower moved their young family to Abilene in the 1890s, they were actually returning to the area where his father had settled in 1878. Jacob Eisenhower, a minister of the Brethren in Christ Church, led a large group of Pennsylvanians to Dickinson County, Kansas, that year and began farming near the town of Hope. His son David chose college instead of farming and went off to Lane University at Lecompton, where he met and married Ida Elizabeth Stover of Virginia. They returned to Hope to open a general store but left again after bankruptcy in 1887–1888. The Eisenhowers moved to Denison, Texas, where he found work as a railroad mechanic. On October 14, 1890, their third son, Dwight, was born.

Early in the decade, the family returned to central Kansas, and David Eisenhower began working at the Belle Springs Creamery in Abilene. After Ida gave birth to two more sons, a larger house became essential for the growing family. In 1898 they purchased a house and three acres of land from David's brother Abraham. Abilene school teacher Ephraim Ellis had built the simple frame house in 1887 and 1888 but soon lost it in the same agricultural depression that bankrupted David Eisenhower's general store. The property reverted to the land developer, who also went bankrupt. Jacob Eisenhower purchased it in 1892 and deeded it to his son Abraham in 1894. When David and Ida bought the house, they also agreed to provide a home for the elder Eisenhower.

Dwight Eisenhower lived with his family in the Abilene house from 1898 until he left for the United States Military Academy in 1911. He attended Abilene High School and, after his graduation in 1909, worked

Eisenhower's boyhood home

for two years with his father as a fireman and refrigeration plant helper at the Belle Springs Creamery. He then went to West Point, from which he graduated in 1915. The following year he met and married Mamie Geneva Doud. For the next two decades he had a variety of military assignments, including positions in the offices of the Assistant Secretary of War and the Army Chief of Staff, and from 1935 to 1939 he was stationed in the Philippines with General Douglas MacArthur.

With Pearl Harbor and American entry into World War II, Eisenhower's responsibilities increased. He was initially appointed chief of the War Plans Division and then of the Operations Division of the War Department General Staff. In 1942, he was promoted to major general and named commander-in-chief of the European theater of operations for the United States. In this position, he commanded the Allied invasion of North Africa and took control of Sicily and Italy. Recognizing both Eisenhower's abilities and his growing popularity and acclaim, President Franklin D. Roosevelt named him commander of the Allied Expeditionary Force in 1943. The following summer he directed the invasion of Europe across the English Channel. Eleven months later the Germans surrendered, and Eisenhower became commander of the United States occupation zone. In June of 1945, he returned to Abilene a five-star general and a genuine American hero.

General Eisenhower served as Army Chief of Staff from 1945 until 1948, when he resigned to assume the presidency of Columbia University. After two years, he took leave from that position to serve as Supreme Commander of the Allied Powers in Europe, establishing the military command of the North Atlantic Treaty Organization.

Looking toward the 1952 presidential race, Eisenhower's admirers began organizing a "Draft Eisenhower" movement in 1951. The popular military hero was reluctant at first, but in early 1952 he resigned from the Army (while remaining president of Columbia) and announced his interest in the Republican presidential nomination. Despite a strong challenge from Senator Robert A. Taft of Ohio, Eisenhower won the nomination on the first ballot at the Republican convention; he selected Senator Richard M. Nixon of California for his running mate. That fall they faced Democratic nominees Adlai E. Stevenson and John Sparkman. Campaigning on "Korea, communism, and corruption," the Eisenhower-Nixon ticket won the largest popular vote in history to that time and returned the Republican party to the White House for the first time in twenty years.

Eisenhower's Kansas "middleness" suited the popular mood of the 1950s. Perceived as a man above politics, he appeared capable of conciliating the social and political conflicts of the day. His moderate Republicanism and restrained approach to government promised a welcome change from the activist New Deal and Fair Deal years. The new president pursued a middle-of-the-road domestic policy in line with his concept of "dynamic conservatism." He tried to limit the role of the federal government but did not dismantle the successful programs of the New Deal. For instance, he advocated an "unregulated" economy but resorted to fiscal remedies to deal with economic declines of the decade; and he sought to restore private enterprise to agriculture but ended up spending six times as much on agricultural programs as Truman had. Despite his apparent business orientation and conservative rhetoric, Eisenhower accepted and in fact legitimized the New Deal framework.

The President took a more aggressive stance on foreign policy matters and, with John Foster Dulles as Secretary of State, proposed a "new look" in foreign relations. In the final analysis, however, the Republicans did not find an alternative to the Truman containment policy and continued to rely on collective security, regional alliances, foreign aid, and support of the United Nations.

Eisenhower's popularity survived the foreign or domestic reverses his administration experienced. Campaigning again with the slogan "I Like Ike," Eisenhower handily won reelection in 1956 in a second contest with Adlai Stevenson. Despite illness and hospitalization in the middle of his tenure, he remained in office until January 20, 1961. Then he and his wife retired to his Gettysburg, Pennsylvania, farm. The former president died on March 28, 1969.

Eisenhower's father died in their Abilene home in 1942, and his mother died four years later. Their sons then decided to give the house to the Eisenhower Foundation to be preserved without change and be open to the public without charge. The family furniture and mementos thus remain as Ida Eisenhower left them at her death in 1946. The house includes the original 1887–1888 structure, two bedroom additions for the Eisenhowers and Jacob Eisenhower, and a small kitchen that dates from 1915. The living room, dining room, parlor, and kitchen and the parents' bedroom on the first floor are open to the public. Upstairs are the children's bedrooms. The small, modest house and its plain and inexpensive furnishings effectively reflect Eisenhower's typical Midwestern background.

While Eisenhower was in Abilene during his campaign in 1952, he broke ground for the Eisenhower Museum. The Eisenhower Foundation financed the project with private funds. Erected on the family's old garden plot east of the house, the Kansas limestone structure was dedicated on Veterans' Day in 1954. The museum contains murals and exhibits relating to Eisenhower's life and work.

In 1955 the Eisenhower Presidential Library Commission was established to raise funds for a library to preserve papers, books, and other historical materials pertinent to Eisenhower's presidency. A two-story modern research facility was completed near the house and museum in 1961 and was dedicated the following year. The Dwight D. Eisenhower Library has been administered by the National Archives and Records Service since its opening; the other two structures came under federal control as well in 1966.

Eisenhower, his wife, and their first child are buried in the Center's Place of Meditation, a chapel erected in 1966. The other structure in the complex is a modern visitor center, built in 1975. At that same time, the area between the Center buildings was landscaped as a mall.

The Eisenhower Center preserves the former president's boyhood home, provides exhibits and programs on his life and career, and maintains research facilities for scholars. These varied programs provide a unique opportunity to learn about this preeminent Kansan and his significant contribution to the history of the state and the nation.

BEECHER BIBLE AND RIFLE CHURCH on state 18 east of Wabaunsee. Built in 1862 by Connecticut Free-State emigrants assisted by Brooklyn preacher Henry Ward Beecher, who sent rifles in crates marked as Bibles.

BOOT HILL MUSEUM 500 W. Wyatt Earp, Dodge City. Cowboy equipment and guns, with historic house, on site of 1870s cemetery.

CHRYSLER HOUSE 104 W. Tenth Street, Ellis. Clapboard house, built about 1889, the boyhood home of famed automobile executive Walter P. Chrysler; with a museum.

CONDON NATIONAL BANK 811 Walnut Street, Coffeyville. Bank robbed by five members of the Dalton Gang before they were killed in 1892.

COUNCIL GROVE NATIONAL HISTORIC DISTRICT near U.S. 56 and state 177, Council Grove. A mission school and other landmarks at the site of one of the most important rendezvous points on the Santa Fe Trail.

DIETRICH CABIN Ottawa City Park, Ottawa. Museum in an 1859 log cabin (one of few remaining in the state).

EL CUARTELEJO (SCOTT COUNTY PUEBLO SITE) west of U.S. 83 in Lake Scott State Park, 12 miles north of Scott City. Ruins of a seven-room stone pueblo occupied by Indians in the late 1600s and early 1700s.

FIRST TERRITORIAL CAPITOL state 18 on the Fort Riley Military Reservation, Pawnee. Where the territorial legislature met in 1855 under pro-slavery auspices.

FORT HAYS FRONTIER HISTORICAL PARK U.S. 183A, south of I-70, Hays. Established as Camp Fletcher in 1865 to protect settlers and railroad workers from Indians; original stone blockhouse, guardhouse, and officers' quarters restored.

FORT LARNED NATIONAL HISTORIC SITE west of Larned on U.S. 156. Well-preserved fort built to protect Santa Fe Trail and used as a base in the Indian wars of the 1860s and 1870s.

FORT LEAVENWORTH NATIONAL HISTORIC LANDMARK Leav-

enworth. Established 1827 as a fort to protect the Santa Fe Trail and the fort at which soldiers were assembled for the War with Mexico; now with a military museum. For 100 years the home of the U.S. Army Command and General Staff College.

FORT SCOTT NATIONAL HISTORIC AREA on U.S. 54, Fort Scott. Founded in 1842 as one of the posts along the "permanent Indian frontier"; active also during the Civil War, when black troops were trained there. Includes restored and reconstructed buildings.

FUNSTON HOME U.S. 169, four miles north of Iola. Home of Frederick Funston, famous in the Philippine insurrection of 1901.

GOODNOW HOUSE 2301 Claflin Road, Manhattan. Residence of Isaac T. Goodnow, who came to Kansas in 1855, participated in constitutional conventions, and played an important role in the development of public education in Kansas.

GRINTER PLACE 1420 S. 78th Street, Muncie. Built in 1857 by Moses Grinter, trader to the Delawares, who operated a ferry in 1831 and later served immigrants to Oregon and California.

HISTORIC WICHITA COWTOWN 1871 Sim Park Drive, Wichita. Village museum with authentic house and items depicting life in Wichita, 1865–1880.

HOLLENBERG PONY EXPRESS STATION near Hanover, five miles north of U.S. 36 via state 15 and 243. Most westerly Pony Express station in Kansas; located in a house built 1856 or 1858 and possibly the only Pony Express station to be left unaltered and in its original location.

INDIAN MUSEUM OF THE MID-AMERICA ALL-INDIAN CENTER 650 N. Seneca, Wichita. Native American art and artifacts.

IOWA, SAC AND FOX PRESBYTERIAN MISSION east of Highland on state 136. Mission operated until 1863 for children of Indians relocated to Kansas from Missouri and Iowa.

KANSAS MUSEUM OF HISTORY Topeka. Extensive collections on Kansas history, including ethnological and archeological materials, art, shop interiors, home interiors, and agricultural, military, and industrial items.

MARAIS des CYGNES MASSACRE MEMORIAL PARK four miles northeast of Trading Post. Where a proslavery group shot eleven free-staters, leaving five dead, in 1858; a violent incident of the Kansas territorial period.

MENNONITE IMMIGRANT HISTORICAL FOUNDATION 202 Poplar, Goessel. Collections of household goods, farm machinery, and other items of the German Russian Mennonites; with tours.

MINE CREEK BATTLEFIELD one mile west of U.S. 69 and state highway 52, Linn County. Where Union troops defeated Confederates in 1864 and saved Fort Scott from attack.

NICODEMUS HISTORIC DISTRICT U.S. 24, Nicodemus. Only remaining all black town founded during the "Exoduster" movement of the 1870s, when many southern blacks moved to the Midwest; site of the first United States post office supervised by blacks.

OLD FORT DODGE JAIL Old Front Street, Dodge City. Museum in building dating from the 1870s, when Dodge City was the scene of vice and violence. Replicas of frontier western buildings nearby.

PAWNEE INDIAN VILLAGE MUSEUM on state 266 eight miles north of U.S. 36, near Republic. Where Republican Band Pawnees lived in earth lodges in the 1820s and 1830s; includes the original lodge floor of one of the largest sites.

PAWNEE ROCK MEMORIAL PARK near U.S. 56, Pawnee Rock. A cliff of red sandstone that was a landmark on the Santa Fe Trail.

PIONEER ADOBE HOUSE U.S. 56 and S. Ash Street, Hillsboro. Built in 1876 by a German-Russian Mennonite; includes a museum.

QUAYLE BIBLE COLLECTION AND OLD CASTLE MUSEUM Baker University, Baldwin City, Kansas. Collection of 600 rare Bibles in the library and a collection of Indian pottery and pioneer artifacts in Old Castle Hall, built in 1858 for the oldest four-year university in Kansas.

SANTA FE TRAIL REMAINS U.S. 50 nine miles west of Dodge City. Still-visible ruts made between 1820 and 1850 in rangeland overlooking the Arkansas River.

SHAWNEE METHODIST MISSION Fairway, 53rd Street, and Mission Road, Kansas City. Established on this site in 1838 on the Santa Fe and Oregon trails and the largest and most important western mission before the Civil War. Three original structures remain.

SPENCER MUSEUM OF ART University of Kansas, Lawrence. Includes American painting as well as decorative art and graphics.

WICHITA ART MUSEUM 619 Stackman Drive, Wichita. Includes Charles M. Russell drawings and sculptures and other American art.

KENTUCKY

CUMBERLAND GAP NATIONAL HISTORICAL PARK Middlesboro.
It has been said that the history of America is in large part the history
of people in motion. Indeed, some of the most time-honored images of
our past are of people coming to America and people migrating from
one part of the country to another. These are images that reflect much
truth. Less than four hundred years ago the continent was virtually empty
of Europeans. *Mayflower* and *Arbella, Goodspeed* and *Susan Constant,
Ark* and *Dove* were only the more famous predecessors of countless
other ships, their names long forgotten, that in the centuries since have
brought thousands to these shores.

Viewed across the space of many generations, few journeys have
ended on the Atlantic coast. By the end of the nineteenth century, those
early immigrants and their descendants—now called Americans—had
moved all the way to the Pacific coast and back again, settling a vast
continental nation as they went. Like some of the ships that first brought
their fathers from Europe, their pathways became legend, remembered
with awe long after the last pioneer had passed. The Oregon Trail, the
Overland Trail, the Santa Fe Trail rank among the great monuments to
human migration and are powerful reminders of an enduring characteristic of the American people.

Yet before any of those overland trails carried their first wagons,
another great pathway—the Wilderness Road—was already well-worn.
It passed through nature's only gateway to the trans-Allegheny West: the
Cumberland Gap. The Allegheny Mountains, which by various names
stretch from Maine to Georgia, for decades rose as a forbidding barrier
to western America. During colonial days, they marked the effective
limit of British settlement and authority. Indeed, at the close of the
French and Indian War the British attempted formally to keep white
settlements separated from the Indian lands beyond. By the Proclamation of 1763, the mountains were to constitute the dividing line; west of
it, white settlement was forbidden.

The policy was at odds with certain realities of American life. Population was growing, and growing hungrier for land. Finally, with the
French threat removed, the lands to the west—especially Kentucky's
storied "Bluegrass"—acted as an irresistible magnet. As the British tried
to define and tidy up their American empire, the Americans had other
ideas and different roads to follow. One of the most important led through
the Cumberland Gap. Today, as then, the Gap (which actually consists
of four geological features) forms a natural doorway through the mountains that divide the eastern seaboard from the interior of the continent.
In the late eighteenth and early nineteenth centuries, before the mountain barrier was pierced by other means, the Gap was a highway of

major social and political importance and a landmark in the westward movement of the new nation. Indians had coveted the rich hunting grounds of Kentucky long before the white man did and had known about the Cumberland Gap through the mountains. Through it they followed the vast herds of buffalo that once teemed here, and rival tribes fought bloody clashes to dominate it. The English first discovered the Gap in 1750, though the French and Indian War, Pontiac's Rebellion, and the British Proclamation Line of 1763 prevented all but small groups of hunters from passing through to the rich country beyond. Among them, however, was Daniel Boone, whose name ever since has been linked with this famous place. In 1769 Boone and several companions passed through the Gap on their way to Kentucky, which they spent two full years exploring.

The early 1770s saw several attempts to settle that beautiful land. Under the treaty of Sycamore Shoals, which secured from the Indians a strip through the Cumberland Gap and land between the Kentucky River and the southern edge of the Cumberland River valley, Judge Richard Henderson established the mammoth and aptly named Transylvania Company on 20 million acres ceded by the Cherokees. To prepare the region for settlement, he hired Daniel Boone to blaze a trail through the Cumberland Gap. In March of 1775 Boone and thirty axmen started work at the Long Island of the Holston (now Kingsport, Tennessee), and within a month they had hacked their way through forest, swamp, and canebrake to the Kentucky River over 200 miles away. Their path, which became known as the Wilderness Road, soon entered history and legend.

The existence of the Road did much to ensure the survival of the early Kentucky settlements and tie them to the East. In 1776, in fact, the Kentucky communities at their own request were organized as the westernmost county of Virginia. During the Revolutionary War the threat of attack by British-backed Indians frequently kept the Gap closed, though troops and supplies did pass through—most notably George Rogers Clark's Virginia and Kentucky expedition en route to its important victories over the British posts at Kaskaskia, Cahokia, and Vincennes. Even so, by the end of the Revolution in 1783, some 12,000 settlers had made the trek to Kentucky—and they were just the beginning. With independence, the last barriers were removed and the tide of immigration swelled. Less than a decade afterward, Kentucky (then with a population of 100,000) entered the Union as the first state west of the mountains. Most of its citizens had traveled there via the Cumberland Gap.

By the end of the century, the Gap had seen 300,000 pass through on their way west. Until 1796, travel on the Wilderness Road was by foot or horseback, but in that year the trail was improved to permit wagon traffic—the ultimate improvement in the late eighteenth century. Through the first quarter century of the new nation's existence, the Gap and the

Cumberland Gap

Road remained a vital avenue linking East and West. Nor was it a one-way route. The thousands who went to Kentucky were farmers and their families; every year they drove or had driven eastward, back over their old route, herds of western livestock bound for eastern markets.

Cumberland Gap enjoyed a prominence bestowed by geography and some of the accidents of history. It was the gateway through a great physical barrier that men craved to cross, but could not by other means. Thus they funneled here, obedient to nature's whim and their own drive to possess the land beyond. But it was not a prominence that could last. Already by the 1820s and 1830s the mountains were yielding passage at other points, and the West was becoming more accessible over other routes: the Erie, the Pennsylvania Main Line, and the Chesapeake and Ohio canals; steamboats traveling up the great interior rivers; and in time the railroads, which respected geography less than any kind of transportation up to then known to man.

Thus the Cumberland Gap faded, if not to complete obscurity, then to a kind of irrelevance reserved for places that time has passed by. Today, though a highway and a railroad pass through it, Cumberland Gap is a quiet place, remote from great centers of population, probably appearing much as it did before westering Americans discovered and made it famous. The Cumberland Gap National Historical Park, administered by the National Park Service, covers portions of Virginia, Kentucky, and Tennessee and offers visitors a variety of opportunities to learn about the area's natural and human history. Aptly featured on its brochure is a print of one of the most famous paintings inspired by the westward movement: George Caleb Bingham's "Emigration of Daniel Boone," which pictures the great frontiersman leading his family and friends through the Cumberland Gap. A Missourian, Bingham too with his family once made that trip, from Augusta County in Virginia, over the Wilderness Road and through the Cumberland Gap.

ASHLAND *(Henry Clay House) two miles southeast of Lexington on Richmond Road.* Horses, bourbon, and bluegrass have long dominated Americans' image of Kentucky and Kentuckians' image of themselves. It is a soft and timeless image of enormous appeal both to those who shared the life it mirrored and to many who did not. The place that gave it birth—the Bluegrass region around Lexington—remains much the same today as in earlier times. Lexington has grown into a small city, and now wide highways pass where quiet country roads once wandered. But the gently rolling landscape, carpeted with bluegrass and marked off with white wooden fences, changes little. Views of grazing thoroughbreds, large horsebarns, and the stately country houses of their owners remain.

Ashland, the home of Henry Clay, is one of the most famous of those country houses. Now surrounded by the city of Lexington, it evokes the spirit both of this region of Kentucky and of a famous figure in American public life. Clay's career covered much of the antebellum era and is identified with some of its most famous events. The years between the American Revolution and the Civil War witnessed the young republic's rapid growth and westward expansion—and the development in the North and the South of two divergent and competing cultures. Its public life, seen through the actions of the national government, revealed Americans from the North and the South and in between searching for ways to balance the conflicting ideals of liberty and union. Only the Civil War finally settled the matter; in the various interim settlements that filled the antebellum years and for a time kept the union together, no one played a larger part than Henry Clay.

Clay's own life nearly spanned those years: born in 1777, just as the Revolution was beginning, he died in 1852, less than a decade before the Civil War. Like many Kentuckians of his generation, he was a native of Virginia (of which Kentucky was once a county). As a young lawyer, he migrated across the mountains to the Bluegrass in 1797 and a year later married Lucretia Hart, the daughter of a wealthy Lexington family. Their union lasted fifty-four years and produced eleven children.

Clay was well connected, clever, and ambitious, and his political star rose quickly. He went to the Kentucky legislature and, filling two unexpired terms in the United States Senate, soon gained experience in Washington. He became a congressman in his own right in 1811, was promptly elected Speaker of the House, and became a leader of the western faction known as the "War Hawks"—eager for war with Great Britain in 1812. He helped negotiate an end to that war as a peace commissioner in 1814 and continued as Speaker of the House of Representatives until 1820 and from 1823 to 1825. While in the House Clay was also influential in the first of the great sectional compromises: the

Ashland

Missouri Compromise of 1820 by which the simultaneous admission of Missouri and Maine maintained the balance between free and slave states. In an attempt to settle the matter for the future, it was also then agreed that in the rest of the Louisiana Purchase, the line 36° 30' north latitude would divide slave states from free.

In 1824, in the first of three tries, Clay became a candidate for the presidency. That year the old political parties were dissolving and the contest was four-way, pitting Clay (who was nominated by the Kentucky legislature) against Andrew Jackson, John Quincy Adams, and William H. Crawford. Clay came in fourth in number of electoral votes, and when the final choice was submitted to the House of Representatives he threw his support to Adams. Although no conclusive evidence supports the charge that Clay made a "corrupt bargain," he did become Secretary of State in Adams' cabinet.

Throughout these years Clay was gaining a reputation as the author and chief supporter of the "American System," a group of policies favoring a protective tariff to encourage American industry and government-financed internal improvements (roads, canals, and improved natural waterways) to expand the domestic market. The policies long remained controversial, as did Clay himself. In 1832 he again ran for the presidency and again was defeated, this time by Andrew Jackson, who became the first westerner (as the word was then understood) to win that office. In 1833, again United States senator from Kentucky, Clay sponsored a compromise tariff that helped keep South Carolina in the union and thus end the Nullification Crisis. Later in the same year he introduced a Senate resolution censuring Jackson for his attack on the second Bank of the United States, which Clay had strongly supported. Clay ran for the presidency for the third and final time in 1844, when the spirit of expansionism gripped the country, and he lost again largely because of his noncommittal position on the Texas question.

Even though he never achieved the nation's highest office, Clay did achieve a permanent and revered place in history, not least for his key role in the last great sectional compromise. Fearing mounting antagonism between the North and the South, Clay in 1850 introduced in the Senate proposals for settling the question of slavery. The debate on them was perhaps the most famous in congressional history; the series of measures enacted later that year, known as the Compromise of 1850, probably bought America another ten uneasy years of peace. The title it earned for Henry Clay—The Great Pacificator or the Great Compromiser—lasted long after his death in 1852.

Throughout his tumultuous public career, Henry Clay returned often and eagerly to his private refuge in Lexington. Named Ashland for the forest of ash trees that once surrounded it, Clay's house was designed by Benjamin H. Latrobe, architect of the United States Capitol. Though extensively rebuilt by his son, Ashland is today much as Clay himself knew it, and indeed it was lived in by Clay's descendants until 1948. A two-and-a-half-story brick Italianate mansion with single-story wings and projecting ells that form a court in front of the house, it reflects both Clay's wealth and the prestige enjoyed by nineteenth-century country squires in the Bluegrass. Though now much diminished, Clay's estate here once totaled some 600 acres. On it were raised hemp, tobacco, corn, wheat, and rye. There was also livestock, especially horses. An avid horseman, Clay imported some of the first Arabian horses to this country and was one of the first men west of the mountains to build a private racetrack.

The house displays many of the furnishings once used by Clay and his family. The dining room china was purchased in Paris and includes a container for ice cream, a delicacy made possible by Ashland's ice house. The dining table of Honduras mohogany seats twenty and was brought by wagon across the mountains from Virginia. Twelve of Ashland's thirteen fireplaces have carved Carrara marble mantels imported from Italy; all burned coal mined near the Kentucky River. The drawing room's gold brocade draperies and the empire-style sofa are French, acquired in 1814 when Clay was abroad negotiating the Treaty of Ghent. In the library, with its walnut chess table and portrait of Clay by Matthew Jouett, Clay met at different times five men who did achieve the high office that always eluded him: James Monroe, Andrew Jackson, William Henry Harrison, Martin Van Buren, and Abraham Lincoln. Upstairs, at the foot of Clay's bed, is the deerskin trunk he used when traveling from Ashland to Washington, a journey that then took ten to fourteen days by stagecoach. The coach presented to him in 1833 by the citizens of Newark, New Jersey, is also on display.

Over the years the city of Lexington encroached on Clay's estate, and today only some twenty acres remain; with the house, they are administered by the Henry Clay Memorial Foundation. But that is more than enough to transport today's visitor back into the time when Clay lived and found refuge here from the political wars that made the name of "The Great Compromiser" from Kentucky renowned throughout America.

SHAKERTOWN AT PLEASANT HILL *Harrodsburg.* The history of religious enthusiasm in America is part of a larger national story. From childhood, when first we learn the story of the Pilgrims' first Thanksgiving, we learn that one of the reasons people came to America was to find religious freedom. So it was with the Pilgrims at Plymouth, with the Puritans at Massachusetts Bay, with the Quakers in Pennsylvania, and much later with the Jews from Germany and eastern Europe.

Some of those who found refuge here belonged to much smaller groups and held much odder beliefs, but they too found refuge here. Among the smallest were the Shakers, who came late in the eighteenth century, prospered for a time, and then quietly disappeared. Wherever their spiritual odyssey might have been taking them, their earthly sojourn unquestionably left behind some remarkable relics. Shakertown at Pleasant Hill is one.

The Shakers were a small Christian sect that sprang up in England in the late eighteenth century. Dissidents from the Quaker Church in England, the group had first been known as the "United Society of Believers in Christ's Second Coming." Later they were called derisively "Shaking Quakers," after the frenetic shaking that characterized their worship, and then simply "Shakers." The Shakers' leader was a self-styled prophetess, Mother Ann Lee, who after a series of mystical encounters claimed to be Christ in female form returned to earth to instruct men in the proper ways of living. That instruction, strictly followed, made at the very least for a unique way of life: sexual abstinence, the holding of property in common, and separation of the faithful from the outside world. But however strange some of their beliefs no doubt seemed to their contemporaries, their gentle, strict, and industrious behavior invariably won them much admiration. In 1774 Mother Ann Lee brought the Shakers to New York, with large hopes for establishing colonies in America. By her death ten years later, plans for eleven were laid down. Over the next five decades or so, the Shakers, whatever their heavenly rewards, achieved in their own austere fashion real earthly success.

The Shaker Village at Pleasant Hill was begun in 1805, the result of the conversion to the faith of three Mercer County farmers, and—minus the Shakers—it is still largely intact. Though one of the key Shaker teachings was separation from "the world," the community at Pleasant Hill grew and prospered with the society around it. The antebellum years in Kentucky's Bluegrass were good ones. Population was rising; the economy was expanding; and sectional strife between North and

South had not yet made border-state Kentucky a land of divided loyalties. By 1820, Pleasant Hill boasted 500 inhabitants and was a prosperous agricultural community. Here it seemed, at first appearance, were Thomas Jefferson's much idolized yeomen farmers: self-reliant, self-sustaining, skilled and diligent in the arts of scientific farming and animal husbandry, quietly living far from the corruption of city civilization.

Appearances, of course, could be deceiving, and this one certainly was. Superb farmers and craftsmen though they were, the Shakers, like utopian groups before and after them, lived very much in a world of their own. Indeed, their "families" were not families of husbands, wives, and children, but "families" of celibate men and women the longevity of which relied solely on the adoption of children and the conversion of those outside the faith. Their farms were not family homesteads, proudly held and defended by staunch individualists, but were rather held and managed in common. They did not, with the virtues supposedly learned from a life spent on the land close to nature, engage in the public life of the young American republic; rather they deliberately disengaged themselves from that life. Their radical concepts of racial and sexual equality, though espoused quietly, placed them far to the left of any society that Thomas Jefferson and many after him ever knew or ever would have approved of.

Yet even in the Methodist, Baptist, evangelical South of the antebellum era, the Shakers were tolerated and even admired despite such heresies. They were, after all, very good at what they did. And some of what they did is still with us. As farmers, they were renowned throughout the region, and not just for exotic attempts to introduce silk production and Chinese sugar cane into Kentucky. Their orchards and nurseries were the finest in the Ohio Valley, and their experiments with feed and forage crops, soils and fertilizers, and farm machinery made Shakertown into a vast if unofficial agricultural experiment station. They were foremost among Kentucky's cattle breeders, by 1870 owning more English shorthorns than any other breeder in America.

If not more remarkable, their inventions and crafts were probably more widely known. Pleasant Hill boasted the first hydraulic water system in Kentucky, and a miniature railway carried feed to stock in the barns. By 1820 the colony also displayed saw, grist, and linseed-oil mills, a blacksmith and wagon shop, and shops for joiners, hatters, and shoemakers. And though they lived apart from "the world," the colonists did not hesitate to trade with it and thus earn their own way. Chief among the Shaker products that by mid-century were much sought after in river towns, and on farms and plantations all down the Mississippi to New Orleans, were garden seed, brooms, and preserves. Shakers annually turned out 50,000 brooms, preserved as much as thirty tons of "sweetmeats," and sold some $4,500 worth of reliable Shaker seed. In the then largely agricultural economy of the South and Mid-west, the name

East Family complex

"Shaker" on such products guaranteed excellence and integrity.

But the early blessings did not last. The Civil War both disturbed the quiet villages at Pleasant Hill and disrupted its Southern plantation markets. As pacifists, the Shakers were obliged to care for the well and wounded of both sides, and by the end of the conflict in this border state their stores and their energies were sadly depleted. There followed a period of decline as marked as the progress of antebellum years. It is not fair to say that the new age was more corrupt and worldly than the one in which the Shakers had prospered, and therefore brought about the demise of this otherworldly sect. Unquestionably, however, something in the delicate balance that had made possible the old life of these folk had disappeared. Fewer orphans were adopted and fewer converts received and, celibate to the end, the Shakers produced no younger generation to carry on. As numbers declined, so it seemed did the skills that once assured prosperity. Debts mounted. Finally in 1910, 105 years after its founding, twelve Shakers disposed of what property remained and Shakertown at Pleasant Hill came quietly to an end.

But many of the buildings remained, and since 1961 efforts by a private preservation group have restored the form—and some of the substance—of Shaker life here as it was before the Civil War. Twenty-seven structures remain and are situated amid more than 2,000 acres of bluegrass countryside, which is now operated as a modern farm. The village is staffed by costumed guides, and food and lodging are provided in original Shaker buildings.

For a community of otherworldly believers far from centers of wealth and population, some of these buildings are magnificent. Drawing on a simple Federal style, they reflect the plain and severe character of their builders and stand today as monuments to another age when, as a matter of course, things were sturdy and well crafted. Most notable perhaps are the graceful twin stairways in the Trustees' House and the intricately notched trusswork in the attic of the Meeting House, supporting a clear-span forty-by-sixty-foot ceiling two stories below. A visit, of an hour or a day, cannot recover the ascetic way of life once lived here. But it can reveal some of the things that the Shakers, now gone to their reward, left behind in this world—and leave us with the feeling that we would have been poorer without them.

ABRAHAM LINCOLN BIRTHPLACE NATIONAL HISTORIC SITE *three miles south of Hodgenville.* A restored log cabin moved to the site of Lincoln's birth, along with a Neoclassical Revival memorial building built 1909–1911.

BARTON MUSEUM OF WHISKEY HISTORY *Barton Road, Bardstown.* The history of whiskey distilling in the United States.

BEREA COLLEGE APPALACHIAN MUSEUM *Jackson Street, Berea.* Culture, crafts, and industry of early white Appalachia.

BUTCHERTOWN HISTORIC DISTRICT *bounded by Main, Hancock, Geiger, Quincy streets, U.S. 42, S. Fort Beargrass Creek, and Baxter Avenue, Louisville.* Residences and businesses dating from 1832, including home of Thomas A. Edison, built 1866–1868.

CHURCHILL DOWNS AND KENTUCKY DERBY MUSEUM *700 Central Avenue, Louisville.* Site of the first derby (1875) and museum related to the derby.

CONSTITUTION SQUARE STATE PARK *Danville.* Site of early constitutional meetings and of signing of Kentucky state constitution.

CORNER IN CELEBRITIES HISTORIC DISTRICT *Frankfort.* Nineteenth-century houses, including Greek Revival-design Orlando Brown House at 202 Wilkinson Street.

EPHRAIM McDOWELL HOUSE AND APOTHECARY SHOP *125–127 South Second Street, Danville.* House and gardens, including medicinal herb garden, built prior to 1830 for McDowell, known as the "Father of Abdominal Surgery."

THE FILSON CLUB *118 W. Breckinridge Street, Louisville.* History museum that includes Indian artifacts as well as items from early pioneer Kentucky life.

FORT BOONESBOROUGH MUSEUM *Fort Boonesborough State Park, state 388, Richmond.* Reconstructed fort near site where Daniel Boone built a fort; with Boone family documents and artifacts.

GRATZ PARK HISTORIC DISTRICT *bounded by 2nd and 3rd streets, the Byway, and Bark Alley, Lexington.* Houses in a variety of architectural styles dating from the eighteenth century, including the 1814 Federal-style home where Confederate raider John Hunt Morgan once lived.

THE HOMEPLACE *Land Between the Lakes, Golden Pond.* An 1850 house, with exhibits of hand tools and household items of that period.

INTERNATIONAL MUSEUM OF THE HORSE *Kentucky Horse Park, Iron Works Road, Lexington.* The history of horses, including worldwide breeds.

J. B. SPEED ART MUSEUM *2035 S. Third Street, Louisville.* Includes European and American decorative arts, painting, sculpture, and graphic arts.

JEFFERSON DAVIS MONUMENT STATE PARK *U.S. 68, state 80, Fairview.* Replica of the birthplace on the site of the birth of Jefferson Davis, Confederate president.

JOHN JAMES AUDUBON MUSEUM *Audubon State Park, U.S. 41, Henderson.* Audubon's paintings displayed on site where he worked.

KENTUCKY HISTORICAL SOCIETY AND MUSEUM *300 W. Broadway, Frankfort.* Museum, restored Old State Capitol (about 1828), and research library, with manuscripts, maps, photos, and state papers of the legislatures and governors.

KENTUCKY LIBRARY AND MUSEUM *Western Kentucky University, Bowling Green.* Log-house outdoor exhibit and tools, musical instruments, toys, and furniture from early frontier life.

KENTUCKY MILITARY HISTORY MUSEUM *East Main Street, Frankfort.* Housed in the Old State Arsenal, built 1850, and containing weapons, flags, uniforms, and photos related to Kentucky.

LIBERTY HALL MUSEUM *218 Wilkinson Street, Frankfort.* Eighteenth-century furniture, silver, and china in a 1796 Georgian house.

LOCUST GROVE HISTORIC HOME *561 Blankenbaker Lane, Louisville.* A frontier Georgian home built by brother-in-law and sister of George Rogers Clark, who retired to the place; with collections dating from 1783–1865.

MARY TODD LINCOLN HOUSE *511 W. Short Street, Lexington.* Girlhood home of Mary Todd, built about 1800–1803 as an inn; guided tours.

MUSEUM OF HISTORY AND SCIENCE *727 West Main Street, Louisville.* Artifacts from early humans down to the space age.

MY OLD KENTUCKY HOME STATE PARK *Bardstown.* An 1818 house where Stephen Foster is reputed to have written the famous song.

OLD FORT HARROD STATE PARK *U.S. 68 and 127, Harrodsburg.* Reconstruction of the 1774 fort that was the first permanent English settlement west of the Alleghenies.

OLD LOUISVILLE RESIDENTIAL DISTRICT *bounded by S. 7th Street, North-South Expressway, Kentucky Street, and Avery Street, Louisville.*

Italianate, Richardsonian, and Beaux-Arts houses built from the 1870s to 1900.

PATTON MUSEUM *4554 Fayette Avenue, Fort Knox.* Tanks, artillery, firearms, and memorabilia related to World War II General George Patton.

RUSSELLVILLE HISTORIC DISTRICT *bounded by 2nd, 9th, Caldwell, and Nashville streets, Russellville.* Mixture of nineteenth-century residential and commercial buildings, including site of 1861 Confederate convention.

UNIVERSITY OF LOUISVILLE PHOTOGRAPHIC ARCHIVES *Louisville.* Temporary exhibitions from the collection of 750,000 photographs.

WASHINGTON HISTORIC DISTRICT *bounded by Hoppe Street, Bartlett Lane, and city limits, Washington.* Early nineteenth-century houses in the state's first incorporated town.

WEST MAIN STREET HISTORIC DISTRICT *three-block area of West Main Street, Louisville.* Riverfront buildings built 1870–1890; site of city's first permanent settlement.

WHITEHALL *seven miles north of Richmond on Clay Lane near U.S. 25.* Late-eighteenth- and early-nineteenth-century house of abolitionist Cassius Marcellus Clay.

WILLIAM CLARK MARKET HOUSE MUSEUM *Second and Broadway, Paducah.* A 1905 building with mementos of Vice President Alben Barkley, antique tools, furnishings, and other artifacts.

LOUISIANA

LOUISIANA STATE MUSEUM 751 Chartres Street, New Orleans. New Orleans—legendary for jazz, fine food, and Mardi Gras—is unique among Louisiana and American cities. European visitors to America often comment that it is the only one that resembles their own. Not only is it old as American cities go, but it also looks old. Visitors' impressions are shaped, of course, by the famous French Quarter or Vieux Carre, actually only a small enclave within a modern metropolis that itself could hardly remind Europeans of home. To most American tourists, too, New Orleans means the French Quarter, its exotic tastes and entertainments unlike anything back home and therefore especially alluring.

But the French Quarter is rightly known as far more than a pleasure emporium. How it looks, not just what it sells, truly distinguishes it. Though the entire Vieux Carre Historic District (as the French Quarter is officially designated) contains hundreds of distinctive balconied buildings that are festooned with wrought iron and surround quiet tropical courtyards, the properties of the Louisiana State Museum are among the best preserved. They offer the history-minded visitor to this exotic place an exceptional sample of architectural history and, through it, the history of early New Orleans. Several are open to the public. None, ironically, is technically French, nor are many of the buildings anywhere in the quarter. New Orleans' history has not been so simple.

The French began it, and their influence endures today over a century and three-quarters after the city passed for the last time from their hands. In between much happened, as these historic buildings testify. The early years under the French rule were hardly auspicious. Founded in 1718 under the auspices of the Company of the Indies by Jean Baptiste le Moyne de Bienville at the place where the Mississippi River and Lake Pontchartrain came closest together, New Orleans was not the first settlement in Louisiana, though it would be the greatest. But greatness was a long way off, and for many years this place grandly named for the Duke of Orleans remained a rude frontier town on the edge of a subtropical wilderness.

Louisiana generally was not a place conducive to easy settlement. Control switched back and forth between the French government and several proprietary companies, all of whom encountered considerable frustration in trying to make Louisiana work. All of them also lost money. To populate the place convicts and prostitutes were sent forcibly from France. When their presence failed to have a sustaining effect, large grants were offered to concessionaires if they could import French agricultural tenants who at least could raise enough food to feed themselves. Good farmers finally were found in war-wracked Germany; many were enticed to Louisiana, and many prospered there. From Africa and the West Indies came slaves, and while they too stayed, they hardly prospered. Though by the 1740s some of the rougher edges had been worn off, the best New Orleans had to offer still could not have been very impressive. It counted probably less than 4,000 whites (800 of whom were soldiers), 2,000 slaves, and a few free blacks. It was not yet a prosperous trading city because the hinterland did not yet produce much that found a ready market in France.

The city's next sovereigns, the Spanish, enjoyed more luck—if only because settlement throughout eastern North America was more secure by the late eighteenth century, and trade coming down the Mississippi River at last made real the long-suspected potential of the town that controlled its mouth. After the Pinckney Treaty of 1795 between Spain and the new American nation gave the United States the right of deposit in New Orleans, the hides, meat, flour, and whiskey of half a continent came floating down to New Orleans. Vigorous Spanish administration and generous land grants finally sparked a tremendous increase in population, and by the late 1790s the successful cultivation of sugar cane and cotton were beginning to make of the Louisiana economy what it would be for years to come.

Thanks to the vagaries of European politics, sovereignty over Louisiana passed briefly back to France in 1800 and three years later (in what has been widely described ever since as the greatest real estate deal in history) to the young United States for the sum of $15 million, or about four cents an acre (the boundaries were somewhat vague). It has remained American (or Confederate) ever since and has grown and prospered with the nation. With them the Americans brought new ways of government and some other new ways of thinking and behaving. With them, as the years passed, New Orleans' and Louisiana's already mixed population and culture made its own distinctive accommodation, as the architecture of the French Quarter reveals. What French buildings there once were, however, were destroyed in the fires that swept the original town in 1788 and 1794, and what we now commonly call French is actually Spanish. The two premier buildings of the Louisiana State Museum properties are excellent examples.

The Cabildo, a massive three-story structure of stuccoed brick, was built between 1795 and 1799, very near the end of Spanish rule. But the Spanish built well, and what once housed their governing council of Louisiana became briefly the French *Maison de Ville,* then public offices under the Americans, and in 1911 the Louisiana State Museum. In its Sala Capitular the French formally transferred New Orleans and Louisiana to the United States. Today the Cabildo houses exhibitions on the settlement of Louisiana during the French, Spanish, and early American periods. On the third floor (a steep-sided mansard roof addition from the 1850s) is the Mississippi River Gallery, which examines the place of that great river in the history of Louisiana and New Orleans.

The Presbytère, flanking St. Louis Cathedral on the other side from the Cabildo, gives the appearance of being the Cabildo's twin, though it

The Cabildo on Jackson Square

was built for a different purpose and is several years older. It was never used as originally intended—as the cathedral rectory—but was leased for commercial shops and during the nineteenth century housed the Louisiana Supreme Court. Today it contains numerous exhibits, including the Louisiana Portrait Gallery. Together, the Presbytère and the Cabildo make one of the most imposing museums in the country and an enduring reminder of the Spanish presence in New Orleans.

Another museum property, located nearby on Dumaine Street, reveals the Spanish period in a different light. Madame John's Legacy (named for a fictitious character linked with the house in a short story by George Washington Cable) is a colonial raised cottage built in the late 1780s. Outside it is restored to its original appearance; inside its galleries and period rooms hold a fine collection of colonial Louisiana furniture and decorative arts. Two other more modest residences dating from the American period are the Creole House in Pirate's Alley and the Jackson House on St. Peter Street. The Creole House, built in 1842 on the site of an old colonial prison, displays the shuttered windows, balconies, and delicate wrought iron that have come to symbolize New Orleans. It is now home for the Friends of the Cabildo. The Jackson House (named for the hero of the Battle of New Orleans), also built in 1842, is of similar appearance and houses additional museum galleries. Just a few doors away, on the site of the Spanish arsenal, stands the American arsenal, built in 1839 and acquired by the State Museum in 1915. When restored it will house transportation and military collections.

After the Cabildo and the Presbytère, the museum's two most imposing properties are the Lower Pontalba and the United States Mint. The

Mint, located at the east end of the Quarter just a block from the river, was built in 1835 during the first presidential term of Andrew Jackson and is today the oldest surviving mint building in the United States. It was also the only mint of the Confederacy. Coinage was minted behind its red brick walls and massive white columns until 1909. Before its recent restoration by the State Museum it served in a number of other roles. The Lower Pontalba on Jackson Square, though comparable in size to the Mint, could hardly be more different in every other respect. The long red brick block between Chartres and Decatur on Jackson Square (and its duplicate across the square) was built by the Baroness Micaela Almonester de Pontalba in 1850 to provide elegant residences on the upper two floors and shops on the street level. The State Museum's 1850 home, in the Lower Pontalba, offers visitors a glimpse of what elegant urban living was like just before the Civil War, during New Orleans' most prosperous era. High ceilings, balconies, fine woodwork, and servants' quarters and private courtyards at the rear distinguished the Lower Pontalba even in a city famous for elegant residences. Today there are still shops on the ground floor, and a section houses the Louisiana State Museum historical research library.

For the visitor to New Orleans' French Quarter, there are many popular attractions. These buildings are perhaps not its most famous. But for the visitor with an eye for historically revealing architecture, they are an excellent place to start exploring the past of this unique place. They are all within easy walking distance of one another. And walking itself is one of the French Quarter's extra rewards.

CHALMETTE BATTLEFIELD, JEAN LAFITTE NATIONAL HISTORICAL PARK St. Bernard Highway, Chalmette. America's first years as a new nation were not easy ones. The military victory that achieved independence from Great Britain was followed by a number of domestic trials. The first system of American government—the Articles of Confederation—proved a dismal failure. The federal Constitution that replaced them, though it survived in the long run, sparked bitter debate and dissension in the beginning. The first system of political parties was established only with much labor and acrimony, and during the crisis over the Alien and Sedition Acts in the late 1790s it appeared that the very idea of loyal opposition might not survive.

Nor did the winning of independence mean that other nations respected the new republic or expected it to endure. The beaten British were far from friendly; and while recognition did come from them and other European powers, none could much sympathize with the principles behind the new American experiment in popular government. The French, America's vital wartime allies, were soon beset by their own revolution, which, as it grew more radical in the 1790s and degenerated into a military dictatorship, alienated much American opinion. And that Revolution soon spread war once again over much of Europe. France under Napoleon dominated the land; Britain ruled the seas. They were

*Chalmette
Battlefield*

locked in mortal struggle more or less constantly for twenty years.

One might have thought that the Great Powers, thus preoccupied with each other, would have left America, remote and harmless far across the Atlantic, well enough alone. But the United States then was very much a maritime nation. Disputes over shipping and neutral rights led to an undeclared naval war with France between 1798 and 1800 and to Thomas Jefferson's ill-fated Embargo of 1807–1809 whereby he sought to use economic pressure to bring the belligerents to terms. He failed; and as the European war dragged on, Britain through her powerful Royal Navy trespassed more and more on American commerce. The specific issue was impressment: the seizure of sailors (many of whom, the British claimed, were British subjects) from American ships for forced service in the Royal Navy. The larger issue, of course, was respect for the American flag: whether the young republic had yet really achieved independence. On land, the British still controlled the vast reaches of Canada, where—according to Henry Clay and other American "War Hawks" in 1810 and 1811—they fomented Indian raids on the frontier. Had not the time come to eliminate the British from North America altogether?

The War of 1812, fought between a badly divided United States (in New England, which lived by trade, there was talk of secession) and a battle-weary Britain, decided it. For the Americans it was a poorly run affair. The navy was small; the regular army was inexperienced and badly administered. Early campaigns to drive into Canada were disasters. The American garrison at Fort Dearborn (future Chicago) was massacred; Detroit fell to the British without a fight; a plan to attack Montreal pitifully fizzled. At sea the news was better, as American seamanship and some skilled commanders bloodied the British in several memorable engagements. But through 1813 neither side could strike a decisive blow.

In April of 1814, however, the overthrow of Napoleon in Europe enabled the British to concentrate new resources on the troublesome war with their old American colonies. Fourteen thousand veterans of the Duke of Wellington's campaigns crossed the Atlantic to finish the business. It was not an easy job. Along the Niagara frontier both sides fought fiercely; Chippewa and Lundy's Lane became famous battlegrounds. On Lake Champlain American naval forces won an important victory, but after the loss of Fort Erie opposite Buffalo in November the Americans abandoned their drive on Canada for good. To the south the British mounted secondary actions in the Chesapeake Bay region and in August 1814, inflicted on the Americans perhaps their greatest humiliation. British troops captured Washington and burned the Capitol and the White House. At Baltimore they met stiffer resistance and finally were stopped at Fort McHenry. Withdrawing to Jamaica, the British prepared for the action that left so many of them dead at Chalmette.

The capture of New Orleans, the British strategists reasoned, would give them control of the entire Mississippi Valley. If they succeeded they could strangle the outlet for western produce that came down the Ohio and Mississippi rivers and effectively dispute American power over the vast lands of Jefferson's Louisiana Purchase. With the stakes so high, they committed much to the effort: fifty ships and an army of 10,000 men sailed from Jamaica for the Gulf Coast. They looked invincible.

But they figured without Andrew Jackson, the American general in charge of the southern frontier, whose ability to rally the diverse and contentious population of New Orleans turned looming disaster into a great victory. The British approached stealthily by way of Lake Borgne and got within nine miles of New Orleans before they were discovered by the Americans. A disconcerted Jackson quickly attacked the gathering British force at the Villère Plantation on December 23, 1814. Though the confused night action was indecisive, it momentarily stalled the British advance and gave the Americans time to organize their real defense of the Crescent City.

For that purpose Jackson chose the Chalmette Plantation three miles upriver from Villère's. The invaders had to pass this way, and it offered good defensive ground. He established his line along the Rodriguez Canal, a shallow ditch along which he hurriedly constructed a shoulder-high rampart of mud and fence-rails. With his flanks protected by the river on the right and an impassable cypress swamp on the left, he had only to meet his enemy head-on. Behind this fortification Jackson gathered his motley army. With him from Tennessee came a loyal band of frontiersmen and Indian fighters, who with other volunteers from Kentucky, Mississippi, and Louisiana formed the core of his command. But he swelled their ranks with black refugees from the Caribbean, Choctaw Indians, released convicts, and—most legendary of all—Jean Lafitte's buccaneers from Barataria Bay. Their ranks totalled roughly 5,000, half the strength of their opponents.

The test came on January 8, 1815, and the result was the most one-sided victory in American military history. Jackson's defenders, many of them excellent marksmen armed with long rifles, commanded a clear field of fire over the Chalmette plantation; along the American line there were also eight batteries of artillery. To the skirl of Scottish Highlanders' bagpipes, the British bravely advanced in rank order, only to be cut down by a withering American fire. With enormous discipline they attacked Jackson's rampart three times. The British general, Edward Packenham, and his second in command were both killed, and in just two hours their force suffered over 2,000 casualties. The Americans lost just seven killed and six wounded. Jackson did not take the offensive, but within ten days the beaten British army left Louisiana forever.

Unbeknownst to any of the combatants, a peace treaty ending the war had been signed in Ghent, Belgium, on Christmas Eve, 1814. Thus this greatest of American land victories had no effect on the war's outcome. But it mattered for other reasons. For the young American nation, the stunning defeat of the British boosted national morale and was a fitting end to a frustrating and divisive war. It made of Andrew Jackson—destined to become president of the United States and a symbol for the age of the common man—a national hero. And it confirmed in the eyes of England and the rest of the world the permanence of the American national experiment. The Battle of New Orleans was also the last battle ever fought between Britain and the United States, two countries that thereafter peacefully went their separate ways. History in time brought them together on other fields of battle—but never again as foes.

RURAL LIFE MUSEUM *Louisiana State University, Baton Rouge.* Of all the southern states, Louisiana may be the most extraordinary. At least its historical image is the most exotic. The familiar antebellum legend of gallant gentlemen, gentle ladies, faithful retainers, all set against a backdrop of white columns, becomes in Louisiana especially seductive. Louisiana historian Joe Gray Taylor writes: "[T]he handsome gentlemen may be speaking French, and the ladies, answering in the same romantic tongue, are small, dark, and vivacious, possessed of all the virtues of their Anglo-Saxon sisters elsewhere in the South, but with the spicy tang of Latinism added." The setting and the supporting cast too are better: "Away from the Big House and the slave quarter stretch endless cotton and cane fields, surrounded by trees bowed down with Spanish moss, and here and there a cabin from which comes the sound of a fiddle playing an Acadian tune, sung by a large, happy illiterate family in an appealing patois." Romantic Hollywood movies once were made with such casts and sets. Part fact and part fiction, it is a tenacious image.

More recently, however, it has been fashionable among historians to debunk the image. It portrays, they argue, the way only a few fortunate Louisianians lived and masks the misery and injustice that was the lot of many whites and most blacks. Perhaps so. But not all the power of the image derives from its romantic trimmings. If it errs in some of its particulars, it is also correct on one of the most important points: it portrays a culture that was profoundly and enduringly rural. The nature of that ruralism could vary considerably. On the rich black alluvial soil that reaches from the Arkansas border down the west bank of the Mississippi, along both banks below the mouth of the Red River and along Bayou Lafourche and Bayou Teche, plantations, some not unlike the romantic image, once flourished. To the north they raised cotton or sugar; south Louisiana was sugar country.

Despite the presence of the great port city of New Orleans and the thousands of Louisianians who were not planters, these plantations dominated the state in the antebellum era. On the eve of the Civil War there were some 1,600 plantations with more than fifty slaves each. Tensas Parish alone counted 118. New Orleans itself was an old-fashioned commercial city whose gentry and thriving middle class serviced the needs of the countryside and profited from handling its products. It moved to rural rhythms, its bankers and merchants busiest during the fall and winter when the plantations' harvest arrived by steamboat from upriver. Probably the most important figure in the city's economy was the cotton or sugar "factor," the planters' business agent in New Orleans. His job was to get the best possible price for the crop and to handle the purchase of supplies needed on the plantations. On the sale of the crop he received a commission, usually two to three percent, and he collected interest on the unpaid balance of accounts carried for his customers. The countryside, too, was dominated by the great plantations. Those 1,600 with at least fifty slaves apiece covered over forty-three percent of the state's arable land, and the many more with at least twenty bondsmen covered an even larger area.

Still, there were many rural people who were not planters. The majority of white Louisiana farmers were more or less prosperous yeomen who worked the soil with their own hands and perhaps the labor of a slave or two. Though they may have planted small amounts of cotton or sugar cane to bring in cash, they were essentially subsistence farmers who raised corn and livestock to support their families. They far outnumbered planters in the hills of northern Louisiana and in the eastern parts of the Florida parishes. The blacks, who were half the people of the state, were also largely rural and nearly all slaves. For them, plantations and even smaller farms meant something different from what they did for the whites. And there were many whites who existed above, but not much above, the mudsill status of the slaves. Poor and landless, they grew in numbers as time went on.

After the Civil War, much changed in Louisiana and the rest of the South. Most notably, slavery disappeared; but, contrary to much popular belief, the plantations did not go with it. Agriculture in the South as elsewhere was growing more commercialized, and landholdings continued to be consolidated in a trend begun before the war. The yeomen as a class lost most. Lack of credit forced them to become dependent on the crop lien system. In time, as they were driven hopelessly into debt, many lost their land and became sharecroppers. The crop lien was an expedient brought about by the reduced value of farmland after the war and the inability of farmers to use it as security for credit. Instead they were forced to use their crops, on which their creditors (frequently the crossroads merchant who sold seed and other farm and household supplies) took a lien or mortgage. The farmer's security was a crop still being grown or perhaps still planned. If it failed to materialize—and the possibility of failure due to sickness, insects, floods, or cold weather was ever present—the consequences could be disastrous. At best the farmer paid dearly for his credit ("from twenty-five percent to grand larceny," it was said).

Sharecropping, meanwhile, began as a transition from slave to free labor, but it ended as an entrenched system of labor for many blacks and whites in the cotton fields. Essentially a substitute for wages, it worked simply enough. Planters who needed labor but could not pay cash for it offered instead a cabin, work stock, tools, seed—and a share in the crops—to the tenants. Tenants bought their own food and supplies from a plantation commissary, on credit because they had no cash, and paid at year's end with the proceeds from their share of the crop. If they owed more than their share covered and went into debt, laws prevented them from moving without the creditor's permission. It was a necessary system initially but one that unfortunately perpetuated itself over several generations.

Today much has changed. Agriculture since World War II has, like so much else, grown modern. The size of holdings still increases and new crops like soybeans outpace old ones like cotton and sugar. Mechanization has spread and fewer hands raise more. Many of the rural people have moved to town, many out of Louisiana altogether. Thus the LSU Rural Life Museum in Baton Rouge is an especially valuable historical resource. In its extensive collection of tools, furniture, and farm

Plantation commissary

implements, today's visitor, who very likely comes from a city, can recapture something of the rural world that most Louisianians, whether rich or poor, once knew.

This major outdoor folk museum spreads over five acres of plantation and includes more than fifteen buildings. There are three distinct areas. The Barn is an exhibit containing the museum's extensive collection of artifacts. These range from a bale of cotton picked and baled by slaves in the early 1860s to a collection of textile machines used in the homes of the nineteenth century; woodworking and blacksmithing tools; and displays on lumbering, hunting and trapping, all common activities of rural dwellers years ago. The Working Plantation illustrates that part of plantation life that is hidden behind the elegant antebellum mansions; this is what made those mansions possible. With the exception of the blacksmith shop and the sugarhouse, all are original nineteenth-century structures. A plantation commissary dating from the 1880s was once a busy general store for sharecroppers. The overseer's house features original *bousillage* walls, a unique Louisiana building technique by which hand-hewn cypress was coated on the inside with a mixture of mud and Spanish moss and then plastered. The sick house was once a slave cabin, of which there are several others on the Plantation. The schoolhouse is furnished with bench-type desks, notebooks, and slates, as it would have been when the children of overseers and yeomen farmers learned their lessons here. The schoolbooks date from the 1870s; notebooks contain French lessons. A cane-grinder and a sugar house recall a key process in sugar manufacturing that once was done on the plantation where the cane itself was raised.

Finally, the museum's collection of folk architecture preserves some of the non-farm buildings once familiar in rural Louisiana. A country church recalls similar structures all over the South. Three of the most common styles of rural house are also on display. The dogtrot house, with its front and rear porches and twin chimneys, is typical of north Louisiana (and much of the rest of the South). The Acadian or Creole house recalls the French-speaking settlers in the southern part of the state. An outside stairway leads to a second-floor room where part of the family slept. In the museum's shotgun house, the rooms are placed distinctively one behind the other. As the attentive visitor no doubt will notice, only the white-columned plantation house is missing. That is by design. Plantation houses (some very much in keeping with the romantic image of the Old South) still abound in Louisiana, and a few actually still are lived in by planters. The LSU Rural Life Museum preserves another rural South—that of both the ordinary people who supported life in the "Big House" and those who aspired to it.

AUDUBON STATE COMMEMORATIVE AREA *state 965 east of St. Francisville.* Receives its name from a short stay by artist John James

Audubon in 1821; includes colonial house, "Oakley," built in 1799.
THE COTTAGE PLANTATION U.S. 61 at Cottage Lane, St. Francisville. Complete early-nineteenth-century plantation with French Colonial house started in 1795.
DESTRAHAN PLANTATION River Road (state 48), Destrahan. A plantation originally devoted to growing indigo and sugar, built in 1787 and representative of area colonial architecture.
E. D. WHITE STATE COMMEMORATIVE AREA five miles north of Thibodaux on state highway 1. A park with the birthplace and home, built about 1790, of a U.S. Supreme Court justice who participated in rulings on the Sherman Antitrust Act in 1911.
FAUBOURG MARIGNY HISTORIC DISTRICT bounded by Esplanade Avenue, Press Street, St. Claude Avenue, and the Mississippi River, New Orleans. Many residences in the Creole, Greek Revival, Victorian, and Edwardian styles.
FORT JACKSON state 23, Buras. A bastioned brick pentagon begun in 1822, active in the Civil War, and used until 1920.
FORT JESUP STATE COMMEMORATIVE AREA state 6 northeast of Many. One original log building remaining of a United States military post established in 1822 on El Camino Real (San Antonio Trace), along with replica of officers' quarters and a museum.
FORT PIKE STATE COMMEMORATIVE AREA U.S. 90E north of New Orleans. Partially restored brick fort built 1819–1821, with historical exhibits on the War of 1812 and the Civil War.
FORT POLK MILITARY MUSEUM Building 917, South Carolina Avenue, Fort Polk. A museum with collections from World War II to the present.
GALLIER HALL 545 St. Charles Avenue, New Orleans. The 1850 Greek Revival New Orleans City Hall designed by James Gallier, Sr.
GALLIER HOUSE 1132 Royal Street, New Orleans. House built 1857–1860 with Renaissance Revival and local French elements, and a museum.
HISTORIC NEW ORLEANS COLLECTION 533 Royal Street, New Orleans. A museum of paintings, maps, and other articles related to Louisiana life, located in the 1792 Merieult House.
HOUMAS HOUSE River Road (state highway 942), Burnside. Greek Revival mansion built in 1840 onto late-eighteenth-century sections; the setting for several movies.
IMPERIAL CALCASIEU MUSEUM 204 W. Sallier Street, Lake Charles. Furnishings and other items from the Victorian period.
KENT HOUSE STATE COMMEMORATIVE AREA Bayou Rapides at Virginia Avenue, west of Alexandria. A country plantation built in 1796 with later additions, reflecting Creole influence; with gardens and antique furnishings.
LONGFELLOW-EVANGELINE STATE COMMEMORATIVE AREA state 31, St. Martinville. An Acadian house built in 1765; with a museum of Acadian crafts.

LOWER GARDEN DISTRICT bounded by Mississippi River, Phillips Street, Saint Charles Avenue, Annunciation Street, Race Street, and U.S. 90, New Orleans. Nineteenth-century residential and commercial buildings with park, canals, and fountains.

MADEWOOD PLANTATION HOUSE Bayou Lafourche facing state 308, Napoleonville. Greek Revival house, built 1840–1848; with antebellum fixtures and furnishings.

MAGNOLIA MOUND PLANTATION 2161 Nicholson Drive, Baton Rouge. Restored late-eighteenth-century house with Federal-period furnishings.

MANSFIELD BATTLE PARK state 175 southeast of Mansfield. Museum with Civil War artifacts on site of 1864 battle where Confederates stopped Union soldiers in Red River campaign.

MARKSVILLE STATE COMMEMORATIVE AREA state 5, Marksville. Museum on site of Indian mounds, earliest from the pre-Christian era; with artifacts from the mounds.

MARSTON HOUSE Bank Street, Clinton. An 1838 Greek Revival house used as a hospital during the Civil War; open by appointment.

MELROSE PLANTATION state highway 119 just east of junction with 493, Melrose. Several houses, oldest dating from 1830s and some with possibly African design, built by free blacks over several decades.

THE MYRTLES PLANTATION state 61, St. Francisville. Begun in 1796 by Gen. David Bradford, who led the Whiskey Rebellion in Pennsylvania; with antiques and furnishings of the early 1800s.

NATCHITOCHES HISTORIC DISTRICT bounded by College Avenue and Texas, Third, and Front streets, and including the Williams Avenue area east of Cane River-Lake, Natchitoches. In an area where French established fort in 1714; oldest permanent settlement in Louisiana, containing buildings from 1700s to 1900s.

OAK ALLEY PLANTATION Great River Road west of Vacherie. House built by French sugar planter 1837–1839 on site where early French settler had planted twenty-eight live oaks in rows—now leading up to Greek Revival house with twenty-eight Doric columns.

OLD STATE CAPITOL North Boulevard and River Road, Baton Rouge. Gothic Revival castle built in 1849, now housing art exhibits and visitors bureau.

OLD URSULINE CONVENT 1114 Chartres Street, New Orleans. Built in 1745 and one of the few buildings with authentic French architecture remaining in New Orleans.

PARLANGE PLANTATION junction of state 1 and 78, Mix. Built about 1750, one of the finest examples of the French Colonial "raised cottage" type of house.

PIONEER HERITAGE CENTER Louisiana State University in Shreveport, Shreveport. Authentic recreation of the pioneer culture of northwest Louisiana, 1830–1860.

PORT HUDSON BATTLEFIELD along U.S. 61, Port Hudson. Earthworks where free blacks and ex-slaves fought Confederate soldiers in 1863.

POVERTY POINT STATE COMMEMORATIVE AREA *state 557 north of Epps.* Unique mound and ridge complex of pre-Christian era, with museum containing artifacts from the site.

ROSEDOWN *state 10 north of St. Francisville.* An 1835 mansion with extensive gardens inspired by French style.

ST. CHARLES STREETCAR LINE *New Orleans.* Laid out in 1835 on the route on St. Charles Avenue to Carrollton; still operates with cars built in the 1920s.

ST. LOUIS CATHEDRAL *Jackson Square, New Orleans.* Begun in 1789 and enlarged in the mid-nineteenth century; still in use.

SHADOWS-ON-THE-TECHE *117 E. Main Street, New Iberia.* Greek Revival house built 1831–1834.

STATE CAPITOL *downtown Baton Rouge.* Built 1931–1932, a 450-foot-tall building inspired by Governor Huey P. Long; with murals in the foyer and an observation tower on top.

MAINE

FORT WESTERN MUSEUM Bowman Street, Augusta. The settlement of Maine in the seventeenth and eighteenth centuries owed much to the entrepreneurial and ecclesiastical imperialism of the Massachusetts Bay Colony. Recognizing the value of a settled frontier to the safety and economic well-being of the Puritan colony, church leaders and provincial officials encouraged the expansion of their "holy experiment" into the forested wilds of the Maine region. One of the earliest such settlements developed around Fort Western on the Kennebec River at present-day Augusta. Part of the old fortification still stands and testifies to Massachusetts' central role in the settlement of the nation's twenty-third state.

Fort Western dates back to 1754, but the site upon which it stands was first developed in the 1620s. Although the Massachusetts Bay Colony eventually dominated Maine much as it did present-day Massachusetts, the first to recognize the northern region's economic potential were residents of Plymouth. They needed income to repay debts incurred in their colonization venture, and trade with the Indians appeared the most likely source. In 1625, Plymouth's Edward Winslow headed an expedition up the Kennebec River and traded the Pilgrims' surplus corn for beaver pelts that they could market in Europe. This lucrative venture convinced the Pilgrim leaders to establish a permanent fur-trading post on the Kennebec, and in 1628 they obtained a patent to an area known as Cushnoc or Koussinoc. Profits from the new enterprise helped the Pilgrims pay off their debts by 1639. Interest in the Kennebec outpost declined thereafter, and in 1661 the colony sold its patent to a group of businessmen organized as the Proprietors of the Kennebec Purchase. The new patentees tried to revive regional fur-trading activity but ended up abandoning the post in 1669.

No attempt was made to reactivate the Kennebec land patent until 1749, when the original proprietors' heirs organized the Proprietors of the Kennebec Purchase from the Late Colony of New Plymouth. The Massachusetts Bay Colony had by that time absorbed both Plymouth and Maine, and the provincial government's commitment to expansion infected the new Kennebec proprietors as well. Plans were made to promote new settlement and develop the Kennebec Valley. As a first step, the proprietors, with support from Boston officials, decided to erect a trading post and fortification on the site of the Pilgrims' earlier outpost. One of the proprietors—Gershom Flagg, of Boston—supervised the construction, which began in July 1754 and lasted at least through the following November. A large garrison house was constructed with logs brought upriver from Fort Shirley (present-day Dresden). The two-story shingle-covered structure provided officers' quarters at each end and storage in the center. At the corners of the fort stood two log blockhouses, each twenty-four feet square, and two smaller watch boxes, each twelve feet square. A timber stockade or palisade enclosed the fort. The use of wood rather than stone in constructing the fortification departed from seventeenth-century practices and reflected both economic considerations and the need to lessen as quickly as possible potential settlers' insecurity about life on the frontier.

Fort Western was one of a series of British military posts erected in the Kennebec Valley to guard new settlements and block French and Indian attempts to take over the river. Others included Fort Richmond, built in 1719; Fort Nolde, erected at Phippsburg in 1734; Fort Shirley, completed in 1752; and Fort Halifax, constructed in 1754 and 1755. Although there were scattered incidents, the anticipated battles did not occur. In fact, Fort Western and its twenty soldiers were never attacked during the French and Indian War (1755–1763).

Fort Western's log garrison house

Once Quebec fell to the British in 1759 and the danger of attack faded, settlers began moving into the area around Fort Western. The fort functioned as the center of the emerging community. The first public religious service in the area was held there in 1763, as was the first marriage. There residents of the area read for the first time the Declaration of Independence, and the fort housed local town meetings as late as 1782.

The richest and most influential figure in the community during the early years was James Howard, the captain in charge of Fort Western through the 1760s. Howard acquired extensive land holdings by the early 1760s, and in 1763 he erected a "Great House" about a mile up the river. This, the first frame house in the area, testified to the wealth he and his family had accumulated through regional trade and commerce. When the Proprietors decided to close Fort Western in 1769, Howard added it and nine hundred acres of land to his holdings. The garrison was subsequently converted for family use and housed a trading post that served the growing community which later became part of Augusta, the capital of Maine.

The Howard family retained ownership of Fort Western for a number of years, but the historic structure eventually passed into other hands and in the late nineteenth century was converted into a tenement. In 1919, William Howard Gannett, one of Howard's descendants, purchased the still-standing garrison house, restored it, and reconstructed portions of the fort. He presented the historic property to the City of Augusta in 1922. The city maintains the property today and sponsors school programs, tours, and other activities that reflect the history of colonial Maine.

Fort Western's history reflects the process of settlement in the Maine region and the influence of Massachusetts on that process. The oldest pre-Revolutionary fort extant in the state, it provides a unique opportunity to learn about the history of colonial Maine.

FORT GEORGE STATE MEMORIAL *Wadsworth Street off Battle Avenue, Castine.* The Fort George State Memorial at Castine commemorates an era that brought independence to both the nation and the state. Occupied by the British during the Revolution and again during the War of 1812, the fort illustrates Maine's direct involvement in both of America's wars for independence. The experience during the War of 1812 proved crucial as well in the movement for Maine statehood, for the downeasters realized that they could no longer depend on the Massachusetts state government to protect their interests. Now administered as a state historic site, the fort provides an important link to this pivotal period in the history of both Maine and the nation.

Located on a peninsula at the head of Penobscot Bay, Castine is one of Maine's oldest and most historic communities. Its first European settler was Edward Ashley, an Englishman who established a trading post there in 1629. The following year the Plymouth Colony took control of Ashley's post, an early indication of Massachusetts' imperialistic tendencies. The French ousted the English by 1635 and established the community of Pentagoet. Although its degree of involvement and interest varied considerably, France's presence remained strong until defeat by the British in the French and Indian War in 1763. Recognizing the strategic as well as the economic advantages of controlling both the bay and the river, the English encouraged settlement in the Penobscot region in the decades prior to the American Revolution.

Castine was still a small village when the British occupied the peninsula in 1779 as part of a larger strategy to defeat colonial rebels. The British recognized that control of the Penobscot would insure access to the region's raw materials, provide a base for shipping operations, and help protect settlements in lower Canada. Consequently, on June 17, seven hundred forty British regulars arrived from Halifax under the command of General Francis McLean and took control from the local patriots. Two weeks later, on July 2, McLean directed construction of a fortification in the center of the peninsula. When the Massachusetts General Court received word of the British plans a few weeks later, the state Board of War hastily made plans to recapture Castine and organized an expedition of over a thousand militiamen and more than forty ships, the largest amphibious expedition of the American Revolution. Meanwhile, informed of the American plans, McLean speeded up construction of the fort and raised the walls to a height of eight feet. When the American convoy arrived on July 24, the fort was still inadequate, and the British were far outnumbered. Although the patriots clearly had the advantage, they failed to take the offensive because of inept leadership and conflicting strategies. Shelling continued until mid-August, when the arrival of British reinforcements shifted the odds against the Americans. In one of the worst naval disasters in American history, the entire Continental fleet was destroyed, captured, or scuttled—a disaster that cost Massachusetts 8.5 million dollars.

The English retained control over Castine through the rest of the war and continued to build and improve Fort George, named in honor of the King of England. Six cannon were in place when the Americans attacked in 1779, and another dozen were mounted during the next few years. Construction was completed as well on the timber-revetted outer walls, the four "arrowhead" bastions, the gun magazines, officers' quarters and barracks, and the deep moat and timber-revetted earthworks that encircled the entire fortification. By the end of the war and British evacuation in January 1784, Fort George stood as an impressive example of eighteenth-century military construction.

Unoccupied, Fort George deteriorated over the next three decades. When war erupted between England and the United States in 1812, Castine's strategic location again became important. The British occupied virtually all of Maine east of the Penobscot River in the summer and fall of 1814 and returned to Fort George in September. After making necessary repairs, they garrisoned the fort and mounted sixty cannon. Maine residents became incensed at the British presence, but the

Powder magazine at Fort George

Massachusetts government did not again finance an expedition to recapture the fort. Recognizing that the state was more concerned with protecting Boston, Maine's political leaders began discussing in earnest the possibility of seceding from Massachusetts and establishing a separate state. The immediate crisis eased shortly, for the Treaty of Ghent ended the war on December 24, 1814. News of the treaty reached Fort George in mid-February, and on April 25, 1815, the British abandoned the fort for a second and final time. The departure of the British eliminated the immediate threat to Maine's safety and welfare, but the movement for statehood gained momentum, culminating in admission to the Union in 1820 as the nation's twenty-third state.

Fort George was decommissioned in 1819 and again deteriorated. The British had destroyed some of the fort before their departure, and the residents of Castine dismantled other portions for building materials. The state finally acquired the property in 1940, but another twenty years passed before serious archeological and historical research was undertaken. By then, little but ruins remained. Now operated by the Maine State Park and Recreation Commission, the Fort George State Memorial includes the earthworks, two restored powder magazines, a restored bastion, and archeological evidence of the palisades, moat, gateway, and ramparts.

A number of other forts were erected in Maine beginning in the seventeenth century, and several have been preserved as state historic sites. The only representation of seventeenth-century fortifications is the reconstruction at Pemaquid's Fort William Henry. A stone tower illustrates military construction in 1692, when the garrison was originally erected. Fort William Henry was one of four that occupied the same site, dating back to 1630. The state maintains several examples of eighteenth-century forts as well. In addition to Fort George, visitors can view the earthworks of Fort Pownall (1759) at Stockton Springs and the breastworks at Fort O'Brien (1775) at Machiasport. The oldest original wooden blockhouse in the United States still stands at Winslow. Part of Fort Halifax, the structure dates from 1754–55. Nineteenth-century forts include Fort Edgecomb (1808) at North Edgecomb, Fort Kent (1839) at Fort Kent, Fort Knox (1844) at Prospect, Fort McClary (1846) at Kittery Point, and Fort Popham (1861) at Popham Beach. All of these fort sites have significance for the state's history, but only Fort George was directly involved in the struggle for independence in late eighteenth- and early nineteenth-century Maine.

MAINE MARITIME MUSEUM *963 Washington Street, Bath.* The history of shipbuilding in Maine dates back to 1607, but the peak of activity did not come until the nineteenth century, when the industry played an integral role in the state's economic growth and development. During the "Great Age of Sail," Maine ranked as one of the nation's leading centers for the manufacture of large wooden sailing ships. Located at Bath—the oldest continuously shipbuilding city in the country—the Maine

Maritime Museum has carefully preserved one of the leading shipyards of that era, Percy and Small, and sponsors a variety of exhibits and programs that tell the story of Maine's maritime culture.

The first European settlers in present-day Maine were also the region's first shipbuilders. Under the sponsorship of the Council for New England, Sir John Popham established a colony at the mouth of the Sagadahoc River in 1607. Although early explorers often carried pre-fabricated boats with them for assembling at their destinations, the settlers of Popham's colony actually constructed vessels of native timber. Using tools and other supplies they had brought with them, ship carpenters built at least one small shallop or workboat and a thirty-ton pinnace during the colony's short life. The framing for the pinnace was completed during the fall of 1607, and the colonists used the finished ship to return to England the following spring. Named the *Virginia of Sagadahoc,* the single-decked, square-sterned sailing vessel carried a single-masted fore-and-aft rig appropriate for coastwise trade in the New World. Although plans for such trade fell through and the entire project collapsed in 1608, the colony had demonstrated clearly the feasibility of colonial boat- and shipbuilding.

Subsequent settlements in Maine's Kennebec region followed the Popham Colony's lead, and by the time of the American Revolution the shipbuilding industry was well established in small coastal towns like Topsham and Georgetown. Although perhaps somewhat refined over subsequent decades, the basic methods and routines established in the industry during that period remained little changed for nearly a century and a half, until the era of wooden shipbuilding ended in the Kennebec region in 1923. Also constant through this era was the focus of construction activity on the town of Bath. Founded in the eighteenth century, Bath became the region's and indeed the state's leading shipbuilding center during the nineteenth-century heyday of the great wooden sailing ships. Even after the day of the clipper ship ended and other shipbuilding centers abandoned the wooden ship, the town's yards continued to produce impressive new vessels that competed successfully with modern steam-powered and steel vessels.

One of Bath's leading shipbuilding firms was Percy and Small. Captain Samuel R. Percy and Frank A. Small formed their partnership in 1894 and took over the offices of Adams and Hitchcock, an older firm that had been dissolved in 1884 upon the death of one of the partners. Percy and Small launched their first ship, the *Charles P. Notman,* in late August of 1894. The four-masted schooner had a capacity of 1,518 gross tons and was constructed in the B. W. and H. F. Morse yard, as were two subsequent Percy and Small vessels. Then in 1897 the partners purchased an old shipyard formerly owned by Daniel Orrin Blaidsell. Their first project in their own yard was the *Alice E. Clark,* a four-masted schooner completed in January 1898. Percy and Small laid forty-six hulls before closing the shipyard in 1920. While some were built for their

Small Craft Center's Restorationshop

own use, the majority were constructed under contract with other shipping firms. A typical construction project began between March and May in order to avoid work in the harsh winter weather. Although the average project was completed in seven or eight months, some took nearly two years. Size had some bearing on construction time, but shipbuilders also encountered delays in the delivery of materials and other logistical problems that slowed down work. In addition to new construction, Percy and Small also repaired vessels, both their own and others. This included routine repair and maintenance, some conversion work, and repairs of damage caused by collison and fire.

Several of the Percy and Small vessels are of particular interest. In 1899 the firm constructed the *M. D. Cressy,* the second five-master launched at Bath and, at 2,114 gross tons, Percy and Small's first big schooner. The following year, work was completed on the firm's eighth ship, the *Eleanor A. Percy,* named for Percy's daughter. This massive six-master was the largest schooner in the world, and its construction took up most of the firm's Bath shipyard, forcing them to use space at the nearby Reed and McDonald yards. The *Eleanor A. Percy* was one of only nine wooden six-masted schooners built on the east coast. All nine were constructed in Maine, seven by Percy and Small. The last and the greatest was the *Wyoming,* a 3,730-ton vessel completed in the firm's shipyard in 1909. It was reportedly the largest wooden sailing vessel in commercial service in the United States. The *Wyoming* project came, however, at a time when business was down, and the firm did not build another schooner until 1912. The situation did not improve by the end of the decade, and in 1920 Percy and Small completed their last vessel, the four-masted *Cecilia Cohen.* This ship was also the last commercial schooner built at Bath, bringing to a close the era of the great wooden sailing ships.

Percy and Small was among many Bath shipbuilding firms, but it is the only one whose shipyards have been preserved as they were during the wooden-ship days. Still standing are the mould loft, an oakum shop, a paint and trunnel shop, a miller and joiner shop, the North Ways, and other structures essential to shipbuilding and repair. Credit for preserving this unique historic site belongs to the Maine Maritime Museum. Organized in 1962 as the Maine Research Society of Bath, the museum has taken the lead in efforts to preserve and document the state's maritime heritage. Another example of this organization's work is the preservation of the *Seguin,* constructed on the Kennebec River in 1884 and now the oldest registered wooden steam tug in the nation. In addition, the Maine Maritime Museum exhibits its extensive maritime collections at the Sewall House, an 1844 mansion that stands at 963 Washington Street, and at its Winter Street Center, a Gothic Revival church erected in the 1840s at 880 Washington Street. It also operates the Apprenticeshop, which offers programs in half-modeling, boatbuilding, and seamanship, and the Small Craft Center–Restorationshop, which produces replicas of traditional craft.

Shipping and shipbuilding played essential roles in Maine's settlement and economic development. Located in Bath, the oldest continuous shipbuilding center in the state, the Maine Maritime Museum ably preserves that history and the maritime culture of the Kennebec region.

ALLIE RYAN MARITIME COLLECTION *Marine Maritime Academy, Castine.* Collections of maritime paintings, prints, and memorabilia with special focus on steamboating. Operated jointly by the Marine Maritime Academy and the Maine State Museum.

ARNOLD TRAIL *from Fort Popham north and west to Canadian border at Coburn Gore.* Traces the route taken by Benedict Arnold and men in 1775 in their march to Quebec; with interpretive panels at Popham, Hallowell, Skowhegan, Solon, Moscow, Stratton, Sarampus, Chain of Ponds, and Coburn Gore.

ASHLAND LOGGING MUSEUM *Ashland.* Machinery and tools of old logging industry in a replica of an early logging camp.

BATES MUSEUM *Hinckley Home–School–Farm, Hinckley.* Indian and pioneer relics and antique farming equipment.

BLAINE HOUSE *Capitol and State streets, Augusta.* House built about 1830, home of James G. Blaine, national political leader in the late 1800s.

BOOTHBAY THEATRE MUSEUM *Corey Lane, Boothbay.* Playbills, stage furniture, costumes, and other material related to theater from the 1700s to present.

BOWDOIN COLLEGE MUSEUM OF ART *Walker   Art   Building,*

Brunswick. Includes American art with Winslow Homer memorabilia and art from ancient times to the present.

BRIDGTON HISTORICAL SOCIETY AND MUSEUM *Gibbs Avenue, Bridgton.* Items from the lumber and textile industries and photos and documents from rural New England of the 1700s and 1800s.

CAMDEN–ROCKPORT HISTORICAL SOCIETY *Camden.* History of Maine, including information on numerous local houses from the 1700s and 1800s.

COLBY COLLEGE MUSEUM OF ART *Mayflower Hill, Waterville.* Winslow Homer watercolors, American folk art, and wide selection of other American art.

EAGLE ISLAND *off Harpswell.* Residence and guest cottage of Arctic explorer Robert E. Peary; with interpretive panels.

FARNSWORTH LIBRARY AND ART MUSEUM *19 Elm Street, Rockland.* Historical materials on Maine as well as continental decorative arts and art from America and Asia.

FORT HALIFAX MEMORIAL *Winslow.* Oldest extant blockhouse in the United States, constructed in 1754 to protect settlers; where Benedict Arnold stayed on his expedition to Quebec in 1775.

FORT McCLARY MEMORIAL *Kittery Point.* Ruins of a fort begun in 1800s and never completed; includes a museum. Nearby, the 1682 William Pepperell House and the 1662 John Bray house.

FRYEBURG FAIR FARM MUSEUM *164 Main Street, Fryeburg.* Equipment and tools used in early agriculture.

ISLESFORD MUSEUM *Acadia National Park, Bar Harbor.* Exhibits from Stone Age inhabitation and colonial periods of the French and English, and maritime artifacts.

KATAHDIN IRON WORKS *on gravel road six miles off state 11, five miles north of Brownville Junction.* Restored blast furnace and charcoal kiln at site of a former iron works.

KENNEBUNKPORT HISTORICAL SOCIETY *North Street, Kennebunkport.* Maritime collection, local crafts, and art.

MAINE HISTORICAL SOCIETY MUSEUM *485 Congress Street, Portland.* Artifacts from Maine history, including art, photos, furniture, and decorative arts.

MAINE STATE MUSEUM *Augusta.* Exhibits on Maine, natural history, and technology. Modern museum building located adjacent to the Maine State House.

MONHEGAN LIGHTHOUSE *Monhegan.* An 1822 lighthouse with a museum of fishing, lobster-trapping gear, and artifacts of local history.

MONTPELIER *Montpelier Memorial Park, Thomaston.* Replica of a 1794 Federal house with furnishings, decorative arts, and other items from the family of General Henry Knox, first United States Secretary of War.

MUSIC MUSEUM *18 High Street, Wiscasset.* Player pianos, crank organs, and other musical machines.

NEW SWEDEN HISTORICAL MUSEUM *state 161, New Sweden.* Furnishings, textile and farm equipment, photos, and portraits of Swedish immigrants in the 1800s.

PENOBSCOT MARINE MUSEUM *Church Street, Searsport.* Ship models, shipbuilding tools, navigation instruments, log books, whaling items, and other gear of the sea.

PHILLIPS HISTORICAL SOCIETY MUSEUM *Pleasant Street, Phillips.* Relics from railroads, households, farms, and schoolrooms of the past.

PORTLAND MUSEUM OF ART *111 High Street, Portland.* American painting, sculpture, and decorative arts, and Japanese prints and swords.

REDINGTON MUSEUM *64 Silver Street, Waterville.* Household items, weapons, photos, and portraits from the 1800s, as well as an apothecary museum.

ROOSEVELT CAMPOBELLO INTERNATIONAL PARK *Lubec.* Summer home of President Franklin Roosevelt, built in 1897; with original family furniture and Roosevelt items.

SEASHORE TROLLEY MUSEUM *Log Cabin Road, Kennebunkport.* Cars, coaches, buses, locomotives, freight cars, and a demonstration railway with a two-mile ride and short trolley-car ride.

SHAKER MUSEUM *Sabbathday Lake, Poland Spring.* Furniture, folk art, and home and farm implements of a nineteenth-century religious community.

SHORE VILLAGE MUSEUM *104 Limerock Street, Rockland.* Weapons, uniforms, and Coast Guard items, including foghorns and lights.

SONGO LOCK *midway between Long Lake and Sebago Lake on the Songo River, next to Sebago Lake State Park, Naples.* Built in 1830, widened in 1911, and still in use.

STEAM ERA RAILROADIANA EXHIBIT AND MUSEUM *Bethel.* Models, pictures, and artifacts of railroading since 1846.

UNIVERSITY OF MAINE ANTHROPOLOGY MUSEUM, *University of Maine, Orono.* Materials on peoples from the northeastern woodlands as well as many other parts of the world.

UNIVERSITY OF MAINE AT ORONO ART GALLERIES *Carnegie Hall, Orono.* Maine art from the past and the present; contemporary American art and graphics.

WILSON MUSEUM *Perkins Street, Castine.* Early tools and artifacts from paleolithic times to the Bronze and Iron ages, Indian artifacts from North and Central America, and local history.

YARMOUTH HISTORICAL SOCIETY *Merrill Memorial Library Building, Yarmouth.* Items from shipbuilding industry, shells, and dolls.

YORK INSTITUTE MUSEUM *375 Main Street, Saco.* Fine arts and decorative arts from the Colonial period.

MARYLAND

HISTORIC ANNAPOLIS Annapolis. As the British settled North America in the seventeenth century, they brought with them many of the tastes and manners and standards of belief and behavior that they had known back home. Though some of them sought greater religious freedom and a wider field for their earthly ambitions, not many wanted to become anything other than what they already were: Englishmen; freer and richer perhaps, but still Englishmen. This conviction persisted among their American-born descendents well past the middle of the eighteenth century. It seemed especially prevalent in the tidewater regions of the Chesapeake colonies, where the image and some of the reality of English country life and landed wealth so easily reproduced itself. The world that these American Englishmen built—or what remains of it today— reminds us of what some of those standards and tastes were. One of the best examples is Colonial Williamsburg in Virginia; another is the National Historic Landmark District of Annapolis in Maryland.

Today Annapolis is probably best known in the rest of the country as the home of the United States Naval Academy; indeed, the two are essentially synonymous. To Marylanders it is their state capital. But it is also a historic enclave of seventeenth- and eighteenth-century houses and public buildings and an excellent example of historic preservation applied to a small city. The site was first settled in 1649 by discontented Puritans who migrated from Virginia to the mouth of the Severn River, but it did not become another dour Massachusetts Bay. The surrounding country was too rich in natural resources, and the prosperity of the planters and merchants who soon populated it in time made Annapolis the great seaport of colonial Maryland. It went at first by other names: Proctor's Landing, Arrundell Towne, Severn, and Anne Arundel Towne. In 1695 it was renamed "Annapolis" after Princess Anne, the Protestant daughter of England's deposed Catholic king, James II. The year before, Francis Nicholson, Maryland's royal governor, had moved the capital from St. Mary's to this more convenient site farther up the Chesapeake Bay, thus securing its political prominence. Prosperity and culture soon flourished.

Annapolis was never a large place, with the happy result years later of leaving its old historic buildings concentrated in a small area. Departing from the then current grid style of town plan, Nicholson laid out his new provincial seat according to a more imaginative baroque plan with streets radiating from two large circles. The effect was charming, if not exactly symmetrical. It remains the dominant organizational feature today. The larger of the two circles was called Public Circle (later renamed State Circle) and occupied a small rise commanding the otherwise flat townsite. It has seen several "government houses." The first, begun in 1696, was destroyed by fire eight years later. Its replacement lasted to the early 1770s, when the cornerstone for the third statehouse, where the Maryland legislature still meets, was laid. Two annexes were added in the nineteenth century but were replaced between 1902 and 1906 by the Colonial Revival additions that exist today. The Treasury, built between 1734 and 1737, still stands as well. The circle also once held an armory, the Anne Arundel County Courthouse, and King William's School, a grammar school that became a part of St. John's College.

Directly west of Public Circle lay Church Circle (whose name has not changed), the site of St. Anne's Church, the principal parish church of the established Anglican church in Maryland. Though at first a modest one-story building, it counted among its regular worshippers the royal governor and such luminaries as Daniel Dulany, a self-made planter, politician, and gentleman who served on its vestry. The original colonial church stood until 1775. The second St. Anne's, not completed until 1792, burned in 1848. The present building dates from 1859 and incorporates some of the second building's walls and tower. It is still an active Episcopal church. The city plan also called for a public market place, which over the years occupied several different sites. It 1784 it moved to its present location by the site of the dock. The building dates from 1858 and was saved from demolition in 1968.

Within Annapolis' charming plan, the colony's rich and ambitious in time built their houses. Between the early 1700s when Ebenizer Cook described a very unpretentious Annapolis in *The Sot Weed Factor* and the American Revolution, the little city was transformed by the elegant Palladian and Neo-Classical houses of Maryland's rising planters, merchants, and politicans. Like much from that era, they were as a matter of course sturdy, well crafted, and clearly built to last. Today many are still in private hands and, as lived-in houses, serve the purpose they were built for. Several have been saved and restored and, as historic house museums, are open regularly to the public. Probably the most

Annapolis harbor

famous is the William Paca house and its adjacent gardens, an excellent example of preservation in action.

A signer of the Declaration of Independence and third governer of Maryland, Paca was an Annapolis grandee whose house befit his stature. He built it between 1763 and 1765, and the result was an elegant thirty-room Georgian mansion with dependencies that was the first of its kind in Annapolis. It overlooked an exquisite formal garden, designed by Paca and probably inspired by those he had seen in England. Within the garden walls were a wide variety of ornamental plants, plus a pond, canal, springhouse, and domed classical pavilion topped with a statue of Mercury. Sadly it was all nearly lost. During the nineteenth century the mansion became a boarding house, and early in the twentieth century a 200-room hotel was built on the site. Along with a parking lot and bus station the hotel engulfed the house and completely obliterated the once glorious garden. When in 1965 the hotel was due for demolition and replacement by a high-rise building, Historic Annapolis, Inc. mounted a campaign to purchase and restore the house and arranged for the state of Maryland to acquire and rehabilitate the garden. Though efforts continue to furnish the interior, today the house and grounds have been returned to a condition that Paca himself would no doubt be proud of.

There are other famous Annapolis houses—the Hammond-Harwood house and the Chase-Lloyd house among them—that likewise recall the grace and opulence of eighteenth-century Annapolis. But it is their preservation together, within a compact historic district, that makes it possible truly to sense what this small provincial city was like at its political and cultural zenith. It then represented a delicate reproduction of eighteenth-century England, adapted no more than necessary to local conditions.

The local conditions however, especially after the American Revolution, changed considerably. And as Annapolis was summoned to new purposes, the old ones known to William Paca and Daniel Dulany could not endure, except in brick and mortar, fine wood-work, and elegant design. Today much of that has been carefully preserved in the historic district where, it is also important to remember, people continue to live and work. "A museum without walls," as it is described by Historic Annapolis, Inc., Annapolis is as alive today as it was in Paca's time, and preserved so that Paca himself might recognize it. Though the sails that still picturesquely ornament the harbor and can be seen from several streets now belong to pleasure craft and not to stout British bottoms bound for London laden with hogsheads of tobacco, the description of Annapolis by a young Englishman, William Eddis, is as fitting today as when he wrote it in 1769:

> The court-house, situated on an eminence at the back of town, commands a variety of views highly interesting; the entrance of the Severn, the majestic Chesapeake, the eastern shore of Maryland, being all united in one resplendent assemblage. Vessels of various sizes

and figures are continually floating before the eye; which, while they add to the beauty of the scene, excite ideas of the most pleasing nature.

FORT McHENRY NATIONAL MONUMENT AND HISTORIC SHRINE *Locust Point, at east end of Fort Avenue, Baltimore.* National anthems should be inspiring songs. Like religious hymns, they should remind the singer and the listener of devotion owed to something beyond, larger than, himself. Some have origins deep in a particular culture. Others are inspired by a particular historical event, itself somehow memorable. "The Star Spangled Banner" is clearly one of these. At once rousing and reverent, it serves admirably as America's anthem—no matter how difficult it may be to sing. The center of events that inspired it, Fort McHenry, near Baltimore, is preserved today as a national monument. To visit it is to visit one of America's true historic shrines.

It is also to visit a historic place that played an important part in the War of 1812 and that records, in its earthworks, masonry, and batteries, a part of the story of American national defense. Over the two centuries since independence, the means of national defense have changed with the changing understanding of America's role in the world and with the technology of warfare itself. In the beginning, defense meant a militia in the "minute-man" tradition of civilian soldiers. Though professional leadership was necessary, a large standing army was thought to endanger as much as to protect American liberties, and for years the country got along without one. A navy built to defend a long coastline and fortifications to guard key ports and harbors largely completed the early American defense establishment. Isolated from potential enemies by vast oceans, enjoying as years went by the friendship of Britain and her powerful Royal Navy, and blessed with weak and friendly neighbors, America long enjoyed great security at little effort. Only at the close of the nineteenth century did Americans project their power through a true ocean navy and begin to take on larger world responsibilities. In the twentieth century, the new age of air power and nuclear weapons, and involvement in two world wars and the troubled peace that followed, brought new meaning and urgency to the idea of national defense. From today's perspective, the needs and means of defense in the first decades of America's history seem especially remote.

Fort McHenry graphically illustrates what they were. It is one of the finest surviving examples of the earliest system of seacoast fortifications in America. It is also one of the few such fortifications that was ever tested under fire—the same fire that inspired Francis Scott Key to write the words for "The Star Spangled Banner" and thus propel Fort McHenry truly into history. Positioned on Whetstone Point on the Baltimore Peninsula, it was designed to protect the approaches to the city from the Patapsco River and Chesapeake Bay. There had been a fortification here during the Revolution, but not until 1794 with the renewal of war in Europe and growing concern over coastal defense in America, was

*Parade ground
and flag pole*

construction on the present fort begun. The federal government appropriated the money ($4,225); the state of Maryland supplied the land.

The result, after several years of work, was a pentagonal masonry
fort with outer batteries. It is a good example of the "star-fort" design
common among European fixed fortification in the eighteenth century.
Its designer, John Jacob Ulrich Rivardi, was a Frenchman, as were many
of the military engineers who served the young republic. The fort was
named for native Marylander James McHenry, once an aide to George
Washington and, from 1796 to 1800, Secretary of War in the cabinet of
President John Adams. Bastions (the points of the "star") protruded
from each corner of the central five-sided enclosure, which contained
a parade, soldiers' and officers' quarters, powder magazine, and underground bombproofs. Later additions included an arch over the sally
port, the cells, the guardhouses, and a V-shaped outwork, known as a
ravelin, outside the walls that protected the sally port. The waterfront
batteries facing the Patapsco River were also outside the walls. The fort
itself was originally encircled by a dry moat, no longer present.

It was all put to the test for the first and last time on September 13
and 14, 1814. Again at war with Britain, this time over questions of
neutral rights and the impressment of American sailors, Americans found
themselves facing an invasion force of some twenty British warships and

several thousand veteran troops, among them "Wellington's Invincibles," fresh from victories over Napoleon on the Continent. The British campaigns in the Chesapeake area had begun gloriously just a month before with the capture and burning of Washington, D.C. Their attention then turned to the larger and commercially more important city of Baltimore. A large British force landed on September 12 at North Point, below Fort McHenry, and began to move toward the city. Though clashing with American troops, they reached within two miles of the city. The next morning the British fleet, anchored in the Patapsco River, began its attempt to reduce Fort McHenry, bombarding it with rockets and explosive mortar shells from aptly named vessels: *Terror, Meteor, Aetna, Devastation, Volcano*. But American resistance was stiffer than it had been at Washington. When early on the morning of September 14 an attempt by sailors and Royal Marines to penetrate the Ferry Branch (a channel of the river on Baltimore's vulnerable south side) was discovered and beaten off, the battle was decided. The river approach blocked, the British withdrew their land forces, who, sadly for them, were destined for a harsher fate several months later at New Orleans.

Fort McHenry—target of a twenty-five hour bombardment of 1,500 to 1,800 shells—had passed the only test it would ever have. The garrison had been stationed mainly in the outerworks, which probably helped keep casualties so low: only four Americans were killed and twenty-four wounded. Meantime, its great forty-two-by-thirty-foot battle flag flew bravely. The man who immortalized that banner (now displayed at the Smithsonian Institution in Washington, D.C.) and Fort McHenry with it was Francis Scott Key, a young Baltimore lawyer then held on a British warship where he was negotating the release of an American prisoner. Inspired on seeing that the fort had not fallen after such a bombardment, he wrote a first version of the familiar words on the back of a letter. Later revised and printed in handbill form, it was soon set to a tune it would keep ever after, "To Anacreon in Heaven"—then, ironically, an English popular song.

Fort McHenry, though never again called up to defend Baltimore, served in other roles for many years to come. During the Civil War its cells housed Confederate prisoners; it was used for a time by the Immigration Service; in World War I it became an army hospital. But its single great moment was past—and its place in history already secured. It was first established as a national park in 1925; the "Star Spangled Banner" became the national anthem six years later.

CHESAPEAKE & OHIO CANAL NATIONAL HISTORICAL PARK

Potomac. Maryland is an oddly shaped state. Its boundaries with Pennsylvania and Delaware are neat, straight, and man-made. But nearly everywhere else, water divides and defines it. That great arm of the Atlantic Ocean, the Chesapeake Bay, separates the Eastern Shore from the rest of the state; the meandering Potomac River marks the line between Maryland and its southern neighbors, Virginia and West Vir-

ginia. From the windswept beaches of Assateague Island to her westernmost mountains in Garrett County is a distance of over 250 miles, but
at two points Maryland is less than ten miles wide. Maryland's history
follows its geography in this respect especially: the settled and refined
eighteenth-century civilization of Annapolis and the Chesapeake shared
little with the mines and mountain farms to the west.

After American independence, the new nation did not long remain
a string of seaboard settlements. Indeed, westward expansion soon
became the great national preoccupation and remained so through the
end of the nineteenth century. How to link that ever growing new West
with the older East therefore also became an urgent question. The first
great obstacle was the Appalachian Mountain chain, which in the days
of travel by horseback and horsedrawn wagon made east-west travel
arduous and transportation for heavy commodities very expensive. Before
steam-powered railways finally solved the overland problem, Americans looked to water-borne alternatives where they could. They improved
river beds and dug canals. One of the most famous was the Chesapeake
and Ohio Canal, most of which lies on the Maryland bank of the Potomac River and is today preserved as a national historical park.

Because at Harpers Ferry it offers one of the few water-level gateways through the mountains, the Potomac River had long attracted the
attention of enterprising men who sensed the need for improved east-
west transportation. George Washington himself was an early promoter
of river and canal transportation up the Potomac Valley. In 1785 he
became the first president of the Patowmack Company, whose purpose
was to make the river navigable as far as Cumberland, Maryland. Though
Washington resigned on becoming the first president of the United States,
the company did by the early 1800s complete a number of projects that
improved the existing river channel. Between Georgetown and Harpers
Ferry five short skirting canals with locks bypassed falls and rapids,

*Along the
canal towpath*

including the Great Falls of the Potomac. But traffic was still hampered by frequently low water, and something more ambitious was clearly called for.

The result was the Chesapeake and Ohio Canal. It consisted not merely of river improvements but of a separate canal channel (entirely on the Maryland side of the Potomac), complete with locks to lift it from sea level at Georgetown to 605 feet at Cumberland and aqueducts to carry it over several tributaries of the Potomac. In addition, there were hundreds of culverts allowing roads and streams to pass underneath, plus seven dams and a number of waste weirs to supply water to the canal and control its level. Perhaps most remarkable, given the technology of that age, was a 3,117-foot tunnel that let the canal pass under a mountain. The canal had a width of fifty to sixty feet at the surface (thirty to forty feet on the bottom) and was built to have a minimum depth of six feet. The locks were nearly a hundred feet long and fifteen feet wide, safely accommodating typical barges of the day. The barges were unpowered and had to be pulled. Thus, along the canal's full length ran a towpath, where mules moved the commerce of the nation at a leisurely pace.

It was an impressive engineering feat, but as a business enterprise the canal was trouble-plagued from the beginning. When construction began, on Independence Day, 1828, George Washington of course was long dead. But his successor several times removed, President John Quincy Adams, made the short trip from Washington to Georgetown to turn the first shovel and speak on the large future the canal portended. Ironically, on that very same day, July 4, 1928, construction was also beginning thirty-five miles north, in Baltimore, on the Baltimore and Ohio Railroad. The "B & O," as it would come to be known, had the same goal as the "C & O" canal: Cumberland, Maryland, and beyond that the rich lands of the Ohio Valley. (In time, there would also be a "C & O" Railroad, connecting the Tidewater with the Ohio Valley, over a more southerly route through Virginia and West Virginia.) What followed was a race of sorts, though in the end it probably mattered less who got to Cumberland first than the kind of service each means offered to shippers and travelers. By the time it finally did get there, the attractions of the canal were much diminished.

By later standards, construction of both the C & O Canal and the B & O Railroad was hardly breakneck, but problems on the canal especially abounded. It required, in addition to the shoveling of many tons of dirt, much skilled labor, which in the rural Maryland and Virginia of that day was not easy to find. The company therefore turned to contract immigrant labor from Britain, Ireland, Germany, and the Netherlands and soon built up the pool of masons, stonecutters, carpenters, and miners (Welsh miners dug the Paw Paw Tunnel) needed for such a project. Working conditions, typical of that age, were harsh, and unrest among laborers (many of whom brought from home old prejudices and rivalries) was not unusual. On occasion there were actual riots. The land itself seemed to throw up obstacles as slate and gravel, undetected by the geological surveys of the time, challenged the energy of the excavators and drained the resources of the company. And the lumber, building stores, and lime for concrete, needed once the ditch was dug, often proved scarce and costly.

But during construction, as later during actual operations, it was competition with the railroad that hurt the C & O most. The B & O proved very aggressive in securing land titles along the proposed right-of-way. One dispute, over rights to the narrow gorge above Point of Rocks, resulted in a bitter court struggle that consumed four years. The canal did not reach Harpers Ferry until November 1833, which was still a year ahead of the railroad, and it opened a section at a time as each was completed. But the railroad beat the financially embattled canal to Cumberland by a full eight years and thence built on into the Ohio Valley. The canal finally reached Cumberland in 1850, and it went no further. Ahead of it, however, stretched years of useful service, if not the true success its planners once foresaw. Through its locks and down its placid channels, the coal, grain, flour, and lumber of western Maryland floated down to Washington. Though the system was nearly ruined by the great flood that swept the Potomac Valley in 1889, repairs were made and the mules continued to plod the towpaths until 1924.

Today much of the canal and its towpath remain, testimony to a major engineering accomplishment and to an idea obsolete almost from its inception. A walk along a short section or a hike over its entire length can suggest for the imaginative visitor earlier times when at least some of the nation's commerce leisurely passed this way. It can also suggest the great effort that men once invested in bridging the mountain barrier. To link the Chesapeake Bay with the Ohio Valley once was thought an undertaking of epic proportion, with the wealth of the American interior the prize. A canal would bind the West to the nation and the nation together. But that job truly belonged to the railroads. So for years the motto of the B & O Railroad, that nemesis of the C & O Canal, proudly maintained: "Linking Thirteen Great States With the Nation." The canal, as fate would have it, never escaped the oddly shaped state of Maryland.

ANTIETAM NATIONAL BATTLEFIELD Sharpsburg. Site of the 1862 Civil War battle; with driving tour, visitor center, and cemetery.
BALTIMORE SEAPORT AND MARITIME MUSEUM Pier 4, Pratt Street, Baltimore. A World War II American submarine and a lightship that houses the museum; collection of maritime artifacts.
BALTIMORE STREETCAR MUSEUM 1901 Falls Road, Baltimore. Contains fourteen streetcars, including two horse-drawn, and provides streetcar rides.
CARROLL MANSION 800 E. Lombard Street, Baltimore. Restored Fed-

eral house built in 1811–1812; museum furnished with period decorative arts.

CATOCTIN FURNACE Cunningham Falls State Park, Thurmont. Late-eighteenth- to early-twentieth-century iron furnace ruins.

CHASE-LLOYD HOUSE 22 Maryland Avenue, Annapolis. Colonial Georgian townhouse built 1769–1774 for Samuel Chase, signer of Declaration of Independence. Privately owned.

CHESTERTOWN HISTORIC DISTRICT   Chestertown. Eighteenth-century residential area with about fifty Georgian and Federal houses.

CLARA BARTON NATIONAL HISTORIC SITE 5801 Oxford Road, Glen Echo. An 1890 clapboard house with an interior like that of a Mississippi steamboat; home of the woman who helped found the American Red Cross.

EMERSON BROMO-SELTZER TOWER 312–318 Lombard Street, Baltimore. A 1911 building inspired by the Palazzo Vecchio in Florence, Italy; constructed for a drug company.

FORT FREDERICK Fort Frederick State Park, Big Pool. Partially restored French and Indian War fortification with living history programs in the summer.

FREDERICK HISTORIC DISTRICT two blocks east and three blocks west of Market Street from South Street to Seventh Street, Frederick. Variety of nineteenth-century residences and business structures; where Francis Scott Key and Roger Brooke Taney once lived.

GATHLAND STATE PARK Gapland. Home of George Alfred Townsend, Civil War correspondent; with several buildings erected 1885 and later.

HAMMOND-HARWOOD HOUSE 19 Maryland Avenue, Annapolis. A 1774 Georgian dwelling with eighteenth-century furnishings and art.

HANCOCK'S RESOLUTION Bayside Beach Road east of Pasadena. Begun before 1700, a rare example of the first Chesapeake Bay farmhouses built in southern Maryland. Privately owned.

JONATHAN HAGER HOUSE AND MUSEUM 19 Key Street, Hagerstown. Museum with eighteenth-century furnishings and other items, housed in the 1740 house of Johathan Hager, founder of Hagerstown.

LOVELY LANE MUSEUM 220 St. Paul Street, Baltimore. Items related to Methodist history, including artifacts from the conference of 1784 establishing the Methodist Church in America (present church building dates from 1884–1887).

MOUNT CLARE MANSION AND MUSEUM Carroll Park, Baltimore. Georgian mansion built about 1763; served as Union headquarters during Civil War. Eighteenth-century items in museum.

MOUNT VERNON PLACE HISTORIC DISTRICT Mount Vernon Place and Washington Place, Baltimore. Nineteenth-century residential district studded with houses designed by famous architects and including a 165-foot-high column topped by statue of George Washington.

NATIONAL COLONIAL FARM 3400 Bryan Point Road, Accokeek. An agriculture museum with outdoor exhibits showing colonial farming practices.

OLD BOHEMIA HISTORICAL SOCIETY Warwick. Museum of furniture, church, and farm items in a building begun in 1792 on the site of an early Jesuit mission.

PEALE MUSEUM 225 Holliday Street, Baltimore. Items related to history of Baltimore, including art of the Peale family; in an 1814 building that was the first museum building in the United States.

PISCATAWAY PARK East 5210 Indian Head Highway, Oxon Hill. On site of large Piscataway village used until 1620; preserves view of Mount Vernon across the Potomac.

POINT LOOKOUT STATE PARK state 5 south of St. Mary's City. On the southernmost tip of the western shore; the site of a Civil War hospital and Union prison camp.

ST. MARY'S CITY. Site of the first permanent settlement under the Calvert family and the first capital of Maryland; tours, exhibits, and living history programs.

SETON HALL HISTORIC DISTRICT bounded by Pennsylvania Avenue and Franklin, Utah, McCulloh, and Orchard streets, Baltimore. Variety of architecture from early to mid-nineteenth century, including St. Mary's Seminary, where Elizabeth Ann Seton founded Sisters of Charity.

SMALLWOOD STATE PARK state 224 near Rison. Restored home, furnished with seventeenth- and eighteenth-century items, of Revolutionary War soldier and Maryland governor William Smallwood.

SOUTH MOUNTAIN NATURAL ENVIRONMENT AREA between Sharpsburg, Burkittsville, Bolivar, and Boonsboro along state 67 and 17 and U.S. 40A. A twelve-mile driving tour of the scattered action sites marking the South Mountain Battle, September 1862, preceding Antietam.

SUSQUEHANNA STATE PARK 801 Stafford Road, Havre de Grace. At the mouth of the Susquehanna, contains Rock Run Grist Mill, built 1794, and the Steppingstone Museum, outdoor living history agricultural museum.

U. S. NAVAL ACADEMY MUSEUM Naval Academy, Annapolis. Art, artifacts, and memorabilia related to United States naval history.

U. S. S. CONSTELLATION Pier 1, Pratt Street, Baltimore. Restored wooden frigate built in 1797; one of the two surviving ships of the original U.S. Navy.

WASHINGTON COUNTY MUSEUM OF FINE ARTS City Park, Hagerstown. American and European art from the sixteenth through the eighteenth century.

MASSACHUSETTS

PLIMOTH PLANTATION Plymouth. The Pilgrims' journey to the New World in 1620 aboard the *Mayflower* has captured the interest of Americans for generations. Even young school children can recount the familiar stories of the founding of Plymouth, the first successful English colony in New England, and the celebration of the First Thanksgiving. But while we are familiar with the pivotal events that shaped Massachusetts' first settlement, few of us know much about what everyday life was like in the early seventeenth century. Plimoth Plantation, an outdoor living-history museum, re-creates the Pilgrim colony of 1627 and brings to life the day-to-day activities and seasonal cycles of this colonial New England community.

The Pilgrims who settled at Plymouth in 1620 were Separatists: that is, they wanted to disassociate themselves from the Church of England and establish a religious community without interference from the authorities of both church and state. Some of the Plymouth settlers had fled English intolerance and harassment over a decade earlier, but they found exile in Holland incompatible with their ideal of a select holy community. America promised the isolation the Pilgrims yearned for, so a group of them secured a land patent from the Virginia Company of London and official sanction for their venture from King James I. The famous *Mayflower* voyage brought them to their new home in December 1620. Before disembarking, forty-one of the ship's passengers signed the Mayflower Compact, a covenant recognizing their isolation in the New World and their mutual interdependence in the tasks that lay ahead of them.

Although they had landed outside the jurisdiction of their land patent, the Pilgrims proceeded with their plans to establish a community. Severe weather, makeshift housing, meager food, and ill health took the lives of half the settlers the first winter, but the survivors persevered the following spring with efforts to put the colony on a surer footing. Central to Plymouth's eventual success was William Bradford's election as governor in 1621. He continued in that post for over thirty years, providing the colony with the leadership it needed to survive famine, Indians, and internal schisms and to establish financial and political autonomy within the developing British empire.

Despite their desire for independence and isolation, the Pilgrims remained Englishmen. Their new colony in many ways re-created the culture they had left behind, and they maintained the agrarian values and traditions of English yeomen farmers. For example, the communal ideal worked for a time and the settlers held land in common, but within the first decade traditional reverence for private property led to permanent allotments. The Pilgrims also soon realized that the colony's survival depended on economic intercourse with other settlements and

with Britain. Farming did not provide a sufficient return for the merchant company that sponsored the venture, and the Pilgrim leaders were
forced to buy them out in 1626. To pay off the resulting debt, the colony
turned to trade, yielding the isolation they had originally sought. The
communal identity suffered further when colonists began moving outside the original settlement about 1630. And of course in the 1630s the
Pilgrims faced the aggressive expansion of the Massachusetts Bay Colony from the north. Indeed, by the end of the first decade many of the
original ideals and plans had fallen by the wayside, as the Plymouth
colony adjusted to the realities of the New World experience.

Plimoth Plantation re-creates the Pilgrim village in 1627, before
changing circumstances altered the basic character of the new community. Established in 1947, the living-history museum complex provides a reconstruction of the village, including the palisade, the fort,
two common or storehouses, and thirteen dwellings associated with
various early families. In this re-created community, costumed staff assume
the names and roles of the original inhabitants and perform the same
everyday tasks and seasonal activities that ordered their lives. The villagers till their gardens, cook meals, repair fences, hunt and fish, tend
to their livestock, and plant and harvest crops. These activities are not
simply craft demonstrations but illustrate the routine tasks that consumed the Pilgrims' days and provided the basic necessities for the
community's survival. In traditional English custom, the villagers also
celebrate Harvest Home, All Hallow's Eve, and Thanksgiving Day and
join together for weddings, funerals, and other occasions that reflect

*Demonstrating the use of
a pit saw*

the centrality of family and religion in the life of the community. By observing the villagers and talking with them, visitors can gain a better understanding of colonial life and of the values and traditions of the men, women, and children who inhabited this village over three and a half centuries ago.

Nearby on the banks of the Eel River is the Wampanoag Summer Settlement. The Wampanoag were the major Indian tribe in the region and played a significant role in the Pilgrims' adjustment to their new home. At the settlement site, Native Americans portray members of an extended family going about their daily activities, parallel to the everyday tasks of their Pilgrim neighbors.

Visitors to Plimoth Plantation can also tour the *Mayflower II,* a reconstruction of the original ship that brought the Pilgrims to America. Assuming the roles of crewmen and passengers, costumed staff tell visitors about the 1620 voyage and their experiences during the first winter. The ship is docked on the Plymouth waterfront, three miles north of the main complex. Nearby stand Plymouth Rock and two waterfront houses also administered by Plimoth Plantation.

Plimoth Plantation operates a reception center and an orientation center as well at the village site. In addition to the living-history program, the Plantation sponsors exhibits, school programs, and a variety of special events that focus on various aspects of colonial life. Open April through November, this unique open-air museum provides an extraordinary opportunity to experience life in seventeenth-century Massachusetts.

BOSTON NATIONAL HISTORICAL PARK *Charlestown Navy Yard, Boston.* European visitors to the United States commonly remark that, compared to their own, large American cities lack distinctive character. Tall steel and glass buildings, intrusive superhighways, great "holes" in city blocks given over to parking seem common to them all—and, to eyes used to different urban vistas, commonly distressing. The exceptions are few, but usually included are three that are themselves far distant and different from each other. New Orleans is probably the most exotic, a French and Creole enclave in an Anglo culture. Its accents, architecture, faith, and food set it apart and enhance its attractiveness not just to foreigners but to tourists from other parts of America who know that in the Vieux Carre things just will not be like things were back home. San Francisco also nearly always qualifies, though for other reasons. The sheer beauty of its physical setting is legendary, and few who have seen it go away unimpressed. In Europe there is nothing quite like it, as Europeans readily admit. About it there is an "end of the rainbow" aura partly shared with all California (the "Golden State") but partly all the city's own. Here the West ended, but through San Francisco's Golden Gate lie even more Wests, more romance, more adventure.

Boston, the third city in the European's scrapbook, is neither especially exotic nor especially beautiful by any conventional measure. It strikes European visitors with something that is simply familiar and therefore welcome in an unfamiliar land. Boston is old. And though it has its share of modern skyscrapers, roaring freeways, and parking lots, it still looks and feels old. It surprises and pleases foreign visitors used to cities of great age, and many Bostonians treasure the quality of age. They and other Americans have made a determined effort to preserve and utilize the city's heritage, and today along Freedom Trail the history-minded visitor can view a concentration of buildings closely associated with the events of the American Revolution. Walking is the best way to see it, and a tour of the entire route can take a full day. As the walker will soon discover, many Boston streets are still narrow and winding, which helps them even more to imagine what an eighteenth-century American (or English) seaport city looked like.

If you begin your tour at Boston Common, a lovely five-sided park in the middle of the city, you will be standing on ground purchased in 1634 as a combined militia training ground and cow pasture. From here British troops embarked for Charlestown and the Battle of Bunker Hill. The red line in the pavement (which marks the whole length of Freedom Trail) leads next to the "new" State House designed by Charles Bulfinch and built in 1795. The Massachusetts Archives next door is the repository for such famous and historical documents as the Charter of the Massachusetts Bay Company under which Massachusetts was founded and the Massachusetts Constitution of 1780. Nearby, the Park Street Church dates from 1809; abolitionist William Lloyd Garrison once preached from its pulpit. Among the noted Americans interred next door in the Granary Burying Ground are John Hancock, Robert Treat Paine, and Samuel Adams, all signers of the Declaration of Independence. The victims of the Boston Massacre also lie here. The original King's Chapel was built in 1688 on Tremont Street. The present structure was built in 1754 and boasted silver and vestments given by Queen Ann and King George III. After the Revolution it became the first Unitarian church in America.

Next door on School Street, Greenough's statue of Benjamin Franklin acclaims one of Boston's most famous sons. Originally built as a private house in 1712, the Old Corner Bookstore became famous only a century and more later when such New England literary lights as Henry Wadsworth Longfellow, Ralph Waldo Emerson, Nathaniel Hawthorne, and Oliver Wendell Holmes gathered here. Old South Meeting House ("Old South") was built as a Congregational church in 1729. It found its place in history when on the night of December 16, 1773, Bostonians angered by the British tax on tea met here and then marched down to the harbor and the escapade known ever since as the Boston Tea Party. The Old State House at Washington and Court streets housed the colonial Massachusetts government. The cobblestones outside mark where British soldiers, taunted by an unruly crowd, opened fire and killed five Bostonians on March 5, 1770, in an event patriots later dubbed the Boston Massacre.

Boston's Old State House

The next stop on the tour is Quincy Market, near the Boston water-front, an excellent example of adapting old buildings for modern use. Its many restaurants and shops have truly restored life to this once bustling market area. Faneuil Hall, one of Boston's most famous buildings, stands directly in front of the Quincy Market area. Peter Faneuil donated it to the city in 1742. It took its present form with enlargement in 1806. Patriot James Otis dubbed its second floor the "Cradle of Liberty" because of protests here by patriots aroused by British colonial policies. The first floor has always been a market; the third houses the Ancient and Honorable Artillery Company Museum.

A walk into Boston's North End reveals two sites which as much as any have been immortalized in the song and story surrounding the American Revolution. Paul Revere's house was built about 1676 and is the oldest surviving house in Boston. In sharp contrast to the stately Georgian buildings that line much of Freedom Trail, this steep-roof wooden structure recalls another era in New England history. While living here from 1770 to 1800, Revere, a silversmith, not only participated in the Boston Tea Party but on the night of April 18, 1775, took the ride that made him famous, warning the residents of Lexington and Concord that the British were coming. Nearby, Old North Church figured importantly in that exciting event. From its steeple, sexton Robert Newman hung the famous lanterns warning that the British were about to cross the harbor on their way to Concord. This is also Boston's oldest standing church, built in 1723 as a "house of prayer for all people." Just down Hull Street and overlooking the Charles River is another of the city's old cemeteries: Copp's Hill Burying Ground, where lie, among others, the famous clergyman Cotton Mather and the builder of the *USS Constitution,* Edward Hartt. The oldest graves here date from the 1660s, but the place has had other uses. In the 1770s the British chose it as the site for a cannon emplacement to bombard the Americans on Bunker Hill.

Bunker Hill itself is one of the two remaining sites, reached by a short walk across the Charlestown Bridge. Here an obelisk marks the place of the first major battle of the Revolutionary War, the one in which the famous order: "Don't fire 'til you see the whites of their eyes" entered the annals of American military history. The area from which the British mounted their assault that June day in 1775 became twenty-five years later the site of the Charlestown Navy Yard. It served for 174 years, through the evolution of naval warfare from the days of wooden-hull square-rigged sailing ships armed with muzzle-loading cannon to the era of guided missiles and sophisticated electronics. As it is now maintained by the National Park Service, the navy yard is actually a vast naval / industrial museum. From the ropewalk building constructed between 1834 and 1837 has come most of the cordage used by the navy. In another building the die-lock anchor chain was invented in 1926. In the foundry, an enormous brick structure with a sawtooth clerestory roof, workmen fashioned molten metal into many of the large castings needed on naval vessels. In 1918 a marine railway was built, capable of hauling tugs, patrol boats, and submarines out of the water for repairs. Perhaps most famous were the shipways, great sloping ramps down which many a new hull was launched, its prow wet with champagne.

Over the years the ships that were built and serviced here made a parade of naval history. The first ship-of-the-line in the U.S. Navy, the *Independence,* was built here in 1814. Built to last, she stayed in the navy 100 years. In the next generation of warships, the steam sloop *Hartford* was launched in 1858 and served in the Civil War as David G. Farragut's flagship during his famous assaults on New Orleans and Mobile. She too was long-lived and stayed in commission until 1938. In the early 1860s the yard built fast steam cruisers like the *Wachusett* to hunt down the great Confederate commerce raiders. Also of Civil War vintage but clearly looking forward to an entirely new age of ship design, the double-turreted iron monitor *Monadnock* was launched in 1863. It saw blockade duty and two years later was the first monitor to round Cape

Horn. The late nineteenth century saw the gradual transition from wood and sails to steel and steam. The *Adams,* a wooden square-rigged steamship launched in 1876, is a good example of the transition. The twentieth century saw a new breed of ship slide down the ways—sleek destroyers and stubby LST's designed for new kinds of warfare in all parts of the world. After World War II many older ships were refitted here for service in the missile age, and into the 1960s a vast array of carriers, cruisers, submarines, and escort vessels could be seen crowding the yards slips and drydocks. Though today the yard is no longer the scene of such activity, two famous warships still are moored here and are open to the public as historic ship museums. The USS *Cassin Young* is a Fletcher class heavy destroyer launched here in 1943, symbolic of many Boston-built ships that served with distinction in World War II and for years afterward. And moored nearby is probably the most famous ship ever to fly the naval ensign: the USS *Constitution,* fondly known as "Old Ironsides." Launched in Hartt's shipyard in Boston in 1797, she remains intact today as a splendid monument to the great age of fighting sail.

LOWELL NATIONAL HISTORICAL PARK *Lowell.* The establishment of Lowell, Massachusetts in 1821 marked the beginning of the industrial revolution in America. The Boston Associates first introduced large-scale mechanization at their Waltham, Massachusetts mills in 1814–1815, but their subsequent venture at Lowell provided the model for the modern industrial city and ushered in an era of economic and social change that transformed American life. The Lowell National Historical Park preserves what remains of the "City of Spindles" and provides a unique opportunity to learn about Massachusetts' pivotal role in nineteenth-century industrialization and urbanization.

Lowell was named for Francis Cabot Lowell, the pioneer manufacturer responsible for construction of the world's first fully integrated textile factory at Waltham in 1814. The success of Lowell's Waltham experiment rested on his duplication and perfection of English power looms, which he had observed in operation in 1811. These machines made possible fully integrated organization of the production process from raw cotton to finished cloth. Lowell's decision to hire young unmarried women from rural New England to operate the looms proved equally significant. The Yankee female operator became crucial to early industrialization, and the recruitment, supervision, and housing of this work force marked the beginning of modern corporate paternalism. The enormous capital investment required for the project led to a third innovation: corporate capitalization. Lowell secured financial support from a group of fellow merchants known as the Boston Associates, and together they organized the Boston Manufacturing Company. The immediate success of the Waltham experiment confirmed their confidence in Lowell and proved the viability of large-scale manufacturing.

After Lowell's death in 1817, leadership of the Boston Manufacturing

Company fell to Patrick Tracy Jackson, Nathan Appleton, and Kirk Boott. Additional mills in 1818 and 1820 increased production and profits, but the physical limitations of the Charles River site hampered further expansion. No less innovative and daring than Lowell, the new leaders of the Boston Associates decided about 1820 to expand their operations and establish a full-scale planned industrial community. After considering a number of potential sites in the region, they decided to locate their new development at the confluence of the Merrimack and Concord rivers, about thirty miles from Boston. The Pawtucket Falls and the Pawtucket Canal provided the necessary power source, and relatively light settlement in the East Chelmsford farming community assured the availability of enough open land to suit their grandiose plans.

Moving quickly, they bought up four hundred acres of land, secured control of the canal and the Merrimack River water rights by purchasing controlling stock in the Proprietors of Locks and Canals, and organized the Merrimack Manufacturing Company as the corporate focus for the new project. Kirk Boott, the company's agent, directed the widening and deepening of the canal, the redesign of the locks, the construction of the Merrimack Canal, and the erection of the first mill, completed in 1823. By the fall of that year, production of cotton cloth had begun. Additional mills came on line in 1824 and 1825, and the company's machine shops relocated there from Waltham. The population expanded dramatically to meet the needs of the new manufacturing complex. East Chelmsford had only about two hundred residents in 1820, but by 1826 over twenty-five hundred lived in the area immediately around the mills. In that year, a four-square-mile area was set apart from East Chelmsford and established as the township of Lowell, America's first company town.

Shortly after initiating the Lowell project, the Boston Associates decided to reorganize the management of the project. They reestablished the Proprietors of Locks and Canals to take control of real estate and canal development and to operate the machine shop, but the Merrimack Company retained control over its developed mill sites and housing.

Trolley in front of the Boott Mill

Other companies were then allowed to purchase mill sites and water power rights. The first to do so was the Hamilton Manufacturing Company, incorporated in 1825. In the next decade and a half, eight more major textile companies located at Lowell. With this expansion of mills and manufacturing, the population of the town swelled to nearly eighteen thousand, and in 1836 Lowell became Massachusetts' third incorporated city.

As at Waltham, the bulk of the machine operators in the early years were unmarried females. To insure the reputation of Lowell as a safe place for rural New England's daughters, the mill companies provided dormitories for them, required regular attendance at St. Anne's Church, and generally attempted to protect both their physical well-being and their moral character. For the other skilled workers and mill managers, the companies provided separate housing that reflected the class distinctions prevalent in the industrial community. Mill influence extended as well to the establishment of churches, schools, and businesses, all essential to the success of the new city. This initial period of development came to a close in 1839 with the chartering of the Massachusetts Cotton Mills, the last of the major textile corporations. By that time Lowell's population had climbed to over twenty thousand, and the dozens of mills had 163,000 spindles and 5,000 looms in operation.

Over the next three decades Lowell's population doubled and the mill companies continued to expand, despite the economic slowdown of the 1850s and the disruption of the Civil War. Maximum capacity on the existing canals was reached in the early 1840s, but construction of the Northern Canal in 1846 and the transition to turbines expanded Lowell's manufacturing potential. As labor needs correspondingly increased, immigrant laborers took the place of the Yankee mill girls. The first immigrants were Irish laborers who arrived in 1822 to dig the canals and build the mills. By the 1860s, a sizable community of French Canadians had located in Lowell as well, and some one-third of the city's population was foreign born. Greeks began arriving in the 1880s, followed by the Portuguese, blacks, European Jews, Poles, Armenians, and Hispanics, all contributing to the city's ethnic and cultural diversity and completing the transition from Yankee town to immigrant city.

Lowell's population climbed to ninety-five thousand by 1900. Steam power provided the key to continued expansion, and a variety of industries and commercial interests broadened the industrial base beyond textile manufacturing. Annual production peaked at $73,000,000 in 1918, as the population reached 113,000. Optimism about future growth and development quickly came to an end, however, in the decade that followed. Major closings and reductions in operations in the 1920s marked the beginning of a general decline in industrial activity from which Lowell has not yet fully recovered.

Awareness of the city's historic role and concern about its continued survival led to efforts in the 1970s to establish an urban cultural park to protect and interpret the city's unique historical resources. The state of Massachusetts established the Lowell Heritage State Park in 1974, and in 1978 the United States Congress authorized the Lowell National Historical Park and Preservation District. The park's 134 acres include 5.6 miles of the canal system, three major mill complexes, and part of the central business district. The National Park Service administers the site in cooperation with the Commonwealth of Massachusetts, the City of Lowell, and other local and private organizations. The Lowell Historic Preservation Commission administers the buffer zone or preservation district. Current programs include a variety of tours and museum exhibits that use Lowell's architectural resources to interpret its history.

As the nation's first industrial city, Lowell stood at the center of the economic and social transformation of American life in the nineteenth century. This unique urban park preserves what remains from that pivotal era and brings to life the drama of American industrialization and urbanization.

ADAMS NATIONAL HISTORIC SITE *135 Adams Street, Quincy.* Includes three eighteenth-century houses associated with two presidents and other members of this illustrious family.

ADDISON GALLERY OF AMERICAN ART *Phillips Academy, Andover.* Collections include paintings by Winslow Homer.

BERKSHIRE ATHENAEUM *1 Wendell Avenue, Pittsfield.* Contains room with works and personal effects of author Herman Melville, who lived in Pittsfield.

BERKSHIRE COUNTY HISTORICAL SOCIETY *780 Holmes Road, Pittsfield.* Housed in home of Herman Melville (built 1780); with Melville memorabilia, period furnishings, and materials relating to industry and early life in Berkshire County.

BOSTON PUBLIC LIBRARY *Copley Square, Boston.* Significant art collections, including works by John Singer Sargent and those of famous printmakers.

BRONSON MUSEUM *8 N. Main Street, Attleboro.* An archeology museum with specimens and exhibits on paleolithic and neolithic New England.

CHESTERWOOD *Stockbridge.* Art museum housed in the summer home and studio of sculptor Daniel Chester French.

EMERSON HOUSE *Cambridge Turnpike and state 2A, Concord.* House built by philosopher Ralph Waldo Emerson; where he lived until his death in 1882.

ESSEX INSTITUTE *132 Essex Street, Salem.* Museum with art and historical objects; also maintains several historic homes dating from 1684 to the 1800s.

FAIRBANKS HOUSE *511 East Street, Dedham.* Oldest frame house in America (1636).

FRUITLANDS MUSEUM Prospect Hill, Harvard. Site of transcendentalist Bronson Alcott's communal experiment in 1843.

HANCOCK SHAKER VILLAGE U.S. 20, Hancock. Restored religious community of 1790, with authentic Shaker items.

HIGGINS ARMORY MUSEUM 100 Barber Avenue, Worcester. Military and arms museum.

HISTORIC DEERFIELD VILLAGE Deerfield. Re-created community of the 1700s and early 1800s, with twelve buildings and furniture, folklore, and decorative arts.

HOUSE OF SEVEN GABLES 54 Turner Street, Salem. House built in 1668 and the inspiration for Nathaniel Hawthorne's famous novel.

ISABELLA STEWART GARDNER MUSEUM 2 Palace Road, Boston. Art museum housed in turn-of-the-century residence.

JOHN F. KENNEDY BIRTHPLACE 88 Beale Street, Brookline. Where the future president was born in 1917 and spent his childhood; restored and refurnished by Rose Kennedy to look as it did in 1917.

LONGFELLOW NATIONAL HISTORIC SITE 105 Brattle Street, Cambridge. Georgian mansion built in 1759 and home of Henry Wadsworth Longfellow for forty-five years.

MASSACHUSETTS HALL Harvard University, Cambridge. Oldest building at the oldest American university—building, 1720; university, 1636.

MERRIMACK VALLEY TEXTILE MUSEUM 800 Massachusetts Avenue, North Andover. Includes tools, machines, swatches, and sample books from the early textile period.

MINUTEMAN NATIONAL HISTORICAL PARK Concord. Where the "shot heard round the world" was fired in 1775, with Daniel Chester French's famous statue and a reconstructed Old North Bridge.

MUSEUM OF AFRO-AMERICAN HISTORY Smith Court, Boston. Housed in the African Meeting House, the oldest existing black church building in the United States; with materials on the history of Afro-Americans in New England.

MUSEUM OF THE AMERICAN CHINA TRADE 215 Adams Street, Milton. Decorative arts from the trade of the United States with China and Japan since 1784.

NEW BEDFORD HISTORIC DISTRICT New Bedford. Sites and buildings from the whaling port of the 1880s, including the Whaling Museum, with models and exhibits.

NANTUCKET HISTORIC DISTRICT Nantucket. Early whaling center and seaport, with historic houses dating from 1686 and Whaling Museum.

OLD SHIP MEETINGHOUSE Main Street, Hingham. The only remaining seventeenth-century church in Massachusetts, built in 1681.

OLD STURBRIDGE VILLAGE Sturbridge. Outdoor museum of living history, with exhibits and demonstrations of crafts, agricultural practices, and cottage manufacturing.

PARTING WAYS 130 Court Street, rear, Plymouth. A museum of Afro-

American history, with material on one of Plymouth's early black families and artifacts showing African influence from a local site.
PEABODY MUSEUM *161 Essex Street, Salem.* General museum with maritime history, enthnology, arts, crafts, and natural history.
PILGRIM HALL MUSEUM OF THE PILGRIM SOCIETY *75 Court Street, Plymouth.* Museum of Pilgrim history housed in Greek Revival structure dating from 1824.
PLYMOUTH ANTIQUARIAN SOCIETY *27 North Street, Plymouth.* Maintains three historic houses spanning the late seventeenth to early nineteenth century.
SALEM MARITIME NATIONAL HISTORIC SITE *Custom House, Derby Street, Salem.* One of the world's great maritime centers in the early 1800s; includes wharf, warehouse, and West India Goods Store.
SANDWICH GLASS MUSEUM *129 Main Street, Sandwich.* Exhibits of famous glass produced locally between 1825 and 1888.
SAUGUS IRONWORKS NATIONAL HISTORIC SITE *east of U.S. 1, Saugus.* Opened in 1648; reconstruction of ironworks, with museum displaying artifacts from the site.
SOCIETY FOR THE PRESERVATION OF NEW ENGLAND ANTIQ-UITIES *141 Cambridge Street, Boston.* Collections on New England architecture, decorative arts, and textiles, with information on numerous historic houses in Boston.
SPRINGFIELD ARMORY *1 Armory Center, Springfield.* Museum with collection of military small arms.
TRUSTEES OF RESERVATIONS *224 Adams Street, Milton.* Information on numerous historic houses throughout Massachusetts.

MICHIGAN

MACKINAC ISLAND Lake Huron. Like the history of many places situated on the edges of what became the United States, that of early Michigan is partly a story of intrigue, competition, and conflict among people who had not yet come to stay. But Michigan was not merely "on the edge." It was in the very midst of the great system of lakes that penetrated from the valley of the St. Lawrence deep into the heart of the North American continent. In the seventeenth century that unknown land lured a variety of ambitious, adventurous, and devout Europeans (chiefly Frenchmen): Brule, LaSalle, Cadillac, Marquette, Joliet. They found there, in addition to the sheer adventure of it all, chiefly two objects of interest: Indians to win for Christianity and a European king, and fur-bearing animals whose coats men coveted then much as they do oil today. The French enjoyed no monopoly, however: as time passed, their great imperial competitors, the British, outdid them. In their turn, amid this wilderness of trackless forests and icy lakes, the British confronted the Americans, its ultimate possessors.

Of those days of the fur trade and fierce international rivalry in the Great Lakes region, probably no other single place is as evocative as Mackinac Island, the great bulk of which is today owned and administered by the Mackinac Island State Park Commission. Located at the eastern entrance to the Straits of Mackinac between Lakes Huron and Michigan, it lay at the center of a far northern contest for influence and wealth that lasted into the first decades of the nineteenth century.

Chief among the island's attractions is Fort Mackinac, today fully reconstructed and offering visitors a number of educational opportunities. It began its career during the American Revolution, when the fearful British commander of Fort Michilimackinac on the tip of the Lower Peninsula moved his garrison across the water to the more defensible Mackinac Island. There in 1780 and 1781 the British built a new fort, "one of the few forts in America—or anywhere else," according to historian Bruce Catton, "that has actual charm, a beautiful contrivance of whitewashed stone going up a green hill to look out over blue water, with unbroken forests on the mainlands to north and south." Their stay was brief, however. By the Peace of Paris, which ended the Revolutionary War, Mackinac Island went to the new American nation, which held it until the second war with Britain in 1812. The British then retook and later held it against American attack until a second peace again returned it, this time for good, to the United States.

Whoever ruled the region, it was the fur trade that truly dominated life there. One of the most famous fur-trade entrepreneurs—John Jacob Astor—built a fortune that made him, for the time, the richest man in America. Astor organized the entire region around the Great Lakes as a vast department of his American Fur Company, with headquarters on

Mackinac Island. From there his deputies, Ramsay Crooks and Robert Stuart, blocked out districts and established outposts on most of the rivers draining this fur-rich hinterland. They reaped a rich harvest of beaver and other pelts, which passed by the thousands through the company's storehouses on Mackinac Island on their way to lucrative eastern markets. Alas, the money and manpower that Astor applied so efficiently proved too much for the beaver, marten, and muskrat, which in much of Michigan eventually were decimated. With them, of course, went the fur business—Astor, with good timing, dissolved the American Fur Company in 1834—and a colorful chapter in the history of Mackinac Island.

The fort remained, however, even though it no longer had either the fur trade to defend or hostile neighbors to deter: the army maintained the garrison until 1894. The buildings, too, once at the heart of the American Fur Company, remained. But in time the island came to be valued just as much for other reasons. As life in the rest of America and in the rest of Michigan grew busier and more crowded, the attraction of Mackinac's remoteness increased, and by the late nineteenth century its character had changed from frontier outpost to vacation retreat. Wealthy families from Detroit, Chicago, and the Twin Cities travelled there by train and ferry, to summer in cottages and elegant houses perched on the bluffs. Others stayed amid the late-Victorian opulence of the Grand Hotel, a mammoth white pine monument built by two railroad companies in 1887 and boasting the longest porch in the world.

Today's history-minded visitor can still recapture much of this rich and varied past. Automobiles are banned on the island, thus preserving much of its charm, but bicycles, horse-drawn carriages, or one's own feet amply suffice to tour the points of interest—and to experience them at much the same quiet pace that earlier generations took. A visit might well begin at the visitor center, downtown near the ferry docks, where park staff will supply information on walking tours and all of the island's public facilities. The fort is just a short walk up the hill. A meticulous reconstruction well interpreted by costumed staff, it recreates army life on this far northern outpost a century and a half ago. All the fort's buildings are open for inspection.

The commissary displays a capsule history of the island, in addition to weapons and original artifacts used by the soldiers who once lived here. Nearby, the post headquarters and quartermaster storehouse reveal in detail how the garrison was maintained. Here salt pork, beef, vegetables, and rum had to be stored in quantities large enough to last through winters that frequently left Mackinac Island isolated by snow and ice for half the year. In the soldiers' barracks and the guardhouse, the daily routine of the ordinary enlisted men assigned to duty here comes to life. The oldest building on the island, the 1781 stone officers' quarters, houses the restored quarters of post surgeon William Beaumont. Beaumont made medical history here when in 1822 he was able to observe

Historic Fort Mackinac

the stomach's digestive process through the unclosed gunshot wound of a voyageur, Alexis St. Martin. Though the garrison never again had to defend itself after the War of 1812, it still stood ready to do so, as the defense triangle formed by three fortified blockhouses indicates. Today they are sites for living-history demonstrations and house a variety of eighteenth-century artifacts.

Below the fort, the town offers the visitor a glimpse of what the fort was meant to protect, particularly the fur trade. On Market Street is the large and handsome house that once belonged to Robert Stuart, one of John Jacob Astor's chief deputies in the American Fur Company. Next door was the place that held the wealth that made possible Stuart's prosperity and Astor's riches. To the Astor Warehouse trappers brought their winter harvest of beaver, mink, muskrat, and otter. There the company's clerk graded the furs for size, fineness, and color and finally cleaned and boxed them for shipment east. There are also a blacksmith shop and the Beaumont Memorial, where the trapper St. Martin accidentally received his famous gunshot wound.

A short walk up from town, away from the fort, reveals the Grand Hotel in all its white wooden majesty, an elegant hostelry today operated by the Mackinac Island State Park Commission. Though guests include few railroad and timber moguls, such as frequented it in the late nineteenth century, today they can still expect to experience the life of a more spacious—and more formal—era. Ever conscious of its dignity, the hotel still requires that gentlemen appear in jacket and tie after six p.m. Beyond the hotel, the privately owned Victorian cottages of West Bluff and Hubbard's Annex likewise recall a vanished age.

In its auto-free quiet, its watery isolation, and its impressively preserved history, Mackinac Island is a rare place in today's world. Thoughtful visitors will find much to bring them back again and again. But they will find it only if they are prepared to put aside the present and be welcomed warmly to this large and living museum.

FAYETTE TOWNSITE *Michigan 149, Fayette.* Michigan historian Bruce Catton writes movingly about the coming of civilization to a land that the Indians and the animals had to themselves for centuries. The key to that process was the relation between the people who came to Michigan and the resources that attracted them. Nature endowed Michigan more richly than many other places. Much of Michigan's story, therefore, is the story of how ambitious and talented men created true wealth from nature's crude abundance.

Furs and forests were resources that nature provided in readily usable form. Beaver pelts and white pine could be transformed from raw material to final product with relative ease and simplicity. Man harvested and finished them, but he did not change their original nature. Iron was different. There was little resemblance between the earthen ore in which nature had deposited it and the iron bars bought by railroads and factories. To convert the dirt to wealth, man had to use more than good traps and sharp saws. He had to use a manufacturing process. In the early years in Michigan, he literally carried that process into the wilderness. At the restored townsite of Fayette on the southern shore of Michigan's Upper Peninsula, today's visitor can see an excellent example of the result.

Fayette was established in 1867 by Fayette Brown, manager of the Jackson Iron Company. He found on the site all the things needed for the profitable smelting of iron ore. A deep, well-protected harbor assured economical transportation of raw iron ore from the company mines at Negaunee. Thick hardwood forests promised an abundant supply of the charcoal needed in the smelting process, and in the limestone bluff along the harbor's eastern edge lay the flux needed to remove impurities from the molten ore. From such raw materials pig iron was made.

The process, though not complicated, did require some heavy hardware. First the ore and limestone were broken up by steam-powered crushers. Then the proper mixture of ore, limestone, and charcoal was hoisted to the top of one of two furnaces and dumped down the stack. Fanned by steam-generated blasts of air (thus the familiar term "blast furnace"), the charcoal ignited and gradually melted the iron ore which, being heavier than limestone, sank to the bottom. Meanwhile, impurities combined chemically with the limestone flux and floated to the top. One set of openings drained the waste, or slag, while another removed the molten iron from the hearth. The iron was then channeled into molds in the casting house, where it cooled and hardened. The bars, or pigs, thus produced then went down to the docks for shipment by water to the major Great Lakes ports.

Fayette's blast furnaces operated for twenty-four years and produced

nearly 230,000 tons of iron, making it one of the most productive smelting operations on the Upper Peninsula. Measured against the much larger
coal- and coke-fired furnaces operating even then in Ohio and Pennsylvania, however, Fayette's output was not grand. But it was the superior
quality of charcoal-smelted over coal- and coke-smelted iron that enabled
it, for a time, to compete successfully. Its success lay with the willingness of the market to support a higher price for a superior product. But
technology was quickly improving the quality of the cheaper coal- and
coke-smelted iron, thus reducing the market for Fayette's charcoal-smelted
product. Production costs meanwhile rose, as wood for charcoal grew
scarcer and as Fayette's machinery succumbed to the technological
obsolescence inevitable in a rapidly changing economy. What had once
been a profitable business was one no longer, and in 1891 the company
quit Fayette for better opportunities.

     But during its stay, there grew up around the smelters a small indus-
trial village, which is preserved today in much its original form. At the
height of smelting operations, it was home to about 500 people and was
in every respect a company town. Though the phrase "company town"
sometimes conveys a negative impression, the Jackson Iron Company
proved generally to be a benevolent and paternal landlord at Fayette.
While certainly not grand, its provision for its employees compares
favorably with the standards of the time. And in its semi-skilled and
unskilled work force is reflected, in small, the image of industrializing
America in the late nineteenth century. Four-fifths were immigrants from
other lands: Canada, Belgium, Ireland, Germany, Scandinavia, and Bohemia. Their languages and faiths were varied, but not (if their behavior
is any guide) their willingness to work hard for low pay and the chance
of something better.

     By later standards theirs was a world with little social insurance against
life's hardships, but it was also a world of strong family and community
ties. From behind the grimy faces of furnace crews captured in photographs now a hundred years old peer men who experienced industri-
alism in its youth. For some, that experience meant pain and failure.
For others—probably many more—it was filled with hope and promise
and satisfaction enough. Some, even in Fayette's small world, worked
their way up. John B. Kitchen was a young Canadian who began with
the company as a bookkeeper and rose to superintendent of the whole
operation in the 1870s. William Pinchin, another who achieved that exalted
position, began as Fayette's chief clerk and postmaster. Others worked
their way out: Edward McNally, an Irish immigrant and general laborer
at Fayette, who ended the owner of a farm in nearby Garden Township;
Fred Louis, a French-speaking Belgian who worked the charcoal kilns
until Fayette closed and in time also owned his own farm.

     These people and the bustling enterprise that once brought them
together are of course long gone, and Fayette, a museum village that
preserves the place where once they worked and lived their lives, is

Snail Shell Harbor

today a ghost town. But even as it reveals many of the original buildings, a walking tour will also evoke their spirit for the sensitive visitor. A stop at the interpretive museum at the entrance to the townsite provides a useful introduction. Follow it past the sites of laborers' log cabins, the machine shop where the heavy equipment was maintained, and the hotel where single workers were housed. The company office was where the books were kept and the workers paid; the "opera" house contained the butcher shop and the apothecary and the town meeting hall. Nine structures remain that were the homes of supervisory employees. The doctor's house and office still stands, as does the large white house that belonged to Fayette's superintendent. Across Snail Shell Harbor lies the heart of the village: the furnace complex—now cold and quiet—that once housed the most advanced charcoal smelting technology, and beyond it the charcoal kilns and limestone quarry. The warehouses that held the iron "pigs" are gone now; but the original dock pilings still line the harbor shore, testimony to the boats and barges that once called here.

In the long story of the interplay of human talents and natural resources, Fayette is hardly a unique chapter. Similar smelting communities grew, prospered, and declined in late nineteenth-century Michigan. Other company towns peppered the landscape all across an industrializing America. About them all, much can be learned generally from Fayette. What is unique about Fayette is that it is still with us in its original form, though as with all historic sites the substance that gave it life is gone. Fayette does not perfectly reproduce a vanished way of life; nor should it. That job belongs partly to the visitor's own imagination, which at Fayette Townsite will be richly rewarded.

HARTWICK PINES STATE PARK AND LUMBERING MUSEUM

Grayling. Nature's abundance, once thought inexhaustible, profoundly shaped Michigan history. To the people who came here, it represented the possibility of wealth or at least of better lives. Nature's abundance and man's development of it also tied Michigan to the rest of the world.

Whether fur-bearing animals, or iron ore, or white pine forests, Michigan was a rich source of materials that man elsewhere wanted. Of these, the harvest of the pine trees probably provided the most vivid episode. Certainly, it left Michigan the most changed.

During the last quarter of the nineteenth century, Michigan produced more lumber than did any other state in the union. The vast white pine forests in the central Lower Peninsula were confronted by men of energy, ambition, and often prodigious physical endurance—all at a time when the national appetite for lumber seemed boundless. The depletion of Michigan's timber wealth was not, however, something that happened all at once. Rather, it was tied to the growth of the nation and its economy, particularly after the Civil War. Once momentum had been gained, the process developed rapidly, and by 1880 the harvest of the forests resembled a "backwoods production line." As historian Bruce Catton points out with irony, lumber technology was perfected just as they ran out of trees. But there were other forests farther west where the techniques brought to Michigan by lumbermen trained in the more easterly portions of the pine belt that stretched from Maine to the Lake states would soon be applied.

In Michigan it all happened, much as it had farther east, in the spirit of cut and run, before the time when forests would be managed scientifically as a cultivated renewable resource. Consequently, the modern face of Michigan is not the same as the one these first loggers knew, though much of it is thickly wooded with second and later growths of timber. Stands of virgin pine like the ones that drew men here are now very rare. Happily, one such stand near Grayling is preserved today as the Hartwick Pines State Park and Lumbering Museum. A visit there can

Virgin white pine

help recapture two key themes in Michigan history: nature's true prod-
igality and man's determination to make use of it.

The process of turning natural abundance into economic wealth was
not, in nineteenth-century lumbering, especially complicated. Indeed,
it was similar to the process for converting the dirt that happens to be
iron ore into pig iron. Ore was dug and then transformed—smelted—
by fairly unsophisticated means into something else: iron bars or "pigs."
Usually the ore had to be transported some distance by water or rail to
the smelter. So with trees: first they were cut, and then they were floated
down a river to a sawmill. There they were changed into something
else: boards. Perhaps because it was so relatively simple, and because
the product literally made possible the physical building of countless
houses, barns, stores, and fences all across America, lumbering in Michigan can easily be seen as a chapter in the epic of national development.
Indeed it was that, but on another scale it was something else too. This
other meaning of lumbering becomes clear at Hartwick Pines.

The entrepreneurs who gambled in a competitive business and a
risky market likely were too busy to think much about their role in the
building of the nation; likewise the ordinary men who cut the trees,
wrestled the logs, and floated them downriver to the mills. Their aim
was to make a living, and logging, physically, was one of the hardest
ways to do it. For years the work was seasonal—possible only when
snow and ice enabled movement of cut logs to some nearby stream or
river. Largely young and unmarried, loggers lived a tough migratory
existence. In the early days, when the logging camps were small, living
conditions could be primitive. Loggers slept in a common shanty built,
naturally, of logs and heated by an open fire. Their food—mostly salt
beef and pork, beans, bread, and strong tea—made up in nourishment
for what it lacked in variety. For men who worked dawn to dusk at
backbreaking labor in Michigan winters, it needed to! Later, as the "production line" brought greater efficiencies to the logging business, conditions improved. Stoves replaced open fires; shanties got proper floors;
and, most notably, the menu grew. Pork and beans remained a standard,
but they shared the table with boiled and fried potatoes, thick beef stew,
fresh bread and pies, and great mountains of pancakes, doughnuts, and
cookies.

In addition to room and board, Michigan loggers earned, for the
time, good wages: about $20 to $25 a month. They earned them, however, only until warm weather made easy movement of logs across snow
and ice impossible. Some then found jobs as rivermen, floating the
great rafts of logs downstream to the mills—the other half of the logging industry's seasonal cycle that filled the spring and summer. Many
more headed for relaxation in one of the lumber towns—Saginaw,
Muskegon, Bay City—or later returned to the farms that began to dot
old cut-over timber lands. One final refinement brought this pattern to

an end, and at the same time greatly increased the speed with which the trees came down. Consequently it also hastened the end of Michigan's "white pine era." In the 1880s and 1890s the sound of narrow gauge steam railways could be heard everywhere in the woods. It meant two things: loggers no longer had to wait on ice and snow to move their bulky product through the woods; and stands of timber once deemed inaccessible because they were too far from water could at last be harvested.

Constant technical improvements in the sawmills made the process of turning timber into lumber even more efficient and, together with increased supply, lowered its price. For the customers at the great lumber yards in Chicago and Omaha, as for the mill owners, timber barons, lumberjacks, and common laborers, improved technology was a good thing. It meant jobs, profits, and an inexpensive product. For years it made Michigan a land of opportunity for people from many other places. Though the chances of business failure and physical injury were great, it brought years of prosperity to many and made possible better lives than they might otherwise have lived.

But it also left the face of Michigan radically changed—indeed, some would say scarred. Where for years stately stands of virgin pine once stood, only the cut-over ugliness of stumps remained. The reality of the "backwoods production line" finally banished the old illusion that nature's abundance was inexhaustible, and from that lesson different attitudes and practices in time arose. Some would say that the lesson was too costly and that for Michigan it came too late anyway. For the thoughtful visitor, Hartwick Pines will raise such questions. It will also recapture some of the recklessness, hardship, and sheer adventure of life in Michigan's woods a hundred years ago.

AFRO-AMERICAN MUSEUM OF DETROIT *1553 W. Grand Blvd., Detroit.* Collection of African and American artifacts, including Paul Robeson items.

ALFRED P. SLOAN JR. MUSEUM *1221 E. Kearsley Street, Flint.* Automotive and Genessee County history; extensive collections of autos; also large figurine collection.

BAKER FURNITURE MUSEUM *E. 6th Street, Holland.* Antique furniture, tools, and carvings in a city noted for furniture manufacture.

CALUMET DOWNTOWN HISTORICAL DISTRICT *bounded by 5th and 6th streets between Scott and Pine streets, Calumet.* Late-nineteenth- and early-twentieth-century commercial buildings with an historic copper industrial district nearby.

CHARLTON PARK VILLAGE AND MUSEUM *2545 S. Charlton Park Road, Hastings.* Reconstructed agricultural village of late 1800s on site of Indian hunting and fishing grounds.

DEARBORN HISTORICAL MUSEUM *915 Brady Street, Dearborn.* Local history and Indian artifacts.

DETROIT HISTORICAL MUSEUM *5401 Woodward Avenue, Detroit.* Extensive collections on Michigan and Detroit history—pioneer crafts; ethnic exhibits; industrial, military, and maritime materials.

DOSSIN GREAT LAKES MUSEUM *Belle Isle, Detroit.* Devoted to maritime history of the Great Lakes.

ELLA SHARP MUSEUM *3225 Fourth Street, Jackson.* Decorative, industrial, and mechanical arts from the pioneer and Victorian periods.

FAIR LANE *4901 W. Evergreen, Dearborn.* The fifty-six-room mansion of Henry Ford, with seventy acres of grounds.

FATHER JACQUES MARQUETTE NATIONAL MEMORIAL AND MUSEUM *Straits State Park, St. Ignace.* National memorial museum relates the life and accomplishments of the seventeenth-century Jesuit explorer.

FORT MICHILIMACKINAC *Straits Avenue, Mackinaw City.* Reconstructed fort on the site of 1715 French settlement.

FORT ST. JOSEPH MUSEUM *508 E. Main Street, Niles.* Contains many items from the fort, established by the French in the late 1600s.

FORT WAYNE MILITARY MUSEUM *6053 W. Jefferson Avenue, Detroit.* American military items, Woodland Indians history, and partially preserved fort, built 1845–1849.

FORT WILKINS STATE PARK *Copper Harbor.* Restored fort of 1840s with nearby copper-mine site and 1866 lighthouse.

GERALD R. FORD MUSEUM *303 Pearl Street, Grand Rapids.* Exhibits relating to the former president from 1948 to the present.

GRAND RAPIDS PUBLIC MUSEUM *54 Jefferson, Grand Rapids.* Extensive collections and exhibits on Indians and on Grand Rapids and West Michigan settlement and industries.

GREENFIELD VILLAGE AND THE HENRY FORD MUSEUM *off Oakwood Boulevard between Southfield and Oakwood, Dearborn.* One hundred historic structures selected to show the inventive genius of Americans, with Henry Ford memorabilia.

HISTORICAL CROSSROADS VILLAGE AND HUCKLEBERRY RAILROAD *G-6140 Bray Road, Flint.* Eighteen buildings in a restored nineteenth-century community; with demonstrations of crafts and an operating narrow-gauge railroad.

IRON MOUNTAIN IRON MINE *U.S. 2, Vulcan.* Displays of mining equipment and tours through underground areas mined 1870–1945.

KALAMAZOO PUBLIC MUSEUM *315 S. Rose Street, Kalamazoo.* Kalamazoo history.

JACKSON MINE MUSEUM *U.S. 41, Heritage Drive, Negaunee.* Buildings and material of what has been called the world's largest underground iron-ore mine.

JOHN JOHNSTON HOUSE *415 Park Place, Sault Ste. Marie.* Log house

of 1822 that is one of oldest existing structures in Upper Peninsula.
KINGMAN MUSEUM OF NATURAL HISTORY *Michigan Avenue at 20th Street, Battle Creek.* Includes both North and South American Indian collections.
LAKE MICHIGAN MARITIME MUSEUM *Dyckman Avenue, South Haven.* Exhibits on commercial fishing in a floating museum.
LINDEN MILL *Tickner Street, Linden.* Gristmill originally constructed about 1850, a good example of the mills built during the state's early industrialization.
LITTLE TRAVERSE REGIONAL HISTORICAL MUSEUM *1 Waterfront Park, Petoskey.* Located in an 1890s railroad station, with exhibits on Indian baskets, Ernest Hemingway, and historian Bruce Catton.
MICHIGAN HISTORICAL MUSEUM *208 N. Capitol Avenue, Lansing.* State museum with exhibits on Indian as well as white history in Michigan and the Old Northwest.
MICHIGAN STATE UNIVERSITY MUSEUM *West Circle Drive, East Lansing.* Natural history as well as history of humans in the Great Lakes region.
MIDLAND CENTER FOR THE ARTS *1801 W. St. Andrews, Midland.* Shops, furniture, and fashion of whites in Midland, with a children's area.
MONROE COUNTY HISTORICAL MUSEUM *126 S. Monroe Street, Monroe.* History of French settlements; Navarre-Anderson trading post; collection of General George A. Custer materials.
MUSEUM OF ARTS AND HISTORY *1115 Sixth Street, Port Huron.* Includes maritime, lumbering, natural, and Indian history as well as items from Thomas A. Edison boyhood home.
NATIONAL SKI HALL OF FAME *Mather Avenue, Ishpeming.* History of skiing, with special exhibit on handicapped skiers.
NETHERLANDS MUSEUM *8 E. Twelfth Street, Holland.* Memorabilia on Dutch settlements in this country and abroad, including Delft Blue pottery.
PIONEER HURON CITY MUSEUMS *7930 Huron City Road, Port Austin.* An entire town composed of museums, showing community in the 1800s.
QUINCY MINE *U.S. 41, Hancock.* Gigantic steam hoist, mining equipment, and narrow-gauge railroad of a former copper mine.
RIVER ROUGE PLANT *3001 Miller Road, Dearborn.* Said to be the largest integrated industrial plant in the world, begun in 1919 and still operating to produce Ford cars.
S.S. KEEWATIN *Tower Marine, Saugatuck-Douglas.* Original passenger steamship, with original furnishings, still afloat.
SAINT BERNARD'S ROMAN CATHOLIC CHURCH *Mack and Lillibridge, Detroit.* Murals on the struggle of blacks to be free, stemming from 1967 riots.

SOO LOCKS *Saint Mary's River, Sault Ste. Marie.* Site of locks making shipping possible between Lake Huron and Lake Superior; still in operation.

UNIVERSITY OF MICHIGAN EXHIBIT MUSEUM *1109 Geddes, Ann Arbor.* Includes North American Indian artifacts.

WHITE PINE VILLAGE *Ludington.* Collection of early Mason County historic buildings with an active interpretive program.

MINNESOTA

GRAND PORTAGE NATIONAL MONUMENT thirty-eight miles north of Grand Marais, Grand Portage. Northern Minnesota brings to mind images of iron mines and frigid snowbound winters. A remote and thinly peopled place, it is far off the well-traveled roads—on the way to nowhere else. The remotest part of it is probably the far northeast corner, where the Pigeon River (the international boundary) flows down off the Canadian Shield into Lake Superior. Indeed, that area is so remote that—as Minnesota historian Solon Buck once complained—cartographers have the unfortunate habit when drawing Minnesota maps of detaching the area from the rest of the state and isolating it in a little insert. Thus pictured as if an afterthought of geography, this part of northern Minnesota would seem largely left out of the state's history as well. But in fact, it figured in the history of the land that would become Minnesota well before white men ever broke the sod on the farming frontier far to the south.

Long before Minnesota became a state in 1858, this small area was the hub of an enormous commercial empire. It stretched 3,000 miles, from Montreal on the St. Lawrence River to Fort Chipewyan in Canada's far northwestern wilderness. Its center was Grand Portage, "the great carrying place." White men first came to this region not to stay, but rather to harvest and market the wealth nature held out for the taking. The wealth came in the form of a homely gregarious animal—the beaver—whose fur, for hats and other garments, was the rage of European fashion in the eighteenth and early nineteenth centuries. An easy prey, the beaver was trapped relentlessly across the Great Lakes and beyond, so that even before the American Revolution trappers had penetrated north and west of Lake Superior to the countless lakes and streams that fed into Hudson Bay and the Arctic Ocean.

The route back to market was by water down through the Great Lakes. To reach it, men sought a connection between the northward-flowing lakes and streams to the northwest and Lake Superior. The Pigeon River was the best such connection, though before it reached the lake, falls and rapids made passage by canoe impossible. Trappers therefore sought a portage and found one on what would become the American side of the river. It started at a small natural harbor on the lake, about eight miles south of the river's mouth, and ran about nine miles north and west to a place on the river above the falls and rapids. Though steadily uphill, the trek was passable and in time became, every summer, a funnel for the wealth of a continent.

The first recorded visit by a European was in 1722, though French traders had likely known of it even earlier. Certainly the Indians had. But the French lost their Canadian empire at the end of the Seven Years War (the French and Indian War in America) in 1763, and it was under their British successors that Grand Portage enjoyed its heyday. As the new masters of North America, enterprising Britons (especially the Scots) quickly exploited the abandoned French trading routes throughout the Great Lakes. They soon found themselves at Grand Portage, where by 1768 independent traders had made a clearing for a meeting place at the Lake Superior end of the trail. The British government in Quebec had opened the fur trade to anyone who applied for a license, and by the 1770s the competition was fierce and sometimes violent. To ease hostilities and make the fur trade more efficient and secure from competition with the well-established Hudson's Bay Company, the Montreal traders experimented with several loose cooperative associations. Finally, in 1779, they established the famous North West Company. Grand Portage became its inland headquarters and the object of a yearly trek by traders up from Montreal and trappers down from the Canadian wilderness.

For several weeks each summer, the Company's stockade was alive with activity. From Montreal the firm's partners came to tally accounts, inspect the year's harvest of furs, pay the men who had trapped them, and make assignments for the season ahead. With them they brought the supplies needed both for the rendezvous itself and by the trappers in the woods in the winter to come. One such inventory, transported in twelve canoes with 102 canoemen, included 1,000 gallons of spirits, 24 casks of wine, 90 bags of ball and shot, 150 guns, 150 bales of dry goods, 12 boxes of iron ware, 12 "nests" of brass kettles, 100 packages of tobacco, 50 kegs of tallow and lard, and 60 kegs of pork. At Grand Portage the small armada of birchbark canoes that plied back and forth across the lakes was maintained, and the beaver pelts were pressed and baled for the long voyage east. Along with the serious business went much revelry, feasting, and exchange of news and stories among men who worked for months and even years in wilderness solitude. The portage itself saw the voyageurs carrying tons of furs and trade goods over the rugged nine-mile path that rose from 600 feet above sea level at Lake Superior to 1,360 feet at Fort Charlotte on the Pigeon River. Each man commonly carried two ninety-pound packs over the trail and two more back, making the eighteen-mile round trip in about six hours. Though later improved so oxcarts could use it, it remained primarily a footpath.

Though Minnesota is rarely thought of in connection with the Revolutionary War, remote Grand Portage saw military activity then. Despite the rebellion in the colonies far to the south and east, the British fur trade through the lakes continued, and in 1778 a small detachment of His Majesty's Eighth Regiment of Foot was dispatched to Grand Portage to show the flag and bolster the loyalty of doubtful traders and Indians. But American independence changed matters in time at Grand Portage. Under the terms of the Peace of Paris, which ended the war in 1783, Grand Portage became American territory, though it did not immediately pass into American hands. The boundary as initially defined was somewhat vague, and for a number of years the British traders of the North West Company conducted business as usual at Grand Portage. Indeed, the 1780s and 1790s saw the height of the fur trade there.

Only after the British at last surrendered their military posts on the Great Lakes to the Americans, and only when American customs inspectors threatened to tax the fur wealth that was being imported duty-free over Grand Portage, did the North West Company decide to look for another route to the interior. In 1803 they moved thirty miles up the shore of Lake Superior, safely inside Canada, to Fort William, whence over the Kaministikwia River and Dog Lake they reached the boundary waters to the northwest. Grand Portage—the stockade on Lake Superior, the trail, and Fort Charlotte on the Pigeon River—subsequently fell back into obscurity, even though John Jacob Astor's American Fur Company continued to use it for several more decades. In time the fur trade itself disappeared, and with it all vestige of what once had been the busiest crossroads in the Old Northwest.

Today a vestige has been recovered and reconstructed. Under the auspices of the National Park Service, archeologists from the Minnesota Historical Society uncovered the location of the Lake Superior stockade and the sites of the major buildings. Several reconstructions now suggest what a great rendezvous post was like. The largest of the buildings is the "Great Hall," the place where the partners of the company came to do their business, feast, and celebrate at rendezvous time. Also at the site are a canoe warehouse that houses two authentic birchbark canoes, a fur press where the beaver pelts were packed tightly into hundred-pound bales, and a kitchen which prepared abundant meals for the partners, voyageurs, and trappers. The stockade, intended as much for privacy as for protection, surrounds the post, and the trail up to the site of Fort Charlotte is open for hiking.

This remote corner of Minnesota, once the center of a vast fur-trading empire, is today a quiet and lonely place, perched bravely between the rocky shore of Lake Superior and the still awesome northwest wil-

Great Hall at Grand Portage

derness. It is an example of a natural pathway once thrust to great prominence by the accidents of geography and the whim of the market. That prominence was fleeting, and, as the little insert maps containing northeast Minnesota suggest, too easily forgotten.

OLD FORT SNELLING *Minneapolis.* The expansion of the new American nation across a whole continent is one of the epic stories of the nineteenth century. Other nations too had undergone territorial expansion, the new lands commonly becoming colonies or provinces governed from afar by older, more settled areas. But in the United States, expansion entailed no such conventional empire-building. Rather, as Thomas Jefferson described it, western America was destined to become an "empire for liberty." It became so through the process of state-making, whereby new territory, after meeting certain standard requirements, was admitted to the federal union on an equal basis with the oldest of the eastern commonwealths. Thus the citizens of North Dakota and Wyoming came to enjoy the same rights and bear the same duties as the citizens of Massachusetts and Virginia.

States were not made all at once, however; and in the preliminary stages whereby the Old Northwest and Minnesota in particular began to move toward statehood, Fort Snelling played a key role. Much of the land that would become Minnesota was part of Thomas Jefferson's famous Louisiana Purchase, by which for $15 million Napoleon sold to the United States some 800,000 square miles of land between the Mississippi River and the Rocky Mountains. Although the deal was struck in 1803, American authority over the vast region awaited a formal American presence. It took some time, but within two decades the Americans effectively took possession of what legally was theirs. In 1804 Jefferson sent explorers Lewis and Clark across his "Purchase," beyond it to the Pacific ocean; a year later Zebulon M. Pike (whose name now graces one of America's highest mountains) was dispatched to explore the upper Mississippi River and scout sites for permanent fortifications. One of them, at the confluence of the Mississippi and Minnesota (then called the St. Peters) rivers, became Fort Snelling.

Fort Snelling actually was part of a larger plan for an ambitious system of outposts and connecting trails that John C. Calhoun, Secretary of War under President James Monroe, hoped would secure this vast territory—and with it the rich fur trade—from British (Canadian) intrusion. But most of the plan remained just a plan, which gave Fort Snelling—alone for nearly thirty years in the Northwest—special significance. The army first arrived in August 1819, under the command of Lt. Colonel Henry Leavenworth. Making their plans known to the local Sioux Indian chiefs, the soldiers began trying to settle in. At first Leavenworth picked a bad spot not far from the southeast end of the modern Mendota Bridge; after a difficult winter he moved to higher ground on a bluff above the Mississippi River. There he began a square log fort, which he never finished. Apparently unsatisfied with Leavenworth's slow start, the army

Living history on the parade ground

abruptly replaced him in the summer of 1820 with Colonel Josiah Snelling. Southeast of the site of his predecessor's wooden fort, Snelling raised the imposing stone structure that to this day bears his name.

"To adapt it to the shape of the ground on which it stands," Snelling used an irregular diamond shape. As much as he could, he built with limestone quarried from the river bluffs. Necessary timber was cut on the Rum River and floated downstream to the fort. A water-powered sawmill at the Falls of St. Anthony converted it to lumber. The fort, which majestically commanded the junction of the two rivers, consisted of a stone wall connecting four corner bastions—one semi-circular, one pentagonal, one hexagonal, and one round—designed to provide the best lines of fire against possible attackers. Inside was accommodation for a garrison of several hundred men and some of their families. The two enlisted men's barracks, one of wood and one of stone, contained married soldiers' quarters, twelve-man squad rooms, the company storeroom, and, in the cellar, the kitchens. Twelve sets of officers' quarters, which housed officers and their families, a separate kitchen, and a large central room for plays and dances, were located across the parade ground. The first hospital and library on the upper Mississippi occupied an adjacent large building, while the fort's commanding officers from Snelling onward enjoyed a substantial house to themselves (with post headquarters on the lower level).

Smaller support structures completed the establishment. A heavy masonry magazine stored in the 1820s some 50,000 musket cartridges, ample artillery shells, and 1,000 pounds of gunpowder. A storehouse with a lift well to each of four storage floors sheltered the food, clothing, and tools that were shipped up the Mississippi every year by steamboat. What could not be imported (and that was much) had to be made and maintained at the fort. Workshops contained a bakery, blacksmith shop, and places for a carpenter, a wheelwright, harness makers, and an armorer. For things not part of army issue, soldiers and their families could go to the sutler's store, which filled the role of a post exchange. There was a school building, which also served as the Protestant church.

A well at first supplied the post's water, which later had to be hauled up from the river. To protect it all, cannon in the pentagonal tower were trained down the north and east walls, while the hexagonal tower guarded the south and the west. The two rivers came under the sights of the semi-circular battery, while a round tower, with musket slits all around, was the fort's defensive strong point. A guardhouse, manned day and night, held the only jail in the territory.

Thus equipped and fortified, Fort Snelling loomed a powerful symbol of the American presence on this northwestern frontier. Though prepared to, it never had to defend itself, which is probably a good measure of how well it met the hopes of its planners. It helped keep the peace both between whites and Indians and among the Indians themselves. Its reassuring walls offered shelter in time of unrest and sociability in a remote and lonely region. It oversaw the largely peaceful process of white settlement that by 1849 won the Minnesota country status as a territory and full statehood just nine years later. It served so well, in fact, that by the late 1850s the army sold it to a private land developer who proposed to build a new city—to be called "Fort Snelling" on the site. The Civil War intervened, however, and the post was soon reactivated as an induction and training center for the thousands of Minnesotans who served the Union cause. Barracks, storehouses, and stables mushroomed until Snelling's old fort grew to five times it original size.

After the war, though no longer a lonely frontier fortress, the fort remained an active post and served as a prime provisioning depot and administrative headquarters for forts farther west on the Great Plains. In 1898 it once again mustered off Minnesota soldiers, this time to the Spanish-American War, and again in the twentieth century to two world wars. By the time the army finally left in 1946, 126 years of hard military service had taken their toll. In 1956 a highway threatened to pass through the old fort grounds. Happily, a determined preservation campaign took hold, and through the combined efforts of local citizens and state government (notably the Minnesota Historical Society, which now administers the site), the site of Old Fort Snelling was set aside as a state historical park and the old fortress meticulously restored and reconstructed. Staffed by costumed guides and featuring a number of living-history demonstrations, it offers today's visitor a vivid glimpse back to the days when this was the far northwestern outpost of American civilization.

That civilization grew in time from thirteen to fifty states, in a unique step-by-step process that assured new territories equal status with old ones. The orderly extension of American power and authority into the western wilderness was the first part of that story. Old Fort Snelling, one of the most powerful symbols of that authority, therefore marks an important moment in the westward growth of the American nation.

SPLIT ROCK LIGHTHOUSE *about twenty miles northeast of Two*

Harbors on U.S. 61. Nature endowed Minnesota more richly than she did many states: fertile farmland, thick pine forests, and enormous deposits of iron ore. Minnesota's history is in part the story of how, from nature's endowment, men made wealth. The wealth was not Minnesota's alone. Minneapolis flour was known around the world; Minnesota lumber built homes and fences far out on treeless prairies; iron from the Mesabi and Vermillion ranges went into the locomotives, skyscrapers, appliances, and automobiles that made the American standard of living a veritable wonder of the world.

Unlike wheat and pine trees, which were transformed into flour and lumber close to home, iron left Minnesota in much of the form that nature had given it. Ore boats carried the reddish dirt down the lakes and rivers to the huge mills at Gary, Detroit, Cleveland, Erie, and Pittsburgh, whence came steel. A crude extractive process, iron mining in northern Minnesota required reliable transportation out of the state. To make it reliable on Lake Superior, some of the most dangerous water in the world, was no easy matter. Split Rock Lighthouse on the treacherous north shore is a symbol of one era's solution.

In addition to containing all the excitement of storms at sea, of ships and sailors dashed helplessly on the rocky shore, and of lighthouse men gallantly keeping the light burning, the story of Split Rock is also the story of economics in the ore business, which by the turn of the nineteenth century was growing prodigiously. The first shipment of 2,000 tons of ore left the harbor of Duluth-Superior in 1892; by 1910 the figure had risen to 25 million tons, with another 5 million tons going from Two Harbors on the north shore. Through the Soo Canal at the eastern end of the Lake passed more tonnage than was handled by the more famous canals at Suez and Panama, while even in its short eight-month season Duluth-Superior was outstripping in crude tonnage both New York and London. The number of vessels on the lake also grew. United States Steel alone operated 112 freighters in 1901, and the companies represented by the Lake Carriers' Association owned over 500 bulk carriers. Although Lake Superior is an enormous body of water and was hardly crowded, it does narrow considerably at its western end between the Chaquamegon Peninsula and Duluth-Superior. Here passed all the ore boats.

Profitable operations in the steel and iron-ore business, as in any other, depended in part on reducing expenses of operation, which entailed some risks. It was known, for instance, that in accord with company policy ore boats commonly ran at high speed even in thick weather: delay meant money and perhaps jobs lost. The boats themselves were designed to carry maximum burden at the most economical fashion and thus were frequently underpowered: larger engines meant less payload. Few ships were insured: exorbitant premiums for such high-risk business meant deeply diminished rewards. The gamble paid off most of the time, though there were times when it threatened not to. One of

Light tower

the most memorable of them was the great gale of November 1905, which drove half a dozen freighters aground on Lake Superior's rocky north shore. Though some were salvaged, the damage cost their owners dearly, and over the next two years the ore carriers mounted a campaign for the cheapest form of protection they knew: a lighthouse and a fog signal to be built and maintained by the federal government in the vicinity of Split Rock.

The result was an appropriation of $75,000 and construction of the imposing lighthouse that still stands at Split Rock. Construction began at the isolated promontory, then accessible only by water, in the spring of 1909 under the direction of Ralph Russell Tinkham, a civil engineer who eventually became chief engineer of the entire federal lighthouse service. Supplies arrived by boat and were either landed in a small cove or hoisted directly up the face of the cliff with a large steam-powered derrick. Trees and brush first were cleared from the site and temporary living quarters then erected, and then work on the station began. The light tower itself rose on a skeleton of steel girders rooted in the rock outcropping and, in the second season of construction, took on its final octagonal brick shape.

Its beacon represented, for the era before radio navigational aids, the latest in technological refinement. Even though electricity was in wide use by 1910, lighthouses, because of their often remote locations, commonly relied on older forms of illumination. No exception, the new beacon at Split Rock employed a powerful incandescent oil vapor lamp whose wickless kerosene vapor flame produced a brilliant white light that was reported visible more than sixty miles away. The twin lens panels consisted of both reflecting and refracting prisms that concentrated the light source into two powerful beams. When rotated, it produced the characteristic lighthouse flash that swept the horizon every ten seconds. Imported from Paris, France, the Split Rock lantern and lens assembly weighed over six tons and, when mounted atop the tower, loomed 168 feet above the surface of the lake. The fog signal equipment likewise relied on non-electric power. Twin gasoline-driven air compressors (one to guard against mechanical breakdown) powered a siren that emitted a thunderous two-second blast three times a minute.

Adjacent to all the magnificent hardware rose the buildings needed to maintain it. The keeper and his two assistants occupied a trio of solid two-story houses, each with three bedrooms, bath, kitchen, pantry, and living and dining rooms. Nearby barns were later converted to garages. In the cove to the west, a dock and boathouse were built to help land supplies, and in 1915 they were joined to the top of the cliffs by an elevated tramway that vastly improved the station's access to the water. Sharing the rock headland with the light tower, the original construction derrick hoisted the bulkiest supplies until the completion of the tramway. Nearby the pillbox-like oil house stored the kerosene burned by the great beacon.

It was all self-contained, solid, and built to last. Physically, much of it did, though as the years passed some things changed. Most notably, the completion of the North Shore highway in 1924 opened the station to access by automobile and quickly ended its isolation. Tourists flocked there and ended the keepers' once quiet life. The Civilian Conservation Corps built a new access road in 1935, and when four years later the Lighthouse Bureau was absorbed by the United States Coast Guard, the Split Rock Station was spoken of as the most visited lighthouse in America. Meanwhile it continued to do the job it was built for, with a few concessions to changing technology. The old flywheel gasoline engines that powered the fog horn were replaced by diesels in 1932. With access by highway well established, the tramway up from the lake was dismantled in 1934. Electricity arrived in 1940 and the oil vapor lamp was replaced by a 1,000-watt bulb. Electric motors rotated the beacon and drove the fog horn. Yet even with such improvements, modern navigational aids were making the station obsolete. The fog signal was discontinued in 1961, and the beacon flashed for the last time in 1969. The site remained a popular attraction, however, and in 1971 was opened to the public as a part of Split Rock State Park. Five years later the Minnesota Historical Society assumed its administration.

Today, the ore boats still pass close by on their way through Lake Superior's narrow western reaches. They still carry Minnesota's red iron-bearing earth down the chain of lakes to the mills and factories where it is transformed into wealth. Radar and other technological marvels guide them. The light at Split Rock has become a relic, though one well worth a visit as a reminder of how dangerous navigation on Lake Superior once was—and sometimes still is.

ALEXANDER RAMSEY HOUSE 265 S. Exchange Street, St. Paul. French Second Empire mansion built in 1872 by first territorial governor of Minnesota; with period furnishings.

ANDREW VOLSTEAD HOUSE 163 Ninth Avenue, Granite Falls. Victorian house of congressman whose name went on national prohibition legislation. Privately owned.

CHARLES A. LINDBERGH HOUSE AND INTERPRETIVE CENTER Lindbergh State Park, Lindbergh Drive, Little Falls. Boyhood home of the famous aviator, built in 1906; with historical materials on the Lindbergh family.

THE DEPOT 506 W. Michigan Street, Duluth. An 1892 French Norman train station housing the Lake Superior Museum of Transportation, with excellent collection of railroad equipment used in Minnesota; St. Louis County Historical Society, with nationally important collection of paintings by Eastman Johnson; and the Chisholm Children's Museum.

FOREST HISTORY CENTER state 76, Grand Rapids. Reconstruction of a turn-of-the-century logging camp; with tours and trail walks.

FORT RIDGELY off state 4, south of Fairfax. Partial reconstruction of an 1855 fort built to defend white settlers against the Sioux; site of an 1862 battle.

GRAND MOUND state 11 west of International Falls. Site of the largest prehistoric burial mound in Minnesota, where the Laurel culture held sway from 200 B.C. to A.D. 800; with exhibits.

HARKIN STORE county 21 northwest of New Ulm. Restoration of a general store from the 1870s.

HULL-RUST-MAHONING OPEN PIT Third Avenue East, Hibbing. An open pit mine on the Mesabi Range of northern Minnesota's iron mining country.

IRON RANGE INTERPRETIVE CENTER off U.S. 169, Chisholm. Geology, ethnic culture, crafts, and industry of the Iron Range.

ITASCA STATE PARK 21 miles north of Park Rapids off U.S. 71. First Minnesota state park (1891); includes prehistoric mounds, log structures, pioneer cemetery, and other buildings.

JAMES J. HILL HOUSE 240 Summit Avenue, St. Paul. The 1889 Richardsonian Romanesque home of the railroad magnate.

JEFFERS PETROGLYPHS county 2 east of Jeffers. More than 2,000 carvings from two periods of Woodland life—beginning 3000 B.C. and ending A.D. 1750.

LAC QUI PARLE MISSION CHURCH R.R. 5, Montevideo. Restored early-nineteenth-century mission established for the Dakota Indians near Joseph Renville's American Fur Company post.

LANDMARK CENTER *75 West Fifth Street, St. Paul.* A preserved turn-of-the-century Romanesque federal court building housing the Ramsey County Historical Society, with major exhibits on topics relating to the history of the state's capital city and surrounding area; also includes galleries of the Minnesota Museum of Art, with exhibits primarily on American art and architecture.

LOWER SIOUX AGENCY *county 2 east of Redwood Falls.* Site of first Dakota attack in war of 1862; with interpretive center on the struggle of the Dakota Indians.

MILLE LACS INDIAN MUSEUM *U.S. 169 on shore of Mille Lacs Lake, Onamia.* Artifacts and dioramas on the Dakota and Ojibway Indians.

MINNESOTA HISTORICAL SOCIETY *690 Cedar Street, St. Paul.* Headquarters of the state's historical program; houses the state's largest history museum and library and provides information about historic sites and resources throughout the state.

MINNEAPOLIS INSTITUTE OF ARTS *2400 Third Avenue, S., Minneapolis.* Extensive collections and exhibits on a wide variety of paintings and other art, including American.

MINNESOTA MUSEUM OF MINING *Chisholm.* Steam shovels, locomotives, and other equipment used in open-pit and underground mining in the Mesabi Range.

MINNESOTA STATE CAPITOL *Aurora between Cedar and Park streets, St. Paul.* Designed by famous architect Cass Gilbert, built 1896–1905. Beaux-Arts Classical building still in use.

NORTH WEST COMPANY FUR POST *county 7 off I-35 at Pine City exit, Pine City.* A reconstructed post of the early 1800s, with utensils and other items showing how the voyageurs worked and lived.

OLIVER H. KELLEY FARM *U.S. 10 east of Elk River.* First headquarters of the organization that spawned the National Grange; in an 1860s farmhouse with late-nineteenth-century items.

PIPESTONE NATIONAL MONUMENT *U.S. 75 north of Pipestone.* Quarries where Plains Indians and others obtained the stone for their ceremonial pipes.

ST. ANTHONY FALLS *Minneapolis.* Site of nineteenth-century milling operations that made Minneapolis the nation's largest flour-producing center.

SCIENCE MUSEUM OF MINNESOTA *30 E. Tenth Street, St. Paul.* Extensive collections in archeology, anthropology, ethnology, and paleontology, as well as other sciences.

SIBLEY HOUSE *Mendota.* Home of the first governor of Minnesota, built 1835–1863; includes a museum containing furnishings of mid-1800s.

SINCLAIR LEWIS MUSEUM AND INTERPRETIVE CENTER *I-94 and U.S. 71, Sauk Centre.* Late-nineteenth-century boyhood home of the author, with his books and family furnishings; visitor center.

SOLOMON G. COMSTOCK HOUSE *Fifth Avenue S. and 8th Street,*

Moorhead. The 1883 Queen Anne home of the banker and politician and of his daughter Ada, president of Radcliffe; includes a museum containing family memorabilia.

TOWER SOUDAN MINE AND STATE PARK U.S. 169 north of Tower and Soudan. Open-pit and underground mine, the first iron mine in the state.

UPPER SIOUX AGENCY STATE PARK state 67 south of Granite Falls. Partially restored buildings at site of agency established 1854 by the United States government to instruct Sioux in farming methods.

W. W. MAYO HOUSE 118 N. Main Street, Le Sueur. Gothic house built in 1859, where Mayo practiced medicine before moving to Rochester and establishing the famous clinic with his sons.

MISSISSIPPI

FLOREWOOD RIVER PLANTATION highway 82 west, Greenwood.
In history and in fiction, plantations and the Old South go together.
Cotton, slaves, and grand houses define them. This image long had
enormous romantic appeal and held a Deep South state like Mississippi
with special power. It contained some truth, but it also raised some
questions. How old really was the "Old South"? What really was a "plantation"? How well did Mississippi really fit the image? A visit to the
Florewood River Plantation near Greenwood helps supply some answers.

The American South is a very large place, and it was not all settled
at once. More than 200 years separate the settlement of the Tidewater
region around the Chesapeake Bay from the settlement of much of the
lower South. Georgia, the youngest of the seaboard southern colonies,
was already a century old by the time large numbers of Americans began
pouring into the virgin lands of Alabama and Mississippi. It may seem
strange to speak of Mississippi in connection with an "Old South" when
parts of that South were so much older. Most people when they think
of the Old South probably have in mind simply the South before the
Civil War. Still, with the probable exception of some Indian artifacts,
nothing in Mississippi before the Civil War was very old, least of all its
plantations.

In the 1820s and 1830s Alabama and Mississippi were the Southwest
of the United States, and for thousands they offered new lands and the
chance for better lives. The great majority came from other and older
southern states: North Carolina furnished the most, followed by South
Carolina, Tennessee, Virginia, and Georgia. Their numbers were
impressive. Between 1830 and 1860 Mississippi's population jumped
from roughly 137,000 to 791,000, an increase almost entirely due to
immigration. Most were plain people—farmers and their families—and
in Mississippi most would remain plain people, wrestling from the new
land a modest prosperity. But for the truly ambitious and the lucky,
there were larger fortunes to be made.

They could be made through planting, and the place where they
were made was on plantations. The difference between planting and
farming and between plantations and farms was essentially one of scale—
and self-image. Historians typically argue over the precise terms, but
one thing is certain: planting entailed more capital than farming. How
much more was open to question. The form that capital took was not:
it was land and slaves. Even by such an easy definition, most Mississippians remained farmers, not planters. Most did not own slaves, though
many non-slaveholders owned their own farms. Perhaps twenty percent
of the state's farm operators loosely qualified as planters, with over 200
acres and more than a few slaves. Those with fifty or more slaves and
over 500 acres of improved land, who might be called great planters,

Plantation owner's home

made up something around eight percent of those who farmed.

Great planters and plantations generally were concentrated in the fertile western part of the state, especially on the rich lands of the Delta. The wealthiest clustered around Natchez and built there some of the most resplendent mansions of the antebellum era. Some still stand and occupy now as then an outsized place in the popular image of the southern plantation. The "Natchez nabobs" were exceptional, and indeed some had significant interests in and profits from things other than agriculture. The far greater number of Mississippi planters, even of those in the Delta, never knew such opulence. They did know the meaning of success; most were self-made men, not far removed from considerably less exalted beginnings. Their plantations were large working farms whose purpose was to make a profit in the business of staple-crop—that is, cotton—agriculture. It took much tending and hard work, and it produced, contrary to the popular image, little luxury.

So a visit to Florewood River Plantation will make clear. Florewood depicts life on a working Delta cotton plantation of the 1850s. It is not the life one might guess at from looking at Natchez mansions or from watching *Gone With the Wind.* Operated by the Mississippi Bureau of Recreation and Parks, Florewood is an outdoor living-history museum comprising a score of buildings situated on approximately 100 acres along the Yazoo River in Le Flore County. Costumed guides demonstrate many plantation activities, and the buildings and crops render a true picture of this venerable southern way of life.

The planter's home owes little to the Hollywood version of southern plantation houses. It does face the river, where once steamboats docked to load bales of cotton, and it is the dominant building on the plantation. But it lacks any imposing white columns and is rather the sort of tasteful white wooden farmhouse one might expect to find in Pennsylvania. As was common, a detached kitchen is adjacent to the planter's house. His office—the only brick building on the plantation, where he kept guns, records, and money—is located between the main house and the river. The carriage house also contained the residence of the plantation tutor, who conducted classes in the plantation schoolhouse. Smokehouse and laundry house were other standard outbuildings, as was the blacksmith shop. The overseer and the driver each had his own house. Slaves lived in the "quarters," an example of which is preserved at Florewood. The common kitchen, where food for the slaves was prepared, was located in the quarters area.

Often plantations are thought of in terms of just such buildings. But it was the land that supported it all, and at Florewood the visitor gets a glimpse of what the land produced. From the planter's vegetable garden behind the smokehouse came good things for the table. Sorghum, peas, and other food crops needed in volume were grown in a big garden west of the main house. Corn fed the field hands and became food for cattle; it was planted abundantly behind the quarters area. But the backbone of it all was cotton, the great white staple. At Florewood some three acres of cotton are planted every year just behind the poultry house. In the gin house, a steam-powered cotton gin removes the seeds from the cotton fibers. The cotton would then be pressed into bales, and moved down to the dock for shipment by steamboat downriver. Nearby, a gristmill converted corn into meal, while a sorghum mill produced thick brown molasses.

Florewood only partly fits the romantic image of the Old South plantation. Many Mississippi plantations were in fact not even this grand. Grace, style, elegance—things so often associated with the plantation image—described a way of life that depended on the success and the taste of the planter. It is safe to say that most Mississippi plantations, carved so recently out of the wilderness, displayed few such qualities. Rather Florewood depicts something more common: the plantation as a method of agriculture, where much of the work was done by black slaves and whose product was cotton.

STANTON HALL AND LONGWOOD *Natchez.* Current scholarly fashion emphasizes the importance of writing history "from the bottom up." The great voiceless majority of human beings who left few written records have histories worth knowing, we are told, and in the last fifteen to twenty years historians have turned with alacrity to workers, women, and blacks and other ethnics as legitimate subjects for their craft. It is a fashion that embodies a strong desire to correct alleged old imbalances, old injustices, or simply old neglect. Old symbols and old pieties are its victims. Nowhere is this more evident than in the history of the South, whose symbols for years were so widely agreed upon and whose pieties were so dearly held. As historians have thrust new settings and new faces to the center of the story (increasingly plain people, black and white, in plain places, city and country), some of the more standard old ones (aristocratic people in white-columned plantation houses, for instance) have suffered their own neglect and considerable debunking of their importance. Long revered by the keepers of the South's past and the South's pride, such symbols are decidedly not now the mode.

Natchez therefore is especially worthy of a visit. Its grand houses were not typical of Mississippi or the South: the lives of its great planters—the Natchez nabobs—tell us little about the daily lives of most southerners. In fact, some of its prominent citizens strongly opposed secession when most southerners were caught up in the wave that swept the old South out of the Union. Even so, Natchez is one of the places that first comes to mind when many people think of the Old South. However atypical in fact, it remains in mind central to the South's image of itself. Because it reflects life as it was lived only by a few of the rich, well-born, and powerful, it is obviously only a partial image. But so is the image of the South reflected in the lives of slaves and yeoman farmers a partial image. Of the small truly wealthy planter aristocracy that built houses like those in Natchez, it can at least be said that they were powerful and influential far beyond their numbers. They left behind houses that extended their influence, in ways they may not have imagined, far beyond their lifetimes.

Even though its great houses were unique and enjoyed by a small minority of Mississippians, the things that made them possible were not unique—only more abundant and profitable in Natchez. The twin features of life that became so typical of so much of Mississippi in the years before the Civil War—cotton agriculture and Negro slavery—fastened themselves first on the Natchez area. Cotton and slavery of course preceded the great mansions; by the time they appeared in the 1850s, Mississippi, though still not far removed from the frontier, was firmly identified with the "Cotton Kingdom." By and large it was a crude kingdom. Natchez was an elegant exception.

Its architectural styles, like its Spanish, French, British, and American heritage, are various. Late Spanish townhouses are reminiscent of their counterparts downriver in New Orleans' Vieux Carré. Wooden cottages with low verandahs resemble a style common through the rural areas of the Lower South. Imposing and fanciful Greek mansions bespeak aspirations of grandeur that were attained barely in time: nearly all of them were built just as the world that produced them was about to be consumed in the Civil War. Some did not survive; of those that did, two especially reflect for today's visitor this unique moment and place in southern history.

Stanton Hall will strike the visitor who has seen southern mansions elsewhere as the most familiar. It is white, handsomely proportioned, with tall columns—the usual ingredients for a stately southern mansion. But this one is more than the usual. For one thing, it is larger and its setting more palatial than most plantation houses. It is not in fact a plantation house at all, but an urban dwelling that occupies an entire city block in the heart of Natchez. No slave quarters or agricultural out-

Stanton Hall

buildings surround it. Rather, tall trees and flowering shrubs separate it from its neighbors and provide a private but not isolated setting. It was built in 1857, four years before Mississippi left the Union, by Frederick Stanton and immediately took its place as one of Natchez' and Mississippi's finest houses. Fronted by four immense Corinthian columns, its white stuccoed grandeur was the product of Natchez architect and builder Thomas Rose and was built entirely by Natchez masons, carpenters, craftsmen, and finishers. Therefore it is a special monument to the unique wealthy civilization that once flourished in this modest river town amid what not long before had been a wilderness.

The entrance aptly sets the tone. Beyond the columns, the front door opens onto a vaulted central hallway seventy-two feet long. To the right, matched front and back parlors open into each other through heavy doors and, like the hallway, extend seventy-two feet. Mirrors at each end make the double room appear virtually endless. Bronze chandeliers hang from high ceilings; heavy molding and woodwork accent the generous spaces. Across the hall are equally spacious library and dining rooms; the grand staircase leads to another ample hallway and six bedrooms upstairs. The fittings are appropriate to the grand setting: magnificent white marble mantelpieces sculpted in New York, massive gold-leaf mirrors imported from France, and silver doorknobs and hinges from England throughout the mansion. Period antiques of rosewood and mahogany fill the rooms much as they did when Frederick Stanton lived here and played cards with his friends in the cupola high on the third floor.

"Longwood," though built in the same place at the same time by a rich man of similar pretensions, is entirely different. Begun in 1859 and unfinished when work halted abruptly two years later, Longwood was imagined by its owner, Haller Nutt, and designed by its Philadelphia architect, Samuel Sloan, as an eight-sided oriental castle adorned to proclaim Natchez' eminence. At least it proclaimed Nutt's singular taste in houses and his architect's considerable skill for concocting from fantastic plans an equally fantastic reality. A first glance at its octagonal shape and sixteen-side cupola topped with a Byzantine onion dome confirms that it is one of a kind. Sloan's drawings for the mansion (which are preserved on some of its walls) envisioned a six-story structure of brick, plaster, and marble with eight rooms on each floor opening onto a rotunda. Though not all of it came to pass, enough did to suggest what Nutt meant when he spoke of Longwood as "the remembrancer of Eastern magnificence which looms up against the mellowed azure of a Southern sky." Three floors plus the cupola were finished and gave the place its strange pagoda-like silhouette. There were even plans to relieve the gloominess of the warren-like interior through a system of indirect lighting via large mirrors high up in the dome. Marble mantels, statuary, stairways, mosaic floors, and splendid tapestries are what would have greeted the nineteenth-century visitor.

As fate would have it, more in fact greets the visitor today than did long ago. Work stopped when Sloan's Pennsylvania artisans returned north with the outbreak of war in 1861. As the conflict wore on, it also deprived Nutt of the wealth he needed to finish the job. Although like many Natchez nabobs he was a Union sympathizer, he saw his plantation overrun and his cotton lands confiscated. When the war came, he settled dejectedly with his family on the incomplete mansion's lower floor; he died of pneumonia in 1864, never to see his fantastic dream completed. His descendants, however, continued to occupy the basement rooms for the next hundred years. While the house never became quite the example of eastern magnificence its builder evidently had in mind, it did endure, attenuated by hard times, as an example of a peculiar kind of Mississippi magnificence. The Natchez Pilgrimage Garden Club has owned it since 1970 (the club also owns Stanton Hall) and maintains it after a fashion that Nutt and Sloan would surely approve of. It is open daily to the public.

Fashions in history, as in other things, change. Current ones venerate ordinariness and look askance at places like Stanton Hall and Longwood, and the men who built them. But places like these last longer than most fashions. Certainly they do not tell us very much about the way most southerners lived. But how most people once lived and how they chose to remember themselves are often very different things. This has been as true in the history of the South as anywhere, and so Natchez proclaims.

VICKSBURG NATIONAL MILITARY PARK *3201 Clay Street, Vicksburg.* Gibraltar, Verdun, Singapore—and Vicksburg—rank among history's great fortresses. On such strategically located places the course of major events has turned. Only Gibraltar, of these examples, has had the good fortune never to be attacked. At Singapore the British were not so lucky. At Verdun the French paid dearly to keep their enemy at bay. At Vicksburg—"the Gibraltar of the Confederacy"—the South too invested much. And, in a hard fight, she lost it.

The contending legions came to this sleepy Mississippi River town through the accidents of topography and grand strategies to win the Civil War. Though the war had begun in the East, and though northern Virginia remained a key battleground from beginning to end, the war in the West occupied an early and important place in the planning of both sides. Thanks to topography the Mississippi River flows south, and down its meandering course before the Civil War had flowed much northern commerce to its natural outlet at New Orleans. With the outbreak of war, the new Confederacy, which straddled the river for a thousand miles, had a potential economic stranglehold on a large part of the North.

But the river was a two-edged sword. Not just a lifeline for the upper Mississippi and Ohio valleys, it was also a dagger thrust deep into the heart of the South. The entire states of Arkansas and Texas and the larger part of Louisiana lay west of it, which meant that if the North could wrest control of its southern reaches the Confederacy would be outflanked and physically divided. The vast agricultural resources of the states west of the river would no longer be available to support the armies in the East, and the South's capacity to carry on the fight would be materially diminished.

The understanding of all this led both sides to Vicksburg in the spring and summer of 1863. Anticipating the Union forces would try thus to use the river, the Confederates had fortified it as best they could. Nevertheless, Federal troops advanced steadily from both north and south. Forts Henry and Donelson in Tennessee fell early in 1862, and after the Battle of Shiloh that April, Confederate forces withdrew into northern Mississippi. Memphis surrendered in June. Meanwhile, far to the south, United States naval forces under Admiral David G. Farragut had captured New Orleans and in an unsuccessful expedition had ranged up the river all the way to Vicksburg, which with the lesser strongpoint of Port Hudson was the only remaining impediment to Yankee control.

It was a major block, however, and removing it took much time and many lives. The job fell to Ulysses S. Grant, who in October of 1862 took command of the Army of the Tennessee with orders to reduce Vicksburg and open the Mississippi. Grant is remembered best for his subsequent determination to engage Robert E. Lee's Army of Northern Virginia until it and the South were soundly beaten. His determined tactics there were foreshadowed in the Vicksburg campaign, which earned him both Lincoln's respect and, in the North, the derisive sobriquet "Grant the Butcher."

The problem of Vicksburg unfortunately afforded no neat textbook approach, and even given the North's superior resources it took a man of Grant's tenacity to prevail. At first he tried attacking from the north while William T. Sherman approached from the river. The two-pronged effort failed when the Confederates destroyed Grant's supply base at Holly Springs. He next tried a series of joint amphibious operations with the navy, often referred to as "Bayou Expeditions." In vain, he foundered about in delta swamps and creeks without finding a passable way around Vicksburg so that he might invade it from the rear. Discouragement and casualties rose, and by early 1863 it was apparent that the fate of the whole campaign, and with it Grant's career, must soon be decided.

Finally, in March, Grant made the decision that would lead to the capture of Vicksburg. At first it took him the long way around. Dividing his army of some 45,000 men into three corps, he moved southward along the western or Louisiana bank of the river to a point near Grand Gulf, twenty-five miles south of Vicksburg, and then a bit farther to Bruinsberg. The navy, which was to supply transportation back across to the Mississippi side, boldly ran the gauntlet past Vicksburg's batteries on the nights of April 16 and 22. Back in Mississippi, Grant struck northeastward, planning to cut the Southern Railroad of Mississippi, which supplied Vicksburg's defenders. But hearing that Confederate reinforcements were approaching Jackson, Grant turned on that city instead and easily captured it on May 14. His rear thus protected, he then got on with the job he had come to do: capture Vicksburg and defeat the army that defended it.

That army, though smaller than Grant's, was formidable: some 31,000 men, well dug in along a crescent-shaped ridge in well-designed fortifications. They were commanded by Lieutenant General John C. Pemberton, a Pennsylvanian by birth and like Grant a graduate of the United States Military Academy at West Point. Venturing out to meet Grant's approach from the east, Pemberton's forces were defeated at Champion Hill and Big Black Bridge. The battle for Vicksburg proper soon began. Their victories en route there had mistakenly led Union officers to believe that Confederate morale had broken and that the city could easily be taken. How wrong they were became clear when the massed infantry assaults of May 19 and 22 were thrown back with heavy losses. Thus deprived of the quick low-cost victory he craved, Grant chose the only acceptable alternative, which was to lay siege to the fortress city. Heavy breeching batteries were brought up to constantly pound the Confederate fortifications, while the navy's gunboats did the same from the river. The Union army dug in and began the process of squeezing the defenders until they quit.

The siege lasted till early July and entailed the countless acts of bravery and sacrifice on both sides that are part of great battles. The battlefield is preserved today in the Vicksburg National Military Park. A visitor center provides an overview of the Vicksburg campaign and its place in the Civil War, and a sixteen-mile tour route along the defensive crescent reveals the sites of the batteries, redoubts, and parapets that Union and

Battery DeGolyer

Confederacy once so fiercely contended over. The Great Redoubt was the object of the Union frontal attack of May 22 that convinced Grant a siege would be necessary. During the siege the field guns of Battery DeGolyer pounded it incessantly. Battery Selfridge mounted heavy naval guns and was manned by Union sailors. At Stockade Redan (a triangular earthwork), federal troops also tried in vain to break Confederate resistance. At the Second Texas Lunette (a crescent-shaped earthwork), Federals burrowed trenches to within fifteen feet of their objective before being forced back. Hovey's Approach gives a good indication of the Federal approach trenches. Beneath the Third Louisiana Redan federal tunnelers exploded two mines in the hope of breaking the Confederate line. The line broke, but the defenders held. Fort Garrott held down the south end of that line; its namesake, Colonel Isham W. Garrott, fell here to a Federal sharpshooter. Fort Hill anchored the left flank and was so formidable that throughout the siege no attack was ever made on it. Guns mounted at the Water Battery just beneath it helped sink the federal ironclad gunboat *Cincinnati.*

In time, constant pounding and continued assaults took their toll. By late June, Pemberton had concluded his command was too weak to either resist another major attack or cut its way out through the encircling Union lines. On July 3 a truce was called, and the next day, July 4, 1863, he surrendered his command to Grant. The Confederates were paroled, and officers were allowed to keep their side-arms and mounts.

With that, the Mississippi River was firmly in Union hands and Confederate hopes of final victory considerably dimmer. The day before,

Confederate forces had also been defeated at Gettysburg. Even two such losses did not break Southern morale, and the fight went on for nearly two more years. Vicksburg did, however, suggest how the war would end—at Appomattox Grant accepted surrender of another Southern army and again allowed officers to keep their side-arms and mounts.

ARMORY REGIONAL MUSEUM *Third Street South, Armory.* Historical exhibits housed in the Gilmore Sanitarium, a former hospital erected in 1916.

BEAUVOIR *200 W. Beach Boulevard, U. S. 90 west of Biloxi.* Greek Revival home of Confederate president Jefferson Davis, built in 1852–1854 and containing the original furnishings.

BILOXI LIGHTHOUSE *U.S. 90 at Porter Avenue, Biloxi.* An 1848 structure fifty-three feet high that guided schooners in the Mississippi Sound and the Gulf of Mexico.

BRICE'S CROSS ROADS NATIONAL BATTLEFIELD SITE *state 370, six miles west of Baldwyn.* Where Confederate General Nathan Bedford Forrest defeated Union soldiers on June 10, 1864.

CAROUSEL *Highland Park, Meridian.* One of the few hand-crafted carousels remaining in the United States; located in a park designed in 1909 in the European tradition.

CARROLLTON Well-preserved example of a prosperous, small, rural county seat and trading center; includes Merrill's Store, a brick structure erected ca. 1834 and used for a variety of public and commercial purposes.

CASEY JONES MUSEUM *I-55 N., Exit 133, Vaughan.* Commemorating famous train wreck; housed in restored depot.

COLUMBUS Important social and commercial center of antebellum Mississippi. Annual pilgrimage includes the Blewett–Harrison–Lee House, Cedars, Gatchell House, and other residences of historical and architectural interest.

CURLEE HOUSE *711 Jackson Street, Corinth.* Greek Revival residence erected ca. 1857 and used as headquarters by both Confederate and Union generals after the Battle of Shiloh.

EPISCOPAL CHAPEL OF THE CROSS *six miles northwest of junction of state 463 and I-55, Madison.* Outstanding example of nineteenth-century Gothic Revival church architecture.

FORD HOUSE *sixteen miles south on state 35, Columbia.* Pioneer dwelling constructed ca. 1810 for John Ford, an early Methodist preacher.

FORT MASSACHUSETTS *south on Ship Island, near Gulfport.* Built ca. 1859 to protect New Orleans; occupied by Union forces in 1861.

GILLIS HOUSE *806 W. Beach Blvd., Biloxi.* A former summer house used by wealthy New Orleans cotton factors from 1838 to 1927.

GOVERNOR'S MANSION *300 E. Capitol Street, Jackson.* Greek Revival house commissioned in 1833, the second-oldest executive mansion in the nation.

HISTORIC JEFFERSON COLLEGE College Street, Washington. Buildings constructed from 1817 to 1937 for the first educational institution in the Mississippi Territory, chartered in 1802.

HOLLY SPRINGS Includes nineteenth-century public and commercial structures and over sixty-five antebellum homes—notably Montrose, an 1858 Classic Revival brick mansion.

ISAIAH T. MONTGOMERY HOUSE Main Street, Mound Bayou. A 1910 house significant as the home of a former slave who was the first mayor of Mound Bayou (1887), a successful early black community. Privately owned.

JACINTO COURTHOUSE state 356, Rienzi. Federal-style courthouse erected in 1854, now restored.

MAGNOLIA HOTEL Rue Magnolia, Biloxi. Resort hotel built in 1847 and now restored as an exhibit gallery.

MANSHIP HOUSE 412 E. Fortification, Jackson. Gothic Revival cottage built ca. 1857 by Charles Manship, mayor who surrendered the city to General Sherman on July 16, 1863.

MERREHOPE 905 Thirty-first Avenue, Meridian. Nineteenth-century clapboard house, restored to 1904 state; one of the four structures to survive in Meridian after Sherman's march in 1864.

MILNER HOUSE / GRASSLAWN 720 E. Beach Boulevard, Gulfport. Two-story frame Greek Revival residence built in 1836 and associated with prominent local families.

MISSISSIPPI STATE HISTORICAL MUSEUM 100 S. State Street, Jackson. Housed in the Old Capitol, built 1833; with art and artifacts relating to Mississippi history.

MONROE COUNTY COURTHOUSE Courthouse Square, Aberdeen. Greek Revival public building erected in 1857.

THE OAKS 823 N. Jefferson Street, Jackson. Restored Greek Revival clapboard house built about 1853.

OLD SPANISH FORT 200 Fort Street, Pascagoula. Mississippi Valley outpost constructed about 1718 and now housing a local history museum.

OLD BRICK HOUSE 410 E. Bayview, Biloxi. One of the oldest buildings in Biloxi, residence of Civil War mayor John L. Henley from 1850 to 1872.

OLD TISHOMINGO COUNTY COURTHOUSE Quitman and Liberty streets, Iuka. Two-story brick Romanesque Revival structure, erected 1888–89.

OXFORD Home of "Ole Miss" and William Faulkner; includes L. Q. C. Lamar House, built ca. 1856 and occupied by the prominent statesman until 1888.

PASS CHRISTIAN SCENIC DRIVE HISTORIC DISTRICT U.S. 90, Pass Christian. "Gold Coast" of elegant beachfront residences.

PORT GIBSON Fine residential and commercial structures that made this town, according to General Grant, "too beautiful to burn."

REUBEN DAVIS HOUSE *803 West Commerce Street, Aberdeen.* Greek Revival mansion constructed 1847–1853 for Reuben Davis, prominent attorney, statesman, and author.

RODNEY *west of Lorman on state 552.* Important nineteenth-century river port, now a ghost town.

ROSEMONT *eight miles east on state 24, Woodville.* Boyhood home of Jefferson Davis, built between 1810 and 1817.

SMITH PARK ARCHITECTURAL DISTRICT *along N. West and N. Congress streets between Capitol Street and State Capitol, Jackson.* Architecturally significant buildings in various styles, built from 1840 to 1940, and focused on a public square that was part of original city plan of 1822.

TULLIS MANOR *947 East Beach Boulevard, Biloxi.* Example of the elaborate vacation homes built on the Gulf Coast in the 1850s.

VICKSBURG River town noted for its many elegant antebellum homes, including Cedar Grove, Planter's Hall, and McRaven.

WAVERLY *junction U.S. 45 and state 50, West Point.* Impressive example of a plantation complex, built ca. 1852.

WINTERVILLE MOUNDS STATE PARK *state 1, four miles north of Greenville.* Built by the temple-mound builders between A.D. 1200 and 1400; one of the largest prehistoric Indian sites in the Mississippi Valley.

MISSOURI

JEFFERSON NATIONAL EXPANSION MEMORIAL St. Louis. The Louisiana Purchase of 1803 doubled the land area encompassed by the nation's borders and assured the United States of dominance in the trans-Mississippi West. On the eastern edge of this vast new territory stood St. Louis, a trading settlement founded by the French in 1764 near the confluence of the Missouri and Mississippi rivers. Ideally situated to serve as a commercial center and transfer point for exploration and settlement, St. Louis reigned as the "Gateway to the West" until the 1870s, when the transcontinental railroad eliminated the city's unique geographical advantages. The Jefferson National Expansion Memorial stands today on the site of the nineteenth-century crossroads and commemorates the era of westward expansion and the explorers and settlers who fulfilled the nation's continental destiny.

Although the territory of Louisiana became part of the Spanish empire in 1762, the settlement of St. Louis two years later reflected continued French dominance in the upper Mississippi region. Pierre Laclede established the village in 1764 as a commercial center for the French fur trading company he represented. Unaware that the Missouri country was no longer part of the French colonial system, he named the new town S. Louis in honor of Louis IX, king of France in the thirteenth century and the patron saint of the reigning Louis XV. Although a Spanish lieutenant governor arrived in 1774 and designated Laclede's settlement as the seat of Spanish government in Upper Louisiana, the French continued to dominate the social and economic life of the region through the rest of the century. In 1800 Napoleon finally forced the weak Spanish monarchy to cede Louisiana back to the French, but St. Louis had scarcely rejoined the French empire before Napoleon sold the territory to the United States.

Ceremonies in St. Louis on March 9 and 10, 1804, marked the transfer of Upper Louisiana to the United States. The American representative was Meriwether Lewis, private secretary to President Thomas Jefferson and, with William Clark, leader of a government-authorized expedition to explore the new acquisition. Lewis and Clark left soon afterwards on a four-thousand-mile journey that took them up the Missouri River to the Great Falls, across the Rocky Mountains, down the Snake and Columbia rivers to the Pacific (well beyond the borders of the Louisiana Purchase), and back east again. The expedition came to a close with a triumphant return to St. Louis on September 23, 1806. Any lingering doubts about Jefferson's bargain with the French vanished with reports from Lewis and Clark of a vast new land rich in natural resources and rife with opportunities.

In the next decades, explorers and fur traders followed the same route that Lewis and Clark had taken along the Missouri River to the

West. Since the trail started at St. Louis, the town naturally prospered as a trading center and home base for western travelers. The arrival of the first steamboat in 1817 greatly expanded the area of trade, and St. Louis became a key transfer point in the growing east-west commerce. The leading beneficiary of the town's strategic location and a key factor in its expanding commercial activity was the fur industry; from 1810 to 1840 St. Louis served as the chief market and supply point for this highly lucrative trade.

Over-trapping and falling fur prices led to a decline in the fur industry in 1840, but business activity actually expanded during the decade that followed. The 1840s marked the beginning of the great westward migration, and St. Louis's strategic location at the head of the Santa Fe, Oregon, and California trails proved highly profitable to local businessmen. Often, after arriving by steamboat from the East, emigrants purchased tools, supplies, guns, and wagons from St. Louis merchants before embarking on the last leg of their journey west. Known as the "Emporium of the West," St. Louis thus functioned as the principal gateway for westward expansion until the 1870s.

Completion of the transcontinental railroad in 1869 significantly undermined that role. As early as the 1840s, local leaders recognized that railroad development would be crucial to the city's future. In 1849 St. Louis hosted the nation's first national railroad convention, chaired by Stephen A. Douglas of Illinois. In a speech in the rotunda of the courthouse, Missouri's Senator Thomas Hart Benton predicted "westward the course of empire" and called for a railroad linking the eastern and western parts of the United States. City boosters felt that St. Louis' strategic location would make it the ideal eastern terminus for such a project, but the selection of a northern route gave the advantage to Chicago and assured the latter's development into the nation's largest railroad center. The railroads quickly replaced the old pioneer trails, and the era of the steamboat and the wagon train came abruptly to an end. The geographic advantages basic to St. Louis' early development held no promise for the future. Recognizing this, city leaders advocated new rail lines to the West, constructed a union railroad station in 1874, and opened an impressive new bridge across the Mississippi that same year. Although these efforts proved crucial to the city's long-term economic health, they did not offset the decline in east-west traffic. By 1875 St. Louis could no longer claim to be the "Gateway to the West."

These developments led to significant changes in the city itself. Since the time of Laclede and the French fur traders, business activity in St. Louis had concentrated along the levee, but the focus shifted uptown in the mid-1870s with the decline of river commerce and the completion of Eads Bridge and the union station. For the next sixty years, the riverfront district declined and decayed. Then in 1935, at the urging of civic leaders, President Franklin D. Roosevelt authorized the development of the old downtown area as the Jefferson National Expansion Memorial

National Historic Site, a tribute to Thomas Jefferson and the significance of the Louisiana Purchase to the nation's westward expansion.

By 1942, over thirty-eight blocks along the riverfront had been acquired and cleared for the project. Only two historic buildings merited saving: the Old Courthouse, erected between 1839 and 1864 on the western edge of the city's business district, and the Old Cathedral, constructed between 1831 and 1834 on property set aside for religious purposes by Pierre Laclede in 1764. The rest of the old waterfront district was cleared for a memorial. Ero Saarinen, a Finnish-American architect, won the 1947 memorial design competition with a proposal for a dramatic stainless steel arch that would symbolize the city's historic gateway role. Constructed between 1962 and 1965, the inverted, weighted catenary-curve arch rises to a height of six hundred thirty feet. A special passenger tram takes passengers to the top for a breathtaking view of modern St. Louis. The Gateway Arch, as it is known, stands astride the visitor center and the Museum of Westward Expansion. The former includes a gift shop and the Tucker Theater, which shows a documentary film on the construction of the arch. Opened in 1976, the museum provides exhibits, guided tours, and special talks on the nineteenth-century American West.

The arch is only the most recent symbol of the city. Mention should be made as well of the Louisiana Purchase Universal Exposition of 1904,

The Arch

more popularly known as the St. Louis World's Fair. Although most of the structures have long vanished, Forest Park—the exposition site—and the Jefferson Memorial Building—now the home of the Missouri Historical Society—still stand from that earlier tribute to Jefferson and the Louisiana Purchase. For decades the city's most prominent symbol was the Eads Bridge, an engineering marvel that still stands astride the Mississippi River adjoining the memorial. But the arch surpasses all. Standing on the riverfront where the city's history began and towering over the modern metropolis, the arch provides a contemporary symbol for the city and sums up its historic role as the gateway to the West.

MARK TWAIN HOME AND MUSEUM 208 Hill Street, Hannibal. Missouri's most famous author, Samuel Clemens, left his home state before the age of twenty; but memories of his childhood in Hannibal provided the inspiration for two of his most famous works, *The Adventures of Tom Sawyer* (1876) and *The Adventures of Huckleberry Finn* (1884). In these two masterpieces of American fiction, Clemens immortalized his idyllic boyhood along the Mississippi River and fixed in the American mind a nostalgic view of Missouri before the advent of the modern industrial age. Several sites in Hannibal associated with his youth have been preserved in tribute to him and his unique re-creation of the Missouri experience.

Samuel Langhorne Clemens was born in 1835 in Florida, Missouri, and grew up in an area of the state known as Little Dixie. Clemens' own family had only recently moved to the Salt River village from Tennessee and, like most of the other residents, still considered themselves Southerners. His father, John Marshall Clemens, hoped to make his fortune at Florida in partnership with a wealthy relative of his wife, but in 1839 he decided to try his luck in the more promising town of Hannibal.

Hannibal typified the small towns that grew up along the Mississippi River during the peak years of river traffic prior to the Civil War. Founded in 1819, the community consisted of only five families in 1827 but expanded significantly during the next as the volume of river trade increased. A pork-packing plant, tobacco factories, flour mills, and sawmills testified to the town's expanding business activity. Other signs of growth and prosperity included a new schoolhouse in 1830, a ferry two years later, a library, and in 1837 the town's first newspaper, the *Commercial Adviser.*

The town's potential for growth induced Clemens' father to try his hand at land speculation. His investment in a quarter block on Hill Street did not pay off, however, and in 1843 he lost title to the property after failing to meet payments. A cousin in St. Louis then stepped in and bought a small lot, which he in turn rented to the Clemens family for twenty-five dollars a year. Here the Clemens erected a one-story three-room house in 1844.

Samuel Clemens was about nine years old then, and his boyhood adventures in and around his family's Hill Street home are reflected in

Mark Twain Home and Museum

his writing. Tom Sawyer did many of the things that Clemens had done as a boy, and his friend Huck was modeled after the author's own boyhood pal, Tom Blankenship, who lived about a block down the alley on North Street. The counterpart to Becky Thatcher was Laura Hawkins, who also lived nearby on Hill Street. Clemens' father practiced law during this period, and one night young Sam Clemens hid in his office to avoid punishment for playing hooky from school. When he climbed in through an open window, he did not know that a murder victim's body was lying in the back room. Upon discovering his company, he jumped out the window, taking the sash with him. Clemens recounted the incident in *Innocents Abroad:* "I didn't need the sash, but it was handier to take it than to leave it. So I took it. I wasn't exactly scared, but I was-ah-considerably agitated."

Samuel and his family lived in the Hill Street residence until 1846, when another bad business venture forced them to give up their home temporarily. They moved across the street to the Pilaster House, where Dr. and Mrs. Orville Grant gave them a place to live in exchange for help in keeping up the house and preparing meals. John Clemens died there in 1847, but later that year his widow and children moved back into their former home across the street. The small quarters became even more crowded in 1851, when Orion Clemens, the eldest son, moved his newspaper publishing business into the front parlor.

Samuel Clemens began his career as an author by writing for his brother's paper, the Hannibal *Journal.* As assistant editor, he wrote news features, local articles, and even "Our Assistant's Column." During this period, a second floor was added to the house to provide additional space. The Clemenses did not enjoy the extra room for long, however, for in 1853 Samuel moved to St. Louis and his mother and brother moved to Muscatine, Iowa.

Clemens went on to become a steamboat pilot, a newspaper reporter again, and of course a celebrated author under the pen name Mark

Twain, but he never forgot his boyhood experiences in Hannibal. Indeed, his recollections inspired both *Tom Sawyer* and *Huckleberry Finn.* In these two masterful novels, he skillfully used characters, settings, and experiences from his youth to provide a nostalgic interpretation of life in mid-nineteenth century Missouri.

The Clemens home, the Pilaster House, and John Clemens' law office still stand today in Hannibal as reminders of Samuel Clemens' ties to the Mississippi River town. The Hill Street house had an assortment of tenants between 1853, when the Clemenses left, and 1911, when Mr. and Mrs. George A. Mahan purchased the structure and presented it to the city of Hannibal. In 1937 and 1938, the house was restored and appropriately furnished. Built flush with the sidewalk, the simple two-story frame building is typical of modest Missouri houses of the period. In the small, low-ceilinged rooms, Clemens' accounts of Tom Sawyer's escapades and his encounters with Aunt Polly come to life. The parlor, the dining room, and the kitchen provided settings for Clemens' tales, and the upstairs bedrooms look just as Tom and Aunt Polly—or Samuel and his mother—would have kept them over a century ago. Adjoining the house on one side is a garden in which stands a statue of Tom and Huck sculpted by Missourian Frederick Hibbard and presented to the city by the Mahans in 1926. A whitewashed fence encloses the garden—just like the famous fence of *Tom Sawyer.* On the other side of the boyhood home is a museum. Opened in 1937, the museum features first editions of Mark Twain's books, personal items, photographs, and even the desk where Clemens wrote *Tom Sawyer.*

Across the street on the southwest corner of Hill and Main stands the Pilaster House. This unusual structure was erected about 1836 or 1837 with prebuilt sections shipped from Cincinnati. The two-and-a-half-story frame structure takes its name from the striking Greek Revival pilasters that adorn the exterior. At one time occupied by the family of the real "Becky Thatcher," the residence housed Dr. and Mrs. Grant in the mid-1840s. Purchased and given to the city by the Mahan family in 1956, the restored building features Grant's office, a drugstore, and a pioneer kitchen on the first floor and living quarters above.

In the mid-1950s, John Clemens' law office was moved into the area from its original site nearer the river. Funds came from Warner Brothers Film Company in appreciation of the town's help while making a movie in Hannibal. The two-story frame structure was restored and dedicated in 1959.

Although later known for its railroad shops, Hannibal remains more closely identified with its most famous native son, Samuel Clemens. His boyhood home, the Pilaster House, and his father's law office provide nostalgic evidence of Clemens' youth in the antebellum river town and bring to life perhaps the most enduring image of nineteenth-century Missouri.

HARRY S. TRUMAN SITES Jackson County. Throughout his years in public life, Harry S. Truman championed the Jeffersonian values and beliefs that had dominated Missouri politics since the time of Thomas Hart Benton. On the Jackson County Court, in the United States Senate, and as vice president and then president of the United States, the "Man from Independence" remained faithful to his roots in rural and small-town Missouri and enjoyed enormous popularity as the plain-speaking defender of the common man. He always preferred the familiar sur-roundings of Jefferson County to the glamor of the White House or world travel: fittingly, the Harry S. Truman Library and Museum stands not far from his former Independence home. This impressive facility and the several historic sites associated with Truman's life together pro-vide a unique opportunity to learn about the life and career of the preeminent Missourian of the twentieth century.

Harry S. Truman was born on May 8, 1884, in his parents' home in Lamar, Missouri, but he spent most of his childhood and youth some hundred miles to the north in Jackson County. Both his father's and his mother's family had settled in the area south of Independence in the 1840s, and the young family returned to live there with Mrs. Truman's parents, Solomon and Harriet Young. They lived on the Young's Grand-view farm until 1890 and then moved to nearby Independence, the county seat. Harry Truman graduated from high school in Indepen-dence in 1901 and worked there and at Kansas City before returning to Grandview in 1906.

For the next ten years, young Truman helped his father operate the family farm. This first-hand experience with the frustrations and demands of farming led to a fuller appreciation of rural life and reinforced the Jeffersonian values that were so much a part of his upbringing. He also

Truman's "Missouri White House"

got his first taste of politics during the years at Grandview. His father's active support of the Democratic party led to the elder Truman's appointment as a precinct election judge in 1906, and he in turn chose young Harry as his clerk. At his father's death in 1915, he succeeded him for a short time as road overseer for the Eastern District of Jackson County and also served briefly as the local postmaster. Through these activities and his involvement in the Kansas City 10th Ward Democratic Club, the Masons, and the Jackson County Farm Bureau, Truman began to develop the wide circle of friends and contacts essential to a successful political career.

Truman left Grandview in 1917 to serve in World War I. At his return in 1919 he married Bess Wallace, and the couple moved into her family's home on North Delaware Street in Independence. He and a partner then opened a haberdashery business, but this venture did not survive the 1921 recession. He emerged from the ordeal heavily in debt and more sensitive to the problems of small business. At the suggestion of a wartime friend, Truman then tried his hand at politics. He won his first race in 1922 and served for two years as the Eastern District judge in the Jackson County Court. His re-election bid in 1924 failed, giving him his first and last electoral loss. He tried again and in 1926 returned to the county court as presiding judge, a position he held until his election to the United States Senate in 1934.

The latter victory in large part reflected the strength of Truman's appeal to the ordinary people of Missouri's villages and farms. He voiced their concerns in a way that only one from among them could do. This appeal carried over into national politics as well. Although his election as vice president in 1944 probably had more to do with Franklin D. Roosevelt's popularity and the war effort, he ably demonstrated the viability of an appeal to the common man in the famous "Whistlestop Campaign" of the 1948 presidential race. But despite his extraordinary political success, the lure of Washington, and the excitement of international politics, Truman preferred the quiet, familiar surroundings of Independence. When he retired from public office in 1953, he returned to the house he and his wife had lived in for over three decades.

Before he left office, Truman began considering the disposition of the papers and other materials accumulated during his years in the White House. Following FDR's lead, he initiated plans for a presidential library that would serve as the repository for his papers and function as both a research institution and a museum. Some 17,000 individuals and institutions contributed to the construction of the library on a thirteen-acre site in Independence, only six blocks from Truman's home. Dedicated on July 6, 1957, it became the second presidential library administered by the National Archives and Records Service. Truman had a deep appreciation of the value of history and remained involved in the library's activities throughout his lifetime. At his death in 1972, he was buried in its courtyard.

The modern limestone structure houses both a museum and research facilities. The museum includes exhibits on Truman's presidency, a full-scale reproduction of his White House Oval office, and even one of the presidential limousines. The lobby features a striking mural entitled "Independence and the Opening of the West," completed in 1961 by famous Missouri artist Thomas Hart Benton, great-nephew of the powerful nineteenth-century political figure. The Truman Library's research collection includes his presidential files, the files of other White House offices, Truman's Senate files, the papers of over 350 official, political, and personal associates, and an assortment of gifts, memorabilia, photographs, and published material. The library also has an on-going oral history program. In 1957 the Harry S. Truman Library Institute for National and International Affairs was established to promote the library and its programs. The Institute sponsors conferences, special research projects, grants-in-aid to scholars, and a book prize.

South of the Truman Library is the Harry S. Truman National Historic Site. The district preserves the character of the neighborhood around the Truman home at 219 North Delaware. Mrs. Truman's maternal grandparents erected the two-and-a-half-story Victorian dwelling in the late nineteenth century, and she and her mother moved there in 1903 after the death of her father. It remained home to her and her husband even through the years in Washington. The President always enjoyed his trips back to the "Missouri White House" and his famous daily walks through the area now included in the historic district.

Another Truman site in Independence is the Independence Square Courthouse. The oldest portion of the structure was erected in the 1830s and subsequently remodeled five times. The last remodeling came during Truman's tenure as chief judge of the Jackson County Court. The Jackson County Parks and Recreation Department has restored and furnished the office he occupied and the courtroom where he presided to their appearance in 1934, just prior to his election to the Senate. No other site is so significant for Truman's early political career.

Also still standing is the Missouri-Pacific Depot used by Truman on his frequent train trips back and forth from Washington. Erected in 1913 in a style typical of period railroad stations, the one-story red-brick structure is popularly known as the Truman Train Station. As the starting point for the 1948 "Whistlestop Campaign," the station commemorates one of the most famous episodes in Truman's political career.

Two other Truman sites are located outside Independence. The house where he was born in 1884 still stands in Lamar, about 112 miles to the south. The modest six-room frame residence was purchased by the United Automobile Workers union and given to the state. Opened in 1959, the Harry S. Truman Birthplace State Historic Site is administered by the Missouri Department of Natural Resources.

Jackson County also owns the farm in Grandview where Truman lived as a young man. A two-story frame farmhouse built by his maternal grandfather in the 1890s still stands on a 5.3-acre section of the original 600-acre farm.

Harry Truman identified closely with his home state throughout his political career and brought considerable fame and attention to Jackson County. The numerous monuments to Truman and his career testify to Missouri's equal pride in him, its only native son ever elected to the United States presidency. The library and museum, the historic district, the courthouse, the railroad station, the birthplace, and the farm each shed life on the man, his politics, and the era in which he lived.

ANHEUSER-BUSCH BREWERY NATIONAL HISTORIC LAND-MARK *Broadway and Pestalozzi streets, St. Louis.* Some original buildings of the innovative brewery established by Eberhard Anheuser and run by his son-in-law, Adolphus Busch.

ARROW ROCK STATE HISTORIC SITE *thirteen miles north of I-70 on state 41, Arrow Rock.* Preserved early-nineteenth-century buildings in a village on the Santa Fe Trail.

BATTLE OF LEXINGTON STATE HISTORIC SITE *state 13A, Lexington.* Where Confederates under General Sterling Price defeated Union troops in 1861; includes the Anderson House, used as a hospital by both sides.

BOLLINGER MILL STATE HISTORIC SITE *state 34 south of Burfordville.* Includes a grist mill undergoing restoration and a wooden covered bridge, both from the 1800s.

BOONE HOME *highway F, Defiance.* Stone house built about 1820 by Daniel Boone and his son, Nathan, with a museum containing furniture and tools of the Boone family.

DEUTSCHHEIM STATE HISTORIC SITE *109 W. Second Street, Hermann.* Includes two houses of early German immigrants; one is the site of a print shop, the other has Greek Revival and Federal details.

DILLARD MILL STATE HISTORIC SITE *off state 49 on Huzzah Creek, Davisville.* A restored water-powered gristmill, built about 1900.

EUGENE FIELD HOUSE AND TOY MUSEUM *634 S. Broadway, St. Louis.* Childhood home of the children's poet, with antique toys and dolls.

FELIX VALLE HOUSE STATE HISTORIC SITE *Merchant and Second streets, Ste. Genevieve.* Federal-style 1818 house; residence and office and storage for fur company trading with Indians.

FIRST MISSOURI STATE CAPITOL STATE HISTORIC SITE *St. Charles.* Where the state legislature met 1821–1826 while the new capitol was being built in Jefferson City; includes restoration of a general store and residences.

FORT DAVIDSON STATE HISTORIC SITE *on state 21 in Pilot Knob.* Earthwork remnants from the 1864 battle in which Union forces bloodied General Sterling Price's Confederate army.

JEFFERSON BARRACKS on the Missouri River ten miles south of St. Louis. Military buildings dating from the 1850s, including a museum; on the site of most important western post 1826–1848.

JEFFERSON LANDING / STATE CAPITOL COMPLEX   riverfront, Jefferson City. Where steamboat passengers disembarked in the 1800s; museum and visitor center in the Lohman Building and an art gallery in the Union Hotel; present state capitol with Thomas Hart Benton murals and the state museum.

KANSAS CITY MUSEUM OF HISTORY AND SCIENCE 3218 Gladstone Boulevard, Kansas City. Natural history museum with materials on prehistoric people, archeology, and paleontology.

MARAMEC MUSEUM Maramec Spring Park, Saint James. A historical and industrial museum with the model of an 1860 village; dioramas of iron works, gristmill, and an early Indian village; and pioneer mementos.

MISSOURI HISTORICAL SOCIETY Forest Park, St. Louis. Museum contains Charles A. Lindbergh collection, artwork, toys, and large costume collection.

MISSOURI STATE MUSEUM State Capitol, Jefferson City. Exhibits on Missouri history, including art and artifacts on pioneer, ethnic, industrial, and Indian settlements.

NELSON-ATKINS MUSEUM 4525 Oak Street, Kansas City. Art museum with American paintings, pre-Columbian works, and an excellent collection of materials of the early Plains Indians and the Far East.

OZARK NATIONAL SCENIC RIVERWAYS Current and Jacks Fork rivers. Includes gristmills, caves, and other landmarks used by both early white settlers and Indians.

PERSHING BOYHOOD HOME STATE HISTORIC SITE one mile north of U.S. 36 on state 5 in Laclede. Home of General John J. Pershing; furnished in style of late 1800s, with displays on his life and career.

PONY EXPRESS STABLES MUSEUM 914 Penn Street, St. Joseph. Original stables of the Pony Express, with exhibits and tours.

STE. GENEVIEVE HISTORIC DISTRICT Ste. Genevieve. French settlement of early 1700s; relocated in 1785 but with distinctive French buildings of the period, including the Louis Bolduc House, open for tours.

TRAIL OF TEARS STATE PARK off I-55 and state 177 ten miles east of Fruitland. On the route of the Cherokees in moving from their southern home to Oklahoma in the 1800s.

VAN METER STATE PARK on state 122 twelve miles northwest of Marshall. Historic Missouri Indians, who gave Missouri its name, lived here; Lyman Archeological Research Center Museum with exhibits on the ancient cultures and burial mounds.

WATKINS WOOLEN MILL STATE HISTORIC SITE six and a half miles north of Excelsior Springs and one and a half miles west of highway

MM, near Lawson. Includes a restored mill and plantation that shows the western edge of industrial revolution; original textile machinery still intact.

WILSON'S CREEK NATIONAL BATTLEFIELD PARK *off U.S. 60 twelve miles southwest of Springfield.* Where Union General Nathaniel Lyon was killed in a Confederate victory of 1861; new interpretive visitor center.

WASHINGTON STATE PARK *state 21 outside of Desoto.* Once part of a ceremonial grounds used by the Indians A.D. 1000–1600; with petroglyphs.

MONTANA

CUSTER BATTLEFIELD NATIONAL MONUMENT fifteen miles south of Hardin. Though a New Englander or a Virginian might disagree, the most epic chapters in the history of American settlement are commonly associated with the West. The landing of Englishmen at Plymouth Rock and Jamestown and their early struggle to survive in an inhospitable wilderness were remarkable accomplishments that men later recorded in suitably inspired accounts. History and legend often blurred. But common to the general memory of these events is the picture of people from afar intent on building in a new land a way of life that was new in some though not all particulars. That way of life was established before the American government ever was, a fact that no doubt helped make the American Revolution so successful. It was a process not just of pushing back the wilderness but also of building civic and political institutions. It took more than 150 years and patient labor of mind and body by many Americans.

But compared with the history of the West, such a slow process lacks the crude grandeur of events played out quickly against a grand physical setting. In America, the vastness of the trans-Mississippi West provided this grandeur. By the time whites went west in large numbers after the Civil War, they took with them the fundamental institutions of government that their forefathers had already worked out. To them fell the rougher work of surviving in a hostile place and of creating wealth where none had been before. In their path lay others, Indians, whose presence set the stage for an epic conflict of cultures. The prize was a vast and beautiful land; a prize too valuable, it turned out, to permit coexistence of two widely differing ways of life. For years the story was largely told in terms of the advance of an irresistibly superior civilization and the demise of an obviously inferior one. Lately, it has been told differently. All agree, however, that by the last quarter of the nineteenth century the Indians were losing the one element crucial to their survival in an age when their contemporaries elsewhere were making industrial revolutions and promoting a vision of the good life filled with factories and farms. They were losing their isolation.

The circumstances leading to "Custer's last stand" afford pertinent illustration. Determined white settlement of the Great Plains waited until after the Civil War and thus actually came after places farther west—California, Oregon, Utah—were settled. Geography, climate, and the Indians were all hindrances, none easily overcome. But the promise of free land under the Homestead Act of 1862 and the building of the railroads enticed many to try life in this high and dry place. The process continued up until World War I. Through it all the Indians beat a steady retreat, though their sad fate initially hardly seemed inevitable. At first, both sides seemed to seek accommodation, and in good faith deals were struck. One of the most famous, the one tied directly to Custer, was the Fort Laramie Treaty of 1868 between the United States government and various northern Plains tribes. It designated as a permanent Indian reservation a large area of present-day western South Dakota and eastern Wyoming and obliged the government to protect the Indians on it "against the commission of all depredations by people of the United States."

But western history, in addition to being played on a grander scale, also seemed to move faster than history had moved in the East. Just six years after the treaty was signed, in 1874, the discovery of gold in the Black Hills of South Dakota—lands sacred to the Sioux and theirs by treaty—showed just how fast. An army expedition led by George Armstrong Custer soon confirmed the presence of gold in paying quantities. Prospectors, those migrant men who relentlessly had followed rumor of gold to California, Idaho, Colorado, Nevada, and Montana, soon arrived in quantity. The army's position was unenviable. At first government policy was to stand by its treaty commitments, and the army, its agent, was given the job of keeping the gold diggers away from the gold. It succeeded imperfectly, and in September 1875 the government tried to buy the Black Hills back from the Sioux, who refused. Seeing the Sioux immovable and the prospectors irresistible, the government stepped aside, effectively opening the area to anyone willing to risk the wrath of the Indians. The Sioux did not attack the miners, but in defiance of a treaty that had been dishonored they did leave the reservation, determined to resist further white encroachment. Hundreds left to join their brethren in the Powder River country, where abundant game meant they did not have to depend on the government for food supplies. From the government point of view, that meant the Indians were out of control.

To the army fell the job of returning them to the reservation if they failed to comply with the government's ultimatum to return. They of course did not comply. The army found itself involved in no mere police action, but another war. That at first it did not realize this led in part to Custer's disaster. The army's campaign began in the spring of 1876, America's centennial year, when Brigadier General George Crook proceeded north from Fort Fetterman, Wyoming, and engaged the Indians in the indecisive Battle of Powder River in Montana. The army next tried a three-pronged strategy, with one force marching west from Fort Abraham Lincoln in North Dakota, another east from Fort Shaw in Montana, and a third up from Fort Fetterman. With luck they were to converge in southeastern Montana on the Indians, who were led by Sitting Bull, Crazy Horse, and other chiefs. Luck was not with them.

The Fort Fetterman force met the enemy first but was so bloodied at the Battle of the Rosebud that it withdrew to Fort Sheridan, Wyoming, to regroup. Unaware of this, the other two columns rendezvoused on the Yellowstone at the mouth of the Rosebud and made plans to engage

Custer Hill

the Indians. The force consisted of both cavalry and infantry. Fearing the enemy might outrun him, commanding General Alfred Terry ordered Lieutenant Colonel George Armstrong Custer's Seventh Cavalry to advance to the Indian camp on the Little Big Horn. They were not to force a battle until the larger force caught up. Custer commanded some 700 men, a large force for Plains warfare and large enough, it was thought, to confront Indians. The Sioux' total strength, so it was also thought, was only about 800, and apparently no one believed they would ever all come together at one time and place. That intelligence was bad; it was the key to the disaster that befell Custer, who thought it safe to divide his regiment into three battalions. On June 25, the one commanded by Custer was attacked not by a few hundred but by thousands of well-armed Sioux and Cheyenne warriors along the Little Big Horn. What exactly happened that day is not certain, though the results were. Overwhelmed, Custer's five companies of some 225 men were annihilated. Indian losses were reported as no more than 100.

But the Indian victory was shortlived. An angry nation demanded revenge, and within two years the power of the northern Plains tribes had been broken. Custer and his cavalry meanwhile had entered the epic history and legend of the West. The Custer Battlefield National Monument on the Crow Indian Reservation today marks the spot. Most of Custer's troopers lie in a common grave around the base of a memorial shaft on Custer Hill. Custer himself was buried in 1877 at the United States Military Academy at West Point. The drama of their "last stand" befit the vast open spaces of Montana. Their reputation as heroes was instantly and permanently secured in part because they were quickly and permanently avenged. To the Indians, whose numbers the army so badly guessed, Custer and his troopers threatened an end to isolation. Before long, not even the remotest corners of the West offered them shelter.

BUTTE NATIONAL HISTORIC LANDMARK *Butte* At three times the size of Pennsylvania, with a single county bigger than the whole state of Connecticut, Montana is a large state once described as "bounded on the west by the Japan Current, on the north by the aurora borealis, on the south by Price's Army, and on the east by the Day of Judgement." Montana is also a rich state. It is rich in a way that men have long understood riches. Beneath its mountains lie gold and silver, metals that since ancient times have been thought to have intrinsic worth, and beneath the same mountains also lie metals of less lofty reputation but whose market worth has proved enormous: lead, tungsten, aluminum, zinc, and most of all copper.

As a visit there will make clear, copper and Butte are one story. It began in the 1860s, a decade that in history books was dominated by the Civil War and Reconstruction and by great moral and constitutional questions about slavery and secession. So it was—in the East. In the West however, such weighty themes had to compete with more immediate matters: in Montana, mining matters. Mining was actually the West's second great attraction for men from the East. The first had been the fur trade, which did not last. Mining did, as a city like Butte boldly testifies. It began there in 1864 with the discovery of gold in Silver Bow Creek. By that time, the West's mineral frontier was well established and well peopled by a migrant population that moved easily about at the newest rumor of precious metal. It was fully fifteen years since the discovery of gold in California had set off the process; since then prospecters had roved through Nevada, Idaho, and the fabulous Pikes Peak diggings in Colorado. A few became rich; many more did not.

About these early days of the mineral frontier there is a romantic image of individual prospecters panning gold from mountain streams with primitive tools and a mule for transportation. The enormous extent of the West's mineral wealth soon changed that, as large forces gathered to harvest it. It required capital and improved transportation and the presence of bold, clever, and sometimes ruthless men. Butte from the 1870s on had all these in abundance.

Marcus Daly arrived in the mid-1870s and quickly smelled Butte's potential. While prospecting for silver he found a vein of copper of unparalleled richness. He had the foresight to sense what it meant. The age of electricity was just dawning, and with it the nation's appetite for copper was bound to soar. High demand made obvious the advantages of large-scale mining, mass-production refining, and cheap rail transportation. With alacrity, Daly set about the risky entrepreneurial tasks of bringing together a product and its market and, in the process, of enriching himself. Two years after his discovery the town of Butte was laid out, and in 1881 the first railroad, the Utah and Northern, reached it. With the backing of outside capitalists, Daly first formed the Anaconda Gold and Silver Mining Company and then, as silver gave way to copper, the Anaconda Copper Company. By the mid-1880s the Anaconda had produced 36 million pounds of copper, and from Daly's smelter on Warm Springs Creek northwest of Butte poured the arsenic-laden fumes that were a smelly symbol of the copper boom. (They were also said to have so coated the grass that local cattle had copper-plated teeth.)

Daly of course was not alone. Given the possibility of such rewards, the competition was quick to gather. William A. Clark soon became Daly's arch-enemy and his political and business rival in the 1880s and 1890s. With both men the mixture of mining and politics was common-place, climaxing in Clark's extraordinary efforts to be elected to the United States Senate in 1898 and 1899. Daly won the Democratic pri-mary in 1898, but through the use (Clark's forces said) of repeat voters herded like sheep to vote the "Dalycratic" ticket. Clark fought back through the state legislature (which, until the Seventeenth Amendment, elected United States Senators), where (with what Daly's forces said was wholesale bribery) he was elected. Daly took his charges to Washing-ton, to the Senate Committee on Privileges and Elections, and pending their decision Clark resigned. Returning to Montana to vindicate him-self, he consolidated his alliances, captured the Democratic party machinery, and won a full term in 1900. It had cost him a bundle, some-thing Clark did not deny. "I never bought a man who wasn't for sale," he is supposed to have said. Marcus Daly meanwhile had died, some

Butte's Broadway

said of a broken heart, and the "copper collar" had been riveted onto Montana politics.

Back in 1889 Daly had reorganized the Anaconda Company as the Amalgamated Copper Company, an enormous holding company controlled by Standard Oil. It was against this giant that Fritz Heinze, the third of Montana's great "copper kings," waged war for over a decade. Heize was educated as a mining engineer, but by nature he was an entrepreneur of the first order. Soon after his arrival in 1889 he built a smelter to cut into the near monopoly of Daly and Clark and, exploiting a law that allowed the discoverer of a mineral vein to follow it downward to any depth beyond its sidelines ("apex law"), he dug high-grade ore from mines others thought were theirs. When they sought injunctions to halt his incursions, Heinze's tame county judges routinely blocked them. In 1900 Heinze and Clark cooperated closely, and after Clark sold out to Amalgamated Heinze continued to battle, picturing it as a David-against-Goliath contest. It was the little man against the corporate giant, he said. To ordinary miners he said: "They will force you to dwell in Standard Oil houses while you live, and they will bury you in Standard Oil coffins when you die."

Although Heinze's "David" pose appealed to many ordinary mining Montanans, it was Goliath who eventually won out. The Copper Trust broke his hold on the local judiciary, and in 1906 he sold out to Amalgamated for $10.5 million. Amalgamated then consolidated its hold on the copper industry and on the state itself. The Anaconda Copper Mining Company, as the new giant was called, was for years the force to be reckoned with in Montana politics and in its economy. Its enterprises were huge: reduction and smelting works in East Helena, Anaconda, and Great Falls, vast coal, lumber, and mercantile holdings—and of course the coppers shafts on Butte Hill: "the richest hill on earth."

The Butte National Historic Landmark today recalls what these early days were like. Among the most famous landmarks is the Copper King Mansion, built by William A. Clark and a fitting memorial to Clark the Copper King. A looming brick Victorian structure of thirty-four rooms, it preserves the opulence of another era in its parquet floors, stained-glass windows, and frescoed ceilings. The Arts Chateau, another turn-of-the-century mansion built with copper wealth, is now a museum and art gallery. The Silver Bow County Courthouse boasts a stained-glass dome, murals nearly two stories high and, aptly, copper-clad doors. The Butte Silver Bow Club (now the miners' union) was once the most exclusive club for wealthy men in Montana. At the World Museum of Mining visitors can see some thirty exhibit buildings recalling every aspect of early mining history. This was the world that Daly, Clark, and Heinze and their miners knew. Although its outward appearance has changed much today, the substance of it has not. Butte Hill still yields up its copper for hungry markets, while the city that grew up around it retains its distinctive character.

GRANT-KOHRS RANCH NATIONAL HISTORIC SITE Deer Lodge.
Montana's none-too-modest nickname is the "Treasure State." Some of
the treasure is obvious. Since ancient times men have treasured gold
and silver, and rumors that Montana guarded large stores of it brought
the seekers of easy wealth in droves to its mountains and valleys after
the Civil War. Copper, though less glamorous, proved an even greater
bonanza as America and the world entered the age of electricity in the
late nineteenth and early twentieth centuries. Zinc, tungsten, lead, and
aluminum later added to the metallic treasures buried in Montana's
mountains. Coal and oil were buried beneath her vast eastern plains,
resources that in the late twentieth century were coveted as much as
gold and silver had been in an earlier era. But nature did not bury all
of Montana's treasure. Tourists and natives know it as "big sky country,"
and its mountain scenery from Glacier Park on the Canadian boundary
down to the Wyoming line is among the most glorious on the continent.
In a crowded world where space itself is a treasure, Montana with 145,587
square miles (the fourth largest state in the Union) is truly richly endowed.

Other treasure was less obvious, and it took a type of man different
from those who sought mineral wealth to harvest it. In its crude form it
was grass, thousands and thousands of acres of it covering Montana's
vast eastern reaches and blanketing countless intermountain valleys. For
centuries before the white man came, it was rich sustenance for great
herds of North American bison that wandered wild and free with no
enemy but Indian hunters. The white man, with a different understanding of nature and how it might be used, changed things. He hunted the
buffalo nearly to extinction and overcame the aboriginal culture, con-
signing its dwindling members to government reservations. The great
bulk of the land he possessed for himself privately, or publicly in the
name of his government. He was not therefore merely a predatory con-
queror or if he was that, he was also other things. He was the carrier of
another kind of civilization and the creater of new kinds of wealth. He
used the grass in new ways, and the Grant-Kohrs Ranch near Deer Lodge
is an example of the result.

This once-mammoth cattle ranch originated with a Canadian trapper
and hunter named Johnny Grant, who settled in the Deer Lodge Valley
in the 1850s before many whites had even heard of the land now called
Montana. With his Indian wife and a large family he prospered, and in
a few years he boasted a herd of 2,000 cattle. They roamed freely on the
unfenced public range, foraging for themselves on the rich grasses. The
cowboys disturbed them only for fall and spring roundups when new
stock was branded and the fattened animals were culled out for market.
It seemed in the beginning a perfect use of nature's bounty, which itself
in the beginning seemed boundless. For the skilled, the patient, and the
lucky, like Johnny Grant, it also produced prosperity, reflected in the
substantial ranchhouse he built in 1862 and 1863. We do not know why
Grant built such a large house in such a rude and empty place, but what

he built lasts to the present day. A log structure constructed by French Canadian Alexander Pambrun, it was sixty-four feet long, thirty wide, and sixteen high—generous dimensions then and now. With a clapboard veneer, green shutters, twenty-eight windows, and two stories, the house was recorded in early accounts as "by long odds, the finest in Montana," appearing incongruously "as if it had been lifted by the chimneys from the bank of the St. Lawrence and dropped down in Deer Lodge Valley."

It may have been incongruous in the beginning, but over its long lifetime the house and its occupants came to dominate the valley. In 1866 Johnny Grant sold his house and ranch for $19,200 to Conrad Kohrs, its second and most famous owner. Kohrs was a Danish immigrant who arrived in the Deer Lodge Valley in 1862. A butcher by trade, Kohrs was also a man whose keen eye for larger opportunities, native talent, and gift of luck made him one of early Montana's most successful entrepreneurs. All around him other men were trying to get rich quick by mining gold. Kohrs more patiently mined nature's other wealth—the grass—and served the market the miners themselves provided. The butchers of Deer Lodge and surrounding settlements needed meat; Kohrs set out to supply it. In the process he became far richer than most of the miners and any of the other butchers. He brought his young wife Augusta to the ranch in 1868 when she was only nineteen, and though she traveled frequently and had a house in Helena, she was a powerful presence in the valley until her death in 1945. Together, the Kohrses and John Bielenberg (Conrad's half-brother and business partner) built a legendary ranching empire whose history illuminates the history of the Montana cattle business as a whole.

The 1860s and 1870s were the heyday of open-range grazing on the public domain. Fences were unknown, and when hungry cattle overgrazed there was always more free grass over the next rise. Eastern markets were expanding, and improved railroad transportation and the advent of the refrigerator car gave western cattlemen easy access to them. Business boomed, and Kohrs profited accordingly. Cautious but with a good sense of timing, he brought to his ranges proven new breeds like Herefords and shorthorns, and as the nature of the beef business changed he deftly changed with it. Like many businesses this one had certain self-correcting features that made for change. Lucrative markets led to overgrazing; and harsh weather in the 1880s led to some disastrous years. As homesteaders pushed west, encroaching on open range that once was the cattlemen's alone, Kohrs purchased and leased huge tracts of land to keep alive, after a fashion, the open-range business. In time higher land values and higher taxes made such holdings untenable, and the cattle business was forced to a new, more intensive form. Less land and fewer but heavier cattle tended more closely by more ranch hands became the trend by the 1920s. Cattle lived not just on nature's grass but on hay and other supplemental feeds. Overgrazed

*Belgian mares
with colts,
ca. 1936*

pasture was replanted, wells dug, fences maintained. The range was managed scientifically. Cattle eugenics became a much studied subject.

Certain fundamentals, however, stayed much the same. This was still a business in which men invested now in the hope of future but always uncertain returns. Patience, hope, and chance still loomed large in it. Weather and the gyrations of the market always threatened quick disaster. A fortunate few, like the Kohrses, succeeded. Their home ranch, virtually all of whose buildings remain today, reflects their success and recalls the old ranching life of their Montana. His successors made a large brick addition to Grant's original house in 1890. With the resulting T-shaped structure came new amenities: running water, central heating, gaslight, a sunlit solarium for Augusta's potted plants. Around it grew up the jumble of other buildings for man and beast that were part of a large cattle ranch. Altogether there are twenty-two, and all are open to public view. Bunkhouse row housed the ranch hands, and though just fifty feet from the main house it was socially a world apart. Large barns, horse stables, wagon sheds, and granaries suggest the kind of activity that once was part of everyday life here.

Outside among the animals under the wide Montana sky, it was very much a man's world. But inside the ranch house it was very much Augusta's. During her long marriage and for the years she was a widow, she was a warm but imposing presence. Her table (always graced with silver, china, and white linen, and at which she always served the meat course herself) featured beef, lamb, veal, roast turkey, heavy soups and stews, rich pies, and always abundant coffee. (Bunkhouse fare was simpler but as abundant.) On birthdays and at Christmas the house was especially festive, the cooks producing even fancier meals. Fresh flowers abounded from beds in the yard, where in summer lilac bushes formed a tunnel where the children ran and played. The interior furnishings, which are all original, reflect the tastes of a lady who traveled frequently to Europe and the East Coast and who brought back with her to Deer Lodge objects that would soften and uplift her life in this remote outland. "There was no show or display, but everything was solid, substantial, in good taste," remembered one visitor in words that well described Augusta Kohrs herself. Both as a wife and as a wealthy widow she entertained generously and decorously. Her philanthropies were considerable, befitting her privileged status. When she came to Montana it was rude frontier. Like her investor, legislator, and rancher husband, she left her mark indelibly on it.

The Grant-Kohrs Ranch thus documents the evolution of the cattle business in Montana and commemorates the personal history of several of the individuals who made their lives and livings in it. It is an important public and private resource and one that will richly reward the history-minded visitor.

BAD PASS TRAIL (SIOUX TRAIL) *along the Big Horn River in Big Horn Canyon National Recreation Area, east of Warren.* Remnants of a trail used by Indians and fur traders, dating back to 7000 B.C., with some 300 rock cairns.

BANNOCK HISTORIC DISTRICT *off state 278, twenty-two miles from Dillon.* Ghost town abandoned in 1938 that was site of state's first gold discovery in 1862; oldest town and first territorial capital.

BATTLE OF THE ROSEBUD SITE *six miles south of Kirby.* Where the Sioux tangled with Gen. George Crook just before the Battle of the Little Big Horn.

BIG HOLE BATTLEFIELD NATIONAL MONUMENT *Wisdom.* National Park Service visitor center, with artifacts from the Nez Perce Indians and United States Army, in the area of the 1877 battle.

C. M. RUSSELL MUSEUM *1201 Fourth Ave. N., Great Falls.* Art of the famous western painter and sculptor, along with art of other western and contemporary artists.

CHARLES W. CLARK MANSION *108 N. Washington St., Butte.* Built in Chateauesque style in 1898–1899 for the son of William A. Clark, the copper king; now an art and cultural center.

CHIEF JOSEPH BATTLEGROUND OF THE BEAR'S PAW *about fifteen miles south of Chinook.* Site of the last battle in the Nez Perce War, 1877, where Chief Joseph surrendered.

CHIEF PLENTY COUPS MEMORIAL *off state 416 west of Pryor.* Log house and store on a farm that is a memorial to the Crow chief who promoted friendly relations between whites and Indians.

COPPER VILLAGE MUSEUM AND ARTS CENTER OF DEER LODGE COUNTY *114 E. Eighth Street, Anaconda.* Artifacts from the area, including trapping, ranching, mining, and Indian life.

DANIELS COUNTY MUSEUM AND PIONEER TOWN *Scobey.* Recreation of a frontier town, with a blacksmith shop, general store, saloon, and other buildings and activities.

FLATHEAD INDIAN MUSEUM *St. Ignatius.* Located on the Flathead

Indian Reservation but with arts and crafts from major tribes throughout the United States.

FORT BENTON MUSEUM *1801 Front Street, Fort Benton.* Located in a mid-nineteenth-century house near the ruins of the fur-trading post; with artifacts from the fur-trade era.

FORT C. F. SMITH HISTORIC DISTRICT *east of Fort Smith in Big Horn Canyon National Recreation Area.* Fort foundations, trail ruts, and other remnants of the fort on the Bozeman Trail destroyed by Red Cloud in 1868.

FORT LOGAN AND BLOCKHOUSE *seventeen miles northwest of White Sulphur Springs.* A complex with log structures, including last log block-house in the West, built 1869–1880 as Camp Baker to protect freight route between Fort Benton and Helena.

FORT MISSOULA HISTORICAL MUSEUM *Building 322, Fort Missoula.* Agricultural, logging, and other equipment from the frontier, housed in the original non-commissioned officers' quarters.

FORT OWEN *one-half mile northwest of Stevensville.* Remnants of log and adobe structures built in the 1850s; the site of the state's first saw-mill, flour mill, and school.

FORT PECK AGENCY *Poplar.* Remains of a nineteenth-century military post that was an Indian boarding school after 1893; now includes some twentieth-century buildings.

GRAND UNION HOTEL *Fourteenth and Front streets, Fort Benton* Built 1881–1882 to accommodate travelers on the Missouri River.

GREAT FALLS CENTRAL HIGH SCHOOL *1400 First Avenue, N., Great Falls.* Built in 1896 and a good example of Richardsonian Romanesque architecture applied to state's schools; now the home of Paris Gibson Square, a community cultural center.

HEARST FREE LIBRARY *Main and Fourth streets, Anaconda.* An 1898 Neoclassical Revival building donated by the mother of William Randolph Hearst, the newspaper tycoon.

HELENA HISTORIC DISTRICT *Hauser Boulevard to Acropolis between Garfield and Rodney streets, Helena.* Mid-nineteenth- to early-twentieth-century buildings, the earliest dating from the city's 1864 gold discovery.

HOCKADAY CENTER FOR THE ARTS *Second Ave. E. and Third Street, Kalispell.* Contemporary art of the Northwest.

J. K. RALSTON MUSEUM AND ART CENTER *221 Fifth S. W., Sidney.* Historic artifacts from the frontier, with art.

KLUGE HOUSE *540 W. Main Street, Helena.* Built by a German immigrant in the 1880s and a rare example of a Prussian-style hewn-log house. Privately owned.

MADISON BUFFALO JUMP STATE MONUMENT *seven miles south of Logan.* Used from 2000 B.C. to the eighteenth century, with two village sites, a trail, and gravesite.

MANY GLACIER HOTEL HISTORIC DISTRICT *west of Babb.* West-

ern Stick Style hotels built by the Great Northern Railroad 1914–1915.
MARIAS MUSEUM OF HISTORY AND ART *First Street S. and Twelfth Avenue, Shelby.* A general museum with cowboy and Indian artifacts and exhibits on oilfields, bottles, and costumes.
MISSOULA COUNTY COURTHOUSE *220 W. Broadway, Missoula.* Built 1908–1910, with Beaux Arts and Neoclassical elements; decorated with murals by Montana artist Edgar S. Paxson.
MONTANA HISTORICAL SOCIETY *225 N. Roberts St., Helena.* Houses major archival, photographic, library, and museum collections that cover prehistory, the cattle industry, farming, mining, politics, C. M. Russell, banking, and other aspects of economic and social history. The society also operates a museum and Montana's Original Governor's Mansion, both located in Helena.
MONTANA TERRITORIAL PRISON *925 Main Street, Deer Lodge.* Built 1892–1918 and used until 1976, the scene of innovative prison reforms during the early period; with a Neoclassical Revival theater that was one of nation's first prison theaters. Now a museum.
MUSEUM OF THE PLAINS INDIAN AND CRAFTS CENTER *U.S. 89, Browning.* Historic and contemporary arts of the Plains Indians, with a gallery shop run by the Northern Plains Indian Crafts Association.
MUSEUM OF THE ROCKIES *Montana State University, Bozeman.* Paleontology, history, art, and natural-science exhibits from the northern Rockies.
MUSSELLSHELL VALLEY HISTORICAL MUSEUM *524 First West, Roundup.* Displays from cowboy, Indian, and frontier life.
PICTOGRAPH CAVE *Indian Caves Park, seven miles southeast of Billings.* A rock shelter used from 2000 B.C. to the nineteenth century; with pictographs.
RANKIN RANCH *Avalanche Gulch.* Built about 1923 and the summer residence of Jeanette Rankin, prominent early feminist and the first woman elected to Congress (1916). Privately owned.
RICHEY HISTORICAL MUSEUM *Richey.* Located in an early-twentieth-century school; with farm tools and ranch items from the area.
ROBBER'S ROOST (DALY'S PLACE) *state 387A, five miles north of Alder.* Built as a roadhouse and stage station in the 1860s and reputedly a hangout of the notorious Henry Plummer gang.
SAINT MARY'S MISSION *North Avenue, Stevensville.* A mission complex built in 1866; one of the state's oldest churches.
SOD BUSTER MUSEUM *Stanford.* Pioneer museum with cowboy and Indian artifacts and original C. M. Russell photos.
SUPERINTENDENT'S HOUSE *east of Philipsburg in Deerlodge National Forest.* A late-nineteenth-century granite house that was the home of mine superintendent Thomas A. Weir, who modernized and improved mining until Granite became a ghost town in 1893.
VIRGINIA CITY HISTORIC DISTRICT *Wallace Street, Virginia City.* Restored and reconstructed buildings from 1863 to the twentieth cen-

tury, notably buildings from 1865–1875 when Virginia City was territorial capital.

WESTERN HERITAGE CENTER *2822 Montana Avenue, Billings.* Housed in 1901 Richardsonian Romanesque library building; with collections of Western Americana.

WORLD MUSEUM OF MINING *end of West Park and Granite streets, Butte.* Located on site of the Orphan Girl zinc and silver mine and containing museum of mining equipment, a turn-of-the-century mining camp, and shops along cobblestone streets.

YELLOWSTONE ART CENTER *401 N. 27th Street, Billings.* Collection of original contemporary graphics, abstract expressionist art, photographs, and western Americana.

NEBRASKA

SCOTTS BLUFF NATIONAL MONUMENT three miles west of Gering on Nebraska 92. Until the completion of the transcontinental railroad in 1869, the principal artery for emigration to the West was the Oregon-California Trail: a route that began on the Missouri River at St. Joseph and Kansas City, followed the North Platte to South Pass, and crossed the Rocky Mountains to destinations in Oregon, Utah, and California. During the era of its greatest use, Nebraska served essentially as a human corridor for tens of thousands who stopped for no more than a rest before moving on. The first important landmark on the trail and a major goal for weary travelers was Scotts Bluff, a towering butte that dominated the North Platte River Valley in the panhandle of Nebraska. The Scotts Bluff National Monument preserves this natural landmark and commemorates the explorers, the fur trappers and traders, the missionaries, the soldiers, the westward emigrants, and the frontier entrepreneurs who traveled Nebraska's nineteenth-century highway.

Scotts Bluff, an erosional remnant of the ancient Great Plains, rises some seven hundred feet above the badlands that separate it from the North Platte River just to the north. Although not the only such formation in the area, it was the first such landmark on the trek west. The earliest known written reference to the bluff and the North Platte Valley route is in the journal of Robert Stuart, a fur trader who passed the land formation as he and his companions returned from Oregon in 1812 and 1813 with dispatches for John Jacob Astor. Despite the discovery of this shorter overland route, the Missouri River route first followed by Lewis and Clark in 1804 and 1805 remained the principal thoroughfare to the western fur territory. Indian trouble on the Missouri in the mid-1820s necessitated a new route, and in 1824 four trappers rediscovered the Platte route. For the next seventeen years, travel along the North Platte related principally to the Rocky Mountain fur trade. Jedediah Smith, William Ashley, William Sublette, and other frontier entrepreneurs passed through present-day Nebraska on their way to and from the famous trappers' rendezvous in the mountains. On a return trip from one such event in 1828, Hiram Scott, an employee of the Rocky Mountain Fur Company, fell ill and, for reasons never clear, was abandoned on the trail to die. When his associates returned in the spring of 1829, they found his skeleton in a spring at the foot of a huge bluff miles from where they had left him. The butte has been known since then as Scotts Bluff, and the legend of this tragic death has become a staple of Nebraska folklore.

Over the next decade, an assortment of fur traders, missionaries, and explorers passed by Scotts Bluff en route to and from the Oregon territory. The first wagons traveled the route in 1830, and in 1836 the first white women made the journey: Narcissa Whitman and Eliza Spalding, wives of missionaries Marcus Whitman and Henry Spalding, pioneer settlers in present-day Washington and Idaho. In 1841, a band of eighty emigrants to Oregon launched the era of the transcontinental wagon migrations. The first mass expedition followed two years later, when Whitman persuaded over one thousand men, women, and children to resettle in the Northwest. In succeeding years the number of travelers increased dramatically, and by 1845 some five thousand emigrants were counted on what had become the principal highway to the West. Diaries and narratives left by these travelers chronicle the slow and wearing pace of wagon travel and the excitement of seeing the bluff, the first landmark on a monotonous journey.

Having encountered hostility in New York, Ohio, Missouri, and Illinois, Mormons under the leadership of Brigham Young set out across Nebraska in 1847 for their promised land, the Great Salt Lake Valley in Utah. Like the Oregon hopefuls, they also followed the North Platte, although along the north bank rather than the south. Travel along the Mormon Trail in 1848 reached four thousand, far exceeding activity on the regular trail. The peak of activity along the latter came after the discovery of gold in California in 1849; nearly 50,000 emigrants passed Scotts Bluff in 1852 alone.

When they reached Scotts Bluff, early emigrants used Roubidoux Pass, eight miles to the southwest, but as early as 1850 some tried to navigate the narrow gap separating the butte from nearby South Bluff. After the army apparently did some necessary excavating, the shorter route was deemed passable. Over 150,000 travelers used Mitchell Pass in the next two decades. It also became the main route for the Pony Express in 1860 and 1861, the first transcontinental telegraph line in 1861, and the Butterfield Overland Mail Company in 1861 and 1862. But despite their geographic advantages, Scotts Bluff, Mitchell Pass, and the Oregon-California Trail lost out to a more politically advantageous route for the transcontinental railroad. The completion of the railroad in 1869 essentially brought to a close Nebraska's central role in western migration. In succeeding decades, Scotts Bluff became a focus for the open-range cattle industry and then homesteading.

Scotts Bluff National Monument stands about five miles southwest of the town of Scottsbluff in the Nebraska panhandle. The National Park Service acquired the site in 1919. Most of the structures and basic improvements date from the 1930s, when the Civil Works Administration, the Works Progress Administration, and the Civilian Conservation Corps constructed Summit Road and the visitor center. The road takes the traveler to the top of the bluff for a breathtaking view of the area. The visitor center houses the Oregon Trail Museum, with exhibits on Scotts Bluff and westward migration. Included in the museum's collections are artifacts from the mid-nineteenth-century trading posts at Roubidoux and Fort John and numerous watercolors, sketches, and photographs by frontier photographer and artist William Henry Jackson.

Mitchell Pass

Programs include orientation talks, hikes, and self-guided trails.

Scotts Bluff still dominates the route west through Nebraska and remains as awe-inspiring today as when the first frontiersmen encountered it over a century and a half ago. For the modern traveler, the landmark provides a link to Nebraska's presettlement history and the era of westward expansion.

HOMESTEAD NATIONAL MONUMENT four miles northwest of Beatrice on Nebraska 4. The Homestead Act of 1862 may or may not have actually opened up the West to settlement by small farmers. But that legislation is closely identified with the westward expansion of the last half of the nineteenth century—and, more broadly, with democracy and equality of opportunity on the frontier. The Homestead National Monument near Beatrice, Nebraska, commemorates the Homestead Act and its impact on the American experience. Located on one of the first homesteads in the nation, this historic site recreates pioneer life in Nebraska and evokes the hopes and hardships of the men, women, and children who settled the western plains in the decades after the Civil War.

President Abraham Lincoln signed the Homestead Act on May 20, 1862, but the law delayed entry of claims until January 1 of the following year. In anticipation of legal entry, Daniel Freeman located on a tract of land along Cub Creek in southeastern Nebraska in June 1862. Although a squatter had prior claim to the property, Freeman paid him off and staked out his own claim to a T-shaped quarter section. Service in the Union Army kept him away for the next six months, but he returned at the end of December to enter his claim at the General Land Office in Brownsville, some sixty miles to the east. En route from an assignment at Fort Leavenworth, Kansas, to a position at St. Louis, Missouri, Freeman did not have time to wait for the claims office to open on January 2 after the New Year's holiday. He convinced a clerk to open the office and filed his claim shortly after midnight on January 1, 1863.

Freeman was thirty-nine by the time he completed his military service and returned to southeast Nebraska to live. Born in Preble County, Ohio, in 1826, he had attended the Cincinnati School of Electric Medicine and practiced medicine in Illinois for eleven years. Before joining the army, he worked for six years as a Pinkerton detective. While he was away on a military assignment, his wife disappeared with their four children. After obtaining a divorce, he was remarried on February 8, 1865, to Agnes Suiter. On March 13 they arrived at the Cub Creek homestead.

To secure full ownership of his claim, a homesteader had to maintain residence on the property and cultivate it for five years. Unlike many of his contemporaries, Freeman had carefully selected a site that promised to be sufficiently productive to support him and his family for the requisite time. His claim included not only typical Nebraska prairie land but also a wooded area along the creek. A good supply of wood and water was a distinct advantage. He planted twenty acres of corn that spring and later tried his hand at wheat and even trees, including peach, apple, pear, plum, hackberry, oak, and cottonwood. By the end of the decade he had "proved up" his entry, and on September 1, 1869, President Ulysses S. Grant signed Freeman's final certificate and land patent.

Freeman lived on the Cub Creek farm for the rest of his life, but he did not depend solely on farming for his livelihood. An itinerant medical practice provided some income, although many of Freeman's patients paid him off in goods or livestock. He fattened the latter, sold them, and unsuccessfully tried his hand at land speculation. He also served as justice of the peace at Beatrice and for three years was sheriff of Gage County. The farm, however, remained central. His pride in the homestead was evident when he submitted a sample of his winter wheat to the Centennial Exposition in Philadelphia in 1876. The sample reportedly won the first premium award for winter wheat at the fair.

Typically, one of the first community institutions established on the frontier was the school, a reflection of the settlers' commitment to basic education and an important cooperative effort in isolated rural communities. Before the school district was organized in Gage County in 1868, Agnes Freeman provided educational instruction on a subscription basis. The first school building, a log structure, was erected in 1871, and the following year a more substantial brick edifice replaced it. Known as District 21, Gage County, Freeman School, the one-room schoolhouse was furnished with manufactured desks at a time when most frontier schools had homemade furniture. The school also provided textbooks as early as 1881, ten years before they were required by Nebraska law. As the parents of eight children, the Freemans took active roles in school matters. Freeman was serving as a director of the school in 1899 when he brought suit against the teacher for conducting religious exercises. Although defeated at first, he eventually won his case in the state courts, establishing a precedent for later battles over prayer in public schools. The Freeman schoolhouse served other community needs as well. In the 1870s, the First Trinity Lutheran Church held services there, and the county used the building as an election polling place for Blakely township. It was also used for a variety of socials, debates, and even a local literary society. Such use of the school as a social and civic center was typical of late-nineteenth-century homestead communities.

Palmer-Epard Cabin

Freeman died at the homestead on December 30, 1908. His wife continued to live there until her death in 1931. Both were buried on the east side of the claim. Nebraska's U.S. Senator George W. Norris, the Beatrice Chamber of Commerce, and others campaigned after Mrs. Freeman's death to have a national monument established on the site. President Franklin D. Roosevelt signed the enabling legislation in 1936, and the first part of the original Freeman tract was obtained in 1939.

The Homestead National Monument includes the original Freeman tract about four and a half miles north of Beatrice. Open to the public year round, the memorial includes a visitor center, the Palmer-Epard cabin, several sites, and a one-and-a-half-mile-long self-guided tour. The visitor center provides exhibits and serves as a starting point for the tour. Visitors see the Palmer-Epard homestead cabin, a log structure erected in 1867 and moved to the site in 1950. Now fully restored, the building contains tools and furnishing's typical of the Nebraska pioneer era. The other major historic structure is the 1872 Freeman school-house, which stands about a quarter-mile west of the visitor center. In use as a school until 1967, the building and its 1.4-acre site became part of the Homestead National Monument in 1970. The structure has been restored to its nineteenth-century appearance and provides an opportunity to learn about a key pioneer institution. Visitors can also view the sites of the original squatter's cabin and the Freemans' first house, the couple's graves, and the restored prairie. Although most of the land was cultivated at one time, care has been taken to reestablish native grasses, including big bluestem, buffalo grass, blue grammo, and Indian grass. The wooded area around Cub Creek also remains, and a variety of wild-life still inhabit the area. Every effort has been made to recreate what the landscape must have looked like to the original homesteaders.

Programs focus on the lifestyles and everyday activities of the pioneers. Living-history demonstrations include spinning, making lye soap, dipping candles, churning butter, and planting and tending the family garden. The annual Homestead Days feature special craft demonstrations, music, and folk art and craft exhibits. Together the historic structures, exhibits, tours, and programs at the Homestead National Monument bring to life the pioneer experience in post-Civil War Nebraska.

GEORGE W. NORRIS HOME McCook. The single most influential individual in the history of modern Nebraska was George W. Norris, congressman from 1903 to 1913 and then United States Senator from 1913 to 1943. Although a Republican through most of his career, he remained independent of partisan control and developed a national reputation for his advocacy of the people's interests. Despite his years in Washington, Norris remained a confirmed Nebraskan and maintained a residence in the small southwest town of McCook. The George W. Norris Home, now a National Historic Landmark, commemorates the life and work of the one of the state's most prominent residents.

George W. Norris was born in Sandusky County, Ohio, on July 11, 1861. There he spent his childhood and youth and completed his education. Admitted to the bar in 1883, he practiced law in Ohio but decided in 1885 to seek new opportunities elsewhere. He wound up in Beaver City, Nebraska, a small town in the south-central part of the state about twenty miles from the Kansas border. There he established a law practice and soon entered local politics. Norris served three terms as Furnas County attorney before his election in 1895 as a judge in Nebraska's fourteenth judicial district. Upon his election, Norris and his family moved some forty miles west to the town of McCook. Here in 1899 he erected a two-and-a-half-story residence that was to remain his Nebraska home for the rest of his life.

Norris served on the state court until 1902, when he won election to the United States House of Representative. He took office the following year and served for five terms. In 1912 he was elected to the United States Senate and served in that body for five terms as well. He thus

George W. Norris Home

represented his adopted home state in Washington for four decades, establishing a reputation as an independent champion of the average citizen.

Norris refused to support his party unconditionally. Convinced that he should represent the people and not party bosses, he supported issues and leaders often with little regard for partisan loyalty. Thus in 1910 he led a group of insurgent Republican congressmen in success-fully reducing the appointive powers and influence of the Speaker of the House. Although this meant antagonizing "Uncle Joe" Cannon, the entrenched Speaker and a powerful "Old Guard" Republican, Norris was committed to eliminating Cannon's virtual dictatorship and restor-ing the rightful role of the people's representatives. This development contributed to the division of the Republican party between Old Guard and New Guard, between supporters of President William Howard Taft and those of his predecessor Theodore Roosevelt. Many insurgents like Norris refused to accept the party's renomination of Taft in 1912 and instead endorsed Roosevelt as the candidate of the Bull Moose Party. This division made possible the election of the Democratic candidate, Woodrow Wilson, that party's first successful contender in two decades.

That same year Norris secured a seat in the Senate. In the three decades that followed, he continued to maintain an independent course, supporting third-party candidate Robert La Follette in 1924 and in 1928 shifting his support to the Democratic presidential nominee, Alfred Smith. He endorsed Democrat Franklin D. Roosevelt in his 1932 race and in his subsequent reelection bids. At least officially, however, he remained a Republican until 1936, when he ran for office as an independent. Nebraskans had little trouble with his lack of partisan loyalty; indeed, his reputation as an independent gained him much valuable support from among the state's Democratic voters.

During his career, the Nebraska politician became identified with a variety of issues that reflected his concern with the interests of the average citizen. He is perhaps best known as the father of the Tennessee Valley Authority, the multiple-purpose river development project established in 1933 as part of FDR's New Deal. Norris advocated government development of power resources, convinced that such projects were in the public interest and held the promise of transforming American life. Similarly, he became an ardent supporter of the Rural Electrification Administration's efforts to establish grassroots cooperatives to extend electrical service into the countryside. Essentially from a rural background himself, Norris was sensitive to the needs of American farmers in the urban nation.

What concerned Norris, however, was not just the plight of rural America but the needs of average citizens, whether rural or urban. In addition to his advocacy of power development and farm relief legislation, he cosponsored the Norris-LaGuardia Anti-Injunction Act. This legislation constituted a major gain for organized labor by forbidding the misuse of injunctions in labor-management disputes. More broadly, his support of the direct primary and the popular election of senators reflected concern with the responsiveness of government to the people. Similarly, he pushed for Nebraska's adoption of a unicameral legislature, convinced that such a course would eliminate waste and inefficiency and insure responsiveness of the state's elected leaders. In a speech at McCook in 1932, Franklin Roosevelt aptly summed up Norris's career: "He has been thinking of the rights and welfare of the average citizen, of the farmer, the laborer, the small business. . . . But especially, it has been an unselfish fight, and directed to the fact that it is the little fellow who has been forgotten by his government."

Norris's former home still stands at 706 Norris Avenue in McCook and testifies to his strong roots in his adopted homestate. Erected in 1899, the residence was remodeled by Norris in the early 1930s in an effort to provide some work for McCook residents hard hit by the depression. The stuccoed exterior has a half-timbered front gable and an arched entrance. Inside are the parlor, dining room, den, kitchen, sunporch, and three bedrooms, all filled with furniture and mementoes collected by Norris and his family during his long political career. The basement contains exhibits on the Nebraska politican and his career. Administered by the Nebraska State Historical Society, the Norris house stands as a fitting memorial to this famous Nebraskan and his distinguished political career.

ARBOR LODGE STATE HISTORICAL PARK Second Avenue, Nebraska City. Mansion of the Morton family, including J. Sterling Morton, creator of Arbor Day; with nearby historic buildings and an arboretum.
ASH HOLLOW STATE HISTORICAL PARK off U.S. 26 twenty-eight

miles north of Ogallala. Interpretive center on site occupied seven to ten thousand years ago, inhabited by whites by 1832; Oregon Trail ruts still visible.

BANK OF FLORENCE *8502 N. Thirtieth Street, Omaha.* An 1856 building that is one of the state's oldest commercial structures; in the former town of Florence, Mormon encampment on trek west in 1846.

BELLEVUE *ten miles south of Omaha on the Missouri River.* Established as trading post in 1823, possibly the state's oldest town, with the oldest church (Presbyterian, 1856–1858) and possibly oldest extant building (log cabin, about 1835).

BROWNVILLE HISTORICAL SOCIETY MUSEUM *Main Street, Brownville.* General history museum on site of the oldest town incorporated in Nebraska.

BUFFALO BILL RANCH *off Buffalo Bill Avenue, North Platte.* Home built by William F. Cody in 1886; with his memorabilia.

CAPTAIN MERIWETHER LEWIS *Missouri River Museum, Brownville State Recreation Area, Brownville.* Steam-powered dredge used by the U.S. Corps of Engineers; now a museum.

CATHER HISTORICAL CENTER *338 N. Webster, Red Cloud.* First editions and manuscripts of Willa Cather.

CATHER PIONEER MEMORIAL *326 N. Webster, Red Cloud.* Childhood home of author Willa Cather, built 1897.

CHAMPION MILL STATE HISTORICAL PARK *Champion Mills.* Water-powered mill constructed in 1890s but no longer in operation.

CHIMNEY ROCK *off state 92 four miles south of Bayard.* Five-hundred-foot column that was a landmark on the Oregon Trail.

DeSOTO NATIONAL WILDLIFE REFUGE *near Blair.* Display of items rescued from the remains of the *Bertrand,* steamboat that sank on the Missouri River in the 1800s.

FORT ATKINSON STATE HISTORICAL PARK *at east edge of Fort Calhoun.* Site in Council Bluffs area where Lewis and Clark camped in 1804 and a military fort existed 1819–1827.

FORT HARTSUFF *near Burwell.* Buildings remaining from the fort, used 1874–1881 to protect against Indians.

FORT KEARNEY *eight miles southeast of Kearney on state 10.* Visitor center on the site of a fort established for protection of travelers on the Oregon Trail.

FORT ROBINSON STATE PARK *Crawford.* Includes restored fort buildings and a museum on fort and local history.

GENERAL GEORGE CROOK HOUSE *Fort Omaha, Omaha.* Museum housed in 1878 residence of frontier Indian fighter.

GREAT PLAINS BLACK MUSEUM *2213 Lake Street, Omaha.* Focus on the underground railroad, with materials on black history and the black cowboy.

HASTINGS MUSEUM *1330 W. Burlington, Hastings.* A local history museum.

HERITAGE HOUSE MUSEUM *Weeping Water.* Local history, including Indian, pioneer, and medical history; on site of the first parsonage of the Congregational church in Nebraska.

JOSLYN ART MUSEUM *2200 Dodge Street, Omaha.* Comprehensive collections from ancient to modern art, with frontier art, decorative art, and Indian artifacts.

KENNARD HOUSE *Nebraska Statehood Memorial, 1627 H Street, Lincoln.* Restored house built in 1869, possibly the oldest in Lincoln, and home of one of three commissioners who selected the site of the Nebraska capital.

MAY MUSEUM *1643 N. Nye, Fremont.* Historical items from the late 1800s in an 1874 house.

MUSEUM OF AMERICAN HISTORICAL SOCIETY OF GERMANS FROM RUSSIA *631 D Street, Lincoln.* Items that German immigrants brought to this Russian-German center, as well as items they used as pioneers.

MUSEUM OF THE FUR TRADE *three miles east of Chadron on U.S. 20.* Reconstructed trading post and museum on the fur-trading period in Nebraska.

NEBRASKA STATE CAPITOL *1445 K Street, Lincoln.* Modernistic structure with Art Deco elements, built 1922–1932, with a 400-foot tower.

NEBRASKA STATE HISTORICAL SOCIETY *1500 R Street, Lincoln.* Extensive exhibits on all aspects of Nebraska and Great Plains history, including art, anthropology, and archeology.

NEIHARDT CENTER *northwest corner of Washington and Grove streets, Bancroft.* House built in the 1890s and used as a study by John G. Neihardt, writer and poet, 1911–1921.

NELIGH MILLS *corner of N Street and Wylie Drive, Neligh.* A restored water-powered mill dating from the late nineteenth century.

PIONEER VILLAGE *Minden.* Collections relating to Nebraska and its history.

PLAINSMEN MUSEUM *210 Sixteenth Street, Aurora.* Mosaics and murals on early regional life from prehistoric times; with period homes including a log cabin and a sod house.

PONY EXPRESS STATION *Ehmen Park, Gothenburg.* Items from the Pony Express days displayed in a log cabin built in 1854 and used as a station.

SARPY COUNTY HISTORICAL MUSEUM *2402 Clay Street, Bellevue.* Local and regional history, with an 1840 log cabin and the remains of the 1835 Baptist mission of Moses Merrill to the Otos.

STUHR MUSEUM OF THE PRAIRIE PIONEER *3133 West U.S. 34, Grand Island.* Restoration of late-1800s prairie railroad town, with fifty-seven houses and farm and business buildings, demonstrations of pioneer crafts, displays of farm machinery, and an operating steam train.

UNIVERSITY OF NEBRASKA ART GALLERIES *Sheldon Memorial Art*

Gallery, Twelfth and R streets, Lincoln. Twentieth-century American art, including sculpture, photos, and graphics.

UNIVERSITY OF NEBRASKA STATE MUSEUM 212 Morrill Hall, 14th and U streets, Lincoln. Natural history museum with extensive exhibits on life in the Great Plains.

WESTERN HERITAGE MUSEUM 801 S. Tenth Street, Omaha. Railroad, telephone, radio, advertising, photography, and other material from early Nebraska history, in the former Union Pacific Station.

NEVADA

MORMON STATION STATE HISTORICAL MONUMENT   *Genoa.*
Mormon entrepreneurs established the first permanent settlement in present-day Nevada nearly a decade before news of the Comstock Lode sparked popular interest in the region. Established in 1850 as a trading post on the California Trail, Mormon Station or Genoa became the region's principal town, the heart of a Mormon colonization effort, and the focus of initial efforts at securing territorial status apart from Utah. The community's importance faded after the discovery of silver and gold near Virginia City in 1859 and the subsequent shift of population to the north. The Mormon Station State Historical Monument commemorates these developments and recreates Nevada's origins in the Carson Valley.

After the discovery of gold at Sutter's Mill in 1848, emigration to California increased dramatically. Despite the hardships of travel across the largely unsettled American West, tens of thousands fell victims to gold fever and journeyed to the new Eldorado. The men who established Mormon Station in 1850 hoped to profit from the gold rush by opening a trading post on one of the most heavily traveled routes to California. As part of a Mormon expedition to the gold fields in 1850, these men knew first hand what emigrants needed as they prepared for the last leg of their journey across the Sierra into California. When their party arrived in Carson Valley in June 1850, Hampton Beattie and six others decided they had found a likely spot for their new business venture.

Carson Valley is located on the eastern slopes of the Sierra Nevada, the last major barrier on the route to California. On the west side of the valley, Beattie and his Mormon associates erected a twenty-by-twenty-foot log cabin. Although this structure was considerably more permanent than the tents that housed other western trading posts, its builders did not expect to stay through the winter and did not even put a roof on the building. With completion of the cabin and an adjoining corral, Beattie and his associates stocked the trading post with sugar, flour, beans, tea, coffee, tobacco, clothing, and other provisions shipped across the Sierra from Placerville. Their relative isolation from competition enabled them to charge incredibly high prices for simple provisions. For example, flour and sugar sold for two dollars per pound. Weary travelers in need of supplies accepted the high prices, often exchanging livestock for essential provisions. As shelves emptied, new supplies were brought in from Sacramento on pack mules. The summer's trading activity proved highly profitable, and by September the entrepreneurs had managed to acquire over a hundred head of horses. Satisfied with this profit, Beattie and company sold out to Stephen Moore and returned to

Mormon Station

Salt Lake City. En route, Indians attacked them and they lost all their horses and supplies.

Back in Salt Lake City, Beattie secured a job in a store owned by John Reese. Intrigued by Beattie's tales and the prospect of a highly profitable enterprise, Reese organized a group to return to Carson Valley. In the spring of 1851, he and eighteen other Mormons set out with ten wagon-loads of flour, eggs, bacon, and other staples to restock the trading post. When they arrived at the Beattie site on July 4, they found the cabin gone. Impressed with the location, however, Reese purchased thirty acres from Moore and erected a two-story log cabin near the site of Beattie's former operations. This L-shaped structure served as both a store and a hotel and formed two sides of a stockade. Known as Reese's Station and then Mormon Station, the trading post eventually included a blacksmith shop, a livery stable, a flour mill, a saw mill, and farming operations. Although the enterprise proved as profitable as he expected, Reese sold out in 1856.

Carson Valley lay within the boundaries of Utah Territory, but the government in distant Salt Lake City had other concerns and did not initially show any interest in the remote settlement. In an attempt to resolve disputed land claims, the settlers took matters into their own hands and established a "squatters' government" at Mormon Station in November 1851. This remained the only government in the area until the Utah Territorial Legislature organized Carson County on January 17, 1854. The following spring, Mormon leader Brigham Young commis-sioned church apostle Orson Hyde to carry out the legislature's will and extend the territory's authority into the region. In addition to his civil functions, Hyde served as spiritual head of the colony of one hundred Mormon families that arrived in Carson Valley on June 15, 1855. Reminded of Genoa, Italy, where he had served as a missionary at one time, Hyde renamed the Mormon Station community Genoa and made it the county seat. By the spring of 1856, the old frontier trading post had become the center of a stable community of some sixty to seventy Mormon families.

The community continued to grow and prosper until mid-1857, when Young called the faithful Mormons back to Salt Lake City to defend it against the threat of government intervention. By October about 450 had left Carson Valley, leaving a population of about 200. For the next two years, Carson Valley was again essentially without government. Residents' attempts to establish a separate Territory of Nevada failed, and in January 1859 Utah reestablished the Carson County government. The non-Mormon population had increased in number and power by that time, however, and Mormon attempts at reestablishing the church's influence proved futile.

The discovery of the Comstock Lode near Virginia City later in 1859 significantly determined the future of both Genoa and the Nevada region. The small trading community could not compete with the newer Comstock settlements. As the population shifted north away from Carson Valley, Genoa's influence in the region waned. In response to the phenomenal growth in population in the mining areas and in recognition of the value of Nevada mineral resources to the nation, the United States Congress finally established the Territory of Nevada in 1861. Although Genoa had played a pivotal role in the early territorial movement, the trading community could no longer claim a leadership role and yielded to the selection of Carson City as the territorial capital. Genoa remained an important transportation and communications center through the 1860s, but even that role was eclipsed by the completion of the Central Pacific Railroad. In the decades that followed, Genoa settled into relative obscurity.

Mormon Station changed hands a number of times in the nineteenth and twentieth centuries before it finally burned down in 1910. Reconstruction began on the original site in 1947. The Nevada State Park System now administers the 2.25-acre Mormon Station State Historical Monument. The site and its exhibits interpret the history of early settlement in Carson Valley and provide an opportunity to learn about the history of frontier Nevada.

VIRGINIA CITY NATIONAL HISTORIC LANDMARK DISTRICT

Virginia City. In 1859 prospectors in Nevada's Gold Canyon discovered the Comstock Lode, the greatest single deposit of silver ever found in the United States. In the next decade the Comstock became the focus of the nation's first great silver rush and provided the catalyst for Nevada territorial organization in 1861 and statehood three years later. Silver mining remained the dominant factor in the state's development until production declined in the late 1870s. The "Queen of the Comstock" was Virginia City, originally a small mining camp but by the mid-1870s one of the largest and most influential cities in the western United States. The Virginia City National Historic Landmark District preserves the most significant structures remaining from the bonanza era and commemorates one of the most colorful and dramatic eras in the state's history.

Optimistic prospectors looking for placer gold gave Gold Canyon its name in 1850. Expectations of a gold strike comparable to that in California proved futile, and only intermittent activity continued in the western Nevada desert country until 1859. In that year, Peter O'Riley and Patrick McLaughlin discovered a quartz vein rich in silver. They named their claim the Ophir Mine, but, thanks to the self-promotion of their partner Henry Comstock, Nevada's richest silver deposit became known as the Comstock Lode.

Although few miners had any real familiarity with silver, news of the discovery triggered America's first great silver rush. By the spring of 1860, some ten thousand eager miners had arrived. Originally just a small mining camp, Virginia City boasted a population of 2,345 by August. The town included forty-two stores, as many saloons, three hotels, six restaurants, 868 dwellings, and an assortment of other structures, all hastily built to meet the needs of the booming community.

During the first years, prospective millionaires established nearly seventeen thousand claims and organized over eighty-five mining companies. Their initial optimism soon faded, however, as it became evident that the surface mining techniques used in California would not work with the Comstock's deep, pocketed fissures of silver. Few could afford the slow and costly mining and milling operations required to

Storefront in Virginia City

extract the silver from the quartz veins. Full development of Nevada's resources was feasible only with large-scale capital investment and efficient management. The Comstock experience was the first example of this kind of enterprise in the West and the prototype for subsequent mining ventures in the region.

The first bonanza period of the early 1860s also owed much to new technology developed specifically to exploit the Comstock Lode. Deep shafts were necessary to work the veins of silver, but existing technology made it impossible to go deeper than about 175 feet without the danger of cave-ins. In 1860, George Hearst, a partner in the Ophir Mine, brought in engineer Philip Deidesheimer to work on the problem. Deidesheimer's square-set timbering plan provided the necessary support and allowed full exploitation of the lode down to 4,000 feet. New drills and blowers for ventilation also made it possible for miners to work in the shafts for longer periods of time. The same year that Deidesheimer began work, Almarin B. Paul arrived in Nevada. By 1862 he worked out a new chemical extraction method and devised an improved stamp mill. At the peak of the initial boom period in 1863, eighty stamp mills were processing the Comstock's rich silver ore.

In recognition of the wealth and resources of the Nevada silver district, Congress hastened plans for statehood, and in 1864 Nevada became the twenty-sixth state in the union. Virginia City's population had reached 15,000 by that time. Saloons, restaurants, theaters, churches, schools, fraternal societies, and a variety of businesses lined the city's crowded streets and served its rowdy citizens. One particularly notable early resident was Samuel Clemens, a *Territorial Enterprise* reporter who became world famous under the pen name Mark Twain. There were also wealthy mining entrepreneurs like William Sharon, acknowledged by his contemporaries as the boss of the Comstock Lode.

The majority of the city's residents were miners, who achieved neither fame nor wealth for their work in the Comstock mines. In an early effort at unionization to improve their situation, these men in 1863 established the Miners Protective Association, which in 1864 became the Miners' League of Storey County. But when hard times hit the Comstock that same year they were forced to temporarily abandon their hopes of securing a standard four-dollar-a-day wage. When prosperity returned, they reorganized and secured the four-dollar wage in 1867 and an eight-hour day in 1872.

The slump in bullion production that began in 1864 proved disastrous for mine owners and mill operators already heavily in debt. William C. Ralston of the Bank of California used the situation to secure a virtual monopoly over milling and transportation in the region. By foreclosing on overdue loans, Ralston secured control over a majority of the stamp mills, consolidated them in the Union Milling and Mining Company in 1867, and relocated them along the Carson River. He then financed and constructed the Virginia and Truckee Railroad to link the mines and his milling facilities. He later extended his rail line north to tie into the Central Pacific–Union Pacific transcontinental railroad at Reno. Through this monopoly of milling and transportation, Ralston brought efficiency and rational organization to the Comstock operations and reigned as the "King of the Comstock" until the mid-1870s.

In 1871 James G. Fair, James C. Flood, John W. Mackay, and William S. O'Brien acquired the Consolidated Virginia and California mines. Convinced that the silver vein grew wider and deeper, they drove deep shafts and in October 1873 struck the "Big Bonanza," a fifty-four-foot-wide lode that was the greatest single bonanza in mining history. The speculative activity that followed broke the power of Ralston and the Bank of California. With a peak annual production of over $38,000,000 in 1876, the Big Bonanza made Fair, Flood, Mackay, and O'Brien the "Silver Kings."

Virginia City reached its zenith during this period, with an estimated population of 20,000. The Great Fire of 1875 destroyed nearly the entire town, but the profits of the Big Bonanza enabled residents to rebuild completely within the next year. The rebuilt "Queen of the Comstock" included opulent homes for the wealthy silver elite, dozens of infamous saloons, an opera house, churches, and an assortment of commercial, residential, and public buildings. But Virginia City's heyday proved short-lived, for the Big Bonanza was worked out by 1878. Within five years production dropped from $38,000,000 a year to only $1,500,000 in 1881. In the decades that followed, mining continued off and on in the Comstock district, but there were no more bonanza years.

While many western mining towns became ghost towns after the area's resources were depleted, Virginia City has displayed remarkable staying power, partially due to the economics of legalized gambling and tourism. Many of the original structures still stand in the Virginia City National Historic Landmark District and provide an opportunity to see how Nevadans lived and worked during the bonanza years.

Virginia City stands on the east face of Mount Davidson about 1,500 feet below the summit. Lettered streets run north and south, named streets east and west. As in the nineteenth century, business activity still centers on C Street. Most of the two- and three-story brick commercial buildings along this street date from the 1870s and 1880s and typically feature tall double-hung windows, doors with transoms, ornate bracketed cornices, and decorative cast-iron pilasters. One of the oldest structures is the Black and Howell Building, which dates from the early 1860s and housed the city's first telegraph office. The Washoe Stock Exchange Board and the Pacific Union Express Company were located here later. The Roos Brothers Building at 20–22 C Street dates from the 1876 rebuilding and originally housed a clothing business. A similar enterprise was located further south in the Banners Brothers Building, now the home of the Crystal Bar (which began operations at a different location in 1867). Adjoining that building is the Gillig Block, an 1876 structure erected for John Gillig's hardware and plumbing supply business. On the east side of C Street stands the Territorial Enterprise Building. The *Territorial Enterprise* dates back to 1854 and was the first newspaper published in the Nevada Territory. An important C Street establishment in the 1870s was the saloon, and a good example stands on the southwest corner of C and Union streets. The building was erected as a saloon in 1876 and by 1898 was known as the Sawdust Corner Saloon. Hotels were also important, and the Molinelli Hotel Building still stands on C Street north of Union.

Scattered through the district are several structures that housed essential community services. The Virginia and Truckee Railroad freight depot dates from 1877 and recalls the importance of transportation to the Comstock mining operations. Water was also essential, and on B Street stands the Water Company Building, erected in 1875 for the Virginia City and Gold Hill Water Company. About a block north of it is the ornate Storey County Courthouse, a two-story brick and stone Italianate edifice constructed in 1876–1877. Another public building is the Fourth Ward School on C Street, just outside the main district. It also dates from 1876, and its impressive size testifies to the city's growth during the bonanza years.

One of Virginia City's most famous structures is Piper's Opera House, at Union and B streets. The original theater burned down in 1883, and this building was completed two years later. Notable features include suspended balconies, a spring dance floor, and a raked (sloping) stage. Famous stars that appeared here included Maude Adams, Edwin Booth, and Lily Langtry. During its heyday it also housed concerts, political rallies, lectures, opera performances, and an assortment of events that appealed to the varied tastes of the city's residents. To the north of Piper's is the Knights of Pythias Building, erected in 1876 for a Virginia City fraternal organization. Further north stands the Miners Union Hall, which at one time housed a library, a ballroom, a chess room, and a meeting hall for the local miners' organization.

Also important to the nineteenth-century community were the Presbyterian church, St. Mary's in the Mountain Catholic Church, and St. Paul's Episcopal Church. The Presbyterian church on C Street was erected in 1867 and escaped the 1875 fire. Stores flanked the frame structure and provided income to support it. The Victorian Gothic St. Mary's Church was built after the fire, as was St. Paul's, a charming pine structure constructed in the Gothic Revival style. Both stand below the main business district on Taylor Street.

A number of fine homes remain from the Comstock period. On B Street at the edge of the main district stands the Castle, a two-story Victorian residence erected in 1863 for Robert Greaves, the superintendent of the Empire mine. Workmen and furnishings imported form Europe insured that Greaves would have a home befitting his status in the community. On D Street stand two other notable houses of the mining elite. At 146 D Street stands the Savage Mansion, a three-story, twenty-one-room edifice erected in 1861 by the Savage Mining Company. This elegant Second Empire structure served as both the residence of the mine superintendent and the mine office. North of the Savage Mansion on D Street stands the Mackay Mansion. Erected in 1860 as the office of the Gould and Curry Mining Company, the two-story, hipped-roof structure became the home of bonanza silver king John Mackay shortly after the 1875 fire.

These are but a few examples of the variety of structures that can be seen today in Virginia City. Some are open to the public as museums, others house businesses, and all can be viewed on walking and driving tours of Virginia City. A driving tour of the Comstock district should include the nearby mining towns of Gold Hill and Silver City as well as Dayton, one of Nevada's oldest towns and an important milling center during the Comstock era. Throughout the old mining communities, old headframes and piles of tailings mark the once profitable silver mines basic to it all. Together these sites bring to life Nevada's history during the bonanza years of the late nineteenth century when silver was king.

NEVADA STATE CAPITOL Carson City. For more than a century the Nevada State Capitol has been the most significant symbol of Nevada statehood. The imposing structure was Nevada's first permanent capitol and has served as the focus of state politics and government since its completion in 1871. The legislation proposed, debated, enacted, and signed into law there has played a central role in Nevada's historical development. Still in use today, the building symbolizes continuity and survival through a turbulent history.

Congress established the Territory of Nevada in 1861, and President Abraham Lincoln appointed James W. Nye the territory's first governor. When Nye arrived in Nevada later that year, he yielded to the influence of local political leader William Stewart and selected the small town of Carson City as the territorial capital, bypassing the larger and more prosperous Virginia City. Founded in 1858 on the site of a trading post, the new capital city was little more than a frontier village when Nye arrived. He, the other territorial officials, and the legislature occupied various quarters for the three years of territorial government that followed. The situation did not improve with statehood in 1864, and the legislature for a time accepted rent-free space at Curry's Hot Springs Hotel in Carson City. It was 1869 before the Nevada State Assembly finally passed the necessary legislation, and on February 23 of that year Governor Henry G. Blasdel signed an "Act to provide for the erection of a State Capitol."

The new structure was to be located on the Plaza, a ten-acre plot near the center of the city. Determined to keep expenses down, the legislature stipulated that the total cost could not exceed $100,000 and that the contractor must use stone from the State Prison quarry. To

Nevada State Capitol

oversee the project, a seven-member State Board of Capitol Commissioners was appointed.

The commissioners selected Joseph Gosling of San Francisco as the architect. For $250, Gosling provided the elevations, sections, and plans for a two-story masonry structure in the form of a Grecian cross. The commissioners then advertised for construction bids and awarded the contract to Peter Cavanaugh and Son of Carson City.

A ceremony marked the laying of the cornerstone on June 9, 1870, and within six months the state legislature occupied its new quarters. Executive offices were occupied in the first months of the following year, and by May 1, 1871, the entire project was completed. The structure, in Renaissance Revival style, measured 148 feet by 98 feet and rested on eight-foot-thick foundation walls. The first-floor walls were three feet thick, the second two and a half feet thick. The dome is sheathed in silver-colored sheet metal. The first floor included offices for the governor, the attorney general, the treasurer, and the comptroller, while the state library, the supreme court, and the legislature occupied the upper floor. Alaskan marble wainscoting, arches, and floors distinguish the public halls. A. V. Higgins of Reno painted a unique decorative frieze on the first-floor corridor walls. Three feet wide and over four hundred feet long, the frieze features borders of grapes and pinecones, garlands suspended from miner's picks, sheafs of wheat, emblems depicting the state's principal industries, and a continuous scroll listing Nevada's leading mineral resources. When it was completed, construction costs totaled nearly $170,000, far in excess of even the highest expectations.

In 1875 the legislature authorized the erection of an iron fence around the Capitol grounds. The bid was won by H. K. Clapp, who turned out to be Miss Hanna K. Clapp, a well-known nineteenth-century feminist and educator. The fence incorporated cast-iron pedestals, rolled rails and pickets, and a sandstone base.

Every governor since Blasdel has occupied the same first-floor office in the Capitol. The structure also housed the state legislature for nearly a hundred years, although not in the same chambers. In 1913 additions on the north and south provided larger quarters for both the state senate and the assembly, as well as additional first-floor office space. The legislature used these chambers until 1970, when a new Legislative Building was erected to the south. The only other major addition was the erection of an octagonal library annex in 1905. Between 1977 and 1979 the entire structure underwent painstaking reconstruction to insure its continued preservation.

For over a hundred years, the State Capitol has stood at the heart of Nevada history. This structure provided the setting for the battles, negotiations, and agreements that have determined the state's development in the nineteenth and twentieth centuries. No action proved more controversial or more crucial than the enactment in 1931 of legislation establishing Nevada's notorious six-week divorce and legalizing casino gambling—both, for good or ill, central to the state's popular image. The structure remains at the center of government and politics today and serves as a vital symbol of Nevada's statehood and history.

AUSTIN HISTORIC DISTRICT U.S. 50, Austin. Some thirteen original buildings erected after an 1863 silver rush; with an historical museum.

BELMONT about forty-five miles northeast of Tonopah via U.S. 6, state 376 and 82. Ghost town from the western mining boom era, including Belmont Courthouse Historic State Monument, Cosmopolitan Saloon, and the Monitor-Belmont Mill.

BERLIN HISTORIC DISTRICT off state 884 near Ione. Some twelve frame buildings remaining from a gold, silver, and mercury mining town during peak years 1900–1918. State-owned; a part of the Berlin-Ichthyosaur State Park, displaying dinosaur fossils nearby.

BOWERS MANSION Washoe Valley, Carson City. Restored 1863 mansion built by gold and silver miner of the Comstock Lode; with period furnishings; county-owned.

EUREKA HISTORIC DISTRICT along U.S. 50, Eureka. Italianate courthouse, opera house, newspaper building, and other structures in a lead and silver boomtown; peak years 1871–1885.

FORT CHURCHILL HISTORIC STATE MONUMENT state 2B about

one mile west of U.S. 95A, seven miles south of Silver Springs. Ruins and reconstructed buildings from a fort built 1860–1869 to protect telegraph lines, overland express, and emigrant routes; with a museum.

FORT McDERMITT *unimproved road about two miles east of U.S. 95 and McDermitt.* Built by California Volunteers in a canyon of the Santa Rose Mountains, used by General George Crook in his 1866–1868 campaign against the Snake Indians, and now part of the Fort McDermitt Indian Agency.

GOLDFIELD *on U.S. 95 twenty-five miles south of Tonopah.* Elegant stone buildings left from an early-twentieth-century gold rush.

HARRAH'S AUTOMOBILE COLLECTION *Reno.* More than 1,000 antique and special-interest vehicles, including cars, motorcycles, boats, and aircraft, in a commercially run museum.

LAS VEGAS MORMON FORT *N. Las Vegas Boulevard at Washington, Las Vegas.* Remains of buildings built by the first settlers, Mormons from Salt Lake City, including an adobe fort.

NEVADA HISTORICAL SOCIETY MUSEUM *1650 N. Virginia Street, Reno.* Exhibits on Nevada history from prehistoric times to the twentieth century.

NEVADA STATE MUSEUM *Capitol Complex, Carson City.* Located in the United States Mint, built in 1869 to handle overload from the Comstock Lode production; with exhibits relating to Nevada history, including railway cars and locomotives and a three-hundred-foot tunnel illustrating mining operations.

NORTHEASTERN NEVADA MUSEUM *1515 Idaho Street, Elko.* Indian artifacts and other historical exhibits, with the Ruby Valley Pony Express Station (1860).

PIOCHE *U.S. 93 north of Caliente.* Two-story courthouse, built in 1871, and a few other buildings remaining from town that underwent a silver boom in 1870.

PYRAMID LAKE BATTLEFIELD SITE *off state 34 about four miles southeast of the southern tip of Pyramid Lake and immediately south of Nixon.* Site of two 1860 fights, one a Paiute ambush that killed forty-six volunteers, the other a three-hour battle in which whites under former Texas Ranger Jack Hays defeated Paiutes.

RHYOLITE *unpaved road four miles west of Beatty.* Surviving buildings from a 1904 gold strike, including impressive stucco passenger depot built in 1907 and ruins of two three-story buildings used as banks and stores.

RUTH MINING DISTRICT *Ruth.* Open-pit copper mine, one mile in diameter and more than 1,000 feet deep, begun in the early 1900s.

SIERRA NEVADA MUSEUM OF ART *549 Court Street, Reno.* Native American baskets and the Great Basin permanent art collection, with historic and contemporary art of the region.

SPRING MOUNTAIN RANCH *west of Las Vegas on Blue Diamond Road.* State recreational park on site of stopping place for travelers on the Old Spanish Trail; later a headquarters for outlaws and then a ranch. Now includes a stone cabin from about 1864, corral complex, bunkhouse, and other buildings.

TONOPAH. The best-preserved of the twentieth-century boomtowns in southwestern Nevada, with a former gambling hall, five-story Mizpah Hotel, and Nye County Courthouse.

NEW HAMPSHIRE

STRAWBERY BANKE Portsmouth. New England, more than any other section of America, is famous for its handsome colonial houses and for its neat and tidy old villages. The scale of them there, as in England itself, seems to be smaller, somehow more pleasant and manageable than in the great urban and suburban civilization that elsewhere supplanted it. It is not surprising that New England's charming towns and villages evoke nostalgia among many of the people who visit and live in them. How one such place prompts anticipation as well is the story of Strawbery Banke in Portsmouth, New Hampshire.

Dating from 1623, the settlement that would become Portsmouth is one of the oldest in America; only Jamestown in Virginia and Plymouth in Massachusetts are older. The wild strawberries that covered the banks of the Piscataqua River inspired its first name: "Strawbery Banke." The town grew and prospered for the next two centuries, first as a farming, fishing,and lumbering center, later as a busy seaport with both foreign trade and shipbuilding. The variety of merchants, mariners, and artisans who lived there built a town of tasteful and substantial stores, houses, and warehouses. Particularly along "Puddle Dock," a tidal creek feeding into the Piscataqua, Portsmouth's sea captains, sailmakers, mast liners, and ordinary seamen congregated in a community that was the heart of this maritime city. In these buildings occurred important events during the Revolutionary War. In December 1774, Portsmouth patriots seized from Fort William and Mary powder supplies later used at the Battle of Bunker Hill. Here John Paul Jones supervised the building of his ship *Ranger* and recruited his crew from Portsmouth sailors. George Washington, the Marquis de Lafayette, John Hancock, and other luminaries passed time here. Later, Portsmouth yards built such famous clipper ships as the *Witch of the Waves,* record-holder for the run to Liverpool. Daniel Webster worked here as a young lawyer.

But in the late nineteenth century, as the great age of sail passed, Portsmouth's own great days seemed to pass with it. Though shipbuilding for the navy continued (134 submarines were constructed at the Portsmouth Navy Yard during World War II), it brought the small city at best only a sporadic prosperity. Meanwhile the old neighborhood around Puddle Dock, once the center of maritime prosperity, had become home for European immigrants, with many old houses divided up into multi-family dwellings. The old wharves rotted, Puddle Dock itself silted up, and the character of the whole place seemed to have changed forever. By the 1950s what was left of old Strawbery Banke was slated for demolition and urban renewal.

At that point, concerned local citizens set out to save what was left and to recover some of what had been lost. The result today is Straw-bery Banke, Inc., a restored urban waterfront neighborhood that captures what a large part of this colonial seaport city once was like. It is the most intact example we have of an early American city. Its buildings are originals, not reconstructions, and most rest on their original foundations. They were not moved here from other places and then grouped together after a later understanding of how such a city must have appeared. Strawbery Banke is in fact the way it was (except, of course, that some buildings simply no longer exist). Only the people are missing, for this is a neighborhood museum and not a living neighborhood. From it, much can be learned about America's earliest urban experience and about the ways that experience has changed over a period of 350 years.

The site covers ten acres, and within it stand thirty-five buildings. Thirty-four are original and all but five stand exactly where they first were built. Five houses are fully restored and furnished in styles current between the Revolution and the Civil War. Dating from about 1780, the Captain John Wheelwright House displays exceptional interior paneling and furnishings from the period of the American Revolution. The Stephen Chase House illustrates the styles of the early nineteenth century, while the Governor Goodwin Mansion is furnished as it would have been when the Goodwins lived in it form 1832 to 1882. The setting for *The Story of a Bad Boy,* by Portsmouth writer Thomas Bailey Aldrich, is preserved in the Thomas Bailey Aldrich Memorial house, built in 1797 and reminiscent of the middle 1800s. The interiors of the other buildings have been adapted to house exhibits on a number of subjects which emphasize that throughout its history this neighborhood had a mixed residential and commercial character. The Peter Lowd House illustrates various nineteenth-century crafts including that of its owner, a cooper. A working blacksmith shop occupies the site where the original once stood, and a boat shop founded in 1793 preserves the art of wooden boat building, including even the use of copper clench nails produced at Strawbery Banke. Two taverns, Stoodley's and the William Pitt, recall the kind of public hospitality the town once offered.

The visitor thus will be impressed both by Strawbery Banke's association with famous people and events and by the pattern of daily life here, as it actually was lived by ordinary people whose names never appeared in the history books. A continuing program of archeological, architectural, and documentary research constantly enlarges this fascinating picture. One house especially makes this point. It is the Joshua Jackson House, built about 1750 and today containing a "Life in Puddle Dock" exhibit. The house itself remains deliberately unrestored and, with its layers of tattered wallpaper, looks the way it did in the 1950s when people lived in it. Exhibits describe its varied inhabitants over two centuries and recall what the whole neighborhood must have been like over the many years when there actually was one.

Much of course no longer exists, or cannot be recovered. Vanished buildings and the vanished Puddle Dock itself are outlined in bluestone

Strawbery Banke Boat Shop

and carpeted with grass—mute reminders of a changing community. But the effect of the Strawbery Banke restoration, like the motives for it, embraces more than nostalgia for handsome colonial houses. The project dramatically saved a distinctive old neighborhood and at the same time raised public awareness about history in the rest of Portsmouth. Thousands from other places visit it every year and see first-hand what the restoration of an entire neighborhood—unlike restoration of a single house—can signify. In the history of New England and of New Hampshire, Strawbery Banke represents a major accomplishment in the preservation of a rich cultural heritage, and its interpretive and educational programs offer excellent opportunities to all history-minded citizens.

HISTORIC MANCHESTER *Manchester*. Massachusetts, its neighbor to the south, takes credit for the development of the modern factory system, but New Hampshire also played a significant role in the launching of the American industrial revolution. The city of Manchester and the mills of the Amoskeag Manufacturing Company incorporated the innovative concepts of industrial organization and management first employed at Waltham and Lowell, and they constituted one of the most significant examples of planned urban-industrial development in the mid-nineteenth century. Although no longer dominated by the textile industry, Manchester remains an important symbol of early industrialization and its impact on the state's economic and social development.

The city of Manchester was originally known as Derryfield, but in 1810 residents renamed the then small village as an expression of confidence in Samuel Blodgett's prediction that it would become comparable to the English industrial city of that name. Blodgett based his expectations on the water power available at the nearby Amoskeag Falls on the Merrimack River. The same year that Derryfield became Manchester, the Amoskeag Cotton and Woolen Manufacturing Company was incorporated and began operating a small cotton mill on a bluff on the west side of the falls, across from Manchester. Over the next two and a half decades, the company erected three more mills, increased its land holdings and water-power rights, and reorganized under the leadership of a new group of investors from Boston. Several of the latter had taken active roles in the Waltham and Lowell mill projects and eagerly turned their attention to the development of this new site. Although the early mills had been located at the village of Amoskeag across the Merrimack from Manchester, the company shifted its attention in the mid-1830s to its substantial landholdings on the east bank, just above the old Derryfield village.

The first mill on the east bank was erected in 1838 for the Stark Manufacturing Company, which leased the land and water-power rights from the Amoskeag Manufacturing Company. The first company housing was also completed that year, and the company proceeded with elaborate plans to establish an entire industrial community comparable to Lowell. Plans for the new company town included broad streets, public parks and commons, ample residential lots, and sites for schools, churches, and cemeteries. The company held its first land sale on October 24, 1838, auctioning off eighty-four lots. Such sales continued annually and sometimes semi-annually, a reflection of the company's interest in promoting the growth of its model industrial community.

In 1839 a second Stark mill was completed, Manchester's first newspaper began publication, and construction proceeded throughout the city. During the following year, the Amoskeag Manufacturing Company constructed its first mill and the population reached 3,325. The new community thus eclipsed not only the earlier industrial village on the west side of the falls but also the older Manchester–Derryfield community. In 1840 residents of the "new village" took control of the town meeting and elected to office their own candidates, pushing aside the old guard. That same year the post office was moved from its old location on Mammoth Road to Elm Street, and then in 1841 the site of the town meeting also changed to the rapidly growing mill community.

Manchester's population reached 10,125 in 1846, the same year the state legislature awarded it a city charter. The city included not only the original central planned community but also numerous villages like Hallsville, Bakersville, and Janesville. It boasted at least ten churches, the Lyceum (a lecture hall), the Atheneum (a library), a high school, several temperance organizations, a police force, a fire company, six newspapers, several banks, and a fine new Town House (or city hall) erected in the latest Gothic style.

The city's phenomenal growth and development of course reflected the successful expansion of industrial activity in the brick mill complexes that lined the canals along the Merrimack. Expansion meant not

*Pandora tower in
Amoskeag millyard*

just new mills and increased textile production but new products as well. The Amoskeag Manufacturing Company began producing locomotives in 1849, steam fire engines in 1859, and even Springfield rifles and sewing machines during the Civil War. Diversification continued until about 1876, when the company returned to its original specialty, the manufacture of cotton cloth. By the close of the nineteenth century, Amoskeag ranked as the largest textile mill in the world.

With industrial expansion came population increases. In the early years, the Manchester mills followed the Lowell example and hired mostly young women as operators. Under the paternalistic eye of the company, the mill girls lived in company-built dormitories, attended church regularly, and generally conducted themselves in a respectable fashion. By 1850 almost a third of the city's fourteen thousand residents were mill girls, clearly the largest single class of workers. Around 1840 immigrant families began moving into the city as well, and the labor force began changing from Yankee to predominantly immigrant. Although immigrants of various nationalities made their way to Manchester, French-Canadians dominated, establishing their own communities within the larger industrial city. By the turn of the century, the Amoskeag work force, both native-born and immigrant, numbered seventeen thousand men and women.

The Amoskeag Manufacturing Company reached its peak in the late nineteenth century and began to decline after World War I. Because of a variety of economic pressures and financial problems, the company finally closed down in 1935. Businessmen and other residents subsequently formed Amoskeag Industries, a realty and promotional organization, to manage the old mill property and bring in new industry. Thanks to those efforts, Manchester remains today an important industrial center and the state's largest city.

While Manchester has changed a great deal over the past century, much of the original fabric of the nineteenth-century city remains. Many of the original Amoskeag Mill buildings still stand, although the canals are gone, and examples of company housing are evident as well. Notable landmarks include the City Hall, constructed in 1844; the Manchester Opera House, which opened in 1881; the Ash Street School, constructed between 1872 and 1874; and the Ezekiel Straw Mansion, an Italianate residence erected in the 1880s for a former state governor and Amoskeag agent. The best starting point for a visit to this historic city is the Manchester Historic Association at 129 Amherst Street. Founded in 1896 during the city's fiftieth anniversary, the association maintains a museum and a library focusing on the history of the Manchester area. In addition to guided and self-guided tours of Manchester's historic areas, it sponsors exhibits, school programs, lecture series, films, and other activities and special events that illuminate the history of New Hampshire's first industrial city.

SAINT-GAUDENS NATIONAL HISTORIC SITE *St. Gaudens Road, Cornish.* Nature and the drawers of boundaries did not endow New Hampshire with especial richness. A small and historically relatively poor state, it has offered opportunities disproportionate to the number of people who sometimes found themselves living there. Wealth has been hard to coax from its textile mills and its rock-strewn hillside farms, and many New Hampshiremen went west to try for a better life elsewhere. But the hilly landscape they left behind held attraction for other sorts of men who saw in it other uses. These were the "summer people."

The lure of the country is an old theme in the history of the western world. In ancient times wealthy Romans built country villas; in more modern eras, the penchant of Englishmen for keeping country houses is renowned. Imitators in America likewise observed the age-old distinction between city and country, seeing (or claiming to see) in woods, fields, and streams a bracing tonic for their lives. Country houses, whether in old Hampshire or New Hampshire, were of course only for the wealthy or at least the comfortably well-to-do. Sculptor Augustus Saint-Gaudens, whose ample country house in Cornish is preserved as a national historic site, was in the latter class. But Saint-Gaudens came to rural New Hampshire in 1885, at a time when, for the first time, others of smaller means were coming, too. The country was prosperous, and for the upwardly mobile middle classes summer vacations away from city and factory were becoming commonplace. To such folk in the industrial and commercial cities of the East, New Hampshire offered a variety of possibilities. Farmhouses with a few extra rooms took in summer boarders who might for a few weeks enjoy simple fare and sit lazily on the front porch soaking up the scenery: as they said, "inviting the soul." Inns and small summer hotels catered to those with a taste for a few more of the solid Victorian comforts, while grander places like the Kearsarge House and the Mount Washington Hotel hosted the fashionable rich with all the amenities of good European resorts.

Others, like Saint-Gaudens, bought houses and made them over into comfortable "summer places." The state's abundance of abandoned farms made it a buyers' market, and many ministers, professors, professionals, and small businessmen found they could afford a place in the country— with woods and a view. Others built from scratch, usually the small inexpensive lakeside cottages that ever since have been a part of the New Hampshire landscape. Meanwhile, atop high hills and along the seashore rose some truly grand country houses complete with servants' quarters, porte-cocheres, manicured lawns, and gardens.

Why they all came (even as over the years they drove up real estate prices) is a fascinating question. Some have suggested that as the pace of life gradually grew more hectic, as it seemed to in the late nineteenth century, more and more people craved some sort of rural restorative. As New Hampshire historians Elizabeth and Elting Morison have written: "They came to get away from whatever it was they were doing—to lose or find or refresh themselves in surroundings that nature and man had conspired to make welcoming, gracious, and lovely." There were, of course, many private reasons too.

Augustus Saint-Gaudens, the Dublin-born son of a French shoemaker, surely had his own. When he first came to Cornish in the summer of 1885 he was already an eminent sculptor, and around him in this beautiful place there gathered over the years an artists' colony that would make it famous. Saint-Gaudens is probably America's best-known sculptor and certainly one of its most accomplished. He believed that success in art sprang from "an uncontrollable instinct toward it"— something that he had in abundance. He had also studied and worked hard. He grew up in New York City and at thirteen was apprenticed to a French cameo cutter, for whom he labored through his teens. He attended art school at the Cooper Union and at nineteen accepted his father's offer to visit the Paris Exposition of 1867. His European education continued over the next several years, during which he honed his already considerable skills and matured as an artist. Three years in Paris were followed by five in Rome, where, among a wide circle of friends, he met his future wife, Augusta F. Homer of Roxbury, Massachusetts.

Back in America, he was commissioned in 1876 to do a statue of

Admiral David G. ("Damn the torpedoes . . .") Farragut that was exhibited in Paris to great acclaim and, cast in bronze, placed in Madison Square in New York City. His star then rose quickly; commissions abounded. This was the great age of Beaux Arts classicism and monumental sculpture, and Saint-Gaudens brought to it unsurpassed conceptual skill and technical competence. His relief portraits were superb, but it was the great monumental pieces that truly captured the spirit of the age and gave his genius full scope: "The Randall," "The Puritan," "The Standing Lincoln." The French government bought his "Amor Caritas" for the Luxembourg Museum in Paris. His "Diana" graced the tower of architect friend Stanford White's Madison Square Garden in New York. His portrait of Robert Louis Stevenson later became part of a memorial in St. Giles Cathedral in Edinburgh.

His grandest work will always be debated by art historians, but there are several pieces sure to be included. His bust of Civil War General William T. Sherman eventually became the powerful equestrian statue that won the Grand Prix in the Paris Salon in 1900 and now stands in New York on Fifth Avenue near Central Park. For fourteen years he worked on the Shaw Memorial for the Boston Common, and for the widowed Henry Adams he created the haunting memorial that stands in Rock Creek Cemetery in Washington, D.C. His heroic figure of the seated Lincoln graces Lincoln Park in Chicago. On a far smaller scale he also applied his talents to the United States coinage, when, at the invitation of his friend President Theodore Roosevelt, he brilliantly redesigned the ten- and twenty-dollar gold pieces. His worldly honors were great. Harvard, Yale, and Princeton gave him honorary degrees; the Royal Academy in London made him a member; the French gave him their Legion of Honor.

Much of the work that earned him such acclaim was done in the quiet backwater of New Hampshire. The site in Cornish that became his home and studio had once been a tavern, known locally as "Huggins Folly." Under his skilled direction it became a small but elegant country estate, whose house, grounds, stable, and studios were inspiration for his own work and center of a colony of sculptors and other artists who gave Cornish a new and lasting reputation. The delights of rural New Hampshire summers and the congenial company of like-minded souls attracted painters such as George de Forest Brush and Maxfield Parrish, poets Percy MacKaye and William Vaughn Moody, novelist Winston Churchill, editor Herbert Croly. Saint-Gaudens also gathered around himself talented students and assistants, including his brother Louis Saint-Gaudens, destined for their own distinguished careers as sculptors.

Today, most of the artists are gone from the Cornish Colony. But a visit to the Saint-Gaudens historic site can still suggest something of what once drew them to this quiet and lovely place. The house, which he remodeled extensively and renamed "Aspet," commands a dramatic

"Aspet"

view across the Connecticut River to Mount Ascutney. The studios reflect the artist's whim and were where he did some of his finest work. The expansive lawn, fountains, and formal gardens where once there was only rough pasture suggest the kind of world—or refuge from the world—that this particular summer resident (he lived here year round after 1900) created in New Hampshire. Its appeal, as thousands of more recent summer people would testify, is as powerful as some of the great statues Saint-Gaudens created here.

BELKNAP–SULLOWAY MILL *Mill Street, Laconia.* Original part built 1823; earliest brick mill still surviving in region.

CANAAN STREET HISTORIC DISTRICT *Canaan.* Commercial, residential, public, and religious buildings from the 1700s and 1800s, including 1796 Town Hall, 1828 Old North Church in Gothic Revival style, and Town Library and Museum, 1839, with Federal and Greek Revival elements.

COLD RIVER BRIDGE *east of Langdon on McDermott Road.* An 1869 bridge, frame with vertical siding; now closed to vehicles.

COLONY HOUSE *104 West Street, Keene.* Includes Hampshire pottery, Staffordshire historical ware, Keene and Stoddard glass, and Revolutionary War documents.

CONCORD HISTORIC DISTRICT *bounded by N. State Street, Horseshoe Pond, railroad tracks, I-93, and Church Street.* Mostly residential buildings dating from the 1730s in the area first surveyed for the town site.

CURRIER GALLERY OF ART *192 Orange Street, Manchester.* American furniture from the 1600s through the 1800s, decorative arts, and American and European painting and sculpture.

DARTMOUTH ROW *Dartmouth College, Hanover.* Four classroom buildings from 1784 in a historic Ivy League college.
EXETER CONGREGATION CHURCH *21 Front Street, Exeter.* Federal-style church built in 1801 with a three-story tower.
FORT CONSTITUTION *near state 1B and Wentworth Street, New Castle.* Site of a fort from the 1600s, scene of a Revolutionary War takeover, rebuilt 1808, now in ruins. Fort Point Lighthouse nearby.
FRONT STREET HISTORIC DISTRICT *Front Street to junction of Spring and Water streets, Exeter.* Buildings from the 1700s, including site of the Town House where the first state government was created.
FROST HOMESTEAD *on state 28 two miles southeast of Derry.* Restored nineteenth-century farmhouse where poet Robert Frost lived and worked 1900–1909.
HARRISVILLE HISTORIC DISTRICT *Harrisville.* Well-preserved buildings of a nineteenth-century textile town that was based on innovative street design.
HISTORICAL SOCIETY OF AMHERST *2 Middle Street, Amherst.* Museum with exhibits from Revolutionary War through the Civil War.
HOOD MUSEUM *Dartmouth College, Hanover.* Art and anthropology museum; with materials on American Indians, American and European art, and other extensive exhibits.
JOHN PAUL JONES HOUSE *Middle and State streets, Portsmouth.* House built in 1758; where the famous naval officer lived in 1782 while supervising the construction of the *America*.
LITTLETON TOWN BUILDING *1 Union Street, Littleton.* An opera house built 1894–1895 with Italianate and Georgian Revival elements.
MacPHEADRIS–WARNER HOUSE *Chapel and Daniel streets, Portsmouth.* Built about 1720 by a Portsmouth merchant, the oldest brick house in Portsmouth, and a well-preserved example of early architecture of New England. Open to the public in the summer.
MOFFATT–LADD HOUSE *154 Market Street, Portsmouth.* Built 1763 or 1764, with nineteenth-century wallpaper and gardens; contains a museum.
MOUNT WASHINGTON COG RAILWAY *Base Station Road, six miles off U.S. 302 from Fabyan–Bretton Woods.* First cog railway ever built (1869), still running three miles to the summit of Mount Washington.
NEW HAMPSHIRE FARM MUSEUM *Milton.* An agriculture museum with farm implements, oral histories, and photos.
NEW HAMPSHIRE HISTORICAL SOCIETY *30 Park Street, Concord.* Museum and library operated by private organization active since 1823.
NEW LONDON HISTORICAL SOCIETY *Little Sunapee Road, New London.* An outdoor museum with barn, blacksmith shop, country store, schoolhouse, and other structures from the early 1800s.
OLD FORT NO. 4 *state 11 just west of junction with state 12, Charlestown.* Reconstruction of a fort that saw action between colonists and

combined French–Indian force, 1747, and again as part of the American Revolution.

OLD POST OFFICE *N. State Street, between Capitol and Park Street, Concord.* Gothic and Richardsonian Romanesque building constructed with local granite, 1884–1889.

PANNAWAY PLANTATION *state 1A just south of Seavey's Creek, Odiorne's Point, Rye.* Where the first white settlement was made in New Hampshire, 1623.

PETERBOROUGH UNITARIAN CHURCH *Main and Summer streets, Peterborough.* Clock and bell tower on a two-story brick church of 1825–1826.

PIERCE HOMESTEAD *on state 31 three miles west of Hillsboro.* Federal-style house built in 1804 by Governor Benjamin Pierce, where Franklin Pierce, his son and later president of the United States, lived until 1838.

PORTSMOUTH ATHENAEUM *9 Market Square, Portsmouth.* Includes models of clipper ships, paintings, early New Hampshire newspapers, and local town histories.

PRENTISS BRIDGE *south of Langdon off Old Cheshire Turnpike, Langdon.* Foot traffic only on this 36-foot single-span bridge built about 1874 as part of the Boston–Canada turnpike.

SALISBURY HISTORICAL SOCIETY *Salisbury Heights, Salisbury.* Museum with collections from the Civil War to the present.

SHAKER VILLAGE *twelve miles north of Concord and west of state 106.* Restored white frame buildings from the colony established in 1792.

STARK MEMORIAL AND HOME *2000 Elm Street, Manchester.* Clapboard house built 1736, moved from original site; boyhood home of General John Stark, leader in Revolutionary War.

THORNE–SAGENDORPH ART GALLERY *Appian Way, Keene State College, Keene.* Includes regional artists.

TUCK MEMORIAL MUSEUM *40 Park Avenue, Hampton.* Antiques and other items from the early history of Hampton, settled 1638.

WEBSTER BIRTHPLACE *off state 127, Franklin.* Restored birthplace and early home of Daniel Webster.

WENTWORTH–COOLIDGE MANSION *off U.S. 1A on Little Harbor, two miles south of Portsmouth.* House first begun 1695; home of the royal governor, 1741–67. Open to the public.

WENTWORTH–GARDNER HOUSE *Gardner and Mechanic streets, Portsmouth.* Georgian house of 1760 built for brother of royal governor; with interior paneling and carved woodwork and Dutch tiles around fireplaces. Open to the public.

WILDER–HOLTON HOUSE *226 Main Street, Lancaster.* Built in 1780, altered later, and used as private residence, meetinghouse, and boardinghouse; contains a museum.

WOODMAN INSTITUTE *182–92 Central Avenue, Dover.* General museum in a 1682 garrison house.

WYMAN TAVERN *339 Main Street, Keene.* Restored clapboard building, original part built 1762 by Minuteman Issac Wyman; site of first meeting of Dartmouth trustees; contains a museum.

NEW JERSEY

MORRISTOWN NATIONAL HISTORICAL PARK Washington Place, Morristown. For New Jerseyans, the American Revolution became a virtual civil war between loyalists to the British Crown and patriotic supporters of colonial independence. Bitter conflict led to violent excesses on both sides, and Governor William Livingston faced the nearly impossible tasks of quelling continued loyalist activity, organizing rebel manpower and material, and establishing a new state government. Indeed, the state might very well have fallen to the British if it were not for George Washington's occupation of Morristown and the consequent consolidation of rebel control. The Morristown National Historical Park commemorates both the activities of Washington and his Continental Army in the Morristown region and New Jersey's larger role in the American Revolution.

When the Revolution began, the village of Morristown consisted of about two hundred fifty residents and fifty or sixty buildings. Around the town green stood the Morris County courthouse and jail, Jacob Arnold's Tavern, and the Presbyterian and Baptist churches. Henry Wick and other area residents farmed the surrounding countryside, growing vegetables, fruit, wheat, corn, rye, and other grains. Lumbering activity supported other residents, while Jacob Ford, Jr., and his family operated iron mines and furnaces in the mountains to the northwest. What attracted George Washington and the Continental Army to the region, however, was the strategic location of the town. The Watchung Mountains to the northeast provided an easily defensible barrier and hence made it possible for the rebels to set up winter camp relatively close to British posts at New York City and along the Jersey coast. From this base, the Continental Army could safely monitor British activities and consolidate patriot control over men and resources in the badly divided state.

Washington arrived at Morristown on January 6, 1777, fresh from victories at Trenton and Princeton that spoiled British hopes of making New Jersey the first colony to return to the loyalist fold. Although the success of the Jersey campaign buoyed rebel hopes, prospects for the Continental Army were not good. Washington's troops numbered five thousand in early January, but the expiration of enlistments soon reduced the total to three thousand. Smallpox threatened to shrink the army further, but Washington wisely ordered inoculations, a bold decision in that day. The Continental Congress promised additional men to fill the ranks, but for several months the Commander-in-Chief had to depend on undisciplined recruits and militia. A chronic shortage of food and clothing and cramped housing in local residences, public buildings, and barns further aggravated the situation. Working from his headquarters at Arnold's Tavern on the Morristown green, Washington tried to make the best of the situation. He sent out details of men to secure provisions and block British access to supplies, engaged in recurrent skirmishes with the enemy, and generally reasserted rebel control over New Jersey.

In the spring, the long-promised reinforcements arrived, raising the army to over eight thousand by May. When the British began moving out of their winter quarters that same month, Washington prepared to evacuate Morristown. Rather than simply abandoning the village and the supply base he had established, Washington ordered the construction of an earthen fortification on the crest of Mount Kemble. The trenches and embankments were completed just before the army broke camp in late May to pursue the British. Originally known as the "Hill," or "Kinney's Hill," the earthwork was later dubbed "Fort Nonsense" by skeptics who questioned Washington's motive in erecting a fortification that was never used.

General Washington did not return to Morristown for another two and a half years. Although the war was far from over, the rebels had secured a stronger position in the north by the time the Commander-in-Chief arrived at the New Jersey village on December 1, 1779. Work began immediately on organizing the campgrounds and erecting housing for the ten to twelve thousand troops assembled there. Washington, his wife Martha, and his aides took up residence in the home of Mrs. Theodosia Ford, while senior officers moved into other private homes. Junior officers joined the soldiers in crude log huts erected in nearby Jockey Hollow. Some six hundred acres of timber were used in the construction of over a thousand huts by mid-February of 1780. These log structures were carefully grouped by brigades in assigned areas that included space for parade grounds, streets, and separate housing for officers and enlisted men. The Jockey Hollow encampment included as well a hospital, a guard house, an orderly room, and a Grand Parade for training, orders, and ceremonies.

Washington faced many of the same problems that winter which had plagued the encampment in 1777. The mounting financial problems of the young republic made it even more difficult to keep the army adequately clothed and provisioned, and discontent mounted within the ranks over short supplies and worthless pay. To top it all off, the Morristown encampment experienced the worst winter of the century. Twenty-eight snowfalls blocked supply lines and exacerbated an already critical problem. For loyalists in nearby New York, conditions seemed perfect for a counter-revolution in New Jersey.

Loyalists led by former New Jersey governor William Franklin convinced the British to launch an attack on June 6, 1780. The British hoped to move swiftly into New Jersey and overcome the Continental Army at Morristown, but on June 7 the New Jersey Brigade of the Continental Army and the local militia combined forces to stop the British at Connecticut Farms. The British and German troops then regrouped and waited for reinforcements led by General Sir Henry Clinton. On

Ford House

June 23 the Royal Army, led by loyalist regiments, advanced to Spring-field but could not penetrate the Watchung Mountains. The British retreat ended the last royal invasion of New Jersey. As the enemy pulled back to Staten Island, Washington ordered his army to evacuate Morristown, ending the town's nearly seven-month reign as the military capital of the American Revolution.

In 1933 the United States Congress designated Washington's Morris-town campsite as the nation's first historical park owned and main-tained by the federal government. The Morristown National Historical Park comprises over one thousand acres divided into three units: Fort Nonsense, erected in 1777; the Ford House, Washington's headquarters in 1779–80; and Jockey Hollow, which includes the Wick House (circa 1750) and reconstructions of the Continental Army's log huts. All three are administered by the National Park Service, which provides markers, tours, exhibits, and other programs on the history of Revolutionary New Jersey.

Conflict and division have played a significant role in New Jersey history, and at no point was this more evident than during the Revolu-tionary War era. Numerous historic sites remain in the state from that pivotal period, but Morristown clearly occupied the center stage. The Morristown National Historical Park brings to life those critical years of the birth of the new republic.

GREAT FALLS HISTORIC DISTRICT *Paterson.* New Jersey has thrived on political conflict throughout its long history, but the Federalist-Jef-fersonian rivalry of the 1790s had particular long-term significance. The Federalists' brief hegemony made it possible for Alexander Hamilton and his associates to secure state support of a plan to establish a man-ufacturing city at the falls of the Passaic River. Jeffersonians decried this modern encroachment on rural New Jersey and staunchly defended agrarian virtues, but the die was cast by the time they forced their opponents out of office. The extraordinary privileges granted to the city's developers by the Federalists in 1791 gave rise to the nation's first planned industrial center, the city of Paterson. The Great Falls of the Passaic / Society for Useful Manufactures Historic District preserves the remnants of this "Cradle of American Industry" and commemorates New Jersey's pivotal role in the shaping of modern America.

Energy, entrepreneurs, and immigrants provided the keys to Paterson's success. The source of energy was the Great Falls of the Passaic River, the second largest falls in the eastern United States. Hamilton first viewed the falls in 1778, while serving as an aide to George Washington in the Revolutionary War. He immediately recognized the site's potential and had it in mind years later when he advocated that the government establish a "national manufactory" to stimulate industrial development in the new republic. Rebuffed by Congress, he took his proposal to the Federalist New Jersey legislature, which promptly gave the project the official support of the State of New Jersey.

Hamilton and his fellow Federalist entrepreneurs incorporated in 1791 as the Society for the Establishment of Useful Manufactures. The New Jersey legislature recognized the group as the sole governing body of the Great Falls project and granted the entrepreneurs exclusive waterpower rights, tax exemption, and other special privileges to insure the venture's success. Despite such initial advantages, the SUM project seemed doomed by 1795 because of financial mismanagement, and the original investors soon abandoned the failing enterprise.

The eventual success of Paterson reflected the tenacity of Peter Colt, who had been hired by the SUM in 1793 to govern the new industrial development. He stayed on despite the project's apparent failure, bought up corporate shares, and took over the SUM. Paterson's time finally came when the War of 1812 cut off access to British manufactured goods and stimulated domestic production. The new manufacturing city boomed in the decades that followed, and Colt became one of the nation's first industrial giants. Although retaining tight control over power development and real estate, the SUM eventually abandoned actual manufacturing activity, thereby clearing the way for a new generation of entrepreneurial leaders who made Paterson an industrial showcase of innovation and invention. This new generation included John Colt, who stimulated textile production by introducing the cotton duck sail in 1821; John Ryle and George Murray, the fathers of the American silk industry; John Clark, the first in a distinguished roster of trained mechanics; Samuel Colt, the inventor of the Colt revolver; Thomas Rogers, the nation's leading locomotive manufacturer; and John P. Holland, the inventor of the submarine. These and many other entrepreneurs and inventors made Paterson the "Cradle of American Industry."

But of course there would have been no factories without workers. Successive waves of German, Irish, Italian, East European, and other immigrant groups in the nineteenth century provided the bulk of Paterson's labor force, working long hours in dangerous and unhealthy workplaces in return for meager pay. Armed with special powers granted by the state legislature, the city's industrial aristocrats attempted to exercise absolute control over the men, women, and children who labored in their factories. Conflict was inevitable. Between 1881 and 1900, Paterson workers staged 137 strikes. Each failed, contributing to increased worker frustration and giving rise to frequent vandalism and rioting. The most famous job action came in 1913, when silk workers went on strike for maintenance of the two-loom system. Despite the supportive activities of the Industrial Workers of the World and noted radical leaders like William D. "Big Bill" Haywood and Carlo Tresca, the workers eventually capitulated. But as before, the strike's failure did not curb labor militancy, and Paterson's workers continued in the next decades to seek redress against the arrogance and indifference of the industrial aristocracy.

The Society for Useful Manufactures continued to operate until 1945, when the city of Paterson purchased its property, assets, charter rights, power plant, and raceway system. In the decades that followed, industrial activity declined because of a range of economic problems, and by the 1960s highway construction threatened the manufacturing district. A citizens' group stopped the proposed demolition and in 1971 established the Great Falls Development Corporation to preserve the old mill structures and promote reuse. Designated a National Historic Landmark in 1976, the Great Falls of the Passaic / SUM Historic District effectively demonstrates the valuable role multi-use development can play

Thomas Rogers Building

in the preservation of our nation's architectural heritage.

Visitors to Paterson can still view the reason for the city's development—the Great Falls of the Passaic River—and the three-tiered raceway system completed in 1846 to harness the water for mill sites located along the banks. Numerous mill structures also still stand in the district, including the Phoenix Mill Complex, erected between 1816 and 1870 and the oldest surviving mill in the district, and the Colt Gun Mill, a portion of the four-story structure used by Samuel Colt for the production of the first commercially successful revolver and then by John Ryle and George Murray for manufacturing silk in the 1840s. Apart from the textile industry, Paterson's leading business was the manufacture of locomotives; several structures remain from the Rogers Locomotive Works, the industry leader. Visitors can also see where some of Paterson's nineteenth-century residents lived, ranging from the John Ryle House on Mill Street to the Irish working-class community of Dublin, just outside the historic district.

The structures that make up the Great Falls of the Passaic / SUM Historical District now house a variety of different businesses, restaurants, and lofts, but the fabric of the nineteenth-century industrial city remains intact. The Great Falls Tour Office provides walking tours and slide lectures on this historic district, and visitors can tour exhibits on the city's industrial past at the Paterson Museum in the Thomas Rogers Building. The programs and activities of the Great Falls Development Corporation insure the continued preservation and development of this unique historical resource.

CAPE MAY NATIONAL HISTORIC LANDMARK DISTRICT   *Cape May.* New Jersey's long history of social, political, and economic conflict should not obscure the prominence and fame of its seashore resorts. In the late nineteenth and early twentieth centuries, any city-dweller in the mid-Atlantic states who could afford it temporarily escaped the trials and tribulations of urban life by a visit to the Jersey shore. Foremost among the seaside havens were Cape May, Long Beach, and Atlantic City, each renowned for its grand hotels, fine beaches, and varied amusements. Few historic structures remain at either Long Beach or Atlantic City, but the Cape May National Historic Landmark District preserves over six hundred hotels, cottages, and other structures from the resort era. The district provides a showcase of Victorian architecture and brings to life this colorful era in New Jersey history.

A Dutch explorer first laid claim to the area around present-day Cape May in 1616, but the cape bears the name of another Dutchman, Cornelius Jacobsen Mey, a representative of the Dutch West Indies Company in the New Netherlands colony in the 1620s. The Dutch surrendered control of the region to the English in 1664, and a decade later New Jersey became a proprietary colony. The leading proprietor in West Jersey was Dr. Daniel Coxe, a Quaker speculator who owned a large tract of land that included Cape Island, as it was then known. Through

Coxe's influence, local government was organized in 1687, but settlement and development of the cape did not actually commence until the early eighteenth century. The first residents were farmers, fishermen, and sea pilots, totaling over six hundred fifty by 1726.

The first paying guests at Cape May were probably pirates and their crews, who took up temporary residence there in the late seventeenth and early eighteenth centuries. It is not clear, however, just when the cape began developing as a resort. By 1801 the tourist trade was such that Ellis Hughes advertised his hotel in a Philadelphia newspaper. Hughes' establishment was probably the first real hotel, although large houses had undoubtedly provided guest accommodations for several decades. By that time, regular stagecoach service from Philadelphia and Camden augmented coastwise travel by sloop and improved accessibility to the cape. But the resort business did not really begin to flourish until after the War of 1812 and the establishment of regular steamboat service between Cape Island and Philadelphia.

Thomas Hughes, the son of early entrepreneur Ellis Hughes, was the first to take full advantage of the cape's natural attractions and newly developed accessibility. In 1816 he began construction of an enormous hotel that he hoped to fill with wealthy visitors from Philadelphia, Baltimore, Delaware, and Virginia. Locals at first dubbed the structure "Tommy's Folly," but Hughes' strategy worked. His hotel, later named Congress Hall, became the basis of a fashionable resort community.

Development of resort facilities on the cape accelerated in succeeding decades. The community had only three hotels and numerous boarding houses in the 1820s, but by the 1850s Cape May, as it had become known, accommodated nearly three thousand visitors a day. Most stayed in large beach-side hotels like Congress Hall, but after the Civil War prominent Philadelphia families began building their own summer cottages. Construction of the West Jersey Railroad also improved accessibility to the cape.

Clearly, the heyday for Cape May came in the decades between 1850 and 1900, when the resort reigned as one of the most popular and fashionable vacation spots on the Atlantic. Distinguished guests included Presidents Franklin Pierce, James Buchanan, Ulysses S. Grant, Chester A. Arthur, and Benjamin Harrison as well as such notable political and social figures as Horace Greeley and John Wanamaker. During this same period, several fires unfortunately damaged many of the older hotels and houses but also made it possible for entrepreneurs and summer residents to erect an exceptional array of Victorian structures that testify to the tastes and fashions of the American gentry in the last decades of the nineteenth century. Although Cape May declined in popularity as a resort in the early twentieth century, its fine old hotels, businesses, and residences survived surprisingly unaltered, and the city now boasts perhaps the greatest concentration of Victorian architecture in America.

Along Beach Drive, opposite the promenade and the beach, Cape

May entrepreneurs erected grand hotels that catered to the needs of the community's wealthy visitors. Thomas Hughes' Congress Hall was the first of these structures, and a successor still bears that historic name. Erected in 1879 at Beach and Congress, the present Congress Hall was constructed of brick in the Second Empire style. It has a striking three-story columned veranda surmounted by a mansard roof with dormer windows. More typical of Cape May was the frame construction of the Windsor Hotel, erected on Beach Avenue at Windsor in 1879 according to plans by Stephen Decatur Button, perhaps the most prolific architect on the cape. Even more striking is the Colonial Hotel, a four-and-a-half-story Second Empire structure erected at Beach and Ocean by the Church brothers in 1894–1895. All the hotels were not built along the coast, however, and two particularly fine examples are the Chalfonte Hotel, erected in 1876 at Sewell Avenue and Howard Street, and Carroll Villa, erected in 1882 at 19 Jackson Street. These two have the fretwork details and bracketed eaves typical of American Bracketed Villa, an American architectural style that gives Cape May much of its distinctive flavor.

Visitors to Cape May expected to be amused, and local entrepreneurs endeavored to meet their needs. There were, of course, bathhouses along the beach, special events like automobile races, and, for a time, a race track on nearby Diamond Beach. But nothing rivaled the popularity of gambling houses. At North and Windsor streets on the lawn of Congress Hall, gambler Henry Cleveland erected in 1845 an establishment that became famous as the Blue Pit. A rival gambling house was Jackson's Clubhouse, built in 1872 at 635 Columbia Avenue. Button also designed this structure in the popular American Bracketed Villa style.

Inland from the beachfront hotels stood the summer homes of Cape May's wealthier patrons. Some were designed by distinguished architects like Button, Frank Furness, and Samuel Sloan, but others reflected the talents of individual carpenter-builders, who turned to pattern books, textbooks, and trade journals for inspiration. While many of these struc-

Emlen Physick House

tures are hybrids of various styles and are more appropriately categorized as vernacular, Cape May also boasts many fine examples of the prevailing architectural styles of the period.

For example, the J. Stratton Ware House at 655 Hughes Street was erected in 1868 in the Gothic Revival style, as was the Eldridge Johnson House (the Pink House), erected in 1882 at 33 Perry Street. The popularity of American Bracketed Villa is evident in the George Allen House at 720 Washington, erected in 1863 according to a design by Samuel Sloan, and in the Neafie-Levy House, constructed in 1866 at 28–30 Congress Street. A fine example of Second Empire style is the George Hildreth House (1882) at 17 Jackson Street. One of the most important residences in the city and an exceptional example of the Stick style is the Emlen Physick House, a sixteen-room structure erected between 1887 and 1889 at 1050 Washington Street. The Mid-Atlantic Center for the Arts now operates the structure as an historic-house museum. A final example is the Dr. Henry F. Hunt House at 209 Congress Place, an elaborate Queen Anne house that dates from 1881. These are but a few from among Cape May's hundreds of fine examples of American Victorian architecture.

The best starting point for a tour of historic Cape May is the Mid-Atlantic Center for the Arts at the Emlen Physick House. Whether by foot, automobile, or trolley, a tour of the city's unique architectural heritage enriches the visitor's appreciation of the Victorian lifestyle. From its grand beachfront hotels to its gingerbread cottages, Cape May typifies the famous Jersey Coast resorts that provided both New Jerseyans and out-of-state visitors with temporary refuge from the accelerating pace of industrializing America.

ALLAIRE VILLAGE Allaire State Park, state 524, Allaire. Preserved 1830 village with Howell Iron Works and Monmouth Furnace.

ATSION VILLAGE U.S. 206, Atsion. Deserted industrial community with foundations of gristmill and several houses from the 1700s, some restored houses and buildings; with a museum.

BATSTO state 542 ten miles east of Hammonton. Restored eighteenth-century village with ironworks and 1800s glassworks and other buildings; visitor center.

CLINTON HISTORICAL MUSEUM VILLAGE Main Street, Clinton. Mill, schoolhouse, lime kilns, and other structures showing rural and industrial life from the eighteenth to the twentieth century.

DEY MANSION 199 Totowa Road, Wayne. House built in 1740 that was headquarters for George Washington in 1780; contains a museum.

EDISON NATIONAL HISTORIC SITE Main Street at Lakeside Avenue, West Orange. Laboratories where Thomas A. Edison made the first motion pictures and other inventions; with tours of both laboratories and Edison's home, Glenmont.

FERRY MUSEUM Washington Crossing State Park, near Titusville. Tavern where Washington rested briefly after crossing the Delaware on Christmas night, 1776.

GROVER CLEVELAND BIRTHPLACE 207 Bloomfield Avenue, Caldwell. Manse of the Presbyterian church where the future president's father was pastor; with Cleveland possessions from childhood to presidency.

HANCOCK HOUSE Hancock's Bridge. Where patriots were ambushed by Loyalists in 1778 during the American Revolution.

HERMITAGE 335 N. Franklin Turnpike, Ho-Ho-Kus. Early Gothic Revival house, rebuilt in 1845; site of visits by Burr, Benedict Arnold, Lafayette, and Washington; with a museum.

HISTORIC GARDNER'S BASIN N. New Hampshire Avenue and the Bay, Atlantic City. Maritime village predating Atlantic City, with twenty-five vessels and maritime artifacts, including whaling gear, exhibits on lobstermen, and exhibits of clammer and sail loft.

INDIAN KING TAVERN 233 King's Highway East, Haddonfield. Built in 1750; where the first New Jersey legislature met in 1777.

LONGSTREET FARM Holmdel Park, Holmdel. A living-history farm depicting agriculture in the 1890s.

MILLER-CORY HOUSE 614 Mountain Avenue, Westfield. A 1740 house with antique furniture and farm implements; demonstrations of open-hearth cooking and colonial crafts September–May.

MONMOUTH COUNTY HISTORICAL ASSOCIATION 70 Court Street, Freehold. Library and museum with records of North American Phalanx, communal society of the 1800s near Red Bank; a number of historic buildings nearby.

MORVEN 55 Stockton Street, Princeton. Built in the early 1750s by Richard Stockton, signer of the Declaration of Independence; headquarters for Cornwallis in 1777 and New Jersey executive mansion 1954–1981; with period rooms and exhibits.

NASSAU HALL Princeton. Completed in 1756 to house the College of New Jersey; occupied by both British and American troops during the Revolution, and the meetingplace for the Continental Congress in 1783.

NEWARK MUSEUM 43–49 Washington Street, Newark. Art and natural history collections; includes the Newark Fire Museum, a schoolhouse from the 1700s, and restored Ballantine House of 1885.

NEW JERSEY HISTORICAL SOCIETY MUSEUM   230 Broadway, Newark. Extensive collections and displays of American and New Jersey history, including maritime, transportation, industrial, and domestic items.

NEW JERSEY STATE MUSEUM 205 W. State Street, Trenton. General museum with fine arts, natural history, decorative arts, and other history.

OLD BARRACKS South Willow Street at Mahlon Stacy Park, Trenton. Building dating from the French and Indian War, now a museum.

OLD DUTCH PARSONAGE 65 *Washington Place, Somerville.* Dutch furnishings in a 1751 house where Rutgers University began.

PRINCETON HISTORICAL SOCIETY 158 *Nassau Street, Princeton.* Period rooms and changing exhibits in a house built about 1766; where the commander of "Old Ironsides" (U.S.S. *Constitution*), William Bainbridge, was born.

SPEEDWELL VILLAGE 333 *Speedwell Avenue (U.S. 202), Morristown.* Where Alfred Vail and Samuel F. B. Morse developed the electric telegraph and gave the first public demonstration in 1838; with an iron foundry and nine historic buildings.

TRENT HOUSE 539 *S. Warren Street, Trenton.* Oldest private house in Trenton, built 1719.

TWIN LIGHTS MUSEUM *Atlantic Highlands.* Where the Navesink lighthouse was built in 1828 and replaced in 1862; with a nautical museum.

VON STEUBEN HOUSE *Main Street, River Edge.* Built about 1695, occupied during American Revolution, and given to General Von Steuben for his services; with a museum.

WALT WHITMAN HOUSE 330 *Mickle Street, Camden.* Where the poet lived 1884–1892; with his furnishings and mementos.

WATERLOO VILLAGE *Waterloo Road, Stanhope.* Restoration of nineteenth-century businesses and homes on site of Andover Forge and Morris Canal.

WHEATON VILLAGE *Millville.* Restored glassmaking community of the 1880s, with museum and glassmaking demonstrations.

NEW MEXICO

CHACO CULTURE NATIONAL HISTORICAL PARK New Mexico 57, Bloomfield. By any measure New Mexico is a very old place. Though it entered into United States history relatively late, its own history reaches far back in time. Europeans—the Spanish—came to New Mexico in the 1540s, long before they arrived in what would become English America. And long before that, other men had made New Mexico their home. We call them "prehistoric" peoples, largely because we commonly think of "history" as beginning with some form of written records to document it, and the Indian peoples who lived here for a millenia left none. But they do have histories that are part of the history of New Mexico. We know them by physical evidence other than writing that they left behind. Archeologists rather than historians read and interpret it, and in New Mexico the evidence is exceptionally rich.

Archeologists have unearthed sites representing an enormous time range: from about 12,000 B.C. to A.D. 1540, the year the spanish arrived. The Sandia Cave is the earliest known archaeological site in the Southwest. The earliest domestic corn in the Southwest was recovered from Bat Cave. Remains of the Cochise and San Jose cultures in the northwestern part of the state have illuminated the preceramic period of the Indian culture. The Mogollon village has provided important clues to the Mogollon culture, one of the most important in New Mexico prehistory. By the close of the first millenium A.D., however, another culture surpassed even the Mogollon influence. These were the Anasazi (Navajo for "ancient ones"), who had sprung from an earlier people, the Basketmakers, in the Four Corners area and who were the direct ancestors of the historic Pueblo of more recent times. Their achievements were prodigious, their moment of glory relatively brief, the reasons for their decline still a mystery.

What they left behind is preserved today in the Chaco Culture National Historical Park in northwestern New Mexico, probably the best example of a concentration of pueblo communities in the Southwest. The monument was established in 1907 thanks largely to the early exploratory efforts of Edgar L. Hewett, of the Museum of New Mexico and the School of American Research. Over the years archeologists have excavated a startling array of buildings testifying to the existence here a thousand years ago of a developed urban-like civilization. Stretching for several miles along the canyon of the Chaco Wash, several distinct areas offer visitors a fascinating glimpse into what this ancient culture must have been like. Well-marked trails wind along the ruin walls which once contained a thriving civilization.

Pueblo Bonito, "the pretty village," was probably the largest single prehistoric Indian building in the Southwest when it was constructed in the middle of the eleventh century. Its excavation began in 1896, and

Pueblo Bonito

the results reveal evidence of some very impressive planning and building. The pueblo covered more than three acres and is characterized by
a symmetry of design that suggests the existence of a clear building plan
adhered to through several generations of builders. It is of course a
ruin, much of which collapsed during the centuries it stood empty and
abandoned. Estimates of its original size therefore remain guesswork,
but we do know that some sections reached a height of five stories.
There may have been as many as 800 rooms, though at any one time
probably no more than 600 were in use. It represents the highest development of Anasazi architecture. The walls generally were made of rough
unshaped stones randomly laid in mud mortar, but the builders did not
stop there. What the visitor sees of many walls, inside and out, is a
veneer of carefully fitted dense sandstone that was quarried about a
mile east and west of the pueblo. Small rectangular openings in the
walls let in light and air, while round holes were sockets for vigas, or
ceiling beams. Subjected to modern techniques of tree-ring dating, these
vigas have been crucial in indicating the age of various parts of the
pueblo.

Near the center of the pueblo is an open area—left by design, we
suppose, to serve as a public plaza or courtyard for the whole community. It probably functioned as a town square, providing a place for
special ceremonial activities as well as much daily domestic activity such
as shelling corn, twisting cordage, scraping hides, firing pottery, and
making tools from stone, bone, and wood. There were two courts separated by a row of small rooms where many grinding stones were found.
This was the pueblo's milling center. Nearby is a large underground
room which served as a religious center. This great kiva is supported
by four rubble-filled masonry columns and contains thirty-four niches
around the wall that may once have held offerings of jewelry and other
valued materials. By the time of excavation all had been opened and
emptied. The west court of the plaza holds another great kiva, which to
some investigators has suggested division into two groups of people

responsible for ceremonies at different times of the year, as is true of many Rio Grande pueblos today. Ordinary kivas were more numerous than great kivas, and thirty-seven have been identified throughout Pueblo Bonito.

Across the canyon on the Casa Rinconada Trail visitors can descend into the largest of great kivas in Chaco Canyon, over sixty feet across at floor level, and can inspect three smaller pueblos. A half-mile east of Pueblo Bonito is Chetro Ketl, the second largest of the great Anasazi pueblos and like Pueblo Bonito built according to some now lost master plan that gives it an architectural balance despite numerous remodelings and additions. Such evidence of an overall plan used through several generations is not found at the famous contemporary cliff dwellings at Mesa Verde, Canyon de Chelly, and the Navajo National Monument. This and other evidence suggest the existence in Chaco Canyon of a more complex social and political system than at the time existed elsewhere.

An important piece of that evidence, and one still shrouded in much mystery, is a complex system of roads extending from the canyon pueblos in four directions for many miles. No mere trails following the easiest way through a difficult landscape, they were true highways, twenty to forty feet wide, graded, and carefully bordered by berms of loose rock or rows of large boulders. Running perfectly straight for miles, they connected most of the pueblos of the Chaco world, about which their existence offers some additional clues. The people who built them obviously had a social organization highly enough developed to command the huge labor force such building must have required. They tell us that these people had some considerable engineering skills not limited to the immediate requirements of domestic architecture evident in the pueblos themselves. They also imply a degree of political and economic cooperation and communication among dozens of communities spread over a wide area, perhaps even a kind of national union similar to that known among the Toltecs and Aztecs in Mexico. Yet they also raise baffling questions too, for when they were built these people had neither draft animals nor wheeled vehicles—and thus no practical need for such ambitious highways. Did they have other symbolic meaning as well?

Such questions still abound. Probably the greatest one is why, during the 1200s, these great Indian communities were gradually abandoned, thus bringing to an end a golden age that has come to be called "classic." What combination of drought, erosion, epidemic, attacks from foreign enemies, and feuding among themselves brought down the society that had produced these large and sophisticated towns and the highways between them? We shall never know for sure. When they left, these prehistoric peoples left behind only the rocks they had built with and the graves of a few of their dead. Much of their history remains safely hidden away from the prying eyes of later centuries.

PALACE OF THE GOVERNORS *Santa Fe*. In the minds of generations of Americans, Santa Fe has symbolized the romance and adventure
of the Southwest. Two things help explain this role: great age and great
remoteness. Many people think of America as having been settled from
the east to west. Beginning at Jamestown in 1607 and Plymouth Rock in
1620, the story goes, Europeans (mainly Englishmen) came to the New
World and slowly built here a new way of life. It was not, of course, new
in all its particulars, but as they slowly advanced westward and possessed the continent, they did adapt to their new environment and
developed in time recognizably American ways of thinking and behaving. There is much truth to the story. But it is not complete, as Santa Fe
boldly witnesses.

Santa Fe was founded before any freedom-loving Englishmen sailed
for Virginia and Massachusetts, and founded by their enemies, the Spanish, at that. Spain's empire-building in the New World proceeded at a
different rate and along a different axis from England's. It began sooner—
from 1492, when Columbus "discovered" America—and it moved faster
and more ruthlessly. With motives that mixed avarice and altruism, the
Spaniards' behavior was forthright enough. They hoped to and in many
cases did enrich themselves with the kinds of riches everyone understood—gold and silver—and they spread the benefits of the Catholic
faith to countless Indians whose old gods they found quite inadequate
to salvation. Together, the helmeted *conquistadores* and holy fathers
seemed irresistible; by the early seventeenth century their empire of
sword and cross reached through South and Central America to Mexico
and north into the present-day United States. Santa Fe was one of its far
northern outposts.

The Palace of the Governors embodies much of the heritage and
spirit of this historic Spanish capital of New Mexico. For more than 350
years, the Palace has stood at the center of Spanish, Mexican, and American life in Santa Fe. "Palace" is something of a misleading term: compared with buildings in the British colonies that also bore that name
(the Governor's Palace in Williamsburg or Tryon Palace in North Carolina, for instance), it is hardly palatial. Despite the riches taken out of it,

Palace
of the
Governors

much of Spanish America remained miserably poor; whatever the Spanish legacy, it was not one of vigorous economic growth and development. This can be seen in the towns and in even the most pretentious buildings.

As constructed in 1610, the *Casas Reales,* or Royal Houses, were a rambling string of one-story plastered adobe buildings, whose style and comfort more reflected surrounding Indian puebloes than they did the glories of Spain or even Mexico City. Though larger than what remains today, the palace originally was plainer, lacking the Spanish-style porch along the front that is familiar to today's tourists as a marketplace for Indian crafts.

The Palace was built as part of the royal presidio of Santa Fe by Don Pedro de Peralta, the second Spanish governor of New Mexico. Until 1680 it served uneventfully enough as offices and living quarters for him and his successors. In that year, the Pueblo Indians revolted against the Spanish, and the palace compound became a refuge for troops and civilians where for a time they held the Indians at bay. When the Indians cut off the water supply, the Spanish were forced to retreat far down the Rio Grande Valley. Their exile lasted for a dozen years, during which the palace belonged to the Indians. When the Spanish finally returned under Don Diego de Vargas in 1692, they came to stay for over a century. They brought with them a paid presidio troop for whom two long rows of barracks were constructed. When completed many years later, these formed a wall enclosing a parade ground, corral, storerooms, and in the southeast corner the original Casa Real. Here there were guardrooms, kitchens and service quarters, two inner patios, and the governor's gallery. The far west end of the structure (demolished in 1866) housed a legislative chamber, jail, and ammunition room.

Spanish rule lasted uninterrupted through the eighteenth century and into the nineteenth, when in 1821 Mexico achieved independence. Mexican officials then replaced Spaniards in Santa Fe and made the old palace their place of official business and their private residence. But their tenure was brief, just twenty-five years. New Mexico was part of the vast territory seized by the United States in the Mexican War. The Mexican flag came down forever on August 18, 1846, when Brigadier General Stephen Watts Kearny occupied the Palace of the Governors in the name of the American republic. Except for a brief occupation by Confederate forces during the Civil War, the Stars and Stripes (and in time the New Mexico state flag) have flown ever since. Under its new masters, the old adobe palace underwent cycles of neglect, repair, modification, and eventually restoration. Its ancient function as the seat of government ended with the construction of a new territorial capitol in 1886, though it continued to be used for office space and until 1909 as the residence of New Mexico's governors. By then nearly three centuries old, the old palace had so deteriorated that there were serious threats to tear it down.

Happily, that fate was averted when in 1909 the state legislature appropriated funds to convert the historic structure into the Museum of New Mexico. Remodeling was completed in 1913 and included replacement of the graceful Victorian-era portal with the Spanish-style porch that has become the building's hallmark. Inside, today the palace serves as the main exhibit building for the history division of the Museum of New Mexico. Period rooms and a variety of exhibitions further our understanding of the history of New Mexico and the Southwest. The Mexican Governor's Office recreates the years of Mexico's occupation and suggests the austerity and isolation of life at this outpost. The New Mexico Chapel, recalling the middle years of the nineteenth century, symbolizes the Holy Faith—*Santa Fe*—that the Spanish also strove from the first to establish in the New World. The American presence is documented in the Merchant's Parlor from the 1860s and 1870s, when Santa Fe bloomed into a prosperous and growing commercial city. The Reception Room of Governor Prince, dating from the early 1890s, recaptures the historic function of the palace as the residence of many governors of New Mexico. Other exhibits located throughout the palace give visitors a glimpse of New Mexico's centuries-long history. Historic paintings and photographs capture other aspects of Santa Fe's and the region's past.

Today a state museum, years before the seat of power and authority, the Palace of the Governors is the oldest public building still in continuous use in the United States. That is fitting, for great age is one of the things that accounts for Santa Fe's historic image. It is also fitting that the palace occupies the north side of the historic plaza of Santa Fe, itself the site of considerable romance and adventure in the minds of many Americans. Here ended the storied Santa Fe Trail from Missouri, and here came the American traders piercing the isolation of first Spain's, then Mexico's, northern empire. They found in Santa Fe less the fabulous riches that they dreamed of than a Spanish-Indian civilization very different from their own and already centuries old. For most of that time, remoteness defined its relation to much of the world beyond. Under the Americans remoteness diminished, but much of the old culture lingered on—as the Palace of the Governors attests.

KIT CARSON HOME *Taos.* As the American nation moved west, history and legend conspired to make the process somehow larger than life. Long before the movies made it so for millions who themselves were many miles and decades removed from it, the West was epic. But it was not so much the West itself as it was America's, especially easterners', image of the West that endowed it with special power to move men in extraordinary ways. The place of New Mexico—already a very old place by the time the wagon trains first rolled in the 1830s—in that image is ambiguous. Others had intruded and settled there long before any Americans from the East arrived with their romantic notions about the West. Spaniards and Mexicans had thought of it as their land for two

Kit Carson House

centuries and had won large parts of it from nature and the Indians. But after the Mexican War, when title passed to the United States, New Mexico too was added to Americans' expansive image of the West. Kit Carson, the great American frontier hero, made his home there in the old town of Taos, and in him two traditions of the West come together.

Carson seemed to fit naturally with the easterners' image of the West. He was born in Kentucky, one of America's very first Wests, in 1809—the same year that Abraham Lincoln was born there. Like Lincoln he moved around, growing up in Missouri, and as a young man of seventeen migrating west over the famed Santa Fe Trail across Kansas and Colorado and into what was then Mexican New Mexico. It was years before anyone thought seriously about truly settling those arid high plains; Carson was a part of that earlier band of adventurers and entrepreneurs who went west as trappers of animals or as traders with the Indians and Mexicans. By the late 1820s Carson had entered the fur trade at Taos, which was a rendezvous point and winter headquarters for many of the mountain men who trapped the streams of the Sangre de Cristo and ranges farther west. As a mountain man, Carson tramped thousands of miles through the intermountain West, earning renown as a tireless guide and authority on this unmapped vastness.

In 1842 he served as hunter and guide for John C. Fremont's trek to South Pass, and in 1843 he guided one group of Fremont's second expedition on a circuitous route that carried them northwest to the Laramie River Valley in what would be southern Wyoming, into Nevada's Great Basin, across the Sierras, and into Mexican California. From Southern California they trekked across the Mojave Desert and over the Spanish Trail to Fort Uintah in eastern Utah. From there the tattered band, Carson in the lead and Fremont following, descended down Crouse Canyon to the Green River Valley in the northwest corner of Colorado. They trailed east and on June 22, 1844, crossed the Continental Divide at Hoosier Pass, 11,598 feet above sea level. From that superb vantage, Carson and cartographer Carl Preuss sat and mapped the headwaters of some of the Rocky Mountain West's great rivers, there only bubbling trout streams: the Rio Grande, the two Plattes, the Arkansas, the Grand (today's Colorado). Another ten days found them back at Bent's Fort on the Arkansas. It was the sort of epic adventure befitting the immense land, and it made legends out of the men who accomplished it.

From such odysseys Kit Carson's image—like the image of the Great West in eastern eyes—grew larger than life. But Carson was a man as well as a legend, and much of his manhood was passed in an intermittently settled fashion in New Mexico. After returning from Fremont's first expedition, he moved to Taos and in 1843 married (for the second time: in 1836 he had married an Arapaho girl who died in childbirth) Maria Josefa Jaramillo, daughter of a prominent family and sister-in-law of trading entrepreneur Charles Bent. Thus Kit Carson the legend entered the local New Mexican gentry. To it, over their twenty-five-year life together, the Carsons gave seven children, six of whom were born in their Taos house. The house was built in 1825, just four years after Mexico achieved independence from Spain. Taos was then on the far northern edge of the Mexican frontier—a frontier that Carson, the Bent brothers, Fremont, and other Americans like them did so much to push back. It was still Mexican territory when Carson and his bride moved in in 1843, but not for long.

The turmoil in the West set off by the Mexican War of 1846–1848 also set Carson roving once more. In 1845 he went with Fremont to the Pacific coast where until 1849 he actively assisted in the American conquest of California. Back in New Mexico, which had also become American territory, Carson briefly took up ranching east of the Sangre de Cristos, but in 1854 he was back in Taos and the family house. There he stayed more or less continuously for seven years, during which he served as Indian agent for the Utes. In 1861 war again disrupted Carson's quiet life in Taos and called him to action that would add to his fame as mountain man and explorer a soldier's laurels.

The Civil War saw New Mexico, remote from the great action in the East, become a minor but momentarily dramatic battleground. Carson, a loyal Unionist, helped organize the First New Mexico Volunteer Infantry and helped thwart the ambitious campaign by Confederate forces under the leadership of Henry H. Sibley to capture the United States' new southwestern territories. Early in 1862 Carson rallied Union forces to hold back the Confederates at Valverde Ford. Suffering a decisive defeat later that spring at Glorieta Pass, Sibley was forced to retreat back toward Texas, and the Confederacy abandoned hopes of capturing the Southwest and California. New Mexico was not yet at peace, however. With settlers distracted by their own civil war, Indian depredations had increased. The new commander of the Military Department of New Mexico gave the nasty job of taming them over to Carson. The Mescalero Apache were the first to feel his wrath, and by 1863 he had harried them into submission and brought 400 warriors and their families to a reservation in southeastern New Mexico. The Navajo were next; and though Carson was reluctant to be the agent of a harsh policy against them, he broke their power and compelled them to move to a reservation. In 1864 and 1865 he fought the Comanche and Kiowa on the eastern plains and concluded his fighting career at the Battle of Adobe Walls in Texas. In 1866 he took command of the army's post of Fort Garland in Colorado. Ill health forced him to resign in 1867; he died less than a year later.

The Carson home in Taos, administered today by the Kit Carson Memorial Foundation, recaptures much of the career of this legendary figure. With adobe walls thirty inches thick, split-level floors, and beamed "viga" ceilings, it originally contained twelve rooms and surrounds a pleasant courtyard. Several rooms are preserved in their original form. Three of them—the parlor, kitchen, and bedroom—are authentically furnished in a combination of Spanish colonial and territorial styles. The fourth features exhibits and artifacts portraying the various phases in Carson's life and adventures. An Indian room recalls the life of earlier residents of the Taos valley. The chapel contains an excellent collection of early Spanish religious articles, including the vestments of the priest who both baptized and married Carson in 1843.

Today a quiet place, the house when the Carsons lived in it was alive with children and was frequented by the great and famous who were family friends. There, amid the old Spanish adobe, the man and legend came together. The legend was largely true: if anyone symbolized the exploration and opening of the West to new influences, Kit Carson surely did. The man partly lived in that legend. He also lived in this old New Mexican town, where things change slowly. What remains of him is still here, buried with his wife in the Kit Carson Memorial State Park at the end of Dragoon Lane.

ACOMA PUEBLO state 23 thirteen miles south of Casa Blanca. On a 350-foot-high mesa with San Estevan del Rey Mission, built 1629–1642, and a pueblo that was built about 1300; now used mostly for ceremonial purposes. Obtain permission before visiting.

ALBUQUERQUE MUSEUM 2000 Mountain Road, N.W., Albuquerque. An art, science, and regional history museum with artifacts from 20,000 B.C. to the present.

AZTEC RUINS NATIONAL MONUMENT one mile north of Aztec on county road. Pueblo ruin on a site occupied from the eleventh through the thirteenth century; one of the largest Pueblo villages of the Southwest.

BANDELIER NATIONAL MONUMENT state 4 twelve miles south of Los Alamos. Cliff ruins, cave rooms, pueblos, petroglyphs, and cave structures inhabited A.D. 1200–1550.

BLUMENSCHEIN HOUSE Ledoux Street, Taos. Eighteenth-century adobe house of artist Ernest L. Blumenschein, who co-founded the Taos Art Colony in 1898.

CHAPEL OF SAN MIGUEL AND BARRIO de ANALCO *in an area bounded by E. De Vargas Street, Old Santa Fe Trail, and the Santa Fe River, Santa Fe.* Buildings of mixed Spanish and Indian construction and narrow winding streets, with a chapel built in 1692.

CHURCH AT CHIMAYO (EL SANTUARIO de CHIMAYO) *south of Truchas in Chimayo.* A Spanish Colonial-design church built in 1816.

CHURCH AT LAS TRAMPAS *Las Trampas.* The church of San Jose de Gracia, completed in 1776 and now possibly the best preserved Spanish Colonial church in New Mexico.

CHURCH AT RANCHOS de TAOS (SAN FRANCISCO de ASSISI MISSION CHURCH) *the Plaza, Ranchos de Taos.* Built 1772–1816 and restored to its present picturesque state.

COCHITA PUEBLO *on the Rio Grande twenty-seven miles southwest of Santa Fe.* Occupied since 1250; with a plaza, mission church, and two kivas. Obtain permission before visiting.

EL MORRO NATIONAL MONUMENT *east of El Morro on state 53.* A mesa point with petroglyphs of Indians and graffiti of European and American passersby since 1605.

FORT SELDEN STATE MONUMENT *eighteen miles north of Las Cruces.* Remnants of an adobe and stone fort built in 1865.

FORT SUMNER STATE MONUMENT *off state 212 southeast of Fort Sumner.* Remains of fort built in 1862 and the state's first Indian reservation; now with a museum.

FORT UNION NATIONAL MONUMENT *on state 477 nine miles north of Watrous.* Ruins of a supply depot built 1863–1869 near the Santa Fe Trail.

GHOST RANCH MUSEUM VISITOR CENTER *U.S. 84, Abiquiu.* A natural history museum emphasizing conservation; with living animals.

GILA CLIFF DWELLINGS NATIONAL MONUMENT *state 11, Gila Hot Springs.* Pueblos occupied from the tenth through the seventeenth century, once housing for 2,000 people.

GLORIETA BATTLEFIELD *U.S. 84–85 ten miles southeast of Santa Fe.* Where the Union preserved the Southwest from the Confederacy in 1862.

GRAN QUIVIRA NATIONAL MONUMENT *state 14 south of Mountainair.* Ruins of pueblo dating from about 1300 and Franciscan mission dating from the early seventeenth century. Other ruins from the same periods are visible nearby at Abo and Quarai.

GUADALUPE CHURCH *100 Guadalupe Street, Santa Fe.* Built in the eighteenth century and said to be the oldest shrine in the United States devoted to the Virgin of Guadalupe; with a museum of Hispanic paintings and murals.

HARWOOD FOUNDATION OF UNIVERSITY OF NEW MEXICO *25 Ledoux Street, Taos.* Art from Taos artists from 1898 to the present, with special collections on Southwest culture and author D. H. Lawrence.

HAWIKUH *twelve miles southwest of Zuni, Zuni Indian Reservation.*

Ruins of the largest of the seven "Cities of Cibola" that Coronado overcame in 1540.

INDIAN PUEBLO CULTURAL CENTER *2401 Twelfth Street, N.W., Albuquerque.* Museum with collections on Pueblo Indians from 1900 to the present.

ISLETA PUEBLO *U.S. 85, Isleta.* One of the largest pueblos in the eighteenth and nineteenth centuries, noted for crops and orchards; includes the Church of San Augustin, built 1709–1710 and one of the oldest remaining in the state.

JEMEZ STATE MONUMENT *state 4, Jemez Springs.* Ruins of a Franciscan mission and pueblo from early in the seventeenth century.

LAGUNA PUEBLO *off U.S. 66 forty-five miles west of Albuquerque.* One of the state's largest pueblos, with one-story stone and adobe structures and the 1701 San Jose de la Laguna Mission.

MAXWELL MUSEUM OF ANTHROPOLOGY *Roma and University, N.E., Albuquerque.* Includes Navajo and other weaving, Mimbres and Pueblo pottery, and Indian basketry and jewelry.

MESILLA PLAZA *south of Las Cruces on state 28, Mesilla.* Not settled until 1848 but of historical significance as a stop on the Butterfield Overland Mail route, 1858–1861, and from being occupied by Confederate sympathizers in 1861.

MILLICENT A. ROGERS MUSEUM *Taos.* An anthropology and art museum with materials on southwestern and Plains Indians and the art of Hispanic New Mexico.

MONTEZUMA HOTEL *six miles north of Las Vegas, in Gallinas Canyon.* A hotel complex built around hot springs, with several structures dating from the late nineteenth century.

MUSEUM OF NEW MEXICO *Santa Fe.* Most important modern cultural institution in the state, including the Palace of the Governors (history), Laboratory of Anthropology (anthropology and archeology), Museum of Fine Arts, and Museum of International Folk Art.

NATIONAL ATOMIC MUSEUM *Kirtland Air Force Base East, Albuquerque.* Nuclear weapons and nuclear energy materials.

NORRIS E. BRADBURY SCIENCE HALL OF FAME *Los Alamos.* Science and technology exhibits stemming from the work of the Los Alamos Scientific Laboratory.

OLD TOWN *one block north of the 2000 block of Central Avenue, N.W., Albuquerque.* Town plaza where Albuquerque was started in 1706, with contemporary shops and galleries and the 1793 San Felipe de Neri Church.

PECOS NATIONAL MONUMENT *on state 63 south of Pecos.* Site of a pueblo active from 1450 to 1838 and a stopping-place of Coronado; now with mounds, restored kivas, and stone and adobe ruins.

PLAZA del CERRO *state 76 east of Riverside and Espanola, Chimayo.* A typical example of a fortified colonial plaza, established in the 1740s; with pitched-roof houses and an Acequia Madre (main ditch).

PUYE RUINS fourteen miles west of Espanola. Remains of 200- to 300-room pueblo of stone blocks atop a mesa, dating from the thirteenth and fourteenth centuries.

ROSARIO CHAPEL old Spanish cemetery, northwest Santa Fe. Built in 1807, with a wooden hand-carved altar screen.

ROSWELL MUSEUM AND ART CENTER 100 West Eleventh, Roswell. Twentieth-century American paintings and sculpture, including works by Peter Hurd and Henriette Wyeth; with collection of southwestern Indian art and the Robert H. Goddard rocket collection.

SALMON RUIN off state 17 nine miles east of Farmington. Chacoan settlement of eleventh century with numerous kivas.

SANDIA LABORATORIES VISITOR CENTER 1515 Eubank, S.E., Albuquerque. A Western Electric company museum on energy development, with a solar tour.

SAN ILDEFONSO PUEBLO off state 4 southwest of Espanola. A living pueblo dating from the eighteenth century, near a village established in 1300. Obtain permission before visiting.

SANTO DOMINGO PUEBLO on Rio Grande south of Santa Fe. A living pueblo on a site occupied before the Spanish period in the largest of the eastern Keresan pueblos. Obtain permission before visiting.

SETON VILLAGE off U.S. 84 / 85 six miles south of Santa Fe. A forty-five-room stone and adobe castle, built in 1930 for naturalist Ernest Thompson Seton and a community devoted to his philosophy.

TAOS PUEBLO three miles north of Taos. A living multi-storied pueblo with portions originating before the first Spanish visit in 1540. Obtain permission before visiting.

TRINITY SITE twenty-five miles south of U.S. 380 on White Sands Missile Range. Where the first atomic bomb was exploded in 1945, now surrounded by a fence and not accessible to public.

TUCUMCARI HISTORICAL RESEARCH INSTITUTE 416 S. Adams, Tucumcari. A history and folk art museum in a 1905 courthouse.

WESTERN NEW MEXICO UNIVERSITY MUSEUM Western New Mexico University, Silver City. Indian artifacts, ranching equipment, mining implements, and photographs; with concerts of folk music.

ZUNI PUEBLO (HALONA PUEBLO) on state 2 and 3 thirty-six miles south of Gallup. On the site of one of six Zuni pueblos existing in Coronado's time. Obtain permission before entering.

NEW YORK

OLD FORT NIAGARA New York 18 north of Youngstown. Along the watery highway that led from the Atlantic Ocean up the St. Lawrence River, through the chain of Great Lakes, to the vast interior of North America, nature placed but one truly mammoth obstacle. At Niagara Falls, waters drained from half a continent plunged 185 vertical feet into a perilous gorge and thence more peacefully flowed northward to Lake Ontario. The whole course of the Niagara River is short—just twenty miles. But, broken by its great Falls and the treacherous rapids of the upper river, it obstructed water passage to the West for centuries. For those who would defy nature, therefore, both banks of the river became a necessary portage. Nowhere along the Great Lakes had nature designed a better chokepoint.

This the Indians had long known. Nor was the fact lost on the French and British empire builders who competed here for treasure and influence. Nor was it lost on the Americans who in time displaced them. That fact placed Fort Niagara at the center of their long North American struggles. Thus contended over for many years, it stands preserved today as an unparalleled cross section of colonial and early American history.

To the French, whose eastern settlements at Quebec and Montreal were widely separated from their western cordon of outposts reaching far down the Ohio and Mississippi valleys to New Orleans, the importance of Niagara as a connecting link was perhaps most compelling. Attempting to secure it, they first (though only briefly) established themselves at the mouth of the Niagara River in 1678. In 1725 they came to stay, finally making good their plans to fortify the river and so secure the fur trade.

A massive stone house, rising defiantly on the shore of Lake Ontario, was the immediate visible result. Later called the French Castle, it still stands and is the centerpiece of Old Fort Niagara today. The French deliberately chose not to build a conventional type of fortification for fear of raising suspicion among the Indians. Rather, they insisted on calling their building merely "a stone house for the purpose of storage," and indeed a trade room where Indians came in large numbers to exchange furs for trade goods occupied a conspicuous place in it. But even though it outwardly resembled a French provincial chateau, it was in fact a formidable fortress designed to withstand attack by hostile Indians—or hostile Englishmen.

In the 1750s the anxious French (who in 1754 again found themselves at war with Britain) strengthened the stronghold with an elaborate system of earthworks, moats, and artillery batteries. But when the test came in July 1759, all their superb effort went for naught. After a siege of eighteen days the French garrison of nearly 500 surrendered to the British. The French never returned. For the British it truly was a prize, for now British guns at Niagara controlled the chokepoint between the two halves of French empire in America.

The French and Indian War in 1763 effectively broke French power, but it did not eliminate British problems. For a time, under the leadership of Sir William Johnson, the British did enjoy the fruits of their victory: increasingly western commerce and the fur trade fell under their control. And Fort Niagara became a center of commercial and political influence as never before. It was in the fort's Old Council Chamber in 1764 that Johnson secured a formal peace with representatives of the Indian tribes all the way from Nova Scotia to the Mississippi. As the years passed, however, peace with their own colonial subjects proved more elusive for the British. The American Revolution was a war that neither side fought in accord with the gentlemanly rules; especially on the frontier where the British made good use of their Indian allies, it could be truly ferocious. Fort Niagara, which remained securely in British hands throughout the conflict, was a center for the numerous Anglo-Indian forays that struck such terror up and down the frontier. Back to Fort Niagara the war parties returned with their American prisoners and more than a few American scalps, while thousands of American loyalists fleeing to Canada sought refuge from their old American neighbors.

After the Revolution Niagara technically became American territory, but the British did not evacuate all their northwest outposts, including Niagara, until 1796. During the "holdover" period, Fort Niagara was a source of succor, law, and order for the Empire loyalists who were

French Castle and British bakehouse

rapidly settling the western or Canadian side of the Niagara River. To this day, the villages they founded under Fort Niagara's protection—Queenston and Newark (later renamed Niagara-on-the-Lake)—remain at the very heart of British Canada.

The Americans finally took possession of the fort in 1796, although it returned once more to British hands during the War of 1812. Both sides saw the Niagara frontier as crucial to victory, and the two forts that guarded the old chokepoint at the mouth of the river (Fort George in Canada, Fort Niagara in New York) were the scene of fierce fighting. In 1813 the British retook Fort Niagara, ravaged Lewiston and burned Buffalo, and left only after the coming of peace in 1815. Two years later, the Rush-Bagot Agreement between the United States and Britain began the process of mutual disarmament on the Great Lakes, a principle that in time resulted in the demilitarization of the entire United States-Canadian boundary. As the prospect of armed conflict thus faded, Fort Niagara was reduced to a peaceful barracks and training post. The Army did not finally leave until 1963, and the Coast Guard still maintains a station there.

The site today is located within the Fort Niagara State Park, and the fort itself, operated by the Old Fort Niagara Association, Inc., offers visitors a moving glimpse of three centuries of American and Canadian history. With Fort Mackinac in Michigan, it ranks as one of the loveliest settings anywhere on the Great Lakes. Most of its buildings are original and were erected between 1726 and 1872. Together they provide a composite picture of the French, British, and American occupation. On the northwest corner, where the Niagara River flows into Lake Ontario, the French built their original "Castle" and it stands today as dominant and as forbidding a presence as it must have been in the 1720s. It was designed as a self-contained fortress and included, in addition to quarters for officers and men, storerooms, bakery, chapel, powder magazine, and a well—reputed to be haunted. During the War of 1812 heavy cannon were mounted in the attic to bombard Fort George across the river. Its massive timbers were cut locally, and much of the stone was taken from the Niagara Escarpment.

Over the years, all three owners extended and elaborated the Castle's landward defenses. The French added a detached powder magazine, whose massive arched ceiling covered by a thick layer of earth enabled it to survive the siege of 1759, when they also constructed the Dauphin Battery. The Gate of Five Nations also dates from the French period and was named by them in honor of the five Indian nations of the Iroquois Confederacy. Both the North and South Redoubts, small fortresses in themselves, were built by the British in 1770 and 1771. The River and Land Defenses, Casemate Walls, and Gallery were American contributions, none ever tested under fire. There are also monuments to the ill-fated French expedition of 1687–88; to the French explorer

LaSalle who established a post here in 1678–79; and to the Rush-Bagot Agreement of 1817.

Three flags still fly here: the Stars and Stripes, the Union Jack, and the vanished Fleur-de-lis of Bourbon France. Musket drills, cannon firings, and costumed staff add to the drama of a visit. But it is also a good place to go on quiet rainy or snowy days when the crowds are absent. At such times it perhaps best evokes the spirit of those lonely voyageurs and frightened soldiers who once passed through this place, perched so bravely on the edge of Lake Ontario, beside the mighty Niagara.

FEDERAL HALL NATIONAL MONUMENT AND CASTLE CLINTON NATIONAL MONUMENT New York. There is much on Manhattan Island that is historic. An early and important settlement in colonial days and a center of culture, wealth, and power ever since, Manhattan has seen much history made. Two places in particular, both now national memorials administered by the National Park Service, illustrate especially well both New York City's crucial role in the founding of the new nation and its own subsequent diverse and constantly changing history. Visitors to Manhattan, then, should be sure to venture south of midtown's famous attractions: Central Park, museums, the theaters, Fifth Avenue shops. It is downtown that they will find the site of New York's earlier history; Federal Hall and Castle Clinton are windows onto much of it.

Of the events associated with the early history of the American nation, two of the most momentous occurred at Federal Hall, on the corner of Wall and Nassau streets in lower Manhattan. The first Congress under the new federal Constitution held its initial session there in March 1789, and on April 30 of the same year George Washington stood on the building's second-floor balcony to take the oath of office that made him the first president of the United States. But even then the place had a history, going back almost to New York's earliest days. The first City Hall, a handsome two-story red brick structure, was built on this site in 1699 and 1700 when the city, though officially English, still bore many marks of its Dutch beginnings. It became the seat of city government and, in 1735, the site of the famous trial of John Peter Zenger, a newspaper publisher accused—and acquitted—of seditious libel in an early landmark case in the history of freedom of the press. Thirty years later, in 1765, City Hall hosted indignant delegates from nine of the thirteen colonies who gathered in what became known as the Stamp Act Congress, to protest what they saw as arbitrary taxation without their consent. During the Revolutionary War when New York was occupied by the British, City Hall saw service as one of several British headquarters buildings.

After the coming of American independence, the government of what was at first a loose confederation of sovereign states finally settled, in 1785, on City Hall in New York as its seat. Four years and one new

Federal Hall

constitution after that, the new federal government took up residence in the newly remodeled building (thence known as Federal, not City, Hall). But in 1790 the national capital moved to Philadelphia and a decade later to the District of Columbia, leaving New York's Federal Hall without the commanding purpose it once had had. As it fell into disrepair, the present Greek-Revival style structure replaced it in 1842. It served first for twenty years as the New York City Customshouse and then as an office of the United States Subtreasury. After the end of the subtreasury system in 1920, the building held offices of several government agencies, while its broad Wall Street steps, dominated by the statue of George Washington, became a favorite place for public rallies, war-bond sales, and patriotic observances. It was designated a national historic site in 1939 and a national memorial in 1955. Today it houses exhibits illustrating the key role of this place in early American history.

Castle Clinton, located on the far southern tip of Manhattan Island, reveals another side of New York's history. It was built in 1811 (after Federal Hall was already fading from eminence), one of several installations intended to protect the city from British attack during the War of 1812. Originally known as the South-West Battery, it had a circular shape it still retains but stood 200 feet out in the river and was connected to Manhattan by a wooden drawbridge. It included twenty-eight guns, a powder magazine, and officers' quarters. The British never came, and at the war's end the fort became headquarters for the Third Military District. It was renamed Castle Clinton for De Witt Clinton, former mayor of New York City and governor of the state. But the place was not destined for a military career. The army moved out in the early 1820s, and only then, after it was deeded to the city of New York, did the old South-

West Battery take on the first of several roles by which millions of New Yorkers and others came to know it.

On July 3, 1824, Castle Clinton opened as Castle Garden—an early and excellent example of adapting a building for uses other than those for which it was originally designed. As a place of public entertainment, it was the setting for concerts, fireworks, and balloon ascensions. The gunrooms, elaborately redecorated, became boxes for eight people to watch the show below. The old officers' quarters were transformed into a bar, while atop the building patrons might stroll on an awning-covered promenade where once sentries kept watch for British ships. Thus reincarnated, it hosted the great and famous: Lafayette, the French hero of the American Revolution; presidents Jackson, Tyler, and Polk; Senator Henry Clay, the "Great Compromiser;" and Louis Kossuth, the Hungarian patriot. A roof was added in the 1840s allowing more formal entertainments including opera and, in 1850, P. T. Barnum's presentation in her American debut of the "Swedish Nightingale," Jenny Lind.

The old fort was soon to welcome other kinds of crowds than theater audiences. Leased to the state of New York, Castle Garden was converted in 1855 to an immigrant landing depot; shortly before, it had been joined to the rest of Manhattan and fenced off from the rest of the Battery. For the next thirty-five years it helped welcome, sort out, and send on their way more than eight million people seeking new homes in America—two out of every three immigrants during this period. For the thousands of Irish, English, and Germans who dominated immigration in those middle decades of the nineteenth century, it was the first glimpse of the Great Republic—built ironically as a defense against the ancestors of some of them. As the flow increased toward the end of the century, Castle Clinton was superseded by the more famous immigrant landing center on Ellis Island; but the old fort had earned a permanent place in the history of immigration (and thus in another part of New York history).

There are still many New Yorkers alive who knew Castle Clinton in its next and final famous role: as the New York City Aquarium. It opened in 1896 and held at first mainly fish from the waters around New York, though as interest grew more exotic specimens soon were added. As during its years as an entertainment park in the 1830s and 1840s, it once again became a favorite place for fun and relaxation for thousands of visitors from New York and afar. The Aquarium finally closed in 1941, and for the next thirty-four years the building remained shut to the public. Moves to raze it failed, and after much restoration Castle Clinton reemerged in 1975 in a form close to the early-nineteenth-century original. Thus "readapted" to its original form (if not its original function), it offers today's visitor a glimpse of New York's existing past. Once filled with artillerymen at the ready, with cheering audiences, with huddled and hopeful masses, and with Sunday-afternoon gazers at exotic fish, Castle Clinton is preserved today for those who would understand these things—and thus New York and American history—better. Along with Federal Hall, it makes lower Manhattan an important stop for the history-minded traveler in New York.

FARMERS' MUSEUM Lake Road, Cooperstown. To many people from other states and countries New York means the Statue of Liberty, Manhattan skyscrapers, and (at least if they honeymooned there) Niagara Falls. Many New Yorkers themselves know better. Between those extremes there is a wide variety of country and city life. The landscape is varied; industry and agriculture abound. Likewise with New York history: it is dominated by familiar images that often hide the real substance. The Farmers' Museum in Cooperstown does much to correct that problem. In a state most famous for the great city it contains, this museum documents a chapter in New York history that, in contrast, was still predominantly rural. In the process, it documents a large chapter in American history as well.

Between the end of the American Revolution and the Civil War, the young American nation busied itself with a number of tasks. It worked out in fact the system of constitutional government that had been established in theory in 1787. Its coastal trading cities prospered as American ships plied the seas. From its first factories came the rumblings of the industrial revolution. But most of all, Americans turned toward the great unsettled interior of their country. And gradually, year by year and generation by generation, they moved west and made it theirs. That process of settling a wilderness meant that at some point nearly all of them were farmers or the families of farmers. How they worked and lived is the subject of this village museum.

The Farmers' Museum focuses on early-nineteenth-century farm life in upstate New York, but the life it depicts was typical of a much larger area. The theme is set in the entrance to the large stone barn exhibit building. There the visitor finds a great log with an old axe sunk deeply in it: a vivid reminder of the farmers' first obstacle—the forest—and how they overcame it. What follows is a tour through America's rural civilization.

That civilization moved as the seasons moved. March, when the sun brought life back into the land, was when the farmers' year began. April saw the sowing of the chief grain crops: oats, barley, wheat, and rye. In May potatoes, corn, sqaush, and beans were started, and perhaps a kitchen garden. Early summer saw constant cultivation and hay-making. Indeed, hay was for years one of New York state's chief crops. Timothy grass and clover were choice feed for the thousands of horses and other animals then found not just on farms, but in the towns and along the turnpikes and canal tow-paths. Cut and first left to cure in the fields, hay was then piled up in large stacks and stored in barns for the winter. On the quantity and quality of the hay crops depended the welfare of the livestock in the months ahead. In poor years cornstalks and grainstraw

*Farmers'
Museum
Main Barn*

could be substituted, but if they proved insufficient, the farmer was obliged to butcher.

The grain harvest filled August and was always an anxious time. As the grain ripened—as the stalks dried and the heads filled and slightly bent over—the farmer had to move quickly. Grain harvested too early would not store well; that left uncut too long was liable to be knocked down by hail or other inclement weather. After a certain amount of drying in the field, the crop was threshed and then stored in bins or carried by wagon directly to market. In the early years, all this was done laboriously by hand, with sickles, scythes, and hand threshing. Later mechanical reapers became common, and later still threshing machines, but none changed the judgment, timing, and good luck that the farmer had to have at this crucial point in his year.

The autumn was filled with other harvests. Hops, used in brewing beer, came in in September and, even more than the summer grains, required much nurture and careful timing. October, traditional harvest time, brought in the corn and vegetable crops. By November the harvest was finished, but not the farmer's work. As temperatures fell, this was the time for butchering meat and hunting wild game. Cattle and hogs were slaughtered, cut up, cured and salted; wild turkeys still were abundant in the woods and, dressed and roasted, were a welcome sight on many a farm dinner table. After the crops were in and food prepared for the cold months ahead, there was still much to do before the snow came. Supplies of firewood had to be seen to and the house and barn sealed up by banking earth and straw around the foundations.

Traditional Christmas and New Years feasts brought welcome brightness to wintertime, while January, the quietest time, often found the farmer trapped by the weather and low on cash besides. Finally, February was marked by preparation for another spring. Tools were sharpened and mended. Old ones, refashioned by resourceful hands, reappeared in new forms. Seed was made ready and, ever anxious to take fullest possible advantage of a short growing season, the farmer carefully watched the wind, the moon, and the clouds for the first signs of spring.

Such was the fundamental pattern of farm life in rural New York. Firmly tied to nature, the farmers and their families were not surprisingly people of largely family and local attachments. But if the scope of their world was narrow, at the same time their independence was great. The home production and preparation not only of all foods, but also of many other necessities was taken for granted. Homespun clothing, homemade shoes and hats, were the rule among people whose self-sufficiency was renowned. Yet as the frontier was pushed back and as population grew and farmers grew more prosperous, a village culture also developed that complemented the self-contained world of the family farm. The Village Crossroads at the Farmers' Museum recaptures what it was like

Here the visitor will see a grey fieldstone school-house typical of those where generations of rural New Yorkers learned to read, write, and figure. A country store displays the array of merchandise that many a farmer, his wife, and his family (for whom the world of "homemade" was more necessity than virtue) came to covet. Buttons, bolts of cloth, pots and pans, shoes, bonnets, candies, lanterns, harnesses, and innumerable "notions" clutter the shelves, illustrating what retail merchandising was like in the rural America of 150 years ago. Other goods and services could be had at the blacksmith shop, the printer's office, and the druggist's.

The doctor's office, filled with bottles, vials, lancets, cups, and splints, gives an idea of what medicine was like in the days before it became "scientific." The practice of law has changed less over the years; indeed, law was the one thing that even on the frontier could not for long be homemade. Some of the special qualities of lawyering in the country, however, can be sensed in the village law office, this one dating from 1829. Two other buildings complete this reconstituted village. The Bump Tavern, an early-nineteenth-century country inn, reveals the accommodations available to a variety of guests, from lady and gentleman travelers to teamsters and drovers to emigrant families on their way west. And the village church—this one Methodist, built in 1791—represents another center of village life and testifies that religion was a part of the "cultural baggage" settlers brought with them to the farming frontier.

The extent of that frontier was enormous, both in space and in time. It moved from upstate New York westward across Ohio and Indiana to Illinois and, in time, to the Great Plains beyond. It lasted more than a hundred years, from the end of the Revolutionary War to just before the First World War, when homesteaders still first were breaking the sod in places like North Dakota. The Farmers' Museum renders the particular quality of that experience in nineteenth-century upstate New York. But it also captures much of what the larger world of rural America once was like.

ADIRONDACK MUSEUM state 28N and 30, Blue Mountain Lake. Indoor and outdoor exhibits on the Adirondack region.

ALBANY INSTITUTE OF HISTORY AND ART 125 Washington Avenue, Albany. Exhibits dealing with the Albany region and Upper Hudson Valley history.

AMERICAN MUSEUM OF IMMIGRATION Statue of Liberty National Monument, Liberty Island, New York. History museum at the base of the famous statue.

CANAL MUSEUM Weighlock Building, Eire Boulevard East, Syracuse. Museum focusing on the history of the famous Erie Canal, parts of which can still be viewed at Rexford Aqueduct and Schoharie Crossing, both state historic sites.

CLERMONT STATE HISTORIC SITE off state 9G, Germantown. Hudson River estate of Robert Livingston, a leader of the Continental Congress and backer of the steamboat *Clermont;* built in 1777.

CORNING MUSEUM OF GLASS Corning Glass Center, Corning. Museum at famous glass-making center.

FORT CRAILO STATE HISTORIC SITE 9½ Riverside Avenue, Rensselaer. Dutch Colonial house built about 1700, the home of the Van Rensselaer family; now a museum of Hudson Valley Dutch life.

FORT ONTARIO STATE HISTORIC SITE E. Seventh Street and Lake Ontario, Oswego. Built in 1839, now a museum showing military life in the nineteenth century.

FORT TICONDEROGA on state 22, two and one half miles south of Ticonderoga. Reconstruction of a fort originally built 1755–1757 by the French, taken by the British, then captured by Ethan Allen and the Green Mountain Boys in 1775. To the north, Crown Point State Historic Site, another focus of French, British, and American military activity in the eighteenth century.

GENESEE COUNTRY MUSEUM Flint Hill Road, Mumford. Museum village of some forty-five structures, including blacksmith shop, print shop, tinsmith, and small-scale farm.

HERKIMER HOME STATE HISTORIC SITE three miles southeast of Little Falls. Built by Revolutionary War general Nicholas Herkimer in the 1700s and used as a tavern on the Erie Canal in the nineteenth century.

HISTORIC CHERRY HILL South Pearl Street, Albany. Former home of the Van Rensselaer family, built in 1787.

HISTORICAL SOCIETY OF SARATOGA SPRINGS MUSEUM AND WALWORTH MEMORIAL MUSEUM Congress Park, Saratoga Springs. Housed in a former gambling casino at one of the most fashionable Victorian resorts.

HUGUENOT HISTORICAL SOCIETY 6 Brodhead Avenue, New Paltz. Administers several historic French Huguenot structures, including the Jean Hasbrouck House.

HYDE PARK, HOME OF FRANKLIN D. ROOSEVELT off U.S. 9, two miles south of Hyde Park. Birthplace and home of President Roosevelt; maintained as at his death in 1945.

JOHN BROWN FARM STATE HISTORIC SITE John Brown Road, about two miles south of Lake Placid. Last home of the famed anti-slavery crusader; located at site of rural black colony know as Timbucto.

JOHN JAY HOMESTEAD STATE HISTORIC SITE Jay Street, Katonah. Early nineteenth-century home of John Jay, governor of New York and first Chief Justice of the United States.

LYNDHURST 635 S. Broadway, Tarrytown. Elaborate nineteenth-century Gothic Revival mansion that was the home of the Jay Gould family.

MARGARET WOODBURY STRONG MUSEUM One Manhattan Square, Rochester. Museum focusing on cultural history and popular taste from 1820 to 1930.

MARTIN VAN BUREN NATIONAL HISTORIC SITE state 9H two miles south of Kinderhook. Home of the eighth president of the United States.

MUSEUM OF THE CITY OF NEW YORK Fifth Avenue and 103rd Street, New York. Exhibits and multimedia presentations on the political, social, and economic history of the city.

MUSEUMS AT STONY BROOK state 25A, west of Main Street, Stony Brook. Includes carriage museum, art museum, and history museum; also blacksmith shop, schoolhouse, and grist mill.

NEW-YORK HISTORICAL SOCIETY 170 Central Park West, New York. Extensive collections relating to the history of the city and the state.

NEW YORK STATE HISTORICAL ASSOCIATION Lake Road, Cooperstown. Housed in the Fenimore House, known for its fine collection of American folk and decorative art.

NEW YORK STATE MUSEUM Cultural Education Center, Empire State Plaza, Albany. Permanent exhibits on the natural and human history of various regions of the state, with temporary exhibits on themes such as technology, decorative arts, and fine arts.

OLD BETHPAGE VILLAGE Round Swamp Road, Old Bethpage. Pre-Civil War farm village, a branch museum of the Nassau County Museum.

PHILIPSE MANOR HALL STATE HISTORIC SITE Dock Street and Warburton Avenue, Yonkers. One of the most extensive manors in the region and the seat of Frederick Philipse III, whose estate once covered a fifth of Westchester County.

ROCHESTER MUSEUM AND SCIENCE CENTER 657 East Avenue, Rochester. Exhibits and programs on the area's natural and human history.

SAGAMORE HILL NATIONAL HISTORIC SITE Cove Neck at the terminus of Cove Neck Road, two miles north of Oyster Bay, Long Island.

Built 1882–1885 by Theodore Roosevelt; his summer White House while president, 1901–1909.

SARATOGA NATIONAL HISTORIC PARK *Stillwater.* Where the Americans defeated the British in 1777, thus preventing General John Burgoyne from successfully invading from Canada.

SCHUYLER MANSION STATE HISTORIC SITE *27 Clinton Street, Albany.* Georgian brick residence of Philip Schuyler, Revolutionary War general and New York political and commercial leader.

SENATE HOUSE STATE HISTORIC SITE *312 Fair Street, Kingston.* Where the first state senate met in 1777.

SHAKER MUSEUM *off state 66, Old Chatham.* One of the finest collections of artifacts made by the religious sect that first settled near Albany over 200 years ago.

SLEEPY HOLLOW RESTORATIONS *150 White Plains Road, Tarrytown.* Administers Philipsburg Manor at North Tarrytown, Van Cortlandt Manor at Croton-on-Hudson, and Sunnyside, author Washington Irving's Tarrytown home.

SOUTH STREET SEAPORT MUSEUM *203 Front Street, New York.* Museum and maritime restoration project.

VANDERBILT MANSION NATIONAL HISTORIC SITE *off route 9, Hyde Park.* Estate built by the financial and industrial leader at the close of the nineteenth century.

WASHINGTON'S HEADQUARTERS STATE HISTORIC SITE *Jonathan Hasbrouck House, 84 Liberty Street, Newburgh.* Eighteenth-century fieldstone house that served as the American commander's headquarters in 1782–1783; nearby at Vails Gate stand the Knox Headquarters, another important Revolutionary command post, and the New Windsor Cantonment, the final encampment of the Continental Army during the winter of 1782–83.

NORTH CAROLINA

TRYON PALACE RESTORATION COMPLEX 610 Pollock Street, New Bern. In the decade before the American Revolution, Tryon Palace in New Bern stood as a symbol of British authority in colonial America. Constructed between 1767 and 1770, the late Georgian structure was the seat of North Carolina's colonial government and the residence of its royal governor and his family until 1775. Tryon Palace's significance did not diminish with independence and statehood, however, for it became home to North Carolina's first state governors and the hub of activity in the transition from royal colony to state. Most of the original structure burned in 1798, just four years after the state capital moved to Raleigh, but a carefully researched and painstaking reconstruction of Tryon Palace now stands as a symbol of this critical period in North Carolina history.

When William Tryon assumed the duties of royal governor of North Carolina in 1765, one of his first acts was to establish the port city of New Bern as the colony's permanent capital. As early as 1711 Baron Christophe von Graffenreid, a land promoter, proposed locating the colonial government at New Bern, which had only recently been settled by Swiss, German, and English emigrants. Colonial assemblies debated the proposal over the next five decades, but the matter remained unresolved until Tryon took office, convinced that the progress of the colony depended on settling this long-standing dispute.

Colonial resistance to the Stamp Act dominated the new governor's first year in office, but by late 1766 crisis and confrontation had abated sufficiently that Tryon thought it time to carry forward his plans for a permanent capitol. In December the assembly approved his request for funds for the erection of a public building in New Bern to house the governor and his family, the meetings of the council and the assembly, and the public records. Tryon had brought English architect John Hawks with him to North Carolina in 1764 with this specific project in mind, and the two men quickly moved forward with contracts and plans for the new structure. They agreed that the building, as the most visible link between the colonies and the distant mother country, should be a reflection of English heritage and tradition. Hawks's solution was a two-story brick structure of fashionable Georgian design, and in the summer of 1767 construction began on a site overlooking the Trent River.

Construction of this new symbol of royal colonial authority continued for the next three years under Hawks's supervision, while Tryon turned his attention to more pressing concerns. He found the controversy over the Townshend Acts particularly frustrating. These tax laws, passed by Parliament in 1767, united outraged North Carolinians and culminated in 1769 in the assembly's adoption of resolutions denying Parliament's right to tax the colonies. The assembly took this action despite Tryon's opposition, so he interpreted the move as an indication of loss of confidence in him.

Intracolonial unity over the Townshend Acts dissolved quickly, however, as conflict increased between the counties to the west and those in the more settled east. Essentially, back-country farmers felt that the eastern-dominated colonial government was not responsive to their needs. Organized as the Regulators, they became increasingly restive after both the governor and the assembly failed to respond to their calls for greater representation, relief from excessive taxation, and reform of local government. When the Regulators rioted in the fall of 1770, Tryon summoned the council to its first meeting in the new palace and alerted military commanders to be on guard. Yet despite rumors that violence might spread to New Bern, the governor followed through with plans for a gala opening of the new capitol on December 5. The threat of violence continued through the winter and spring and stymied efforts to resolve the Regulators' grievances. Tryon finally took action when he received evidence of actual plans for armed insurrection. He called out the colonial militia and on May 16, 1771, defeated the Regulators in the battle of Alamance Creek.

Tryon had little time to enjoy either this hard won peace or his fine new home, for he left the colony shortly thereafter for the post of royal governor of New York. His replacement, Josiah Martin, arrived in New Bern on August 11, 1771. Governor Martin and the colonial assembly quickly became embroiled in a clash of wills that lasted throughout his tenure. The antipathy intensified in 1774 in the controversy over North Carolina's response to Parliament's Coercive Acts and the call for a Continental Congress. Martin failed to block the meeting of a provincial congress, and his authority as governor further deteriorated in the spring of 1775 as hostility to British colonial power mounted. In May he and his family were forced to flee the Palace and New Bern, just over a

*Main building
of Tryon
Palace*

month after the Battles of Lexington and Concord launched the colonies' fight for independence. The Palace stood vacant until January 1777, when North Carolina's first state governor, Richard Caswell, was sworn in. Caswell took up residence in the Palace, and the former colonial capitol became a hub of Revolutionary War activity. As the war continued, the state government fled New Bern and the threat of British attack, but on June 17, 1783, the Palace Square was filled with celebrants rejoicing over the signing of the Articles of Peace. By that time, however, Tryon's Palace had become somewhat shabby through years of neglect. The state legislature continued to hold meetings in the deteriorating structure off and on for the next decade, but in 1794 the state government officially moved to a newly constructed capitol in Raleigh. Tryon's building survived only four more years until a fire on February 27, 1798, destroyed all but the west wing.

Interest in reconstructing Tryon Palace first surfaced in 1925, but the project languished for lack of adequate funding until the early 1950s, when the North Carolina state legislature appropriated funds for the purchase of the Palace property and two trust funds and a bequest by Mrs. James Edwin Latham provided major funding for its restoration, reconstruction, and furnishing. Extensive archeological and documentary research preceded the restoration of the west wing and the rebuilding of the remaining portions of the eighteenth-century structure. For the latter, noted architect William G. Perry relied on John Hawks's original drawings and plans, which were found in the New-York Historical Society Library and the Public Record Office in London. Furnishing of the house began in 1957, using as a guide an inventory of Tryon's furnishings made after his move to New York. In April 1959, the restored and reconstructed Tryon Palace opened to the public as a state historic site managed through the Tryon Palace Commission. Costumed guides take visitors through the Council Chamber, the governor's library, the dining room, the parlor, the upstairs family rooms, the colonial secretary's office, the kitchen, and various support rooms essential to the maintenance of a home of this size. All have been furnished to reflect as accurately as possible the Palace at the end of Governor Tryon's tenure. Also included in the Tryon Palace Restoration Complex are elaborately landscaped gardens and lawns, appropriate outbuildings, and two other historic houses: the John Wright Stanly House, which dates from the 1780s, and the Stevenson House, a Federal-style structure erected in the early nineteenth century. In addition to guided tours, palace events include historical dramas, school programs, and an annual symposium on the decorative arts. No other site provides such rewarding opportunities to learn about the history of North Carolina as both colony and state.

ZEBULON B. VANCE BIRTHPLACE STATE HISTORIC SITE
911 Reems Creek Road, Weaverville. In Reems Creek Valley, nestled

*Vance's
reconstructed
homestead*

in the Blue Ridge Mountains of western North Carolina, stands the Zebulon B. Vance Birthplace State Historic Site. The Vance family occupied the homestead for thirty-five years prior to Zebulon Vance's birth there in 1830. The reconstructed house and outbuildings now commemorate Vance's central role in the state's historical development and, more broadly, provide a glimpse of the Appalachian Mountain folk culture, a distinctive component of the North Carolina character.

Between 1785 and 1790, David Vance and his wife Priscilla Brant Vance moved to Reems Creek Valley from Quaker Meadows in North Carolina's Catawba Valley. In 1795 they secured title to the 328-acre homestead that would remain the Vance family home for the next half-century. An officer of the Continental Army during the Revolutionary War, Vance helped organize Buncombe County and was appointed clerk of the court for the county. He also served in the North Carolina General Assembly and on the commission that established the North Carolina–Tennessee boundary in 1799. The Vances had two sons, David Vance, Jr., and Robert Brant Vance, who inherited the homestead upon their father's death in 1813. Robert, a physician and politician, died in 1827 of wounds received in a duel with a political opponent, and his brother became sole owner.

After serving as an officer in the War of 1812, David Vance returned to the family homestead and became a successful farmer and merchant. He and his wife, Mira M. Baird Vance, had two sons, Robert B. Vance, born April 26, 1828, and Zebulon Baird Vance, born May 13, 1830. The family continued to live at the homestead until after the death of Priscilla Vance in 1836. The next year David Vance moved the family to Lapland (present-day Marshall). Seven years later he, too, died and was buried near his father in Reems Creek Valley. In 1846, Mira Vance sold the farm, which by then encompassed 950 acres.

Although the Vances moved away from the family farm in 1837, they did not leave the back country of western North Carolina. Located no more than ten miles to the northwest of Reems Creek, Lapland was very much a part of the frontier region, as was Asheville, the family's home after 1846. In these mountain communities, Zebulon Vance attended several schools, including Matthew Woodson's on Flat Creek, Miss Jane Hughey's at Lapland, and Washington College in East Tennessee. He was at the last when his father died in 1844. He returned to Tennessee and moved with his mother to Asheville, where he attended Newton Academy. At the age of twenty-one, Vance began reading law before undertaking formal course work at the University of North Carolina in Chapel Hill. He obtained his law license in December 1851, was elected Buncombe County solicitor the following March, and in May began practicing law in Asheville.

On August 3, 1853, Zebulon Vance married Harriet Espy at Quaker Meadows, near where his grandfather had first settled before the Revolution. Five sons kept Mrs. Vance busy while her husband pursued a career in politics. He won a seat in the North Carolina House of Commons in 1854 at the age of twenty-four, but he failed in subsequent bids for the state senate and the United State House of Representatives. Vance finally won a seat in Congress in 1858, only to relinquish it three years later when North Carolina seceded from the Union.

Initially a moderate Unionist, Vance accepted secession as the only viable course of action in the face of President Abraham Lincoln's call for militia support to put down the Southern rebellion. In mid-April 1861, he urged his fellow North Carolinas to join him in fighting for the South. Within the month, he organized the Rough and Ready Guards, a company of backcountry volunteers headed by himself as captain. In September he was promoted to colonel and put in command of the Twenty-Sixth North Carolina Regiment. He served less than a year in that capacity, however, before resigning to take office as the state's governor. He occupied the governorship for the remainder of the war, and his efforts on behalf of his fellow North Carolinians earned him renown as the "War Governor of the South."

A popular leader, Vance managed to mobilize the state in behalf of the war effort but without sacrificing individual rights. His staunch defense of the latter and his refusal to cooperate fully in the Confederate cause made him unique among rebel governors but also protected the sovereignty and general welfare of his home state. His reelection in 1864 indicated popular support of his policies, but Robert E. Lee's surrender of the Confederate troops at Appomattox Courthouse on April 9 cut short his second term. Just over a month later, he was arrested and jailed in the Old Capitol Prison in Washington, D.C. Paroled in less than two months, he was finally pardoned on March 11, 1867.

Zebulon Vance's popularity remained substantial after the war, and in 1870 he was elected to the United States Senate. Disqualified from holding office by the Fourteenth Amendment, he was forced to give up his seat. After Congress reversed the disabilities, Vance made a second, unsuccessful, bid for the Senate in 1872. Four years later, however, he won election to a third term as governor. He took office in 1877 but resigned in 1879 after finally securing election to the Senate. Reelected to second and third terms, he remained in the Senate until his death on April 14, 1894. He was buried in Riverside Cemetery in Asheville.

Ownership of Vance's birthplace in Reems Creek Valley changed hands several times after his mother sold the property at public auction in 1846. When the State of North Carolina finally secured ownership of the house and surrounding 2.28 acres in 1957, major alterations had significantly changed the structure's appearance. The original brick chimney remained from the 1790s and served as the basis for reconstruction of the Vances' two-story log house. The reconstructed house, completed in 1960, was furnished to reflect the years between 1790 and 1840 when the Vance family resided there. In 1960 and 1961, the state also reconstructed a springhouse, a loomhouse, a tool house, and a slave house. A corn crib and smokehouse were moved to the site and reconstructed in 1963. A modern visitor center / museum was dedicated in 1965.

Open to the public since 1961, the Zebulon B. Vance Birthplace commemorates the life and career of the notable North Carolinan. Exhibits at the visitor center focus on Vance's role in the state's history. The site also depicts the lives of early settlers in the Appalachian Mountains. While the backcountry frontier was neither as heavily populated nor as influential as the more settled areas to the east, the traditions and culture of the western region constitute an integral part of the North Carolina experience. Through its annual Pioneer Living Days, the Zebulon B. Vance Birthplace preserves many of the basic skills and crafts of the Appalachian Mountain folk culture. Special programs include living-history demonstrations of open-hearth cooking, woodcraft, leather making, whiskey distilling, weaving, and other daily pioneer activities. The site and its programs and activities provide a fitting memorial to Zebulon Vance and to his origins on North Carolina's mountain frontier.

DUKE HOMESTEAD STATE HISTORIC SITE 2828 *Duke Homestead Road, Durham.* The development of the modern tobacco industry played a key role in North Carolina's impressive economic growth in the late nineteenth and early twentieth centuries, and the history of that industry is integrally tied to the history of the Duke family of Durham. The Dukes began modestly in 1865 to manufacture smoking tobacco on their farm near Durham. By the end of the century the family controlled the largest tobacco company in the world. Their innovative and aggressive business leadership made North Carolina the center of tobacco culture, manufacturing, and merchandising. The Duke Homestead State Historic Site preserves the farm where this all began and provides programs and exhibits on the history of the Dukes and of tobacco farming and manufacturing in North Carolina.

Duke family's farmhouse

When Washington Duke turned to tobacco cultivation after the failure of his cotton crop in 1859, he was one of many North Carolina farmers hoping to profit from the recent discovery of a procedure for producing bright tobacco, a mild-flavored yellow variety preferred by consumers. When coupled with the availability of rail transportation and the opening of tobacco-manufacturing facilities at nearby Durham, bright tobacco held considerable promise as the cash crop that would finally bring prosperity to the area. The Civil War temporarily disrupted these hopes and plans; but the war also widened the market, for soldiers who passed through the region returned home after the war to tell of the superior quality of Durham tobacco. As postwar recovery began, the stage was set for the emergence of the modern tobacco industry.

The Civil War had been particularly disruptive for the Duke family. When drafted into the Confederate army in late 1863 or early 1864, Duke had sent his family to stay with relatives and had rented his farm to tenants. He returned from the war in 1865 to find his farm abandoned and a good part of his stored tobacco gone. Penniless and with four children to support, Duke put the family to work processing what was left into smoking tobacco. He and his sons had surprising success peddling their products in towns and villages in eastern North Carolina and decided to continue manufacturing smoking tobacco on a part-time basis. While still farming tobacco, wheat, corn, oats, and other subsistence crops, the Dukes used crude hand processes to manufacture 15,000 pounds of their "Pro Bono Publico" brand in 1866. The slow process began with curing the tobacco to a lemon-yellow color over a charcoal fire. Then the cured tobacco would be flailed, forced through a sieve, weighed, and packaged in bags that bore the family brand name. As the demand for their tobacco increased, they expanded their farm complex to include a second factory, formerly a stable, and by 1870 a third, a new two-story frame building that was the first erected specifically for tobacco-factory use. With additional workers, production increased in 1873 to 125,000 pounds of smoking tobacco annually.

As early as 1868 Washington Duke's son Brodie suggested moving the family operation to nearby Durham. The elder Duke did not see the necessity of moving, but he helped his son set up a small factory in town by 1870. As the family business expanded over the next few years, the advantages of locating in Durham, nearer shipping facilities and the farmers' tobacco market, became obvious even to Washington Duke. So in 1874 the Dukes moved their tobacco business from the homestead in Durham. The small family-oriented business was well on its way to becoming a modern large-scale tobacco company.

By that time Durham had become a tobacco manufacturing center. The Dukes' stiffest competitor was W. T. Blackwell and Company, the manufacturer of "Bull Durham" smoking tobacco and the largest company of its kind in the world. The Blackwell firm dated back to 1858 and had a well-deserved reputation for a superior product. To improve their company's competitive position, the Dukes secured additional capital by adding a non-family partner in 1878. Renamed W. Duke, Sons and Company, the firm in 1881 started manufacturing a new product, cigarettes, which were then beginning to increase in popularity in the United States. To cut costs, the company in 1884 successfully experimented with the first mechanical mass production of cigarettes. Lower production costs and aggressive advertising resulted in the Dukes soon dominating the market.

Washington Duke's youngest son, James Buchanan "Buck" Duke, became convinced that continued competition between the large-scale tobacco manufacturers was too costly and inefficient, and in the mid-1880s he developed a plan to combine the top five companies. He approached the Dukes' four closest competitors and in 1890 secured their agreement on the proposal. The five then merged to form the American Tobacco Company, and James Duke became head of the largest tobacco company in the world with a virtual monopoly on the market. Popularly known as the "tobacco trust," the American Tobacco Company eventually came under fire for violation of antitrust legislation, and in 1911 the United States Supreme Court ordered dissolution of the company. Out of this came Liggett and Myers, P. Lorillard, R. J. Reynolds, and a new American Tobacco Company.

The Duke homestead changed owners several times before Duke University purchased it in 1931 with gifts from Duke family and friends. The university maintained the property until 1974, when the homestead was deeded to the state of North Carolina to be administered by the State Division of Archives and History. Now open to the public, the Duke Homestead State Historic Site preserves forty-three acres of the original farm complex. The simple two-story frame farmhouse that Washington Duke built for his family in 1852 is the oldest structure at the site. The Dukes' third factory, the two-story frame building erected about 1870, also remains, and the first factory has been reconstructed. Other structures include a curing barn, a tobacco pack house, and outbuildings. A modern visitor center houses the Tobacco Museum with its exhibits on the Duke family and the history of tobacco culture. Special programs include a film on tobacco culture and living-history demonstrations of tobacco farming and manufacturing. Together, the restored and reconstructed farm complex, the exhibits, and the programs bring to life North Carolina's modern tobacco history.

ALAMANCE BATTLEGROUND state 62, eight miles southwest of Burlington. Visitor center and monuments giving vivid account of the 1771 battle between Colonial Governor William Tryon's militia and rebellious frontiersmen.

AYCOCK BIRTHPLACE Fremount. Visitor center and 1840 home that is the birthplace of Charles B. Aycock, early 1900s governor who laid the foundations for modern state educational system.

BATH HISTORIC DISTRICT Restored and original structures, including the Palmer–Marsh House (ca. 1744) and the Bonner House (ca. 1830), in the first incorporated town in the province; visitor center.

BENNETT PLACE off I-85 west, Durham. Tours on the site of surrender negotiations between Confederate General Joseph E. Johnston and Union General William T. Sherman, 1865; visitor center.

BENTONVILLE BATTLEGROUND Newton Grove. Battlefield where 80,000 Union and Confederate soldiers fought in one of the last major battles of the Civil War; nearby, the Harper House, where wounded from both sides were treated; visitor center.

BETHABARA Bethabara Road, two miles northwest of Winston-Salem. Church and sites of first cabin and fort of a 1700s Moravian settlement; founding place of the Wachovia Colony.

BILTMORE two miles south of Asheville on U.S. 25. Museum of art and history in the nineteenth-century mansion of Cornelius Vanderbilt; gardens designed by Frederick Law Olmsted.

BRUNSWICK TOWN off state 133 south of Wilmington (adjacent to Orton Plantation). Excavated foundations of the town that was the largest North Carolina port in the Colonial period; visitor center.

CAPE HATTERAS NATIONAL SEASHORE near Manteo. Visitor center and sea museum near the tallest lighthouse in the United States, with the "graveyard of the Atlantic" offshore.

CUPOLA HOUSE 408 S. Broad Street, Edenton. One of the South's finest examples of Jacobean architecture; built about 1725 and now included in the Historic Edenton tour.

FORT FISHER four miles south on U.S. 421, Carolina Beach. Remains of the Confederate earthen fort that kept the port of Wilmington open to blockade runners; taken by the Union in 1865; visitor center.

FORT MACON Bogue Point, four miles east on Fort Macon road, Atlantic Beach. Restored fort with a museum on a military post dating from 1826; site of a Civil War battle in 1864.

FORT RALEIGH four miles north on U.S. 158, Manteo. Site of first

English settlements, 1585, including the "Lost Colony," with reconstruction of original earth fort and a visitor center.

GUILFORD COURTHOUSE six miles northwest of Greensboro near U.S. 220. Military park where Lord Cornwallis won the battle in 1781 but lost enough men to weaken his forces before Yorktown.

HAMPTON MARINERS MUSEUM 120 Turner Street, Beaufort. Ship models, marine artifacts, library on boatbuilding.

HISTORIC HALIFAX Halifax. Restored buildings and exhibits present a picture of life in the Roanoke Valley; where the Halifax Resolves and the state's first constitution were adopted; guided walking tours include four restored and furnished historic buildings.

MINT MUSEUM OF ART 501 Hempstead Place, Charlotte. Housed in an 1835 building that was the first branch of the U.S. Mint; exhibits of minting operations and gold coins plus European and American art.

MINT MUSEUM OF HISTORY 3500 Shamrock Drive, Charlotte. Local and regional materials—furniture, decorative arts, costumes—in a home built about 1774.

MOORES CREEK NATIONAL MILITARY PARK twenty-five miles northwest of Wilmington on state 210. Visitor center, exhibits, and tours on the site of the 1776 battle where patriots defeated the British.

MUSEUM OF THE ALBEMARLE Elizabeth City. Indian artifacts, farm exhibits, lumbering items.

MUSEUM OF THE CHEROKEE INDIAN U.S. 441, Cherokee. Audiovisual and other exhibits relating the story of the Cherokee from hundreds of years ago to the present.

MUSEUM OF EARLY SOUTHERN DECORATIVE ARTS 924 S. Main Street, Winston-Salem. Items from the South before 1820—architecture, furniture, paintings, ceramics, textiles, metal wares.

NORTH CAROLINA DIVISION OF ARCHIVES AND HISTORY 109 E. Jones Street, Raleigh. Archives, manuscripts, museum, historic sites, junior history, and publications on state history; period of collections from sixteenth century to present.

NORTH CAROLINA MUSEUM OF ART 2110 Blue Ridge Boulevard, Raleigh. European and American art, including sculpture, decorative arts, and ethnic art.

NORTH CAROLINA MUSEUM OF HISTORY 109 E. Jones Street, Raleigh. General history museum with emphasis on North Carolina history and including photography, paintings, and graphics as well as other materials.

OCONALUFTEE INDIAN VISITOR CENTER Great Smoky Mountains National Park, Cherokee. Cherokee guides and crafts people recreate a village of two hundred years ago.

OLD EAST University of North Carolina campus, Chapel Hill. Remodeled building of 1795, called the first structure on the campus of the first state university in the United States.

OLD SALEM HISTORIC DISTRICT Salem College campus and area near Salem Square, Winston-Salem. More than thirty restored structures of the German community of the 1700s.

POLK MEMORIAL Pineville. Commemorates significant events in the administration of the 11th president of the United States; reconstructed farmstead provides a glimpse of James K. Polk's early life in North Carolina; visitor center.

REED GOLD MINE off state 200 about thirteen miles southeast of Concord. First authenticated discovery of gold in the United States, in 1799; tour includes mine shafts and stampmill; panning area and visitor center.

SANDBURG HOME Flat Rock. An 1838 house that was the home of poet Carl Sandburg from 1945 to 1967, with his personal and literary effects.

SOMERSET PLACE Pettigrew State Park, near Creswell. Restored plantation and grounds of one of the most notable estates in North Carolina in the early 1800s.

STATE CAPITOL Raleigh. Greek Revival building erected 1833–1840 and still being used.

TOWN CREEK INDIAN MOUND nine miles southeast of Mount Gilead. Reconstruction of a ceremonial center built by Indians of the Pee Dee culture in fifteenth century A.D.; visitor center.

WOLFE MEMORIAL 48 Spruce Street, Asheville. The twenty-eight-room boarding house made famous by writer Thomas Wolfe; original house and furnishings preserve the flavor of Wolfe's boyhood home.

WRIGHT BROTHERS NATIONAL MEMORIAL Kill Devil Hills, Kitty Hawk. Memorial, markers, and reproduction of the craft and the camp where the Wrights flew the first power-driven passenger-carrying plane in 1903.

NORTH DAKOTA

FORT UNION TRADING POST NATIONAL HISTORIC SITE and FORT BUFORD STATE HISTORIC SITE Williston. The popular image of western forts in the years after the Civil War owes much to Hollywood. Fort Apache is probably the classic example: a wooden stockade with guardhouses, massive gates, cannon, and the flag proudly waving. Inside and all around, hard-riding and hard-fighting cavalry troopers stand at the ready and patrol against redskin hostiles. Usually, too, such forts are seen as objects of fierce attack and the site of much heroism. The image is not false in all its particulars, though for the sake of dramatic effectiveness it does depart somewhat from history.

Many western outposts, for example, were not bastions of military power at all, but rather commercial entrepôts that existed to trade, not fight, with the Indians and seldom saw a soldier. Not all forts were located in the rugged deserts and canyonlands of the Southwest, where the movies commonly picture them. Many of the forts that were in fact military in nature were garrisoned not by dashing cavalry but by lowly foot soldiers. And most forts never saw an Indian attack, their buglers never summoning the brave (and always outnumbered) defenders amid warwhoops and whizzing arrows.

Such places were Fort Union and Fort Buford, today national and state historic sites located twenty-five miles southwest of Williston near the confluence of the Missouri and Yellowstone rivers. Together, they illustrate the true character of many western outposts in the nineteenth century, and something of the cultural evolution of the northern plains region. Their histories are consecutive, together spanning some six and a half decades. In the beginning, in 1829, when Fort Union was established, the plains belonged to the buffalo and the Indians. In 1895, when Fort Buford was deactivated, they belonged to homesteaders and railroads. Cattle, not buffalo, roamed there, and the Indians, their numbers greatly diminished, were on reservations. North Dakota had become a territory and finally a state, soon to settle down to an agricultural prosperity that its frontier beginnings barely hinted at.

Fort Union was a trading post, not a military base, and it represents a stage in the West's development when there existed a comfortable truce between the Indians and the relatively few white men on the plains that was based on trade. Since the late eighteenth century fur trappers had penetrated the land that would become North Dakota. Many were French and Scots who came down from Canada, hunting and trapping on their own or trading for furs with Indians. With them, these first whites lived easily enough; some even took Indian wives and wandered with the nomadic tribes. As the demand for furs grew and trade increased, however, more ambitious entrepreneurs came on the scene. Such men built Fort Union. The site, on the Missouri River just a few miles from the mouth of the Yellowstone, commanded the water route into the region of the interior fur trade, and it was a natural meeting place for the upper Plains Indians and white traders hungry for furs. Furs were big business, and the long arm of John Jacob Astor's New York-based American Fur Company reached all the way to North Dakota. Its experienced agent or *bourgeois,* Kenneth McKenzie, began Fort Union in 1829 and four years later completed it to his satisfaction. For an outpost 1,900 miles from its sources of supply down the Missouri in St. Louis, it was an impressive place. Its walls were cottonwood logs twenty feet high, grounded in stone foundations. On two corners stout stone bastions, twenty-four feet square and thirty feet high, stood ominous guard against potential intruders. The purpose of the fortifications was to discourage trouble before it happened, and in that they succeeded very well. The Indians who came to trade—Assiniboin, Crow, Blackfoot, and Sioux—camped in their tepees on the plains around the fort, and when tempers flared among them (as was not uncommon) it was McKenzie's policy to leave well enough alone. Inside the stockade were

Ford Buford Powder House

all the facilities needed to sustain life in the wilderness and carry on trade with the Indians: a warehouse and retail store, a press room where the furs were packed for shipment by steamboat downriver, cooper's and blacksmith's shops, milkhouse and dairy, a stable, and an icehouse. The *bourgeois* enjoyed a large one-and-a-half-story house. Here, McKenzie (known as "King of the Upper Missouri") and his successors lived and entertained in a style surprisingly elaborate for so remote an outpost.

Other fur entrepreneurs followed Astor and McKenzie; Pierre Chouteau, whose St. Louis trading company bought the fort in 1834, was the most famous. For another twenty years he and the post prospered thanks to a brisk demand for buffalo robes that followed the earlier craze for beaver. But that too dwindled in time as hunters decimated the great herds and as the Indians grew more hostile. It was to contain them that Fort Buford, a different type of fort, was built just three miles away. In the first years after the Civil War, the army established a chain of forts along the Missouri River to protect the western trails from Indian attack. Fort Buford was one of them.

The new fort was begun in 1866. Its first years were passed in a state of semi-seige, as Indians raided woodcutting and hunting parties, rustled livestock, and harassed mail coaches. But though it was less well fortified than the old Fort Union (from which the army salvaged materials to build the new fort), it was never directly attacked. It was however a center of military activity. It served as a main provisioning base in the army's numerous campaigns against the northern Plains tribes in the 1870s and 1880s. A number of famous figures in frontier history passed through, among them Sitting Bull, the great Sioux chief who had defeated Custer and the Seventh Cavalry at the Little Bighorn. But mostly duty for the 270 or so men garrisoned here was routine—as it was on most frontier posts most of the time. Cavalry and infantry units patrolled the international boundary to the north, guarded railroad construction crews, and tried with mixed results to curb illegal trade with the Indians in whiskey, guns, and ammunition. Inevitably much of the average soldier's time was spent trying to combat the boredom of peacetime garrison duty. Post commanders encouraged musical and theatrical performances, use of the post library, and participation in fraternal organizations. Inevitably, too, soldiers found their own diversions in sports, picnics—and drinking.

As a military post, Fort Buford was agent of the same western culture that Fort Union had been, but at a later stage. This is why the history of the two together is so illuminating. From the fur traders at Fort Union, the northern Plains Indians received their first sustained glimpse of another civilization. Both sides saw advantages in contact, though sometimes the results were disastrous as when smallpox epidemics wrought havoc among the Indians. But in the nineteenth-century West nothing stayed the same for long, and the civilizations that touched so tentatively in the 1830s and 1840s clashed violently just twenty years later. By then the whites came in larger numbers and with other things in mind than trade. By the time Fort Buford was abandoned in 1895 they had overwhelmed the Indians and were well on the way to changing permanently the face of the northern plains. What the Indians—the losers—thought about it all is hard to know. They themselves left no written records, and the accounts of them written by traders and other white visitors were naturally weighted in favor of what to them were the superior claims of their own more compelling civilization.

The history of Forts Union and Buford measures the steady inroads of that civilization. Neither bears much resemblance to the popular image of such places; but then the popular image of the West generally has seldom accounted for North Dakota history at all. These two very different forts illustrate an important true chapter in the history of the state and region.

THEODORE ROOSEVELT NATIONAL PARK *Medora*. North Dakota
is on America's far northern frontier. Its place in the history of the nation has not been large—at least not by the standards of a Virginia or a New

York. Its landscape and climate have lured relatively few people, and not all of them came to stay. Among those who did not, perhaps the most famous later became the twenty-sixth president of the United States. But when he first came to this severe, beautiful land, Theodore Roosevelt was a less exalted personage. He claimed that the time he spent here was some of his happiest. Today, nearly a century later, the land has hardly changed, and the imaginative visitor to the national park named for him can still see why he found it so appealing.

In Roosevelt's sojourn in the Badlands several themes in the history of North Dakota and the West are joined with the larger history of a rapidly growing and changing American nation. He came first as a hunter for the wild game the West had long been famous for. But when he arrived in the fall of 1883, a young sportsman from New York eager for a buffalo hunt, most of the bison had already been slaughtered for their hides and for sport. Roosevelt's "big game" days still lay ahead, on another continent. Here in Dakota the West was changing, and with his characteristic enthusiasm Roosevelt hoped to be a part of the process.

As a guide on his none too successful hunt, Roosevelt hired a local cowboy named Joe Ferris, whose brother Sylvane and a partner, William J. Merrifield, operated a few miles south of Medora a cattle ranch named, romantically, the Maltese Cross. During his brief stay, even as his enthusiasm for buffalo waned, his excitement rose over the prospects for the cattle industry on the northern plains. Not one to hesitate, he worked out a contract with Sylvane Ferris and Merrifield whereby he would buy into the Maltese Cross and stock it with 400 head of cattle. His partners would operate it for seven years.

Back in New York Roosevelt's political fortunes rose, but on February 14, 1884, his personal life was shattered by the deaths of both his wife and his mother. For solace he soon returned to North Dakota, then experiencing a cattle boom that persuaded the young widower to invest in another 1,000 head of cattle and a second ranch: this one, the Elkhorn Ranch, situated on the Little Missouri River about thirty-five miles north of Medora. Though his idea perhaps to devote his full time to ranching never materialized, he did build a substantial ranch house at the Elkhorn and by 1885–1886 was the owner of 3,000 to 5,000 cattle.

The open-range cattle industry on the high northern plains was risky, and fortunes could change as quickly as the weather. The weather in the spring and summer of 1886 was exceptionally hot and dry, the winter that followed exceptionally severe, with ice and heavy snow burying the summer's only marginal crop of grasses. To make matters worse, drought-plagued cattlemen from the southern plains had driven their herds northward in search of forage, further overstocking the crowded ranges of North Dakota and Montana. The result was a disaster for the starved and frozen beasts, and ruin for many a rancher. Roosevelt himself lost half his herd—and lost in the process much of his enthusiasm for the cattle business. Meanwhile, his life back East was moving in

Caprock erosional features

other directions: he had remarried in 1886 and was growing ever more embroiled in politics and public affairs. In the early 1890s the Elkhorn Ranch was abandoned and the headquarters moved to the Maltese Cross. In 1898 (by which time Roosevelt was secretary of the navy and about to become governor of New York) he sold out entirely and put his cattleman days behind him.

Though hardly a success as a rancher—a wealthy man, he did not have to be—Roosevelt judged his North Dakota sojourn to have been of enormous importance to him personally. While he may have overstated that importance when he wrote later that "I would never have been President if it had not been for my experience in North Dakota," the interlude there surely did show him a remote, wild, and delicate world he had not known before and that he treasured long afterward. Simultaneously the rancher and the politician, he also styled himself a writer and historian, roles at least partly inspired by his western experience. At the Maltese Cross he wrote *Hunting Trips of a Ranchman* (1885) and at the Elkhorn most of his biography of Missouri senator Thomas Hart Benton. His more famous *The Winning of the West* also reflected and idealized his experience on the ranching frontier.

Roosevelt learned about more than cows, and took more away with him than romantic memories of hard days in the saddle and comradely nights around the campfire. He learned about the wilderness, which the Badlands of North Dakota then were and still are. Though remembered as champion of the "strenuous life," typically and famously pictured gun in hand beside a dead rhino, Roosevelt was also an early and influential voice for conservation. During his eight years as president, he made the cause of resource conservation and management respectable public policy. Under his aegis, the United States Forest Service was established. As president he set aside 150 million acres of timberland and more than fifty wild-game refuges. He established sixteen national monuments, including Arizona's Grand Canyon, and doubled the number of national parks.

Today the national park that bears his name is a special monument to conservationist policies and to the New Yorker who did so much to advance them. The "barren, fantastic and grimly picturesque deserts of the so-called Bad Lands," as he described them, have changed little since TR galloped over them. Though now more accessible, large areas remain isolated and untamed—a remainder of how harsh nature still can be. That of course is just the point that Roosevelt learned here to appreciate and respect, and it is the lesson that today's visitor too can learn with profit.

The park consists of a north and a south unit. Each offers scenic drives and back-country trails through the forbidding, undisturbed Badlands landscape. Tablelands, buttes, canyons, and rugged hills broken by the meandering Little Missouri offer unsurpassed scenic loveliness and, for the visitor interested in geology, a large and spectacular display. At the entrance to the South Unit, directly adjacent to the town of Medora, the National Park Service maintains a visitor center that is a good place to begin a tour. A diorama in the visitor center provides an accurate reproduction of the Elkhorn site. Nearby is the restored Maltese Cross cabin, the only surviving building from either of Roosevelt's ranches; the furnishings are representative of the 1880s and a few are original Roosevelt items.

Within the park itself, a large variety of wildlife make their home as in Roosevelt's time, and a glimpse of some of them in this open and natural setting is well worth some vigilance and patience. Probably most impressive are the buffalo. The restored and protected herds today are reminders of the millions of these wandering beasts who once dominated the Great Plains. Also greatly reduced by the intrusion of civilization but now thriving in the park are pronghorn antelope and Rocky Mountain bighorn sheep. Coyotes, badgers, and rare blackfooted ferrets can be found here. Prairie dogs, gregarious inhabitants of extensive underground "towns," abound.

Today many of these animals survive and increase because of man's deliberate conservation efforts. But man was also the chief disturber of the balance that once naturally sustained them. The ranching frontier, in which Roosevelt briefly invested, saw cattle graze where buffalo once lived. As the disastrous seasons of 1886 and 1887 showed, however, this harsh land and climate limited even what man could do here. Adjacent to the south unit of the Theodore Roosevelt National Park, there is a historic memorial to another man's grand plans—and the limits they confronted. In spirit and in fact it is very much related to the park that preserves Roosevelt's Badlands, and the visitor there will not want to miss it.

In 1883 the Marquis DeMores, the first-born son of a French duke, launched a daring venture in the western range-cattle industry. As novel as his background, his plan called for the slaughtering of beef cattle in the Badlands and then shipping the dressed meat in refrigerated railroad cars to eastern markets. The advantage over the normal procedures, he believed, lay in eliminating the weight loss and injury common to the shipping of live cattle east for slaughtering. The meat packer's costs would thus be lower, with savings reflected in lower prices for the customer. DeMores picked a site near the Little Missouri River, and in the summer of 1883 he constructed a slaughterhouse and packing plant. The first beef went east on the Northern Pacific Railway that October. For a time success seemed at hand, and around the packing plant a bustling town, named "Medora" after the Marquis' beautiful young wife, soon sprouted. The Marquis planned to make his permanent home in the Badlands; on a high hill overlooking the packing plant he built a 26-room house, ever since called the Chateau DeMores, to which he brought Medora in the spring of 1884. Elegantly furnished, it hosted many of the Badlands' eastern and European visitors, among them the young Theodore Roosevelt.

The venture did not prosper for long. It depended entirely on grazing cattle year-round on the open range. But without supplemental feeding, not even those rich grasses assured herds large and fat enough to sustain the Marquis' large and expensive packing plant and his extended distribution system. What had begun so hopefully in 1883 was ended just three years later. The Marquis and Medora soon left North Dakota for France, where more grand schemes—and failures—awaited. His last adventure ended violently at the hands of angry Arabs in the Sahara Desert in 1896. His wife lived on in France until 1921.

With them went much of the town of Medora's prosperity, though today it prospers as gateway to the south unit of the park. The State Historical Society of North Dakota administers the DeMores site. A visitor center and the Chateau are open to visitors; the foundations and one towering smokestack are all that remain of the packing plant. Refrigerator cars still pass through on the Northern Pacific (now the Burlington Northern), but they no longer load beef—or even stop—at Medora.

INTERNATIONAL PEACE GARDEN Dunseith. There is something special about gardens in dry places. Anyone who has lingered for more than a short time in America's more arid regions discovers how many of the people who live there cherish their little green spaces. Many westerners, or their ancestors, once migrated from greener, more well-watered places back east. As they moved out onto the plains (long thought of as the Great American Desert) and beyond in the late nineteenth and early twentieth centuries, they did their best to make more hospitable—more like home—the hard land they settled. To live, they grew wheat and raised cattle. To make life more livable, they planted hollyhocks, columbine, and cottonwoods. Today nearly a hundred years later, almost all of those first comers are gone, and indeed many of the cottonwood groves they started have likewise thinned with age. But on the family farms and in the small towns, around white clapboard houses and newer, more pretentious brick ones, come July and August (harvest time in much of North Dakota) there is a predictable profusion of flowers.

People everywhere enjoy flowers and plant flower gardens. The English, who live in one of the greenest, most well-watered countries in the world, probably have the keenest reputations as gardeners. But something else can be ventured about the farming folk who lived and live in the northern plains and who keep gardens. First, the land and climate there make life itself a constant battle and prosperity something of a miracle. Natural evidences of beauty, color, and life are therefore especially treasured. When winters are long and harsh, summers signify in a way they do not to the south and west. Flowers and high summer go together in North Dakota, and neither lasts long. Second, this is an agricultural place where most people depend directly on the land for their livelihood. They sow seed; from their harvest comes their own and the nation's daily bread. They put up hay and fatten cattle, which though handsome to see grazing under a vast western sky are even more handsome on dinner tables in distant cities. In essence these people garden for a living; joining their labor and intelligence to nature's endowment, they grow things they and others need. Perhaps therefore they are especially fascinated in their spare moments with flower gardens that have no similar practical use. For them non-utility is a luxury, and for a couple of months each summer they indulge it fiercely.

It is fitting, therefore, that North Dakotans have on their northern boundary one of the country's finest public gardens. They share it with their Canadian neighbors in Manitoba; it is called the International Peace Garden. Its beginning was remote from North Dakota. It originated with an idea of Henry J. Moore, a Canadian attending a gathering of gardeners in Greenwich, Connecticut, in 1928. Moore was intrigued by the thought of a garden somewhere on the international boundary "where the people of the two countries could share the glories found in a lovely garden and the pleasures found in warm friendships." Those were conventional enough sentiments that most gardeners and other people surely shared. But the location selected for the garden was a remote one, where few people had ever been, though in time it became an attraction for thousands and an apt embodiment of its founders' wishes.

The site is not far from the geographical center of the North American continent, and it encompasses some of the loveliest land on the northern plains. It includes the rolling terrain of the Turtle Mountains and part of the Manitoba Forest Preserve and has, for this dry region, a surprising number of streams and lakes. With 50,000 people in attendance, the park was dedicated on July 14, 1932. A cairn of native stone had been erected and still stands, flanked by American and Canadian flags. The inscription reads: "To God in His Glory, we two nations dedicate this garden and pledge ourselves that as long as men shall live, we will not take up arms against one another." The pledge has been a sound one: the United States-Canadian boundary remains the longest undefended international boundary in the world.

Such large meanings aside, the garden has evolved over the years into a large-scale edition of what many North Dakotans strive for in their own front yards—manicured splashes of color in a harsh dry place. The centerpiece is a 160-acre formal garden that straddles the boundary line, extending down from the entrance gate to a pond and then uphill toward the Peace Chapel. That size of garden, in a place with slight rainfall, requires much planning and tending. Currently there are a head gardener and a dozen or so caretakers. The fruits of their labors are evident. The formal garden is laid out in tiers which have been labored over for a number of years. Within its carefully tailored beds there are fountains, small pools, and man-made streams. The flowers themselves are likewise the product of both nature and nurture. While snow and cold still grip the ground outside, in a greenhouse gardeners start some 22,000 plants a year, all sprung from seed or slips of old plants. Later in spring all are carefully transplanted to their assigned places outside. In

Peace Chapel

addition perennials abound in the park gardens: iris, peonies, roses, day lilies bloom year after year. Flowering shrubs, evergreens, and deciduous trees enclose it all. The current style of plantings follows an English model emphasizing contrasting blocks of color: gold marigolds, pink and red petunias, blue and white border plants.

Planting is only a part of the job. The season is short at this latitude, and while it lasts much must be done. Weeding, pruning, and hand-digging are constant chores that no machine can accomplish. Watering, as anyone who has been to North Dakota in the summer knows, is even more important. In the absence of an irrigation system, Peace Garden gardeners do it the old-fashion way, filling tanks with the lake water and hauling it to garden plots. All of this work builds up to what many visitors find is a remarkably short climax. Those from warmer places who arrive early in the season expecting to find a profusion of color in a famous formal garden go away disappointed. Colors usually peak in mid-August, and while they last they are as impressive as any in the land. Some of the people who come to see them are serious gardeners from around the world, eager to take notes on the kinds and arrangements of plantings and to compare them with formal gardens they have visited elsewhere. More of the people who come are summertime gardeners from surrounding North Dakota and Manitoba. They come to see here on a much grander scale the same things they work at in their own front yards. Many farm for a living and find in this well-trimmed, well watered place confirmation that this remote and forbidding part of the world is a different and a better place for their having come here.

In recent years, the Peace Garden has attracted other people too. The International Music Camp, one of the leading summer schools of fine arts in North America, meets here annually. Its productions are featured throughout the summer. A staff of 130 instructs and supervises some 2,500 students, and a specially selected band and choir each year tour the United States, Canada, and abroad. The Royal Canadian Legion sponsors and operates an athletic camp where over 100 physical education teachers provide summer instruction in a wide variety of team and individual sports. For the general visitor there are scenic hiking trails across the natural wooded country northwest of Lake Storman, which are accessible not only by foot in summertime, but by skis and snowshoes in the winter, when nature takes on a different kind of beauty. The Peace Tower and the Peace Chapel remind visitors of the unique relationship that exists between the United States and Canada and makes the park itself possible. An amphitheater, auditorium, and lodge and the Canadian Centennial Pavilion contain dining and meeting rooms that attract thousands here each year for business as well as pleasure.

For years North Dakota license plates have proclaimed North Dakota as the "Peace Garden State," which is something of a mystery to people from other parts of the country. But this is in keeping with North Dakota's image generally. The state is little known and less talked about—except as the butt of jokes about the weather and rural remoteness. Its chambers of commerce for years have tried hard to combat this weatherman's image and simply the great void that comes to many people's minds when they hear the words "North Dakota". To an extent they fight in vain, which is partly a good thing. For if the world ever truly discovered North Dakota it would become a different and less pleasant place. Certainly its Peace Garden would be less peaceful. Nature decreed that their land should not support many people as either residents or visitors, and thus far remoteness and a harsh climate have enforced that decree. For those who do know it, the Peace Garden stands out as gardens in more congenial places do not. Its two or three months of bloom require such planning and effort as the first pioneers here summoned merely to survive. But survival for them, as for most men, was not enough. Thus in addition to wheat fields they planted flower gardens. And the Peace Garden—one of the handsomest gardens of all—is especially at home here.

BALDWIN'S ARCADE *Steele Avenue and Third Street, Hope.* An 1881 clapboard building that typified the boom town and is the county's oldest commercial building; now a museum administered by the Steel County Historical Society.

BONANZAVILLE *West Fargo.* Re-created pioneer village and museum telling the story of life in Cass County and the Red River Valley since the Indian era.

BUFFALO TRAILS MUSEUM *Epping.* Interpretive displays, dioramas, and exhibits in several buildings to tell history of the plains pioneers and early Indians.

CAMP HANCOCK STATE HISTORIC SITE *West Main Street, Bismarck.* On the site of Camp Greeley, established in 1872 to protect work gangs on the Northern Pacific Railroad; with a remaining 1873 building and an interpretive museum.

CHATEAU DeMORES STATE HISTORIC SITE *Medora.* French villa built in 1883 by a visionary entrepreneur, the Marquis DeMores.

DIVIDE COUNTY MUSEUM *Crosby.* Twenty-two buildings from throughout the county moved onto one site to create a pioneer village.

DOUBLE DITCH INDIAN VILLAGE STATE HISTORIC SITE *seven and a half miles north of the I-94 bridge over the Missouri.* Ruins of a large Mandan Indian earthlodge village inhabited A.D. 1675–1780; with two fortification ditches.

FORT ABERCROMBIE STATE HISTORIC SITE *eastern edge of Abercrombie.* One original building and reconstructed blockhouses and palisade from the military post situated here 1857–1878; with a museum.

FORT ABRAHAM LINCOLN STATE PARK *state 1806, south of Mandan.* A museum, reconstructed Mandan earthlodges, and blockhouses located on the site of the fort commanded by George A. Custer in 1876 and an Indian village dating from before Lewis and Clark.

FORT CLARK STATE HISTORIC SITE *near Stanton.* North Dakota's largest state historic site; includes the remains of a large Mandan and Arikara earthlodge village and several fur-trade forts.

FORT TOTTEN STATE HISTORIC SITE *Fort Totten.* Well-preserved remains of a fort built 1868–1871 and used after 1891 as an Indian industrial school; interpretive center.

GEOGRAPHICAL CENTER HISTORICAL SOCIETY *Rugby.* Pioneer village with twenty-six buildings and farm machinery, cars, and buggies; on the site of the geographical center of the North American continent.

GINGRAS TRADING POST STATE HISTORIC SITE *one and a half miles east of Walhalla.* Restoration of mid-nineteenth-century log store and home of prominent trader Antoine B. Gingras.

HATTEN-EIELSON MUSEUM *Hatton.* Pioneer furniture and memorabilia commemorating Carl Ben Eielson, famous Arctic flyer, in his family's 1907 home.

KNIFE RIVER INDIAN VILLAGES NATIONAL HISTORIC SITE *Lewis and Clark Trail, Stanton.* Largest of three Hidatsa Indian villages dating from 1750–1845, with more than 108 earthlodge depressions and several fortification trenches; a stopping place for Lewis and Clark.

NORTHERN PACIFIC RAILWAY DEPOT *701 Main Street, Fargo.* An 1898 Richardsonian Romanesque and Shingle style depot designed by architect Cass Gilbert.

RICHLAND COUNTY MUSEUM *Wahpeton.* Pioneer artifacts with a pioneer street and an extensive collection of Rosemeade pottery.

STATE HISTORICAL SOCIETY OF NORTH DAKOTA *North Dakota Heritage Center, State Capitol Grounds, Bismarck.* The official state museum and archives, including facilities for public programming, a library, an historic preservation program, archeological collections, and the state historicsites program.

STUTSMAN COUNTY COURTHOUSE *504 Third Avenue, S.E., Jamestown.* An 1883 Gothic Revival building that is the oldest courthouse in the state; with sheriff's residence and jail.

TRAIL COUNTY MUSEUM *Hillsboro.* Contains household furnishings and agricultural implements from the 1800s, Indian artifacts, and Norwegian immigrant items.

WADESON CABIN STATE HISTORIC SITE *two miles east of Kathryn.* Restored log-cabin home built by Scandinavian settlers in 1878; served as community hall and country store.

WHITESTONE HILL BATTLEFIRLD STATE HISTORIC SITE *southwest of Merricourt.* Site of a battle between United States troops and the Sioux in September 1863; with memorials and a museum.

OHIO

CAMPUS MARTIUS MUSEUM 601 2nd Street, Marietta. The Land Ordinance of 1785 and the Northwest Ordinance of 1787 established the basis for American settlement of the Northwest Territory, that area northwest of the Ohio River roughly occupied by present-day Ohio, Indiana, Illinois, Michigan, and Wisconsin. This legislation did not, however, solve the problem of Indian resistance to white encroachment, and the residents of Marietta, the first authorized settlement in the Ohio Country, found it necessary to erect a stockade for protection. A portion of that fortification, the Rufus Putnam House, has been preserved within the Campus Martius Museum at Marietta. The restored log structure and other exhibits at the museum together provide a unique opportunity to learn more about the frontier Ohio experience.

The United States secured control of the region northwest of the Ohio in the Treaty of Paris concluding the War of Independence in 1783. At first, New York, Virginia, Massachusetts, and Connecticut each pressed claims to the region, but by 1786 all had ceded their rights to the federal government. It was hoped that these western lands would provide much-needed revenue, and in 1785 and 1787 legislation was enacted to assure the territory's orderly settlement. The Land Ordinance of 1785 established procedures for the survey, subdivision, and sale of the land; the Northwest Ordinance of 1787 provided the basis for organizing the territory under congressional supervision and established the terms for admitting new states to the union. Although devised specifically for this region, these acts set important precedents for subsequent land policy and territorial organization in the expanding nation.

Foremost among the advocates of the ordinances was the Ohio Company of Associates, a group of land investors who wanted the government's assurance that squatters and adventurers would not take control of the new territory. The company was established in 1786 by Revolutionary War veterans who had heard about the virtues of the Ohio Country from their commanding officer, General George Washington. Washington had traveled through the region before the war and suggested it might serve as a suitable refuge if the British won. Although his pessimism proved unfounded, the Ohio Country's attractions still intrigued his listeners after the war's end, and a group of them proposed to the federal government that they would exchange their severance pay of continental scrip for land in the territory. Both would benefit: the government would be reducing its indebtedness, and the veterans would be getting a new start. Although their offer of about ten cents an acre in specie fell far short of the one dollar-per-acre minimum established in the 1785 ordinance, Congress yielded to their persuasive arguments and agreed to sell the company over a million and a half acres of land along the Ohio River in the Muskingum and Hocking river valleys.

The Ohio Company immediately organized an expedition to the new territory. Under the leadership of Rufus Putnam, one of the company's founders, a forty-eight-man party crossed the Alleghenies to Sumrill's Ferry, traveled down the Ohio River, and arrived at the mouth of the Muskingum River on April 7, 1788. Since Fort Harmar, erected in 1785 to keep out squatters, occupied the west bank of the Muskingum, the Ohio Company expedition set up camp on the east side of the river. The small community was named Marietta in honor of Marie Antoinette and her assistance to the American Revolutionary cause. Concerned about hostile Indians, Putnam decided the settlement was too vulnerable and shortly began making plans for a permanent fortification on a more secure, elevated spot above the village, about one mile up the Muskingum from the Ohio. Following Putnam's instructions, Jonathan Devol proceeded with construction of a stockade, essentially a 180-foot hollow square of dwellings. A blockhouse stood at each of the four corners and row houses filled in between, their backs forming the outside curtain walls of the fortification. The company took responsibility for the block-houses, but individual settlers constructed the row houses for themselves and their families, who began arriving by August. Because of his concern about the consequences of any delay, Putnam gave the men only thirty days to complete their individual sections. Anyone who did not meet the deadline relinquished his right to build within the fort. Evidence of this haste was the absence of chimneys—it simply took too

Rufus Putnam House

long to mold and dry the necessary bricks. The new fort was still not completed by July 1788 and the arrival of General Arthur St. Clair, the first governor of the Northwest Territory. He was quartered temporarily at Fort Harmar before taking residence in the southwest blockhouse of the Ohio Company stockade.

The completed fort, named Campus Martius (Latin for "Field of War"), included a row of pointed stakes leaning out from the curtain wall as well as an outer palisade. The residents of Marietta obviously wanted to make sure that their refuge would be secure should Indians attack. St. Clair tried to negotiate a treaty with the various tribes in the region, but hostility turned to war by 1790. Campus Martius had been built to house between fifty and sixty families or three to four hundred people, but over nine hundred crowded into the stockade during the Indian troubles. Although the fort was never actually attacked, the Indians' defeat of American troops in western Ohio in 1790 and 1791 placed the entire territory in a vulnerable position. Then in 1793 General Anthony Wayne launched a massive new assault that culminated in a decisive victory at the Battle of Fallen Timbers on August 20, 1794. The various tribes agreed to give up their claims to most of the Ohio Country and on August 3, 1795, signed the Treaty of Greenville.

With the end of Indian hostility, the Campus Martius stockade was no longer needed, and the settlers moved out, many actually dismantling their houses and moving them to lots in Marietta. Rufus Putnam decided to stay put, however, and purchased the fort site from the company. He substantially enlarged his residence with lumber from an adjoining blockhouse and resided there until his death in 1824.

The Putnam house is the only portion of the original fort still standing. Owned by the Ohio Historical Society since 1917, the historic structure is now enclosed in a museum building erected in 1931. The structure deteriorated over the years, but major restoration work between 1966 and 1972 returned it to its appearance in the late eighteenth century. Visitors can see the original four-inch timbers that formed Putnam's portion of the curtain wall and examine the hand-hewn mortise and tenon construction. The addition constructed after 1795 is now shown incomplete, in the process of being framed. Some original Putnam family furniture and other appropriate period pieces furnish the parlor, kitchen, and second-floor bedrooms as they would have during the early 1790s.

Behind the museum building stands another historic structure, the Ohio Land Company office. This clapboarded one-room log structure dates from 1788 and was used as an office by Rufus Putnam. In addition to the two historic buildings, the Campus Martius Museum also includes exhibits on the history of the fort, Marietta, and the Northwest Territory. Special activities include the pioneer-living program, designed to acquaint students with various aspects of frontier life within the setting of the Putnam house. The old stockade structure and the museum's other

facilities provide an excellent context for learning more about this pivotal period in the settlement of Ohio and the Northwest Territory.
PIQUA HISTORICAL AREA Ohio 66, one mile north of Piqua. Ohio's growth and development in the first half of the nineteenth century hinged on the successful linking of local farms and factories with distant markets. By the time of the Civil War, a network of roads, canals, and railroads crisscrossed the state, removing restraints on full realization of its great agricultural, commercial, and industrial potential. One link in this transportation system was the Miami and Erie Canal, erected between 1825 and 1845. A portion of it has been preserved in the Piqua Historical Area, an historical complex that depicts life in the western part of the state during this pivotal era in Ohio history.

In the mid-eighteenth century, the Piqua area was a center of frontier rivalry. The principal town in the Ohio Country was Pickawillany, on the Miami River, and French and English rivalry for influence with the Indian population in the region culminated in a devastating raid on the town by the French in 1752. Conflict between Native Americans and encroaching white civilization continued until 1795, when General "Mad Anthony" Wayne and the chiefs of twelve Ohio Indian tribes signed the Treaty of Greenville, which opened two-thirds of present-day Ohio to white settlement.

One of the supply posts for Wayne's military campaign was Fort Piqua, not far from the old Indian village of Pickawillany. John Johnston, one of the men hauling supplies at the fort, recognized the region's agricultural potential but had to go back home to Philadelphia after the conclusion of his work. He did not return to the Old Northwest until 1802, when he took charge of the trade affairs at the Fort Wayne Indian Agency. Soon thereafter he learned that the Fort Piqua site was now in private hands and managed to purchase 235 acres in 1804 and 1805 when the owner defaulted on the payment of federal land fees. He kept his post at Fort Wayne through the rest of the decade but began making improvements on the Fort Piqua property by 1808. He first had a log house and barn erected, and then in 1810 construction began on a larger brick residence. The following year he resigned his agency post, and he, his wife Rachel, and their children moved to the old Fort Piqua farm.

Over the decades that followed Johnston became an invaluable member of the Piqua community. He served from 1812 to 1830 as the federal Indian agent for western Ohio and had a significant role in the Indians' neutrality during the War of 1812. Because of his good relations with the area tribes, he was called upon in 1841 to negotiate the purchase of the Wyandot lands, the last tract of land in the state held by the Indians. His service to the community and state was not confined to Indian relations, however. He took an active role in politics, supporting the ambitions of his close friend William Henry Harrison; served as a trustee of Miami University for twenty-five years; and took a seat

Johnston's house and farm

on the state commission that built the Ohio canal system.

The last was particularly important to Johnston, for his farming enterprise required access to markets. The state's fertile soil proved highly productive in the first decades of the nineteenth century, but few farmers were able to transport their surplus produce to regional markets. Indeed, this inadequacy threatened to stunt the state's overall economic growth. Such a grim prospect inspired Ohioans to embark upon the construction of an extensive canal system. In 1825 work began on two separate canals. The first, the Ohio Canal, completed in 1833, linked Lake Erie and the Ohio River via the Scioto and Cuyahoga valleys. The second, the Miami and Erie, was not finished until 1841, when it finally linked the Ohio River at Cincinnati with Lake Erie at Toledo. This second canal followed the Miami, Auglaize, and Maumee river valleys, including a portion that ran along the east edge of Johnston's farm. Easy access to the canal and hence to the Cincinnati market contributed to Johnston's focus on commercial farm production rather than on subsistence agriculture. Marketability obviously influenced his decision to raise sheep and hogs and produce dried apples and cider. To enhance his farm's productivity and hence profitability, the former Indian agent also adopted the latest mechanical devices and kept abreast of new scientific agricultural developments.

After the death of his wife in 1840, Johnston lost interest in farming and eventually left Piqua to live with his daughters in Cincinnati and Dayton. When he died in 1861, he was buried in the family cemetery next to his wife and eight of their fifteen children.

The Piqua Historical Area centers on Johnston's farm. Within the 174 acre park stand his two-and-a-half-story, gambrel-roofed brick home, erected between 1810 and 1815; the large double-pen log barn constructed in 1808; a two-story brick springhouse erected after 1810; a reconstructed fruit kiln stand for drying apples; and a reconstructed cider house. Nearby a portion of the Miami and Erie Canal has been restored and visitors can take a canal ride on the *Genl. Harrison,* a cargo boat typical of the 1840–1850 period but actually a modern reproduction built by the Ohio Historical Society. The park area also includes the Historic Indian Museum, a facility important for its focus on the experiences of Native Americans during the historic period. Now owned and operated by the Ohio Historical Society, the Piqua Historical Area brings together various cultures and currents from early Ohio history.

RUTHERFORD B. HAYES PRESIDENTIAL CENTER *Hayes and Buckland Avenues, Fremont.* In the late nineteenth and early twentieth centuries, Ohio represented moderation and stability, the "normalcy" that native son Warren G. Harding advocated for the nation in the early 1920s. This image proved a significant factor in the political successes of the seven Ohio Republicans who held the presidency of the United States during this period. None more clearly reflected these values than Rutherford B. Hayes. The Rutherford B. Hayes Presidential Center, the nation's first presidential library and museum, commemorates the life and work of this famous Ohioan and symbolizes the state's central role in post-Civil War American politics.

Rutherford Birchard Hayes was born in Delaware, Ohio, in 1822. He was raised by his widowed mother, Sophia, and her bachelor brother Sardis Birchard, a prominent merchant in Lower Sandusky (later Fremont), Ohio. Educated at Kenyon College in Gambier and at Harvard Law School, Hayes joined the Ohio bar in 1845 and shortly thereafter began practicing law in Lower Sandusky. Hoping that his nephew would settle there permanently, Birchard in 1846 purchased land on which he planned to build a house for Hayes. The latter soon decided that his prospects in Lower Sandusky were limited, however, and in 1849 he moved to Cincinnati. His first years in the Queen City were spent establishing a law practice and courting Lucy Webb, whom he married on December 30, 1852. His skill as a criminal lawyer enabled him to build a substantial practice by the middle of the decade. Eager to advance his career, he joined the Literary Club of Cincinnati and the Odd Fellows, campaigned for the Republican party, attended various social functions, and gradually established a wide circle of friends and associates.

Hayes secured his first political office in 1858, when the City Council appointed him to fill a vacancy in the office of city solicitor. He ran successfully for a full term the following year and then met defeat with other Republicans in 1861. He returned to private practice briefly before volunteering for the Union Army. During his four years of service with the Ohio Volunteer Infantry, Hayes was wounded four times and rose to the rank of brevet major general. As stories of his military exploits circulated around Cincinnati, Hayes became a popular local figure. Despite his refusal to campaign and his insistence that his first duty was to the army, Hayes was elected to Congress in 1864 from the Second Congressional District in Cincinnati. He took office at the end of the war and served the Thirty-Ninth and Fortieth congresses. Reelection in 1866 indicated constituent approval of his support of the Fourteenth and Fifteenth amendments, congressional Reconstruction, and full payment of the public war debt. Hayes did not serve the second term but resigned in mid-1867 to run in the Ohio gubernatorial race. He defeated his Democratic opponent that fall and won reelection again two years later. His four years as governor were marked by defense of Republican principles and advocacy of sound fiscal policy. He refused to run for a third term as governor but made an unsuccessful bid for his old congressional seat in 1872.

Then, with his uncle in ill health, Hayes decided to retire from public life. The family moved in 1873 to Spiegel Grove, the estate his uncle had purchased for Hayes in 1846. "Spiegel" means "mirror" in German, an allusion to the pools of rainwater that reflected the wooded setting and reminded Birchard of German fairy tales. After Hayes's move to Cincinnati in 1849, Birchard had erected a summer retreat, a two-and-a-half-story brick house with a veranda across the front facade. Hayes and his family moved into the house in 1873. The Hayeses had six children by then, so a one-story frame wing was added on the west. Hayes managed Spiegel Grove and his uncle's affairs and then inherited the estate upon his uncle's death the next year. His retirement from public office proved rather brief: in 1875 he made a successful bid for a third term as governor of Ohio.

Hayes's unblemished personal and political reputation, military service, and record as governor of Ohio proved attractive to national

Spiegel Grove

Republican party leaders in search of an antidote to the scandals and rumors surrounding the administration of another Ohioan, Ulysses S. Grant. At the national convention in Cincinnati in June 1876, the party selected Hayes as its presidential nominee. He did not resign from office and in fact only left the state once during the campaign. In the fall election his Democratic opponent, Samuel J. Tilden, won the popular vote, but the Republicans contested the electoral votes in Florida, Louisiana, and South Carolina. The crisis remained unresolved until the infamous compromise of 1877 cleared the way for Hayes. Throughout, he refused to comment on the situation, and he continued to serve as governor until just a few days before Inauguration Day, when the congressional election commission awarded the disputed votes to him and thereby made him the next president. He took the oath of office privately two days before the public ceremony on March 5.

As president, Hayes withdrew the last federal troops from the South and launched a new era of reconciliation between North and South. He also advocated strengthening the national currency and fought the agrarian groups that saw coinage of silver as a solution to their mounting economic problems. Most important, he restored public confidence in the presidency. In sharp contrast to the Grant administration, he became a champion of civil service reform and attempted to end the spoils and waste that had become associated with the federal government. In so doing, he reasserted the powers of the presidency and restored the traditional balance of power. The absence of alcohol and wine from the Hayes White House further testified to the Ohioan's moral rectitude. Although critics made fun of "Lemonade Lucy," the First Lady's insistence on total abstinence proved a welcome relief from the excesses of the day and gained much public support for the Hayes family.

During his presidency, Hayes expanded the Spiegel Grove house. A brick addition that repeated the original gable more than doubled its size. This remodeling also included enlarging the rooms and adding a three-story projecting bay and a cupola. The changes made the house more comfortable for the Hayes family when they moved back to Ohio in 1881. (Hayes had pledged in his 1876 campaign that he would serve only one term and refused to consider a reelection bid.) In retirement, Hayes remained a popular public figure and maintained an active speaking schedule until his death in 1893.

Spiegel Grove stands today essentially as it was at Hayes's death. The last alteration to the house was made in 1889, after the death of Mrs. Hayes. The former president had the 1873 addition torn down and erected a new two-and-a-half-story wing that housed a formal dining room, kitchen, and bedrooms. These alternations completed the process of remodeling and renovation that adapted the structure to the changing tastes and needs of the Hayes family and make it today a fine example of a Victorian family residence.

In 1910 the Hayes family presented Spiegel Grove to the state of

Ohio as a memorial to the former president. Although the house was retained for family use for many years, it is now open to the public. Nearby stand the Hayes library and museum. The first section was completed in 1916, and an addition was dedicated six years later on the centennial of Hayes' birth. Additional east and west wings date from 1967. This Neo-Classical Revival sandstone structure houses the nation's first presidential library and museum and the only one not owned and operated by the federal government. The library's collections include over 100,000 volumes, over a million manuscripts, and a variety of photos, scrapbooks, and other memorabilia. The museum provides exhibits on the Hayes family and life in late-nineteenth-century America. Also within the Spiegel Grove property stands the Vermont granite tomb of Hayes and his wife. The six entrance gates to the center came from the White House.

The house, library-museum, and tomb together make up the Rutherford B. Hayes Presidential Center, which is affiliated with the Ohio Historical Society and governed by the Rutherford B. and Lucy Webb Hayes Foundation and the Hayes Historical Society. The center provides an opportunity to learn about both the private life and the public career of the nation's nineteenth president.

Other Ohio sites and museums commemorating presidents of the United States from the state include Grant's Birthplace State Memorial in Point Pleasant, the Ulysses S. Grant Boyhood Home in Georgetown, the James A. Garfield Home in Mentor, the Garfield Memorial in Cleveland, the McKinley Birthplace Memorial in Niles, the William McKinley Tomb in Canton, the William Howard Taft National Historic Site in Cincinnati, and the Warren G. Harding Home, Museum, and Memorial in Marion.

ADENA STATE MEMORIAL Adena Road, Chillicothe. Home built 1806–1807 by Thomas Worthington, Ohio's first senator and sixth governor; many original furnishings.

ALLEN COUNTY MUSEUM 620 W. Market St., Lima. General museum with Indian artifacts, railroad manuscripts, and photographs; nineteenth-century fire-fighting equipment and 1890s MacDowell House on grounds.

ARMS MUSEUM 648 Wick Ave., Youngstown. Artifacts related to the history of the Mahoning Valley, with Arms family possessions, in late-nineteenth-century residence of Wilford Arms.

ARMSTRONG AIR & SPACE MUSEUM I-75 and state 198, Wapakoneta. Artifacts related to career of the first man on the moon; exhibits dealing with other Ohio contributions to aviation history.

CINCINNATI FIRE MUSEUM 315 W. Court St., Cincinnati. Fire fighting artifacts from the late 1800s to the present, housed in 1906 fire house.

CINCINNATI HISTORICAL SOCIETY *Eden Park, Cincinnati.* Library with extensive collection of pictures, manuscripts, and maps pertaining to Cincinnati and Ohio River Valley.

DELTA QUEEN *Public Landing, Ohio River, Cincinnati.* Sternwheel steamboat built in 1926 and still carrying passengers from the Ohio to the Cumberland and Mississippi.

DITTRICK MUSEUM OF HISTORICAL MEDICINE *11000 Euclid Ave., Cleveland.* Exhibits on dentistry, pharmacy, nursing, and the practice of medicine in the 1800s and 1900s.

DUNBAR HOUSE *219 Summit St., Dayton.* Museum with memorabilia of black writer Paul Laurence Dunbar, who lived here from 1903 until his death in 1906.

EAST LIVERPOOL MUSEUM OF CERAMICS *400 E. 5th St., East Liverpool.* Large collection of regional ceramics and local-history artifacts in 1908 city post office.

FORT MEIGS STATE MEMORIAL *near intersection of U.S. 25 and state 65, Perrysburg.* Largest reconstruction of a fort in America; originally built by William Henry Harrison in the War of 1812.

THE GEORGIAN *105 E. Wheeling St., Lancaster.* Restored 1830s Federal-style house with furniture, tools, glass, Fairfield County historical items.

GRANT'S BIRTHPLACE *state 232, Point Pleasant.* Restored house and museum where Ulysses S. Grant was born.

GREAT LAKES HISTORICAL SOCIETY MUSEUM *480 Main St., Vermilion.* Collections on all aspects of Great Lakes history, with ship models, photographs, and marine engines, in 1909 residence on shore of Lake Erie.

HALE FARM AND WESTERN RESERVE VILLAGE *2686 Oak Hill Road, Bath.* Houses and other buildings from the 1800s; craft and agricultural demonstrations.

HARDING HOME AND MUSEUM *380 Mount Vernon Ave., Marion.* House built by Warren G. Harding in 1890, from whose front porch he campaigned for president in 1920; with Harding furnishings and family items.

LAWNFIELD *8095 Mentor Ave., Mentor.* One-story farmhouse of 1832 with additions of 1870s and 1880s; the home from which James A. Garfield ran for president in 1880 and won; contains a museum.

McGUFFEY HOUSE AND MUSEUM *401 E. Spring St., Oxford.* Home of William H. McGuffey, who wrote the famous reader; with a museum containing textbooks by him and others in the 1800s.

McKINLEY BIRTHPLACE *40 N. Main St., Niles.* Exhibits related to President William McKinley in a building on the site of a school he attended.

McKINLEY MUSEUM OF HISTORY, SCIENCE AND INDUSTRY *749 Hazlett Ave., N.W., Canton.* General museum with "Streets of Yesteryear" exhibit, historic vehicles, canal-boat replica, dolls, toys, and watches.

MONTGOMERY COUNTY HISTORICAL SOCIETY 7 *N. Main St., Dayton.* General museum with artifacts related to Miami Valley history; housed in 1840s Greek Revival county courthouse.

MOUND CITY GROUP NATIONAL MONUMENT 16062 state 104, Chillicothe. Museum with artifacts from the Hopewell culture, on the site of mounds built 200 B.C. to 500 A.D.

NATIONAL ROAD / ZANE GREY MUSEUM 8850 E. Pike, Norwich. Transportation artifacts, including vehicles; Ohio art pottery; and personal items once belonging to western writer Zane Grey, who grew up in the area.

OHIO HISTORICAL CENTER & OHIO VILLAGE 1-71 and Seventeenth Ave., Columbus. Extensive exhibits on all aspects of Ohio and midwestern history, including glass, crafts, and industry; Indian artifacts; military items; and natural history; recreated 1850s Ohio Village nearby.

OHIO RIVER MUSEUM AND STEAMER W. P. Snyder, Jr., Front St., Marietta. Artifacts related to all aspects of the history of the Ohio River; 1918 sternwheel steamer nearby.

PERRY'S VICTORY AND INTERNATIONAL PEACE MEMORIAL Put-in-Bay, South Bass Island, Lake Erie. Marks Commodore Oliver Hazzard Perry's naval victory over the British in 1813 and more than 150 years of peace between Canada and the United States.

PRO FOOTBALL HALL OF FAME 2121 Harrison Ave., N.W., Canton. Photos, films, and relics from notable players and games.

ROSCOE VILLAGE 381 Hill St., Coshocton. Restored canal town, with museum, operating shops, homes, and full-scale operating replica of a canal boat.

ROSS COUNTY HISTORICAL MUSEUM 45 W. 5th St., Chillicothe. Historic house containing many artifacts from Ohio's early history; several other restored historic houses nearby.

SCHOENBRUNN VILLAGE STATE MEMORIAL U.S. Rt. 250, New Philadelphia. Restoration of nineteen log structures of Moravian mission to Indians; Ohio's first settlement.

SERPENT MOUND STATE MEMORIAL state 73 South, four miles north of Locust Grove. Largest serpent effigy mound in the United States built by prehistoric Indians.

SHARON WOODS VILLAGE OF THE MIAMI PURCHASE ASSOCIATION state 42 (11500 Lebanon Pike), Sharonville. Historic village with restored farm houses, railroad station, and doctor's office, with decorative arts and furnishings from the 1800s.

STAN HYWET HALL 714 N. Portage Path, Akron. Built for the founder of the Goodyear Tire & Rubber Company, Frank Seiberling, 1911–1915; with Tudor and Stuart furniture, Flemish tapestries from 1500s and 1600s, other rare items and extensive gardens.

TAFT NATIONAL HISTORIC SITE 2038 Auburn Ave., Cincinnati. Where President William Howard Taft was born and raised, with Taft furnishings.

UNITED STATES AIR FORCE MUSEUM *Wright-Patterson near Dayton.* Some 150 planes and missiles with space hardware and foods.
WARREN COUNTY HISTORICAL SOCIETY MUSEUM *105 S. Broadway, Lebanon.* Early artifacts from southwestern Ohio with large collection of Shaker furniture.
WESTERN RESERVE HISTORICAL SOCIETY *10825 East Blvd., Cleveland.* Extensive exhibits on all phases of Ohio history, including pioneer objects, decorative arts, antique cars, and early planes.
ZOAR STATE MEMORIAL *Zoar.* Seven restored buildings of German religious sect; village established in 1817.

OKLAHOMA

CHICKASAW COUNCIL HOUSE Tishomingo. The Indian Territory of nineteenth-century Oklahoma was originally set aside for the Five Civilized Tribes: the Cherokees, Chickasaws, Choctaws, Creeks, and Seminoles. Removed from their homelands in the southeastern United States in the 1830s and 1840s, these Native Americans preserved their distinctive heritages and cultures by establishing separate tribal nations within their new western home. Among these was the Chickasaw National Council, whose first and last council houses still stand on Court House Square in Tishomingo. These structures reflect the growth and development of the Chickasaw nation prior to statehood and commemorate the broader Native American experience in Oklahoma's Indian Territory.

The infamous Indian removal policy of Andrew Jackson's presidency forced thousands of Native Americans to migrate to a newly established Indian Territory west of the Mississippi River. From Mississippi came the Choctaws, from Alabama and East Georgia the Creeks, from northern Mississippi and western Tennessee the Chickasaws, from Georgia the Cherokees, and from Florida the Seminoles. Although some went peacefully and others resisted the white man's coercion, all ended up following the "trail of tears" to the West. When the Chickasaws arrived in present-day Oklahoma, they found that they were to share the southeast part of the Indian Territory with the Choctaws. Although the tribes were related, co-occupation did not work out. For one thing, the Choctaws had arrived first and established farms and settlements in the eastern portion, forcing the Chickasaws to settle to the west, where they were more exposed to hostile Plains Indians. Furthermore, attempts at unified government proved unsuccessful, for each nation insisted on maintaining its separate identity and tribal organization. In 1848 the Chickasaws wrote their own constitution, and then in 1855 the two tribes officially parted ways, each setting up independent governments. The treaty also divided the lands, giving the Chickasaws control over 4,707,903 acres.

The elective council of the Chickasaw Nation first met at Post Oak Grove but in 1855 established its permanent capital at Good Spring on the Pennington Creek—the present site of Tishomingo, named for the last Chickasaw war chief in Mississippi. The first Council House or capitol was a simple one-room log house, but in 1858 the council moved into a more substantial two-story brick building. That building burned down in 1890, however, and the Chickasaw National Council erected a third capital at Tishomingo. The council occupied the new Victorian stone structure in November 1898 and continued to meet there until 1907, when the independent Chickasaw nation came to an end with Oklahoma statehood.

*Original log
Council House*

Just as the Indian removal policy reflected the interests of white Americans, so statehood reflected the influence of white settlers in the Oklahoma region. In 1889 the federal government yielded to demands that the Indian Territory be opened to white settlement and allowed homesteaders to establish claims in an area known as the Unassigned Lands. Situated in the heart of the Indian Territory, this white enclave organized the Oklahoma Territory the following year. In the decades that followed, additional sections in the western part of the territory were opened up as part of an allotment process that eliminated lesser tribal nations. Then in 1898 Congress passed the Curtis Act, which authorized allotment of the remaining portion, the lands of the Five Civilized Tribes, and dissolution of the Indian Territory and the tribal nations. Native American leaders still hoped to avoid absorption by the white-led Oklahoma Territory and petitioned Congress for the Indian Territory's admission to the union as the state of Sequoyah. Their appeal was ignored, however, and in 1907 the Oklahoma Territory and the Indian Territory were joined as the state of Oklahoma. Under the new state government, the former capitol of the Chickasaw nation became the Johnston County courthouse.

The first Council House was moved in the late nineteenth century from its original site to the country home of R. M. Harris, then governor of the Chickasaws. In the 1930s it was moved back to Courthouse Square in Tishomingo and then in 1964 relocated to its present site, a few hundred yards east of its original location. The Oklahoma Historical Society acquired the historic structure in 1969 and subsequently erected a cover structure to protect the deteriorating building and provide space for exhibits on the tribal culture and the Chickasaw Nation. Nearby stands the three-story granite Victorian structure that served as the Chickasaws' last capitol. Although there has been some modernization to accommodate the county government, this edifice also remains much the same as in the period before statehood. Together these structures reflect the growth and development of the Chickasaw Nation and call to mind the larger Native American experience in the Indian Territory of nineteenth-century Oklahoma.

GUTHRIE HISTORIC DISTRICT Guthrie. In 1889 the United States Congress yielded to pressure from both land-hungry white settlers and railroad and financial interests and authorized the first land run into Indian Territory. Thousands joined the race to claim homesteads on April 22, and by that afternoon a small stop on the Santa Fe Railroad had become the city of Guthrie, Oklahoma's largest settlement. Although made up of only tents and temporary structures at first, Guthrie blossomed over the next two decades as territorial and then state capital. The Guthrie Historic District preserves the turn-of-the-century city and brings to life the Oklahoma experience in the critical transition from settlement to territory to statehood.

In the first Oklahoma land run on April 22, 1889, thousands of homesteaders rushed to claim farm land, but an equally impressive number headed for a townsite about eight miles south of the Kansas border. Named Guthrie in honor of a director of the Santa Fe Railroad, the townsite had only one complete structure when that day began: a small frame station that served as a watering stop and section house for the railroad. Construction had begun nearby on a federal land office, but the building was not complete by the time the first train rolled in packed with eager new residents. Others followed on subsequent trains; some came by wagon, horseback, and foot; and by sunset the town claimed a population of fifteen thousand. The federal government had restricted the new town to a half-section of land or 320 acres, but that area could not begin to satisfy the newcomers' demand for town lots. The shortage was quickly eased by simply establishing four adjoining townships. Thus, until consolidated over a year later, the new city of Guthrie actually comprised four separate legal entities.

The new residents wasted little time. Construction of more permanent buildings began that first afternoon with lumber brought in by rail, and within the month the first brick edifice was occupied. Following the city's most well-worn path, a central business district soon developed from the railroad station east to the land office. Oklahoma and Harrison avenues became the two principal commercial arteries, lined with a variety of stores, businesses, banks, hotels, boarding-houses, and saloons established by ambitious entrepreneurs catering to the needs of the booming territorial society. Among the most successful was Frank Greer. Greer arrived in Guthrie on the opening day, set up business in a tent, and that same afternoon published the territory's first newspaper, the *Oklahoma Daily State Capital.* He also took on job printing and soon moved into a small frame building on Oklahoma. As business increased, Greer's State Capital Company moved to a third and finally in 1902 to a fourth larger home on Harrison. By the early twentieth century he owned Oklahoma's three most widely circulated newspapers and one of the largest printing and bookbinding operations in the Southwest.

When Congress authorized the land run in 1889, no provision was included for organizing and governing the territory. Consequently, for the first year the residents governed themselves. When the territory was finally established in May 1890, Guthrie was designated the capital. The first territorial legislature convened that fall, and one of the first bills to gain approval called for relocating the territorial government to Oklahoma City, a rival city also established in the 1889 land run. The territorial governor vetoed the proposal, but the controversy over the capital's location continued for decades. When Oklahoma secured statehood in 1907, Congress temporarily settled the issue by designating Guthrie as the capital until 1913, when a popular referendum would determine the permanent location. Oklahoma Democrats, whose power base was further south around Oklahoma City, viewed that clause in the enabling act as an attempt by Republicans in Washington to control the state's politics. By 1910 the Democrats, led by Governor Charles N. Haskell, and the Republicans, led by Guthrie newspaperman Greer, were openly at odds over the issue. Haskell finally decided to take action and convinced the legislature to hold a referendum on the capital location in June 1910. Voters could choose among Guthrie, Shawnee, and Oklahoma City. Just after the polls closed, Haskell declared Oklahoma City the winner and had the state seal secretly transferred there. Greer and other Guthrie residents challenged the validity of the referendum, but the United States Supreme Court upheld Haskell's action.

Guthrie's growth and development ended with the capital's relocation in 1910. As a result, few of the buildings were significantly altered, and the city today appears much as it did in the first decade of the twentieth century. In fact, the city was placed on the National Register of Historic Places as the only intact territorial and state capital remaining in the United States.

Of particular interest in the historic district are the Oklahoma Territorial Museum and the State Capital Publishing Museum, both administered by the Oklahoma Historical Society. The Oklahoma Territory Museum occupies the old Carnegie Library and a modern adjoining building. The library, constructed in 1902 and 1903, was the site of the inauguration of the last territorial governor and the first state governor and of Statehood Day ceremonies on November 16, 1907. This last included the symbolic wedding of Mr. Oklahoma Territory and Miss Indian Territory. Visitors can now see portions of the historic library as well as exhibits on Oklahoma's territorial period. The State Capital Publishing Museum occupies the last home of Greer's famed printing business. Erected in 1902 according to a design by Joseph Foucart, the structure contains many original furnishings, vintage letterpress printing equipment, and exhibits on the company and the printing industry.

Gray Brothers Building

In addition to the museums, visitors to the district can see a rich assortment of historic structures erected during the city's heyday. These include the Gray Brothers Building, home of the Bank of the Indian Territory until 1905; the Logan County Court House, constructed in 1902 and used as the state capital until 1911; and the Atchison, Topeka and Santa Fe Railway Company Station, built in 1902 on the site of the original Guthrie Station. These and the other historic buildings in the district effectively recall Guthrie's pivotal role in Oklahoma's transition from territory to statehood.

FRANK PHILLIPS HOME 1107 S. Cherokee, Bartlesville. Oklahoma's most famous resource is oil. First commercially tapped in 1897, the state's oil reserves fueled the dramatic growth and development of the Oklahoma economy in the twentieth century. A leading figure in the establishment of the petroleum industry was Frank Phillips, founder of the Phillips Petroleum Company at Bartlesville. His home still stands there as a monument to him and the other oil entrepreneurs who played such pivotal roles in shaping the twentieth-century Oklahoma experience.

The town of Bartlesville was established toward the end of the nineteenth century in northeastern Oklahoma, between the Osage Hills and the Caney River. Its founder was Jacob Bartles, who purchased a grist mill there in 1875 and operated a trading post on the north bank of the

Frank Phillips Home

river. The town remained a relatively insignificant rural settlement until 1897, when the Cudahy Oil Company drilled Oklahoma's first commercial oil well, the Nellie Johnstone No. 1, on the banks of the Caney. The arrival of the Santa Fe Railroad two years later led to expanded operations in the oil field, but full exploitation was hindered for a time by legal technicalities related to Indian land allotments. Determined entrepreneurs secured leases one way or another by 1901, and the oil boom spread from Bartlesville throughout Indian Territory. By 1905, 255 producing wells had been drilled in the territory, and by 1907 the new state of Oklahoma led the Southwest in the production of crude oil—a position it retained until 1928 and the Texas oil boom.

One of the early entrepreneurs in the Oklahoma petroleum industry was Frank A. Phillips. He was born in rural Nebraska in 1873 and grew up on his family's farm in Creston, Iowa. His education ended at the age of 14, when he began working in a local barbershop. Ambitious and determined to make his way in the world, Phillips purchased that barbershop and the town's other two as well by his early twenties. In 1897 he married Jane Gibson, daughter of Creston banker John Gibson. Phillips' new father-in-law persuaded him to try his hand at bond sales, and he again demonstrated an amazing entrepreneurial talent in moving bond issues that had frustrated more experienced salesmen.

Just after the turn of the century, Phillips heard about the oil strikes around Bartlesville. He and his brother, L. E. Phillips, traveled to Oklahoma and investigated the investment possibilities in 1903 and 1904. Convinced of the potential for enormous profits, the Phillipses decided to join the oil boom. John Gibson and several associates provided capital for the organization of the Anchor Oil and Gas Company, and by early 1905 the young entrepreneurs had settled in Bartlesville, opened an office, and hired a driller. Oil drilling lacked the scientific exactitude of present-day operations, and the Phillips' first three wells proved dry. With only enough money for one more try, the brothers drilled a fourth well near the Caney River on property leased from Anna Anderson, a young Delaware Indian girl whose grandfather had secured the land for her as her allotment in the division of tribal property. On September 6, 1905, the Anna Anderson No. 1 came in, yielding two hundred fifty barrels of crude oil a day. The Phillips brothers made eighty more consecutive strikes after that and soon had Anchor Oil and Gas on a sound competitive footing within the developing petroleum industry.

By 1915, the price of crude oil had dropped from $1.05 to $.35 per barrel. Phillips, still active in banking and finance, decided to sell most of his oil holdings. Then with increased demand during World War I, the per-barrel price of crude oil shot up to $3.50. The remaining tag ends of the old oil leases became valuable again and the brothers resumed oil drilling operations. On June 13, 1917, they incorporated the Phillips Petroleum Company, using as assets $3,000,000 in oil leases. The company expanded dramatically over the next decade and in 1927 diversified with the purchase of a refinery in Texas. That in turn led to direct marketing, and in November 1927 the Phillips company opened its first service station in Wichita, Kansas. Marketed at first in the Midwest and West, Phillips 66 products were on sale in all fifty states by 1968. Frank Phillips died in 1950, but the company he founded remains an innovator and leader in the energy and chemical industries.

The Frank Phillips Home at 1107 Cherokee Avenue in Bartlesville was erected by the oil entrepreneur in 1909. The two-and-a-half-story Greek Revival building, designed by Walter Everman, is constructed of brick with sandstone trim and an imposing two-story portico supported by white columns. Its twenty-nine rooms include a gameroom, a library, a sunroom, and seven bedrooms decorated with the Phillips' furniture, art, and other decorative objects. Opened to the public in 1973 and administered by the Oklahoma Historical Society, the home serves as a monument to Frank Phillips and his pivotal role in the development of the Oklahoma oil industry.

Visitors to Bartlesville can see several other sites related to the oil industry as well. On the banks of the Caney River in Johnstone Park stands a replica of the wooden oil derrick that once marked the Nellie Johnstone No. 1, the state's first commercial oil well. Southwest of the city is the Woolaroc Museum and Ranch, a museum of southwestern culture located on Frank Phillips' four-thousand-acre ranch. And in downtown Bartlesville on the second floor of the Phillips Building is the Phillips Exhibit Hall, which depicts the company's history, activities, and products. Still headquartered at Bartlesville, the present-day Phillips Petroleum Company testifies to the impact of the oil industry on twentieth-century Oklahoma.

BOGGY DEPOT SITE *fourteen miles southwest of Atoka.* Faint outlines of streets with building foundations, abandoned wells and cisterns, and cemetery of 1838 settlement by Chickasaws; important in the days of the California gold rush and Butterfield Overland Mail.

CHEROKEE NATIONAL HISTORICAL MUSEUM *Cherokee Heritage Center, Tahlequah.* Village museum with re-creation of villages from the 1600s and late 1800s; Cherokee culture and history.

CHEROKEE STRIP HISTORICAL MUSEUM *one-fourth mile east of Fir Street exit off I-34, Perry.* Exhibits on the agriculture and culture of the Cherokee Strip.

CHISHOLM TRAIL MUSEUM *605 Zellers Avenue, Kingfisher.* General history museum with exhibits on agriculture and Indian life; information on the 1892 mansion of Gov. Abraham J. Seay.

CREEK NATIONAL CAPITOL *Old Creek Indian Council House, Okmulgee.* Displays of Indian craftwork and weapons and the history of the Creeks since their removal from Georgia and Florida; in the 1878 Victorian capitol.

DAVIS GUN MUSEUM *Fifth and U.S. 66, Claremore.* Besides guns, swords, and knives, includes saddles, steins, animal horns.

FERGUSON HOUSE *521 N. Weigel Street, Watonga.* Clapboard house built about 1902, and home of Thompson Benton Ferguson, newspaperman and governor of Oklahoma Territory; where Edna Ferber worked on novel *Cimarron;* state-owned.

FIVE CIVILIZED TRIBES MUSEUM *Agency Hill on Honor Heights Drive, Muskogee.* Art in traditional style by Cherokees, Choctaws, Chickasaws, Creeks, and Seminoles; housed in 1875 Indian agency building.

FORT GIBSON *Fort Gibson.* Reconstructed log buildings and stockade and restored original stone buildings from fort of 1837–1857 used in Indian conflicts and as a trade center.

FORT WASHITA *southwest of Nida on state 199.* Restored buildings from an 1842 fort established by Zachary Taylor to protect Chickasaws; a stop on the Overland Trial.

GILCREASE INSTITUTE OF AMERICAN HISTORY AND ART *1400 N. 25 West Avenue, Tulsa.* Displays on the Five Civilized Tribes and other Indians from Alaska to Mexico, the American frontier, and American art.

MARLAND MANSION *Monument Road. Ponca City.* Coursed stone house with Mission Style elements, built 1928–1941 for E. W. Marland, wealthy oil man; with a museum.

MURRAY-LINDSAY MANSION *south of Washita River, Erin Springs.* Vernacular Neoclassical Revival house built in 1880 by a cattle king.

MURRELL HOME *Park Hill.* Clapboard house built 1843–1844 that was social center and school for the community; with a museum.

MUSEUM OF THE CHISHOLM TRAIL *U.S. 81 and state 70, Waurika.* Exhibits on pioneers and the famous cattle trail through the area.

MUSEUM OF THE WESTERN PRAIRIE 1100 N. Hightower, Altus. General museum with early farming implements and cattle-ranching equipment.

NATIONAL COWBOY HALL OF FAME 1700 N.E. 63rd Street, Oklahoma City. Collection of Russell and Remington art and displays on cowboys and historic trails.

NELLIE JOHNSTONE NO. 1 Johnstone Park, Bartlesville. Replica of the 1897 oil well that was the first commercial well in the state; first oil well on private land near Wapanuck, drilled 1885–1888.

NO MAN'S LAND HISTORICAL MUSEUM Sewel Street, Goodwell. Collection of Indian artifacts and exhibits from anthropology, archeology, agriculture, and natural sciences.

OKLAHOMA STATE MUSEUM Historical Building, Oklahoma City. Galleries on the Plains Indians, Five Civilized Tribes, pioneer, territorial, and statehood aspects of Oklahoma, transportation, military life, Indian art, and aviator Wiley Post.

OLD TOWN MUSEUM Pioneer Road and U.S. 66, Elk City. General museum with restored first house in Elk City, early school, wagon yard, chapel, and rodeo setting.

OVERHOLSER HOUSE 405 N.W. 15th Street, Oklahoma City. Built 1903 by rich pioneer and merchant.

PRICE TOWER Dewey Avenue and Sixth Street, Bartlesville. Office building housing headquarters of the Phillips Petroleum Company; designed by Frank Lloyd Wright, built 1953–1956, showing adaptation of skyscraper for openspace setting.

SOD HOUSE four miles north of Cleo Springs on state 8. Frame and sod house built by homesteader, the only existing homestead sod house in Oklahoma, with furnishings of the 1890s era.

THORPE HOUSE 704 E. Boston Street, Yale. Clapboard house built 1916–1917 where Jim Thorpe, first competitor to win both pentathlon and decathlon in the Olympics (1912), lived; state-owned.

TOM MIX MUSEUM Dewey. Memorabilia of the famous movie star, who was once a Dewey marshal; with a silver-studded black leather saddle on a life-size replica of Mix's horse, "Tony."

WESTERN TRAILS MUSEUM 2229 Gary Freeway, Clinton. Exhibits from anthropology and archeology.

WILL ROGERS MEMORIAL one mile west of Claremore on state 88. Grave and personal belongings of the famed humorist.

OREGON

FORT CLATSOP NATIONAL MEMORIAL Route 3, 4.5 miles south of Astoria. The Lewis and Clark expedition was the first official United States exploring expedition, and it may have been the most important. From the vast northwestern region traversed during that great adventure, several American states were eventually formed: the Dakotas, Montana, Idaho, Washington—and Oregon. It was Oregon's distinction to lie at the farthest reach of Lewis and Clark's journey. It was in the Oregon Country, not far from the mouth of the Columbia River, that the expedition made its home during the winter of 1805–06. Today, the Fort Clatsop National Memorial marks that place and helps the visitor understand a key episode in the history of the young American nation and the Pacific Northwest.

The spirit and curiosity of no less a man than Thomas Jefferson himself lay behind the expedition. After one false start, it finally got under way in May 1804, captained by army officers Meriwether Lewis (Jefferson's private secretary) and William Clark (brother of Revolutionary War soldier George Rogers Clark). It traversed some 3,555 miles round-trip from St. Louis and did not return until September 1806. Its leaders were charged by President Jefferson to follow the Missouri River to the watershed of whichever westward-flowing river promised "the most direct and practicable water communication across this continent for the purpose of commerce" and to investigate the Indians, flora, fauna, and mineral resources of the region. Even though "water communication across this continent" proved elusive, the expedition in general well satisfied the expectations of its famous patron. The information it brought back added greatly to the vague knowledge about the lands contained in Jefferson's Louisiana Purchase and the country beyond it. It raised Americans' awareness of the continental scope of their new national experiment, and it began the process of exploration, possession, and settlement that in time made the Northwest American.

By the late autumn of 1805, Lewis and Clark's little "corp of discovery" had reached the middle portion of the Columbia River on its course through Oregon. From The Dalles, they proceeded by water and overland to the river's mouth, where they crossed from the Washington to the Oregon side in search of salt, better hunting grounds, and a satisfactory site for their winter encampment. On December 7, 1805, they settled on a place three miles up the present Lewis and Clark River that they called Fort Clatsop after a friendly local Indian tribe. It stood safely above the river, offered fresh-water springs, and was protected from ocean gales by forest cover and hills. Construction of a shelter began immediately, and by Christmas the whole lonely company was under roof. That "roof" (a reconstruction of which is on the site today) was not a large one. A mere fifty feet square, it consisted of two long facing

Parade ground

buildings joined on the sides by palisades, creating a small parade ground in between. Divided into seven rooms, this was home for three months for thirty-one men, one woman, and a baby.

Much of the party's time during that long wet winter was spent making preparation for the return journey in the spring. Almost every day's entry in Lewis and Clark's journals contains references to the hunt. And though game was plentiful, it was often lost to wild animals or Indians who helped themselves before the meat—mostly elk—could be carried back to the fort. The expedition traded eagerly with the Indians for berries, roots, and fish (especially the Columbia's abundant and flavorful smelt) and even developed some taste for a staple of the Indian's diet—dog—that Lewis for one claimed he preferred to either venison or elk. The need for salt, both to make their current fare more palatable and to preserve food for the long journey ahead, was critical and drove them to set up a salt-making camp fifteen miles to the southwest near present-day Seaside, Oregon. There they hiked in shifts, to laboriously boil large kettles of seawater from which they were able to extract about three quarts of salt a day. The place, known as Salt Cairn, is now marked with a structure of boulders and native clay with five kettles placed on it.

Adding to the problems of chronic food shortage, rain fell on all but 12 of the 106 days they spent there. Dry wood was almost impossible to find. Meat and leather clothing rotted, colds and rheumatism grew chronic, and fleas flourished. Despite the hardship, Lewis and Clark put the long days of their Oregon sojourn to good use. At Fort Clatsop they reworked the detailed journals they had kept since the beginning of the expedition. They organized their already voluminous notes on the people, plants, and animals in the vast territory they had thus far traversed, and they collected local specimens from around the fort. And, of course, they carefully planned their eastward journey. Given the monotony and discomfort of their winter in the wet Oregon wilderness, the beginning of that trip back to civilization was something everyone eagerly anticipated. Though it was delayed by inclement weather, on March 23, 1806, the party once again paddled out into the Columbia and headed east toward home. Behind them they left their soggy log fort, which was a parting gesture Lewis and Clark gave to Chief Comowool, a friendly Clatsop.

Time and neglect soon took their toll. The Indians probably used the fort as a hunting lodge for a few years, but by the time American settlers arrived in the 1850s few traces remained, and subsequently even those vanished. The fort today, which is believed on or very close to the original site, is a replica built in the 1950s as a result of efforts by several state and local historical and service organizations. After its acquisition by the National Park Service, the 125-acre site was developed and improved. It now includes a visitor center housing an auditorium and interpretive exhibits that tell the story of the expedition and its residency at Fort Clatsop. In addition, a living-history program offers to summertime visitors actual demonstrations by costumed staff of some of the skills necessary to the expedition's survival: candle-making, tanning, making moccasins, splitting shakes, and curing jerky. Maintained forest trails lead to a spring about fifty yards behind the fort, which was probably the party's main source of fresh water, and to the canoe landing on Netal Creek where Lewis and Clark are thought to have stepped ashore on December 7, 1805. There, today's visitor can see demonstrations of trapping and canoe building.

The Fort Clatsop Memorial stands as a vivid reminder of one of the world's great exploring adventures. But the adventure did not end with Lewis and Clark. Just as their famous expedition ever after inspired the nation's awe, so the Oregon Country, which they only scouted, in time evoked the nation's imagination and tempted its ambition. From the valleys of the Ohio, the Mississippi, and the Missouri, wagon trains of ordinary people trekked over the Oregon Trail seeking a new and better setting for their lives. As Gordon Dodds has written in his thoughtful history, Oregon for Lewis and Clark was still, in 1805 and 1806, a place on "the outer limits of rival empires." Within just a few decades it became a place that promised to thousands of settlers if not a totally new life, then at least a better old one—"if not quite a Garden of Eden, at least a mightily improved Missouri."

JACKSONVILLE HISTORIC DISTRICT *Jacksonville.* Historic sites and historical museums preserve artifacts from earlier times, evoking the spirit of the past. They may be interesting because they tell us something about our roots and thus about who we are, or simply because they remind us of how different from us people just two or three generations ago could be. But they often share a common problem that requires some imagination to overcome. Part of the meaning of any site or artifact is lost when people cease to use it for its original purpose. The well-preserved western cavalry outpost is no longer home to the cavalry, itself long vanished. The famous tycoon's mansion is no longer

Jacksonville Museum

a mansion in the sense that no one lives there anymore. The old railroad station where there are no trains is not really a railroad station.

There are some places where continued use and awareness of a place's historical importance sustain some of the substance as well as the spirit of the past. Historic districts, usually under varied ownership, are good examples of how this can work. In the Skidmore / Old Town District in Portland, for example, a number of late-nineteenth-century commercial structures still stand and are still used by businesses of various sorts. Other cities boast similar districts. In such settings the past and the present truly come together. Although historic districts are often found in cities where buildings are more concentrated, they are not found only there. Historic Jacksonville is an excellent case in point. That Jacksonville is so well preserved is due partly to the efforts of diligent preservationists, partly to history itself.

Like many towns in the West, Jacksonville owed its beginnings to gold, which was discovered early in the 1850s in Rich Gulch on Jackson Creek in southern Oregon's Rogue River Valley. Aptly enough, two California prospectors made the first strikes; from the subsequent rush of others to get rich quick, the town of Jacksonville quickly grew. As in the California goldfields just a few years earlier, a bedlam of tents, crude shanties, and log cabins mushroomed overnight, and the Rouge River Valley took on all the appearance of the mining frontier elsewhere. The gold was important for Oregon, which up to then lacked any reliable medium of exchange. With it capital accumulated, transportation improved, and the territory began to grow. So, on a smaller scale, did Jacksonville. Frame buildings and then brick ones soon replaced the tents and log cabins, and the place began generally to take on an air of permanence. In 1853 it became the county seat with a respectable population for that remote region of about 900.

The gold boom in Jacksonville, as in other places all over the West, was a fickle thing, and Jacksonville in time had to find other ways to sustain itself. The first years were tumultuous. Indian attacks and the Rogue River Indian War interfered with mining, and in 1873 fire destroyed much of the business district. But gradually the town evolved into a small agricultural center and settled down to its own quiet prosperity. It never grew greatly, never became the metropolis some of its early boomers no doubt envisioned. In 1884 the Oregon and California Railroad bypassed it in favor of Medford, which was a great blow in an age when railroads symbolized growth and progress. Years later, in 1927, the county seat too moved to Medford.

Such misfortune also had a good side. Rapid growth and development often mean that old buildings quickly make way for new ones. As fashions change, prosperous places feel obliged and are able to change with them. This has been especially true in American cities and towns, which—being of no great age—have few traditions of keeping and using things from the distant past. Thus, to the extent that such things in America have been saved, it has been because circumstances disadvantageous to change have kept things the same. In this sense Jacksonville—bypassed by the railroad, abandoned by the county government, the gold long since played out—has been lucky. Its last boom is a distant memory, but it never became a ghost town, the fate of so many western mining towns. It would be recognizable today to people who knew it a hundred years ago. They were, after all, the ones who built much of it.

Today there are in Jacksonville about sixty nineteenth-century buildings still standing and in good condition. Most of them are still being used for their original purposes. Together they comprise Historic Jacksonville, a National Historic Landmark. Many properties are in private hands. Most of the town's old houses are still just that: houses where people make their homes. Others, owned by Jackson County and administered and maintained by the Southern Oregon Historical Society, are open to the public. A visit can provide a vivid glimpse of what life here once was like. A walking tour around the town suggests how little in some respects it has changed.

The Beekman House dates from 1876, America's centennial year, and is a good example of the country gothic architecture typical of many small western cities and towns. It was built by Wells Fargo agent C. C. Beekman, who was also Jacksonville's first banker. With its white picket fence, high gables, and clapboard exterior, it reflects the solid but modest prosperity that made Jacksonville the place it is. Inside are similar modest comforts of a Victorian home in Oregon. The parlor was used by the family only on formal occasions, as its furnishings make clear. A gilt-framed pier glass mirror hangs in the small entry hall leading into the parlor, where a walnut étagère, a settee, and matching chairs of cherry-wood upholstered in satin damask announce that this was a formal place. Battenberg lace curtains hang at the windows. In the dining room the table is set with Haviland china and Venetian glass finger bowls. Decanters and a silver tea service grace the oak sideboard. The kitchen features an ornate Superior wood cook stove, a wooden icebox, and a pie safe with pierced tin inserts. The pantry just off the kitchen stores crockery, glassware, boxed and tinned foods. In the adjacent maid's room (she might have been called the "hired girl") are an old-fashioned iron bedstead, an armoire, and a Singer treadle sewing machine inlaid with mother of pearl.

Also open to the public view, the Catholic rectory was originally built as a small clapboard house in the 1860s. It served as a rectory until 1908, when the Jacksonville parish became a mission of Medford; it then once again became a private home. Restoration began in 1976, and today in the front part of the house visitors can see representative living quarters of a Catholic priest from the 1870s. The 1891 addition reflects the style of the 1890s.

The Old Courthouse, constructed in 1883 as the seat of government in Jackson County, is rather different. It cost some $38,000, even then a modest sum for a substantial Italianate building like this one. Faced with sandstone from Kanaka Flat on nearby Jackson Creek, it rises two and a half stories and is topped by a classical cupola. Elaborate decorative detail can be noted throughout. Today the courthouse houses the Jacksonville Museum of the Southern Oregon Historical Society. Young people especially will enjoy the Old Jail, which is now designed as a children's museum. It contains a variety of exhibits of interest to young people and many things that they can touch and handle. A butter churn, mine sluicebox, old kitchen appliances can all be operated. In the garage old tires, tools, and license plates bring back the early 1900s. In the barbershop children can sit in the chair and weigh themselves on tall scales. There is even an old telephone switchboard; only the operator who said "Number please" is missing. In the general store children can get a firsthand idea of how different shopping was before the era of the supermarket.

But what makes Historic Jacksonville truly special are not just—or even especially—its historic buildings open to the public as historical museums. Jacksonville's particular historic buildings happen to be very good and are important historical resources. But it is the large number of other nineteenth-century houses and businesses throughout the town that makes the historic district mean more than any single historic site. Here are houses, shops, and other businesses occupying their original buildings—still lived in and used by ordinary people in the course of their daily lives. Therefore a visit here is somewhat different from a visit to a famous old cavalry post, immaculately preserved and cared for. Here past and present literally come together in a special way. Most of Historic Jacksonville has been preserved for use by the people who live there today. They have made of their small town an excellent example of preservation in action in the best sense. In some ways history did not deal especially kindly with their early Oregon gold town. Some of the good things and much of the growth coveted here and elsewhere clearly passed it by. But with what it did have, Jacksonville created something unique and, we suspect, as lasting as more conventional kinds of attractions. It cares for its past, something that cannot fail to impress visitors from other places—many of which do not.

SKIDMORE / OLD TOWN *Portland.* The story of Portland in the nineteenth century begins with the story of competition with other towns that also aspired to commercial eminence. In time Portland became Oregon's only metropolis, and until it was eclipsed by Seattle after the turn of the century, it dominated the commerce of the Pacific Northwest. It had to fight for its supremacy, and like other successful cities elsewhere it proclaimed its achievement with solid business and residential buildings. Some still stand and are reminders to today's visitor and resident alike of the era when Portlanders first built for permanence.

Although Oregon was the first great goal of the wagon trains moving west from Missouri in the 1840s, it was at first a "promised land" only in a very limited sense. To the legendary rich lands of the Willamette Valley trekked farmers from the Ohio and Mississippi valleys, intent on reproducing in a new place a better version of an old way of life. They were cautious and conservative farmers whose success, in Missouri or in Oregon, was modest—like their hopes. Indeed, from their own labors and nature's crude endowment they grew an abundance of the food and fiber which in that agricultural world was wealth.

But one of the reasons for Oregon's great allure was also one of its great problems. Extraordinarily remote from the centers of American civilization, it afforded many people the chance for a truly fresh start at the same time it denied them sustenance from older areas. It was destined for many years to be a colony of the East—an exporter of raw materials and an importer of everything else. But in the beginning it was too isolated to be even that. Rather it was an outpost, separated from an older America by fearsome plains and mountains, whose passage in the years before the railroad only the hardiest undertook and which raised the costs of trade to prohibitive levels. Thus what grew in Oregon at first stayed there. Subsistence rather than economic abundance was its lot, though the subsistence it offered was often as not decent enough.

Oregon's evolution to another stage of development was triggered by gold, discovered first in California in the late 1840s and in Idaho, Montana, and eastern Oregon itself in 1860 and 1861. The California gold rush was legendary and quickly brought west thousands of argonauts eager to get rich quick. It also momentarily depopulated Oregon's farms as laborers rushed south to try their luck. But other more typical Oregonians quickly saw that more certain returns could be made from "mining the miners." Here was a market that was not half a continent away, and whose demand for the products of field and forest found in Oregon its natural supply. It also brought, in the form of gold, Oregon's first reliable medium of exchange and unit of account. Capital began to accumulate; with it transportation improved, and towns and villages grew.

It was not long before the small Columbia and Willamette valley settlements of the 1840s and 1850s began to vie with each other for position as Oregon's economic hub. Oregon City, as the territorial capital and largest place between California and Alaska, seemed to have good prospects. Its immediate location at the falls of the Willamette River gave it two special attractions: water power and the cartage business springing from the need to get goods around the falls. In the 1840s it grew to be the largest town in the territory. Farther down the Willamette, however, the town of Milwaukie touted its own advantage of better deep-water navigation. Linn City made the same claim; and St. Helens, nearer yet to the mouth of the Columbia, offered even shorter travel time to the ocean. But none of these places was destined for the supremacy each craved. That distinction went instead to Portland, whose victory came not just because it was a good seaport.

Portland managed what other places did not: it firmly established itself as the link between the sea and the great wheat-producing Tualatin Plains. Transportation to the interior continued to be a crucial factor in Portland's growth long after the discovery of gold in the upper Columbia Basin in the 1860s. Portland businessmen moved quickly to secure their city's position as magnet for the miners' gold dust and as supplier of their food and shelter. Meanwhile Portland continued to enjoy its position as import-export center for the northwest coast region. The Oregon Steam Navigation Company and later the railroads connected Portland, the port and commercial center, with the region's vast hinterland and in time assured its lasting success.

By the 1870s, 1880s, and 1890s Portland's prosperity was evident from the shape of the city itself. Handsome residential districts bespoke the confidence and prosperity of its entrepreneurs; social and cultural amenities proclaimed how far Portland had traveled from its rude frontier beginnings. But it was probably Portland's commercial building in this era that most clearly mirrored present success and affirmed the city's faith in the future. It was built to last; and though fashions inevitably changed and later generations pulled much of it down, a surprisingly large amount remains preserved today in the Skidmore / Old Town Historic District. But the district is not only a monument to the success of early Portlanders. It is also a monument to several significant architectural styles and a distinctive, now rare, building material: cast iron. In the 1870s around the present Skidmore Fountain area there began to appear blocks of Italianate commercial structures, which by the turn of the century were joined by others in the high Victorian Italianate and Richardsonian Romanesque styles. The entire period of Portland's first great commercial growth coincided with the great era of cast-iron building in America. It was with cast iron that architects and builders developed the techniques of modular construction that made possible the modern steel skyscraper. In the last half of the nineteenth century whole cast-iron structures were prefabricated in foundries, shipped by rail to building sites all across the country, and there assembled much as prefabrication is done today with other materials. Portland enjoyed block after block of these buildings whose cast-iron Italianate facades, columns, arches, and decorations are a distinctive architectural heritage. With over twenty-five such buildings still standing, the Skidmore / Old Town District has one of the largest collections in the country.

A walking tour through the district, once the heart of Portland, best reveals the rich variety of these old buildings. Though some have been remodeled over the years, hints remain of their former shapes. Guide material produced by the Junior League of Portland helps the imaginative visitor reproduce what Portland's most prosperous business area once looked like. Besides, much still remains intact and unspoiled by the years and changing tastes. The Hallock and McMillan Building, built in 1857, is the oldest surviving brick building in Portland. The Deilschneider Building, built two years later, was once the home of the Oregon Iron Works and is the fourth oldest standing structure in the city. Handsomely restored, the Failing Building (1886) exhibits a variety of building materials: wood, plaster, sheet metal, in addition to cast iron. Built for $24,000 in 1883, the F. B. Simon Building is an especially good example of cast-iron architecture. The cast-iron embellishments—lions' heads, female faces, acorns, and grape clusters—of the Blagen Building (1889) recall those that decorated hundreds of other commercial block fronts along Portland streets a century ago. Typically, the date of construction and the owner's name appear on the pediment above the roof line. Blending classical, Romanesque, and gothic motifs, the Glisan Building even has a wrought-iron parapet. It dates from 1889 and was the last cast-iron building constructed in Portland. The same year, the Skidmore Block went up, by its quite different Richardsonian design indicating that the Victorian age was nearing its end. The same new style can be seen in the New Market Annex, where heavy brick and stone fronts have replaced the more delicate ornamental facades once fabricated from cast iron. Richardsonian Romanesque dominated the 1890s; the stone Hazeltine Building is an excellent example.

Old Portland's two most famous architectural landmarks are in the district. One is the New Market Theater, built in 1872. An arcaded mar-

Skidmore Fountain

ket with marble stalls was located on the street level; above was an
elegant red plush theater. The second is not a building at all, but a
fountain. The Skidmore Fountain (1888), which still sits on its original
site in the heart of Portland's old business district, was the city's first
piece of public art. A gift of Portland pioneer Stephen Skidmore, it
beautifies the city as much today as it did long ago.

The preservation of this historic district is in keeping with one
observer's early assessment of the growing city. Wrote Samuel Bowles,
editor of the *Springfield* (Massachusetts) *Republican* in 1869: "Oregonians have builded what they have got more slowly and more wisely
than the Californians: they have . . . less to unlearn; and they seem sure,
not of organizing the first state on the Pacific Coast, indeed, but of a
steadily prosperous, healthy and moral one—they are in the way to be
the New England of the Pacific Coast."

BYBEE-HOWELL HOUSE Howell Park Road, Sauvie Island. Restored
Greek Revival house built in 1856, and the oldest building on Sauvie
Island.

CAPE MEARES STATE PARK south side of Tillamook Bay, west of U.S. 101. Cape discovered in 1778 by English Captain John Meares and still in its natural state.

CHAMPOEG STATE PARK VISITOR CENTER St. Paul. Visitor center with artifacts from early history, in the historic French Prairie where western agriculture was first practiced.

COLLIER STATE PARK LOGGING MUSEUM U.S. 97 thirty miles north of Klamath Falls. Pioneer logging equipment, photographs, and locomotives.

COLUMBIA RIVER MARITIME MUSEUM Sixteenth and Exchange streets, Astoria. Marine artifacts, ship models, and navigation instruments.

CRATER LAKE NATIONAL PARK Crater Lake. Natural and human history in the area of an extinct volcano.

DEADY HALL University of Oregon, Eugene. Second Empire building constructed 1873–1876, the first building on the university campus.

DOUGLAS COUNTY MUSEUM Fairgrounds Exit off I-5, Roseburg. Collections include Native American and fur-trapper material, agricultural tools and equipment, logging artifacts, and photographs.

FORT DALLES Fifteenth and Garrison Streets, The Dalles. Gothic Revival surgeon's quarters remaining on the former site of fort in operation 1850–1867.

FORT KLAMATH MUSEUM state 62 two miles south of Fort Klamath. Reconstructed guardhouse of the original fort of 1863; with photo displays and memorabilia.

GEORGIA-PACIFIC MUSEUM Georgia-Pacific Building, 900 S.W. 5th St., Portland. Artifacts, including old films, of the lumber industry.

HORNER MUSEUM Oregon State University, Corvallis. Natural and human history from Oregon, with tours and exhibits.

KAM WAH CHUNG COMPANY BUILDING Canton Street, John Day City Park, John Day. Museum in a stone building of about 1866 that served as a combination trading center, doctor's office, and social center for Chinese immigrants.

KLAMATH COUNTY MUSEUM 1451 Main Street, Klamath Falls. Exhibits on Modoc Indian war and Klamath and Modoc Indians; also administers Baldwin Hotel, pioneer western hotel restored with original furnishings.

LEE HOME AND METHODIST MISSION PARSONAGE Thomas Kay Historical Park, Salem. Restored buildings from the mission founded in 1834 by Jason Lee and others.

McLOUGHLIN HOUSE NATIONAL HISTORIC SITE 713 Center Street, McLoughlin Park, Oregon City. Restored clapboard house built 1845–1846 for Dr. John McLoughlin, chief factor of the Hudson's Bay Company.

OREGON HISTORICAL SOCIETY MUSEUM 1230 S.W. Park Avenue, Portland. Extensive collections and displays on the Oregon country, including art, anthropology, ethnography, archeology, maritime history, and photos.

OREGON MUSEUM OF SCIENCE AND INDUSTRY *Washington Park, Portland.* Includes planetarium and hands-on exhibits.

OREGON TRAIL MARKER *U.S. 26 at Laurel Hill.* Shows where the famous route of immigrants came over the Cascades and connected with the Old Indian trail.

PACIFIC UNIVERSITY MUSEUM *Old College Hall, Pacific University, Forest Grove.* Collections on Native American, pioneer, and Oriental culture in the Oregon Country; housed in oldest building in continuous educational use west of the Rockies.

PIONEER COURTHOUSE *520 S.W. Morrison Street, Portland.* A restored Renaissance Revival building of 1869–1873 that is the oldest federal building in the Pacific Northwest.

TIMBERLINE LODGE *six miles north of Government Camp in Mount Hood National Forest.* Built 1935–1938 by WPA architects in an indigenous style called "Cascadian."

UNION COUNTY MUSEUM *311 S. Main Street, Union.* Chinese items, Victorian room, photographs, and small library, housed in 1881 bank building; several fine examples of Queen Anne houses in town.

VILLARD HALL *University of Oregon, Eugene.* A Second Empire-style building rare for Oregon, built 1885–1886.

WESTERN FORESTRY CENTER *4033 S.W. Canyon Rd., Portland.* Exhibits on the history and practice of forestry.

WOLF CREEK TAVERN *about twenty-two miles north of Grants Pass, Wolf Creek.* An 1857 house that was a stagecoach inn on the original Territorial Road and hosted Jack London, Mary Pickford, and Rutherford B. Hayes.

PENNSYLVANIA

INDEPENDENCE NATIONAL HISTORICAL PARK bounded by Walnut, 6th, Chestnut, and 2nd streets, Philadelphia. Probably no other historic site evokes the spirit of the struggle to establish the American nation as well as Independence National Historical Park in Philadelphia. Though there are many places up and down the eastern seaboard that figured significantly in that story, none quite matches the broad historical significance of the Independence Park, nor is any other associated with so many specific momentous events. All countries have national shrines: the scenes of great battles, the homes of great leaders, the sites of great moral or political contests that shaped the character of a nation. America has its share, and Independence Park is one of the finest. But it is also more. The men and the deeds that made it famous were at the time objects of attention far beyond American shores, and the system of government that they established whereby free men might best rule themselves has remained so ever since. What happened here in the late eighteenth century is one of the great chapters in the history of political thought, something for all to marvel at, no matter how poorly adapted some other political cultures were to it. In this sense, it is like Runnymede in England where with the signing of Magna Carta a new fundamental principle governing rulers and ruled was defined: a principle that could be transferred and adapted elsewhere. It introduced something new into a forthcoming age that was permanently changed by it.

The specific events that so distinguish this part of old Philadelphia include the meetings of the First and Second Continental Congresses, the signing of the Declaration of Independence, the labors of the Constitutional Convention, and George Washington's second inauguration as president. Philadelphia also served as the second capital of the United States under the Constitution during the 1790s. The park covers some twenty-two acres in downtown Philadelphia and consists of a number of handsome as well as historic buildings.

Independence Hall on Chestnut Street is certainly the most famous. It antedates American independence by many years and is a monument as much to the symmetry and taste of eighteenth-century colonial civilization as to the revolution that brought America's colonial history to an end. It was originally designed as the State House for the Province of Pennsylvania. Ground was broken in 1732; it was finally completed in the 1750s. The result befit its status as a government seat and Philadelphia's standing as one of the largest and most important cities in the first British Empire. A stately two-and-a-half-story red brick structure with two symmetrical wings and imposing bell tower, it was and is one of the most beautiful eighteenth-century public buildings in the Georgian style in America or anywhere else. Equally famous and lovely, its interior was the setting for the signing of the Declaration of Indepen-

Independence Hall

dence and the drafting of the Constitution. The events and the room were superbly matched. It is a generous forty feet square and twenty feet high. Along the east wall twin segmentally arched fireplaces flank the speaker's dais; massive fluted pilasters adorn the wall itself. A heavy Doric entablature borders the plaster ceiling. Here in the hot summer of 1787, sitting in Windsor chairs around green baize-covered tables, that remarkable assembly gathered to hammer out a constitution that is still America's fundamental law.

With just a few absentees like Thomas Jefferson and John Adams, who were abroad on diplomatic assignments, those fifty-five men made up an aristocracy of political talent and wisdom unique in American history. Wrote a French observer: "If all the delegates named for their convention at Philadelphia are present, we will never have seen even in Europe, an assembly more respectable for the talents, knowledge, disinterestedness, and patroitism of those who compose it." The living symbol of American nationhood, George Washington, solemnly presided from the high-backed "rising sun" chair so dubbed by the aged Benjamin Franklin, who at the end of the convention saw in its outstretched rays the portent of a new and hopeful day for the United States. The rest of the furniture has been duplicated, with the exception of the original silver ink stand and quill box that were used by the signers of the Declaration and the Constitution.

Nearby in other stately buildings other history was made. Carpenters' Hall, built in 1770 as a guild hall by the Master Carpenters of Philadelphia, was the scene for the meeting of the First Continental Congress in 1774. This gathering of patriots irrevocably set the aggravated colonies on the radical road to independence. Its handsome spaces resounded with eloquent words conveying to the world a new idea: that from twelve (later thirteen) colonies an American nation was about to be born. Here Virginia's Patrick Henry (already of "Give me liberty, or give me death" fame) declared that the "distinction between Virginians, Pennsylvanians, New Yorkers, and New Englanders are no more. I am not a Virginian, but an American." Although profound local distinctions lasted for a long time and indeed still remain, the bold assertion of a new sovereignty was a revolutionary—and to the British a treasonous—act. It shortly precipitated a bloody war. In 1775 the second Continental Congress met in the Pennsylvania State House (Independence Hall), appointed George Washington commander in chief to general American resistance, and took steps to organize a government.

The Revolutionary War was a close thing; it required not just perseverance and hard fighting (Valley Forge and Saratoga) but skillful diplomacy and the French alliance to win it. Before that happened, Britain several times seemed near to reclaiming her wayward colonies, and during the winter of 1777–78 she actually chased the Americans out of Philadelphia and the handsome Georgian building that housed their fledgling government. Victory came at last late in 1781 at Yorktown and was made formal two years later. Back in Philadelphia, at Independence Hall, the Continental Congress adopted the Articles of Confederation drafted during the war as the nation's first form of government. They did not last; dissatisfaction at their inadequacies led to the calling of the Constitutional Convention that met in Independence Hall in 1787, and whose work received Franklin's final sage approbation.

In 1790 Philadelphia became the capital of the young federal republic; the government remained there for ten years before taking up its new and permanent quarters on the Potomac. During that time it found a home in two new buildings immediately adjacent to Independence Hall. Both were red brick with cupolas, solid Georgian in style. The new congress met in the Philadelphia County Courthouse, which became Congress Hall. The new supreme court held its deliberations in the Philadelphia City Hall, which is still known as Old City Hall. In Congress Hall George Washington was inaugurated for his second term, and John

Adams for his only term, the latter occasion marking the first transfer of executive power in American history.

When the capital moved to Washington, the power and glory of government went with it. But the grand buildings in Philadelphia where it had had its beginnings found other uses. Congress Hall housed federal and state courts. Old City Hall reverted to the city government. In 1802 artist Charles Willson Peale opened a museum in Independence Hall, and his paintings of Revolutionary War heroes became the basis of the park's present collection. The city of Philadelphia bought the building from the state in 1818 and has preserved it ever since.

Throughout the park there are many other buildings of related historical importance. The First Bank of the United States on Third Street was built between 1795 and 1797 and is probably the oldest bank building in the country. The Second Bank of the United States on Chestnut was designed by William Strickland in the Greek Revival style and built between 1819 and 1824. Today it houses the park's portrait gallery. Philosophical Hall on Independence Square and Library Hall just across Fifth Street are both associated with the American Philosophical Society, founded in 1743 by Benjamin Franklin and the oldest learned society in America. Philosophical Hall dates from the late 1780s and is still occupied by the Society. Library Hall was built originally for the Library Company of Philadelphia and now houses the Society's own collections. New Hall once was used by the War Department and as reconstructed is the United States Marine Corps Museum. Next door, Pemberton House contains the Army-Navy Museum. In the Graff House, built originally in 1775 (the present house is a reconstruction), Thomas Jefferson drafted the Declaration of Independence. The Free Quaker Meeting House is the oldest in Philadelphia. St. George's Church is the oldest Methodist church in the United States. Christ Episcopal Church has the distinction of having buried in its cemetery seven signers of the Declaration of Independence, including Benjamin Franklin.

And finally there is the Liberty Bell, for years located in Independence Hall and now housed in a special pavilion on Independence Mall. The liberty proclaimed in its famous inscription (from Leviticus: "Proclaim Liberty throughout all the land unto all the Inhabitants Thereof") at first had nothing to do with American independence. Cast in England in 1751 when the colonies were still quite content, the great bell was ordered by the colonial assembly to commemorate the fiftieth anniversary of the granting of William Penn's Pennsylvania Charter of Privileges. But it became Pennsylvania's and America's official bell. Its association with the events of the American struggle for independence—it was rung at the first reading of the Declaration to the citizens of Philadelphia in Independence Square on July 8, 1776—proved its inscription prophetic.

DRAKE WELL MUSEUM *on Pennsylvania 36 three miles southeast of Titusville.* In recent American history, oil has probably commanded more attention than any other natural resource. It has done so because the circumstances surrounding it have changed. Our habitual way of thinking about oil has been disrupted. For decades abundant domestic supplies more than met domestic demands; the market worked well. As the fuel that powered the automobile revolution in personal transportation, oil (in the form of gasoline) took on the aura of one of life's basic necessities. Like food, shelter, clothing, and medical care, its possession was taken for granted.

That depended on cheap sources of supply, many of which in the years after World War II lay beyond America's shores. In 1953 the nation became a net importer of petroleum. The price of reliance on foreign sources at first seemed low, though unreliable foreign suppliers and the disruption of long ocean supply lines was always a threat. Fears became fact in the wake of the 1973 Arab-Israeli war. Since then Americans have not thought about oil in quite the same old ways. They still crave and depend on it, but they have embraced public policies and private initiatives to enhance domestic production. And they have conserved. They have become more deliberate about their use of oil and generally about "energy", a word whose meaning has blurred considerably with increased use. Still, oil's future in America will likely remain large. Americans will continue to rely on it to run their cars, heat many of their houses, and produce much of their electricity.

This was not always the case. Indeed, to look at the beginning of the oil business in this country is to be impressed by how the same natural resource is coveted over the years for a number of different reasons. A good place to look at that beginning is the place where in fact it began: the Drake Well Museum in Titusville, Pennsylvania.

As seen by historian Thomas C. Cochran, Pennsylvania played a central role in the business and industrial revolutions that destined America for great power and wealth. William Penn's colony was a thriving mercantile emporium, and early in the years after independence the new commonwealth, particularly Philadelphia, became the nation's financial center. As the nation moved west, Pennsylvanians carved out a great home market and, especially after the Civil War, built vast inland empires of manufacturing and energy. Titusville was an early and important part of that story.

As the site of the world's first successful oil well, it is also a place of some larger historical importance. When Edwin L. Drake struck oil here in 1859, oil was hardly an unknown substance; but what was known and how it was used foretold little of petroleum's enormous place in America's future. Reports of oil-like matter bubbling to the earth's surface here and there date from Biblical times; in America, Frenchmen discovered an oil spring near Cuba, New York, in the seventeenth century. In the eighteenth century Seneca Indians reportedly traded small quantities of oil gathered from springs with white men; for a time it was known as "Seneca Oil." A map of the Middle Colonies published in

*Drake's Well House
and Derrick*

1755 also indicated the presence of oil in Pennsylvania. Settlers along Oil Creek in the northwestern part of the state knew it was there in the 1840s; like the Indians before them, they harvested small amounts by either skimming or soaking it up with a flannel cloth. Also like the Indians, they valued it for what they believed were its medicinal properties.

Whatever those might have been, it was not as medicine that men truly needed the oil. The big market was for cheap and safe fuels for lighting. To that age-old market the Industrial Revolution was adding another: for lubricants to keep the nation's growing number of machines running. By later standards of consumption, even this was small business, but at the time it was enough to spur ambitious and imaginative men to find ways to bring up the oil and transform it into usable forms. By the 1850s a dwindling supply of whale oil was already being supplemented by oil distilled from coal, which was the business of some fifty American companies. Petroleum from western Pennsylvania, which was often a byproduct of salt wells, was also finding its way into the lucrative new markets. There seemed great potential: experiments had clearly shown that the petroleum could be refined into an effective illuminant. The problem was to provide a large and constant enough supply to justify major refining operations and to convince the operators of coal-oil refineries to convert to petroleum. The solution was to drill for it directly.

Edwin L. Drake, whose name is most commonly associated with the well at Titusville, was actually only agent for a group of shareholders of the Seneca Oil Company and its relative, the Pennsylvania Rock Oil Company, the first petroleum company in the world. With his commission to find and produce oil, Drake (a former railroad conductor who had fallen in with the oil entrepreneurs in 1857) arrived in Titusville in May 1858. He knew where to look—the site of an oil spring on the Hubbard farm—and after several weeks spent unsuccessfully excavating a pit, he learned how to look. He needed to drill. That decision caused delay, but by the spring of 1859 he had assembled the materials and the men he needed: a six-horsepower steam engine with a stationary tube body to power the drill, and William A. Smith, a salt-well driller from Tarenton, Pennsylvania, who agreed to do the drilling for $2.50 a day. It was a new technology, and there were problems. Smith discovered that ground water caused the hole to collapse. Only by sinking several sections of cast-iron pipe, which had to be brought from Erie, down about thirty-two feet to bedrock could he proceed. Drilling resumed and on Saturday afternoon, August 27, they reached a crevice at a depth of sixty-nine feet. The drillers then went home for Sunday, and not until the next afternoon did Smith notice a dark fluid on top of the water just a few feet below the derrick floor. It was the first time oil had been struck by drilling.

The technique lasted, with many improvements over the years. But the real meaning of Drake's well became clear only with time. Though it was hardly a "gusher" such as Texas would boast forty years later (it flowed at a rate of only eight to ten barrels a day), it did demonstrate that a steady supply of petroleum could be obtained by drilling. And that was the assurance that risk-conscious entrepreneurs needed. They quickly gathered in the oil business, which in Pennsylvania was closely allied with the railroad business. Applying talent and energy to the job of bringing together a product and its market, men like John D. Rockefeller, Thomas A. Scott, Andrew Carnegie, and J. Edgar Thomson wrote a bold new chapter in the history of Pennsylvania and America. As epic as that story was however, it was actually only prologue to the story of oil in the twentieth century, when Spindletop and hundreds of other Texas oil fields spewed forth black gold for new markets in industry and transportation that truly dwarfed the market for lamp oil and axle grease which Drake and his cohorts once had gambled on.

The record of this pioneering effort is preserved today at the Pennsylvania Historical and Museum Commission's Drake Well Museum in Titusville. There visitors will find a full-size replica of Drake's enginehouse and derrick on the site of the original well. The largest drilling rig used in Pennsylvania and replicas of early railroad tank cars are also on display. A museum of petroleum history contains tools and artifacts of the early oil industry, together with working models and dioramas. Today it is a quiet place, its boom long over. But the industry and way of life it gave birth to are with us still. A visit to the Drake Well Museum makes clear just how small its beginnings were.

***STATION SQUARE** Pittsburgh.* The city of Pittsburgh symbolizes a part of Pennsylvania history that is far removed from Quakers, Benjamin

Franklin, and momentous events of the Revolutionary War. Though its origins date back to the eighteenth century—it was named for a famous British statesman—its real story belongs to a much later time. Economic growth and development, not the search for religious and political freedom, was its great theme.

Pennsylvania as much as any state reaped enormous benefits in the late nineteenth and early twentieth centuries. Abundant natural resources, especially coal and iron, met with entrepreneurial talent of a high order. With derision some have called it the age of the robber barons, when the ruthless few exploited the helpless many for profit and savaged the earth around them. With awe, others have called it the age of enterprise, when captains of industry and finance created wealth where none had been before and in the process brought prosperity (or at least better prospects) to millions of ordinary people. Whichever, there was wide agreement as to the symbols of the age: railroads, dignified office blocks, and factories with smokestacks spewing honest black smoke that meant progress.

Pittsburgh's prosperity rested on coal, iron, and steel. From them its people built a great industrial city. By the turn of the nineteenth century it was part of the industrial heart of the United States and one of the most industrialized regions in the world, reaching from southern New England through New York and Pennsylvania westward along the southern shore of the Great Lakes to Chicago. To the observant it foretold a future of unprecedented wealth and power.

Railroads tied it together. Trains captured the imagination of the age; the Pennsylvania—the "Standard Railroad of the World"—and the mighty New York Central were the wonders of the business world. Their freights linked resources to factories and factories to markets. Their famous "limiteds" opened a new age of deluxe land travel. Their monumental terminals became landmarks of America's cities for years to come.

Along with the giants like the "Pennsy" and the "Central," smaller lines proliferated and on a less grand scale left their mark on industrializing America. One was the Pittsburgh and Lake Erie Railroad, begun in 1877 to connect Pittsburgh, the coal and coke resources of southwestern Pennsylvania, and the port cities on Lake Erie. It was not a long railroad, but once allied with the New York Central in 1882 it was an important and profitable one. Coal freight and boxcar leasing were the mainstays of its prosperity, but it also ran a large passenger service for profit and prestige. The great terminal built to house it and the company headquarters just across the Smithfield Street Bridge from Pittsburgh's Golden Triangle has today been preserved by the Pittsburgh History and Landmarks Foundation. It is an excellent example of saving a building designed for one age by adapting it for the uses of another one.

The building was begun in 1899 and opened in 1901, at what some have called the height of America's imperial age. Its architecture certainly had imperial pretensions. The station is essentially a classical cube six stories high from the street, with a ground floor at train level. It had 80,000 square feet of floor space, which made it smaller than the competing Pennsylvania Station across town, but its decoration, particularly on the inside, was second to none. The style is probably best described as neo-baroque. The street-level entrance leads to a large two-story vestibule from which plunges a wide and graceful staircase. The staircase hall is particularly magnificent and prepares the visitor for the main waiting room, which occupies the bottom of the court at the rear of the building. It too is two stories high, but above that soars a great coffered tunnel vault of stained glass. Beyond, a vestibule opened the way to a cavernous and now vanished train shed. Thus from curbside to trainside one was led from one part of the building sensibly to the next—awed all the way by a profusion of Edwardian decor.

By the sterner standards and antiseptic tastes of another era, it is all incredibly extravagant, but it has an indisputable grandeur all the same. From the Renaissance arcades of the entry down to the brass escutcheon plates elaborately initialed "PLERR," every detail reveals this as a place of both monumental and functional purpose. It was meant to announce to the world the railroad's image of itself and efficiently to accommodate the daily flow of thousands of passengers through its imposing spaces. In both it succeeded remarkably.

Such buildings, however, were the creatures of their times, and as times changed so did they. Monumental railroad stations were the victim of changing patterns in public travel in the 1950s and 1960s, as cars and airplanes increasingly replaced trains. As the grand waiting rooms stood empty, the value of the urban real estate where they stood commonly soared. Many made way for more modern profit-producing replacements. The old Pennsylvania Station in New York is only the most famous example, but there were many others, some in Pittsburgh.

Terminal Building

In the years after the Second World War the Wabash, Federal Street, and East Liberty stations were demolished. Passenger traffic on the Pittsburgh and Lake Erie all but disappeared, but its grand baroque station (which was and still is company headquarters) happily did not. Its resurrection to a new life was due largely to the efforts of the Pittsburgh History and Landmarks Foundation.

Through an agreement with the railroad whereby it would continue to occupy the top six floors, the Foundation, relying largely on local private investment, undertook to adapt the grand old building and surrounding railroad facilities. The result is today known as Station Square, a forty-acre restaurant, shopping, and office complex where once steam whistles, coal smoke, and cinders reigned supreme. The centerpiece today as in its earlier life is the station, whose barrel-vaulted waiting room has been transformed into an elegant restaurant. The stained glass was painstakingly cleaned and every other detail of the first designers meticulously seen to, so that the station has returned to what it must have been like in 1900. Only the travelers are missing, but other people spending money for things other than railroad tickets have assured its success. Adjacent, the old railroad freighthouse has been converted to an area of specialty shops. The old Shovel Warehouse nearby will become an office building. The massive old trainshed that extended beyond the station along the river was taken down in 1935 because of maintenance problems; on stub tracks beneath it, where heavy steel coaches, Pullmans, and club cars once waited, there are now more shops, historic railroad exhibits, and parking for Station Square visitors. Beyond a new hotel and convention center have risen.

Station Square is not an historic site in the same sense as a president's boyhood home or a Civil War battlefield. It has not been preserved merely as a shrine where we can learn something about how things once were. It has been preserved for use—just as it first was built for use. The uses have changed, though P&LE freight trains still rumble by outside and there are still P&LE offices upstairs. We can however still learn from it how some things in Pittsburgh once were. To learn it requires some curiosity and imagination. For the visitor so equipped, Station Square presents an image, necessarily changed with time, of a younger Pittsburgh and a younger America. As the gilt and marble and stained glass testify, its style in monumental architecture and in much else was rather different from our own. But just that the place still stands and is still used by the people of Pittsburgh and America is to make the style of that age partly our own. We are certainly richer for it.

AFRO-AMERICAN HISTORICAL AND CULTURAL MUSEUM 7th and Arch streets, Philadelphia. Sculpture, art, and artifacts, including materials on the slave trade, black churches, Reconstruction, and civil rights movement.

AMERICAN SWEDISH HISTORICAL MUSEUM 1900 Pattison Avenue, Philadelphia. Materials on the Swedish contribution to American life.

THE ATHENAEUM 219 S. 6th Street, E. Washington Square, Philadelphia. Library and art collections relating to nineteenth-century social and cultural history.

ATWATER KENT MUSEUM 15 S. Seventh Street, Philadelphia. History of the Delaware Valley, with art and botanical garden.

BALCH INSTITUTE FOR ETHNIC STUDIES 18 S. 7th Street, Philadelphia. Materials made and used by ethnic cultures in America—costumes, printed materials, decorative arts and crafts.

BARTRAM'S HOUSE AND GARDEN 54th Street and Eastwick Avenue Philadelphia. Home of John Bartram, American botanist, built in 1731; with period furnishings and a botanical garden.

BRANDYWINE BATTLEFIELD U.S. 1 near Chadd's Ford. Site of Washington's defeat by the British on September 11, 1777; with restored quarters of Lafayette and reconstructed headquarters of Washington.

BUSHY RUN BATTLEFIELD state highway 993 near Jeanette. Where British Colonel Henry Bouquet won over Pontiac-led Indians in 1763; with marked battle sites and a museum.

CALEB PUSEY HOUSE Race Street, Upland. Built by Caleb Pusey, an English Quaker, in 1683 and restored as the oldest existing English-constructed house in Pennsylvania.

CANAL MUSEUM Hugh Moore Park, 200 S. Delaware Drive, Easton. Museum, exhibits, films, locktender's house, canal, and operating lock.

CLIVEDEN Germantown Avenue between Johnson and Cliveden streets, Germantown. House built by the Chew family in 1763 and the site of the British repulse of Washington's troops in the Battle of Germantown, October 4, 1777.

CONRAD WEISER HOMESTEAD U.S. 422 near Wolmesdorf. Restored home of Conrad Weiser, who was important as an intermediary with the British and the Indians in the 1700s.

CORNWALL IRON FURNACE north of Lebanon in Cornwall. Nineteenth-century iron furnace with exhibits related to all phases of the iron-making process.

DANIEL BOONE HOMESTEAD secondary road one mile north of Baumstown, in Birdsboro. Boone family homestead where Daniel Boone lived until the age of 16; now occupied by a stone farmhouse on site of original cabin, other restored buildings.

ECKLEY MINERS' VILLAGE near Hazelton. A company coal mining town with more than fifty houses, churches, and other buildings, showing how anthracite workers lived in the nineteenth century; museum exhibit building; complex also includes the Anthracite Museums at Ashland and Scranton.

EPHRATA CLOISTER 632 W. Main Street, Ephrata. Eighteenth-century communal religious village museum, with twelve buildings in medieval German style and decorative arts collections.

FLAGSHIP NIAGARA *foot of State Street Erie.* 1813 brig commanded by Commander Oliver Hazard Perry in the Battle of Lake Erie; exhibits related to the battle.

FORKS OF THE OHIO *downtown Pittsburgh.* Where the English first built an outpost in 1754, the French Fort Duquesne, and the British-Americans Fort Pitt; today Point State Park contains the original Bouquet Blockhouse and Fort Pitt Museum.

FORT LIGONIER *S. Market Street, Ligonier.* Reconstruction of a fort built by the British, 1758–1759, with a museum.

FORT MIFFLIN *on Delaware River at foot of Fort Mifflin Road, east of Philadelphia airport.* Preserved fort begun in the 1790s and used until World War II.

FORT NECESSITY NATIONAL BATTLEFIELD *on U.S. 40 eleven miles east of Uniontown in Farmington.* Reconstruction of stockade, storehouse, and entrenchments on a site where Washington built a fort in 1754; with several restored historic houses.

GETTYSBURG NATIONAL MILITARY PARK *Gettysburg.* Visitor center, tours, markers, and several museums interpret the July 1863 battle where the Confederacy reached its zenith.

GOVERNOR PRINTZ PARK *corner of Taylor Avenue and 2nd Street, Essington.* Site of Printzhof, built in the 1640s, the first permanent white settlement in Pennsylvania and the center of "New Sweden."

GRAEME PARK *County Line Road, Horsham.* Fieldstone gambrel-roof house constructed in 1721–1722 by Sir William Keith, a provincial governor of Pennsylvania.

GOLDEN PLOUGH TAVERN AND GATES HOUSE *Market Street and Pershing Avenue, York.* Restoration of a half-timber Germanic tavern and a house that was once the headquarters of American General Horatio Gates.

HISTORIC BETHLEHEM INCORPORATED *510 Main Street, Bethlehem.* Collections focusing on 1700 to 1850; housed in six eighteenth- and nineteenth-century restored buildings.

HOPE LODGE MATHER MILL *Bethlehem Pike, Fort Washington.* 1750 Georgian house with collection of eighteenth-century decorative arts.

HOPEWELL VILLAGE NATIONAL HISTORIC SITE *five miles south of Birdsboro.* Restoration to a nineteenth-century period of an ironmaking village established in 1770.

JOSEPH PRIESTLEY HOUSE *Priestley Avenue, Northumberland.* 1794 home of Joseph Priestley, furnished with antique scientific equipment, fine art, decorative arts, and furniture of the period of Priestley.

LAKE SHORE RAILWAY MUSEUM *North East.* Locomotives and railroad passenger cars in the Pullman collection, with photographs from railway history.

LANCASTER MENNONITE HISTORICAL MUSEUM *2215 Millstream Road, Lancaster.* Library and museum with collections on Pennsylvania Mennonites from 1710 to the present.

MERCER MUSEUM OF THE BUCKS COUNTY HISTORICAL SOCIETY *Pine and Ashland streets, Doylestown.* Collection of 40,000 pre-industrial era tools and products housed in a concrete structure of 1916; also nearby are Fonthill, home of Henry Chapman Mercer, and the Moravian Pottery and Tileworks.

MORTON HOMESTEAD *state 420 in Prospect Park.* Late seventeenth-century log house that was the home of John Morton.

MOUNT PLEASANT *Fairmont Park between East River Drive and Columbia Avenue, Philadelphia.* Built 1761–1762 in the late Georgian style with elegant interior workmanship; furnished in period style.

MUSEUM OF AMERICAN JEWISH HISTORY *55 N. Fifth Street, Independence Mall East, Philadelphia.* Documents, artifacts, ceremonial objects, and memorabilia from the Colonial period to the present.

OLD ECONOMY VILLAGE *14th and Church streets, Ambridge.* Communitarian village, the last home of the Harmony Society; preserved buildings from 1824 to 1831, furnished with decorative arts, textiles, and furnishings of the period.

OLD POST OFFICE *Pittsburgh History and Landmarks Museum, One Landmarks Square, Pittsburgh.* Extensive collections on all aspects of regional history and a program of tours and lectures; housed in an 1897 post office building.

PENNSBURY MANOR *on the Delaware River south of Morrisville.* Reconstruction of the seventeenth-century country plantation of William Penn; furnished buildings, restored gardens, farm, and agricultural interpretation.

PENNSYLVANIA FARM MUSEUM OF LANDIS VALLEY *2451 Kissel Hill Road, Lancaster.* History of rural life, with emphasis on German farming areas; buildings preserved from 1700s and 1800s and furnished appropriately.

PENNSYLVANIA HISTORICAL AND MUSEUM COMMISSION *Third and North streets, Harrisburg.* William Penn Museum, a general museum with history, science, and decorative and fine arts collections in permanent and temporary exhibits.

PENNSYLVANIA LUMBER MUSEUM *Galeton.* History museum interpreting logging tools and equipment, a sawmill, logging camp, and other exhibits related to the lumber industry.

PENNSYLVANIA MILITARY MUSEUM *Boalsburg.* A general military museum exhibiting military equipment and uniforms from Pennsylvania units from the French and Indian War through the present.

PHILADELPHIA MUSEUM OF ART *26th Street and Benjamin Franklin Parkway, Philadelphia.* Comprehensive art museum with American period rooms, Pennsylvania German decorative arts, American furnishings, and the Alfred Stieglitz photography collection.

POTTSGROVE MANOR *West King Street, Pottstown.* 1752 historic house; furnishings and paintings from the period 1680 to 1800.

RAILROAD MUSEUM OF PENNSYLVANIA *Strasburg.* A comprehensive museum of railroading with collections interpreting transportation, railroad history, locomotives, railroad cars and models, tools, and lamps.

S-BRIDGE *just off U.S. 40 six miles west of Washington.* One of the last remnants of the National or Cumberland Road built in the early 1800s.

SCHWENKFELDER MUSEUM *Seminary Street, Pennsburg.* Early Americana as preserved by one of the German sects that populated eastern Pennsylvania in the 1600s and later.

VALLEY FORGE NATIONAL HISTORICAL PARK *Valley Forge.* Site of the 1777–1778 encampment of the Continental Army; historic houses, period furnishings, original headquarters of General Washington, and reconstructed huts of the other soldiers.

WASHINGTON CROSSING HISTORIC PARK *Washington Crossing.* Site of the embarkation of the Continental Army for the crossing of the Delaware River prior to the Battle of Trenton in 1776; historic houses, period furnishings, wildflower preserve, and park facilities.

WHEATLAND *1120 Marietta Avenue, Lancaster.* Residence of president James Buchanan.

RHODE ISLAND

NEWPORT HISTORIC DISTRICT Newport. From the late seventeenth century until the American Revolution, Newport reigned as one of the leading ports in colonial America. The city's flourishing coastwise trade and highly profitable international commerce stimulated the Rhode Island economy and inspired an urban elegance rivaled by Boston only in the mid-eighteenth century. Beautiful homes constructed in the latest styles and filled with elegant furnishings testified to the affluence of Newport's entrepreneurs, and the erection of equally fine public buildings further demonstrated pride in the city's wealth and power. Newport's golden age of commerce came to a close with the War for Independence, but an amazing number of the structures from that period survive today in the Newport Historic District, a National Historic Landmark. The district preserves Newport's colonial past and commemorates Rhode Island's emergence as a major commercial center in the British empire.

Roger Williams' insistence on religious tolerance made colonial Rhode Island a haven for dissenters. One such group from the Massachusetts Bay Colony established the town of Newport in 1639 on the south coast of Aquidneck Island. From the first, activity centered around the deep water harbor. Newport's first street, Thames, was laid out parallel to the harbor, and a dock was constructed at the end of Marlborough Street later that first year. Over the next decades the community developed in a rather haphazard fashion that reflected immediate needs rather than any formal plan. By 1680, over four hundred structures stood along the narrow streets around Washington Square, a commons area that became the heart of the colonial settlement. By that time entrepreneurs had also constructed the Long Wharf at the foot of the square, and a burgeoning maritime industry assured the settlement's success.

Although shipbuilding began at Newport as early as 1646 and remained an important industry throughout the period, shipping and commerce provided the catalyst for the settlement's growth prior to the Revolution. Before the close of the seventeenth century, Newport's commercial activity expanded from coastwise trade with other colonies to trade with the West Indies and Europe. Ships arrived at the Newport harbor with manufactured goods from Britain, whale oil from New Bedford and Boston, and spices, sugar, molasses, and slaves from the West Indies. Exports ranged from such local products as rum, spermacetti candles, and hemp to finely crafted furniture, clocks, and silver. The most profitable commercial activity was the triangular trade in molasses, rum, and slaves. By the beginning of the eighteenth century, fifty to sixty Newport-based ships were engaged in this activity, and Newport had become the center of the New England slave trade. Much of the city's growing wealth and influence was due to this highly profitable but notorious activity. In fact, an import tax on slaves between 1707 and 1732 financed the construction of bridges and the paving of Newport streets.

Maritime activity provided a solid economic base for the city's growth and development. By the mid-eighteenth century, Newport flourished as one of the most prosperous ports in the colonies and the economic center of Rhode Island. Affluent merchants and sea captains erected stylish new homes and filled them with finely crafted furnishings. Craftsmen and small tradesmen built more modest homes and shops along the streets that lined the bustling harbor. Churches and civic buildings incorporated the best of Georgian style and stood as symbols of the town's wealth and power. Only Boston equalled the stylish grace and urban sophistication of Newport in the decades prior to the Revolution.

This golden age of Newport's prosperity ended with the war. Newport never fully recovered from wartime cessation of commerce, and economic leadership shifted to Providence in the 1780s. Although the city did not regain its position as a commercial center, its popularity as a resort for the wealthy brought economic revival by the mid-nineteenth century. Summer visitors largely avoided the old colonial city, however, and consequently many of the historic structures escaped significant alteration and demolition. Indeed, no comparable collection of colonial buildings exists today in the state or perhaps in the nation. The Newport Historic District constitutes a unique historical and architectural legacy.

Few buildings survive in Newport from the seventeenth century. The best example of housing that remains from that era is the Wanton–Lyman–Hazard House at 17 Broadway. Built by Stephen Mumford about 1695, the two-and-a-half-story frame structure uses medieval construction techniques but details and ornamentation are suggestive of the later Georgian style. The White Horse Tavern at 26 Marlborough Street dates from at least two decades earlier. William Mayes began operating a tavern in this two-story frame building in 1687, and it now boasts of being the oldest such business in continuous operation in the United States. Across Farewell Street stands an early symbol of Newport's tradition of religious diversity—the Meetinghouse of the Society of Friends at 30 Marlborough Street. The original portion was erected in 1699 by Quakers from Connecticut and Massachusetts. Subsequent enlargements in the eighteenth and nineteenth centuries marked the growth of the Quaker community and its growing influence in Newport commerce.

Eighteenth-century structures clearly predominate in the district. The most distinctive are the Georgian civic buildings and churches designed by Richard Munday and Peter Harrison. Munday, a local master carpenter, designed the Colony House, the center of early Rhode Island government. Erected in 1739 at the east end of Washington Square, this structure housed the colonial and early state governments and was the scene of numerous historic occasions, including Rhode Island's ratification of the Declaration of Independence and the Constitution. At the west end of Washington Square at the head of the Long Wharf stands the Brick Market, a market house constructed in 1726 at the peak of Newport's commercial development. Designed by noted amateur architect Peter Harrison, this structure and the Colony House reflect the commercial and civic activity that made Washington Square the heart of colonial Newport. Harrison also designed the Redwood Library at 50 Bellevue Avenue and Touro Synagogue at 72 Touro Street, two important edifices whose histories reflect Newport's tradition of religious tolerance.

The basic fabric of the district, however, is residential. Whether of grand design or the simplest plan, most houses in eighteenth-century Newport were constructed of wood. As late as 1793, only six brick structures stood in the city, including the Colony House and the Brick Market. Small frame houses give the district much of its charm and distinctiveness today, and several particularly interesting examples stand west of Thames Street in an area known as Easton's Point. There tradesmen and craftsmen erected houses and shops accessible to the harbor and shipping facilities. Among the craftsmen were the Townsend and Goddard families, leading Newport cabinetmakers known for their exceptionally fine furniture. The Townsends had several shops and residences along Bridge Street, including a house–workshop complex built for Christopher Townsend in 1725 at 74–76 Bridge Street and another erected before 1758 at 68–70–72 Bridge by Job Townsend. John Goddard, an apprentice to Job Townsend, later became an accomplished cabinetmaker himself and resided in the house at 81 Second Street.

As Newport prospered in the mid-eighteenth century, wealthy merchants and sea captains built larger and more elegant homes alongside these modest residences. The Jonathan Nichols–Hunter House at 54 Washington Street is typical of the houses erected along the harbor for wealthy shipping entrepreneurs. Like many other waterside residences, the Hunter House originally had adjoining wharves and shops in order to take full advantage of the location. Erected in 1748, it has a pineapple-crowned pediment above the entrance, a symbol of Newport hospitality and a reflection of the city's West Indies trade. Once called Shipwrights Street because so many ships' carpenters lived and worked there, Bridge Street later became known for the sea captains that resided there at the close of the eighteenth century. The Captain Peter Simon House at 25 Bridge Street, a sea captain's residence erected before 1727 and altered prior to the Revolution, is typical.

These are but a few examples of the many fine colonial structures that line the streets of the Newport Historic District. Their preservation and restoration reflect the efforts of the Newport Historical Society, the Preservation Society of Newport County, the Newport Restoration Foundation, Operation Clapboard, the Oldport Association, and numerous

Hunter House

other individuals and groups. Now carefully restored through their efforts to its eighteenth-century elegance, the colonial city of Newport recaptures an era of commercial wealth and maritime power unequalled in modern Rhode Island history.

SLATER MILL HISTORIC SITE *Roosevelt Avenue, Pawtucket.* Industrialization, the factory system, and mass-production technology shaped the history of Rhode Island and indeed of the nation in the nineteenth and twentieth centuries. The turning point in the transition from cottage handcrafts to factory machine production came in 1790, when Samuel Slater and his associates at Pawtucket successfully produced machine-spun cotton thread for the first time in the United States. Three years later, they opened what came to be known as the Old Slater Mill, the nation's first successful cotton factory and the progenitor of the modern industrial plant. The Slater Mill Historic Site preserves this historic building and commemorates both the beginnings of textile manufacturing and industrialization in Rhode Island and the birth of the American Industrial Revolution.

The example of British industrialization inspired numerous attempts at establishing manufacturing in the United States in the decades after the American Revolution. These efforts failed at first because of lack of capital and inadequate knowledge of the machinery and the production process. In the late 1780s, however, Moses Brown, a wealthy Quaker merchant from Providence, decided to try his hand at textile manufac-

Mill complex on the Blackstone River

turing. Brown had the necessary capital, but none of the machines he acquired matched the reputed performance of the spinning machinery developed by Richard Arkwright in England in the 1760s. Brown, his son-in-law William Almy. and his nephew Smith Brown sought someone with firsthand knowledge of the Arkwright mills, but they had little success because of British restrictions on the emigration of skilled mechanics. At about this same time, Samuel Slater came to the United States from England. As a former apprentice to Jedediah Strutt, one of Arkwright's partners, Slater had the expertise that Smith and his associates needed to make their enterprise a success. After an exchange of correspondence, Slater and Brown met in 1790 and agreed to join forces.

Slater was far from impressed by the assortment of machinery Brown had assembled in a fulling plant at Pawtucket. Brown's spinning machines did not measure up to the Arkwright equipment Slater was familiar with, and the Americans clearly had no perception of the requirements of the production process. With the help of local mechanics like Oziel and David Wilkinson and Sylvanus Brown, Slater rebuilt the spinning frames, constructed drawing and roving frames, and completed work on a carding machine. While these improvements in the machinery were important, Slater's most significant contribution was his understanding of the whole production process. Because he had been apprenticed as an overseer, he was familiar not just with individual machines but with how they functioned as a system. He knew how to set up a mill and maintain continuous production flow without bottlenecks and waste. Although historians have long emphasized Slater's role in duplicating the Arkwright machines, his expertise in organizing and managing machines proved more significant to the development of the modern system of factory organization and production.

In December 1790, Slater and his associates finally completed installation of the machinery and began production of the first machine-spun cotton thread. Located in rented space in a Pawtucket fulling mill, this first textile factory clearly demonstrated the profitability of spinning yarn and convinced Slater, Almy, and Moses' son Obadiah Brown to construct a new mill building to house an expanded textile factory. In 1793 they erected a simple two-and-a-half-story, timber-framed structure. Although constructed of wood rather than stone, as Slater was accustomed to in England, the mill was solidly built to withstand the wear and tear of factory use. Well-scaled Neoclassical details enhanced the exterior and made the edifice more acceptable at a time when manufacturing was still viewed with suspicion by the public. Innovations included a trap-door monitor on the gabled roof and open interior spaces. The former provided a source of light in the attic and became a distinguishing feature of early American factories. The open interior on each floor provided flexibility in organizing the mill. With the machinery from their rented quarters installed in the new building, Almy, Brown, and Slater began operating in 1793 the nation's first successful water-powered cotton manufactory.

In 1797, Slater established a partnership with his father-in-law Oziel Wilkinson and several brothers-in-law and erected a new, larger mill across the Blackstone River. His former associates also established new mills, and until 1803 the three entrepreneurs together owned all the spinning factories in the United States. Competitors entered the field after 1803, and by 1815 Rhode Island had over one hundred mills in operation.

Although mechanized spinning had become commonplace, weaving remained a cottage industry at Pawtucket until 1815, when David Wilkinson constructed a workable power loom based on a design by William Gilmore. By that time Francis Cabot Lowell and the Boston Associates had taken the lead in the textile industry by integrating the production process from raw cotton to finished cloth. Although Rhode Island remained a strong competitor in the textile industry for some time to come, Pawtucket's era ended in 1829 when the major companies folded in the wake of a national economic collapse.

Over the next decades, the various owners of the Old Slater Mill used it for different purposes. When demolition threatened the historic structure in 1921, the Old Slater Mill Association was established to preserve it. The structure was restored in 1924 and 1925, but not until 1955 was it opened as a museum of technology and industry. The present mill includes the original 1793 building as well as additions made in 1801 and 1812 through 1817. Although much altered over the years, the building has been restored to its 1835 appearance. Exhibits focus on the evolution of the textile industry and the transition from cottage handcrafts to machine production.

In 1973 two additional historic structures, the Wilkinson Mill and the Sylvanus Brown House, were also opened to the public. At the Wilkinson Mill, erected in 1810, visitors can see a recreated nineteenth-century machine shop and the restored power system. The Sylvanus Brown House, which dates from 1758, has been restored and furnished as an example of a skilled artisan's home in an early urban–industrial community.

Public programs at the Slater Mill Historic Site include guided tours, exhibits, craft demonstrations, and a variety of educational programs. The visitor to the site learns not just about machines, technology, and water power but also about factory life, the workplace, and living conditions in an early industrial village. No other site is so historically important or offers such valuable insight into the industrial experience in Rhode Island at the dawn of the Industrial Revolution.

ALDRICH HOUSE *110 Benevolent Street, Providence.* The zenith of Rhode Island economic development and political power came in the decades between 1860 and 1910. The dominant figure of this golden age was Nelson W. Aldrich, United States Senator from Rhode Island from 1881 to 1911 and a symbol of the integral relationship between business and politics in this period. His Providence home still stands as a reminder of his impressive career. In light of his impact on the state's history, it is fitting that the structure now houses the Museum of Rhode Island History of the Rhode Island Historical Society.

Nelson Aldrich was fully committed to the conservative, pro-business philosophy that guided the Republican party in the last half of the nineteenth century. He was convinced that establishing a favorable climate for business growth and development was the essential function of the government, and his career reflected this single purpose. He refused to become simply a spokesman for Rhode Island business and insisted that his constituents' interests would best be served if he focused his attentions on harmonizing the needs of American business broadly. In this broker role, Aldrich became one of the most powerful men in the nation and amassed a fortune consistent with his intimate relationship with the American business and industrial community.

Aldrich's political career began in 1869, when he won election to the Providence Common Council. Although initially an Independent Republican, he soon aligned himself with the party faction headed by Henry Anthony, the "boss" of Rhode Island politics until his death in 1884. After five years on the city council, Aldrich advanced (with Anthony's assistance) to the state legislature in 1875 and to the United States House of Representatives in 1878. Then in 1881, the Anthony-controlled state legislature selected Aldrich to succeed the late General Ambrose Burnside in the United States Senate. After Anthony's death his successor, Charles R. Brayton, continued the tight political operation that kept Aldrich in the Senate for three decades.

Appointed to the Senate Finance Committee, Aldrich became a leading Republican strategist on economic policy. From 1883 to 1909, he played a major role in every tariff bill that came before the Senate. Basically he tried to mediate between conflicting interests and work out compromises within the context of the protectionism he and his colleagues were convinced was essential to continued economic growth.

Aldrich House

In 1888 he took the lead in Senate opposition to a Democratic-sponsored proposal for tariff reduction. Aldrich's counterproposal became a cornerstone of the Republican platform in the presidential race that fall and two years later served as a model for the highly protective McKinley tariff. Aldrich guided the latter through the Senate in 1890. Public reaction against high tariffs gave the Democrats a temporary majority in Congress in the mid-1890s, but Aldrich still managed to hold off significant downward tariff revisions in the Wilson–Gorman act of 1894. He remained an unyielding advocate of high tariffs and in 1909 cosponsored the controversial Payne–Aldrich tariff. Insurgent Republicans had secured party endorsement of tariff reform in the 1908 platform, but the 1909 act did not deviate from traditional Republican protectionism and clearly indicated Aldrich's unassailable power. Public reaction against Payne–Aldrich contributed to the erosion of party support in 1910 and 1912 elections, but Aldrich refused to compromise his position and remained an ardent protectionist and spokesman for powerful Old Guard Republicanism.

After the Panic of 1907, the Rhode Island senator became concerned with the inflexibility of the currency. In 1908 he sponsored the Aldrich–Vreeland Act, which provided emergency currency during financial crises such as that in 1907. More important, the act created the National Monetary Commission. With Aldrich as chairman, the commission studied the currency problem and in 1909 proposed the "Aldrich plan" for a strong central bank. The senator retired before Congress took action, but his plan did provide the basis for the current Federal Reserve System.

During his three decades there, Aldrich became in many ways the "boss" of the Senate. His leadership on central economic issues explains part of this, but the rest of the explanation rests with his skills as a politician. He manipulated his colleagues not through speeches but through persuasion, trade-offs, and the like. With seniority, his influence expanded, and his chairmanship of both the Senate Finance Committee and the Steering Committee placed him in a position to discipline party members. He worked closely with an inner circle that included William B. Allison of Iowa, John C. Spooner of Wisconsin, and Orville H. Platt of Connecticut. Together these men dominated the major Senate committees and maintained tight control over their Republican colleagues. In an era of weak presidents, this legislative power was crucial. When Theodore Roosevelt attempted to restore the power of the presidency after the turn of the century, even he had to make concessions to the boss of the Senate.

Aldrich had been a successful businessman prior to entering politics, but while a public servant he became a multimillionaire. His political power and business contacts gave him access to profitable investments in sugar, tobacco, rubber, banking, street railways, gas, and electricity. In the 1890s his wealth enabled him to purchase an impressive house on Benevolent Street in Providence and to develop an estate at Warwick Neck. He retained both until his death in 1915 at the age of 73. Ownership of the Providence residence remained with the family until 1974, when they deeded it to the Rhode Island Historical Society.

The house at 110 Benevolent Street dates from 1821–1872. John Holden Green designed the Federal-style mansion for Robert S. Burroughs, and several others owned it prior to Aldrich's purchase in the 1890s. The three-story structure has a clapboard exterior, a low-pitched hipped roof and cupola, and a small portico supported by Doric columns and pilasters at the main entrance. Interior features have been retained whenever possible, but the house does not contain period rooms. Instead, this historic structure provides a handsome setting for the Museum of Rhode Island History, the state's first comprehensive history museum. The structure houses both exhibits and a variety of educational and interpretive programs. Other facilities of the Rhode Island Historical Society include the John Brown House, an eighteenth-century historic-house museum, and the Rhode Island Historical Society Library on Hope Street.

THE ARCADE *130 Westminster Street, Providence.* Three-story shopping arcade in the Greek Revival style, built in 1827 and recently renovated; one of the earliest enclosed arcades in America.

BABCOCK-SMITH HOUSE 124 Granite Street, Westerly. A mansion built in 1832 for Dr. Joshua Babcock, town postmaster and physician, active in state politics.

BRICK SCHOOL HOUSE 24 Meeting Street, Providence. One of Providence's first schools, and an early school for black children; now the headquarters of the Providence Preservation Society.

BRISTOL HISTORICAL AND PRESERVATION SOCIETY 48 Court Street, Bristol. Museum in the 1828 town jail, including costumes, toys, furniture, Indian artifacts, military items, and other collections.

COGGESHALL FARM MUSEUM Colt State Park, Bristol. A working eighteenth-century farm with restored buildings and demonstrations of crafts and agricultural practices.

COLLEGE HILL HISTORIC DISTRICT Providence. The heart of the original town settlement, including many well-preserved public buildings and private homes from the eighteenth and nineteenth centuries.

ELEAZER ARNOLD HOUSE 449 Great Road, Lincoln. Seventeenth-century stone-end house, typical of Rhode Island vernacular architecture.

FIRST BAPTIST CHURCH IN AMERICA North Main Street, Providence. Built in 1774 and 1775 by the congregation founded by Roger Williams; restored colonial church was also the site of Brown University's commencement ceremonies.

FORT ADAMS Fort Adams State Park, Newport. The second-largest bastioned fort in the United States, covering twenty-one acres, begun in 1799.

GOV. STEPHEN HOPKINS HOUSE Hopkins Street, Providence. Home of an early governor and signer of the Declaration of Independence, and one of the oldest homes surviving in Providence; period herb gardens.

INTERNATIONAL TENNIS HALL OF FAME AND TENNIS MUSEUM Newport Casino, Bellevue Avenue, Newport. Center of public life during Newport's gilded age and site of the first national tennis tournaments.

JAMES MITCHELL VARNUM HOUSE 57 Pierce Street, E. Greenwich. Carefully restored Georgian house built in 1773 for General Varnum, Revolutionary War commander, lawyer, and congressman.

JOHN BROWN HOUSE 52 Power Street, Providence. Georgian mansion built in 1786 by one of Providence's most prominent merchants; headquarters of the Rhode Island Historical Society and noted for collection of Rhode Island furniture.

NAVAL WAR COLLEGE MUSEUM Coasters Island, Newport. In Founders Hall, location of the world's first naval war college (1884); exhibits on naval warfare and the Navy in Narragansett Bay.

NEWPORT HISTORICAL SOCIETY 82 Touro Street, Newport. Exhibits on Newport and Rhode Island history, including decorative arts, maritime collection, toys, and textiles.

OLD STATE HOUSE 150 Benefit Street, Providence. Site of the renunciation of Rhode Island's allegiance to King George III, May 4, 1776.

PRESCOTT FARM Route 114, Middletown. Collection of colonial farm buildings, including a working windmill and post-and-beam house with seventeenth-century furnishings.

PRESERVATION SOCIETY OF NEWPORT COUNTY *Mill Street, Newport.* Maintains and operates seven historic properties in Newport and one in Portsmouth, spanning over 150 years of the county's history.

PROVIDENCE CITY HALL *Kennedy Plaza, Providence.* Beaux Arts-style building (1875–1878), recently restored; elaborate interior stencilling.

RHODE ISLAND BLACK HERITAGE SOCIETY *1 Hilton Street, Providence.* Archive and museum collection documenting the life of blacks in the state from the earliest slaves to recent immigrants.

ROGER WILLIAMS NATIONAL MEMORIAL *North Main Street, Providence.* Site of the original (1636) settlement of the town.

SMITH'S CASTLE *U.S. 1, N. Kingstown.* Early trading outpost, enlarged during the era of Rhode Island plantation system in the eighteenth century.

SOUTH COUNTY MUSEUM *state 2, N. Kingstown.* Exhibits of early Rhode Island rural life and industry, including tools, farming implements, and vehicles.

UNIVERSITY HALL *Brown University, Providence.* Built 1770–1771, the oldest building at Brown; used as a hospital and barracks during the Revolutionary War.

WHITEHALL *311 Berkeley Avenue, Middletown.* Home of George Berkeley, philosopher and minister, his family, and others sent from England in 1729 to prepare to found a college in Bermuda.

WHITEHORN HOUSE *416 Thames Street, Newport.* Federal-period home that houses the collections of the Newport Restoration Foundation.

WILBOR HOUSE AND BARN *West Main Road, Little Compton.* Decorative arts and agricultural collections from three centuries of Little Compton's history, including artifacts from the development of commercial poultry production.

SOUTH CAROLINA

CHARLES TOWNE LANDING—1670 *1500 Old Towne Road, Charleston.* Located across the Ashley River from modern-day Charleston, Charles Towne Landing is a historical park marking the site of the first permanent English settlement in South Carolina. Comprising some 200 acres and including a large exhibit pavilion, gardens, an animal forest, and a reproduction of a sailing ship of the seventeenth century, Charles Towne Landing offers much to history-minded visitors with an interest in South Carolina's and America's colonial beginnings. For large and small groups, a variety of formal educational services are available. Short or long, formal or informal, a visit will provide a richer understanding of the early decades of South Carolina history, particularly of Charleston and the Low Country.

The Spanish and French made early, unsuccessful efforts at settlement here, but the real story begins with the English who, coming decades later, also came to stay. From their settlement on the site today marked by the Charles Towne Landing park grew the prosperous and sophisticated colony of South Carolina and that distinctive Low Country civilization symbolized by what historian Louis B. Wright has called the Venetian-like city-state of eighteenth-century Charleston.

In 1663 King Charles II, newly restored to his throne, granted Carolina to eight of his key supporters during his years of exile in France. Their names loomed large in the history of that day: George Monck, Duke of Albemarle; Edward Hyde, the Lord Chancellor of England; William, Earl of Cravan; Lord John Berkeley; his brother, William Berkeley, governor of Virginia; George Carteret; Sir John Colleton; and Anthony Ashley Cooper. It was six years before these Lords Proprietors actually were able to start a settlement, and by then it was Anthony Ashley Cooper, later the Earl of Shaftesbury, who had assumed the leading role.

Judging from the "Fundamental Constitutions" drawn up by Shaftesbury and his secretary and personal physician, John Locke, the Proprietors hoped to create in Carolina a "balanced government," with a landed aristocracy (bearing the old Continental titles of Landgrave and Cassique) ruling in conjunction with the more numerous smaller landholders. That plan eventually collapsed, but only in form. As prominent families acquired vast tracts of land and established large plantations worked by slave labor, they became in fact an aristocracy that shaped South Carolina's history for two centuries.

In August 1669, a fleet of three small ships finally set sail from England, bound for Carolina. Not all of them reached it. A storm sank the *Albemarle* in Barbados; the *Port Royal* grounded in the Bahamas. The *Carolina,* the largest ship, and a replacement sloop rented in Bermuda reached the mainland coast in the vicinity of Port Royal in March 1670. Although that was their original destination, the English were persuaded by the chief of the local Kiawah Indians and by reports of an exploratory party to settle instead on a small sheltered peninsula a few miles up the Ashley River. There they landed early in April (on May 23 a third ship, the *Three Brothers,* finally joined them), and there a total of 148 people established what became the first lasting English settlement in Carolina.

The settlement (called by the settlers Albermarle Point but soon renamed "Charles Town" by the Proprietors in honor of the King) remained at the site for ten years until, having grown much stronger, it moved across the Ashley River to Oyster Point. There the second, permanent, Charles Town grew to wealth and eminence. But the early foundation laid by the Lords Proprietors and the first settlers on the original site made later success possible, and it is that effort and that experience especially that the visitor will find richly portrayed at Charles Towne Landing.

An initial visit to the central exhibit pavilion will provide a useful overview of South Carolina's colonial history, from the austere beginning to its later years of wealth and sophistication. On the circular ramp leading to the lower level are situated large wrought iron replicas of the coats of arms of the eight Lords Proprietors who controlled the colony until 1729. Below, in the exhibit area, artifacts and illustrative displays contrast what life was like in the early years with what it became just half a century later when Charleston had grown to be one of the leading cities in colonial America.

The colonists' need to adapt to a strange natural environment demanded the practice of subsistence agriculture from the beginning. Their ambition truly to prosper soon turned them also to the great staple crops of the low country: rice, indigo (valued as the source of dark blue dye), and long-staple cotton. Lending themselves to large-scale production, these highly marketable crops and the horde of slave labor needed to cultivate them became the centerpiece of the great plantation system for which the Low Country was renowned. Here at Charles Towne Landing exhibits on rice, indigo, and cotton, including implements actually used, underscore the agricultural foundation of the colony's prosperity.

On that foundation and the trade that sprang from it, the glories of the "city-state" of Charleston eventually were built. What it was like—its theater, opera, music, and horse-racing—is suggested through a number of special exhibit techniques, including "sound pods" offering samples of period music and illustrations on large moving belts and lighted panels. Also on display is a hand-crafted scale model of the ship *Carolina,* the largest of the three vessels to set out for Carolina from England in 1669 and the only one actually to reach Charles Towne.

But the bulk of the Charles Towne Landing park consists of history-related displays out of doors. Immediately adjacent to the exhibit pavilion the visitor will find a replica of the first experimental crop garden

Settlers' Life Area

in America. It was begun at Charles Towne in the first year of settlement at the behest of the Lords Proprietors, who wrote to their agent, Joseph West: "Planting is both our design and your interest. . . ." And so it was, though certainly not all of the crops experimented with finally rooted themselves on Carolina's plantations. The rice and indigo were enough, however, to justify the efforts. The records of flourishing (if only briefly) orange, lemon, lime, pomegranate, and fig trees, of mulberries and grapes from which grew dreams of silk production and mellow Carolina vintages, provided a colorful episode in the colony's early history.

A short walk toward the end of the peninsula reveals the site of the original fortified area at Charles Towne. Early records indicate that fear of attack by Indians and Spaniards led the early settlers to enclose and fortify by means of ditches, moats, and palisades an area of about ten acres. What can be seen today is the result of a major "dig" undertaken by historical archeologists in the late 1960s. Beginning with information supplied from the earliest known map of the town and other early records, including the reports of a Spanish spy, the excavation uncovered tell-tale traces of early abandoned settlement beneath land that, for centuries afterward, had been plantation. This original fortified area is now preserved for future archeological exploration, but to today's imaginative visitor the site will clearly suggest one of the keys to understanding the early Charles Towne and indeed all early American settlements: the insecurity of life on the edge of an awesome wilderness.

Happily, the fortifications were never put to the actual test of attack by hostile Indians or Spaniards. Instead, the local tribes were generally friendly to the English newcomers in those first years, and the threat from Spanish Florida to the South largely remained only that. As security increased and agriculture prospered, the English thus were able to turn their energies to trade with other English colonies (and, illegally, with the colonies of other European nations). Encouraged by the Proprietors, small sailing vessels plied the eastern seaboard to trade with the chain of colonies that by the late seventeenth century stretched all the way from Carolina to Massachusetts. They sailed as well into the West Indies, laden with the products of farm and forest. They returned with rum, sugar, and wine. A full-scale reproduction of the type of vessel typically used in such trade will be found just a short walk beyond the fortified area. Built in 1970, it was crafted from woods indigenous to Carolina and christened *Adventure,* a name popular for trading vessels of the period. A large ketch requiring a crew of six and capable of carrying about twenty tons of cargo, the *Adventure* is fully seaworthy and is sailed periodically in Charleston harbor. Along with a small punt meant to be towed behind the *Adventure* (fashioned from a 500-year-old cypress long and weighing 1400 pounds), it is moored in Old Town Creek. Visitors are welcome on board.

The park offers two other attractions rounding out the visitor's picture of colonial South Carolina. In a twenty-acre animal forest, trails and pathways reveal in its natural habitat much of the wildlife native to the region 300 years ago. The absence of zoo-like obstructions enables a view of raccoons, bobcats, deer, bison, and elk similar to the one that the seventeenth-century settlers once had. It is not difficult to appreciate the sense of wonder at the land's natural bounty expressed by men used to the tamer and more peopled landscape of Europe. One of them, English explorer William Hilton, wrote in the 1660s of "woods stored with abundance of deer and turkey everywhere . . . also partridges great store, cranes abundance, conies (rabbits) . . . great stores of ducks, teal, widgeon, and in the woods great flocks of parrakeeto's." Charles Towne Landing's animal forest preserves much of this feeling.

As fascinating as forest and wild game clearly were, few European settlers of the North American continent contented themselves with such natural features for long. With great energy they remade large parts of the landscape into a friendly pattern of farms and plantations. They also fashioned another landscape form that, in South Carolina, reached its zenith: the English park garden. Thanks to the work and dedication of Mrs. Joseph I. Waring, whose family, the Legarés, acquired the Old Towne Plantation in the mid-nineteenth century, the visitor today will find here one of the finest examples of such a garden anywhere. Through the eighty acres of gardens and surrounding woodland and marsh wind seven miles of bicycle and foot trails, affording easy access. Guide-driven touring cars are also available in the garden area.

No historic site fully recreates the way life was in the distant past. Nor can it. Part of that job belongs to the visitor, who must bring curiosity and some imagination to it. The visitor who comes to Charles Towne Landing thus prepared will be well rewarded. The park does not offer a perfect replica of a vanished seventeenth-century settlement, though it does preserve some of its physical artifacts in an exemplary way. But it explains, through many means, the motives and pattern of English settlement in South Carolina and suggests the reasons for its growth and change.

KINGS MOUNTAIN NATIONAL MILITARY PARK northwest of Bethany on South Carolina 161. The dominant images of the Revolutionary War include minutemen at Lexington and Concord, Washington at Valley Forge, Lafayette and Cornwallis at Yorktown. They are all images associated with the East; indeed most of the war's great engagements took place in the East, where nearly all Americans lived in the late eighteenth century. On the barely settled frontier beyond the Appalachian Mountains, Britain's Indian allies brought fear and destruction to many a lonely log cabin, but, as both sides knew, the real contest lay elsewhere. The war in the South and in South Carolina likewise was eastern, both sides contending over the population centers and the resources that made resistance possible. Therefore what happened at Kings Mountain on October 7, 1780, was special and a sharp reminder that the West had to be reckoned with. In the history of South Carolina, it is a reminder of the contentiousness and internal divisions that even then marked this place.

In the fall of 1780 the Revolutionary War was already five years old, and up to then the British appeared still to have a good chance of winning it. With the war in the North fought to a stalemate, the British turned their attention south and were rewarded at first by stunning military success—and, as they had hoped, with the rediscovered loyalty of thousands of South Carolinians. In May 1780 they received the surrender of a large American army at Charleston and proceeded quickly to reassert royal authority throughout the colony. Their victory just three months later at Camden seemed to assure their domination of the Low Country and much of the piedmont. To take fullest possible advantage of the tide in his favor, the British commander, General Charles Cornwallis, determined to enlist as many Americans as possible in a strong loyalist militia. He entrusted that responsibility to seasoned Scots veteran, Patrick Ferguson. Ferguson did not fail—at least not at first. Ranging up and down the backcountry, "Bull Dog" Ferguson (as he was called by his officers) recruited several thousand American loyalists. With them he proceeded to harry and hunt down recalcitrant patriots.

It was the kind of brutal, irregular campaign that was sure to inspire retaliation. From the mountains to the west and the thinly settled coves and valleys beyond in Tennessee, an even more irregular American militia did not hesitate to engage him. So Musgrove's Mill, Thicketty Fort, and Cedar Spring were added to the list of the hundreds of small but fierce skirmishes typical of a conflict that in many ways was a civil war. But the British still had a larger strategy: to carry the war northward to Virginia, Cornwallis' real goal. After the great British victory at Camden, the way seemed clear at least into North Carolina. Cornwallis headed

United States Monument erected 1909

for Charlotte and dispatched Ferguson's loyalist militia to protect his flank on the west and at the same time scour the mountain country for more recruits. Ferguson established headquarters at the hamlet of Gilbert Town and from there issued a stern challenge to all of the "backwater men," as he called the overmountain patriots in the West. They were to "desist from their opposition to the British arms, and take protection under his standard" or he would "march his army over the mountains, hang their leaders, and lay waste their country with fire and sword."

The men Ferguson challenged were the special products of a remote and independent civilization. Safely west of the mountains around the headwaters of the Holston, Watauga, and Nolichucky rivers, they had lived until then largely free from any but their own local authority—unthreatened and unconcerned by the war for independence raging in the East. But suddenly Ferguson's invasion threat changed all that. The time had come, they realized, to meet and end that threat before it could be carried out. That meant assembling and marching a large force eastward across the mountains, finding Ferguson and his hated Tory militia, and fighting them to the finish.

Despite the "minute-man" reputation enjoyed by these fiercely independent pioneers and by many like them elsewhere, the particular task before them required more than savage energy and the readiness to fight. Fortunately there were real leaders among them, men whose names figured largely in the early history of this region: Isaac Shelby, William Campbell, Charles McDowell. But more than any other, it was John Sevier who legend and fact most firmly tie to the Battle of Kings Mountain. As a leader, probably his only equal that day was his enemy, Patrick Ferguson.

The course that brought them together led the overmountain men from their assembling point on the Watauga River at Sycamore Shoals on a snowy five-day march southeastward to Quaker Meadows near present-day Morganton, North Carolina. Reinforcements swelled their numbers to over 1500 as they moved within striking distance of the loyalists. Ferguson was not, however, to be taken by surprise. Informed by spies of the Americans' presence and fearing their superior numbers, he fell back toward the main body of Cornwallis' army. Just thirty-five miles from safety, he found the spot where he believed he could successfully turn and meet his pursuers.

The place was a ridge some 600 yards long, 60 to 120 feet wide, shaped rather like a human footprint. Its slopes were heavily wooded, its summit boulder-strewn and nearly treeless. Ferguson thought the terrain at the top offered ideal natural fortification, the open space being perfect for use of the bayonet in which he had trained his men so well. Ironically, the wooded slopes surrounding it became the perfect terrain for the patriot attackers. Hunters and backwoodsmen, they were deft with the long rifle and from the thick cover Kings Mountain obligingly provided, these marksmen took a quick and heavy toll on Ferguson's defenders, who rapidly found themselves exposed on all sides. Their bayonet charges and their disciplined volley fire were a poor match for the Indian tactics so skillfully employed by the mountain men. Ferguson, who no doubt saw disaster coming, nonetheless fearlessly rallied his officers and refused to surrender. With two horses shot from under him and blowing his shrill silver whistle to the last, he finally fell, a bullet in his head, both arms broken, his hat and clothing shot to tatters.

The Tories soon surrendered, though their foes, who were not professional soldiers but aroused citizens filled with all the hate and revenge that civil strife can bring, for a time refused them quarter and continued the killing. Later, after it was over and the toll counted—just 28 mountain men killed to 225 loyalists, all the rest of whom were wounded or captured—the strategic meaning of Kings Mountain became plain for all to see. Even though the patriot army soon dissolved back into the western wilderness, Ferguson's defeat badly frightened Cornwallis. Only a week later the General retreated south from Charlotte, effectively stalling his earlier plans. As a result, the American forces in the Carolinas found the breathing space they so badly needed.

Of the effect of Kings Mountain on the king's cause in America, one

Englishman later wrote that it "so encouraged the spirit of rebellion in the Carolinas that it could never afterward be humbled." It was, as he said, "the first link in a chain of evils that followed each other in regular succession until they at last ended in the total loss of America." Today, this quiet place still evokes the spirit of the brave men—all Americans, save Ferguson—whose war cries and death blows here changed the course of the American Revolution.

FORT SUMTER NATIONAL MONUMENT Charleston Harbor, Charleston. What state has been more contentious than South Carolina? Few if any, believes historian Louis B. Wright. Early in its history, South Carolina was a sparring ground for French and Spanish explorers. During the Revolutionary War, native-born patriots and loyalists turned it into a bloody battleground. After independence the new state of South Carolina displayed old divisions between the Low-Country aristocracy and the upcountry democracy. Later, divisions between blacks and white, populists and Bourbon conservatives, sustained the reputation of a contentious commonwealth—made so by overweening individualism and the sin of excessive pride.

As they have been among themselves, so have South Carolinians have sometimes been with others. Fort Sumter, one of the most famous historic places in America, commemorates the most noted display of that contentiousness. The occasion was nothing less than the beginning of the Civil War. It seemed fitting that South Carolina, the home of John C. Calhoun and other philosophers of secession, should be the general scene. It seemed fitting too, that Fort Sumter, a symbol of federal authority, should provide the immediate setting.

It is one of history's little ironies that things once deemed highly desirable later become, to the same people, quite the opposite. So it was with a federal fort in Charleston Harbor. During the War of 1812 when the British Navy freely roamed the long and largely undefended American coastline, residents of many port cities (and their congressional representatives) clamored for better protection. Civilian and military authorities responded, recommending in 1821 that an elaborate chain of fixed fortifications be built to protect the Atlantic and Gulf coasts from seaborne attack. Some forty forts were proposed, and among those actually completed, armed, and manned, Fort Sumter (named after Thomas Sumter, a South Carolina Revolutionary War patriot) was destined to be remembered long after such places had outlived their military usefulness.

Essentially completed by 1860, it was a formidable supplement to the older Forts Moultrie and Johnson. It sat on a small sand island, located strategically at the entrance to Charleston harbor, which had been reinforced with granite from as far away as Maine. Its brick walls, five feet thick, rose nearly fifty feet above low tide. Four of its five sides, 170 to 190 feet long, were designed to carry three tiers of guns commanding all approaches to Charleston from the sea. The full battery was to number 135 guns, though when the fort first saw action in 1861 only 60 were in place. The fort included officers' quarters, enlisted men's barracks, a parade ground, and a powder magazine. A sally port opened onto a quay. The city of Charleston was three and a half miles away at the end of the peninsula.

Thus built to defend Charleston, Fort Sumter in its first test under fire was called on to defend itself from Charleston. As the Southern states drifted out of the Union during the tense winter of 1860–61, the position of federal forts and arsenals throughout the South grew ever more uncertain. A contentious South Carolina was the first to go, just before Christmas 1860. Responding to the presidential election of Abraham Lincoln, candidate of the anti-slavery and exclusively Northern Republican Party, a state convention meeting in Columbia passed without dissent the historic first ordinance of secession, declaring that "the union now subsisting between South Carolina and the other states, under the name of the 'United States of America,' is hereby dissolved." Though the leader, South Carolina was not alone for long. Within six weeks, the six other states of the lower South—Mississippi, Florida, Alabama, Georgia, Louisiana, and Texas—had left the union. Early in February, representatives of the seceded states met in Montgomery, Alabama, to draw up a constitution for the Confederate States of America.

Moves to halt the spread of secession and the drift to civil war failed. A peace convention held at the urging of Virginia (which had not yet left the union) came to nothing. And the worried South took little comfort from Lincoln's first inaugural address. Though he foreswore the use of violence and reaffirmed his intention not to interfere directly or indirectly with the institution of slavery in the states where it already existed, Lincoln also declared that secession was intolerable. "Physically speaking," he said, "we cannot separate. . . . No state, upon its own mere action, can lawfully get out of the Union." Meanwhile, Fort Sumter in Charles-

Giant cannon used to defend Fort Sumter

ton harbor threatened the crisis Lincoln said he hoped to avoid.

Most of the other federal installations scattered throughout the South had already capitulated peacefully to the Confederate states, and shortly after South Carolina's secession, Robert Anderson, the federal commander in Charleston, evacuated the older harbor defenses and withdrew his garrison to the more formidable Fort Sumter. What to do about Sumter thus became the first test of the Lincoln administration, and despite contrary advice, the new president at least appeared determined to hold it. Early in April 1861 he dispatched a relief expedition—solely, he said, to provision the fort—and he so notified the South Carolina authorities. Ever distrustful, the South Carolinians chose not to wait and demanded Major Anderson's immediate surrender. When he refused, shore batteries commanded by Pierre G. T. Beauregard opened fire at 4:30 on the morning of April 12, 1861. The bombardment continued for 34 hours before Anderson ran up the white flag; it provided a dramatic show for Charleston society, which came down to the Battery to view it. Though bloodless, the action quickly precipitated other events that made war inevitable. On April 15 President Lincoln issued a call for 75,000 three-month volunteers to suppress armed disorder. Seeing this as a commitment to coerce the South, Virginia left the union two days later and was soon followed by Arkansas, Tennessee, and North Carolina.

The long war that followed observed little of the gentlemanly etiquette that had marked the dispute over Fort Sumter. The Civil War was the first in American history to suggest the awful possibilities of "total war." It also saw the first application to warfare of some new nineteenth-century technologies: the railroad, the telegraph, the repeating rifle and the Gatling gun, and iron-clad warships. Indeed, when federal naval forces tried to force open Charleston harbor in April 1863, ironclads led the way. But not even they could retake Fort Sumter, which remained firmly in Confederate hands until the advance of Sherman's army from Georgia forced evacuation early in 1865.

Fort Sumter has never again fired a shot in anger or been forced to defend itself. At the end of the war its battered and crumbling masonry bore little resemblance to the original design, and over the years its contour was altered even further. Today, as long ago, it is accessible only by boat. Though the technology of warfare has long since passed it by, it still stands its vigil at the mouth of Charleston harbor, a moving memorial to a war begun in a contentious South Carolina that left the state, contentious still, a permanent part of the American nation.

AIKEN COUNTY HISTORICAL MUSEUM *226 Chesterfield, Aiken.* History museum housed in Old Aiken County Jail Building.
CAMDEN BATTLEFIELD *five miles north of Camden on county road just west of U.S. 521 and 601.* Where the British under Cornwallis

defeated the Americans under Horatio Gates in 1780; marked by a road-side marker and a monument.

CHARLESTON MUSEUM 360 Meeting Street, Charleston. A general museum, with natural science, art, and history, emphasizing South Carolina and the Southeast; also administers the Heyward-Washington House and the John Manigault House.

THE CITADEL Charleston. Important military college established in 1842; museum displays military artifacts and equipment.

COWPENS NATIONAL BATTLEFIELD off state 110, Chesnee. Visitor center interprets the Battle of Cowpens, 1781.

DRAYTON HALL on state 61 twelve miles west of Charleston. Called the finest example of the Colonial plantation house in the state; built in 1738.

FORT HILL Clemson University, Clemson. Antebellum home of famous South Carolina politician and statesman John C. Calhoun.

FRENCH PROTESTANT HUGUENOT CHURCH 136 Church Street, Charleston. Gothic-style church built in 1845; no longer a living congregation, but now restored.

GIBBES ART GALLERY 135 Meeting Street, Charleston. Art museum containing an excellent collection of portraits and miniatures of South Carolinians.

HISTORIC CAMDEN U.S. 521 north of I-20, Camden. Reconstructed colonial village; four restored historic houses include the Kershaw-Cornwallis Mansion.

HISTORIC CHARLESTON FOUNDATION 51 Meeting Street, Charleston. Administers two house museums: Nathaniel Russell House, 1809 and Edmonston-Alston House, 1828–38.

HISTORIC COLUMBIA FOUNDATION 1616 Blanding Street, Columbia. Foundation administers three house museums: Robert Mills House, 1823; Hampton-Preston Mansion, 1818; and Woodrow Wilson Boyhood Home, 1872.

JOHN MARK VERDIER HOUSE 801 Bay Street, Beaufort. Historic house built in 1790; displays Federal-style furnishings.

LEXINGTON COUNTY MUSEUM 230 Fox Street, Lexington. History museum depicting everyday life in Lexington County in the nineteenth century.

McKISSICK MUSEUMS University of South Carolina, Columbia. General museum specializing in South Carolina history, geology, contemporary art, the history of University of South Carolina, and Movietonews.

MIDDLETON PLACE Ashley River Road, Charleston. Remaining wing of original eighteenth-century plantation house built by the renowned Middleton family.

OLD SLAVE MART MUSEUM 6 Chalmers Street, Charleston. Located in an 1852 building where slaves were bought and sold; exhibits on the slave trade and African art and artifacts.

PENDLETON DISTRICT HISTORICAL AND RECREATIONAL COMMISSION 125 E. Queen Street, Pendleton. History museum interpreting the South Carolina upcountry.

POTTERSVILLE MUSEUM Rt, 2, Box 4, Edgefield. Specially interested in the documentation of Edgefield pottery.

THE RICE MUSEUM Lafayette Park, Front & Screven streets, Georgetown. History museum that interprets the rice culture of the Carolina Low Country.

SAINT MICHAEL'S EPISCOPAL CHURCH 80 Meeting Street, Charleston. Mid-seventeenth-century Georgian church with a large portico and a solid spire rising 185 feet.

SOUTH CAROLINA STATE MUSEUM 2221 Devine Street, Columbia. General museum with the history, natural history, art, science, and technology of the state as its focus.

SOUTH CAROLINA DEPARTMENT OF PARKS, RECREATION AND TOURISM 1205 Pendleton Street, Columbia. Administers Andrew Jackson State Park, Lancaster; Hampton Plantation State Park, McClellanville; Hunting Island State Park, Frogmore; Keowee-Toxaway State Park, Sunset; Lansford Canal State Park, Catawba; Old Dorchester State Park, Summerville; Redcliffe Plantation State Park, North Augusta; Rivers Bridge State Park, Ehrhardt; Rose Hill State Park, Union.

STAR FORT AND VILLAGE OF NINETY SIX on state 246 two and one-half miles south of Ninety Six. Site of a trading post established in 1730; remains of a British fort built in 1780.

WALNUT GROVE PLANTATION near Spartanburg. Circa 1765 Georgian-style manor house; home of Kate Moore Barry, a scout for General Morgan at the Battle of Cowpens.

SOUTH DAKOTA

BADLANDS NATIONAL PARK Interior. The struggle and the partnership between man and nature is one of the great themes in the history of the West. Nature—incredibly vast open spaces, rugged mountains, the great dome of blue sky—is very large in the region. Man's numbers were very small. Survival had not been easy for the Indian tribes who contended among themselves long before white men ever arrived in the West; it was not easy for the whites who later contended with the Indians and competed among themselves. In the Dakotas, beset by extremes of heat and cold and blessed with relatively little moisture, this has been especially true. Prairie—a sea of waving grass untouched by plow or fence—covered the region, and for centuries supported only well-adapted wildlife.

In South Dakota the prairie vastness was broken by only a few natural features. The great Missouri River on its long course down the Montana to the Mississippi enters South Dakota halfway between the northeast and northwest corners and then flows southeastward to the southeast corner of the state. Though the prairie lies on both sides of the river, social and cultural differences in time clearly distinguished the "East River" from the "West River." The river is still a dividing line. Far to the west, the pine-covered Black Hills rise forbiddingly out of the prairie. With the discovery of gold there in the nineteenth century, they became the site of much adventure and considerable controversy among the Sioux to whom they were sacred, the prospectors to whom the gold was sacred, and the army whose job was to keep the peace. The Black Hills in the twentieth century have attracted another kind of outsider as a constant stream of tourists come to savor the rugged beauty of the place, to visit old gold-rush towns like Deadwood, and to stand in awe before the great stone monuments of Mt. Rushmore. Elsewhere, nature long ago carved her own sculpture to break the prairie's sameness. Known to the Indians and then to the whites plainly enough as the "badlands," her handiwork today is preserved in the Badlands National Park. It reminds us of nature's immense and continuing power in ways that are less apparent in greener, more peopled places.

The Badlands story begins perhaps 25 to 35 million years before man arrived here. As best the geologists can tell, this was once a vast inland sea. As it slowly receded, it left behind a broad marshy plain crossed by slow-moving streams flowing down off the highlands to the west. Wet and warm, it became the home of a wide variety of plant and animal life, long since vanished. We know them by their fossilized remains, which in the Badlands constitute the world's greatest fossil bed from the Oligocene Epoch of the Age of Mammals. Some are legendary, like the fearsome sabre-tooth tigers and the dog-sized three-toed horses. Others are more exotic, like the oreodont, a small cud-chewing creature, and titanothere, a large rhinoceros-like creature. Their sojourn here was far longer than man's yet has been, but it too was fragile. As the climate changed they vanished, and as the land changed they were replaced by other creatures, some of whom still inhabit it. A once green and humid place became brown and dry as, so the scientists speculate, new dry winds from the north reduced the rainfall and evaporated the lakes and marshes. Only grass grew where once there had been swamps. Volcanic ash, probably from the Yellowstone region, added distinctive white layers to Badlands soil. Streams and small rivers still flowed down from the western highlands, but they began to cut into the soft sedimentary rock with its fossils of long extinct plants and animals. The result was the startling display of rocky pinnacles, spires, ridges, and ravines that became the Badlands. Even today the process steadily continues. Beneath the top layer of sandstone, wind or water may erode the underlying clay, leaving a cave or creating a delicate archway that itself will probably not last for many generations. The landscape is changing as much today as it did millions of years ago.

That much of the Badlands story was and is oblivious to the presence of man, who is a recent intruder. It is, therefore, "prehistory." The early human story here, of which there are no written records, is also prehistory and cloaked in mystery. One archaic Indian site is known to be 7,000 years old, and there is clear evidence that by A.D. 1000, numerous nomadic tribes, subsisting by hunting and gathering, were at least frequent visitors here. During the eighteenth century the Arikara from the Missouri River hunted as far west as the Black Hills, and around the middle of the century the Oglala and Brule tribes of the Teton Sioux moved west of the Missouri to the lands along the Bad and White rivers, north and south of the Badlands. Once a forest people, these Sioux, with horses acquired from other tribes and guns from the whites, adopted a new way of life based on buffalo hunting. The first whites to disturb them were occasional fur trappers like Jedediah Smith. They noted the land's spectacular geological features and extensive fossil beds, and at Fort Pierre on the Missouri River they established a main distribution point for trade throughout the Upper Missouri region. From there, a trail led west and south through the west end of the Badlands and eventually on to Fort Laramie in Wyoming. Wagon ruts still remain in the area.

As more whites intruded more frequently, deals were struck with the Indians who had preceded them. Treaties in 1856 and 1865 recognized the region as Indian Territory, and in 1868 the Treaty of Fort Laramie reserved for the Sioux virtually all of the land west of the Missouri in what is now South Dakota. But with the discovery of gold in the Black Hills, Indian lands steadily shrank; the land between the Cheyenne and White rivers, which they were forced to relinquish in 1889, became the location of the original Badlands National Monument, today the north unit of the national park. Conflicts with the army were com-

Castle Butte

mon as the Indians did not always go peacefully. They culminated with the Ghost Dance religion and the incident at Wounded Knee Creek on December 29, 1890, the last major clash between the tribes and the army. Several thousand Sioux of the Ghost Dance cult found refuge in the fall and winter of 1890 in the Stronghold Table area, now in the park's south unit.

In many parts of the Great Plains the end of Indian resistance prefaced the beginning of large-scale permanent white settlement. In the 1890s and early 1900s homesteaders brought thousands of acres of prairie under the plow. Between 1900 and 1910, as railroads penetrated the area, many people even tried to settle in the forbidding Badlands. Few succeeded, and those who survived the first difficult years frequently met defeat in the notorious dry years of the 1920s and 1930s. At the same time it was becoming evident that this harsh land might be valuable for other purposes. As early as 1909 the South Dakota legislature petitioned the federal government to establish a national park in the area, but it was twenty years before the Badlands National Monument was authorized. Land acquisition and road construction took another ten years. As established in 1939 the monument comprised some 150,000 acres, reduced over the years to 111,000. The South Unit, during World War II a U.S. Army gunnery range on the northwest corner of the Pine Ridge Indian Reservation, added another 133,000 acres to the monument in 1968. The national monument finally became a national park ten years later.

For today's visitor it preserves large areas of virgin prairie, exceptional geological formations, and great fossil resources. As it was to the early Canadian fur trappers who described the region as *les mauvaises terres à traverser*—bad lands to travel across—it is still a desolate land. But it is also strangely beautiful and teeming with life. On high buttes golden eagles nest their young. Clumps of cottonwood and wild rose shelter small birds and animals. Prairie dogs build their towns—and attract their predatory enemies: coyotes and badgers. There are jackrabbits and cottontails, racers and rattlesnakes. Pronghorn sheep, whitetail and mule deer timidly graze on prairie grass. Finally there are bison—once so numerous they darkened whole sections of the prairie. The largest North American land animal, they have no natural enemy except man, who a hundred years ago hunted them nearly to extinction. Today, in a different mood, he has helped to bring them back. The Badlands herd, reintroduced in 1963, now numbers about three hundred.

FORT SISSETON STATE HISTORIC SITE *southeast of Britton.* The most famous forts in the history of the West lie far beyond Fort Sisseton, cozily nestled away in northeastern South Dakota. Fort Laramie, Fort Bridger, Fort Apache, Bent's Old Fort all have about them an aura of adventure and romance, part real and part the product of free-wheeling Hollywood producers. Certain ingredients are standard to the image: a wind-swept wilderness setting, usually with mountains looming nearby; a log stockade with blockhouses, cannon, and waving flag; hard-riding cavalry troopers ever ready to charge or chase hostile Indians. Sometimes (as with a trading fort like Bent's Old Fort) there were mountain men, Mexicans, and other "exotics" whose presence lent to such places an added air of the foreign, the truly remote, the fantastic. Action too was important: these were places where brave men proved themselves and did their duty. In the movie versions, that invariably entailed fighting off Indian attacks and riding to the aid of women and children huddled in besieged wagon trains.

Thus in the popular image the fact and the fancy blurred. There were some forts, however—probably the vast majority—that did not fit the image at all and whose careers no film maker ever bothered to embellish with the ingredients of a good western. They lacked glamor and seldom knew excitement. Most are now abandoned. But it is just such ordinariness that enhances their importance. The old West—the Great Plains especially—was not nearly the romantic place we who never knew it sometimes imagine. The records left by the people who actually settled it tell a different story—a story of drabness and monotony, of a hard life in a hard place. Their success, like their hopes, was modest and required strength, endurance, and few illusions. They stuck, through good times and bad. They nurtured a lot from a little. They raised new generations. The strongest are still there.

This, the ordinary West, is evoked by a place like Fort Sisseton. Daily routine and service, not exciting events, describe it. Fort Sisseton (first named Fort Wadsworth) was established in 1864 as the Civil War still raged in the East. Government preoccupation with that conflict and neglect of its treaty obligations with the Indians led to a Sioux uprising in southern Minnesota in 1862. Much blood was spilled. To see that it did not happen again, the army planned a network of border forts to discourage further Indian unrest and to protect settlers if hostilities again broke out. Fort Sisseton was first supposed to be built on the James River, a major watering place for the huge buffalo herds that the Sioux depended on. But on the advice of scouts and fur traders who knew the eastern Dakota region well, a site on the Kettle Lakes where there was abundant water, timber, fuel, and clay was selected instead. As a result, most of the buildings were built of South Dakota materials: stone quarried in the area, bricks kilned from clay found near the lakes, oak from wooded lakeshores and coulees.

It was built by the soldiers who were to garrison it. Officers doubled as engineers and foremen; enlisted men were the common laborers, woodcutters, and quarrymen. An earthen embankment with a ditch in front took the place of a wooden stockade. Inside rose the array of buildings needed to house and service a frontier outpost. The two barracks buildings were enormous, measuring 45 feet wide by 182 feet long and designed to house two companies of soldiers (about 150 men). They were constructed of split fieldstone gathered nearby. Beginning in 1873 the South Barracks was used as a commissary where a twelve-month stock of supplies was stored for the garrison. The stable, roughly the same size, sheltered the garrison's mounts. A magazine (distinctive in its crow-step gables) stored small-arms ammunition and cannister and shot for artillery pieces. A guardhouse provided a jail. In the adjutant's office north of the magazine, this administrative assistant to the post's commanding officer kept track of the paperwork that passed back and forth between his office and the War Department in Washington. The commander himself enjoyed use of a substantial two-story brick building that at times was divided and shared by other officers as well. Quarters for married officers and their families were nearby. There

Parade ground and restored buildings

were two blockhouses, part of the standard image of the western fort, over twenty-eight feet square and built of logs; they were never called up to defend against an enemy. Of more use was the post hospital, where an army surgeon dealt with typhoid, tuberculosis, pneumonia, and an occasional gunshot wound, along with less exotic problems like frostbite and malingering. For the women and whatever troopers might be interested there was a combination library-schoolhouse, which housed in addition the post telegraph office. Outside the compound toward Kettle Lake were a sawmill, carpenter, blacksmith, and wheelwright shops, an ice house, and the kiln where thousands of bricks were made, the raw materials for which are still abundant nearby. Timber for the sawmill, however, was quickly depleted and troops had to haul logs from as far away as Sica Hollow, twenty miles northeast. The most important of the auxiliary buildings was the sutler's store or trading post, another standard feature of western military posts. The trader's was a coveted position—in such isolated garrisons he virtually monopolized the market for luxuries and supplies not furnished by the army. A clever and politic man could make a good living at it.

Most of these buildings are preserved today, thanks mainly to the combined efforts during the 1930s of the National Park Service and the Works Progress Administration. The ordinary soldiers and their families who once stood guard here are of course missing. But the records of their routine give an idea of the kind of lives they once lived in these sturdy but rude buildings. For the troopers, hard work never ended. They chopped wood and hauled water; they cut and stored ice from the lakes during the winter for use in the summer; they kept gardens and put up hay for the stock. This was all in addition to their official duties, which, though seldom involving fighting, still required training and discipline. They routinely patrolled the trails and, maintaining a show of force, deterred potentially hostile Indians. They provided security for railroad survey and construction crews who were penetrating the Dakotas in the 1870s and 1880s and escorted wagon trains of settlers and gold-seekers toward the western edge of the Dakota Territory. It was not glamorous—just necessary work.

The pay was modest, though the army then as now offered a kind of security in compensation. Under the scale in effect in the 1870s privates received $13 a month, corporals $15, sergeant majors $23; there was incentive pay for men who stayed in the service more than three years. Dakota winters were fierce, and the army issued troops special cold-weather clothing including blanket-lined greatcoats, buffalo overshoes, and woolen mittens. It was customary on frontier posts to have laundresses attached to each company to tend the washing and mending of enlisted men's clothes; every company was permitted up to four. At Fort Sisseton the role usually fell to the wives of non-commissioned officers. There was also a tailor to alter ill-fitting army-issue uniforms. Daily rations were generous if monotonous: twelve ounces of pork or canned beef, or twenty of fresh beef, or twenty-two of salt beef; eighteen ounces of soft bread or twenty of cornbread; plus peas, beans, potatoes, onions, and coffee. Post menus typically were heavy with starch and red meat: roast beef, fried pork and bacon, turnips and mashed potatoes, bread pudding, biscuits, pancakes, and molasses. For men engaged in hard outdoor work it was suitable fare—and no less varied than what many civilians then enjoyed.

After twenty-five years of service and after the frontier had moved far beyond it, Fort Sisseton, like so many other posts, was abandoned. In 1889, the year it closed, the land around it was safe and was becoming settled. But other lives awaited it. Control of the military reservation passed to the new state of South Dakota, which in the 1920s leased the remainder that had not been taken up by settlers to a wealthy Chicagoan for use as a hunting lodge. Game (except for buffalo) still abounded, and grouse, prairie chicken, wild geese, canvasback, mallard, and pheasant provided sport for city hunters and mouth-watering fare in the lodge's dining room. Restoration of the fort as an historic site was undertaken in the 1930s by the National Park Service with labor supplied by the WPA. Later a local horseman's association leased it and made good use of the splendid stables. It became a state historical park in 1959 and offers today's visitor an honest view of what the ordinary—and important—forts of the old West really were like.

DEADWOOD HISTORIC DISTRICT AND LEAD HISTORIC DISTRICT *Deadwood and Lead.* The discovery of gold in 1874 along French Creek in Dakota Territory launched perhaps the most colorful era in South Dakota history. The Black Hills gold rush brought thousands of fortune seekers to this remote area in the late nineteenth century, and the notorious personalities and dramatic events of those boom years inspired countless romantic legends of the Old West. South Dakota's gold-rush days still live at Deadwood, one of the most famous of the frontier mining cities. Now restored to its appearance during the era of Calamity Jane, Poker Alice, and Deadwood Dick, the historic city provides a fascinating opportunity to experience the excitement of South Dakota's bonanza years.

Credit for publicizing the region's rich mineral resources must go to George A. Custer of Little Big Horn fame. In July 1874 he commanded a military expedition to the Black Hills in search of new sites for fortifications. His expedition included a miner named Horatio W. Ross, who discovered gold while camped along French Creek in the Black Hills. Earlier accounts of gold in the region, some dating back to the 1830s, had gone largely unnoticed, but the report by the colorful military leader attracted nationwide attention. Despite a treaty with the Sioux Indians prohibiting prospecting activities, would-be millionaires soon invaded the territory and began staking claims. Among the first were a group of prospectors led by John Gordon. The Gordon party erected a stockade on French Creek in late 1874 but had little time to survey the region's mineral wealth before the army evicted them.. Still more gold seekers quickly took their places, however, and by 1875 thousands of miners had set up camp around the discovery site.

Then in the spring of 1876 news spread of gold strikes some sixty miles to the north in an area known as Deadwood Gulch. Less than a hundred miners could be found in the North Hills area in early 1876, but by the end of the year the number in the gulch area rose to between three and ten thousand. The first mining settlement was Elizabethton, but internal bickering led to the establishment of a new townsite, more appropriately named Deadwood. Ike Brown, Craven Lee, J. J. Williams, and several others platted the new town on April 26, 1876. Four days later, Brown and Lee opened the first saloon and store, and other entrepreneurs soon joined them. Before long, an assortment of log cabins, board shacks, and tents lined the gulch's main street. By June, Deadwood had its first newspaper, the *Black Hills Pioneer,* and the gold rush community also boasted banks, a stage station, lodge halls, various saloons and stores, and a host of other establishments to serve the mining community.

Deadwood

In the fall of 1876, Deadwood's citizens decided to establish a local government to bring order to the increasingly unruly boomtown. Deadwood already had a well-deserved reputation as a tough and rowdy mining town, overrun with saloons, gambling, and loose women. Part of the town's reputation was due to the legendary and often notorious figures popularly associated with it.

Perhaps the most famous name from the Old West associated with Deadwood was Wild Bill Hickok, the famous frontier scout and lawman. Hickok came to the Black Hills town in mid-1876 to do some serious gambling and, while absorbed in a poker game at the #10 Saloon, was murdered on August 2 by Jack McCall. Wild Bill's poker hand—black aces and eights—became known as the "Dead Man's Hand." With Preacher Smith officiating, he was buried in Deadwood's "Boot Hill" on Mount Moriah. The Preacher himself, another colorful character from the boom era, was ambushed by Indians outside town a few weeks later and was buried in the same graveyard.

Another Old West figure associated with Deadwood was Calamity Jane. Although best known for her decidedly nonladylike expertise as a scout, bullwhacker, and soldier, she apparently also had something of a local reputation as a woman of easy virtue. Among the many stories associated with her are her exploits as a pony express rider between Deadwood and Custer and her assistance to victims of a smallpox epidemic in 1878. Upon her death, she was buried beside Wild Bill Hickok on Mount Moriah overlooking Deadwood. Other legendary figures included Potato Creek Johnny, who discovered the biggest gold nugget in the Black Hills; Poker Alice, a notorious faro dealer and madam; Deadwood Dick, a black cowboy actually named Nat Love; and lesser-known characters like Kitty the Schemer, Mustache Maude, and China Mary. From such legends came Deadwood's reputation as South Dakota's most notorious boomtown.

Deadwood stood at the center of what has been described as the richest hundred square miles on earth. That reputation rests primarily on one claim: the Homestake. Fred and Moses Manuel and Hank Harney discovered an outcrop of gold-rich ore on April 9, 1876, and immediately staked claim to the Homestake Lead, as it became known. A lead, pronounced "leed," is an outcrop or ledge, and the term was used as the name for the mining camp soon established nearby. In 1877 a group of California investors bought up the Manuel and Harney claims and established the Homestake Mining Company. The new company systematically developed the rich ore deposits and expanded its control to eight thousand acres of claims. Although other mines worked out, the Homestake has remained productive and is now the oldest and largest operating gold mine in North America. It produces nearly a third of all gold mined in the United States. Lead may not have Deadwood's colorful past, but it does reflect the long-term importance of Custer's 1874 discovery to the state's growth and development.

Now designated a National Historic Landmark, the city of Deadwood looks much as it did in the days of Wild Bill Hickok and Calamity Jane. Visitors can see the #10 Saloon and other historic buildings, visit the Mount Moriah cemetery, tour the exhibits at the Adams Memorial Museum, pan for gold at the Bobtail Placer Mine, and see what underground mining was like at the Broken Boot Gold Mine. Special events include the reenactment of the trial of Hickok's killer Jack McCall and an annual rodeo. And at nearby Lead, visitors can take a surface tour of the Homestake for a more contemporary view. Together, these various opportunities bring to life a colorful and exciting chapter from South Dakota history.

ADAMS MEMORIAL HALL MUSEUM 54 Sherman, Deadwood. Artifacts from mining and frontier days, including "largest [gold] nugget in the world" and gun collection.
AGRICULTURE HERITAGE MUSEUM South Dakota State University, Brookings. Includes material on homesteading, farm machinery, claim shanty.
BUECHEL MEMORIAL LAKOTA MUSEUM St. Francis Indian Mission, St. Francis. Rosebud and Pine Ridge Sioux ethnographic materials, including early photographs.
CENTER FOR WESTERN STUDIES Augustana College, Sioux Falls. Local western art and Native American art, including Alfred Ziegler bronzes and Herbert Fisher watercolors; research collections.
CENTRAL CITY MINING TOWN Central City. Foundations and a few surviving structures from the 1870s mining town.
CRAZY HORSE MEMORIAL five miles north of Custer off U.S. 16. Giant sculpture (641 feet long and 563 feet high) of Sioux chief, being carved; visitors able to view sculptor Korczak Ziolkowski at work.
DACOTAH PRAIRIE MUSEUM 21 S. Main Street, Aberdeen. General museum with pioneer and Indian artifacts, crafts, and some art.
DAHL FINE ARTS CENTER 713 Seventh Street, Rapid City. Art museum known for its 200-foot cyclorama showing history of the United States; with regional prints as well.
FORT MEADE on state 34 about two miles east of Sturgis. Parade ground, stone stables, and other buildings constructed during the life of the fort, 1878–1944; military center during Wounded Knee unrest; now veterans' hospital.
FORT RANDALL just off U.S. 18 on west bank of the Missouri River below the southwestern corner of Fort Randall Dam, across from Pickstown. Site of fort established in 1856; now only stone shell of the 1875 chapel, cemetery, and ruins of foundations and cellars remain.
INGALLS HOUSE 210 Third Street, W., De Smet. Clapboard house built 1887; childhood home of Laura Ingalls Wilder, author of *Little House on the Prairie.* Privately owned.

LA VERENDRYE SITE Third Avenue near Third Street, Fort Pierre. Where French explorers buried a lead plate in 1743 to note their attempt to find the Northwest Passage; marker on site and lead plate in Robinson Museum, Pierre.

MINNILUSA PIONEER MUSEUM West Boulevard between Main Street and St. Joe, Rapid City. Displays on Black Hills and western Dakota history, including natural history and fur trapper era.

MOUNT RUSHMORE NATIONAL MEMORIAL Keystone. Famous granite carving of the heads of four American presidents: George Washington, Thomas Jefferson, Abraham Lincoln, and Theodore Roosevelt.

OAHE MISSION SCHOOL AND CHAPEL west side of Missouri River atop east end of Oahe Dam. Congregational church, built 1877, moved to the top of the largest earthen structure in the United States.

OVER MUSEUM University of South Dakota, Vermillion. Regional history, ethnology of Plains Indians, and contemporary Sioux art.

PINE RIDGE AGENCY Pine Ridge. Center of the Ghost Dance activities of 1890 that resulted in the Battle of Wounded Knee: now mostly modern buildings.

PRAIRIE VILLAGE Madison. Forty restored buildings from late 1800s and early 1900s, with furniture, steam tractors, threshing machines, and other equipment depicting plains life.

ROBINSON MUSEUM Memorial Building, Pierre. Exhibits on the Plains Indians, white settlement, military life, and industry; the Verendrye Plate.

ROCHFORD Pennington County. Ghost town on site of gold discovery of 1876 that was active until the 1880s.

ROSEBUD AGENCY Rosebud. Agency serving the Brule Sioux since 1870s.

ROUBAIX Lawrence County. Small town originating in gold rush of 1876 and in operation until the 1930s.

SIOUX INDIAN MUSEUM AND CRAFTS CENTER Rapid City. Historic and contemporary art, with a crafts shop and tours.

SIOUXLAND HERITAGE MUSEUM 200 W. Sixth Street, Sioux Falls. Folk arts, oral history, and other regional history of the Dakotas.

SLIM BUTTES BATTLEFIELD state 20 about two miles west of Reva. Monument and markers where force under General George Crook attacked Sioux village after battle of Little Big Horn in 1876, killing Chief American Horse.

SOUTH DAKOTA MEMORIAL ART CENTER Medary Avenue at Harvey Dunn Street, Brookings. South Dakota art of the 1800s and 1900s.

SOUTH DAKOTA STATE HISTORICAL SOCIETY Memorial Building, Pierre. Research collections on Dakota and genealogy.

SPEARFISH HISTORIC COMMERCIAL DISTRICT portions of Main, W. Illinois, and Fifth streets, Spearfish. Turn-of-the-century buildings in town founded in the 1876 gold rush.

SPIRIT MOUND just west of state 19 about eight miles north of Ver-

million. Where natives believed devils lived; a site visited by Lewis and Clark in 1804; now private farming land.

WAY PARK MUSEUM *Fourth Street and Rushmore Road, Custer.* Located in an 1875 log cabin, one of first permanent buildings in the Black Hills; originally located a short distance away.

WOUNDED KNEE BATTLEFIELD *secondary road about sixteen miles northeast of the town of Pine Ridge, on Pine Ridge Reservation.* Site of the last battle of the Indian wars, where more than 150 Sioux and 25 white soldiers were killed; with markers.

YANKTON HISTORIC DISTRICT *bounded by Marne Creek and Fourth Street, and including both sides of Cedar and Mulberry streets, Yankton.* Nineteenth-century residences in the territorial capital of Dakota.

TENNESSEE

ROCKY MOUNT Piney Flats. In the late eighteenth century, Tennessee stood on the western frontier of the new nation. A central issue in that early period was the relationship of the transmontane frontier settlements to the mother state, North Carolina. Resolution of conflicting claims came only with the establishment of the Southwest Territory in 1790 and statehood for Tennessee in 1796. The most significant symbol of this pivotal period in the state's history is Rocky Mount, the log house in Washington County that served as the first capitol of Tennessee and the first territorial capitol west of the Allegheny Mountains. Preserved today as a state historic site, Rocky Mount commemorates Tennessee's territorial period and effectively interprets everyday life on the eighteenth-century frontier.

Rocky Mount stands at the fork of the Holston and Watauga rivers, the heart of the earliest permanent settlement in Tennessee. William Cobb was not in the first group that arrived in the Watauga Valley in 1790, but he, his father, his brother, and their families came later that same year from their homes in eastern North Carolina. The Cobbs settled in present-day Washington County near William's sister and her husband, Henry Massengill, one of the founders of the Watauga community. Between 1770 and 1772, William Cobb erected the two-story nine-room house that he named Rocky Mount, a reference to the limestone outcroppings on his property. Constructed of white-oak logs hewn, notched, and chinked with clay, the house featured a gabled roof with oak shingles. The stair rail was walnut, but the mantels, panelling, and other interior woodwork were pine. Rocky Mount's glass windows were a rarity on the frontier and reflected the status and wealth of the house's owner, who owned a number of slaves and considerable property in the region. In the decades that followed the house's construction, the Cobbs' hospitality became well known and visitors to Rocky Mount included Daniel Boone, John Sevier, and Andrew Jackson—who stayed there for six weeks while awaiting a license to practice law in the nearby town of Jonesborough. According to tradition, Cobb even provisioned the frontier soldiers that passed through the valley in 1780 on their way to the Battle of Kings Mountain, a turning point in the War for Independence in the South.

When the North Carolina legislature established Washington County in 1777, William Cobb served as justice of the peace. He also helped lay out Jonesborough, the state's oldest town, and served in several minor offices. But in contrast to his brother-in-law Henry Massengill, he did not become involved in the controversial Watauga Association, an attempt to establish self-government in the region in 1772. He also apparently did not take part in establishing the State of Franklin in 1784. Residents of the Holston-Watauga area set up the state after North Carolina ceded its western lands to the federal government. Although North Carolina repealed the cession shortly thereafter, the overmountain settlers proceeded with plans to organize a state government and secure admission to the union. Failure to gain recognition from the federal government and internal dissension brought the venture to an end after 1786, but tension over the statehood issue continued until the North Carolina legislature enacted a second cession law in December 1789. The next spring Congress accepted the transfer of land and, on May 26, 1790, created the Territory of the United States South of the River Ohio, or the Southwest Territory.

The legislation establishing the new territory provided for government under the provisions of the Northwest Ordinance of 1787, with an amendment to permit slavery. The ordinance called for the federal appointment of a governor, a secretary, and judges, who would act as the territory's governing body. For the influential position of governor, President George Washington appointed William Blount, a wealthy North Carolina politician and land speculator with extensive holdings in the new territory. Blount had campaigned actively for the appointment, which was also sought by John Sevier, General Anthony Wayne, George Mason, and others. Blount, however, knew Washington from his service as a North Carolina delegate to the Constitutional Convention of 1787 and therefore had an advantage over the other candidates.

On October 23, 1790, Governor Blount arrived at Rocky Mount and decided to establish his headquarters there. He may have chosen Rocky Mount because of the Cobbs' well-known hospitality or the two former North Carolinians may have had common friends. The governor began his duties by calling together citizens of the area and explaining what territorial status meant. He then established the boundaries for Washington County and appointed local officials, retaining Cobb as justice of the peace. He repeated the procedure in Sullivan, Greene, Hawkins, Davidson, Sumner, and Tennessee counties, the other areas of significant settlement. With the basic framework of the territorial government firmly in place, he returned to Rocky Mount in December.

For eighteen months Rocky Mount served as the capitol of the Southwest Territory. Then in March 1792, Blount established a permanent capitol at White's Fort, which he renamed Knoxville in honor of Secretary of War Henry Knox. Blount's home there served as the territorial capitol until June 1, 1796, when Tennessee became the sixteenth state in the union. This second territorial capitol is open to the public as an historic house museum.

Sometime between 1795 and 1797, ownership of Rocky Mount changed from the Cobbs to the Massengills. In the years that followed the house became a stop on the Baltimore-to-Memphis stagecoach route and even served as a post office from 1838 to 1847. The Massengills retained ownership throughout and made several alterations to meet their family's needs. Interest in preservation of the structure began in

Rocky Mount, Tennessee's first capitol

the 1930s, but it was 1959 before the state of Tennessee finally purchased the property from the family. Restoration began the following year. Weatherboarding and recent additions were removed, a chimney was rebuilt, and walls were stripped to the original pine panelling. The fully restored structure was then furnished in a style appropriate to the late eighteenth century. Original furniture includes a Brewster chair, a huntboard, and a Hepplewhite chest. The Massengill family provided additional funds for reconstruction of the kitchen and scullery and a slave cabin and for the construction of the Massengill Museum of Overmountain History. Open to the public since 1961, Rocky Mount is administered by the Rocky Mount Historical Association. Current activities include guided tours, exhibits on regional history, school programs, a library, craft days, and a variety of special events and programs that bring to life Tennessee's frontier heritage.

THE HERMITAGE *on U.S. 70 North, twelve miles east of Nashville.* No figure more clearly symbolizes the frontier theme of Tennessee's history than Andrew Jackson. Born in a log cabin in rural North Carolina, Jackson rose from relative obscurity as a Middle Tennessee lawyer, businessman, and farmer to become a national military hero, standard-bearer of the Democratic party, and seventh president of the United States. Historians often refer to the period from 1824 to 1840 as the "age of Jackson" in recognition of the dominant role he played as champion of the common man and as a pivotal figure in restructuring both the American political system and the office of the presidency. Jackson's home, the Hermitage, stands today as a monument to him and the central role he played in shaping the history of antebellum America.

Jackson lived and worked in the Nashville area for about sixteen years prior to his purchase of the Hermitage property in 1804. During those early years he married Rachel Donelson Robards, established himself in the community as a lawyer and farmer-businessman, and tried his hand at politics. He proved particularly able in the last regard, moving quickly from the Tennessee state constitutional convention in

Columned portico of Jackson's Hermitage

1796 to the United States House of Representatives, the United States Senate, and finally the state judiciary in 1798. His business ventures proved less successful, however, and apparently necessitated the move in 1805 from a fine frame house at Hunter's Hill to the first Hermitage, a rather modest two-story log structure located about twelve miles east of Nashville. The house contained only three rooms, but a trio of one-story cabins nearby accommodated visiting relatives and friends such as Aaron Burr and James Monroe. The Jacksons lived in this first Hermitage for nearly fifteen years. Here they raised their adopted son and several wards, and here Rachel Jackson waited for her husband's return from the military exploits that made him a national hero. Today only a fragment of the main house and one of the smaller cabins remain on the Hermitage grounds.

By 1818 Jackson had decided to build a home more befitting his newly won prominence and his success as a cotton planter and businessman. His wife selected a site not far from the log Hermitage, and construction began the next year on a two-story house. The simple design provided four rooms on each floor opening off central hallways. For their new home, the Jacksons purchased fine furniture and silver in New Orleans and even hired an English landscape designer to lay out a formal garden. Over the next decade, they entertained numerous family, friends, and dignitaries—including the Marquis de Lafayette, who stopped at the Hermitage during his tour of the United States in 1825. More historically significant were the visits of Jackson's friends and confidants to plan strategy for his 1828 presidential race. Old Hickory, as many of his admirers called him, met frequently with John Overton, John H. Eaton, William B. Lewis, and others instrumental to his victory in that bitterly fought contest. The efforts of this new generation of political leaders to organize the electorate in 1828 constituted the first evidence of the emergence of a modern American party system at the national level.

The triumph in the presidential race was soon overshadowed by the death of Rachel Jackson on December 22, 1828. Only a simple stone slab marked her grave in the corner of the garden until 1831, when Jackson had a domed and columned tomb erected as a memorial to his beloved wife. At his death, he was buried beside her in the tomb that still stands southeast of the Hermitage.

In January 1829 Jackson left the Hermitage for Washington and his inauguration as president. His nephew Andrew Jackson Donelson and Donelson's wife Emily accompanied him. Donelson served as his private secretary, and his wife assumed the duties of First Lady in the Jackson White House. The Donelsons' home, Tulip Grove, was completed in the mid-1830s on a tract of land adjoining the Hermitage. This two-story brick structure remains today as part of the Hermitage complex.

Although he spent most of his time in Washington during his eight years as president, Jackson's ties to the Hermitage remained strong. In 1831, two years into his first term in office, he had the house remodeled and enlarged with one-story wings on the east and west sides and porches on the north and south facades. He left day-to-day details, however, to his adopted son, Andrew Jackson, Jr., and his son's wife, Sarah. They had moved to the Hermitage shortly after their marriage in 1831 and occupied the bedroom across from Jackson's on the first floor. Jackson had just returned to Washington from a visit with them at the Hermitage in the summer of 1834 when he received news that a fire had gutted the house. Reconstruction began early in 1835, using the stable core structure and rebuilding the interior according to the 1831 floor plan. Alterations included a two-story columned portico across the front facade, which was painted white to cover the smoke damage from the fire. The furniture on the first floor had been rescued from the fire and was put back in place after the reconstruction, but Sarah Jackson purchased new furniture for the second floor. The house and furnishings remain essentially the same today.

Jackson returned to the Hermitage in 1837 at the conclusion of his second term as president. He continued to correspond with his political associates and enjoyed the company of his family for the remaining eight years of his life. He died June 8, 1845 at the Hermitage. His bedroom remains as it was at his death.

Andrew Jackson, Jr. inherited the house and 1,050-acre plantation. Not a particularly wise businessman, Jackson was forced to sell the house in 1856 to cover his debts. The state of Tennessee purchased it with the idea of donating it to the federal government for use as a national military academy. Sectional rivalry and the Civil War thwarted this plan, and the Jacksons ended up living on at the Hermitage as caretakers for the state. Jackson died in 1865, but his widow continued to live in the house until her death in 1887. Their son Andrew Jackson III and his family were living in the Hermitage in 1889 when, at their suggestion, the Ladies' Hermitage Association was established to take responsibility for the preservation of the historic structure. The state deeded the house and surrounding acreage to the group, which continues to maintain the properties that now comprise the Hermitage complex. In addition to the remnants of the first Hermitage, the Hermitage, the Jacksons' tomb, and Tulip Grove, properties include several out-buildings, a slave cabin, the old Hermitage Church, and a small museum. Together they provide insight into both the public career and the private life of one of Tennessee's most significant historical figures.

VICTORIAN VILLAGE DISTRICT *Adams and Jefferson streets, Memphis.* In the last half of the nineteenth century, the city of Memphis survived war, epidemics, and financial reverses to emerge in 1900 as Tennessee's largest urban center. The survival and growth of the city in the face of adversity reflected the determination of its core of business elites to make Memphis a commercial center for the cotton South. As evidence of their optimism and faith in the city's future, these men built impressive homes along fashionable Adams and Jefferson avenues. Several of these homes have been preserved in the Victorian Village historic district and together constitute the most effective symbol of the entrepreneurial talent and business leadership crucial to Memphis' emergence in the twentieth century as a major metropolitan center.

Memphis' growth and development in the nineteenth century depended on the cotton economy. Initially only a minor entrepot on the Mississippi River, the West Tennessee settlement became a transportation center for the Mid-South cotton trade and by the 1850s the principal river port between St. Louis and New Orleans. The coming of the railroad in that same decade augmented the city's value to regional commerce, and by the time of the Civil War Memphis claimed to be the biggest inland cotton market in the world. The Civil War and Union occupation temporarily disrupted the Memphis cotton trade, but after the war cotton again assumed its central role in the city's economy.

Both before and after the war, the city's cotton trade depended on factors or commission merchants, who served as the middlemen between the planters and the markets. These men acted as the planters' agents, marketing their crops and providing the credit and supplies essential to continued operation. The latter functions provided the catalyst for local banking and the wholesale and retail grocery business. The profit from these activities proved substantial, and cotton factors and their associates ranked among the wealthiest and most influential of the city's residents by the late 1860s. When the city hosted the Commercial Convention of 1869, Memphis business leaders viewed with optimism the continued growth of the cotton economy in the coming decade.

The 1870s, however, proved all but disastrous for the bluff city. In 1876, the city felt the impact of a nationwide financial panic and suffered through a yellow fever epidemic, but those trials paled in comparison to the events of 1878. Another epidemic of yellow fever struck the city in the early fall of that year. Although many, particularly the wealthy, fled the city, over five thousand Memphians died, nearly thirty percent of those that remained. The consequent disruption of economic activity aggravated the city's deteriorating financial standing, and on January 31, 1879, Memphis declared bankruptcy and surrendered its charter back to the state. When rumors spread that the city would repudiate its debts, prominent Memphians organized as the Committee of Fifteen to come up with a compromise that would salvage the city's standing in national financial circles. The committee also developed a plan to clean up the city and eliminate the sources of disease. Concerted action by the city's business leadership was essential to the resumption of economic growth and development in the coming decade.

Cotton continued to dominate the city's economic life in the 1880s and 1890s. Ensconced in the Cotton Exchange, founded in 1873, and in the warehouses of Front Street's Cotton Row, the city's factors and commission merchants controlled the cotton trade and hence retained leadership of the business community. Their influence extended to banking, the wholesale-retail grocery business, and allied industries and services such as Merchants' Cotton Press and Storage Company, the leading compress and warehousing firm, founded in 1870. When the South Memphis Land Company began developing a suburban industrial site at the turn of the century, cotton processing and storage still dominated. Despite proposals in the late nineteenth century to diversify the city's economic base, business leaders remained convinced that cotton was the key to the city's future.

The men who ran the cotton firms, banks, grocery houses, and allied cotton businesses ruled the city's social as well as economic life. They dominated the social register and consolidated their positions by interfamily marriages. Many of them built fashionable homes along Adams and Jefferson avenues, away from the worst of the city but only seven or eight blocks from the Front Street cotton market. Some even built their homes with towers, from which they could watch for incoming steamboats and other signs of activity along Cotton Row. Although many of these homes gave way to the wrecking ball of urban renewal, a few still stand along Adams and Jefferson avenues between Neely and Orleans streets. Ranging in style from Neo-Classic to Late Victorian, the houses of the Victorian Village historic district reflect the varied tastes of their owners and convey the wealth and influence of the city's business elite in the last half of the nineteenth century.

The oldest house in the district is the Massey house at 664 Adams Avenue. The one-story frame house dates from 1844 to 1849 and is one of three pre-1850 houses surviving in the city. Neo-Classic features include Doric columns and a pedimented porch. Further east at 707 Adams stands the Pillow-McIntyre house, built between 1852 and 1856. This

*Mallory-Neely house
at 652 Adams*

two-story Greek Revival mansion features characteristic Corinthian columns supporting a large pedimented porch. General Gideon Johnson
Pillow acquired the house in 1876. Pillow, a Mexican War hero and
former Confederate general, practiced law in the city with former Tennessee governor Isham Green Harris until the former's death in the
1878 yellow fever epidemic. The next owner was Peter McIntyre, a
prominent merchant married to Ella Goyer, daughter of Charles Wesley
Goyer, who lived at 690 Adams.

Prominent Memphis businessmen built the Victorian mansions that
flank the Massey house. Banker Isaac B. Kirtland erected the house at
652 Adams Avenue in about 1855. The second owner was Benjamin
Babb, a cotton factor, who lived in the imposing brick and stucco residence from 1864 to 1883. He sold the house to James C. Neely, one of
the city's most influential merchants and cotton factors. Neely remodeled the house in 1885, adding a third floor and a front tower. After
their marriage in 1900, his daughter Frances ("Daisy") and her husband, Barton Lee Mallory, resided in the three-story Italianate Victorian
house. Mallory was vice president of W. B. Mallory and Sons, a wholesale grocery firm established by his father, and was a principal figure in
the South Memphis Land Company, the Memphis Compress and Storage Company, and the Memphis Merchants Exchange, a commodities
market organized in 1881. After Mrs. Mallory's death in 1969, the house
was given to the Daughters, Sons, and Children of the American Revolution. With its original 1890s interior and furnishings, the house provides a rare opportunity to experience the Victorian lifestyle.

On the other side of the Massey house stands the Fontaine house.
Prominent banker and businessman Amos Woodruff built this three-

story French Victorian mansion in 1870. Architects Edward Culliatt Jones and Mathias Harvey Baldwin designed it with a floor plan nearly identical to that of the Neely-Mallory house, which Woodruff apparently admired. The house is named after its second owner, Noland Fontaine, a partner in Hill, Fontaine and Company, the city's largest cotton and supply firm. Fontaine purchased the house in 1883 and hosted there some of the city's most lavish parties—including a banquet in 1892 celebrating the completion of the bridge across the Mississippi, the first constructed below St. Louis. The house is now part of the James Lee Memorial, administered by the Association for the Preservation of Tennessee Antiquities.

To the east of the Fontaine house stands the Lee house. The oldest part of this house dates from 1848, when lumberman William Harsson erected a two-story farm home outside the city limits. His son-in-law, Charles Wesley Goyer, added on to the original structure in 1865 and again in 1871, completing the present three-story front facade. Jones and Baldwin, the architects for the Fontaine house, also designed this high Victorian addition. The house was sold in 1890 to Captain James Lee, Jr., of the Lee Line, one of the most successful shipping firms on the Mississippi River in the late nineteenth century. The APTA also owns this house.

Across the street from the Fontaine house at 679 Adams stands the Mollie Fontaine Taylor house. Noland Fontaine erected this high Victorian brick structure between 1886 and 1890 as a wedding gift to his daughter at her marriage to Dr. William W. Taylor. Further west stands the Eldridge Wright house, a two-story frame Victorian house named for a recent owner. At 688 Jefferson Avenue stands the Wright carriage house. This structure apparently was erected prior to the Civil War as a farm home but was converted after 1866 to a carriage house to serve a larger home owned by Luke E. Wright, a prominent Memphis lawyer and diplomat. His home has been demolished. Two other noteworthy Victorian houses stand at 669 and 671 Jefferson Avenue. Nearby at 756 Jefferson stands the Lowenstein house, built in 1890–1891 by merchant Elias Lowenstein. Also close by, at 700 Poplar Avenue, is St. Mary's Episcopal Cathedral and Chapel, the cathedral church of the diocese since the late nineteenth century.

The Victorian Village historic district preserves the only significant remnant of late-nineteenth-century Memphis. These imposing homes illustrate the lifestyle of the city's business and social elites in the Victorian era and symbolize the entrepreneurial leadership that established the city as the urban center of the Mid-South at the turn of the century.

AMERICAN MUSEUM OF SCIENCE AND ENERGY *Tulane Avenue, Oak Ridge.* Science and technology museum at the site of the world's first full-scale nuclear reactor and the nation's principal atomic research laboratory.

ANDREW JOHNSON NATIONAL HISTORIC SITE *Depot Street, Greeneville.* Includes 1830s frame tailor shop, two-story brick house, and grave of Andrew Johnson, controversial Tennessee politician who became the nation's seventeenth president at the death of Abraham Lincoln in 1865.

BELLE MEADE MANSION *Harding Road at Leake Avenue, Nashville.* Nineteenth-century Greek Revival residence, once the center of the nation's largest thoroughbred farm.

BLOUNT MANSION *200 W. Hill Avenue, Knoxville.* Tennessee's second territorial capitol, erected in 1792 as the office and home of William Blount, the first governor of the Southwest Territory.

CADES COVE OPEN-AIR MUSEUM *Great Smoky Mountains National Park, Gatlinburg.* Preserves early water-powered grist mill and other structures typical of early-nineteenth-century Southern Appalachia.

CARTER HOUSE *1140 Columbia Avenue, Franklin.* Residence erected in 1830 and used as the Union command post during the Battle of Franklin, November 30, 1864.

CHILDREN'S MUSEUM OF OAK RIDGE *461 W. Outer Drive, Oak Ridge.* Museum collections and programs focused on Appalachian life.

C. H. NASH MUSEUM-CHUCALISSA *1987 Indian Village Drive, Memphis.* Archeological museum and reconstructed prehistoric Indian village.

COUNTRY MUSIC HALL OF FAME AND MUSEUM *4 Music Square East, Nashville.* Includes museum that chronicles the development of country music and Studio B, one of the city's (and country's) most historic recording studios.

CRAGFONT *Highway 25, Gallatin.* Two-story Georgian house erected between 1798 and 1802 for General James Winchester, the first speaker of the Tennessee legislature and founder of Memphis.

FORT DONELSON NATIONAL MILITARY PARK *Highway 79, Dover.* Commemorates the Confederate defeat on February 16, 1862, by federal forces under the command of General Ulysses S. Grant.

FORT LOUDOUN STATE HISTORICAL AREA *Vonore.* Reconstruction of important frontier garrison from the pre-Revolutionary War period.

JACK DANIEL DISTILLERY *Lynchburg.* Nation's oldest distillery complex in continuous use.

JAMES KNOX POLK ANCESTRAL HOME *301 W. 7th Street, Columbia.* Residence erected in 1816 for the family of James K. Polk, who served the state as congressman and as governor before his election as the eleventh president of the United States (1845–1849).

LOOKOUT MOUNTAIN *Chattanooga.* Site of the Battle above the Clouds, an important Civil War engagement, and now part of the Chickamauga and Chattanooga National Military Park.

MARBLE SPRINGS *Neubert Springs Road, Knoxville.* Log home erected

1783–1815 for John Sevier, a leader in the movement for self-government in the Tennessee territory and the state's first governor.

MEMPHIS PINK PALACE MUSEUM *3050 Central Avenue, Memphis.* Cultural and natural history museum focusing on Memphis and the Mid-South.

MISSISSIPPI RIVER MUSEUM *Mud Island, Memphis.* Museum complex focusing on the culture and history of the Mississippi River Valley.

RED CLAY STATE HISTORICAL AREA *Cleveland.* Site of the last capitol and council ground of the Cherokee nation in the East prior to the 1832–1838 removal.

RUGBY COLONY *State Highway 52, Rugby.* Cooperative community established in 1880 by British author and reformer Thomas Hughes.

RYMAN AUDITORIUM *116 Opry Place, Nashville.* Constructed in 1889–1892 as a revival tabernacle but most famous as the former home of the Grand Ole Opry.

SHILOH NATIONAL MILITARY PARK *Shiloh.* The site of an important victory in General Ulysses S. Grant's campaign to establish Union control of the Mississippi River.

STONES RIVER NATIONAL BATTLEFIELD *Old Nashville Highway, U.S. 41, Murfreesboro.* Site of important Civil War engagement, December 31, 1862–January 2, 1863.

TENNESSEE STATE CAPITOL *Capitol Hill, Nashville.* Impressive Greek Revival structure erected between 1845 and 1859 to house the state government.

TENNESSEE STATE MUSEUM *Polk Cultural Center, 505 Deaderick, Nashville.* Exhibits on the history and culture of Tennessee.

TIPTON-HAYNES LIVING HISTORICAL FARM *Erwin Highway 19 W., Johnson City.* Outdoor museum complex that includes a two-story main house, slave quarters, and various outbuildings from the late eighteenth century and a law office erected about 1850.

TRAVELLER'S REST MUSEUM HOUSE *Farrell Parkway, Nashville.* Two-and-a-half-story brick residence built in the early nineteenth century by Judge John Overton, a prominent lawyer and political associate of Andrew Jackson.

TEXAS

PANHANDLE-PLAINS HISTORICAL MUSEUM   2401   Fourth   Avenue, Canyon. The Great Plains are one of the truly striking features of the American landscape. Stretching in a broad belt from Montana and North Dakota south to Texas, they define where the West begins. Their vast treeless expanse sweeps gradually upward to the eastern ramparts of the Rocky Mountains, a juncture of landforms as dramatic as any in the world. The land is flat or undulating, drained by shallow rivers that flow east and south to the Mississippi and the Gulf of Mexico. The climate is semi-arid, the contrast in seasons typically extreme. Hot summers, freezing winters, and fierce winds chasten the region. Such a land supports life grudgingly. For centuries nomadic tribes followed the wildlife, which followed the grass. By the mid-nineteenth century, the new American nation had pushed to the plains' eastern edge, where many a settler and his family waited, bound for some promised land.

For most of them, the promised land lay much farther west, and the Great Plains were just an obstacle to be crossed en route there. From the reports of earlier explorers, Americans had an image of the plains as "The Great American Desert," a place unfit for human habitation. Thus on to Utah, California, and Oregon they hurried, leaving on the plains only wagon ruts and the graves of the dead.

Until then the process of settling the continent had proceeded in a more or less orderly fashion. One region was settled before people moved on west to the next. The process took place in gentle increments, not all of equal length. It took nearly 200 years, for instance, before settlement east of the Appalachian Mountains was ready to spill over into the great interior valleys of the Ohio and the Mississippi. But between the American Revolution and the Civil War it was possible to conceive of the Americans as on a rapid march westward, settling and civilizing everything in their path. The pattern held until they reached the plains, which, though well traveled over, were generally settled after places farther west.

That process of later settlement and the natural and Indian history that preceded it are the subjects of the Panhandle-Plains Historical Museum in Canyon, Texas. The high plains reaching northward from the Texas Panhandle through parts of Oklahoma, Kansas, Colorado, and Nebraska are the Great Plains in pure form. They rise to an elevation of some 3900 feet above sea level. Only grasses grow on their windswept vastness; only structures built by men punctuate their flatness. Life there has never been easy, and maintaining a balance with nature, today as in the past, is the key—and a constant challenge.

Exhibits at the Panhandle-Plains Historical Museum interpret this continuing process from prehistoric times to the present day. All the groups of men who have ever lived here have depended ultimately on

*Main
museum
building*

the kinds of flora and fauna this dry land would support. Some types grew naturally, such as the rich prairie grasses that prompted early visitors to visualize the region as a sea of waving grass. Well adapted to the dry climate, they supported a surprising population of wild things, from the lordly buffalo and lithe antelope to prairie dogs and prairie chickens. The animal population rose and fell and moved around to nature's rhythms. Dependent on the grass which nature grew just so much of, its numbers were limited and subject to hardship and sudden death. Natural history exhibits graphically depict these forces.

Indians were the high plains' first human inhabitants. They have inhabited the Panhandle-Plains region probably for 12,000 years. Most of that time the tribes were nomadic hunters who followed the game, though agriculturalists with a more settled way of life were known to have existed along some streams and rivers. In the museum's Hall of the Southern Plains Indians, visitors can glimpse the culture of the Cheyenne, Comanche, Kiowa, and Arapaho who once lived here. Exhibits include life-size replicas of Indian dwellings and artifacts depicting how these peoples dealt with their harsh environment.

Their demands on it were in fact small. But so were their numbers, and the Indians eventually gave way before the compelling force of another civilization. The cattlemen who came next saw the land differently and produced from it very different results. The Hall of Ranching suggests what these were. Cattle had been in Texas long before the 1870s and 1880s, the peak of the range-cattle business. Cattle and Spanish missions had spread across Texas together; as early as the American Revolution thousands of head of cattle ranged on haciendas on either side of the Rio Grande, especially in the low chaparral between the Rio Grande and the Nueces. Later the cattle moved north. After the Civil War, when the railroads running west into Kansas opened lucrative eastern markets to western beef, enterprising Texans made the range-cattle business into something from which legends grew. But the Texas trinity of mustangs, longhorns, and cowboys was fact, not legend. On the rich grasses and open range of the Panhandle, cattle flourished and fortunes were made. It did not last, however. Ranchers overstocked the range and destroyed the grass, and eastern tastes changed to favor better beef than what trail-driven sinewy longhorns could provide.

Cattle of course would still be raised in Texas—by the millions—but after the 1880s they no longer would have the plains to themselves. By the turn of the century the farmers had arrived. For the first time, the sod was broken and the land fenced, and with hard work and much patience thousands of new pioneers made the land yield new kinds of wealth. Their disputes with the cattlemen over fencing of the open range are famous, but in time both came peacefully to share this high dry place. Along with the farmers and their families came the towns. Not wild and woolly places like Dodge City and Abilene, these were the domestic creations of ordinary folk who were settling in. In the Panhandle-Plains region few towns were even founded before 1890, and their schools, churches, retail blocks, and grain elevators foretold a new and more lasting chapter in the history of the high plains.

The state of Texas made it easier for citizens to buy public land, and railroads and land promoters did their best to lure people here. Some came from East Texas and the eastern United States; others from farther afield. Clinging to each other, Poles, Germans, German-Russians, Czechs, and Scandinavians dotted Northwest Texas with communities—actually "folk islands"—that to this day preserve much of the Old World culture. The "Panhandle Town" exhibit depicts typical town life as it emerged around the turn of the century when farming was beginning to displace large-scale cattle-raising. The exhibit is an actual replica of a town, with five streets and fifteen full-size buildings furnished with period artifacts.

Thus the Panhandle-Plains Historical Museum interprets the history of this high plains region as part of a continuing process. The relation of man to nature has always been a basic part of that process. Nature has not been generous here, which is why in the history of western settlement settlers came here later than to places much farther away. When finally they did come, they learned what their predecessors too had had to know: partnership with nature would yield more than war with her. Some of the details of that partnership have changed with changing markets and new technologies. The necessity for it has not.

SPINDLETOP MUSEUM *Lamar University, Beaumont.* Spaciousness—the sheer expanse of a physically enormous state—is one of the great themes of Texas history. But for all its great size, much of the land of Texas is inhospitable. Though East Texas is green and well watered like the Lower South, Texas farther west is dry and forbidding. East or west, it took time to settle such a vast place. Despite their popular hell-for-leather, larger-than-life image, most Texans for many years built up their state as others built up theirs: slowly, steadily, and, as Texas historian Joe Frantz relates, always willing to pray for miracles but not really expecting any.

Pots of gold at rainbow's end are rare anywhere, anytime. Though nature endowed America more richly than she did many lands, much of that endowment required application of much human talent before it became economic wealth. True windfalls have been relatively few. One of the most famous was the discovery of gold in California in 1849. Another was the discovery of oil under the Spindletop dome in Texas in 1901.

That the oil was in Texas was especially fitting. It gave to Texas spaciousness a new dimension; great wealth overnight joined great space in Texas history. It had always been possible to coax wealth from Texas' thousands of square miles and countless quarter sections, and some did so. But oil was different. From it wealth flowed faster and with less nurture. The risks and rewards therefore were more enormous than ever before. The process began near Beaumont, Texas, on the very first day of the twentieth century, and it quickly changed the way that Texas looked and in time the way that America lived. Today some of what it first looked like is recaptured in the Spindletop Museum and reconstructed Gladys City Boomtown, operated by Lamar University in Beaumont.

In the late nineteenth century petroleum geology was still an infant science, but what knowledge there was about where oil might be found said the Gulf Coast was not the place. Since the 1860s America's major oil-producing region had been in Pennsylvania, where Edwin L. Drake had drilled his pioneer well in 1859. The geology there and the geology of East Texas could hardly have been more different, so many experts claimed there could be no oil under Beaumont. It took a local real-estate man with an educated hunch and considerable persistence to prove otherwise. Patillo Higgins had long suspected that beneath Spindletop Hill, where cracks in the ground emitted gaseous vapors and sulfurous water, lay a vast pool of oil. To find out he formed a partnership with others who owned land on the hill and began the Gladys City Oil, Gas, and Manufacturing Company (its namesake, Gladys Bingham, was a student in Higgins' Sunday School class at the First Baptist Church of Beaumont). Thinking big, Higgins drew up plans for the elaborate model city he hoped to build there, and of course he drilled for oil.

But the drilling technology was not adequate to the local geology. The hill was actually a large salt dome with a rock cap. To get below the cap required drilling through layers of quicksand and gumbo to depths far greater than had been necessary in eastern oilfields. Three dry holes and much frustration resulted. Higgins seemed on a fool's errand. But he would not give up and searched far afield for the drilling know-how that might release the oil he still believed was there. He found it through the help of an Austrian immigrant and mining engineer, Anthony F. Lucas, who agreed to pay for new drilling in return for a ninety percent share in the partnership. At first Lucas too turned up a dry hole, and he went for help to the Pittsburgh drilling firm of James

M. Guffey and John H. Galey. Guffey secured $300,000 backing from Philadelphia banker Andrew W. Mellon, and together Guffey and Galey hired the Corsicana-based drilling team of Allen, Curt, and Jim Hamill to get on with the work.

They began in October 1900, but by Christmas still had not struck oil. Spindletop's quicksands were a constant problem, though by a new technique of introducing mud into the hole they were able to stabilize it and to lubricate their rotary drilling bit. On January 10 they had reached a depth of about a thousand feet, and as they had done often before they withdrew the drill bit to change it. What followed had not happened before: the drill pipe itself began to rise out of the hole straight up through the top of the derrick. A thousand feet, some six tons of it, rose up and fell back to the ground in great sections, wrecking much of the drilling equipment as it came. There was a great roar of escaping natural gas—and then the oil. The drilling derrick was eighty-four feet high, and the geyser of thick greenish-black oil reached a hundred feet above that. The "Lucas Gusher" spewed out of control for nine days before the Hamills succeeded in capping it. The flow probably measured 80,000 to 100,000 barrels a day, creating a colossal mess and a serious fire hazard but also giving clear notice of what really was down there.

Lucas Gusher, Spindletop

The word spread fast, and overnight Spindletop Hill sprouted a forest of oil derricks and a bedlam of shanties and buildings that bore little resemblance to Higgins' paper-planned city. (In two years the population of Beaumont itself soared from 9,000 to 50,000.) Higgins had been vindicated, however, even though he did not number among the millionaires created by Spindletop. Within a year more than 400 wells had been sunk; in short order between 500 and 600 oil companies were chartered. Not all lasted, and as the field's production peaked in 1903, a gutted market drove the price of crude oil down to just three cents a barrel. Fortunes were more easily lost than made, and by 1908 many felt that Spindletop had played out. It had not. In 1925 the little-known Yount-Lee Oil Company of Beaumont brought in a successful well on the flank of Spindletop and over the next five years pumped some fifty million barrels. In the late 1940s the formation began to be tapped for vast sulfur deposits up to then ignored. Gas too was harvested.

From Spindletop grew some of the world's greatest petroleum companies. Guffey's oil company later became Gulf. Magnolia Petroleum became Mobil, the Texas Company Texaco. Sun Oil still keeps its original name. Exxon, the largest, also traces its ancestry to Spindletop. Spindletop and other places like it were destined to make the production of petroleum the biggest industry in Texas. In West Texas it became possible to ride for 150 miles and never lose sight of oil derricks. In the east, gas flares turned night to day. Texas led the nation in oil production by 1928, pumping a quarter-billion barrels; by 1951 it pumped a billion. And despite the corporate giants that flourished here, so did many independent producers of modest means who were responsible for eighty percent of new discoveries.

The ultimate effect it all had on Texas is apparent in a city like Houston and the brash free-swinging confidence of the men—many of them oilmen—who have built it. "Wealth is meant to be used in calculated risks," writes Joe Frantz, "and if it's lost, so what? The once-wealthy entrepreneur who is broke knows he will rise again, and (uniquely) his acquaintances also think he will. . . . He may own them next month."

It is not therefore really so great a distance from the weathered wooden shanties and oil derricks of the reconstructed Gladys City Boomtown to Houston's sleek glass towers and booming business activity. Both sprang from Texas' special windfall: oil. Oil clearly made Texas in the twentieth century a different sort of place from the one it was becoming in the nineteenth. It also made the state even greater in the eyes of the rest of the nation than its size alone ever had. Some Americans no doubt resented that. But for Texans used to spaciousness, it seemed natural enough.

LYNDON B. JOHNSON NATIONAL HISTORICAL PARK *Johnson City.*
One of the most enduring and endearing beliefs about America is that the path to the highest office in the land is open to all comers, no matter how lowly their origins. We are proud that in America power is not

reserved for members of a privileged caste, class, or party. Neither wealth nor family name, we believe, is a relevant qualification for the presidency. On the contrary, humble beginnings bestow special favor. The president who has moved from log cabin to the White House is proof that opportunity is real, and that character and performance can transcend early hardship. Probably the most popular image of this deeply held national faith is that of the young Abraham Lincoln reading by the light of a fire in his family's wilderness cabin.

There is much truth in the image. Except for the "Virginia Dynasty," a ruling aristocracy if ever America had one, few American presidents have come from families whose wealth, education, and influence might be expected to produce figures large in public life. Though in recent times those who have become president have been men of some financial substance, their backgrounds generally have been anything but privileged. The log cabin and the firelight may be gone, but other symbols of ordinary origins have been an important part of the modern president's public image. Many nations routinely enshrine their great men, but America's fascination with their birthplaces and boyhood homes is something special.

Lyndon B. Johnson, the thirty-sixth president of the United States, was born and raised a Texan. The places in Texas where he was born and grew up and where later he kept his home reveal something both about the private man and about the nation he served as a public one. The Lyndon B. Johnson National Historical Park, two separate locations fourteen miles apart, documents Johnson's lifelong connection with Texas.

Johnson's western frontier roots were real and enduring. His forebears first came to the region in the 1860s when his great-uncle Tom and his grandfather, Sam, began a cattle-driving business. Not farmers or ranchers themselves, these men drove other men's cattle north from the open Texas ranges over the legendary Chisholm Trail to the railheads in Kansas. Until the competition gathered, the profits were good. Later, as conditions changed, Sam Johnson's nephew and former ranchhand bought the property and made it into a working cattle ranch. To the original dogtrot log cabin he added a two-story frame house (destroyed by fire in 1918) and a smokehouse. James Polk Johnson died young, at forty, but his success and involvement in the local affairs of Blanco County lived after him; he was the founder and namesake of Johnson City. At the Johnson Settlement, these and other buildings of the period and an exhibit center recapture much of what the Texas ranching life once was like.

In Johnson City itself, Lyndon Johnson's own boyhood home has been restored and with an adjacent visitor center preserves the actual setting of Johnson's growing up in the 1910s. It is a modest white clapboard house like thousands of others all across America. Johnson's parents, however, were exceptional: Sam Ealy Johnson, Jr. was a self-reliant and ambitious man who served as a Texas state legislator, from whom Lyndon learned some of his first lessons about political life. His mother, Rebekah Baines Johnson, was a rarity for that time and place: a college-educated woman. She was also a devoted mother who imparted to Lyndon, his brother, and three sisters the virtues of hard work and the value of education. Johnson's formal education began at the local schoolhouse in 1912 when he was just four. Later he taught high school and worked his way through Southwest State Teachers College in San Marcos.

From then on he learned by doing, and his record became increasingly a public one. He first went to Washington in 1932, as secretary to a Texas congressman, and quickly discovered that he thrived in public life. The mid-1930s saw him state director of the National Youth Administration, one of Franklin Roosevelt's New Deal agencies, and in 1937 he was elected to a vacant seat in the United States House of Representatives. Except for naval duty during World War II, he stayed in the House until 1949 and then moved up to the Senate. It was as a young senator in 1951 that Johnson and his wife acquired the house that over the next two decades became famous as the LBJ Ranch and the Texas White House.

Located along the banks of the Pedernales River fourteen miles west of Johnson City, it had belonged to Johnson's aunt and uncle. When Johnson acquired it from them, the "big house" needed much work. But over the years it was remodeled and expanded to meet the demands of a prominent public man. Henceforth Johnson thought of it as home; his widow still lives there. It is also the heart of the other unit of the Johnson historical park, which straddles the banks of the Pedernales.

Visits begin on the side of the river opposite the LBJ Ranch at a visitor center in the Lyndon B. Johnson National Historical Park. From there bus tours depart. Though it is not open to the public, the ranch house is on the tour route. It is not hard to imagine times in the 1960s when, as the Texas White House, this rambling wooden building was the scene

Texas White House

of incredible activity. But when he came here as senator and later as chief executive, Johnson came to relax as well as to work. He made of the place a working cattle ranch and took much pleasure in tending it. He also took great joy in the rolling Hill Country itself, and the visitor here will not fail to see why.

This is also the site of Johnson's birthplace, a small farmhouse that has stood by the Pedernales since 1889. It was reconstructed as a guesthouse in 1964 just as he was beginning his presidency. He served in that office until 1969, through some of the most tumultuous years of American history, and when he retired to this lovely place he was older than his years and had well earned his rest. He died four years later and was buried in the family cemetery on the banks of the river beside his parents, grandparents, aunts, uncles, and family friends.

Together, the several parts of the Johnson historical park tell the story of one American who made the trek from obscure and humble beginnings to great fame and power. To know that story is also to know something else. Though Johnson was born in the twentieth century, not that many years separated him from real frontier events. In 1908, the year of his birth, the last great cattle drive out of the Hill Country was just eighteen years in the past; the last Indian battle in Blanco County, just thirty-six years; admission of Texas to the Union just sixty-three years. Johnson literally was close to the formative years of his community. Obviously, for someone from a place older than Johnson City, such ties were more rare. But the larger truth it points to applies as much to the native of Massachusetts or Virginia as to the man from the Texas Hill Country.

Americans like their presidents at least to appear to be people like themselves, even if in fact they are quite different. For years, to be like the people was to be or once to have been close to the land and the life of the soil. That has changed, but not the fundamental requirement that those who would be president must be close to the common experience of the nation—whatever that happens to be. However Johnson the president ultimately will be judged, Johnson the man was close to that experience for his time. For that reason there will probably be no more presidential parks quite like his—with its ranch house, log cabin, chuck wagon, and herds of Hereford cattle.

ALAMO *Alamo Plaza, San Antonio.* Established in 1718 as San Antonio's first mission, San Antonio de Valero; site of famous battle for Texas independence.

ALIBATES NATIONAL MONUMENT *southwest of Fritch on the Canadian River.* Flint quarries from about 9000 B.C. and ruins of pueblos built A.D. 1250–1450.

AMON CARTER MUSEUM OF WESTERN ART *3501 Camp Bowie*

Boulevard, Fort Worth. Collection of American paintings, focused on the works of Remington and Russell.

ANTIOCH MISSIONARY BAPTIST CHURCH *313 Robin Street, Houston.* Built 1875–1879 and one of the oldest buildings in downtown; home of city's oldest black congregation.

ASHTON VILLA *2328 Broadway, Galveston.* Italianate residence constructed in 1859 for an important community leader.

CHAMIZAL NATIONAL MEMORIAL MUSEUM *800 South San Marcial, El Paso.* An historic site with exhibits and theater of the performing arts dedicated to the exchange of ideas between Mexico and the United States; commemorates the peaceful settlement of boundary dispute between the United States and Mexico.

CONFEDERATE AIR FORCE MUSEUM *Harlingen International Airpark.* Exhibits fifty-eight airworthy aircraft from World War II era; air show each year in October; displays of aircraft and military artifacts.

ELISSA *Pier 22 near the Strand, Galveston.* An iron barque built in 1877 and now on the National Register of Historic Places; restored as an operational sailing ship and maritime museum.

FORT CONCHO NATIONAL HISTORIC LANDMARK *213 East Avenue D, San Angelo.* Twenty-two original structures built from 1867 to 1889, including barracks, headquarters, chapel, schoolhouse, and officers' quarters; exhibits reflect the role of the Army in the settling of West Texas.

FORT DAVIS NATIONAL SITE *state 17 just north of town of Fort Davis.* Restored fort dating from 1854 and the largest in Texas; bugle calls and a formal retreat ceremony daily.

FORT LANCASTER *off U.S. 290 ten miles east of Sheffield.* Established as frontier fort in 1855 and key post on the Chihuahuan Trail; ruins of old fort and interpretive center with exhibits.

FORT McKAVETT STATE HISTORIC SITE *Fort McKavett.* Many of original structures of fort established in 1852; interpretive center with exhibits.

FORT LEATON *on farm-to-market 170 four miles east of Presidio.* Remains of a private fort built of adobe, occupied from the 1830s until 1927.

FORT RICHARDSON *U.S. 281, southern edge of Jacksboro.* Most northerly Texas fort, built to guard against Indians; restored, with a museum.

FORT WORTH STOCKYARDS *from Twenty-third to Twenty-eighth street, between Houston and railroad tracks, Fort Worth.* Partially restored remains of the livestock complex that established the city as the leading livestock center of the Southwest in the late 1800s and early 1900s.

GRANBURY *thirty-six miles southwest of Fort Worth.* Historic town square and restored opera house.

GOVERNOR HOGG SHRINE STATE PARK *518 South Main Street,*

Quitman. Honeymoon cottage and museum devoted to the Jim Hogg family, commemorating the 1890s reform governor and his philanthropist daughter Ima.

GOVERNOR'S MANSION 1010 Colorado Street, Austin. An 1856 Greek Revival building that was the state's second home for governors.

HUECO TANKS El Paso vicinity, twenty-five miles east on highway 62-180. Three granite outcrops forming natural cisterns, with pictographs of Indians; a stop on the Butterfield Overland Mail.

INSTITUTE OF TEXAN CULTURES 801 South Bowie at Durango Boulevard, San Antonio. An historical research institute of the University of Texas, with guided tours and gallery talks.

JFK MEMORIAL Main and Houston streets, Dallas. Near the site where President John F. Kennedy was assassinated on November 22, 1963.

JEFFERSON HISTORIC DISTRICT Jefferson. Fifty-six commercial and residential buildings, dominated by one-story Greek Revival style.

KING WILLIAM DISTRICT San Antonio. Affluent German residential district; primarily Victorian homes, built 1870–1900.

LYNDON B. JOHNSON SPACE CENTER NASA Road 1, Houston. Collection of spacecraft and flight artifacts as well as exhibits about American space flight program.

MISSION SAN JOSE 6539 San Jose Drive, San Antonio. Queen of the Missions, established 1778; Renaissance ornamental facade with famous rose window; exhibits relate to use of mission.

MISSION PARKWAY San Antonio. Three missions founded between 1720 and 1731 echo the Spanish heritage of the area: Mission Nuestra Senora De La Purisma Concepcion at 807 Mission Road, Mission San Francisco De La Espada on Espada Road, and Mission San Juan Capestrano at 9101 Graf Street; built as fortifications as well as churches.

MISSION ESPIRITU SANTO Goliad State Park, Goliad. Reconstructed on the ruins of original mission; exhibits on Spanish, Indian, and Republic of Texas history.

MOSQUITO FLEET BERTH Pier 19, Galveston. Site of wharf since 1818 and traditional port of the shrimpboats of Galveston.

MUSEUM OF TEXAS TECH UNIVERSITY and RANCHING HERITAGE CENTER 4th Street at Indiana, Lubbock. Large interpretive complex, housing collections that focus on the environment, history, and culture of the Southwest.

NAVARRO HOUSE 228 South Laredo Street, San Antonio. Historic building, home of one of the two native-born Texans to sign the Texas Declaration of Independence.

OLD SAN ANTONIO BREWERY 110 Jones Avenue, San Antonio. 1895 neo-Romanesque industrial complex; now restored, housing San Antonio Museum Association Museum of Art.

SUNDAY HOUSE 406 West San Antonio, Fredericksburg. Typical of town residences used by ranchers and farmers on weekends when attending church or when a member of the family needed to be near the doctor.

TEXAS CAPITOL *Congress and Eleventh streets, Austin.* One of the largest nineteenth-century state capitols, made from Texas granite and other native stone.

TEXAS MEMORIAL MUSEUM *2400 Trinity, Austin.* History and natural history museum, with exhibits on paleontology, archeology, and the history of Texas.

U.S.S. TEXAS *state 34 southeast of Houston, San Jacinto State Park.* Built 1911–1914, the only surviving United States battleship with reciprocating steam engines; served as Eisenhower's flagship on D-Day, 1944.

VEREINS KERCHE *112 West Main, Fredericksburg.* Replica of German church built in 1847 and used as a church, school, and meeting hall.

WASHINGTON-ON-THE-BRAZOS STATE PARK *Washington.* Park contains Star of the Republic Museum and Anson Jones Home, residence of last president of the Republic of Texas.

WINEDALE HISTORICAL CENTER *of the University of Texas at Austin, four miles east of Round Top, Farm-to-market Road 2714.* Tours of restored Texas German farmstead; hand painted wall and ceiling decorations in a Greek Revival farmhouse; outbuildings.

UTAH

TEMPLE SQUARE *Salt Lake City.* Mormon leader Brigham Young selected the site for Temple Square on July 28, 1847, only four days after arriving in the Valley of the Great Salt Lake. The haste with which Young made that decision reflected his and his followers' determination to proceed with their mission of building a "Kingdom of Zion" in the Utah desert. In the years that followed, the ten-acre square not only provided a reference point in laying out the new city but also became the hub of community life and the revered center of the Church of Jesus Christ of Latter-day Saints. Still the heart of the Mormon community, Temple Square stands as a monument to Mormon determination, industry, and achievement in establishing a new home in the intermountain West.

The first structure erected on the square in 1847 was a bowery or open-air shelter of poles, branches, and brush. As the size of the community increased, a new larger bowery was built on the grounds, and in December 1851 work was completed on the first tabernacle, a sandstone and adobe edifice with a sloping, shingled roof. A third bowery to the north handled the overflow from the various religious services and public meetings held at this tabernacle prior to 1867. For the sacred ordinances and ceremonies of the church, the Mormons erected in 1854 the Endowment House. This two-story adobe building provided a temporary location for these religious activities until 1889, three years before the completion of the Temple. The other project completed on the square during its first decade was the erection of a wall around the entire site. Constructed between 1852 and 1855, the sandstone and adobe wall stood fifteen feet tall and extended a full city block in each direction. Four wooden gates, later replaced with iron grillwork, provided entrances from the streets that bordered the square—South Temple, West Temple, North Temple, and Main streets. The wall still stands as a reminder of that first decade of settlement and construction.

From the first, Young's plans for Temple Square centered on the construction of a "temple of our God," which he had seen in a vision when he selected the site in 1847. He decided on the size, the general shape, and some details for the structure but left the design details to Truman O. Angell, a church architect who had helped build earlier temples at Kirtland, Ohio, and Nauvoo, Illinois. After several years' delay, the four cornerstones were put in place on April 16, 1853, the twenty-third anniversary of Joseph Smith's organization of the church. Although original plans called for adobe and sandstone construction, church leaders decided that granite would be more durable. That decision slowed construction considerably, for the enormous stone blocks had to be hauled by oxen twenty miles from a quarry at Little Cottonwood Canyon. A proposal to dig a canal to ease the burden fell through, but the construction of the Utah Central Railway provided an even better solution.

The completion of spurs from the main line to the quarry and to Temple Square in 1873 made it possible finally to speed up construction. In 1877, the year Brigham Young died, the walls stood twenty feet tall. Angell died in 1887, and Young's son Joseph Don Carlos Young took over the project. The capstone was finally put in place on April 6, 1892. Upon completion of the elaborate interior, dedication ceremonies were held on April 6, 1893, forty years after construction began.

The Temple measures 186 feet by 118 feet, and the tallest spire reaches 210 feet in height. The sixteen-foot-wide foundations extend sixteen feet into the ground, and the walls taper from a thickness of nine feet at the base to six feet at the top. The basic style is Gothic, but with Romanesque and classical details. The most notable features are those that reflect Mormon theology and organization. Brigham Young proposed the two sets of three spires, the shorter west set representing the Aaronic Priesthood and the taller set to the east representing the Melchizedek Priesthood. Atop the tallest spire, the center one on the east, stands a twelve-and-one-half-foot-tall statue of the angel Moroni, who according to Mormon doctrine appeared before Joseph Smith in 1823 and revealed to him the location of the gold plates upon which were written the Book of Mormon. Cyrus E. Dallin, a Utah-born sculptor, fashioned the statue of hammered copper overlaid with gold leaf. He also sculpted the bronze figure of Brigham Young that stands at Main and South Temple streets, the southeast corner of the square. Stone carvings on the exterior illustrate various Mormon concepts and beliefs. For example, carvings of the sun, moon, and stars represent the three

Aerial view of Temple Square

degrees of glory to be rewarded after death. Such details enhance the structure's significance as the symbolic focus of the Mormon church. Because it is used for sacred ordinances and ceremonies, the Temple is not open to the public.

A second tabernacle was erected west of the Temple between 1863 and 1867. The basic concept for the building came from Brigham Young, but the actual construction reflected the architectural and engineering talents of William H. Folsom and Henry Grow. The latter's experience in bridge building proved essential in constructing the huge elliptical dome. The unusual roof rests on forty-four cut sandstone pillars at the perimeter of the structure. Otherwise, the dome is supported by an elaborate wooden lattice truss framework similar to that used in building suspension bridges during the 1860s. No nails or iron were used in constructing the framework, only wooden pegs or dowels and rawhide bindings. The building was completed in October 1867 in time for the semiannual meeting of the General Conference of the Church. In contrast to the Temple, the tabernacle is open to the public and has been used for a variety of functions, including political speeches, pageants, and concerts by the Utah Symphony. It is perhaps best known as the home of the Mormon Tabernacle Choir. The Sunday morning program of the 375 member choir was first broadcast on radio on July 15, 1929, and is the oldest continuously broadcast noncommercial program in the history of the medium. The building also houses one of the finest organs in the world. Joseph Ridges, an English carpenter and cabinetmaker, used pine logs hauled three hundred miles from southern Utah to build the tabernacle's first organ in the 1860s. Over the years it has been rebuilt and improved several times but retains some of the original cabinetry and pipes. The tabernacle's unique design makes it an architectural and engineering landmark, and its exceptional accoustical qualities have assured it a pivotal role in Utah's cultural history.

The third historic building in Temple Square is the Assembly Hall, erected in 1880 on the site of the first tabernacle. This semi-Gothic structure was designed by Obed Taylor and constructed of granite blocks reputedly left over from the construction of the Temple. The building has four gables, with ornamental spires atop each gable and at each corner. It was constructed and is still used as a non-sectarian place of worship.

The grounds also include several monuments and memorials that relate to Mormon history. East of the Assembly Hall is the Sea Gull Monument. Erected in 1913, this monument commemorates the gulls that flew in from the Great Salt Lake in 1848 and devoured the crickets that had nearly ruined the Mormons' first grain crops. To the south stands a memorial to the Handcart Pioneers of 1856. South of the temple stand memorials to Joseph Smith, the first Prophet and President of the church, and his brother Hyrum Smith, the Patriarch, both of whom were murdered by an anti-Mormon mob in Carthage, Illinois, in 1844.

To the east stands a monument to the "Three Witnesses to the Book of Mormon." Another monument southeast of the North Visitors Center commemorates the restoration of the Aaronic Priesthood by John the Baptist to Joseph Smith and Oliver Cowdery on May 15, 1829. Two visitor centers also provide exhibits and programs that focus on the Mormon experience.

Salt Lake City's Temple Square stands today as an impressive symbol of the Mormon experience. No other site so clearly reflects the tenacity and individuality of the church's members or so ably commemorates their achievements in establishing a new home in the Utah desert.

CAMP FLOYD STATE HISTORICAL SITE one-half mile south of *Fairfield.* The arrival of federal troops in Utah in 1858 broke the relative isolation that Mormon settlers had enjoyed for a decade. Although not the first outsiders to venture into the Mormon stronghold, the soldiers, officers, and various camp followers who settled at Camp Floyd constituted the first sizable gentile community in the territory. Furthermore, the establishment of the installation demonstrated Washington's determination not to allow Utah to continue to pursue a path inconsistent with that of the rest of the nation. Although the troops withdrew after three years, the episode marked the beginning of an era of adjustment and accommodation that culminated in the integration of Mormon Utah into the larger national experience. The Camp Floyd State Historical Site preserves the remnants of the installation and commemorates these pivotal developments in Utah history.

In 1857, President James Buchanan ordered troops sent to Utah Territory to quell rumored plans of a Mormon insurrection against the federal government. Although the veracity of the president's informants was questionable, a demonstration of federal authority did seem advisable to many Washington leaders, given the Mormons' unorthodox beliefs and practices. Polygamy was less acceptable than slavery to many mid-nineteenth-century Americans. Thus in May 1857, General Winfield Scott issued orders for the Utah Expedition.

General W. S. Harney, the commanding officer of the Department of the West, initially took charge of the expedition, but duties in troubled Kansas necessitated shifting command to Colonel Albert Sidney Johnston in August 1857. Altogether, some 2,500 troops were assembled, including the Fifth and Tenth Infantry, the Second Dragoons, and the Fourth Artillery. Along the way they were joined by another thousand civilians, including sutlers, teamsters, and laundresses.

The Mormons also made plans. They had had too many terrifying encounters with anti-Mormonism in New York, Ohio, Missouri, and Illinois to sit back and wait for events to unfold. Brigham Young put the territory under martial law and then met with other leaders to develop a defense strategy. The elders of the church and the officers of the Nauvoo Legion, the territorial militia, agreed on the importance of taking the initiative before the federal troops arrived. Pooling resources,

Camp Floyd Cemetery

they outfitted 1,100 "raiders" to harass and delay the army expedition. These guerrilla tactics proved effective and forced federal authorities to make some basic concessions. Presidential amnesty and a pledge that the army would not disturb Salt Lake City relieved some fears, but the Mormons still faced the establishment of a federal army installation within their Kingdom of Zion.

Johnston and his troops finally arrived at Salt Lake City on June 26, 1858. They found the territory's largest city virtually uninhabited, its residents under orders from the church to avoid any contact with the intruders. From there the troops proceeded south about forty miles to Cedar Valley, a location that provided access to both Salt Lake and Provo, the territory's second largest city. Johnston ordered a permanent camp set up at Fairfield, a small town founded a few years earlier by John Carson and six other Pennsylvania Mormons. Lieutenant Colonel D. Ruggles laid out the installation, including camp headquarters, living quarters for officers and enlisted men, and the necessary storehouses, stables, corrals, workshops, and the like. Construction began in July, and on November 9, 1858, the post officially opened. Named Camp Floyd in honor of Secretary of War John B. Floyd, the installation brought nearly 3,500 soldiers and civilians into the small Mormon community and transformed it virtually overnight into the territory's third largest city.

Despite the Mormons' worst fears, the army did not wreak havoc and violence. For the most part, its activities were confined to escorting wagon trains through the territory, chasing down outlaws, and pacifying Indians in the area. Mutual suspicion did lead to occasional incidents of violence between individuals, but church leaders were more concerned about the long-term effects of the gentile presence. Soon after the troops arrived, the first challenge to Mormon hegemony came with the publication of *Kirk Anderson's Valley Tan,* the territory's first gentile (and blatantly anti-Mormon) newspaper.

Critics could be dealt with, but Mormon leaders found it more difficult to combat the deleterious effect of the gentile community on community morals. Gamblers, prostitutes, and assorted other purveyors of leisure activities accompanied the troops into Utah and set up shop in Fairfield and eventually even in Salt Lake City. One count found seventeen saloons in "Frog Town," as Fairfield became known.

Yet at the same time, the Mormons profited significantly from the army's presence. Some found employment as carpenters and mechanics, and others supplied the adobe bricks used in constructing most of the camp structures. The Mormon church took its share of the profits as well through the sale of lumber from church-owned mills. Others sold grain, fuel, hay, livestock, and produce or bartered for surplus army supplies, particularly manufactured goods that were scarce in the isolated western territory. The more enterprising actually set up business. The Walker Brothers established a general store at the camp in 1859 and went on to become influential figures in Utah's mercantile and financial communities. In short, the installation stimulated the essentially stagnant Mormon economy and established the basis for more extensive entrepreneurial activity in succeeding years.

Command of Camp Floyd shifted to Colonel Philip St. George Cooke in 1860. Cooke had led the Mormon Battalion in the Mexican War and thus proved more acceptable to territorial leaders. When the Civil War proved a greater threat than polygamy, plans proceeded for the abandonment of Fort Crittenden, as it was named after Floyd's desertion to the Confederate cause. The first surplus sale had been held in July 1859, and Cooke disposed of the remaining supplies and equipment after he took command. The biggest sale came in May through July 1861, when four million dollars' worth of supplies sold for only a hundred thousand dollars. Meanwhile Cooke also cut the number of troops, leaving about seven hundred men. Then after razing the cabins and other buildings, Cooke and the last of the troops abandoned the Utah installation on July 27, 1861. The Fairfield-Camp Floyd population had reportedly reached seven thousand in 1860, but by September 1861 only eighteen families remained.

Development of the Camp Floyd State Historical Site began in 1959. The park focuses on the restored old commissary, the old cemetery, and the restored Stagecoach Inn. The latter structure was erected by Fairfield founder John Carson to house prominent visitors to the camp. Built on the site of the Carson family's house, the two story adobe and frame structure became a major stop on the route to California laid out by Captain J. H. Simpson, senior engineer at Camp Floyd. The inn continued in operation until 1947, and in 1958 Carson's son gave the structure to the Utah State Park and Recreation Commission. Now fully restored and furnished, the structure is open to the public as a museum.

While brief in duration, Johnston's expedition had significant long-term impact on the development of Mormon Utah. Gentile settlers and new economic opportunities opened up the church-based community to a broader range of experiences, and federal occupation clearly demonstrated the necessity of Mormon integration into American government and society. The Camp Floyd State Historical Site commemorates these developments and their significance for the complex relationship between state and nation.

TINTIC MINING DISTRICT Eureka. Exploitation of Utah's rich mineral deposits played a central role in the state's historical development. Gold, silver, lead, and copper mining provided unprecedented economic opportunities for Mormons and non-Mormons alike and brought new people and new influences into the relatively closed religious society. Indeed, mining activity contributed significantly, to the integration of the Mormon state into the American nation. The Tintic Mining District in central Utah preserves a portion of one of the state's most productive mining sites and provides the opportunity to learn first-hand about this vital economic activity and its impact on the people and history of Utah.

The Tintic Mining District occupies the west and east slopes of the central portion of the East Tintic Mountains in Juab and Utah counties. The mountains and the region were named for an Ute Indian chief who resisted white settlement in the 1850s. After he and his followers were finally subdued in the Tintic War in 1856, cattlemen moved in and occupied the land. The area held little interest for most Utahns, however, until the discovery of ore in 1869. By December of that year, mining operations had commenced. Although the full potential of the mineral resources at Tintic and elsewhere was not realized for several decades, 1869 marked the beginning of a turbulent era of economic exploitation and development in Utah.

The first claim, the Sunbeam, was followed shortly by the discovery of other ore runs, including the Mammoth, Eureka Hill, and Bullion Beck. The mines required labor, and camps sprang up over night to accommodate both Mormon and gentile miners. Immigrants from northern and western Europe dramatically increased the non-Mormon contingent during the first decades, and the population became even more ethnically diverse with a large influx of southern and eastern Europeans by the close of the century. While most were common laborers, the new Utahns also included an assortment of colorful mining entrepreneurs who hoped to make their fortunes with bonanza discoveries. And of course there were storekeepers, saloon operators, prostitutes, and other assorted individuals who made their livings not in the mines but by catering to the needs of the mining community.

As activity increased in the Tintic mines, temporary camps turned into towns. Early settlements included Diamond, Silver City, Mammoth, and Eureka, each located near productive ore runs. Laid out to conform with the hilly topography of the region, these towns had little grace or style but gave focus to the business, social, and institutional activity that accompanied the expansion of mining activity in the 1880s and 1890s.

The extension of the Utah Southern Railway into the Tintic region in 1878 significantly improved the accessibility of the mines and made increased ore production more profitable. New mines like the Iron Blossom opened up in the next decades, and considerable capital was invested as well in deeper mining of older ore runs. At the same time, improved milling and smelting operations improved the capacity of the surface mine plants.

The peak period of activity came between 1890 and 1926. By 1899 the Tintic district led Utah in the value of ore production, and activity did not slacken off until after 1925, when the total value of production peaked at $16,200,000. By that time, mounting capital requirements had led to the consolidation of many individual operations into large-scale mining companies, notably the Chief Consolidated, Tintic Standard, and North Lilly. Chief Consolidated continued to work its Tintic mines until the 1950s, but the depression of the 1930s and depleted ore runs led to a drastic decline of mining activity in the region. With the economic base vanishing, the population dropped dramatically, and entire towns disappeared, buildings and all.

Today only about 750 residents remain in Eureka City, at one time the mining district's center with a population of over three thousand. The Tintic Historical Society, a local organization that sponsors tours of the area and operates the Tintic Mining Museum in the Eureka City Hall, has led efforts to preserve what remains of the historic mining community. While much has been lost, visitors to the district can still view mine headframes, the remnants of surface plants, various commercial and institutional structures, and a variety of vernacular residences erected to house the miners, mining entrepreneurs, merchants, and numerous others who played significant roles in the region's development. The structures of the Tintic Mining District were the product of a pivotal era in Utah history. Here Mormons and non-Mormons worked together to develop the region's unique natural resources and realize its potential for economic growth.

Eagle and Blue Bell Mine

ANASAZI INDIAN VILLAGE STATE MONUMENT Boulder. Site of an excavated village from the Anasazi culture, about A.D. 1050–1200; with a diorama.

BEAVER COUNTY COURTHOUSE 90 E. Center Street, Beaver. Built 1876–1882 with Victorian eclectic elements; has a clock tower and dome with bull's-eye windows.

BINGHAM CANYON MINES Bingham Canyon. Site of a gold, silver, and lead rush in 1862; then the first open-pit copper mine, begun in 1904 and still in operation; viewing area.

BOX ELDER STAKE TABERNACLE Main Street between Second and Third South Street, Brigham City. A Late Gothic Revival building constructed in 1896 and representative of Latter-day Saints Church (and other) architecture of the period.

BRIGHAM YOUNG UNIVERSITY FINE ARTS COLLECTION Harris Fine Arts Center, BYU, Provo. Includes examples of Mormon art as well as other American, pre-Columbian, Indian, and European art.

BRIGHAM YOUNG WINTER HOME Dixie State Park, St. George. Museum in a home built in the early 1870s and used by Young until his death in 1877.

CAPITOL HILL HISTORIC DISTRICT Salt Lake City. Includes capitol building, Council House (1864–1866), Ottinger Hall (1900), and homes from the early twentieth century.

CORINNE METHODIST EPISCOPAL CHURCH Colorado and South Sixth Street, Corinne. An 1870 building that was possibly the first church in this non-Mormon town.

COVE FORT two miles east of I-15 on state 4. Restored fort built by Mormons in 1867 to defend against Indians.

DAUGHTERS OF UTAH PIONEERS MUSEUM 300 N. Main, Salt Lake City. Displays of items from the 1800s in Utah.

DOMINGUEZ-ESCALANTE TRAIL Spanish Fork. Markers showing where the Spanish Fathers journeyed in their expedition of 1776 to find a Santa Fe-to-California route.

EDGE OF THE CEDARS STATE HISTORICAL MONUMENT Blanding. Museum displaying artifacts excavated on the site of Anasazi culture, A.D. 800–1250.

EMIGRATION CANYON LANDMARK east edge of Salt Lake City on state 65. Where Brigham Young and his party first viewed the valley where they would settle permanently, in 1847, and the route taken by Donner party and others later; marked by "This Is The Place" monument.

FORT BUENAVENTURA STATE PARK Ogden. Log trading post and fort established by Miles Goodyear in 1846, re-created at original site.

FORT DOUGLAS Fort Douglas Military Reservation, Salt Lake City. Early-twentieth-century installation, with buildings remaining from the fort established in 1862 to monitor Mormons and protect against Indians; with a museum.

FORT DUCHESNE-UTE TRIBAL MUSEUM *U.S. 40, Fort Duchesne.* On the site of a fort of the 1800s, a museum with items from the fort as well as Indian artifacts and art.

GOLDEN SPIKE NATIONAL HISTORIC SITE *Promontory Summit, state 83 thirty-one miles west of Brigham City.* Where the golden spike was driven to mark the completion of the nation's first transcontinental railroad line in 1869.

GOVERNOR'S MANSION *603 E. South Temple Street, Salt Lake City.* Built by mining tycoon-publisher-senator Thomas Kearns in 1902; located in the South Temple Historic District, which includes the Lion House, Beehive House, and fine turn-of-the-century mansions.

GUNNISON MASSACRE SITE *six miles southwest of Hinckley on the Sevier River.* Where Utes killed seven men in a surveying party in 1853.

HAMBLIN HOME *Dixie State Park, west of Santa Clara on U.S. 91.* Restored house built by Jacob Hamblin, Mormon missionary to Indians, in 1863; with a museum.

HAMPTON FORD STAGE STATION *northwest of Collinston on state 154 at Bear River.* Site of a toll ferry, 1853; bridge, 1859; and house and barn, 1867–68; only house and barn remaining.

HELPER MULTIPLE RESOURCE DISTRICT *on Denver Rio Grande and Western Railroad and U.S. 50-6 in southeastern Utah.* Reflects role of coal mining and railroading.

HOVENWEEP NATIONAL MONUMENT *off state 163 southeast of Blanding.* Indian dwellings from the early Pueblos, A.D. 400–1300.

KIMBALL STAGE STOP *I-80 east of Salt Lake City, near Park City.* One of few remaining original stations of the Overland Stage.

LAKE POWELL *Colorado River.* Built for reclamation and recreation, a controversial project that covered natural wonders and some historic sites.

MAN AND HIS BREAD MUSEUM *Utah State University, U.S. 89-91 south of Logan.* An agriculture museum with steam tractors, gear for horse-drawn vehicles, and other equipment from the turn of the century.

MANTI TEMPLE *north edge of Manti on U.S. 89.* Latter-day Saints Temple erected 1877–1888. Excellent example of Victorian monumental architecture.

MOUNTAIN MEADOWS MASSACRE SITE *on state 18 seven miles south of Enterprise.* Where Mormons reputedly killed about 100 people during the Utah War in 1857.

OLD IRONTOWN *about twenty-two miles west of Cedar City off state 56.* Remains of a Mormon iron foundry dating from about 1869.

OLD MAIN *Utah State University, Logan.* Built 1889–1902 and the state's oldest building continually used for higher education.

OLD SPANISH TRAIL Moab and Green River on U.S. 50-6. River crossings of the trail used in the 1800s to carry on trade between New Mexico and southern California.

OLD STATE HOUSE off I-15 at Fillmore. Pioneer relics in the building that was the first territorial capitol, 1855–1858.

PARK CITY Where mining began in 1869 and still continues, in gold, silver, lead, copper, and zinc.

PIONEER VILLAGE Farmington. Museum with weapons, relics from early frontier days, and some historic buildings.

PIUTE COUNTY COURTHOUSE Main Street at Center Street, Junction. A 1903 courthouse, restored in 1943, with Jacobean Revival elements.

SILVER REEF one and a half miles off I-15, sixteen miles north of St. George. Ruins of a mining town that boomed in the 1870s and 1880s.

TOPAZ WAR RELOCATION CENTER SITE sixteen miles northwest of Delta. Site of 1942–1943 concentration camp where more than 8,000 Japanese-Americans were imprisoned during World War II.

UTAH STATE HISTORICAL SOCIETY MUSEUM AND LIBRARY 300 S. Rio Grande Avenue, Salt Lake City. Peoples of Utah Museum and research collections including photographs, manuscripts, and other documents on Utah history.

WASHINGTON COTTON FACTORY I-15, Washington. Stone building, now in private hands, from the 1865–1870 attempt of the Mormons to establish their economic independence.

WHEELER HISTORIC FARM 6351 S. 900 East, Salt Lake City. An 1898 farmhouse with other buildings from the period, as well as equipment, showing Utah agriculture at the time.

WILLARD HISTORIC DISTRICT downtown Willard. Mormon town planned according to a Joseph Smith plan, with many Gothic Revival and other buildings from the 1800s.

VERMONT

OLD CONSTITUTION HOUSE 16 North Main Street, Windsor. In 1791
Vermont became the nation's fourteenth state, the first to join the original union of thirteen. The new state's tardiness in joining the young
republic did not indicate any lack of patriotic zeal but rather reflected
the tangle of maneuvers, threats, and negotiations that had complicated
the would-be state's status. Indeed, for the fourteen years prior to
achieving statehood, Vermont functioned as a separate independent
republic, refusing to yield to British allegiance but unwilling to accept
its neighbors' claims to jurisdiction. The constitution of this "Free and
Independent Republic of Vermont" was adopted on July 8, 1777, at a
tavern in Windsor. Now preserved as the Old Constitution House, this
historic structure commemorates the struggle for independence and
identity in eighteenth-century Vermont.

Between 1750 and 1764, Benning Wentworth, the royal governor of
New Hampshire, made grants of nearly three million acres of land in
the region west of the Connecticut River and north of Massachusetts.
His actions proved highly controversial and provoked decades of dispute between the local residents and the governments of New Hampshire, New York, and Massachusetts. The settlers who obtained the land
from Wentworth's grantees in the 1760s staunchly defended the legality
of the New Hampshire official's actions despite the questionable nature
of that colony's claim to jurisdiction over the region. In fact, New York
clearly had the stronger case and attempted in the late 1760s and early
1770s to secure control over the area that had become identified as the
Hampshire Grants (or, simply, the Grants). To counter those actions,
Ethan Allen organized the settlers in 1770 to protect their titles. Known
as the Green Mountain Boys, this organization took the lead in pushing
for the independence of the Hampshire Grants from any other colonial
government.

The quarrel between the Grants and New York continued right up
to the Revolution. When Allen and his men captured the British Fort
Ticonderoga in 1775 shortly after Lexington and Concord, they acted
less out of rebel zeal than from a desire to maintain a strong bargaining
position with both the patriots and the crown. Meeting at Dorset in
January 1776, representatives of the Grants decided to support the Revolution—but not at the cost of yielding autonomy to either New York
or New Hampshire. So instead of joining the Continental Congress, the
Grants declared its independence in a convention at Westminister on
January 16, 1777, and adopted the name "New Connecticut."

On June 4, 1777, seventy-two delegates convened at Windsor to frame
a constitution for the new republic. Dr. Thomas Young, a radical patriot
from Philadelphia and close friend of Ethan Allen, sent the convention
a copy of the Pennsylvania Constitution, apparently hoping they would

Elijah West's tavern

follow suit and produce a truly revolutionary document. Young also suggested a different name—Vermont. The delegates were amenable to both suggestions. When they convened on July 2 at Elijah West's tavern, they framed a constitution much like that of Pennsylvania but with two unique features: the prohibition of slavery and the establishment of universal manhood suffrage. On July 8, 1777, the day after the only Revolutionary War battle on Vermont soil, the delegates adopted the new constitution and referred it to the voters for ratification. Despite some questionable aspects of the vote, the constitution was ratified the following March, and Vermont became an independent republic—a status it retained until 1791, when it was admitted to the United States.

Elijah West's tavern was still relatively new when the constitutional convention met there in July 1777. The two-story clapboard structure was erected apparently around 1775 for use as a tavern and continued as such until about 1848. After that it housed retail shops and small manufacturing and in 1870 was converted into tenement housing. By 1914 it was used as a warehouse. In that year, William M. Evarts and the Old Constitution House Association rescued the historic structure and moved it to its present site. The Association restored the building and operated it until 1960, when the property was deeded to the State of Vermont. Collections on exhibit include eighteenth- and nineteenth-century furniture, American paintings and prints, and Vermontiana.

Now known as the Old Constitution House, Elijah West's tavern was once the scene of one of the most significant meetings in Vermont history. Truly this site merits the cherished nickname "Birthplace of Vermont."

SHELBURNE MUSEUM *U.S. 7, Shelburne.* The Shelburne Museum in the northwestern part of Vermont brings together an amazing array of objects and structures that reflect the variety of the state's historical experience. Electra Havemeyer Webb, who founded the museum in 1947 with her husband J. Watson Webb, wrote that she hoped the museum "would depict the manner of living in Vermont . . . during the early days and that the buildings and the collections housed therein would show the fine crafstmanship and ingenuity of our forefathers." The museum's thirty-five historic structures and "collection of collections" ably fulfill Mrs. Webb's expectations and provide the visitor with an extraordinary opportunity to learn about the culture and society of the Green Mountain State.

The Webbs reportedly decided to establish the Shelburne Museum in order to preserve a Webb family carriage collection, but equally important was Mrs. Webb's interest in opening to the public her own extensive collections of art and Americana. Regardless of which initially motivated the project, the two needs led to a common solution—a museum. The couple purchased an eight-acre lot in the Burlington-Shelburne area, where the Webb family country estate was located. Weed House, a two-story brick structure standing on the property, became the museum's first gallery. Then a new structure, a great horeshoe-shaped barn, was erected to house the carriage collection. The first year, the Webbs also moved to the property a one-room schoolhouse, erected in 1830 at Vergennes, Vermont. Badly deteriorated when they found it, the structure was rebuilt and restored to its nineteenth-century appearance. Although not the original intention of the couple, the preservation and restoration of other similarly endangered historic structures became one of the museum's central missions in the decade that followed.

The Shelburne Museum complex now encompasses thirty-five structures in a forty-five-acre parklike setting. They range in age and style from an eighteenth-century Massachusetts saltbox to the Greek Revival-style Electra Havemeyer Webb Memorial Building, opened in 1967. Within the restored and reconstructed buildings, visitors can view one of the most important collections of American folk art in the world. Collections include quilts and textiles, hunting decoys, advertising signs and figures, weathervanes, hand tools, toys and dolls, as well as fine furniture and art from all over the world. Of particular interest are the structures and objects with Vermont origins, for they provide invaluable insight into how Vermonters lived in the past.

The majority of Shelburne's historic structures were relocated there from elsewhere in Vermont. The oldest residence is the Dutton House, a saltbox erected in 1782 in Cavendish. When discovered in 1949, it had survived almost unaltered. Now reconstructed and restored, it houses a collection of furniture typical of that accumulated by a family over successive generations. In contrast, the Vermont House, erected at nearby Shelburne in 1790, contains period rooms furnished with fine American Queen Anne and Chippendale furniture, as would have been typical of a retired sea captain's home. A third and quite different example of

Dorset House

Vermont housing is the Sawyer's Cabin, a crude structure built about 1800 with square-hewn logs, typical of early settlers' dwellings in the northwestern timber region. The Little Stone Cottage was only a bare stone shell when discovered in South Burlington in 1947, but it has been skillfully reconstructed and furnished as a typical farm family home in mid-nineteenth-century Vermont. A final example of a Vermont residence is the Dorset House, a Greek Revival frame structure built in 1840 in East Dorset and now housing the museum's exceptional decoy collection.

The Shelburne Museum complex includes a variety of nonresidential structures as well. Typical of small-town Vermont are the Vergennes School; the Charlotte Meeting House, a Methodist church erected at Charlotte in 1840; the Stagecoach Inn, also from Charlotte and dating from 1783; the Tuckaway General Store and Apothecary Shop, erected in 1840 and now standing only a quarter-mile from its original site; the Castleton Jail, a slate and brick structure dating from 1890; and the Up and Down Sawmill, originally constructed at South Royalton in 1787. Particularly intriguing are the structures and collections associated with transportation. The museum was founded to preserve a carriage collection, and thus it is fitting that the complex includes a blacksmith and wheelwright shop complete with a forge, tools, shoeing frame, and wagon patterns just as it had in 1800 when it was erected at nearby Shelburne. Visitors to this structure can see artisans demonstrating nineteenth-century blacksmithing. Another structure associated with travel is a covered bridge originally constructed in 1845 across the Lamoille River at Cambridge. Shelburne acquired it in 1949 when the state Department of Highways decided to replace it, and it now provides a picturesque entrance to the museum.

More modern technological advances have not been neglected either. One of the museum's most popular structures is the *S.S. Ticonderoga,* the last remaining example of a vertical-beam side-paddle steamboat. Designed for the luxury tourist trade, the *Ti* was built in 1906 at the Shelburne Shipyard and traveled Lake Champlain for forty-seven years before its retirement and restoration at the museum in the mid-1950s. Near the historic steamboat stands the Colchester Reef Lighthouse, a substantial frame structure that stood guard in Lake Champlain for eighty-one years before the museum acquired it in 1952. And of course, there is the railroad. Visitors can tour the Shelburne Depot, built in 1890 by Webb's father, Dr. W. Seward Webb, then president of the Rutland Railroad. Under a nearby shed stands the *Grand Isle,* a luxurious private railroad car built about 1890 by the Wagner Palace Car Company (of which Dr. Webb was also president) and presented to Edward C. Smith, the governor of Vermont at that time.

Many of the collections also contain objects with Vermont origins, including quilts, hooked rugs, weathervanes, folk sculpture, painted furniture, paintings, and farming and homemaking implements. These collections and the historic structures together depict the folk culture of early Vermont.

In addition to tours the Shelburne sponsors public lectures, school field trips, and a variety of other programs. Open from mid-May through mid-October, the museum brings together the varieties of the Vermont experience.

CALVIN COOLIDGE HOMESTEAD *Plymouth Notch Historic Site, off Vermont 100A, Plymouth Notch.* The peaceful, orderly transfer of political power—a rare process at many times and in many places—fortunately is a well-established habit in the United States. Ever since Thomas Jefferson succeeded John Adams as president in 1801, political parties and presidential aspirants have cycled in and out of office in obedience to the will of the electorate. In America the opposition has been a loyal opposition; only once, in 1860 and 1861, did a significant number of Americans conclude that the price of loyalty was too high.

*Coolidge
Homestead*

The office of vice president was provided to protect against disruption in the executive branch. Elected at the same time (and since 1804 on the same party ticket) as the president, the vice president stands ready to serve in the event of the sudden death or incapacity of the president. Provision for such an office was a wise precaution, and over the history of the Republic several vice presidents have thus constitutionally inherited the presidency. John Tyler was the first, when William Henry Harrison died just a month after taking office in 1841. More famously, Andrew Johnson succeeded the murdered Abraham Lincoln in 1865; likewise Lyndon Johnson followed John Kennedy nearly a century later. In between, there were others. Assassins' bullets also made presidents of Chester A. Arthur in 1881 and Theodore Roosevelt in 1901. In 1945, when a cerebral hemorrhage claimed the life of Franklin D. Roosevelt, Harry Truman stood in line for the job. In 1923, when Warren G. Harding died suddenly in San Francisco, Vermont's Calvin Coolidge was that man.

"Vermont is a state I love," Coolidge wrote near the end of his presidency, expressing in typically few words one of his abiding feelings. It is appropriate therefore that his own small part of Vermont has been preserved today. Plymouth Notch Historic District is an excellent example of a late-nineteenth- and early-twentieth-century rural village. Coolidge's boyhood home, however, made it famous. While the boyhood homes of many other presidents have also been preserved, only at Coolidge's did the boyhood and the presidency so dramatically come together. In this white clapboard house, where his family had moved in 1876, Vice President Coolidge became President Coolidge forty-seven years later.

John Coolidge, Calvin's father, bought the house with several acres and the blacksmith shop across the street for $375. ("He was a good trader," Calvin later remarked.) The elder Coolidge was something of a model, versatile Vermonter—selectman, road commissioner, school teacher, deputy sheriff, justice of the peace, legislator, agent for Dun and Bradstreet, among other things—and was much admired by his son. He was also long-lived, and he lived the balance of his eighty-one years in this house. Calvin also remembered his mother with great affection, perhaps in part because he lost her when he was a boy of twelve. Just five years later, in 1889, his young sister Abigail died in the same room, a victim of appendicitis. But grief, like other emotions, was something that the quiet Vermonter kept locked tightly within himself. He also was to lose one of his own sons, Calvin, Jr., while in the White House.

The house was an excellent place to spend a boyhood and later a vacation, but unlike his father Calvin Coolidge sought his future and fortune in the larger world beyond Vermont. In this, he was joining the long line of people who for years were Vermont's chief export. As New England's agricultural prosperity declined and as cities and industries grew up elsewhere, thousands of young and not-so-young Vermonters left their native state in search of a better life elsewhere. Diligent and hard-working folk, many of them found it. In the process, they educated other Americans in steady Vermont virtues. From a stern faith and a hard land they had learned that from self-control and self-reliance comes self-respect. Of such virtues there was no better representative than Calvin Coolidge.

He went to school at Amherst College, one of the country's finest, and in the late 1890s practiced law in Northampton, Massachusetts. But then this reticent man took to the public life. Joining the Republican party, he served in the Massachusetts General Court (legislature) in 1907 and 1908, was mayor of Northampton in 1910 and 1911, and was state senator from 1912 to 1915. His political fortunes rose steadily; by 1916 he was lieutenant governor of Massachusetts, by 1919 governor. In that office Coolidge first gained national attention by his firm handling of the Boston police strike in 1919. In 1920 the Republican national convention chose him as Warren G. Harding's running mate.

The theme of Harding's front porch campaign that year was "return to normalcy," and the voters, weary from the great domestic and foreign crusades of the Wilson years, responded with an overwhelming mandate. As the "roaring twenties" began, the Republicans were swept into office, Calvin Coolidge with them. But though its beginning was propitious, the Harding administration was a sad one. Some of Harding's cabinet appointments were excellent (Herbert Hoover as secretary of commerce; Charles Evans Hughes as secretary of state), but others were disastrous. His attorney general, Harry M. Daugherty, and his secretary of the interior, Albert B. Fall, involved the administration in major scandals involving violation of the prohibition statutes and the lease of naval oil reserves to private interests. The president was probably innocent of any direct complicity, but the burden of his friends' misdeeds fell heavily on him. When he died suddenly in August 1923, he was a sad and tragic figure.

Vice President Calvin Coolidge was his successor. Never close to Harding's "Ohio Gang," Coolidge was untouched by scandal. Indeed, his reputation for probity helped put the country and the government on a new and steadier path. He was elected in his own right in 1924, a year that found the Democratic opposition in disarray and a major third-party campaign mounted by Robert La Follette's Progressives. Running on a platform of lower taxes and reduced government expenditure, Coolidge and the Republicans won handily. The balmy days of the "Coolidge Prosperity" followed, with the quiet man from Plymouth Notch quietly presiding over a country contentedly at peace abroad and contentedly pursing its own business at home.

Neither Coolidge nor anybody else knew that it would not last, but happily for him the blame for the dark times ahead fell on others. Though it was generally assumed that he would seek a second full term, Coolidge surprised the nation over a year before the election with this terse and famous announcement: "I do not choose to run for President in 1928." Publicly that was all he ever said, but what he said he truly meant. His reasons, this shy and private man kept safely hidden away. The sudden death of his son, Calvin, Jr., may have had something to do with it; perhaps too he simply had decided that his duty was done and it was time for others to take their turn. In retrospect, his timing was good. The unenviable title of "depression president" fell not on him but on his unfortunate successor, Herbert Hoover. Coolidge died in January 1933, two months before Franklin D. Roosevelt (who as a Democrat also had run for vice president in 1920) took office.

Coolidge was not unlike many Vermonters who left their native state for a larger life elsewhere. But he is the only Vermonter ever to have reached the White House. The presidency came to him in part by accident, and it came fittingly while he was in Vermont. When Harding died in August 1923, Coolidge was vacationing at the family homestead at Plymouth Notch. In the small hours of the morning of August 3, his father brought him the telegram with the news of the president's death. Legally, the peaceful succession had already taken place. But it was shortly confirmed when at 2:47 A.M., by lamplight, Coolidge took the presidential oath of office administered by his father, who among other things was a notary public. The next day he left by private train for Washington. The simple wooden house and the quiet little village that he left behind suddenly were different from all the others in Vermont. Coolidge always said that this was where he had come from and was the place he would return to. Ten years later he joined earlier generations of Coolidges in the Plymouth Cemetery just down the road.

AMERICAN PRECISION MUSEUM *Windsor.* An industrial museum displaying machines from the period when New England produced the highest quality guns and other items in the country.
BENNINGTON BATTLE MONUMENT *off U.S. 7 at Monument Circle, Bennington.* A 306-foot stone monolith and a diorama; commemorates the 1777 victory of Americans over the British.
BENNINGTON MUSEUM *W. Main Street, Bennington.* Exhibits and art on Vermont and New England history, including "oldest Stars and Stripes," Bennington pottery, early American glass, Grandma Moses paintings and mementos.
BRATTLEBORO MUSEUM AND ART CENTER *Old Railroad Station, Brattleboro.* Photos, art, and Estey organs in a 1915 railroad station.
BROOKFIELD VILLAGE HISTORIC DISTRICT *Brookfield.* Churches, houses, and commercial buildings from the 1800s, and an unusual floating pontoon bridge.
DISCOVERY MUSEUM *51 Park Street, Essex Junction.* A children's museum, including natural history, in an 1850 school.

ETHAN ALLEN BURIAL PLACE *Colchester Avenue, Burlington.* Cemetery and marble statue of the Revolutionary War hero.
EUREKA SCHOOLHOUSE *Springfield.* A 1785 school, a covered bridge, and items from the period.
FAIRBANKS MUSEUM AND PLANETARIUM *Main and Prospect streets, St. Johnsbury.* General museum, largely on natural history but with ethnological artifacts and toys, tools, furniture, and other material made in the region.
FARRAR-MANSUR HOUSE *the Common, Weston.* House built about 1797 with museum of antiques, dolls, portraits.
FRANKLIN COUNTY MUSEUM *St. Albans.* Local history items including maple exhibit and material on the Civil War raid on St. Albans, in a nineteenth-century school.
GENERAL JOHN STRONG MANSION *state 17, Addison.* Elegant 1795 brick house with many period furnishings.
HILDENE *Manchester.* Robert Todd Lincoln home, with items from the family of Abraham Lincoln.
HUBBARDTON BATTLEFIELD *Castleton-Hubbardton Road and Old Military Road, Hubbardton.* Where Americans, including the Green Mountain Boys, fought a rear-guard action against the British in 1777; museum with an electronic re-creation of the battle.
JOSEPH SMITH MONUMENT *state 14 east of Royalton.* Where the Mormon founder was born; museum and granite monument.
KENT TAVERN MUSEUM *County Road, Calais.* Brick 1817 stage stop with attached country store in preserved rural setting; with Vermont furnishings, decorative arts, tools, and spinning and weaving rooms.
MATTESON TAVERN MUSEUM *East Road, Shaftsbury.* Farmhouse and tavern built in the late 1700s, containing period furniture and agricultural and woodworking equipment.
MORRILL HOMESTEAD *Strafford.* Seven outbuildings and Gothic Revival homestead of Justin Smith Morrill, congressman and senator who wrote the act establishing land-grant colleges; with original furnishings.
MOUNT INDEPENDENCE *six miles west of Orwell off state 73-A.* Remains of Revolutionary War fortifications, including stockade, blockhouses, gun batteries, and hospital.
OLD STONE HOUSE *Brownington.* Antique furniture, farm equipment, and household items in a large 1836 stone academy building.
PARK-McCULLOUGH HOUSE *North Bennington.* General history museum in large Victorian house built in 1865; home of two governors.
ROKEBY *U.S. 7, Ferrisburgh.* The home of author Rowland Robinson and a station on the underground railroad, built about 1784.
ROUND CHURCH *Bridge Street and Cochran Road, Richmond.* Sixteen-sided clapboard church built 1812–1813, serving as community church and town meeting center.
RUTLAND HISTORICAL SOCIETY *101 Center Street, Rutland.* Located

in old bank building; changing exhibits on the development of the Rutland area.

ST. JOHNSBURY ATHENAEUM *30 Main Street, St. Johnsbury.* Public library and art gallery with nineteenth-century works, predominately from the United States, in original nineteenth-century building.

SCOTT COVERED BRIDGE *West River, state 30, Townsend.* Built in 1870, 165.7 feet long; called the longest single-span bridge of its type in the world.

SHELDON MUSEUM *1 Park Street, Middlebury.* Nineteenth-century furnishings in an 1829 house.

VERMONT HISTORICAL SOCIETY *Pavilion Building, Montpelier.* General Vermont history museum with pewter, furniture, glass, Indian artifacts, and other items; historical library.

VERMONT STATE HOUSE *State Street, Monpelier.* Granite state capitol erected in 1859; contains paintings, portraits, and original furnishings, as well as a brass cannon captured from Hessians during the American Revolution.

WILLARD HOUSE *Middlebury College campus, Middlebury.* House now the admissions office for Middlebury College; where Emma Willard opened a school with an innovative curriculum for women, 1814.

WOODSTOCK HISTORICAL MUSEUM *26 Elm Street, Woodstock.* General museum in an 1807 house; with period furnishings, material on naturalist George Perkins Marsh, sculptor Hiram Powers, and United States Senator Jacob Collamer.

VIRGINIA

COLONIAL WILLIAMSBURG Williamsburg. Of the thirteen original colonies, Virginia is by several years the oldest. Founded at Jamestown in 1607, it was an English colony longer than any other place in North America. Virginia was also the home of many of the Founding Fathers of the new American nation, and the Commonwealth was a key actor in the war for American independence. Not only is its history long, but its heritage for Virginians and other Americans is exceptionally rich. It is fitting therefore that Virginia should be home to one of the nation's premier historic areas: Colonial Williamsburg.

Colonial Williamsburg today covers some 173 acres of the original eighteenth-century town of Williamsburg, the capital of Virginia from 1699 to 1780. Through its many restored and rebuilt structures and its extensive educational and cultural programs, it recaptures and explains to modern visitors the vanished eighteenth-century world of Virginia's great planters and yeoman farmers, of its skilled craftsmen and slaves, and of its political leaders. But even as Colonial Williamsburg invites visitors almost literally to step backward into those times, visitors will find that, to fully appreciate this unique place, they must be prepared to leave at the gate much of the baggage from their own urban, industrial, and democratic experience. They should be prepared imaginatively to engage the history of another age—an age far different from their own.

The colony of which Williamsburg was for decades the social and political center was an overwhelmingly rural civilization of planters, farmers, slaves, and their families. Settlement in the eighteenth century still lay largely east of the Blue Ridge and was oldest and thickest in the Tidewater. Virginia's great rivers flowed to the Chesapeake Bay and thence to the Atlantic Ocean, providing a trade route to England. Its great staple cash crop, tobacco, followed that path and for years tied it as closely to the mother country as to any of its sister colonies. Travel and communication were slow, while the land itself was fruitful and pleasant—factors that made the Virginians of two and a half centuries ago a remarkably self-contained and self-centered lot. The buildings of Williamsburg's historic area—eighty-eight of which are actual survivors from the eighteenth and early nineteenth centuries—reflect that quality. They are tasteful, sturdy, and well-crafted and, like their models in Georgian England, clearly were built to last.

But many of the buildings in this eighteenth-century town were built for purposes that did not last, and thus they stand today as especially important historical documents. Several examples, which nearly all visitors will see, demonstrate the distance between our world and that of Colonial Williamsburg. The Governor's Palace on the Palace Green at the northern edge of the town was originally constructed between 1706 and 1720 (the present building is a reconstruction). As the residence of Virginia's royal governors, it was the center of official "court" life in the colony. Royal governors were appointed by the king as his legal representatives. The "palace," however, was erected with local revenues and, by the time of its completion, was the object of some local resentment. A handsome Georgian building flanked by brick officers' quarters and guardrooms and set amid formal gardens with an artificial canal and holly maze, it befit its exalted residents and impressively symbolized royal authority.

The Revolutionary War erased the very idea of kingship from American public life for all time, but during the years of Williamsburg's eminence it was an acceptable idea. But royal authority was for many years, on local matters at least, symbolic. Real power resided in another building close by: the Capitol, which with the Palace today plays an essential part in the interpretation of the historic events in Williamsburg. Here sat the high court and the Governor's Council and, most important, the House of Burgesses. The Burgesses was the first representative legislative assembly in America, but the resemblance between it and modern law-making bodies, whether local or national, is pale indeed. The Burgesses was an institution of representative, not democratic, government; its members, gentlemen of property and standing chosen by the few, not the many (only landholders could vote), to rule. They constituted, along with their peers who elected them, a public aristocracy of talent and virtue that expected and received the deference of other classes. In return, they generally ruled well and in the public interest, even though phrases like "we, the people" and "one man, one vote" would have struck them as strange indeed.

Similarly suggestive of the enormous distance history has traveled since then are the restored Bruton Parish Church, built between 1710 and 1715, and the many craft shops scattered through the historic area. Religious devotion was not one of the qualities for which eighteenth-century Virginians were especially noted. They did highly value a sense of public respectability rooted in part on private piety. Bruton Parish Church, where a young George Washington and Thomas Jefferson once worshipped, recalls that quiet comfortable union between the affairs of God and the affairs of men.

Just as remote was the world of colonial craftsmen, which is depicted today at Williamsburg in probably the world's largest program of diversified eighteenth-century crafts. Thirty-six crafts are practiced, including the apothecary, baker, cabinetmaker, jeweler, cooper, miller, silversmith, wheelwright, and wigmaker. In the score of small shops are sold a variety of hand-made products from toasting forks and iron hinges to corn meal and gingerbread men. But demonstration, not manufacture, is the chief purpose of the crafts program. It demonstrates how a vital segment of the colonial population worked and what they made, and it reveals a world vastly different from the more familiar one of machines

The reconstructed colonial Capitol

and assembly lines. Many Williamsburg craftsmen still spend years
learning a skill—beginning craftsmen serve four to seven years as
apprentices. The tradition of apprentice training is now producing its
fourth generation of competent journeymen; a few artisans have risen
to the rank of master of their craft. As with the politics and religion of
this eighteenth-century civilization, this replication of what was essentially cottage and small commercial industry will propel visitors backward in time and open to them ways of living now long lost.

Colonial Williamsburg thus richly renders the history of a culture
remote both in time and in many of the particulars of its everyday life.
The visitor cannot but come away impressed by that remoteness. But
Colonial Williamsburg also preserves a heritage that is more familiar.
The visitor is constantly aware that George Washington, Thomas Jefferson, Patrick Henry, and George Mason walked these streets. This was a
place where great deeds were bravely undertaken—deeds ever since
remembered and revered by all Americans. In this Capitol Patrick Henry
thundered his defiance of King George III during the Stamp Act Crisis
in 1765. Here too in May 1776 the Virginia Convention urged the Continental Congress to declare the colonies free and independent of Great
Britain. And a month later it adopted George Mason's Virginia Declaration of Rights, which later became the basis for the Bill of Rights of the

United States Constitution. This was the town where in 1760 Thomas Jefferson came to attend the College of William and Mary and where in 1779 he became the last governor to live in the Palace before the capital moved to Richmond.

Today's visitor, whether from Virginia or some other state, will find at Colonial Williamsburg both history and heritage. Restored through the generosity of the late John D. Rockefeller, Jr., the old city lives today much as it did in the era of its greatness two centuries ago. Its buildings, gardens, and people (there is a staff of 3,000) welcome over a million visitors annually. They offer one of the world's finest examples of painstaking historic restoration and provide unique opportunities for firsthand education in the history of Virginia's and America's colonial past. Colonial Williamsburg stands as a reminder of the enduring presence of men whose actions and ideas long outlived them.

MONTICELLO *On Virginia 53 two miles south of Charlottesville.* Virginia looms large in American history, not least of all because of its reputation as the "mother of presidents." Four of the first five were Virginians: Washington, Jefferson, Madison, and Monroe. All have been variously memorialized by their state and nation. All lived in houses that have survived to the present and are today shrines to their famous former owners: Washington's Mt. Vernon, Jefferson's Monticello, Madison's Montpelier, and Monroe's Oak Hill.

Of these homes (and indeed of any other "president's house" through the rest of American history), none more precisely reflects the character of its master than Jefferson's beloved Monticello, administered today by the Thomas Jefferson Memorial Foundation. Indeed, there are few other houses in America that so well embody the grace and symmetry of the eighteenth-century world that produced Jefferson and his fellow Founding Fathers.

Monticello (pronounced Mont-ti-chello, from the Italian meaning "little mountain") sits atop an 867-foot rise two miles southwest of Charlottesville. The location was unique, since most great country seats of that era were situated near rivers and the water transport they afforded. Between 1769, when Jefferson began construction, and his death fifty-seven years later, the house and grounds were the chief private pride and joy of an extraordinary public man. During his long years of service to Virginia and the nation—as a member of the Continental Congress, governor of Virginia, minister to France, secretary of state, vice president, and president of the United States—it was his home and refuge. For the legion of his admirers it was—and is—the place to pay him homage.

"Architecture is my delight and putting up and pulling down one of my favorite amusements," Jefferson wrote, and so his hilltop house underwent much building and remodeling. The original house—the west front of the final structure, constituting Jefferson's bedroom, the parlor, and the dining and tea rooms—was Palladian in design, a significant departure from the Georgian style so dominant in Williamsburg,

*Monticello,
home of
Thomas
Jefferson*

whose buildings Jefferson regarded as "rude, mis-shaped piles." To this
unfinished beginning Jefferson brought his bride in January 1772, and
through the troubled years of the American Revolution he pushed the
work forward.

But after only ten years of married life Martha Jefferson died, leaving
a disconsolate husband who soon lost himself in public affairs. Appointed
American minister to France in 1784, Jefferson was away from Monticello for five years. While abroad, he visited some of France's great
architectural monuments; he brought back to Virginia ideas for the rebirth
of Monticello, which gradually became the splendid example of Roman
classicism we know today.

Inspired by the modern houses of Paris, particularly the Hotel de
Salm, Jefferson set out in 1789 to double the size of the old house by
adding new rooms to the east, raising ceilings, and relocating staircases.
The result gives the appearance of an essentially one-story structure—
there are actually three—incorporating a mixture of three-dimensional
forms illustrated by his use of a spherical dome atop an octagonal base.
The decorative motifs of the rooms, porticoes, and friezes reflected various orders—Corinthian, Doric, Ionic—and rhetorical models of Roman
art. But the most striking aspect, and what today gives Monticello a warmth
not typical of many neoclassical buildings, was not Jefferson's copying
but rather his gift for combining different classical motifs into something fresh and inviting. Matching that gift was Jefferson's conviction that
taste and virtue were keys to successful republican government. Classical architecture could elevate taste; within its symmetrical forms, he
believed, a distinctive American architecture could best be developed.

The distinctiveness of Monticello was not accomplished overnight.
The demands of public life constantly diverted the energy and attention
of the private man, and not until 1809—twenty years after remodeling

was begun—was the house completed, essentially as it stands today. The main entrance is through the great portico on the east front, which opens into a large square room partly surrounded by a balcony. Jefferson called it, sensibly, the entrance hall, but it also served as something of a museum. Today as then, it contains paintings and statuary plus natural and Indian artifacts, some the fruits of Lewis and Clark's expedition to the Northwest during Jefferson's presidency. Over the entrance door still hangs Jefferson's famous seven-day clock, whose weights are Revolutionary War cannon balls. The weights hanging on the north wall control the striking of the copper gong on the roof; those on the south wall fall imperceptibly with the ticking and indicate the day of the week.

Directly beyond the entrance hall and separated from it by glass doors lies the parlor, the most formal room in the house. In the shape of a semi-octagon, it was the setting for marriages, christenings, and family musicales. The Louis XVI furnishings are similar to those Jefferson brought back with him from Paris. A door at the north end of the parlor leads to the dining room, which is painted blue to match the Wedgewood medallions set in the mantel. A pivoted door facilitated the serving of dishes from the kitchen, and a dumbwaiter to the wine cellar below is concealed at the end of the fireplace. Beyond, in what Jefferson called his "most honourable suite," the busts of numerous American heroes adorn the walls of the tea room.

In addition to the "public rooms," the first floor housed several guest bedrooms, Jefferson's own bedroom, and the library suite. Jefferson's room, unlike the other bedrooms, was high ceilinged and connected across his alcove bed, which was open on both sides, with the cabinet in the library suite. The furniture is original and includes his famous revolving chair. Jefferson died in this room on July 4, 1826, the fiftieth anniversary of the signing of the Declaration of Independence. His library of about 6,000 volumes, once housed just beyond, was sold in 1815 to the government and became the nucleus of the Library of Congress.

Monticello's second and third floors (which contain more bedrooms and the dome) are not open to the public, though the two twenty-four-inch-wide stairways leading to them are visible. Jefferson believed that large central staircases wasted space and were expensive, and when he remodeled he had these two unobtrusive ones added just off the north and south passages. The dome room on the third floor, which one visitor said might have been made "the most beautiful room in the house," probably served only as a playroom and, after Jefferson's death, for storage. Far below, two L-shaped wings, the "dependencies," reach out along the brow of the mountain to form a symmetrical U open to the west. Together with the basement of the main building, they house the array of facilities necessary for the functioning of a grand country house: servants' quarters; kitchen; laundry; stables; wine, beer, and rum rooms. Surrounding it all lie the acres of grounds and gardens and the elaborate system of roads that Jefferson so meticulously designed and strove so hard to maintain.

There are today two distinct though related reasons to visit Jefferson's Monticello. It is without question one of the great architectural masterpieces of its place and time—indeed, of any place and time. It is also the house of Thomas Jefferson, one of the chief molders of the new American republic and, two centuries later, an enduring presence in our national life. If a place can be said to evoke a man's spirit, surely Jefferson's home evokes his. To Jefferson's famous epitaph (which he wrote himself) "Author of the Declaration of American Independence, of the Statute of Virginia for religious freedom, and father of the University of Virginia," it is tempting to add "the Master of Monticello." But then he also stipulated "not a word more."

APPOMATTOX COURT HOUSE NATIONAL HISTORICAL PARK *on Virginia 24 three miles northeast of Appomattox.* Virginia holds an important position in the history of the United States and of the South, and particularly in the history of their wars. Two of the most important—the Revolutionary War and the Civil War—ended on Virginia soil. But it is the Civil War that most often conjures the name "Virginia." Richmond, its capital, was also the capital of the Southern Confederacy. Robert E. Lee, Thomas "Stonewall" Jackson, Joseph E. Johnston, and J. E. B. Stuart were all Virginia's native sons. The war's first great land engagement, First Manassas or Bull Run, was fought there in July 1861. Over the next four years, Virginia was the scene of thousands of skirmishes and some of the fiercest, most decisive battles of the war. Its great interior valley, the Shenandoah, was known as the breadbasket of the Confederacy, and it paid dearly for that reputation. From the Virginia fields and forests that lay between Richmond and the Potomac, the sound of guns and marching men was never long absent. And in a backwater village in Virginia's "Southside," the war and the dream of Southern independence finally ended. Today that village, Appomattox Court House, is the site of a national historical park that offers a moving glimpse back into the South's last desperate days. The ranks of men that once assembled here—Lee's tattered Army of Northern Virginia and Grant's serried legions—stayed but a few days and soon were gone forever, but not so the sad and quiet memory of what it was that led them to this place. What they did here and why are the questions that attract today's visitor.

In the century and more since its end, the Civil War has generated many historic sites and preserved battlefields: Harpers Ferry, Fort Sumter, Shiloh, Gettysburg, Fredericksburg, Chickamauga. They are worthy places, and most are well known to thousands of visitors for whom the tragedy and heroism of common soldiers, the tactics and strategy of the generals, the thunder of guns and charging horses, hold enduring allure. But Appomattox Court House is different. Within its precincts there is a small cemetery that contains the graves of a few Confederate and Union soldiers killed in skirmishes before the surrender—the only men to die here. There are no grand fields where thousands contended, only a small village of nineteenth-century and reconstructed buildings. To it the visitor will need to bring a different set of expectations.

Appomattox Court House—the name of the village, not just the building—witnessed the quiet end of the Civil War. Located in south-central Virginia between Richmond and Lynchburg, the village is today administered by the National Park Service and appears much the way it did in April 1865. It was then that Robert E. Lee judged that his disintegrating Army of Northern Virginia could neither fight nor run any more. His decision to surrender it to the Union forces commanded by Ulysses S. Grant marked the end of practical, large-scale Southern resistance and thus the effective end of the Civil War. When Lee reached that conclusion, he met with Grant at Appomattox Court House, and there the decision to end the war was finalized.

In that hamlet (Lee's headquarters were just to the south of Appomattox Court House; Grant's just to the west), the most suitable house where the two generals could talk terms belonged to Wilmer McLean, a merchant and resident of Appomattox Court House only since 1863. He and his family had lived previously near Manassas, where twice, in 1861 and 1862, their home had been part of a battlefield. McLean expected Appomattox Court House to be an out-of-the-way refuge from the contending armies. But on April 9, 1865, the war again intruded. In McLean's front parlor Lee and Grant met, agreed, and signed the instrument of surrender.

Grant's terms were generous and are well known; Lee's response was grateful. Straightaway, 25,000 rations were distributed to the hungry Southerners and visits among old friends in the ranks were quietly exchanged. Said one participant: "There was no theatrical display about it; it was the simplest, plainest, and most thoroughly devoid of any attempt at effect, that you can imagine." Arrangements were made for the printing of paroles for the surrendered army and for the formal surrender ceremony on April 12, at which neither Grant nor Lee was present. On that morning, the Army of Northern Virginia filed down the old Richmond-Lynchburg stagecoach road, lined with Union troops, to stack their weapons for the last time. Union General Joshua L. Chamberlain ordered his troops respectfully to present arms. The Confederates, commanded by General John B. Gordon, returned the salute, "honor answering honor." There were no drums, trumpets, or booming guns—only "an awed stillness rather, and breathholding, as if it were the passing of the dead."

The stillness remains among these restored and reconstructed brick and wooden buildings and along quiet gravel paths. Today a visitor center occupies the reconstructed courthouse. Guides and exhibits help explain the events of April 2–12, 1865, and it is the best place for a visit

McLean
House at
Appomattox

to start. Outside in the village itself, the McLean House, where the surrender took place, is the chief attraction. Also a reconstruction (the
original, built in 1848, was dismantled as part of an abandoned project
to move it for permanent display to Washington, D.C. in the 1890s), it
is a handsome, three-story brick structure, decorated and furnished in
the style of the mid-nineteenth century and in a manner thought to be
typical of the way the McLeans would have kept it. A gazebo, ice-house,
kitchen, and servants' quarters surround it, providing a complete reproduction of a prosperous rural dwelling of the place and period. Other
buildings include the Clover Hill Tavern where many of the paroles
were printed (today a model of the village will be found inside), its
guest house (a restored structure dating from 1819), and its kitchen
(also restored, and containing a shop selling books and souvenirs relating to Appomattox Court House). A law office, a country store (also the
post office), a county jail, and several period houses (some of which are
open to the public) can also be seen.

Lee and Grant and their soldiers did not stay long in this quiet place.
Here they brought to an end the bloodiest war in American history, an
occasion both wished quickly to put behind them. But the spirit of the
times is kept alive at Appomattox Court House and will tempt the visitor
to linger awhile longer.

ARLINGTON HOUSE—THE ROBERT E. LEE MEMORIAL   *Arlington National Cemetery, Alexandria.* Custis-Lee Mansion, constructed by
George Washington Parke Custis between 1802 and 1818 and the home
of Robert E. Lee from 1831 to 1861.

ASH LAWN *Charlottesville.* Frame residence erected in 1799 by James

Monroe, fifth president of the United States (1817–1825) and the last of the Virginia presidential dynasty.

BERKELEY PLANTATION *Charles City.* Birthplace of Benjamin Harrison V, a signer of the Declaration of Independence and Virginia governor, and of William Henry Harrison, ninth president of the United States (1841).

BLUE RIDGE INSTITUTE *Ferrum.* Museum focusing on the folklore and folklife of the Blue Ridge Mountains.

BOOKER T. WASHINGTON NATIONAL MONUMENT *State 122, Hardy.* Museum at the site of Burroughs Plantation, the birthplace and early childhood home of Booker T. Washington, noted black leader and educator.

CARLYLE HOUSE *121 North Fairfax Street, Alexandria.* Georgian residence erected in 1752 and prominent in the social and political life of pre-Revolutionary Virginia.

COLONIAL NATIONAL HISTORICAL PARK *Yorktown.* Includes part of Jamestown Island, site of the first permanent English settlement, and the Yorktown Battlefield, the scene of the last important conflict of the Revolutionary War.

CYRUS H. McCORMICK MEMORIAL MUSEUM *Steeles Tavern.* Museum of agricultural technology and history.

FREDERICKSBURG NATIONAL MILITARY PARK *Fredericksburg.* Includes parts of four major Civil War battlefields—Fredericksburg, Chancellorsville, Wilderness, and Spotsylvania.

GADSBY'S TAVERN-CITY HOTEL *134 North Royal Street, Alexandria.* Eighteenth-century coffee house and inn used as a meetingplace by political leaders during the colonial and national periods.

GUNSTON HALL PLANTATION *Lorton.* Georgian residence erected between 1755 and 1758 for George Mason, author of the Virginia Declaration of Rights.

JAMESTOWN NATIONAL HISTORIC SITE *Jamestown Island.* Portion of the site of the oldest permanent English settlement in America, established in 1607.

JOHN MARSHALL HOUSE *Ninth and Marshall streets, Richmond.* City's only surviving eighteenth-century brick house, erected in 1790 for John Marshall, influential Chief Justice of the United States (1801–1835).

MANASSAS NATIONAL BATTLEFIELD PARK *Manassas.* Scene of the first major engagement of the Civil War, the battle in which Stonewall Jackson earned his famous nickname.

MARINERS MUSEUM *Museum Drive, Newport News.* Museum of maritime and naval history in one of the nation's leading shipbuilding centers.

MEADOW FARM MUSEUM *Mountain and Courtney roads, Glen Allen.* Living historical farm that reflects life in nineteenth-century southeastern Virginia.

MOUNT VERNON *George Washington Memorial Parkway, Mount*

Vernon. Impressive Georgian estate overlooking the Potomac River and home of George Washington from the 1750s until his death in 1799.

NATIONAL TOBACCO-TEXTILE MUSEUM *614 Lynn Street, Danville.* Museum housed in 1880 tobacco factory.

PETERSBURG NATIONAL BATTLEFIELD *Petersburg.* Scene of important Civil War campaign that led to the fall of Richmond and the eventual defeat of the Confederacy in 1865.

RICHMOND NATIONAL BATTLEFIELD PARK *3215 E. Broad Street, Richmond.* Commemorates Union attempts to capture the Confederate capital during the Civil War.

RISING SUN TAVERN *1306 Caroline Street, Fredericksburg.* Important eighteenth-century meetingplace, where the Statute of Virginia for Religious Liberty was first outlined.

SCOTCHTOWN *State 685, Beaverdam.* Federal-style house erected about 1719 and later the home of Patrick Henry, Revolutionary War leader and the state's first governor. Also childhood home of Dolley Madison.

STONEWALL JACKSON HOUSE *8 E. Washington Street, Lexington.* Residence of General Thomas J. "Stonewall" Jackson prior to the Civil War.

STRATFORD HALL *State 214, Stratford.* Noted example of early Georgian architecture, erected 1725–1730. Birthplace of Robert E. Lee, Confederate general, and of Richard Henry Lee and Francis Henry Lee, both signers of the Declaration of Independence.

UNIVERSITY OF VIRGINIA *Charlottesville.* Founded in 1819 by Thomas Jefferson, who also designed its first buildings.

VALENTINE MUSEUM *1015 E. Clay Street, Richmond.* Museum rich in the decorative arts of historic Richmond.

VIRGINIA STATE CAPITOL *Capitol Square, Richmond.* State capitol designed by Thomas Jefferson and Louis Clerisseau, erected 1785–1792, and used as the seat of government for the Confederacy during the Civil War.

WOODROW WILSON BIRTHPLACE *20 N. Coalter Street, Staunton.* Birthplace of Woodrow Wilson, twenty-eighth president of the United States (1913–1921).

WASHINGTON

FORT VANCOUVER NATIONAL HISTORIC SITE 1501 E. Evergreen, Vancouver. Trends in fashion sometimes have large historical consequences. The early-nineteenth-century fashion in gentlemen's clothing for beaver hats certainly did. As much as any grand, abstract schemes of empire, this fashion impelled white men far into the North American interior. The land was immense, and its ultimate resources could hardly be guessed by these early European intruders. But fur-bearing animals, especially the beaver, were an obvious resource.

A gregarious animal, the beaver was easy prey and even before the American Revolution had been trapped relentlessly across the Great Lakes and beyond to the countless lakes and streams that fed into Hudson Bay and the Arctic Ocean. For much of the area, the route back to market was by water over Grand Portage and down through the Great Lakes to Montreal. It was a long and arduous trek and a hard way of life. From it sprang a mixture of history and legend that still has enormous appeal. The images of fur trappers spending long winters in the wilderness (to stalk the beaver when the fur was thickest) and then paddling their pelt-laden canoes down to distant rendezvous points contain much truth. Certainly the history of westward expansion in both the United States and Canada would have been different without them.

One of the most famous names in the history of the fur trade is the Hudson's Bay Company. A British trading company chartered in 1670, it was a major influence all through Canada and much of what became the northwestern United States. Under its unofficial auspices British influence was projected far ahead of any formal British government presence. In fact, the Hudson's Bay Company established a fur-trading post in what would become the Oregon Territory and then the state of Washington several years before there was any considerable American presence in that part of the world. Between the time Lewis and Clark had traveled to the mouth of the Columbia in 1805 and the later 1830s when immigrants began to arrive over the Oregon Trail in large numbers, Oregon was largely undisturbed except for the trappers whose natural ties were with the company and through it to England. Spain and Russia too once had claims in the northwest region, but it was Britain and the United States who emerged as the serious contenders in the region. In 1818 they agreed to joint occupation of the Oregon Country until a boundary could be agreed on.

Meantime, the Hudson's Bay Company post at Fort Vancouver was the commercial and social center of the region. The company's first headquarters in the Department of the Columbia had been at Fort George at the mouth of the Columbia, but they were moved 100 miles upriver in the early 1820s in an attempt better to secure Britain's de facto claim on the Oregon Country. Inside what is now the city of Vancouver, Wash-

Bastion
at Ford
Vancouver

ington, near the river, soon rose an impressive fort and trading post
that radiated influence for the next twenty years. Its success was due in
no small part to the dominating personality of the company's chief factor, Dr. John McLoughlin. From Fort Vancouver McLoughlin skillfully
organized brigades of trappers who ranged as far south as the Great
Salt Lake, gathering furs in winter and trading them in summer. Company ships sailed up and down the coast collecting furs; when holds
were full, they sailed for home and the final market. But the fort itself
was the immediate place of exchange between the trappers who supplied the furs and the company that demanded them. Its warehouses
brimmed with supplies for the fur brigades and trade goods for the
Indians. Most supplies were imported by ship from England, then a
months-long sea voyage on the other side of the world, but the post
was a partly self-sufficient economic community. There was little that
post carpenters could not make. Bakers provided bread and biscuit for
some 200 to 300 fort employees. Farmers built fences enclosing more
than 2,500 acres where peas, oats, barley, wheat, and garden vegetables
grew in abundance in the damp, mild climate. The Northwest's first
orchard was planted with the apples, pears, peaches, and plums for
which in time the region would be renowned. Cattle, horses, sheep,
and goats made up substantial livestock herds.

It all gave the appearance of a prosperous trading and agricultural
community, which in a way it was. But it was also in these years an
outpost, and a remote, lonely one at that, of British civilization. It existed
to expedite the harvest of a form of nature's wealth then much in demand
back home; it did not serve as the nucleus for settlement or colonization of the region. The area beyond its immediate vicinity remained a
wilderness filled, as Europeans had feared since first coming to the New
World, with wild beasts and sometimes even wilder men. Appropriately,
a fifteen-foot-high stockade of Douglas fir posts surrounded it, affording
mainly privacy but also, if need be, protection.

Ironically, the greatest threat to Fort Vancouver came ultimately not from the surrounding wilderness but from other white men who were competing ever more strenuously for it: the Americans. In the late 1830s and 1840s the number of them immigrating to the Willamette Valley rose greatly, and McLoughlin's attitude toward them was ambivalent. The well-stocked British post was a natural way station for the wagon trains completing their long overland trip from Missouri, and in time of trouble many early American settlers found refuge there. Their presence and McLoughlin's willingness to deal with them (to some he even extended Bay Company credit) did not endear him to his superiors in Montreal. In particular, Sir George Simpson, governor-in-chief of the company, was not pleased with what he saw as (and what clearly was) the dilution of British influence in the region. The gap between the two men widened and led to McLoughlin's resignation from the company in 1846—and to his decision to take up residence in the American settlement of Oregon City, south of the Columbia. But that very same year a treaty was signed between Great Britain and the United States that ended their joint occupation of the Oregon Country and established an international boundary at the forty-ninth parallel, the present boundary between Washington and British Columbia. Fort Vancouver thus found itself deep inside American territory, and part of its original mission—the spread of British influence—an anachronism. Its other purpose—to gather the furs for beaver hats back home—also disappeared as fashions inevitably changed. For a few years the fort continued its old trade with the settlers and the Indians, but returns dwindled and by 1860 it finally closed its gates.

Other lives, however, awaited it. As early as 1849 the United States Army established a base nearby. Known variously as Camp Vancouver, Columbia Barracks, Fort Vancouver, and Vancouver Barracks, it became a key military headquarters and supply depot until after World War II. When the company abandoned Fort Vancouver in 1860, it turned the land and abandoned buildings over to the army. The buildings of the original fort soon burned, but the site stayed a busy one for years. It was a troop marshaling point and command post during various Indian wars and until 1920 headquarters of the army's Department of the Columbia. During the Spanish-American War and both world wars troops mobilized and trained here. Some of the army's most famous officers, including Ulysses S. Grant, Philip H. Sheridan, and George C. Marshall, spent a part of their careers here. The army finally deactivated the post in 1946 but retained sixty-four acres for reserve training. The rest went to the city of Vancouver, the Washington National Guard, and the National Park Service, on whose ninety-eight acres has been established the Fort Vancouver National Historic Site.

Since 1966 the Hudson's Bay Company stockade and five major buildings have been reconstructed on their original locations. A bakery produced hundreds of loaves and biscuits for fort employees, the fur brigades, and ships' crews. A kitchen, adjacent to the chief factor's house, provided meals for the mainly British clerks and officers of the fort and for their special guests. The chief factor's house itself, long occupied by John McLoughlin, was an elegant one for the time and place, with white clapboard siding and a wide front porch. Grapevines climbed on iron trellises and two spiked cannon stood silent sentinel in the front yard. It was the scene of parties and dances and the place where the fort's gentlemen took their meals. In a less hospitable spirit, a bastion was built in 1845 to protect the fort from threats of American intrusion, and atop its three stories were mounted eight three-pound cannon. These structures have been replicated. What cannot be literally recaptured, however, is the wilderness setting of the original outpost; today a modern city surrounds its replica. Thus history-minded visitors are still obliged to imagine a world different from the one they will see here today. The effort will be worthwhile and will suggest that history since John McLoughlin's day has entailed both gain and loss.

WHITMAN MISSION NATIONAL HISTORIC SITE *off U.S. 410 six miles west of Walla Walla.* The conflict of cultures between Indians and whites gives the history of the West an especially epic quality. It was a profound conflict, amenable to little compromise. The stakes—a vast land and the survival of a way of life—were too high. For years it was fashionable to write about it as if all the right were on the side of the whites: the advance of democracy and a settled agricultural civilization obviously justified the dispossession of heathen aborigines who had made little use of the land they claimed. More recently it has been just as fashionable to see the whites as crude aggressors and their advance as the aggrandizement of a people who knew little of the West and cared less for the people already there. The Indians, in this view, held the morally superior position. They saw themselves in partnership with nature rather than at war with it, and they were victims to boot. That there might be merit in the competing claims of both sides is harder for many to see. The history of the Whitman Mission in southeastern Washington—as emotionally charged as any episode in the history of the West—affords a pertinent illustration.

It has all the ingredients that at the time and ever since have raised fierce feelings. The story in outline is this. In the 1830s America stood poised on the edge of its second great wave of territorial expansion. The first, which finally took it across the Appalachians and into the great valleys of the interior, had occurred in the first decades after independence. The second, which would take the nation across the Mississippi, the Great Plains, and the Rockies to the Pacific Coast, occupied the rest of the nineteenth century. An immense area with many obstacles to settlement, the West demanded much fortitude, and it exacted high costs.

Marcus and Narcissa Whitman found themselves at the beginning of this second wave. Both were New Yorkers and devout Presbyterians; both were dedicated to the cause of spreading the Gospel to the Indians

*Old
Oregon
Trail*

of the Far West. To that fertile (or so they thought) field they bravely set out under the auspices of the American Board of Commissioners for Foreign Missions in 1836. Their journey to the Oregon Country, documented in Narcissa's journal, is one of the great stories of the West. It took them over what would become the legendary Oregon Trail: northwest from St. Louis along the Missouri and Platte rivers to Fort Laramie, over South Pass to Fort Hall, along the Snake River to Fort Boise, then to the Columbia and Fort Vancouver. Narcissa Whitman and Eliza Spalding (wife of companion missionary Henry Spalding) were the first white women to cross the continent overland. But as arduous as that trek was, even harder life awaited them. Whitman had been west in 1835 to scout the location for a mission, and now with his recent bride he settled north of the Walla Walla River at Waiilatpu ("Place of the people of rye grass"). There they bravely set about planting a new vineyard for the Lord.

In time the mission station took on the appearance of success. There was a large adobe mission house which contained the Whitmans' living quarters, kitchen and store rooms, and an "Indian room" in and out of which the Cayuse, whose souls the Whitmans sought to save, constantly wandered. Later as more and more wagon trains from the East passed by, they built a shelter for immigrants, a gristmill, a blacksmith shop, and—twenty-two miles away—a sawmill. But appearances are sometimes deceiving, and these certainly were. More energetic and zealous missionaries than the Whitmans would be hard to imagine, but the Cayuse proved more than a challenge even for them. For the Indians, the mysteries of Christian redemption, at least as it was presented by the Whitmans, seemed to have limited attraction. There were no mass conversions, and the permanence of those that were converted was always in doubt. This was something that Marcus Whitman found especially troubling and that underscored the doubly difficult nature of the work he had cut out for himself.

He had some success in getting the Indians into the Christian tent, but to keep them there he believed it was necessary to change their ways of behaving along with their ways of believing. He wanted them to abandon their old nomadic culture, settle down, and become farmers. Domestic arrangements more regular than those the Indians seemed to practice were, Whitman believed, vital to the faith. His was a disciplined if not terribly imaginative vision, and what had worked for him and many other white Americans he had no difficulty believing would also work naturally for red Americans. He may have been right, but the test was never really tried. The Cayuse did not take up farming. Instead, each year they disappeared periodically, as they had for generations, to the buffalo country or the salmon fisheries in search of food. How much of their new religion they took with them we can only guess. We do know that what they brought back was a source of bitter frustration to devout Marcus and Narcissa Whitman.

By 1842 word of their still very limited success and of dissension among Whitman and other Protestant missionaries had reached back to the mission board, which saw little future in the effort and ordered the Whitmans' and several other missions closed. In response, Whitman determined to plead his case personally and set out on a harrowing midwinter journey back east. He left Waiilatpu in October 1842 and took six months to reach St. Louis via Fort Hall, Bent's Fort, and Taos. In this instance his single-mindedness paid off, and the board rescinded its decision. But the future of the mission still lay in fact with Whitman, who promptly returned west over the Oregon Trail, working his way as physician and guide with a wagon train in the Great Migration of 1843. The expedition stopped at Waiilatpu to rest and replenish, as did others to follow. Even though the main branch of the Oregon Trail bypassed the mission after 1844, the sick, the destitute, and the stragglers still found kind and generous treatment there.

As for the mission itself, the reprieve granted by the board had little effect on the situation in the field. The missionaries bickered less among themselves, but they got on no better than before with the Indians whom they had come to rescue. The larger and more frequent wagon trains were part of the problem. Though most were just passing through en route to the Willamette Valley farther west, the Cayuse feared quite reasonably that the time would come when whites would cast covetous eyes on their lands too. Their fears were well founded but still just fears. Another problem was more real and more immediate.

However they may have resisted the white man's religion, the Cayuse were powerless to resist his diseases. As they heard of frightful scourges spread among the other tribes apparently from the wagon trains, they grew more and more suspicious of Whitman and other whites among them. Finally in the autumn of 1847 a measles epidemic spread to their lodges, and within about two months about half the Cayuse were dead. Whitman (who was trained as a medical man, not as a clergyman) tried in vain to relieve their suffering, but when his medicines appeared to work for whites but not for Indians (who, never having been exposed to the disease, had developed no natural immunity to it), he was blamed more than ever for bringing black times among the Indians. His own life meanwhile had grown dark with discouragement and personal tragedy. The years of seemingly fruitless struggle were taking their toll, as the increasingly melancholic entries in Narcissa's diary reflect. She grew less well, he more harried. Their two-year-old daughter, Alice Clarissa, the first American child born in the Pacific Northwest, earlier had died in a tragic drowning accident.

Deliverance came swiftly and decisively in late November 1847, eleven years after the Whitmans began their mission effort. Without warning (though discontent was evident everywhere) a small band of Cayuse attacked the mission. Whitman was their first victim. Within a short time Narcissa and eleven others died. Forty-nine more, mostly women and children, were taken captive. Two, both young girls sick with measles, soon died. The results of the massacre, aside from the end of the Whitmans and their mission, were two. When news of the disaster was carried back to Washington, D.C., it helped hasten the creation of an official Oregon Territory, the first formal territory west of the Rockies. And it led to a war of the settlers in the Willamette and Columbia valleys against the Cayuse, who were defeated decisively. They never again threatened the whites, who as they had feared came quickly and to stay.

The massacre thus assured the Whitmans' place in history. But what were their motives? Were they merely the agents of a harsh cultural imperialism that in less than a century decimated the Indian tribes of the West and consigned the survivors to reservations? Were they the missionaries of a religion that preached humility and practiced arrogance? Were they martyrs—or just fools whose sad fate was lamentable but not unjust? Whatever the answer, it is wise to remember that the Whitmans' attachment to religious doctrine and principles of personal morality—matters they deemed universal and as applicable to the Cayuse as to the Presbyterians—was as common in their age as it is uncommon today. If they were deluded, they were not alone. But how, one wonders, did they themselves see it? Surely they wanted to save the Indians' souls in the next world. To do so, they were convinced (not unreasonably) the Indians must change their way of living in this one. The result was to prepare any Indians who listened for the way things actually turned out in the West. Indian civilization did largely give way to a more compelling one, of which the Whitman mission was precursor. The Whitmans knew no more for sure than any men what the future held.

But they probably made a fair guess. Whether theirs was vision or delusion is a question best left to individual judgment. A visit to the site of their mission—and their deaths—will not fail to raise it.

PIONEER SQUARE HISTORIC DISTRICT *Seattle.* In 1890 Seattle was a modest town of about 42,000 people. In 1910 it was a significant metropolis of nearly a quarter of a million. Its growth during those years was attended by all the tensions and dislocations, the ambitions and sharp dealings natural to times of rapid development. It eclipsed Portland as the trading emporium of the Northwest and took on the industrial character that set it apart from surrounding mountains, woods, and waters. It knew its share of robber barons and progressive reformers, and its opportunities beckoned thousands of ordinary people whose prospects, if not income, told them they were no longer poor. Its growth and development promised mobility to the multitudes and, to the lucky who were so inclined, gentility as well.

This much could be said of many other American cities of that age. They were exciting—and risky—places to be. But in Seattle one particular episode raised the excitement and the risk to another, higher order of magnitude. The key events occurred hundreds of miles away and were in fact a throwback to a time when wealth was something one dug out of the ground. Seattle's future, ironically, was in other directions—

Park headquarters in Pioneer Square

where wealth was being created in men's hands and minds and multiplied far faster than anyone could dig gold. Still, the discovery of gold in the Klondike district of Canada's Yukon gave to growing Seattle an extra fillip, a glamor and romance that many places craved and few attained. The city profited because of what the economists call "place utility": it was squarely on the way to another place where thousands suddenly wanted to go. Moreover, it was the last place on the way there, which made it the jumping-off point for a great adventure, and its merchants and purveyors of various amenities the happy beneficiaries of the adventurers' needs.

Gold fever was nothing new in the West. Ever since the California strikes in the middle of the nineteenth century that sent thousands of "forty-niners" west in search of a quick fortune, rumors of the magic metal had lured prospectors all over the West. Nevada, Colorado, Montana, Idaho, and Oregon all in turn were invaded by the army of migrant argonauts. Some indeed made great fortunes; many more did not. In Seattle, too, talk of gold had been common for thirty years before the Klondike strikes. But talk was cheap, and little prosperity was built on it. The economic hard times following the Panic of 1893 made news of real substance especially welcome.

It came on July 17, 1897, when the steamer *Portland,* out of St. Michael at the mouth of the Yukon River in Alaska, docked at Seattle with more than two tons of Klondike gold on board. The gold had been gathered over the previous entire year by dozens of prospectors already in Alaska. Two Indians and a white man—Skookum Jim, Tagish Charlie, and George Washington Carmack—made the first strike along a small tributary of the Klondike River on August 14, 1896, and in the next several months the best river-bottom claims near the confluence of the Yukon and the Klondike began to yield up their treasure. When the ice went out the next spring, the men took the paddle steamer down to St. Michael and then larger boats like the *Portland* back to the States.

There definite word of rich gold strikes spread quickly. As quickly, Seattle began to reap the rewards. It was the beginning of two out of the three possible routes to the Klondike. There was an all-water route from Seattle across the North Pacific and Bering Sea to St. Michael, and thence up the Yukon to the gold fields. It was the easiest and also the most expensive; only a few could afford it. By far the most popular route was north from Seattle via sea to Skagway or Dyea in southern Alaska, by trail over the coast ranges to Whitehorse, and thence by boat downstream to the Klondike. The third, all-Canadian route which went north through Alberta and the Northwest Territories was so arduous that few who used it ever reached the gold fields. But the other two brought the vast majority of stampeders first to Seattle, which quickly learned that mining the miners promised fortunes less risky than those to be made far away in the cold Canadian North.

As gold rushes went, this one was relatively well regulated—at least to the extent that the gold was located in Canada, where the famed Northwest Mounted Police (the future red-coated Royal Canadian Mounted Police) exercised a greater influence for law and order and good sense than was usually known in the American West. Given the harsh climate and wilderness conditions in the gold fields, one of their best-considered requirements was that no one would be allowed entry to Canada unless he carried a full year's supply of food and equipment. It was a wise rule and no doubt prevented much suffering in the Klondike area, where provisions could not be had for any price.

It was also very good business for Seattle merchants, or "Alaska outfitters" as many came to call themselves. The price of a year's outfit could vary from $300 to $2,000 depending on individual tastes and budgets, but on whatever was spent Seattle merchants reaped good returns. Certain things were basic. As much as 400 pounds of flour, 100 of beans and potatoes, 200 of bacon, 100 of sugar, 25 of coffee, 15 of salt, and 25 cans of butter per miner was not unusual. There were portable stoves, cooking and eating utensils, picks, axes, shovels, and gold pans to add to the load. A miner's wardrobe for a year was simple but substantial and might include a heavy mackinaw overcoat, several suits of heavy underwear, a dozen wool socks and mittens, heavy shoes and rubber boots, overalls, and blankets. It all had to be floated and carried many miles north to a remote place few had ever heard of before, where no returns were guaranteed. Still, there was no shortage of people willing to take the risk. Within two weeks after the *Portland* docked in Seattle with proof that the rumors of gold were true, would-be miners spent some $325,000 on outfits from Seattle merchants. As the months went by it began to add up. Stacks of supplies along sidewalks in what is now the Pioneer Square Historic District vividly demonstrated to a city that was economically hard pressed the fundamental attraction of supply and demand. By the spring of 1898 some $25 million worth of goods had changed hands, and the rush was not yet over.

With their new-found wealth Seattle businessmen established and built new concerns and buildings, expanded and added onto old ones. Some companies that sprang up with the gold-rush trade long outlived it and still prosper. There are even still some that were established by successful miners with gold brought back from the Klondike. Some of those that did not survive left behind buildings where miners once flocked for a variety of goods and services. Pioneer Square, which is the heart of gold-rush Seattle, has been extensively restored and offers to today's visitor a vivid glimpse of the old city that was the embarkation point for one of the West's last great adventures.

The Seattle Unit of the Klondike Gold Rush National Historical Park consists of a visitor center located in the Union Trust Annex building (1898) within the historic district and commemorates the role played by Seattle in those events. (Other units of the park are located in Skagway, Alaska, and Whitehorse, Yukon Territory, revealing what awaited the miners at the other end of their trek.) A visit best begins there and should be followed by a leisurely walking tour through the surrounding area. Many original buildings are still in use as restaurants, art galleries, bookstores, and antique shops. The waterfront where the *Portland* docked with the exciting first news is nearby.

Several buildings are especially notable. The Lippy Building on First Avenue South was built in 1900 by Thomas Lippy, who brought $2 million back from the Klondike and was one of the few miners really to strike it rich there. The Schwabacher Building (1890) antedates the gold rush and housed one of the major Alaska outfitting firms. The Olympic Block was the site of Cooper & Levy, another large gold-rush outfitter. The Metropole Building (1895) housed the G. O. Guy Drug Company, where miners could buy—among other things—a specially designed unbreakable waterproof medicine kit. The Butler Block (1890) was famous as the location of the Butler Hotel, then a center of Seattle social life. The Post Hotel (1893) was another famous hostelry. The Maynard Building (1890) stands on the site of Seattle's first bank. The Merchants Cafe, whose interior has changed little over the years, is the oldest standing restaurant in Seattle. Here miners once bought beer for five cents a glass and upstairs might avail themselves of a high-class brothel.

The Klondike gold rush did not last long, but while it did it changed the face of Seattle, as Pioneer Square today testifies. Seattle continued to change, most notably as the main business district moved north, leaving the old gold-rush area for years destitute and neglected. Today, however, it is an excellent example of urban restoration in action as well as an important artifact of one of Seattle's and the Northwest's most exciting eras.

CAMP SIX *Point Defiance Park, Tacoma.* Logging exhibit within a natural forest, with original equipment moved to site to show steam logging camp.

CENTRAL WHIDBEY ISLAND HISTORIC DISTRICT *south of Oak Harbor, about six miles either side of Coupeville.* Many nineteenth-century buildings, including blockhouses, wharves, docks, lighthouse, and fort.

CHENEY COWLES MEMORIAL MUSEUM *2316 First Avenue, Spokane.* General museum with Indian and pioneer artifacts, frontier firearms, and traditional and contemporary art.

FORT NISQUALLY *Point Defiance Park, Tacoma.* Oldest existing building in Washington, erected 1843, and part of the Hudson's Bay Company trading post here; with other reconstructed buildings.

GLOVER HOUSE *W. 321 Eighth Avenue, Spokane.* Frame and granite Stick-style house built in 1888 for James N. Glover, businessman and "founding father" of Spokane. Privately owned.

LaCONNER HISTORIC DISTRICT *waterfront, LaConner.* Nineteenth-century buildings in a shipping and supply point during the steamboat era.

LEWIS AND CLARK INTERPRETIVE CENTER *Fort Canby State Park, Ilwaco.* Collections and exhibits focusing on the historic expedition and on coast artillery.

MAKAH INDIAN NATION MUSEUM *Neah Bay.* Collections based on archeological dig at Ozette.

MUSEUM OF HISTORY AND INDUSTRY *2161 E. Hamlin Street, Seattle.* General museum with permanent and temporary exhibits on northwestern Americana and maritime, aeronautics, industrial, mining, transportation, and sports history.

NAVAL SHIPYARD MUSEUM *Washington State Ferry Terminal Building, Bremerton.* Displays on the Puget Sound Naval Shipyard and tours to the *U.S.S. Missouri,* scene of Japanese surrender at the end of World War II.

NORTH CENTRAL WASHINGTON MUSEUM *127 S. Mission, Wenatchee.* Collections include pioneer artifacts, farm equipment, and other material of local historical interest.

PORT TOWNSEND NATIONAL HISTORIC DISTRICT *bounded by Scott, Blaine, Walker, and Taft streets and the waterfront, Port Townsend.* Well-preserved nineteenth-century seaport community located at the entrance of Puget Sound.

ROCKY REACH DAM *Columbia River, Wenatchee.* First dam constructed on the Columbia; with a museum.

SAN JUAN ISLAND NATIONAL HISTORICAL PARK *300 Cattle Point Road, Friday Harbor.* Museum with artifacts from the Pig War of 1859, with restored military buildings.

SPOKANE HOUSE INTERPRETIVE CENTER *Riverside State Park, Spokane.* Site of 1810 trading post, with displays on the early history of Spokane and the Washington country.

STATE CAPITOL MUSEUM *211 W. 21st Avenue, Olympia.* Materials on pioneer and Indian life, fine arts, and natural science, in a 1920 mansion.

THOMAS BURKE MEMORIAL WASHINGTON STATE MUSEUM *University of Washington, Seattle.* Exhibits on Northwest Coast Indians and ethnology of the Pacific Rim and Islands.

WASHINGTON STATE HISTORICAL SOCIETY *315 N. Stadium Way, Tacoma.* Exhibits on Pacific Northwest, including art and pioneer exhibits.

WING LUKE MEMORIAL MUSEUM *414 Eighth Avenue South, Seattle.* Clothing, art, photographs, and documents on early Asian-Americans in Seattle.

YAKIMA VALLEY MUSEUM *2105 Tieton Drive, Yakima.* Includes recreated pioneer kitchen, blacksmith shop, and early post office.

WEST VIRGINIA

POINT PLEASANT BATTLE MONUMENT STATE PARK   *Point Pleasant.* Over two hundred years after the Battle of Point Pleasant, the causes of "Lord Dunmore's War" remain clouded in controversy. But whether the product of British duplicity or simply the white man's greed for land, the battle constituted a landmark in West Virginia's frontier history, establishing peace in the trans-Allegheny West on the eve of the American Revolution. The Point Pleasant Battle Monument commemorates this engagement and its significance to early settlement in present-day West Virginia.

At the close of the French and Indian Wars, England attempted to prevent a recurrence of hostilities by establishing the Proclamation Line of 1763, which basically prohibited white settlement west of the Alleghenies, thereby preventing further encroachments on Indian lands and lessening the likelihood of renewed Indian-white hostilities. Nevertheless both speculators and settlers continued to cross the mountains and claim land in the region east and south of the Ohio River. After the Iroquois and the Cherokee gave up their claims to the area in a series of treaties in 1768 and 1770, the settlement line shifted farther west, and white activity in present-day West Virginia increased dramatically. Indeed, the route that roughly followed the James and Kanawha rivers became the principal pathway west for squatters, settlers, surveyors, and speculators in the decade preceding the Revolution. But the 1768 and 1770 treaties had not included the Shawnees and other Ohio tribes, who still hunted the region and grew angry at white encroachment. In early 1774 Indian-white hostility finally flared in "Lord Dunmore's War."

Historians have long disputed Lord Dunmore's role in the frontier war. On the one hand, he is portrayed as an emissary of the British parliament attempting to distract the colonists with a back-country Indian war, while on the other he is credited with a significant role in opening up the Northwest Territory and stabilizing the frontier. What is clear is that Dunmore faced a difficult situation when he became royal governor of Virginia in 1771. He had to deal with not only Indian-white hostility but conflicts between speculators and settlers and Pennsylvania's rival claim to the region.

The turning point came in 1774, when outraged Indians finally turned to violence. While their anger reflected long-standing hostility to white encroachment, a more immediate cause was the slaughter on April 30 of the household of Logan, a friendly Mingo chief, by a group of unidentified whites. Seeking revenge, Logan and the Mingo killed settlers and speculators alike along the Virginia and Pennsylvania frontiers. Before long other Ohio tribes joined the Mingo, and Shawnee chief Cornstalk assembled an army of warriors from throughout the region. Alarmed at the escalating conflict, Lord Dunmore ordered the border militia organized, and he and Andrew Lewis, a veteran of the French and Indian Wars and member of a prominent frontier family, took charge of separate divisions. Dunmore marched north to Fort Pitt, which his agent John Connolly had claimed for Virginia earlier in the year, and then proceeded down the Ohio toward a planned rendezvous with Lewis at Point Pleasant, the confluence of the Ohio and Kanawha rivers.

Meanwhile Lewis led his men from Fort Union up the Kanawha, gaining strength as new volunteers swelled the division to 1,100 militiamen. Upon arriving at Point Pleasant, Lewis set up camp and awaited Dunmore's arrival from the north. Meanwhile, Cornstalk and his warriors decided to take the offensive and attacked the lone division at Point Pleasant on October 10, 1774. The two sides were apparently relatively evenly matched in numbers, and fighting continued through most of the day. Finally Cornstalk withdrew to the west through the Scioto Valley.

Dunmore's failure to arrive and complete the pincer movement aroused considerable question, and some critics even charged that he had instigated the conflict to begin with and then deliberately held back, expecting defeat of Lewis' militia to distract Virginians from their complaints against the mother country. In that context, the engagement was not so much a battle between whites and Indians as a conflict between colonists and British allies. Thus the Battle of Point Pleasant is often termed the "First Battle of the Revolution." Whether or not such charges are well founded, the battle did bring peace to the frontier and free Virginia from a troublesome problem that might otherwise have interfered with its role in the Revolution. Moreover, the engagement contributed to Virginia's claim to the Allegheny region after the war.

In 1980 the United States government recognized the importance of this engagement by erecting an eighty-four-foot granite shaft at the battle site. At its base stands a statue of a uniformed Virginia frontiersman. Also located within the two-acre Tu-Endie-Wei Park is the Mansion House,

Mansion House

a two-and-a-half-story hand-hewn log house, the first in the county. Walter Newman erected the building in 1796 for use as a tavern, and the Daughters of the American Revolution have restored and furnished it to illustrate the lifestyles of early settlers in the trans-Allegheny West. No other site is so integrally tied to the history of settlement on the West Virginia frontier.

HISTORIC HARPERS FERRY *Harpers Ferry.* Harpers Ferry is a beautiful place. Steep hills, rolling rivers, and a backdrop of blue mountains distinguish it even in a region famous for agreeable scenery. Wrote Thomas Jefferson of the view when it was still part of Virginia in 1783: "You stand on a very high point of land [since called "Jefferson Rock"]. On your right comes up the Shenandoah, having ranged along the foot of the mountain a hundred miles to seek a vent. On your left approaches the Patowmac, in quest of a passage also. In the moment of their junction they rush together against the mountain, rend it asunder, and pass off to the sea." It was, he said, a scene worth crossing the ocean to see. Himself a connoisseur of fine settings who built one of America's finest houses atop a small mountain near Charlottesville, Jefferson spoke the truth. Later with more extensive human settlement, the place and the cozy town that grew here were subjects of many lithographs and romantic Currier & Ives-style calendar art. Today Harpers Ferry, its glory long gone, is a manicured ruin. For a time it had a turbulent history that such appearances belie—a history tied close to the history of West Virginia and the nation.

Geography in part determined it. The Harpers Ferry gap is one of the few water-level gateways through the Blue Ridge Mountains, and as restless Americans began to look west in the late eighteenth and early nineteenth centuries it naturally attracted attention. Its first settler, Peter Stephens, arrived in 1733. Fourteen years later a millwright named Robert Harper, foreseeing the potential of the site at the confluence of the Potomac and the Shenandoah, bought "Peter's Hole," as it was called, and built a mill. He also began a ferry service: thus the name of the place ever since, even though the ferry is long gone. But it was transportation through the mountain gap, not across the river, that really mattered, and in time Harpers Ferry became a sort of funnel for people and goods moving back and forth across the Blue Ridge barrier.

At first they moved by water, the only cheap means of transportation in colonial America. Even before American independence, interest ran high in improving navigation along the Potomac Valley; George Washington himself was an early promoter. With his help the Patowmack Company was organized in 1785, and though Washington soon went on to other larger responsibilities, the company did make progress. By 1802 navigation of a sort was possible all the way to Cumberland, Maryland, thanks to five short skirting canals and locks around the falls and rapids between Georgetown and Harpers Ferry. The one at Harpers Ferry had three locks. Other, more ambitious works followed. In 1828 construction began on the more efficient towpath Chesapeake & Ohio Canal on the Maryland side of the river. Though progress was excruciatingly slow, and though it was never the great commercial success its promoters had hoped, it continued in use until the 1920s. Its major difficulty was that it came too late. The railroad age was just dawning, and the Valley of the Potomac and the Harpers Ferry gap were as attractive a route for trains as for canal boats. Indeed, the builders of the C & O Canal and the Baltimore & Ohio Railroad raced each other westward in the 1820s and 1830s. The canal reached Harpers Ferry in November 1833, a full year ahead of the railroad, but from there on it fell behind and over the years diminished in importance. The canal never went beyond Cumberland (which it reached eight years after the railroad), while the railroad went all the way to Chicago and St. Louis. The B & O still passes through Harpers Ferry on its way west. More recently, modern highways have followed the same old route that once had been Indian trail and colonial wagon road.

But Harpers Ferry was more than just a place to pass through on the way somewhere else. Since Robert Harper built his first mill there, the site's industrial potential had beckoned. It offered much that early industry required: waterpower, supplies of iron, hardwood forests for making charcoal, and a river for floating goods down to market. It was a prospect that both politicians and entrepreneurs appreciated and that in the nineteenth century gave Harpers Ferry an industrial present foreshadowing the rest of West Virginia's industrial future. In 1795, with the advocacy of Virginia and then-President George Washington, it was chosen as the site for the second of the new nation's two federal armories (the other was at Springfield, Massachusetts). It began production in 1801 and by 1810 was turning out 10,000 muskets a year. Guns became the town's chief business, and the buildings devoted to their fabrication sprang up along the narrow strips of flat land near the rivers. The federal armory consisted of a twenty-building complex along the Potomac (now all vanished) and an arsenal on Shenandoah Street (ruins remain) where finished weapons were stored and displayed. Production at the federal armory reflected old craft techniques and fell behind that of its Massachusetts counterpart. Not until the 1850s was the principle of interchangeable parts fully incorporated into the manufacturing process. But the government's were not the only factories here. In 1819 a Maine gunsmith and inventor, John Hall, was awarded a government contract for 1,000 modern breech-loading rifles, and over the years Hall's Rifle Works, located on Virginius Island along the Shenandoah, produced thousands more. It was in Hall's factory that the mass-production techniques of modern industrial production were most fully applied.

By the 1850s the factories (there were a variety of other kinds of water-powered factories on Virginius Island, some of whose ruins remain) dominated the life of the town and gave it the physical shape that later would typify many other West Virginia towns and cities. The factories,

Restored buildings on Shenandoah Street

shops, and railroad lines (and later the highways) hugged the small open spaces near the rivers. Houses, churches, and everything else climbed the slopes too steep for anything else. Harpers Ferry, like the many other coal towns that would follow the pattern, had its share of company houses, dominated from the grander hilltops by those of the armory superintendents and perhaps the master armorer or the paymaster. By the standards of the time, these early factories sustained a passable way of life for workers and the townspeople who depended upon them. Though the security of the corporate and the public welfare state lay far in the future, paternalism and attitudes left over from the age of craft manufacturing probably cushioned somewhat the lives of these early industrial workers. It was a way of life that for many of them, in return for the risks, offered reasonable rewards.

It was just such prominence as a transportation and arms manufacturing center that put Harpers Ferry at the center of events that fixed forever its place in history—and, ironically, also assured its own rapid decline. The Civil War brought disaster to many a once-prosperous town that fell in its path, but in few was the result so dramatic as in Harpers Ferry. Harpers Ferry also enjoyed distinction as the site of that war's harrowing preview. It happened on the night of October 16, 1859, when abolitionist John Brown led the daring raid that brought him martyrdom and Harpers Ferry permanent fame. It was Brown's fantastic plan to seize the federal arsenal there, free and arm Virginia slaves, and from the mountain fastness conduct guerrilla warfare against the South and its peculiar institution. Though he captured the town easily, the plan quickly went awry and cost the lives of an already free black man, the white mayor of the town, and several of Brown's little band of raiders. Brown finally barricaded himself in the armory guardhouse, where he was captured by troops commanded by Robert E. Lee and J. E. B. Stuart. Two months later in Charles Town, after a trial that observed "the judicial decincies," John Brown was hanged for murder and treason against the Commonwealth of Virginia. Whether he was a madman or just a fool, Brown and his raid set the country's temperature rising. Southerners were universally outraged; many Northerners openly praised his bravery and lamented only his failure. Mad or not, he certainly sought martyrdom and at Harpers Ferry found it.

But the war that John Brown at least symbolically began did not leave Harpers Ferry alone. In 1861 Federal troops burned the armory and arsenal to deny them to the Confederates, who the next year captured the town and its entire 12,700-man Union garrison. The Confederate general, Thomas J. "Stonewall" Jackson, had been present (in another uniform) at John Brown's execution. With the arsenal gone and the threat of more fighting always real, many townspeople left, never to return. Those who did come back found a different place, on which fortune never really shone again. Its strategic location had made it one of the war's sorrier victims. In the late 1800s devastating floods of the two rivers that once made for its prosperity dashed its hopes for industrial revival. Thus cut down in the bloom of youth, large parts of it today are preserved as a national historical park that affords a unique view back on early industrial West Virginia. Harpers Ferry still remains a very lovely place—lovelier perhaps than it might have become had history not so arrested its development. It records, however, how many other West Virginia towns looked in their beginnings too.

WEST VIRGINIA INDEPENDENCE HALL *Market Street, Wheeling.* In 1861 Unionists in northwestern Virginia refused to accept the Commonwealth's secession from the United States and took action that culminated in the establishment of the separate state of West Virginia on June 20, 1863. The various debates and conventions that dealt with the statehood issue took place at the Custom House in Wheeling, the principal city in transmontane Virginia and a focus of Unionist activity. Now known as West Virginia Independence Hall, the historic structure has been restored and opened to the public as the birthplace of the Mountain State.

Separated by the Blue Ridge Mountains, the eastern and western sections of Virginia experienced different settlement patterns, developed divergent economic and political interests, and generally evolved into two very different entities bound together as the Commonwealth of Virginia. Over the years various efforts were made to reconcile the often conflicting regional interests, but by the mid-nineteenth century little headway had been made. This simmering pot finally came to a boil in the secession crisis of 1860–1861.

Virginia initially refused to join the secession movement and instead led border-state efforts to secure an acceptable compromise that would preserve the Union. The state's neutrality abruptly ended in mid-April 1861, when the exchange of gunfire at Fort Sumter, South Carolina, opened the Civil War and forced Virginia to choose sides. Unwilling to take up arms against a sister state, delegates to a convention in Richmond adopted a secession ordinance on April 17. Refusing to acquiesce in such rash action, Unionists—predominantly from the western part of the state—met shortly thereafter at Clarksburg and agreed to reconvene the next month at Wheeling, whose panhandle location and openly Unionist sympathies would assure them protection from their secessionist opponents.

The first Wheeling Convention met May 13–15, 1861, in the federal courtroom in the Wheeling Custom House. Although considering independent statehood, the delegates moved cautiously. Initially, action focused on organizing to oppose ratification of the secession ordinance. Then when the convention met again on June 11, the delegates re-established the state government and filled the state offices vacated by the secessionists. This "Restored Government of Virginia" encompassed thirty-two counties in northwestern Virginia. While not satisfying ardent separatists, the step was crucial, for it provided the means of securing Virginia's official permission for the creation of a separate state.

The first real step toward separation took place the following October, when voters approved a dismemberment ordinance, by that time encompassing thirty-nine counties. The next month a third convention assembled in Wheeling to write a constitution for the new state. Delegates debated the state's borders, which were expanded to include eleven more counties; slavery, which was essentially left alone; and the actual

Former Wheeling Custom House

form of government, which drew significantly on the experience in neighboring Ohio. The convention finally completed work on the constitution in February 1862 and duly submitted it to popular ratification. With voter approval, action then shifted to Washington, D.C. In reviewing the new constitution, Radical Republicans in Congress objected to the mild slavery provision and insisted on an amendment providing for gradual emancipation. Accordingly, delegates reconvened in Wheeling in February 1863 and adopted the Willey Amendment. By that time President Abraham Lincoln had signed the bill for admission to the Union, and on June 20, 1863, West Virginia became the thirty-fifth state.

The new state government continued to occupy the Custom House for a time but eventually moved into new quarters. Then in 1885 the capital was relocated permanently to Charleston in the center of the state. The federal government sold the old Custom House in 1912, and it underwent various remodelings and alterations before the West Virginia Independence Hall Foundation convinced the state to purchase the historic building. Designed by Ammi B. Young and constructed in 1859, the three-story Italian Renaissance Revival building has been carefully restored and now appears much as it did during the pivotal 1861–1863 period. Visitors today can tour the Governor's Offices and other rooms associated with the debates and negotiations of those years, see a film on the building's history, and view changing exhibits that highlight the West Virginia experience. Administered by the State Department of Culture and History, West Virginia Independence Hall stands as a symbol of the state's controversial origins in the mid-nineteenth century.

BERKELEY SPRINGS STATE PARK *S. Washington and Fairfax streets, Berkeley Springs.* Spa popular in the 1700s and 1800s, built around hot mineral springs; some historic structures.

CAMPBELL MANSION *east of Bethany on state 67.* Restored 1793 house that was the home of Alexander Campbell, founder of Disciples of Christ denomination and of Bethany College.

CAMP WASHINGTON-CARVER *Clifftop.* A 4-H camp built 1939–1940 for blacks, with what is called the largest chestnut building in the state and one of the largest log structures in the United States; exhibits and demonstrations.

CASS SCENIC RAILROAD *from Cass to Bald Knob.* Tourist railroad built to haul lumber in early 1900s.

CENTER WHEELING MARKET *Market Street between 22nd and 23rd streets, Wheeling.* Called the oldest cast-iron market in the United States; an important social center. First structure in market built 1853.

DELF NORONA MUSEUM AND CULTURAL CENTER *801 Jefferson Avenue, Moundsville.* Exhibits on the site of Mammoth Grave Creek Mound, one of largest mounds in United States, dating from 500 B.C.

DROOP MOUNTAIN BATTLEFIELD STATE PARK west side of U.S. 219 between Droop and Hillsboro. Breastworks, graves, and monuments on the site of the 1863 battle where Union General William Averell defeated Confederate General John Echols.

EBENEZER CHAPEL Ohio Avenue S. at Hillsview Drive, Marmet. Methodist church built about 1836; exhibits show how early circuit riders traveled through mountainous communities.

GREENBRIER off U.S. 60, White Sulphur Springs. Resort complex that includes 1816 President's Cottage, where several presidents visited in 1800s, and 1913 Georgian Revival main building; still in use.

HUNTINGTON GALLERIES 2033 McCoy Road, Huntington. Art museum with American paintings and sculptures from 1800s and 1900s, graphics, American glass, pre-Columbian ceramics, American decorative arts, and a regional collection.

INDIAN CREEK COVERED BRIDGE one and one-half miles south of Salt Sulphur springs on U.S. 219. An 1898 covered bridge with a museum.

JACKSON'S MILL state 1 east of Jackson Mill. Museum at an 1837 stone mill with wooden gears; where Stonewall Jackson spent his first twelve years.

JEFFERSON COUNTY COURTHOUSE N. George and E. Washington streets, Charles Town. Site of John Brown's trial in 1859.

LIGHTHORSE HARRY LEE CABIN west of Mathias in Lost River State Park. Museum in the log house built in 1800 by the Revolutionary War cavalry leader.

MASON-DIXON SURVEY TERMINAL POINT two and one-fourth miles northeast of Pentress on state 39. Monument at the western terminus of the line marked in 1767.

MOTHER'S DAY SHRINE Andrews Methodist Church, E. Main Street, Grafton. An 1873 church that was the starting-place in 1914 for the campaign to designate Mother's Day as a national holiday.

MUD RIVER COVERED BRIDGE off U.S. on state 25 over the Mud River, Milton. Picturesque 112-foot bridge built in 1875–1876.

OGLEBY INSTITUTE-MANSION MUSEUM Ogleby Park, Wheeling. Collections of Wheeling glass and china and period rooms with decorative art.

OLD BETHANY CHURCH Main and Church streets, Bethany. An 1852 church that housed the congregation led by Alexander Campbell, founder of the Disciples of Christ denomination and Bethany College.

OLD JUDY CHURCH ten miles south of Petersburg on U.S. 220. Restored log clapboard church built in 1848 that illustrates the nineteenth-century frontier church.

OLD STONE CHURCH Church and Foster streets, Lewisburg. Limestone church started in 1796 and added to in 1830, still in use.

OLD SWEET SPRINGS state 3, Sweet Springs. Buildings from a spa used since the 1700s.

PEARL S. BUCK BIRTHPLACE U.S. 219, Hillsboro. An 1858 restored house that was the birthplace of the writer; now with her memorabilia and family furniture.

REBER RADIO TELESCOPE *National Radio Astronomy Observatory, on state 28, northeast of Green Bank.* First radio astronomy telescope, 1937, used to make first radio map of Milky Way.

RICH MOUNTAIN BATTLEFIELD *off U.S. 250 six miles south of Elkins.* Where Union General George McClellan defeated Confederates in 1861.

SISTERVILLE HISTORIC DISTRICT *Chelsea to the Ohio River between Catherine and both sides of Virginia streets, Sisterville.* Buildings from 1890–1915 in a town associated with discovery and development of oil.

SUNRISE MANSION *746 Myrtle Road, Charleston.* Domestic Neoclassical Revival house built in 1905 for Governor William McCorkle; now with a museum.

WATTERS SMITH FARM *off U.S. 19 west of Lost Creek, Smith Memorial State Park.* Site of an 1876 farm of an early settler, with frame farmhouse and numerous outbuildings.

WEST VIRGINIA CULTURAL CENTER *Capitol Complex, Charleston.* Extensive exhibits on all phases of West Virginia history, including settlement and Civil War periods, folk arts and crafts, early industrial tools, and household goods from the 1800s.

WHEELING SUSPENSION BRIDGE *Ohio River from Tenth Street, Wheeling, to Virginia Street, Wheeling Island.* First bridge over the Ohio and the longest suspension bridge in the world when completed; first erected 1849, with later rebuilding.

WISCONSIN

MADELINE ISLAND La Pointe. By the standards of many countries, America's history is not very long. At least the part of it that records Europeans' sojourn here reaches back only a few hundred years. When we think of their discoveries and early efforts at settlement, we think quickly of places like St. Augustine in Florida, Jamestown in Virginia, or Plymouth in Massachusetts—coastal places where, sensibly, settlers who had come by sea from Europe first perched themselves. The vast interior of North America still belonged to the Indians, its possession by whites to await, so we commonly believe, the great westward movement of the nineteenth century.

That belief is largely correct. From their first arrival until late in the eighteenth century, Europeans penetrated little beyond the barrier of the Appalachian Mountains and ventured not far from the Gulf Coast. Civilizations and cultures are not easily transplanted. Despite the old schoolbook stories about persecuted Europeans yearning for freedom in the New World, few of them sought something radically new. Rather they hoped to re-establish here, perhaps with a few changes, civilization as they always had known it. They were colonists, not revolutionaries. Colonies take time to grow, and for years these particular ones huddled close to the sea that linked them with home.

There were, however, two exceptions. The Spanish, America's first great colonizers, in the sixteenth century built an enormous empire in South and Central America that extended along the southern edges of what would become the United States. It was an empire of sword and cross, and in the decade before the English founded Jamestown, Spanish soldiers and friars penetrated deep into New Mexico.

Far to the north, bearers of the same cross but servants of a different king laid claim to another vast hinterland. There, French priests and explorers probed up the St. Lawrence and Ottawa rivers and into the chain of enormous lakes—inland seas almost—that reach far into the interior. Some of their names are well remembered: Jean Nicolet, Père Jacques Marquette, Louis Jolliet, Samuel de Champlain. Others, as important, have vanished into obscure legend. One of them, a young Frenchman named Etienne Brulé, was probably the first white man to explore the south shore of Lake Superior—a lake so big, Brulé said, that the Indians at the Soo had never seen the end of it. But Brulé had, and along the way he passed through the Apostle Islands and viewed the Chequamegon Peninsula and what many years later became Wisconsin. Employed by Samuel de Champlain, the governor of New France, Brulé was a harbinger of the great changes that white men would bring to this region.

Like their Spanish counterparts to the south, the French had several things in mind. One was glory and adventure. Though dangerous,

Museum and log stockade

exploring and empire building could be exhilarating, to say nothing of the rewards such activities might earn from grateful monarchs back home. Another was riches, something that the Spanish sought in the form of gold and silver, the French in furs. Brulé's friendship with the Indians had helped Champlain entice them down from the high country to Montreal, their birchbark canoes laden with furs. Traded for pots, pans, powder, and guns, the furs then went in larger boats to lucrative markets in France.

But Brulé's wanderings had also demonstrated that white men could go to the places where the Indians got the furs, and it was not long before French Canadian *coureurs de bois,* or "woods runners," followed in his path. Trappers and traders at once, these hearty creatures produced a gratifying quantity of furs. True to good mercantilist policy, the French government tried to regulate the business for the enjoyment of favored monopolists, something hard to do in the vast unpoliced wilderness. But whether they were licensed or not, the fur trappers and traders had entered the history of the region. They stayed there much longer than the French.

Finally, the French had in mind religion. Although somewhat less ferocious about it than their fellow Catholics in New Spain, the French were nonetheless absolutely serious in their belief that the empire and the faith necessarily advanced hand in hand. Its agents were the Jesuits—

or, as they were then known, the Black Robes. As hearty as any *coureurs de bois,* these missionaries advanced with them. They offered the Indians something rather different, however—not trade goods in return for beaver pelts, but baptism and salvation for nothing. Few then thought it cultural arrogance to convert the heathen to Christianity. Certainly the French saw it as a sacred duty, and to their credit they generally conducted themselves in a manner befitting the gentle precepts of their faith. Persuasion, not force, brought to their altar the Indians who came.

All of these things came together at Madeline Island, three miles off the Chequamegon Peninsula where Brulé once explored. After his visit early in the 1620s, other whites too may have wandered there. But there is record that in 1659 (twenty-seven years after Brulé was killed by the Indians) Pierre Radisson and Medard Chouart des Groseilliers, both trappers, built a cabin on Chequamegon Bay. Six years later Jesuit Father Claude Allouez founded a mission at La Pointe, the first Christian church in what later became Wisconsin. The westernmost of two Jesuit outposts on the south shore of Lake Superior (the other was at L'Anse at the base of Keweenaw Peninsula), the mission was understandably small and weak, many of the Indians surrounding it not at first being amenable to friendly persuasion. But the Jesuits were brave souls, and observant too. They had heard the same tales of fabulous copper deposits along the south shore that had tempted Champlain, and Allouez actually brought back to the Soo samples of copper ore picked up on the Keweenaw Peninsula. More famous by far was his successor at the La Pointe mission, Père Jacques Marquette, who in the company of Louis Jolliet later explored far down the Mississippi River.

French soldiers arrived in 1693 and with Pierre La Sueur set up a trading post; it and Grand Portage on the north shore serviced the western Lake Superior fur trade. The trade prospered and Frenchmen profited from it until their North American empire fell to the British in the French and Indian War. The Madeline Island trading post then flew the Union Jack, and the fur trade continued to flourish under the great North West Company. Later, under American sovereignty, it was John Jacob Astor's American Fur Company that well into the nineteenth century funneled the wealth of a continent back through warehouses on Mackinac Island to the east. Its agents used the trading post at La Pointe for their headquarters in the Chequamegon region.

But fashions changed, the beaver disappeared, and the fur trade did not last forever. For the rest of the nineteenth and into the twentieth century logging and commercial fishing dominated life in northern Wisconsin. Madeline Island was touched by both, as it was by the great age of the *coureurs de bois* and the Black Robes. Today, they too have greatly declined and have been replaced with new wealth in the form of thousands of tourists and summer residents.

The collections of the Madeline Island Historical Museum document the island's and the area's history from the Indians onward. Materials on the voyageurs and explorers, on the missionaries, on logging and fishing are included. The exhibits are arranged on the site of the old American Fur Company post. The four structures that comprise the site—one the last remaining building of the American Fur Company—are all made of logs and are enclosed by a log stockade similar to the one used by the American Fur Company. La Pointe itself is one of the oldest settlements in Wisconsin and remains a pleasant village on the shore of the world's largest lake. Life is easier there today than when Frenchmen first wandered this way three and a half centuries ago. But for the imaginative visitor a visit to the Madeline Island Historical Museum can recapture something of what it once was like, when visions of empire, wealth, and salvation first brought Europeans to this remote northern place.

OLD WORLD WISCONSIN Eagle. America is a nation of nations. In 1600 it was virtually empty of Europeans. By 1750 the seaboard colonies east of the Appalachians had become proud replicas of European civilization adapted to the American environment. By 1850 (two years after Wisconsin became a state) immigrants and their American-born children had settled the great interior valleys of the continent. By 1900 their communities spanned the continent. They numbered in the millions, and their coming here is one of the great episodes in the history of human migration.

Their reasons for moving, like their numbers, were many. With the exception of the Africans who came involuntarily as other men's slaves, these people came freely, as individuals and families, seeking somehow a better life. Some sought to escape religious oppression; others fled from political tyranny and the ravages of famine and war. Nearly all sought greater economic opportunity than the Old World had offered. And there were countless personal reasons—bothersome relatives, bad debts, military conscription, and simple wanderlust—that might cause men to forsake old familiar ways and places for new and unknown ones. Risks abounded.

The result was the making of a new nationality—the Americans—from many old ones. For the immigrants themselves, survival and success in a new land meant adapting to its ways of thinking and behaving. As years passed, their American-born children more and more found the new ways the natural ones. Yet these people shaped the new land as much as they were shaped by it. Their "Americanization" was a slow and sometimes painful process. For security and encouragement, like commonly clung to like, thus preserving something of the old culture, language, and faith. Remnants survive even today.

Ethnic settlement in Wisconsin, as illustrated at Old World Wisconsin, offers an excellent example of how immigrants at once took up new ways and kept alive old ones. Though far inland, Wisconsin's rich farmlands and forests early attracted thousands of immigrants from many European countries. Foreign-born made up thirty-six per cent of the new state's population in 1850. Fifty years later, still nearly a quarter of all Wisconsin residents had been born abroad. Most came from Germany, the British Isles, and Scandinavia. From Switzerland, Poland, Bohemia, and the Low Countries came more. In Europe the great majority had been farmers and the families of farmers, and so they remained in Wisconsin. Their settlement, however, was in keeping with their own unique national habits and ways of doing things. Their buildings particularly showed this. Germans commonly built half-timbered houses and barns resembling those in their homeland, where the technique of building with fitted square timbers and birch or clay-straw nogging in between went back to the Middle Ages. Norwegians built with logs as they had in their own forested homeland. Finns followed an old tradition of squaring the sides of logs but rounding the tops and hollowing the bottoms to assure a better fit. Cornishmen built sturdily of stone as once they had in the treeless west of England. Russians topped their churches with onion-shaped domes.

The old cultures survived in other ways too. Food was one. Norwegians still baked their lefse and relished their lutefisk. Germans brewed beer and made in their new home sausage and sauerkraut as fine as any in the Fatherland. The Danish brought kingle, the Swedish meatballs. In time the cheesemaking knowledge of the Swiss helped make cheese and Wisconsin to many Americans virtually synonymous. Keeners sang at Irish wakes; Bohemian polkas and Polish mazurkas were danced at American barn dances. Dutchmen crafted wooden shoes. Icelanders fished the cold waters off Washington Island as once they had fished the cold North Atlantic. Bilingualism flourished in the ethnic enclaves of cities like Milwaukee, signs in shop windows commonly proclaiming: "English spoken here." And the Europeans brought old names to their new land: Kiel, Friesland, Denmark, Berlin, Cumberland, and Cambridge.

Not all of Wisconsin's pioneers came from so far, however. Many were native-born Americans from places farther east. Their Anglo-American roots reached back to New England, where overcrowded and underproductive farms forced many to seek better opportunities elsewhere. First they moved to more abundant lands in neighboring New York State, but with the opening of the Erie Canal in 1825 more and more continued their journey into the lands of the old Northwest Territory and the states being carved from it. Ohio, Indiana, Illinois, Michigan, and finally Wisconsin all came to bear the imprint of these industrious "Yankees." By 1850 some 103,000, roughly a third of Wisconsin's population, were of eastern origin. Half were New Yorkers; ten thousand had come from Vermont, whose people were already its chief export. Names on the present-day map of Wisconsin testify that these people came to stay; Genesee, Rochester, Palmyra, Troy, Burlington.

Places names, however, were sturdier than many of the original farmsteads that these agricultural people once built. Much of the dis-

*Kortesmaa Barn on the
Finnish Farmstead*

tinctive architecture and way of life of Wisconsin's immigrant pioneers threatened to disappear as times and tastes changed and as the process of Americanization separated younger generations farther and farther from their European origins. To preserve and bring together as much as possible of what remained was the idea behind the founding of Old World Wisconsin. The result today is a 576-acre outdoor museum near Eagle, in southeastern Wisconsin, dedicated to documenting and displaying the world of Wisconsin's pioneers. A joint venture of the State Historical Society of Wisconsin and the Wisconsin Department of Natural Resources, Old World Wisconsin was conceived according to a long-range master plan calling for a museum of 136 buildings representing sixteen ethnic groups, including twenty-one farms and a typical Wisconsin crossroads village of the 1870s.

Today over forty buildings are complete and others are under construction. Visitors will find German, Finnish, Danish, Norwegian, and Yankee farmsteads, plus the crossroads village and a visitor center. All are connected by pleasant paths that wander through the Kettle Moraine State Forest. The buildings are all original and have been carefully moved to Old World Wisconsin from many parts of the state. Painstaking research has assured that each is the actual product of one or another part of Wisconsin's immigrant heritage. The Koepsell House in the German area was built in 1858 in Washington County and is an excellent example of the half-timber architectural style. The Dahlen Corncrib in the Norwegian area is made of hewn logs; the Raspberry School, built in Bayfield County, was used by Norwegian and Swedish children until 1914. The Danish Pederson House was brought from Polk County, as was the adjacent Jensen Barn. In the Finnish area Henry Kortesmaa's Granary illustrates how one farmer stored feed grains for his animals. The Ronkainen Sauna, built in 1919 in Douglas County, represents an essential building that the Finns made famous. A log outhouse has been preserved from the town of Oulee in Bayfield County. In the visitor center the Clausing Barn, built in 1897 in Ozaukee County, houses an exhibit hall and an ethnic restaurant.

The history that Old World Wisconsin thus preserves and celebrates is the history not of a single place and people, but of a process. It preserves the colorful distinctiveness of Wisconsin life at a time when pioneers from many lands were building new lives here. But, faithful to the earnest desire of those people truly to become Americans, it does not celebrate ethnic distinctiveness for its own sake. Wisconsin's immigrant farmers and their families left old lives and old places for compelling reasons to seek in America something better. Most of them found it and willingly paid the price of adopting new and unfamiliar ways of living. They were a part of that process whereby from the people of many old nations one new nation grew: *E Pluribus Unum,* as it says on the coins. But these immigrants also shaped the life they found here and, as Old World Wisconsin shows so well, vastly enriched it.

CIRCUS WORLD *Baraboo.* Popular entertainment has changed greatly over the years. Today, if any one thing dominates Americans' efforts to divert and amuse themselves, it is television. Millions pass much of their leisure time before its flickering images. Relatively cheap for the viewer, television, like the other great forms of popular entertainment before it, is widely accessible and greatly enjoyed. In one respect, however, television differs radically from its predecessors. The entertainment it affords can be had, and indeed usually is had, in solitude, apart from other people seeking entertainment in just the same way. Whether one watches a lot or a little, chances are that one watches in small company—or alone.

By contrast, going to the movies, the vaudeville theater, or the circus was something one never did alone. Indeed, it was not so long ago that the most common forms of popular entertainment routinely summoned people together. Of all those assemblies, the circus may have been the most memorable, romantic, and odoriferous. At the Circus World Museum in Baraboo, Wisconsin, the great now-vanished era of the circus comes to life, preserving an important chapter in the state's and the nation's popular history.

As historian Richard N. Current relates, Wisconsin has been the veritable "mother of circuses." The area around Delavan first became associated with circuses when in the late 1840s a New York-based circus, the Grand Olympic Arena and United States Circus, made a nearby farm its winter headquarters. Performers and promoters soon congregated there, and some struck out on their own. Two of the most enterprising were William Cameron Coup and Don Costello. With the backing of Phineas T. Barnum, "The World's Greatest Showman," they established a traveling circus eventually famous as "Barnum and Bailey—The Greatest Show on Earth." At first, like its smaller predecessors, the show traveled by horse-drawn wagon, but at Coup's instigation it took to the

Nineteenth-century circus parade wagon

rails in a string of special railroad cars. Their arrival in towns and cities all across the country, along with colorful posters that proclaimed ever more (and ever more amazing) acts and animals, heralded for thousands of Americans, young and old, long-awaited fun and excitement.

It was Baraboo's Ringling brothers, however, who won for Wisconsin its greatest circus fame. Their father was a German immigrant who changed his name from Ruengeling to Ringling. As he migrated about the Midwest, beginning and ending in Wisconsin, his seven sons and one daughter were exposed to the traveling entertainment of the day. Returning to Baraboo, Al, the oldest, and four of his brothers organized a small variety show. At first they called it a "classic and comic concert company"; then, after 1884, a circus. The circus premiered in front of the Sauk County Jail in Baraboo in May of that year. It was a modest affair—just twenty-one hands including the Ringlings themselves and all the hired help (Al's wife, Louise, performed as the snake charmer). The work was hard and the long night-time wagon treks over rutted country roads were wearing, but persistence, talent, and no doubt some luck brought them success.

As they plowed their profits back into the business and added new acts, animals, and equipment, their reputation spread beyond the likes of Black Earth, Mt. Horeb, and New Glarus. By 1890 they were prosperous enough to mount the show on their own circus train, which, though still not large compared to some of the competition (like Barnum and Bailey), put them in the big time. They soon grew from one "ring" to three, and their tours reached all the way to the Atlantic coast. The mid-1890s saw them open in Chicago (they were by then too big to play Baraboo at all) and move on to St. Louis and New England. By the turn of the century their shows ranged coast to coast and had become the rival of the once "Greatest Show on Earth," Barnum and Bailey. When both Barnum and Bailey died early in the 1900s, the Ringlings bought their circus. In time they added its name to their own, and in the "Ringling Brothers and Barnum and Bailey Combined Shows," they truly did have the "Greatest Show on Earth."

Meanwhile the circus spent the winters in Baraboo and, not surprisingly, made its mark on the little Wisconsin town. Along the Baraboo River rose large brick barns to shelter both the exotic animals and the thousand horses needed to move the heavy circus wagons; here a baby elephant was first born to a captive mother. There were blacksmith shops, shops to repair wagons and railroad cars, buildings to store countless costumes. Local residents found work here as roustabouts, bookkeepers, and performers. Related businesses too grew up, like the Moeller Brothers, which built the elaborate wagons that were the basic unit of every circus parade. And, one imagines, not a few of the town's children caught the circus fever hanging about such an exciting place and went home to dream dreams of when they too might leave Baraboo and live that gay and romantic life.

It all continued until 1918, when the last brightly colored circus train left Baraboo—almost for ever. From then on the show wintered first in Bridgeport, Connecticut, and finally in Sarasota, Florida. It came back to Baraboo only once, in 1933, to mark the fiftieth anniversary of the Ringling Brothers' fabulous enterprise. And fabulous it had become. The Ringling Brothers, Barnum & Bailey routebook for 1936 recorded 1,540 employees, some ninety railroad cars in four trains, and a "Big Top" the size of two football fields. But times and fashions in entertainment changed. Among the casualties after World War II were the great railroad-borne circuses, and though circuses still can be seen in America—usually in indoor coliseums and auditoriums—much of their romance is gone. Finding their excitement in other ways, today's leisured Americans are not the same people as those who once flocked so eagerly to the Ringlings' and a hundred others' tents, to be thrilled by "the only black camels ever exhibited in Europe or America," a "two-horned rhinoceros," an array of such peerless human performers and curiosities as "Madame Dockrill, empress of the Arena and her Four-Horse Act," "Col. Goshen, the Giant of Giants," and "Little Queen Mab, the smallest and prettiest dwarf ever exhibited."

It was all nearly lost but for the efforts of John M. Kelley of Baraboo, for years legal counsel for the Ringlings and a dedicated fan of everything connected with the circus. With the support of other private citizens, service clubs, circus historians across the country, and the State Historical Society of Wisconsin, something quite remarkable was saved. Circus World Museum is the result of those efforts to preserve Wisconsin's and America's circus heritage. It does so in a lively fashion worthy of its subject. Forty acres and twenty-seven buildings contain an enormous array of original circus equipment: 150 superb wooden circus

wagons, chariots, bandwagons, dens, cages and coaches, a steam cal-
liope, and railroad advertising car. But the artifacts are not merely preserved: they are preserved for use. Indeed Circus World Museum is just
that: a small living version of the actual world of the circus. The horses
and elephants and tigers are real—and so are the smells. Real jugglers,
clowns, trapeze artists, and lion tamers perform for audiences beneath
a real "Big Top." Hotdogs, popcorn, peanuts, cotton candy, and pink
lemonade tempt children now just as they did many years ago. And
every summer, to celebrate the Fourth of July, a genuine steam-powered circus train travels the 125-mile route from Baraboo to Milwaukee
and back again, drawing thousands of happy spectators all along the
way.

In the history of popular entertainment in America, the circus was a
uniquely happy chapter. True to that history, the Circus World Museum
is a uniquely happy place. But it is so in ways that no mere amusement
park furnished with wild animals possibly can be. Rather, it evokes in
lively fashion the fun of another era, which (perhaps despite ourselves)
is still fun for us.

---

*BARRON COUNTY HISTORICAL MUSEUM on Museum Road one
and one-half miles west of Cameron, Barron.* Pioneer street with a
farmstead, dentist's and doctor's offices, general store, etc.
*BARTLETT MEMORIAL HISTORICAL MUSEUM 2149 St. Lawrence
Avenue, Beloit.* Limestone farmhouse from circa 1850, outbuildings, and
a one-room schoolhouse; with local history exhibits.
CHIPPEWA VALLEY MUSEUM Carson Park, Eau Claire. Historical
collections from the Chippewa River Valley.
*DOUGLAS COUNTY HISTORICAL MUSEUM 906 East Second Street,
Superior.* Local history exhibits housed in 1890 Martin Pattison Mansion.
*FIRST CAPITOL STATE PARK MUSEUM Yellowstone Lake State Park,
Blanchardville.* Restored supreme court and council house, the first
state capitol; with exhibits.
*FORT CRAWFORD MEDICAL MUSEUM 717 South Beaumont Street,
Prairie du Chien.* Medical and dental collections, and exhibit of Dr.
Beaumont's famous experiments on the human digestive process.
*GALLOWAY HOUSE AND VILLAGE 336 Old Pioneer Road, Fond du
Lac.* Victorian household items and historic structures related to the
county's history.
HAWKS INN 428 Wells Street, Delafield. Furnished 1848 stagecoach
inn.
HERITAGE HILL STATE PARK 2640 S. Webster Avenue, Green Bay.
An outdoor museum with buildings on early Wisconsin—Tank Cottage,
built 1776 and oldest known building in state; Fort Howard buildings;
fur trader's log cabin; and more.

HOARD HISTORICAL MUSEUM 407 *Merchant Avenue, Fort Atkinson.* Includes 1864 Hoard House, 1841 Dwight Foster House, and Dairy Exhibit Building.

KENOSHA COUNTY HISTORICAL MUSEUM 6300 *Third Avenue, Kenosha.* Local museum housed in 1895 residence.

LA CROSSE COUNTY HISTORICAL MUSEUM 429 *N. 7th Street, La Crosse.* Housed in Hixon House, erected 1857.

MANITOWOC MARITIME MUSEUM 809 *South Eighth Street, Manitowoc.* Collections related to Great Lakes shipping and submarine construction during World War II in Manitowoc.

MARATHON COUNTY HISTORICAL MUSEUM 403 *McIndoe Street, Wausau.* Exhibits on state and local history.

MAYVILLE HISTORICAL SOCIETY Bridge and German streets, Mayville. Historic properties including an 1873 wagon shop and an 1881 cigar factory.

MID-CONTINENT RAILWAY MUSEUM North Freedom. A railroad museum with a steam train taking passengers on a nine-mile route.

MILTON HOUSE MUSEUM state 26 and 59, Milton. Historic buildings ranging from an 1837 log cabin to an 1876 buggy shed.

MILWAUKEE COUNTY HISTORICAL SOCIETY 910 *Third Street, Milwaukee.* A general museum with brewery, early settler, marine, transportation, and decorative-arts materials.

MILWAUKEE PUBLIC MUSEUM 800 *W. Wells Street, Milwaukee.* The largest natural history museum in the state, and a major museum in the United States.

OCTAGON HOUSE, CARRIAGE HOUSE MUSEUM, AND GARDEN HOUSE 1004 *Third Street, Hudson.* An 1855 house furnished from the period; with blacksmith shop and country store.

OLD WADE HOUSE STATE PARK state 23, Greenbush. A clapboard house with Greek Revival elements, built 1847–1851, that served as a stagecoach inn; now restored, with outbuildings.

OSHKOSH PUBLIC MUSEUM 1331 *Algoma Boulevard, Oshkosh.* Local nineteenth-century social and cultural history.

PENDARVIS 114 *Shake Bag Street, Mineral Point.* A group of restored Cornish miners' houses built nearly 150 years ago; with tours and items from the period.

PIONEER PARK 32 *11th Street, Clintonville.* Includes History House, Stovewood House, and 1869 log cabin.

PIONEER VILLAGE OF OZAUKEE COUNTY HISTORICAL SOCIETY Hawthorne Hill County Park, County Trunk 1, Cedarburg. A ten-acre restoration of an early village.

STATE HISTORICAL SOCIETY OF WISCONSIN MUSEUM Madison. Special displays and other exhibits on the history of Wisconsin.

STONEFIELD Nelson Dewey State Park, Cassville. Re-creation of an 1890s village and a farm museum on the estate of Wisconsin's first governor.

***TALLMAN RESTORATIONS** 440 N. Jackson Street, Janesville.* Includes the restored Italianate villa of lawyer and abolitionist William M. Tallman, an 1842 stone house, carriage house, and local history museum.

***VILLA LOUIS** St. Feriole Island, Prairie du Chien.* An 1843 mansion furnished with the lavish mahogany furniture, chandeliers, silver, and French stemware of the wealthy Dousman family.

***WATERTOWN HISTORICAL SOCIETY** 919 Charles Street, Watertown.* A furnished fifty-seven-room octagon house.

***WAUKESHA COUNTY HISTORICAL MUSEUM** 101 W. Main Street, Waukesha.* Local history exhibits housed in 1893 county courthouse.

WYOMING

FORT LARAMIE NATIONAL HISTORIC SITE three miles southwest of Fort Laramie. The "winning of the West" is probably one of the most romantic phrases in American history, suggesting exciting images of Indians, trappers, soldiers, and settlers. Behind the romance lies much reality, for the American West, particularly the Great Plains and the Rocky Mountains, did indeed have to be won from a none too hospitable nature and from often decidedly hostile residents. It did not happen all at once: much of the nineteenth century was consumed by the effort. When it was over, thousands of people from the green valleys of the Ohio and the Mississippi found themselves and their children transplanted to the high plains and the higher mountains. Thousands of people who had been there first found themselves there no longer, or at least they found their bands and their lands much diminished. Their old tribal hunting civilization gave way to the stronger and more compelling one that finally and firmly won the West for America and for a modern age.

In time, that grand process of settlement generated a vast historical literature. It also left behind no small trail of artifacts. The preserved forts, battlefields, boom towns, and memorials to great treks can still be found in the West in abundance, and each evokes its own special sense of what a particular moment in western history (usually a rather dramatic moment) was like. The Fort Laramie National Historic Site in Wyoming is one of those places, but also one whose history spans—as few others do—the entire process of western settlement. The visitor there will become acquainted with several "Wests," in all of which, as the nineteenth century unfolded, Fort Laramie figured importantly.

Other than explorers Lewis and Clark, fur trappers were the first white men to venture into the wilderness that composed Thomas Jefferson's Louisiana Purchase. Through the 1810s and 1820s solitary and enterprising trappers tracked the lush beaver country east and west of the Continental Divide. Most of their names have vanished, but a few like Jim Bridger and Jedediah Smith gave lasting substance to their image as "mountain men." With their harvest of pelts, they rendezvoused each year, commonly in the valleys of Wyoming's Green and Wind rivers, to which St. Louis traders had sent supply trains up the North Platte. It was en route to such a rendezvous in 1834 that William Sublette and Robert Campbell built a first stockade near the mouth of the Laramie River. The American Fur Company soon bought this first Fort Laramie and made it into a major trading post where trappers and Indians came to barter furs for trade goods. As the rendezvous system declined, the importance to trappers (who were dwindling along with the beaver) of fixed supply posts was enhanced, and in 1841 Fort Laramie was rebuilt as a more substantial adobe-walled structure—just in time, it seemed, for the fur trade to decline.

Historic buildings around parade ground

But the strategic location that made the fort important to the mountain men also made it a familiar landmark to their successors. It sat at a crucial point astride the Oregon and California trails, which, between the 1840s and the coming of the transcontinental railroad after the Civil War, were the way west for thousands of immigrants in search of promised lands west of the Rockies. The first of the great Oregon migrations passed through in 1843, led by Marcus Whitman. The numbers quickly swelled as Mormons, searching for their place apart, were followed by gold-seeking "forty-niners" bound for California. For the fabled trains of covered wagons, Fort Laramie was the jumping-off point beyond which lay the truly fearsome part of their journeys. Most paused there just long enough to make repairs and resupply—at exorbitant frontier prices. But they passed through in a steady stream, watched by the bands of Sioux, Cheyenne, and Arapaho Indians camped around the fort, attracted by the white man's dry goods, tobacco, and whiskey.

Soldiers sometimes passed through too, but Fort Laramie was still a fort without an official military presence. That changed with its transfer in 1849 from the American Fur Company to the United States government, which proceeded to make it into the key army post protecting the wagon trains from hostile Indians. Over the next decade, the old trading post became a sprawling military base, parts of which are preserved today. It was one of the largest such installations in the West and was active longer than most. It provided the logistical and transport support for posts farther west, and though it was never attacked, it served as command headquarters for the numerous campaigns against the Indians in the 1860s and 1870s. Councils with the Plains tribes were held and treaties signed here.

As the Indians, either beaten in battle or pacified on reservations, ceased to be a military threat, so Fort Laramie's mission changed again. In the late 1870s and 1880s not everyone was just passing through en route to California and Oregon. The great interior of the West—the northern plains and Rockies of which Fort Laramie lay at the heart—

was beginning to attract settlers who stayed. These ranchers and home-steaders created the state of Wyoming, and their descendants still shape its character. In those early years Fort Laramie was looked to as a guarantor of law and order on a frontier that was still home to many an outlaw and cattle rustler.

The Bureau of the Census declared the frontier officially closed in 1890—the same year, coincidentally, that the army deactivated Fort Laramie, and the year that the last organized Indian resistance ended at Wounded Knee in South Dakota. The West, if not yet truly "settled," was well on the path to becoming so—and to becoming an integral part of the American nation. Montana attained statehood in 1889, Wyoming and Idaho in 1890, Utah in 1896. As that happened, a distinctive chapter in American history ended, and many of the places associated with it soon passed into oblivion or were changed to meet the needs of life in a new age.

Fort Laramie, fortunately, was not one of those. Though allowed to decay for fifty years after the army abandoned it, it is today preserved as a national historic site and offers the visitor a moving glimpse back to the West's early days. Located just southwest of the town of Fort Laramie in eastern Wyoming, twenty-one of the fort's historic structures still stand. Grouped around the parade ground, those open to the public include the post trader's store, which is refurnished today in the style of the mid-1870s. Here soldiers and civilians found a wide array of merchandise from farm implements to household items to weapons. The lieutenant colonel's quarters, built in 1884, reveal the very comfortable accommodations provided for this senior officer and his family. The old guardhouse, constructed in 1866, contains quarters of the guard and, in the basement, the fort's jail. In the old bakery, the post baker (who lived in the building) produced between 1876 and 1883 300 to 500 eighteen-ounce army loaves every day. The most famous building at Fort Laramie is also the oldest. "Old Bedlam," a rambling two-story white frame structure with a broad porch, dates from 1849, the year the army moved in. Though intended as officers' quarters, it has served many roles. Three—bachelor officers' quarters, the post headquarters, and the post commander's headquarters—are displayed in today's restoration.

Much of the original fort no longer stands, though there are visible ruins and foundations enough to suggest how expansive it once was. Either when they approach or when they leave, visitors will be struck by something else about it. The land and sky that surround it are incredibly more vast. Fort Laramie is a lonely windswept place, just as it surely was when it was a working fort. Viewing it amid that endless prairie, it is not difficult to imagine with what eagerness men sought its walls a hundred and more years ago.

FORT BRIDGER STATE MUSEUM *Fort Bridger.* In the romantic history of the old West, army forts are a common image. It is an image that reflects much truth. Although not all of them were home to the heroic horse soldiers celebrated by Hollywood, military outposts were vital in the settlement of the region. In novels and the movies, however, they usually serve as the setting for an exciting Indian attack, with gallant bluecoats lining the stockade wall defending to the last man their women and children from the yelping savages. Or perhaps wagon trains, hotly pursued by hostile bands, race for the gates and the sheltering guns of the army, arriving just in time.

The real history of the forts seldom matched the image. Fort Bridger, one of the most important, affords a pertinent example. It owed its beginning to commercial, not military impulses; it was garrisoned primarily by infantry, not cavalry; it had no protecting stockade and apparently needed none—like most forts, it was never attacked. Its story begins just as the great era of the fur trade in the West was ending. In its heyday, that trade had produced an extraordinary group of individuals. Remembered as "mountain men," they were the first white men to track the beaver into the Rockies' far reaches, learning as they went the secrets and the dangers of this vast and beautiful land. One of the most famous of these pathfinders, whose life and legend even then seemed inseparable, was Jim Bridger. Unlike some others, Bridger stayed on after the fur trade dwindled, confident that the future wealth of the West lay with people coming into it—as once it lay with beaver pelts going out of it. A canny fellow, he soon saw history prove him right.

Early in the 1840s Bridger built a small log stockade on Blacks Fork of the Green River, in what would become southwestern Wyoming. The site straddled four of the greatest paths of westward immigration: the Oregon, the California, the Mormon, and the Arkansas trails. The 1840s saw the first great Oregon migration, and for ten years Bridger and his business partner Luis Vasquez operated a prosperous trading post that serviced—for a price—the needs of westward migrants. The discovery of gold in California in 1849 swelled the tide and their business. The Mormons were another kind of immigrant. Hounded in the 1840s and

Fort Bridger Museum

1850s from the East and driven by their own special revelation, the Saints trekked west to the Great Basin, there to build up Zion and wait for the Lord. They sought a world isolated from gentile corruption, and for a while in Utah they found it.

Unfortunately for Bridger and Vasquez, who emphatically were not Mormons, their unpretentious but prospering outpost lay within the new Utah Territory, something the Mormons would not countenance. In 1853 the Saints attempted to force Bridger out and, failing, set up their own post called Camp Supply several miles to the south. Eventually they bought Bridger's fort, though Bridger himself later claimed that he had received no compensation. In any case, it embittered him against the Mormons, whose firm subjection to federal authority he subsequently campaigned for.

The result of this and other Mormon-gentile conflicts was the short and virtually bloodless Mormon War of 1857–1858, in which an army expedition commanded by Albert Sidney Johnston (who later died a Confederate general at Shiloh) was dispatched to Utah to elicit the loyalty of the Salt Lake Saints. Receiving word of the column's approach, the Mormons put both Camp Supply and Bridger's post to the torch and destroyed the massive stone houses and fortifying walls they had built. The army therefore spent the first of its many winters there in a crude temporary camp, a far cry from the relatively soft life later garrisons would enjoy. The war meanwhile ended through negotiations that saw a new United States military presence established within the Salt Lake Valley at Camp Floyd. But the army was also at Fort Bridger to stay, with only one short interruption, for over thirty years.

Those decades to 1890 marked the "winning of the West," and in virtually all phases of that epic adventure—except actual battles with the Indians—strategically located Fort Bridger played a part. During the Civil War the post lost its regular army troops, but in the late 1860s it became a base of military operations throughout southwestern Wyoming and northeastern Utah. It welcomed the immigrants who continued to flood the trails, some of whom in time stayed and settled the region. Its troops patrolled the trails that old Jim Bridger knew would bring people west. It housed a station on the short-lived but legendary Pony Express; it guarded the stagecoaches and the transcontinental telegraph line. Not far to the north passed the Union Pacific Railroad, and soldiers from Fort Bridger were assigned to protect its laborers and supplies. It was Fort Bridger's good fortune, in its relations with the Indians, to deal with the peaceful Shoshone tribe, with whom treaties were signed at the fort in 1863 and 1868.

Some of the garrison was sometimes reassigned for fighting purposes to other posts, but Fort Bridger itself was not directly involved in any of the great Indian campaigns of the 1870s. Indeed, so peaceful had things become that the post was temporarily abandoned in 1878. Reactivated two years later, the fort entered the happiest, the most redundant, and the last phase of its career. It became in the 1880s—a decade when the largely pacified West was growing pleasant and prosperous—a model sort of place, known as a soft-duty assignment by the men who served there. Comfortable and improved quarters for officers and their families went up on the east bank of Blacks Fork, which flowed through the parade ground. On the other side was a new guardhouse and new stone barracks for enlisted men. For the commanding officer a commodious Victorian house was provided, where military dignitaries, public officials, and railroad moguls became frequent visitors. Trees were planted; the regimental band played in a gazebo; the hunting and fishing were excellent.

Though the army named the post after Jim Bridger early in its occupation, another man was far more associated with the fort's actual history. He was William Alexander Carter, the post sutler or trader. An enduring presence on the military frontier, the sutler was a civilian merchant, appointed by the army, whose job it was to provide for the garrison's numerous commodity needs beyond the absolute necessities that came through the post commissary and quartermaster. He served a market essentially without competition and, if clever, stood to profit greatly. It was at the sutler's store (one is preserved at Fort Bridger) that soldiers bought tinned food, candy, ready-made clothing, tobacco, beer, and whiskey. But it was for services other than serving this captive market that William Alexander Carter and sutlers like him occupy an important place in the development of the West.

As the West was settled, people other than soldiers and Indians came to live there. From a restricted economy concerned of necessity with subsistence and self-sufficiency there evolved in time a more sophisticated, specialized, and commercial one where different people, doing different things, required different kinds of services. The sutler provided many of them. He was an entrepreneur and a banker, a link between the West and the centers of financial and industrial power in the East, and often—as was clearly the case with Carter at Fort Bridger—a principal architect of the commercial life of the region and a prime shaper of its evolution. Between 1857, when he arrived with Johnston's column, and his death in 1881, Carter became an influence to be reckoned with in almost every phase of economic life in the Rockies and the Great Basin. In addition to his mercantile business, he delved into freighting, ranching, and farming. He served as postmaster and probate judge. Thousands from many walks of life—wagonmasters, teamsters, miners, politicians, speculators, farmers, ranchers, tourists, and just plain adventurers—knew and were known by him. As much as any of its military commanders, this businessman secured Fort Bridger's place in history.

Today the fort is maintained as a historic site by the state of Wyoming and offers the history-minded visitor a vivid look back at the real western military frontier. No epic battles were ever fought here. But thousands of ordinary people did pass this way, en route sometimes to promised lands and better lives and sometimes to disappointment. Their stories make up the true history of the westward movement, and in many of them Fort Bridger is one chapter.

YELLOWSTONE NATIONAL PARK *Mammoth Hot Springs.* The very words "national park" conjure up visions of high mountains, rugged canyons, and wild, remote seashores. The words "Yellowstone National Park" most commonly bring to mind the Old Faithful geyser and tourists (against the advice of the park rangers) feeding the bears. The national parks in general, Yellowstone among them, are indeed places that people visit largely for their natural attractions—for their scenery. They are not therefore "historic sites" in the same sense that Fort Sumter or Mount Vernon or the Statue of Liberty is. They exist not to remind us of some famous event or series of events in human history but rather to preserve distinctive natural places as they were before human history touched them.

Yellowstone does that for sure; its natural wonders are legion, and they are famous around the world. But as the very first national park established in the United States or anywhere else, Yellowstone has special historic significance. The bill creating it was signed into law by President Ulysses S. Grant in 1872. In the century and more since then, many other places in America have been set aside as various sorts of natural preserves to be managed by a professional park service for the benefit of all the people. Many foreign countries have done likewise. Understanding the reasons for this remarkable movement, though not as simple as it might seem, can add immensely to one's visit to this beautiful place and to one's knowledge of American history.

It is fashionable today to view the national parks (especially the older and grander western ones) as evidence of a decades-old "prophetic public ecological conscience" similar to that of many modern-day environmental groups. Many such places have in time come to embody such a conscience, but in the early days this was not the case. The earliest park, Yellowstone, suggests why. The act establishing the park spoke not of nature's delicate balances and man's relation to them. It said nothing about "ecology." It simply declared that a tract of land lying near the headwaters of the Yellowstone River in what were then the territories of Wyoming and Montana "is hereby reserved and withdrawn from settlement, occupancy or sale . . . and dedicated and set apart as a public park or pleasuring ground for the benefit and enjoyment of the people." It was intended that the place should be used by people, not just preserved for animals. What people might find there were the things that had overawed the relatively few white men who then had seen the place: an incredible display of nature's beauties—and some of its oddities. High mountains, rugged canyons, and especially the spectacular steaming geysers and boiling mud were the kinds of natural phenomena that had to be seen to be believed. For a nation then learning to love remarkable scenery, Yellowstone was a lesson not to be missed.

Old Faithful Inn

Though remote and at first nearly inaccessible, Yellowstone soon became a tourist attraction. Its establishment in fact probably owed not a little to lobbying by the Northern Pacific Railway, whose tracks led that way and which became Yellowstone's first concessionaire. With the Civil War ended and the West opening to settlement, America in the late nineteenth century was possessed by a new feeling of nationalism and pride. It became common to boast that American cities were the greatest, American railroads the longest, American farms and factories the most productive—and American scenery was the grandest. America's grandeur compared more than favorably with Switzerland's, something that a spectacular display like Yellowstone clearly demonstrated.

For years, however, Yellowstone largely was left for curiosity-seekers to discover for themselves. The act that established this vast "pleasuring ground" had provided for a superintendent to look after it. But so casual was the intent and so strong the conviction of some lawmakers of the park's economic worthlessness that few funds were available to do the job. In 1866 the responsibility passed to the United States Army, which stayed for thirty-one years.

The period of the army's administration brought significant improvements. The Corps of Engineers completed important public works, including the park's roads, while soldiers and scouts stationed strategically through the park established respect for law and order. The army's headquarters—Fort Yellowstone, at Mammoth Hot Springs—is also today the park's headquarters. Its dignified stone buildings are a reminder of the growing conviction that this truly was an American showplace. Wrote post commander John Pitcher: "This post is seen and visited by many distinguished people from all over the world and for this reason, if for none other, it should be a model post in every way."

And so it was as the years passed. But also, as the years passed, a problem arose, one apparent in the very language of the legislation that in 1916 established the National Park Service as the new custodian of Yellowstone and America's other national parks. The Park Service was established "to conserve the scenery and the natural and historic objects and the wild life" in the national parks, as well as "to provide for the enjoyment of the same in such a manner and by such means as will leave them unimpaired for the enjoyment of future generations." That has proved to be a tall order, for it says that the national parks must serve not one but two broad purposes not always perfectly compatible: preservation and use. Yellowstone was at first valued as a natural curiosity and partly as a source of spiritual inspiration for busy people who no longer lived very close to nature: "The glory of this territory is its sublime solitude," declared a congressman from New Jersey in 1886. "Civilization is so universal that man can only see nature in her majesty and primal glory, as it were, in these as yet virgin regions." Yellowstone is still treasured as a place of wonderful and mysterious beauty and, in the language of modern preservationists, as a place where nature's own ecosystems remain undisturbed by man.

It is also a place (like all the national parks) that, by statute and popular consensus, remains open to human use. Tourism and commercial recreation are as much a part of Yellowstone as Old Faithful and the bears. As the nation's population has grown and its leisure time increased, the pressures on Yellowstone have risen commensurately. How best to balance the twin demands of preservation and use thus remains a key concern for those who administer Yellowstone and the other national parks as public trusts. It is a concern that likely will intensify in the future. For the thoughtful American, whose national park this is, a visit to Yellowstone is a good occasion to consider this old dilemma.

It is also, of course, a chance to marvel at nature's beauty and some of her curiosities—and to go home, as the old naturalists understood so well, refreshed by the wilderness.

BUFFALO BILL HISTORICAL CENTER *720 Sheridan Avenue, Cody.* Consists of four separate museums: Plains Indian Museum; Buffalo Bill Museum, including the boyhood home of William F. Cody; Whitney Gallery of Western Art; and Winchester Arms Museum.

FETTERMAN FIGHT SIGHT *U.S. 87 just northeast of Story.* A Federal marker where Red Cloud laid an ambush for the unwise Captain William J. Fetterman and eighty others and annihilated them in 1866.

FORT CASPAR MUSEUM *Fort Caspar Road, Casper.* Military museum located in a reconstructed 1863 fort where the Mormon and Oregon trails crossed the Platte; named for Lt. Caspar Collins, who lost his life near there in 1865 while attempting to aid an army supply train under attack by the Indians.

FORT D. A. RUSSELL *Francis E. Warren Air Force Base, Cheyenne.* Site of a military reservation established in 1867 to protect railroad construction crews, later a logistical base for Indian wars; more than 200 neo-Colonial red-brick structures, built in the late 1880s, still standing. Museum and tours available to the public.

FORT FETTERMAN on Orpha Cutoff via I-25 about seven miles west of Douglas. Founded in 1867 on the Bozeman Trail and the base for the 1876 Indian War campaigns; now with restorations of two buildings and a small museum.

FORT WASHAKIE town of Fort Washakie. Named in honor of the renowed Shoshoni leader in 1878; today, the administrative headquarters of the Wind River Indian Agency.

FRONTIER DAYS OLD WEST MUSEUM North Carey Avenue, Frontier Park, Cheyenne. Exhibits and artifacts from the cowboy and ranching era.

GRAND ENCAMPMENT MUSEUM COMPLEX Grandview Park, Encampment. Once a turn-of-the-century copper boom town; now modern museum and several historic buildings.

GRAND TETON NATIONAL PARK MUSEUM Moose. Includes the Colter Bay Indian Art Museum, Moose Visitor Center with fur-trade history items, 1892 Menor's Ferry, and other historic structures.

GUERNSEY STATE PARK MUSEUM Guernsey. General museum with collections on agriculture, anthropology, ethnology, history, transportation, and the military.

HISTORIC GOVERNOR'S MANSION 300 E. 21st Street, Cheyenne. Constructed in 1904 and home of twenty Wyoming governors; materials on the governors and period furnishings.

INDEPENDENCE ROCK sixty miles southwest of Casper on state 220. Outcropping on the Sweetwater River where pioneers traveling west on the Oregon Trail carved and painted names.

J. C. PENNEY HOUSE Union Pacific Park, Kemmerer. Nineteenth-century house where J. C. Penney lived 1904–1909.

LARAMIE PLAINS MUSEUM 603 Ivinson, Laramie. General museum with items from Indian and frontier history; housed in Ivinson Mansion, constructed 1892.

MEDICINE WHEEL twenty-five miles west of Burgess Junction on alternate U.S. 14. Loose circle of limestone rocks with spokes radiating from a central hub measuring about seventy-five feet in diameter; located on top of the Big Horn Mountains. Purpose unknown; one of the most mysterious remains of late period culture in the United States.

OREGON TRAIL RUTS south side of North Platte River, one mile south of Guernsey. Half-mile section of Oregon Trail worn two to six feet deep into sandstone; a few yards north is grave of Lucinda Rollins, an early immigrant.

REGISTER CLIFF south bank of North Platte River three miles south of Guernsey. Limestone precipice that was a landmark on Oregon and California trails; names and dates carved into the rock, which rises 100 feet from valley floor.

SOUTH PASS CITY *about thirty-four miles south of Lander on state 28.* Several surviving buildings from the town built in 1867 in the Sweetwater gold region; where Esther Morris became the world's first female justice of the peace in 1870.

TRAIL END HISTORIC CENTER *400 Clarendon Avenue, Sheridan.* Historical and Indian artifacts in a mansion built 1908–1913 for John B. Kendrick, former governor of Wyoming and United States senator.

WAGON BOX FIGHT SITE *one and one-half miles southwest of Story.* Where Sioux and Cheyenne warriors in 1867 attacked twenty-eight infantrymen, who hid behind overturned boxes of wood-hauling wagons.

WYODAK COAL MINE *four miles east of Gillette along U.S. 14-16.* Gigantic open-pit mine in operation since 1924; an illustration of energy resources in Wyoming.

WYOMING STATE MUSEUM *Barrett Building, 22nd and Central avenues, Cheyenne.* History and art museum with materials on historic and prehistoric Indians and Wyoming and western history.

Index